THE CARAVAN & CAMPING GUIDE
2025

Published by AA Publishing, a trading name of AA Media Limited, whose registered office is Grove House, Lutyens Close, Lychpit Basingstoke, Hampshire RG24 8AG. Registered number 06112600

© AA Media Limited 2024

57th edition 2024

AA Media Limited retains the copyright in the current edition © 2024 and in all subsequent editions, reprints and amendments to editions. The information contained in this directory is sourced entirely from the AA Media's information resources. All rights reserved. No part of this publication may be reproduced, stored in a retrieval system, or transmitted in any form or by any means – electronic, photocopying, recording or otherwise – unless the written permission of the publishers has been obtained beforehand. This book may not be sold, resold, hired out or otherwise disposed of by way of trade in any form of binding or cover other than that in which it is published, without the prior consent of all relevant publishers.

The contents of this publication are believed correct at the time of printing. Nevertheless, the publishers cannot be held responsible for any errors or omissions or for any changes in the details given in this guide or for the consequences of any reliance on the information provided by the same. This does not affect your statutory rights.

Assessments of the AA campsites are based on the experience of the AA Caravan & Camping Inspectors on the occasion(s) of their visit(s) and therefore descriptions given in this guide necessarily contain an element of subjective opinion which may not reflect or dictate a reader's own opinion on another occasion. See pages 10–12 for a clear explanation of how, based on our Inspectors' inspection experiences, campsites are graded.

AA Media Limited strives to ensure accuracy of the information in this guide at the time of printing. Due to the constantly evolving nature of the subject matter the information is subject to change. AA Media Limited will gratefully receive any advice from our readers of any necessary updated information.

For any enquiries relating to this guide, please contact Caravan.Camping@aamediagroup.co.uk

Website addresses are included in some entries as specified by the respective establishment. Such websites are not under the control of AA Media Limited and as such AA Media Limited has no control over them and will not accept any responsibility or liability in respect of any and all matters whatsoever relating to such websites including access, content, material and functionality. By including the addresses of third party websites the AA does not intend to solicit business or offer any security to any person in any country, directly or indirectly.

AA Media Limited would like to thank the following for their help in the compilation of this guide:
Tracey Freestone, David Hancock, Lauren Havelock, Nicky Hillenbrand, Lin Hutton, Julia Powers and Victoria Samways.

Country and county opening page descriptions: Nick Channer.

Cover design: The berkshire design company

Photographs in the preliminary pages and gazetteer are provided by the named establishments. Credits for other images used are as follows:
24 Hadspen Glamping – Owen Howells Photography
323 courtesy of Old Oaks Touring & Glamping.

Following images sourced from www.unsplash.com:
52 Cambridge – Jean Luc Benazet; 53 Little Moreton Hall – David Griffiths; 55 Chester Cathedral – Ian Kelsall; 61 Tintagel – Lasma Artmane; 92 Furness Abbey – Matt Newton; 104 Mam Tor – Benjamin Elliott; 115 Dawlish – Anthony; 133 Cerne Abbas Giant – Joe Percival; 140 Forde Abbey – Annie Spratt; 148 Weymouth – Benjamin Elliott; 150 Egglestone Abbey – Annabeth Robinson; 161 Carisbrooke Castle – Paul Arky; 189 Blickling Hall – Andrew Hall; 191 Bamburgh Castle – Benjamin Elliott; 192 Northumberland NP – Jonny Gios; 213 Glastonbury Tor – Niklas Weiss; 226 Hastings – Ben Guerin; 255 York – Scott Precious; 276 Castle Kennedy – Ben Sugden; 279 Glen Nevis – Migle Siauciulyte; 280 The Uplands – Niklas Weiss; 283 Loch Earn – Martin Bennie; 298 Barmouth Beach – Anthony VB Dains ; 302 Caernarfon Castle – Neil Mark-Thomas; 306 Alex Holt; 313 Powis Castle – Marian Florinel; 315 Rhossili Bay – Kaijia; 317 Jose Llamas

50; 152; 167; 178; 221; 257 AA/James Tims

Every effort has been made to trace the copyright holders, and we apologise in advance for any unintentional omissions or errors. We would be pleased to apply any corrections in a following edition of this publication.

Maps prepared by the Mapping Services Department of AA Publishing.

Maps © AA Media Limited 2024.

Contains Ordnance Survey data © Crown copyright and database right 2024.

Ireland map contains data available from openstreetmap.org © under the Open Database License found at opendatacommons.org

A CIP catalogue record for this book is available from the British Library.

Printed by Stamperia Artistica Nazionale – Trofarello – TORINO – ITALY.

ISBN: 978-0-7495-8428-3

A05887

Discover all AA-rated caravan and campsites at RatedTrips.com

Opposite: Polmanter Touring Park, St Ives

Contents

Welcome to the *AA Caravan & Camping Guide*	4
How to use the guide	6
Guide to symbols	9
The AA classification scheme	10
VisitEngland Quality Assessment	13
Pledge to make the countryside bloom	14
The Best of Britain Parks	15
Useful information and campers' checklist	16
AA Campsites of the Year 2024–25	20
Spotlight on The Quiet Site and 'going green'	26

Site recommendations

The best sites for…	32
5-Star Platinum Parks	38
5-Star Premier Parks	39
AA Holiday Parks	42
Adults only – no children parks	44
Glamping sites	45

The sites

ENGLAND	48
CHANNEL ISLANDS & ISLE OF MAN	258
SCOTLAND	262
SCOTTISH ISLANDS	286
WALES	288
NORTHERN IRELAND	318
Atlas	323
Index	351

Welcome to the AA Caravan & Camping Guide 2025

Despite the 'cost of living' challenges easing gradually during early 2024, many camping and caravanning sites experienced a quiet summer period due to the residual effects of rising costs, with the trend for very late bookings as budgets for breaks away continued to be squeezed. Aligned with an unusually wet spring, it was a difficult period for some sites, especially those in far-flung locations. However, the return of warmer, sunnier weather during late July and August saw business levels return to the seasonal norm and parks busy with happy families enjoying valuable time away. Hopefully, the economy and weather will be kinder during 2025 and see the return of full capacity sites for much of the season.

Who's in the Guide
Within these pages you'll find simple rural campsites, beautifully landscaped parks with top quality toilet facilities and excellent security and customer care, and self-contained Holiday Parks that offer a wide range of sport, leisure and entertainment facilities. All have touring facilities for caravans, motorhomes and tents, and a growing number also have glamping areas. There are also glamping-only sites offering quirky and luxury stays in safari tents, yurts, posh pods, shepherd's huts, and even treehouses, and Holiday Parks that only offer holiday caravans and lodges for hire.

Our award-winning parks
Following nominations by our inspectors, we award an overall winner from England, Scotland, and Wales and five regional Campsites of the Year, a Holiday Park of the Year and a Glamping Site of the Year — all are selected for their outstanding overall quality and high levels of customer care. Our three special awards recognise the best Small Campsite, the Most Improved Campsite, and NEW for 2025, the Best Sustainable Campsite. Tyddyn Isaf Caravan Park on the beautiful Anglesey coast is the stand-out Wales and Overall winner for 2025. See pages 20–25 for this year's award-winning parks.

From Pennants to Stars for 2025
Star ratings, while already well established for Hotels and B&Bs, have replaced the AA pennant ratings for the Caravan and Camping scheme in 2025. Reflecting the marketplace and consumer demand, we have also recalibrated the star ratings from 3 to 5 Stars, with 1 and 2 Pennants being replaced by 'Quality Assessed'. In addition, we have refined the main categories of parks to Caravan and Camping Parks, Holiday Parks, and Glamping Sites. See pages 10–13 for more information about the revised AA Classification Scheme.

Top Sites – Gold and Platinum Stars
Our best parks are awarded Gold Stars if they receive a quality score of 90% and above. Our elite collection of parks with Platinum Stars are 5-Star rated parks that have achieved 95% or above following an inspection. See pages 38–40 for the full list of Platinum and 5-Star rated parks in this year's guide.

Campsites – Best For…
We have added informative notes to our quick reference 'Best For…' lists, highlighting the inspectors' favourite 'stand-out' sites for waterside pitches, for families and for the best eco-friendly sites. See pages 32–37 for these featured sites.

Spotlight on the very eco-friendly Quiet Site in Cumbria, winner of AA Campsite of the Year 2023–24
Our main feature this year focuses on how Daniel Holder's commendable ethos on sustainability over the past 20 years has transformed The Quiet Site. This exemplary park, set high above Ullswater in the Lake District with fabulous views across the lake and surrounding fells, is now one of the greenest parks in the country. In 2020, The Quiet Site was the first holiday park to win the Queens Award for Enterprise: Sustainable Development.

Old Oaks Touring & Glamping, Glastonbury

Join us at RatedTrips.com
You can find all AA-rated establishments, including caravan, camping and glamping sites on RatedTrips.com. All sites and parks listed on the website link to local pubs, restaurants, local walks, places to visit and things to do in the area. Plus, you'll find plenty of travel inspiration for your next UK holiday.

How to use the AA Caravan & Camping Guide

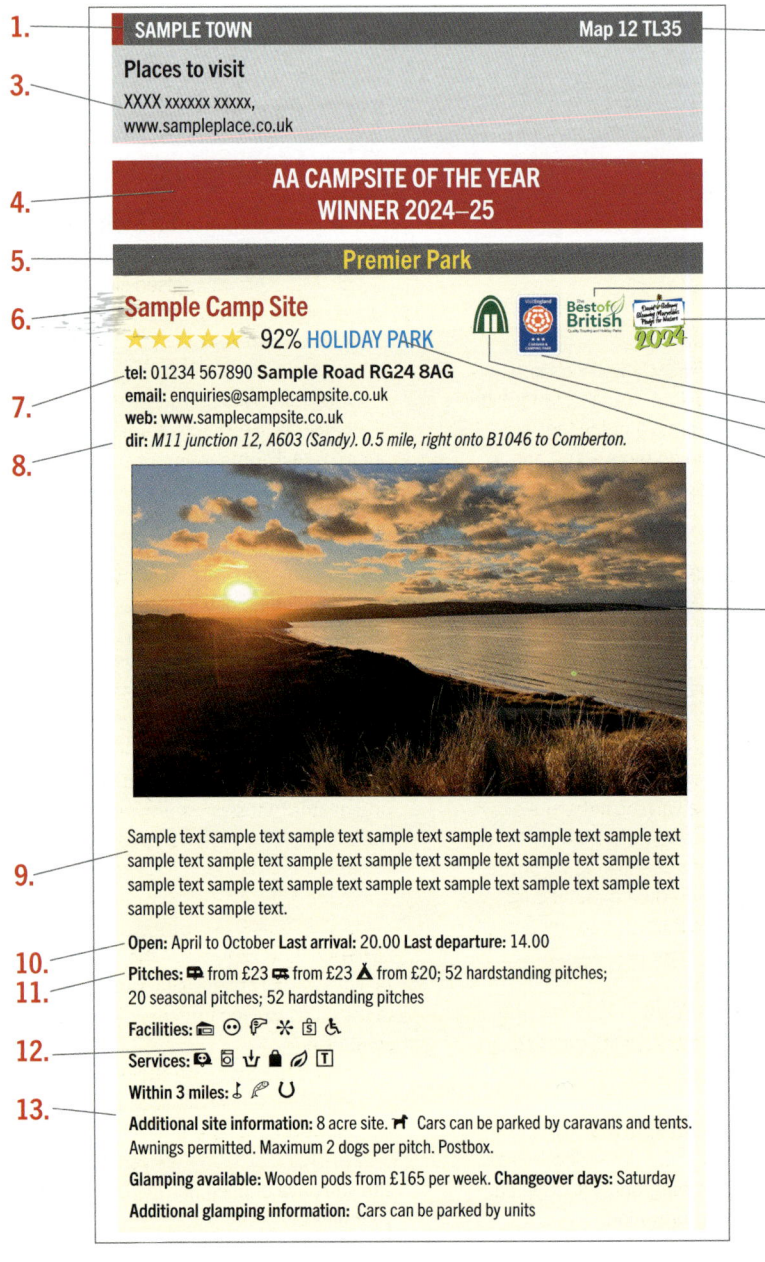

1. Location
Place names are listed alphabetically within each county.

2. Map reference
Each location is given a map reference so you can find it easily in the atlas section at the back of the guide. The map reference comprises the guide map page number, the National Grid location square and a two-figure map location reference.
For example: **Map 19 NZ90**.
19 refers to the page number of the map section at the back of the guide.
NZ is the National Grid lettered square (representing 100,000sq metres) in which the location will be found.
9 is the figure reading across the top or bottom of the map page.
0 is the figure reading down each side of the map page.

3. Places to visit
Suggestions of nearby places to visit for adults and children. Unfortunately, sometimes places have to change their opening times at short notice. It is always best to call ahead and check before visiting.

4. Award winner
A banner here indicates if the site is an AA Campsite of the Year Award winner 2024–25.

5. Top rated parks
Premier and platinum parks are highlighted here. For an explanation of categories see page 12.

6. Site name and rating
★ Campsites are listed in descending order of their Star rating. Sites are rated from 3 to 5 Stars (which can be platinum, gold or black) and are also awarded a score ranging from 50 to 100% according to how they compare with other parks within the same Star rating. For further explanation see pages 10–12.

7. Contact details

8. Directions
Brief directions from a recognisable point, such as a main road. Please contact the individual site for more detailed directions or use the AA Route Planner at **www.theAA.com**, and enter the site's postcode.

9. Description
Descriptions are based on information supplied by the AA inspector at the time of the last visit.

Please note: The AA Star rating is based on the touring pitches and the facilities only. AA inspectors do not visit or report on statics or chalets for hire under the AA Caravan & Camping quality standards scheme. However, the AA has a category of **HOLIDAY PARK** and any static caravan, chalet or lodge-only parks are inspected.

10. Opening, arrival and departure times
Parks are not necessarily open all year and while most sites permit arrivals at any time, checking beforehand is advised (see page 16).

11. Pitches
Rates given after each appropriate symbol 🚐 (caravan), 🚙 (motorhome), ⛺ (tent) are the minimum overnight cost for one unit. The prices can vary according to the number of people in the party, but some parks have a fixed fee per pitch regardless of the number of people. Please note that some sites charge separately for certain facilities, including showers; and some sites charge a different rate for pitches with or without electricity. Prices are supplied to us in good faith by the site operators and are as accurate as possible at the time of going to press. They are, however, only a guide and are subject to change during the currency of this publication. The glamping symbol () indicates that the campsite offers one or more types of glamping (see also point 13, below).

*If this symbol is shown before the prices it indicates that the prices are from 2024.

12. Symbols
These are divided into Pitches, Leisure, Facilities, Services and Within 3 miles sections. A guide to the symbols can be found on page 9 and at the bottom of most pages throughout the guide.

13. Additional site information
This includes information about the size of the site, whether dogs are accepted or not, whether cars can be parked by a caravan or tent, and whether awnings are permitted. We also include any restrictions and any additional facilities the site would like their visitors to be made aware of. If the site offers glamping, further information is shown at the end of the entry. As most sites now accept credit and debit cards, we only indicate those that don't accept cards 💳.

14. Photograph
Optional photograph(s) supplied by the campsite.

15. Other categories
These are: Quality Assessed, Holiday Park or Glamping-only Site. See page 12 for further information.

16. Glamping
The campsite offers one or more types of 'glamorous camping' accommodation, i.e. wooden pods, tipis, yurts, bell tents, safari tents, shepherd's huts, vintage caravans etc. Details are provided in the entry description and at the bottom of the entry.

17. VisitEngland
The campsite has accreditation to VisitEngland scheme. For further information see page 13.

18. The David Bellamy Blooming Marvellous Pledge for Nature
Many AA recognised sites have signed-up to an exciting new initiative that shows their commitment to helping Britain's wildlife.

The symbol we show indicate parks signed-up to the Pledge at the end of June 2024. For more details see page 14.

19. Best of British
A group of around 50 parks, both large and small, which focus on high quality facilities and amenities. See page 15 for more details.

Facilities for disabled guests
The Equality Act 2010 provides legal rights for disabled people including access to goods, services and facilities, and means that service providers may have to consider making adjustments to their premises. For more information about the Act see: www.gov.uk/definition-of-disability-under-equality-act-2010

If a site has told us that they provide facilities for disabled visitors their entry in the guide will include the following symbol: ♿

The sites in this guide should be aware of their responsibilities under the Act. However, we recommend that you always phone in advance to ensure the site you have chosen has facilities to suit your needs.

Guide to symbols

Pitches
- Caravan
- Motorhome
- Tent
- Glamping accommodation

Leisure
- Indoor swimming pool
- Outdoor swimming pool
- Tennis court
- Games room
- Separate TV room
- Children's playground
- Kids' club
- Stables & horse riding
- Golf course
- Boat hire
- Cycle hire
- Cinema
- Entertainment
- Fishing

- Mini golf
- Watersports
- Gym
- Sports field
- Pitch n putt
- Spa facility

Facilities
- Electric vehicle charging
- Baths/showers
- Electric shaver sockets
- Hairdryer
- Ice packs facility
- Baby facilities
- Disabled facilities
- Shop or supermarket on site or within 200 yards
- BBQ area
- Picnic area
- WiFi available
- Car hire can be arranged

Services
- Café or restaurant
- Fast food/Takeaway
- Electric hook-up
- Motorhome service point
- Launderette
- Licensed bar
- Calor Gas
- Campingaz
- Battery charging
- Toilet fluid

Other
- Dogs accepted
- No dogs permitted
- No credit or debit cards

Opposite: Witches Craig Caravan & Camping Park, Blairlogie

The AA classification scheme

AA parks are now classified by a three, four or five Star rating according to their style and the range of facilities they offer. As the number of Stars increases, so the quality and variety of facilities is generally greater.

NEW Star ratings and standards

Star ratings, while already well established for Hotels and B&Bs, replaced the AA Pennant ratings for the Caravan & Camping scheme in 2025. Reflecting the marketplace and consumer demand, we also recalibrated the star ratings to 3 to 5 Stars, with 1 and 2 Pennants being replaced by Quality Assessed (see below) and 3 Star requirements becoming the minimum rating.

The quality standards used to assess all parks have been fully updated to reflect the marketplace, the ever-increasing diversity of product in the industry and a greater flexibility in service provision — acknowledging the growing use of technology and other innovations in the guest experience.

What can you expect at an AA-rated park?

All AA parks must meet a minimum standard: they should be clean, well maintained and welcoming. In addition, they must have a local authority site licence (unless exempt) and satisfy local authority fire regulations. See the opposite page for requirements.

The AA inspection

Each park that applies for AA recognition receives an unannounced visit each year by one of the AA's highly qualified team of inspectors. They make a thorough check of the site's touring pitches, facilities and hospitality. The sites pay an annual fee for the inspection, recognition and rating, and receive a text entry in the *AA Caravan & Camping Guide* and on the AA Rated Trips website. AA inspectors pay when they stay overnight on a site. The criteria used by the inspectors in awarding the AA Star rating is shown on this and the opposite page.

AA quality percentage score

AA-rated Campsites, Caravan Parks, Holiday Parks and Glamping-only sites are awarded a percentage score alongside their Star rating. This is a qualitative assessment of various factors including customer care and hospitality, toilet facilities and park landscaping. The score runs from 50% to 100% and indicates the relative quality of parks with the same number of Stars. For example, one 3-Star park may score 70%, while another may achieve 90%. The percentage score is reassessed annually.

Quality Assessed

This accreditation involves a full inspection, testing all services to ensure minimum quality standards are met, but without Stars being awarded. It will promote businesses where they have been fully inspected and assessed against the standards but prefer to be marketed without a Star rating.

Opposite: Killerby Old Hall Caravan Park, Cayton

The AA Star Criteria

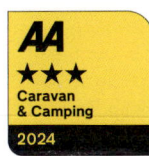

Three Star Parks
These parks are of a very good standard and offer the following as a minimum:
- Facilities, services and park grounds are very clean and well maintained, buildings in good condition
- Attention paid to customer care and security
- Evenly surfaced roads and paths
- Decent, modern or modernised, heated toilet blocks (lit all night) to contain mirrors, shelves and hooks, shaver/hairdryer points, waste bin with lids in female toilets, well maintained toilet seats, soap, clean towels and/or hand dryer
- Modern shower cubicles, ideally with doors, with free hot water
- Automatic laundry with some drying facilities, separate from toilets (one washing machine and one tumble dryer) or laundrette facilities close by to the park with full information including directions and opening times
- Several electric hook-ups
- Several hardstandings, wheel runs and/or firm, level ground
- Children's playground with equipment, games rooms and/or recreation area unless park is geared towards adults
- Warden's hours and 24-hour contact number clearly signed
- Free hot water for dishwashing
- Reasonable efforts at on-site security and supervision

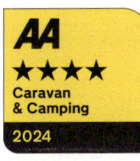

Four Star Parks
Parks with this rating have achieved an extremely high standard in all areas. As well as fulfilling all the criteria for 3-Star rated establishments, 4-Star Caravan and Camping Parks must offer additional facilities:
- Quality shop on site (or within reasonable distance)
- 24-hour warden
- Reception area open during the day, with tourist information available
- Spacious vanity unit-style washbasins or similar, including some in lockable cubicles
- Fully tiled or equivalent shower cubicles with doors, dry areas, shelves and hooks
- Some combined toilet and washing cubicles, or a fully serviced cubicle for use as a family room
- All toilet blocks heated October to Easter
- At least half of all pitches must have electric hook-ups
- Minimum 10% hardstandings, where necessary

- A late arrivals enclosure or pre-arranged agreement for late arrivals
- Good security and supervision
- Motorhome service point with access for a large unit

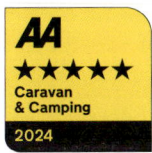

Five Star Premier Parks
Premier Caravan and Camping Parks are of an extremely high standard, set in attractive surroundings with mature landscaping, and have exceptional facilities, security and customer care. They would be expected to have the following:
- Several designated self-contained cubicles, ideally with toilet, washbasin and shower/bath
- Several fully serviced pitches (minimum 25%)
- Electric hook-ups to most pitches (minimum 75%)
- Hardstandings where necessary, at least 20% of total amount
- Excellent supervision and security, including barrier (pin code or automatic number plate recognition (ANPR)) and CCTV at entrance, ideally across the whole park

5-Star Premier Parks may also provide:
- Heated swimming pool and some leisure facilities
- Quality shopping facilities
- A café or restaurant, as well as a bar
- A designated walking area for dogs (if accepted)

Glen Nevis Caravan & Camping Park, Fort William

HOLIDAY PARKS

In this category we distinguish parks that cater for all holiday needs including cooked meals and entertainment. Some are static-only parks offering holiday caravans, chalets or lodges for hire. They provide:

- A wide range of on-site sports, leisure and recreational facilities
- Supervision and security at a very high level
- A choice of eating outlets
- Facilities for touring caravans that equal those available to rented holiday accommodation (if provided)
- Clubhouse with entertainment
- Laundry with automatic washing machines

Star ratings range from 3 to 5 stars.

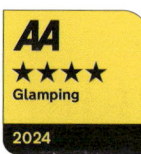

GLAMPING-ONLY SITES

These sites, offering a different camping experience from touring with caravans, motorhomes and tents, are also inspected and rated from 3 to 5 Stars. This is an assessment of the quality and variety of the facilities a site offers.

Platinum Stars ★★★★★

Platinum Stars are awarded to camping sites scoring 95% and above with a 5-Star rating. See page 38.

Gold Stars ★★★★★

AA Gold Stars are awarded to camping sites scoring 90% and above within the 3 to 5 Star ratings. See pages 39–40 for parks with 5 Gold Stars.

Lynmouth Holiday Retreat, Lynton

VisitEngland Quality Assessment

VisitEngland has an assessment service for Holiday Parks and Caravan & Camping sites, which assesses parks as Quality Assessed or with a three, four or five Star rating (see detail below).

What can you expect from a VisitEngland rated park?
All parks graded under the VisitEngland quality standards must meet all legal obligations, achieve a minimum standard of facilities and reach a high score for housekeeping.

The VisitEngland Assessment process
All applicants will receive an unannounced annual visit by one of our highly qualified assessors. All areas of the site will be checked, and paperwork verified to ensure legal obligations are met. A site will pay an annual fee for participating in the VisitEngland standard. Feedback and advice will be given to the site.

VisitEngland Quality percentage score
All sites, whether they are Holiday Parks, Holiday Villages or Camping & Caravanning sites will have all areas on site assessed annually, with individual scores awarded and an overall percentage calculated. This will include any aspect on site, including physical aspects, the welcome and any hospitality areas and, of course, the cleanliness across the site. A rating will then be awarded based on both physical requirements and the sectional scores awarded.

VisitEngland Quality Assessed Parks
'Quality Assessed' parks receive a full assessment and have to achieve a minimum standard and meet all of the legal criteria. These sites may not have the criteria to meet a Star rating (e.g. having several electric hook ups) or may just prefer to market their business without a Star rating.

VisitEngland Three Star rating
Awarded to sites which may offer a quieter stay with limited facilities and who have achieved a Quality score of between 60% and 74% in all aspects on site.

VisitEngland Four Star rating
Awarded to sites which will likely have more facilities on site and who have achieved a Quality score of between 75% and 86% in all aspects across the site.

VisitEngland Five Star rating
Awarded to sites which have outstanding facilities, including leisure aspects, who have achieved a Quality score above 87% in all aspects.

VisitEngland Gold Award
Available to any site rated Three to Five Star who may be limited in facilities, but offer outstanding service, hospitality, housekeeping, facilities and physical aspects.

To find out more about VisitEngland Quality Standards and assessment visit
www.visitenglandassessmentservices.com

Pledge to make the countryside bloom

The David Bellamy Blooming Marvellous Pledge for Nature celebrates the work that camping, caravanning, holiday and home parks across the country are doing for wildlife. Formerly the David Bellamy Conservation Award, it's a new way to highlight those parks that are committed to doing the right thing:

The pledge is an exciting initiative that lets holiday and home parks show the world how dedicated they are to helping Britain's wildlife.

All parks that make the pledge commit themselves to:
- ✔ Improving their existing habitats for wildlife
- ✔ Creating new wildlife habitats and features where possible
- ✔ Managing their green space in as environmentally friendly a way as possible
- ✔ Involving their guests and staff in wildlife conservation
- ✔ Engaging with local conservation bodies and projects

Each year, the parks must also commit to starting at least one big project to help nature. Past challenges include projects such as tree planting, creating a pond, putting up bird boxes, championing a specific species and putting in a pollinator patch.

The Blooming Marvellous Pledge builds on the amazing work done by parks under the David Bellamy Conservation Award Scheme, which ran for over 25 years. The Scheme was set up by the British Holiday and Home Parks Association (BH&HPA) and Professor David Bellamy, who was one of the UK's leading environmentalists. The Pledge honours his legacy and his practical and pragmatic approach to nature conservation. David dedicated his life to encouraging people to get out into the countryside so that they could experience and value nature. The pledge continues this vital work.

Over 400 parks have signed up to the pledge this year. To discover some of those parks which have, look out for the pledge logo (shown below) throughout the guide. The symbol we show indicate parks signed-up to the Pledge by the end of June 2024

For more information, visit:
www.ukparks.com/bellamy-parks.php

The Best of British Parks

The Best of British Touring and Holiday Parks Group is an elite group of prestigious privately owned parks throughout the UK, providing you with a variety of holiday options – touring pitches for caravans, motorhomes and tents, glamping, self-catering camping pods or lodges and caravan holiday homes to hire or own – all with the reassurance of The Best of British brand and exceptional customer service.

The Best of British parks are family-run and committed to providing the highest level of quality and customer service to their visitors. You will experience first class service as well as clean, well maintained facilities throughout. With almost 45 holiday parks, caravan and camping sites, you won't be short of options for somewhere new to explore on your next camping trip. From clifftop campsites on the Jurassic Coast, to luxury holiday parks hidden away in the Welsh valleys, you will discover an exciting new spot for your upcoming trip in the UK. There are more than 15 parks in coastal settings and a multitude set in the countryside.

Best of British quality criteria includes:
- Offering high quality facilities and amenities.
- Assuring the highest standards of customer service possible.
- Providing customers additional and special attention to make them welcome on arrival at the park and throughout their stay.
- Maintaining either a 5 star award from their Tourist Board, or an AA 5 Star award with a percentage score of 85% or more.

A commitment to providing the highest quality standards is a prerequisite for membership of Best of British and all member parks undergo a quality inspection.

Look out for the logo, shown right, throughout the guide to find which parks are Best of British members. For more information, visit www.bob.org.uk

Wooda Farm Holiday Park, Bude

Useful information

Booking information
It is advisable to book in advance during peak holiday seasons and in school or public holidays. It is also wise to check whether or not a reservation entitles you to a particular pitch. It does not necessarily follow that an early booking will secure the best pitch; you may simply have the choice of what is available at the time you check in.

Some parks may require a deposit on booking which may be non-returnable if you have to cancel your holiday. If you do have to cancel, notify the proprietor at once because you may be held legally responsible for partial or full payment unless the pitch can be re-let. Consider taking out insurance such as AA Travel Insurance: visit theAA.com/travel-insurance for details. Some parks will not accept overnight bookings unless payment for the full minimum period (e.g. two or three days) is made.

Last arrival Unless otherwise stated, parks will usually accept arrivals at any time of the day or night, but some have a special 'late arrivals' enclosure where you have to make temporary camp to avoid disturbing other people on the park. Please note that on some parks, access to the toilet block is by key or pass card only, so if you know you will be late, do check what arrangements can be made.

Last departure Most parks will specify their latest departure time. Do check with the park if this is not given. If you overstay the departure time you could be charged for an extra day.

Chemical closet disposal point
You will usually find one on every park, except those catering only for tents. It must be a specially constructed unit, or a toilet permanently set aside for the purpose of chemical disposal and with adjacent rinsing and soak-away facilities. However, some local authorities are concerned about the effect of chemicals on bacteria in cesspools etc, and may prohibit or restrict provision of chemical closet disposal points in their areas.

Complaints
If you have any complaints speak to the park proprietor or supervisor immediately, so that the matter can be sorted out on the spot. If this personal approach fails you may decide, if the matter is serious, to approach the local authority or tourist board. AA guide users may also write to:

The Caravan & Camping Scheme Co-ordinator,
AA Media, Grove House, Lutyens Close,
Lychpit, Basingstoke RG24 8AG

AA Media may at its sole discretion investigate any complaints received from guide users for the purpose of making any necessary amendments to the guide. AA Media will not in any circumstances act as representative or negotiator or undertake to obtain compensation or enter into further correspondence or deal with the matter in any other way whatsoever. AA Media will not guarantee to take any specific action.

Dogs
Dogs may or may not be accepted at parks; this is entirely at the owner's or warden's discretion (assistance dogs should be accepted). Even when the park states that they accept dogs, it is still discretionary, and certain breeds may not be considered as suitable, so we strongly advise that you check when you book. Some sites have told us they do not accept dangerous breeds. (The following breeds are included in the Dangerous Dogs Act 1991 – Pit Bull Terrier, Japanese Tosa, Dogo Argentino, Fila Brasileiro and XL Bully). Dogs should always be kept on a lead and under control, and letting them sleep in cars is not encouraged.

Electric hook-up
Many parks have electric hook-ups on some, or all, of their pitches; if you need an electric connection you should request it when making your booking. Generally the voltage is 240v AC, 50 cycles, although this can vary slightly according to the location. The supply can vary considerably from 5 amps to 16 amps although 16 amps is becoming the norm – again you should check with the campsite if this is important to you. Remember, if your consumption is greater than the supply the electricity will trip out and need resetting.

Electric hook-up connections are now standardised in the UK with the blue coloured safety connectors. However, it is good practice to always connect your cable to your caravan, motorhome or tent electric distribution unit **before** connecting to the hook-up supply.

It is also important that tents or trailer tents have a Residual Circuit Device (RCD) for safety reasons and to avoid overloading the circuit. Caravans and motorhomes have RCDs built in. You should remember that if your RCD trips out at 16 amps and the campsite supply is say 10 amps you can easily overload the supply and cause the hook-up to trip out.

It is quite easy to check what demands your appliances can place on the supply at any one time. Details are normally available in the caravan or motorhome handbooks which show the wattage of appliances fitted.

The amperage used is based on the wattage of appliance divided by the supply voltage.

The following table is a quick check of electrical consumption, depending what is switched on.

Average amperage (based on a 240v supply)	
Caravan fridge (125 watts)	0.5 amps
Caravan heater set at (500 watts)	2.1 amps
Caravan heater set at (1000 watts)	4.2 amps
Caravan heater set at (2000 watts)	8.4 amps
Caravan water heater (850 watts)	3.5 amps
Kettle (domestic type) (1500 watts)	6.3 amps
Kettle (low wattage type) (750 watts)	3.1 amps
Hairdryer (2100 watts)	8.8 amps
Microwave (750 watts)	3.1 amps
TV (flat-screen LED type) (30 watts)	0.13 amps
Battery charger (built-in type) (200 watts)	0.8 amps

Island locations
The island locations listed in this guide may have different rules and regulations for caravanning and camping. If unsure, always call ahead of your trip to check.

Motorhomes
At some parks motorhomes are only accepted if they remain static throughout the stay. Also check that there are suitable level pitches at the parks where you plan to stay.

Overflow pitches
Campsites are legally entitled to use an overflow field which is not a normal part of their camping area for up to 28 days in any one year as an emergency method of coping with additional numbers at busy periods. When this 28-day rule is being invoked site owners should increase the numbers of sanitary facilities accordingly. In these circumstances the extra facilities are sometimes no more than temporary portacabins.

Parking
Some park operators insist that cars are left in a parking area separate from the pitches; others will not allow more than one car to be parked beside each caravan, tent or glamping unit.

Park restrictions
Many parks in our guide are selective about the categories of people they will accept on their parks. In the caravan and camping world there are many restrictions and some categories of visitor are banned altogether. Where a park has told us of a restriction/s this is included in the notes in their entry.

On many parks in this guide, unaccompanied young people, single-sex groups, single adults, and motorcycle groups will not be accepted. AA Media takes no stance in this matter, basing its Star classification on facilities, quality and maintenance. On the other hand, some parks cater well for teenagers and offer magnificent sporting and leisure facilities as well as lively entertainment events; others have only very simple amenities. A small number of parks in our guide exclude all children in order to create an environment aimed at holidaymakers in search of total peace and quiet (see page 44).

Seasonal touring pitches
Some park operators allocate a number of their hardstanding pitches for long-term seasonal caravans. These pitches can be reserved for the whole period the campsite is open, generally between Easter and September, and a fixed fee is charged for keeping the caravan on the park for the season. These pitches are in great demand, especially in popular tourist areas, so enquire well in advance if you wish to book one.

Shops
The range of provisions in shops is usually in proportion to the park's size. As far as AA Star requirements are concerned, a mobile shop calling several times a week, or a general store within easy walking distance of the park is acceptable.

First time campers checklist

Key: C = caravans   M = motorhomes   T = tents

Before you leave home or the site (hitching)

★ Before you go away for the first time practise putting up your tent; hitching and unhitching your caravan; reversing your motorhome or towed van into an enclosed space. **(CMT)**

★ Make a list of all the essentials you need to take with you. Mains lead, gas cylinder, levelling ramps and/or chocks... all the way through to small essentials like a box of matches, spare fuses, and a torch (check batteries). **(CMT)**

★ Check all interior items are safely stored, cupboards closed, all interior electrics are set correctly, turn off gas bottles, make sure roof lights and windows are closed and the external door is locked. **(CM)**

★ Empty fresh and waste water containers and toilet cassettes. **(CM)**

★ Check that corner steadies are raised tightly, and chocks and steps stowed. **(C)**

★ Connect tow bracket electric plugs, check that the breakaway safety cable is connected and, if used, that the anti-snake device is fitted correctly. **(C)**

★ Check the caravan's noseweight. **(C)**

★ Adjust the hitch height – i.e. above the car's towball. **(C)**

★ Secure the hitch on the towball. **(C)**

Trevalgan Touring Park, St Ives

★ Use the jockey wheel to raise the car about 2.5cm to ensure the caravan and car are properly coupled. If fitted, also check the tow hitch indicator (green = correctly coupled). **(C)**

★ Raise the jockey wheel and lock in position. **(C)**

★ Check that the caravan number plate is secure (and that it replicates the towing vehicle's number plate). **(C)**

★ Ask another person to stand behind the caravan or motorhome to check all the lights and indicators work. **(CM)**

★ On leaving a site disconnect the hook-ups and make that final check of the empty pitch. **(CMT)**

Arriving at your destination (unhitching)

★ Tell the site this is your first time. They're more likely to go out of their way to help. **(CMT)**

★ Listen to what the site staff tell you when you arrive (if you're a family, it's a good idea for you all to step into reception — that way you all understand the same message). **(CMT)**

★ Check caravan handbrake is on, chocks are in place and corner steadies are lowered. **(C)**

★ Lower jockey wheel and level the caravan and then lock in place. **(C)**

★ Give everyone in the family designated tasks when you arrive on site (finding the way to the toilet block, locating the nearest fresh water point etc). **(CMT)**

★ Get to know your surroundings. An early-evening stroll around any campsite is a great opportunity to check out the facilities. **(CMT)**

★ Say hello to your neighbours. They might just come in handy, and who knows you might a make a lot of new friends. **(CMT)**

DON'T churn up the grass. You're only ruining things for subsequent visitors. If you have a bit of a mishap, let the staff know so they can rectify things as soon as possible.

And finally **DON'T** be afraid to ask. All the campsites in this guide are adept at helping first-timers — most will happily guide you to your pitch if you ask. Although you'll soon find your fellow campers are happy to chip in and help out, too.

There's even more useful information on how to safely tow a caravan or trailer at: www.theaa.com/driving-advice/safety/how-to-tow-a-caravan

Broadhembury Caravan & Camping Park, Ashford

AA CARAVAN & CAMPING AWARD WINNERS 2024–25

WALES & OVERALL CAMPSITE OF THE YEAR

TYDDYN ISAF CARAVAN PARK
★★★★★

DULAS, ISLE OF ANGLESEY, page 292

This is a beautifully situated family park on rising ground adjacent to a sandy beach with magnificent views overlooking Lligwy Bay. A memorable holiday destination, it has been in the Mount family since 1975, with daughter Haley and husband Simon continuing the family tradition of excellent hospitality and service. Due to the undulating nature of the park, quality hardstanding pitches, most fully serviced and offering excellent privacy, have been created ensuring all have stunning coastal and country views – the sunsets here are particularly spectacular. In addition to superb amenity blocks, all with excellent privacy cubicles, guests can unwind and indulge at very smart Grazing Ground, a new coffee lounge and bar serving pastries and snacks all day, best enjoyed on the alfresco terrace with views of the Anglesey coastline. A fabulous reception building opened in 2024, with a shop, the Y Mochyn Bach takeaway offering wood-fired pizzas, and upstairs is a gym and a business centre, with high-speed internet. Sustainability and conservation are taken very seriously – there are 200 solar panels powering all the buildings, and 8,500 trees were planted in 1992, and this now mature woodland is a peaceful haven for guests to discover the rich flora and fauna. Wildflower meadows and a private footpath to the beach complete the impressive picture.

SCOTLAND & NORTHERN IRELAND

WITCHES CRAIG CARAVAN & CAMPING PARK
★★★★

BLAIRLOGIE, STIRLING, page 285

In an attractive setting, deep in 'Braveheart' country, this extremely well-presented park stands at the foot of the dramatic Ochil Hills, which form an impressive backdrop to the park. Witches Craig has been tastefully developed by the Dewar family, and the mature landscaping and beautifully maintained grounds continue to impress our inspector, with the terrific displays of colourful shrubs and plants, all lovingly cared for by Veda Dewar. The attention to detail across the park is superb, especially within the immaculate toilet block, and the quirky metal statues and themed carvings from tree trunks that stand around the park. The touring pitches are all on large hardstandings and set in small areas to provide a feeling of seclusion, while tents are in a large, well-drained field to the rear of the site, replete with cooking shelters and picnic benches. First time visitors or campers that have been visiting the site since childhood, as many customers have, are guaranteed of a warm and friendly welcome from Veda and her staff. A regular local bus service to Stirling passes the site entrance and many of the historical sites are just a short drive away. This is not a big site (it does have a bar and swimming pool) but a very popular family-owned park that attracts customers on a regular basis to this stunning area.

Following nominations by our inspectors, we award an overall winner from three national finalists, five regional winners, a holiday park winner, glamping-only site winner plus a NEW sustainable park winner – all selected for their outstanding overall quality and high levels of customer care. Our two special awards recognise the best small campsite and the most improved campsite.

ENGLAND & NORTH WEST REGION

SKELWITH FOLD CARAVAN PARK
★★★★★

AMBLESIDE, CUMBRIA, page 92

In the grounds of a former mansion, hidden away in a beautiful setting close to Lake Windermere, Skelwith Fold is very much in tune with the 130 acres of natural oak woodland in which it sits and through which a network of paths has been created for guests to enjoy. Very high quality is at the forefront of every aspect of the park, which, aligned with year-on-year investment and excellent maintenance standards, continues to impress our inspector at every annual visit. The needs of tourers are met through generously sized hardstanding pitches in peaceful woodland glades, and there are first-class toilets for the able and less able, as well as outstanding private family facilities. The views of nearby Loughrigg Fell from the five-acre family recreation space are truly outstanding, as is the children's adventure play area. Wildlife watching (private tarn and nature hide) and walking are readily available within the park, and the luxurious Safari Suites (with hot tubs) and Hideaway pods, with every amenity, are in a prime location for watching wildlife; all are for hire. Skelwith Fold is a unique blend of sublime rural idyll and modern and extremely high-quality amenities that deliver exactly what the discerning visitor is looking for in the beautiful Lake District National Park. There truly is something for everybody here. Worthy winner of the AA England & North West award.

NORTH EAST ENGLAND

COTE GHYLL CAMPING & CARAVAN PARK
★★★★★

OSMOTHERLEY, NORTH YORKSHIRE, page 249

A quiet, peaceful site secluded in a pleasant valley within walking distance of pretty Osmotherley village and just minutes from the glorious North Yorkshire Moors. It is the perfect base for active guests, with pony trekking, mountain biking and excellent moorland walking (Cleveland Way, Coast-to-Coast Path, Lyke Wake Walk) on the doorstep. It is also a great place to relax, as the park is south facing, well landscaped and divided into terraces bordered by woodland. It offers a good mix of grass and hardstanding pitches, with very spacious fully serviced pitches for larger units, and popular grass or hardstanding pitches for solo travellers. The well-appointed amenity blocks have underfloor heating, good privacy cubicles, and well-equipped family bathrooms; Cedar block was refurbished with an impressive new look for 2024. Youngsters can let off steam on the two first-class play areas, and Cod Beck, which flows through the park, is a great and safe place for children to paddle and have fun. Mature trees, shrubs and an abundance of seasonal floral displays create a relaxing and peaceful atmosphere, and the whole park is immaculately maintained. Under the same ownership, Cote Ghyll Mill near the park entrance houses a youth hostel and has a café/restaurant serving breakfasts and evening meals. This is an impressive park run by dedicated family owners.

AA CARAVAN & CAMPING AWARD WINNERS 2024—25

HEART OF ENGLAND

LONGNOR WOOD HOLIDAY PARK
★★★★★

LONGNOR, STAFFORDSHIRE, page 217

Off the beaten track down a long drive and enjoying a secluded and very peaceful setting in the heart of the Peak District National Park, this spacious adults-only park is a hidden gem. Surrounded by meadows and beautiful rolling countryside and sheltered by woodland where there are walks to enjoy and lots of wildlife to observe. In 2022, the owners of AA 5-star rated Herding Hill Farm (camping and glamping) in Northumberland bought this park and have since invested in significant improvements, although they did keep the same management team, including James O'Neill, son of the former owner. Guests can expect a warm, friendly welcome and a high standard to customer care. A large lodge has been transformed into smart games room with a professional-grade pool table, darts board and a selection of classic board games, and there's also a modern, fully equipped gym. Recent developments include a sauna, available for the exclusive hire of two adults, and the luxury one-bedroom Chatsworth Lodges with hot tubs. The excellent facilities are well maintained and include a spotlessly clean amenity block with privacy cubicles, a good range of spacious hardstanding pitches (nine fully serviced), and high levels of security. Dogs are very welcome — they can stay for free in the glamping pods, static caravans and some of the lodges, and there's a dog wash and 4-acre dog walk.

SOUTH EAST ENGLAND

CONCIERGE CAMPING
★★★★★

CHICHESTER, WEST SUSSEX, page 228

A stunning park occupying two meadows adjoining Guy and Tracey Hodgkin's home close to Chichester Harbour and the South Downs. Developing the innovative and ground-breaking 'Concierge' concept has been a labour of love for the past 10 years. The result is a first-class, small park for 37 units and the attention to detail throughout is hugely impressive. Everything is high spec, from very spacious pitches and the reception, replete with a shop that sells local produce, coffee, drinks, late-arrival and breakfast hampers, to the smart covered rear terrace with adjoining bar and excellent Notso & Notdough, a twist on Asian and Japanese street food, and the state-of-the-art amenity block. Here, you'll find ultra-efficient rain showers, piped radio, Ratham Estate toiletries and an excellent disabled/family room. Gladiator pitches have a mini-safari tent living space with a wood-fired oven, Smart TV and a Nespresso machine. Ten unique Emperor pitches were added in 2024 for the ultimate 'Concierge' experience. Set in an adjoining meadow, they come with a stunning day-living cabin with en suite bathroom, a stylish, fully fitted kitchen with log-burning cooker, and spacious dining areas inside and outside on a decked area. A tranquil wooded area next to the stream has been cleared to create a natural, shady outside 'lounge area' — a real treat for guests. This is one of Britain's top parks.

SOUTH WEST ENGLAND

WOODOVIS PARK
★★★★★

TAVISTOCK, DEVON, page 127

Peacefully located at the end of a private, half-mile, tree-lined drive in a remote woodland setting on the edge of the Tamar Valley, Woodovis Park offers superb on-site facilities and high levels of customer care from the family owners who really care deeply about the place. Our inspector commented "no surprise to find the whole park in excellent shape, exemplifying the diligence and commitment which underpins all aspects of the operation". All developments are carefully considered and in keeping with the relaxed and natural feel of the park. Upgraded to 5-Star Platinum status in 2022, the park continues to impress thanks to the dedicated, hands-on approach of Anthony Ell and his excellent team, and sound investment across the park. Recent additions include a Doggie Spa, with organic shampoo, warm water and a hairdryer for canine visitors; a bike wash with jet wash and bike-cleaning tools; and a Snack Shack serving evening food and breakfast rolls at weekends. The toilets are immaculate, plus there is an indoor swimming pool, sauna, well-stocked shop, good information and games rooms, a campers' kitchen with pizza oven, and children's activities such as circus-skills workshops and storytelling, all creating a friendly atmosphere. There's a real commitment to sustainability here too, with their own fresh water bore hole and a solar farm producing enough power for the whole park.

NEW – SUSTAINABLE PARK OF THE YEAR

OLD OAKS TOURING & GLAMPING
★★★★★

GLASTONBURY, SOMERSET, page 212

'Wow! What an excellent offering paired with great pride from James and Tara White, a real pleasure to visit' stated our inspector. Located close to Glastonbury Tor and with panoramic views towards the Mendip Hills, Old Oaks Touring & Glamping is an exceptional, adults-only park divided up into several beautifully landscaped areas with superb touring pitches, luxury glamping accommodation and top-class facilities. Sustainability is at the heart of the business; James and Tara have developed the park with ecology at the forefront of everything that they do, minimizing the impact on resources while enhancing the natural environment in and around the park. The smart facility blocks have been built using traditional materials and the latest energy efficient technologies, including solar thermal hot water systems, heat recovery systems, air source heat pumps, and low energy LED lighting. The solar farm generates 60% of the park's electricity. A Victorian-style reed bed, a predecessor to their new sewage treatment plant, filters wastewater from the plant in a natural, chemical-free process whilst providing an excellent habitat for wildlife. Their commitment to the environment also includes using electric park vehicles and mowers; locally-sourced shop produce; and beekeeping courses. It's the perfect 'get away from it all' spot where you can enjoy outdoor pursuits or simply relaxing.

AA CARAVAN & CAMPING AWARD WINNERS 2024–25

HOLIDAY PARK OF THE YEAR

TREVORNICK
★★★★★

HOLYWELL BAY, CORNWALL, page 66

Having bought Trevornick Farm in the early 1960s and inherited the annual Scout Jamboree camp in the dunes behind Holywell Bay, owner Mike Hartley soon realised what a plum spot he'd acquired. The site was nudging the beach and Newquay was a burgeoning surf town. He welcomed his first paying customers to camp on the farm in the summer of 1963 and, as they say, the rest is history. Sixty years on, sons Robert and Richard continue the family tradition, but much has changed since those early days. Making the most of its stunning coastal location, just a 15-minute footpath walk to the beach, it's now a large seaside complex with a focus on offering a full holiday experience for all the family. The breadth of appeal is a significant asset here with something for everyone and all budgets, allied with an exceptional array of facilities, from a children's club, indoor and outdoor play areas, amusement arcade, forest trail to a superb pool complex with spa room, evening cabaret and a range of eating venues. There's a real sense of pride underpinning all aspects here and year-on-year improvements highlight the progressive approach and continued investment across the park. There's an excellent range of touring and camping pitches, 36 ready-erected Euro tents and luxury static caravans for hire. Well worthy of its 5 Platinum Stars and the award of Holiday Park of the Year.

GLAMPING SITE OF THE YEAR

HADSPEN GLAMPING
★★★★★

CASTLE CARY, SOMERSET, page 209

'Disconnect with city life, reconnect with nature and unwind in luxury' sums up the ethos of this idyllic, get-away haven deep in the Somerset countryside close to Castle Cary. Set on a hillside with stunning views, the three beautifully furnished canvas eco-lodges welcomed their first guests in May 2023. Sustainability is at the heart of this unique off-grid glamping experience, successfully providing all the comforts of home without mains gas or electricity; the lodges are lit with solar power and heated with sustainable wood-fired stoves and LPG gas. Firewood comes from their own woodland, water from a private borehole, and there is no WiFi. Each lodge is individually designed and decorated — Horscombe sleeps up to four; Lime Kiln up to five; Grisway up to seven; and all have outdoor wood-fired hot tubs. They have very stylish open-plan living areas, fully equipped kitchens, en suite shower rooms, and a veranda with a barbecue. There's excellent food (breakfast/picnic) and drinks' hampers, sourced from local farm shops, which can be pre-booked when finalising your stay. Next door is the award-winning Newt (membership required), set in the grounds of Hadspen House, with its garden café, farm shop and magnificent gardens. Pick-ups and drop-offs from Castle Cary Station (2.8 miles) can be arranged. Hadspen is our stand-out glamping site for 2024–25.

SMALL CAMPSITE OF THE YEAR

KILLERBY OLD HALL COTTAGES & CARAVAN SITE
★★★★

SCARBOROUGH, NORTH YORKSHIRE, page 251

Set within 13 acres of parkland between the coastal resorts of Scarborough and Filey, Killerby Old Hall, with its courtyard holiday cottages, luxury lakeside lodges and beautifully maintained small caravan park is the ideal destination for a relaxing rural break in the Yorkshire countryside. Run by Shaun and Babette Pye, the peaceful 47-pitch caravan park is tucked away at the rear of the hall and is sheltered by mature trees and shrubs. All pitches are spacious, well-presented hardstandings, of which 28 are fully serviced, and all have electric hook-ups and a digital TV feed. The modern amenity blocks are well equipped and there's also a laundry room, and a large, easy to access motorhome service point. The outdoor children's play park is a special feature, and the indoor heated swimming pool situated within the beautiful grounds can be booked for an extra charge. The Nine Eighty Bistro & Bar is a cosy, comfortable and appealing space with characterful decor. It's a real bonus having this eatery on site – it serves breakfast, brunch and baked items every day; cocktails, pizzas and small plates Thursday to Saturday evenings; and traditional Sunday lunches too. The glamping field is a beautiful and serene space with six large, well-spaced and smartly equipped en suite lodges set around a small lake.

MOST IMPROVED CAMPSITE

PARK FOOT HOLIDAY PARK
★★★★★

POOLEY BRIDGE, CUMBRIA, page 99

In a stunning location, surrounded by dramatic fells and overlooking Lake Ullswater, Park Foot Holiday Park provides the perfect base for exploring the Lake District. Set on the shores of Ullswater, it offers a superb and memorable holiday destination for families who wish to enjoy a range of activities in a naturally beautiful area, whilst benefiting from excellent on-site facilities. Serious ongoing investment by the Allen family, who have owned Park Foot since 1951, has resulted in significant improvements across the park during 2023/24 to enhance guests' experiences. A well-designed lodge development is a recent addition which expands the accommodation on offer, and a new toilet and shower block in Lakeside Field will be open for the 2025 season. A lakeside jetty was built to improve the launching facilities for boats, canoes and paddle boards, while the 2024 season saw the opening of the Ninja Trail adventure playground and the creation of fully serviced super pitches in Sandall Field. There is a new outdoor seating area with a stone bridge that provides a link to the shop and reception; two electric vehicle chargers installed near the reception, and wildflower planting and beehives have added further interest. Although well-established owners, the Allen family are still investing in the future and improving the overall quality of the park.

SPOTLIGHT ON

THE QUIET SITE
Overall Campsite of the Year 2023–24 and 'going green'

TURNING DOWN THE VOLUME ON
ENVIRONMENTAL IMPACT

Is The Quiet Site England's greenest holiday park? David Hancock visited the park to find out how they are achieving exceptional results when it comes to 'going green'.

A meandering narrow road gently climbs up from the banks of Ullswater, creating a real feeling of anticipation, and on arrival at the aptly named Quiet Site – winner of the AA England & Overall Campsite of the Year 2023–24 – you'll find a wonderful park where you can savour the stunning views of the lake and surrounding fells.

Equally impressive as gaining the AA's top accolade, is owner Daniel Holder's commendable ethos to sustainability and for achieving such exemplary standards in transforming The Quiet Site into one of the greenest parks in the country. In 2020, it was the first-ever holiday park to win the Queens Award for Enterprise, Sustainable Development. The standards reached by Daniel and his team are exemplary and have totally transformed this site.

Going quietly greener – developing a sustainable park

Following a successful career in electrical engineering, developing lithium batteries, Daniel bought The Quiet Site in 1985 and has since transformed it from a simple campsite to one of AA's award-winning 5 Platinum Star parks, with sustainability at the heart of everything he has achieved on the park.

Daniel says 'We have spent the last two decades making both business and investment choices based on a desire to be fully sustainable. In doing so, we consider our place in the community, our impacts on biodiversity as well as our embedded and operational footprints.'

To achieve his goal, Daniel has invested heavily in green technology, so the park is now 90% energy self-sufficient by using solar panels, a biomass boiler and three ground-source heat pumps, all smartly hidden,

Recycled 30% of site's grey water

Reduced energy use by 20% (over 10 years)

Reduced water use by 6%

Reduced site waste by 15%

Planted over 10,000 trees

which heat all the water used across the site. The last gas boiler was replaced with a sustainable heat pump in June 2023 and Daniel believes biomass is now a transitional fuel which will be replaced with hydrogen within the next decade.

The 20-year sustainable journey

Time invested in innovative ways to become increasingly ethical, responsible and sustainable has had a very positive impact in limiting both the guests' and site's carbon footprint. It must be said that the results are very impressive. The park has achieved carbon neutral status: they have reduced energy use by 20% in the last 10 years, they recycle 30% of the site's grey water, they have reduced water use by 6%, despite growing the business and occupancy, and have reduced waste from the site by 15%.

In addition, The Quiet Site team has planted over 10,000 trees, installed four reed beds, created wildflower meadows and nature corridors, built bird boxes and bee hotels and significantly increased biodiversity across the site. There is also an off-grid wood-fired takeaway, The Quiet Bite, serving bacon rolls and pizzas, an excellent recycling zone, electric vehicle charging points, bike hire, and a zero-waste shop selling only local produce and ethical, sustainable products.

Carbon neutral glamping

In addition to offering spacious terraced pitches — with glorious fell and lake views — for caravans, motorhomes and tents, there are fantastic glamping options be found at the top of the park, including posh camping pods and cabins, 15 unique Glamping Burrows (Hobbit Holes), and 15 quirky Gingerbread Houses. All were built by Daniel and his on-site team.

Many of these units are energy positive. This simply means they generate more energy than they use, having been designed to operate efficiently in both hot and cool weather. Good insulation, heating by solar panels and shade from hedges means that during recent heatwaves the temperature inside the units was close to half that of the outside. By contrast, the humble static caravan, designed over 50 years ago and now dominating the industry (and the landscape), is difficult to heat sustainably in the winter, and they become an uninhabitable heat trap in the summer, which will only get worse as the climate warms up.

Virtually invisible within the gorgeous Lake District landscape, unless you know where to look, are the bespoke glamping units called the Burrows — large underground living spaces with amazing views over the Ullswater Valley; all are very secure, superbly insulated by soil and grass, and very energy efficient. Equally unusual as these units are the Gingerbread Houses, added in 2021. These carbon positive spaces have photovoltaic (PV) panelled roofs, triple insulation and ground-source heating. They are also surrounded by a ginger beech hedge.

Zero waste shopping

The shop on the site sells a wide range of items, from bamboo toothbrushes to house plants, and there's no plastic packaging to be seen. Milk and orange juice comes in reusable glass with a European-style deposit scheme. Local cheeses have their own wax skins, and a gravity dispenser is used for cereals, rice, nuts and dried fruit — just bring your own containers or use a provided paper bag.

Sustainable Integrated Transport Ullswater (SITU)

SITU was formed in 2021 by Ullswater residents who wanted to see a sustainable and integrated transport system for the Ullswater Valley that would benefit residents, local businesses and visitors to the area. Daniel is a key member of this forward-thinking group who are actively working on a variety of projects with local communities, farmers, landowners, local authorities and relevant agencies to reduce the adverse impact that transport can have on the environment and its residents, as well as increasing road safety.

> "...we consider our place in the community, our impacts on biodiversity as well as our embedded and operational footprints."

Having created the five-mile Eamont Way footpath that links Penrith railway station and Pooley Bridge, the Ullswater Bus was launched in July 2023, initially as a weekend-only scheme. In 2024, the service expanded to two buses that run from late March to early November, including weekends and bank holidays. The 16-seater buses follow three routes that are designed to link with the valley attractions and various accommodation sites, including The Quiet Site, and with the 508 Stagecoach service between Penrith and Windermere, and the Ullswater Steamers.

You can pick up the bus from the entrance of the park and wind down the narrow lanes to Pooley Bridge or stay on the bus to Lowther Castle and spend the day exploring the castle and its surrounding 130 acres. Then, either return by bus, or walk over Askham Fell back to Ullswater, and then wait for the bus to take you back to The Quiet Site for a well-earned meal in the bar.

Ultimately, the aim is to significantly reduce the number of cars using the roads in the Ullswater Valley, especially in the busy summer months, encouraging people to arrive by train or to park in Penrith and explore Ullswater by 'Bike, Boot, Bus or Boat'.

A green vision of 'quiet' sustainability

As Daniel says 'Designing to abolish waste and pollution, keeping materials in use for longer and using renewable energy sources doesn't sound too hard, does it? There needs to be a balance between how we operate our business, our customers' behaviour towards the environment, and the community in which we are located. Operating as a carbon neutral business is just the beginning of our quest to become truly sustainable.'

An ambition we're sure he'll achieve before very long.

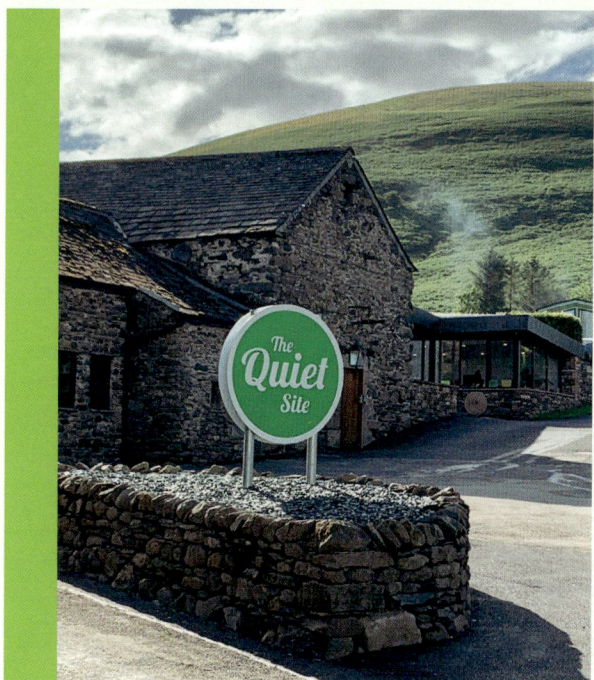

The best sites for...

If you're looking for a site with a specific feature or quality, check out the following recommendations

THE BEST ECO-FRIENDLY CAMPSITES

Reduce your carbon footprint as these green campsites and glamping sites — all are very eco-conscious, with conservation and sustainability at the heart of the business. Some are off-grid, using solar power and LED lighting and wood sourced from their land; others have state-of-the-art amenity blocks, are heated by biomass boilers or ground source heat pumps, have farm shops selling home-reared or local produce, and a growing number now offer electric car charging points.

THE QUIET SITE
Watermillock, Cumbria, page 101
A lovely site with stunning views across Ullswater from terraced pitches, camping pods and comfortable Hobbit Holes. Sustainability is at the heart of the park; solar, biomass and ground source heat energy; reedbed water treatment; wild meadow walks and a zero-waste shop.

WOODOVIS PARK
Tavistock, Devon, page 127
A stunning park in a remote woodland setting on the edge of the Tamar Valley. There's a real commitment to sustainability here, with their own water bore hole, and solar panels that produce enough power for the whole park.

FEN FARM CARAVAN SITE
Mersea Island, Essex, page 151
Set beside the Blackwater Estuary, Fen Farm has a unique atmosphere with a mixture of meadow, woodland and marine shore, and varied wildlife to match each environment. There are two excellent solar-heated toilet blocks, a woodland dog walk, and an electric car charging point.

EYE KETTLEBY LAKES
Melton Mowbray, Leicestershire, page 173
A haven for lovers of coarse fishing and walking, this quality touring and lodge park has very impressive eco-credentials — notably a wind turbine and solar farm (300 panels) providing electricity, air-source heating in the toilet blocks and excellent planting and wildlife schemes.

HADSPEN GLAMPING
Castle Cary, Somerset, page 209
'Disconnect with city life, reconnect with nature and unwind in luxury' at this idyllic Somerset haven next door to The Newt country estate. Three individually decorated, off-grid, canvas eco-lodges use solar power, LED lighting, and firewood from the estate heats the hot tubs.

BROOK LODGE FARM
Cowslip Green, Somerset, page 210
In a sheltered Mendip Hills setting, this peaceful park is run by owners who are keen on preserving the site's environment and to increase both the flora and fauna in a natural habitat. Green tourism award

Hadspen Glamping, Castle Cary

Old Oaks Touring & Glamping, Glastonbury

winners, they have a wildlife corridor, bat boxes, a tree conservation area, and solar-powered heated water.

OLD OAKS TOURING & GLAMPING
Glastonbury, Somerset, page 212
An exceptional, long-established touring and glamping park built around a strong green ethos. Facility blocks use the latest energy efficient technologies, and the former Victorian-style reedbed treatment area has been transformed into stunning wildlife area for guests to enjoy.

CONCIERGE CAMPING & GLAMPING
Chichester, West Sussex, pages 228–229
A stunning, high-spec park developed with meticulous attention to detail by forward-thinking owners. It has an impressive, state-of-the-art amenity block with solar panels, innovative heat pump technology and sensor showers, plus electric car charging points and a shop selling only local produce.

LORDSTONES COUNTRY PARK
Chop Gate, North Yorkshire, page 241
A privately-owned country park high in the North York Moors with a quality farm shop selling estate produce, a café-restaurant and a small camping-cum-glamping park — bell tents, bothy tents, yurts and luxury wooden pods — surrounded by ponds and wildlife.

FLAXTON MEADOWS
York, North Yorkshire, page 254
Eco-conscious Flaxton Meadows provides a peaceful retreat in a natural environment close to York. All the electricity, hot water and heating for both the tourers' amenity block and the luxury lodges (with hot tubs) are supplied by solar panels and ground source heat pumps.

RUNACH ARAINN
Kilmory, Isle of Arran, page 286
Hidden away in a secluded woodland setting, just a 15-minute walk from a lovely beach, this off-grid glamping site offers superb yurts with stylish interiors and private facilities for a truly exceptional stay. Fire pits and outdoor cooking facilities add to the overall charm.

CAERFAI BAY CARAVAN & TENT PARK
St Davids, Pembrokeshire, page 308
Magnificent coastal scenery can be enjoyed from this delightful site set on an organic farm. There are first-class solar-heated wetsuit shower rooms and toilet facilities, low level lighting to enable stargazing and an excellent farm shop too.

THE BEST FAMILY SITES

Many AA rated campsites, touring and holiday parks are ideal places for a family holiday experience. Here's our pick of the top-rated sites that have great facilities for children, and plenty for the grown-ups to do too.

Polmanter Touring Park, St Ives

TREVORNICK
Holywell Bay, Cornwall, page 66
A large seaside holiday complex full of entertainment for all the family, from a children's club, indoor and outdoor play areas, a sports field and amusement arcade to a forest trail and outdoor heated swimming pool. A sandy beach is just a 15-minute footpath walk away.

POLMANTER TOURING PARK
St Ives, Cornwall, page 82
Polmanter is an excellent choice for family holiday close to St Ives beaches. High quality is evident everywhere, from the soft play area for toddlers and the teenage hangout in the games room to the outdoor swimming pool and hard tennis courts, there's somewhere for guests of all ages to enjoy.

PARK FOOT HOLIDAY PARK
Pooley Bridge, Cumbria, page 99
A gorgeous location right beside Ullswater and the wonderful fells, this quality park is the perfect family holiday destination in the Lakes. As well as entertainment for all the family, children can enjoy the play areas, pony-trekking and water sports plus there are bikes to hire.

RIVER DART COUNTRY PARK
Ashburton, Devon, page 108
Set in 90 acres of magnificent parkland, this peaceful, hidden-away touring park offers numerous outdoor activities for all ages — abseiling, canoeing, bike trails, zip wire, play fort — plus Dartmoor is only a few minutes away.

CREALY THEME PARK & RESORT
Clyst St Mary, Devon, page 113
A quality family park situated adjacent to the popular Crealy Theme Park — free or discounted entry is available for all campers. There are luxury safari cabins and

spacious lodges with hot tubs for all the family to enjoy, and adventure golf and a multi-use games area.

WOODLANDS GROVE CARAVAN & CAMPING PARK
Dartmouth, Devon, page 114
Geared for families and set in an extensive woodland environment, this quality park offers free entry to the adjoining Woodlands Family Theme Park (fun rides and attractions across 11 play zones), which makes an this an excellent package holiday for families.

FRESHWATER BEACH HOLIDAY PARK
Bridport, Dorset, page 133
A family holiday centre sheltered by a sand bank and enjoying its own private beach. The park offers a wide variety of leisure and entertainment programmes for all the family, plus the Jurassic Fun Centre with an indoor pool, gym and six-lane bowling alley.

TANNER FARM TOURING CARAVAN & CAMPING PARK
Marden, Kent, page 163
At the heart of a 150-acre Wealden farm, this spacious and very peaceful touring park is perfect for families as it has two play areas, a football field, a recreation/wet room (with TV) and excellent country walks directly from the park. Marden station is three miles away for trips to London.

SILVERDALE HOLIDAY PARK
Silverdale, Lancashire, page 172
A superb family holiday destination overlooking Morecambe Bay. Children are well catered for whatever the weather with a 17-metre indoor swimming pool and toddler pool, a bowling alley with

amusements, a soft play area and two outdoor adventure playgrounds.

SEARLES LEISURE RESORT
Hunstanton, Norfolk, page 188
A long-established family-owned holiday complex with well managed facilities, adjacent to the sea and beach. Wide ranging indoor and outdoor activities include a kid's daytime programme, archery, outdoor adventure play parks, excellent swimming pools, and entertainment for all ages.

ORD HOUSE COUNTRY PARK
Berwick-upon-Tweed, Northumberland, page 193
Set within the grounds of 18th-century Ord House, this very well-run park really caters for youngsters — there's a fantastic adventure playground, mini golf, a football field, and a soft toy play area.

BEECRAIGS CARAVAN & CAMPING SITE
Linlithgow, West Lothian, page 282
Located on hills with unrivalled views towards the Forth Bridges, Beecraigs Country Park has an excellent caravan and camping site. There are extensive walks and cycle trails and a very large play area where kids can let off steam.

BLAIR CASTLE CARAVAN PARK
Blair Atholl, Perth & Kinross, page 282
An attractive site set in impressive seclusion within the Atholl Estate. Woodland walking and cycling trails (bike hire), family pods, and a huge central area with a children's play area, football pitch and putting green.

HOME FARM CARAVAN PARK
Marian-Glas, Isle of Anglesey, page 292
A first-class park set in an elevated and secluded position close to sandy beaches and with views of Snowdonia. There is a family bathroom, excellent indoor and outdoor play facilities, a tennis court, and a recreation and ball games area.

AERON COAST CARAVAN PARK
Aberaeron, Ceredigion, page 294
A well-managed family holiday park on the edge of the attractive resort of Aberaeron, with direct access to the beach. On-site facilities include an extensive outdoor pool complex, a multi-activity outdoor sports area, an indoor children's play area, a games room and an entertainment suite.

Crealy Theme Park & Resort, Clyst St Mary

THE BEST FOR WATERSIDE PITCHES

Spending time by a body of water, whether it be a lake, a river or the sea, is a great way to unwind and get in touch with nature. Here's a selection of great campsites that offer just that, a chance to pitch up by the water.

FIELDS END WATER CARAVAN PARK & FISHERY
Doddington, Cambridgeshire, page 51

A stunning, meticulously planned and well-executed park with a newly developed area set around a peaceful lake. Twenty fully serviced pitches and four en suite glamping pods are located beside the water, and a footbridge across the lake links one side with the first-class facilities block.

PORTH BEACH HOLIDAY PARK
Newquay, Cornwall, page 69

You can drink in the views and watch the Atlantic waves roll in from this attractive park set in a sheltered bay adjacent to Porth Beach. It's a stunning setting on the coast path close to Newquay – enjoy fabulous cliff walks or spend time surfing on nearby Fistral Beach.

SOUTH END CARAVAN PARK
Barrow-in-Furness, Cumbria, page 93

Situated on Walney Island, a small island off the beautiful Cumbrian coastline, this family-owned park makes the most of its stunning location – it's next to the sea and the marshes (abundant with birds) and enjoys fine views of the Lake District fells.

RIVERSIDE CARAVAN & CAMPING PARK
South Molton, Devon, page 126

A family-run park set alongside the River Mole and in 70 acres of landscaped parkland with 10 acres of woodland and riverside trails. Book one of the premium fully serviced or large grassy pitches set beside the river or one of the three large, peaceful fishing lakes.

GOLDEN CAP HOLIDAY PARK
Chideock, Dorset, page 136

A grassy site overlooking the sea and beach at Seatown and surrounded by National Trust land. The pitches closer to the sea at this uniquely placed park enjoy a spectacular outlook. The stunning cliff walks, notably the coast path up Golden Cap, are not for the faint-hearted though.

DACRE LAKESIDE PARK
Brandesburton, East Riding of Yorkshire, page 236

A large lake popular with water sports enthusiasts is the focal point of this grassy site, which offers seasonal and touring lakeside pitches. The stylish Bert's Pizzeria & Gelato overlooks the six-acre lake used for windsurfing, sailing, kayaking, canoeing and fishing.

NABURN LOCK CARAVAN PARK
Naburn, North Yorkshire, page 248

A mature, hedged park set beside the majestic River Ouse from where the river bus to nearby York leaves from a jetty beside the park. The riverside towpath provides excellent walking and cycling opportunities, and there's fishing from the private riverbank.

SLENINGFORD WATERMILL CARAVAN CAMPING PARK
North Stainley, North Yorkshire, page 248

The old watermill and the River Ure make an attractive setting for this touring park within easy reach of

Fields End Water Caravan Park & Fishery, Doddington

Golden Cap Holiday Park, Chideock

Harrogate and the Dales. Premium riverside pitches, scenic waterside walks, canoeing and fly fishing are available, plus the chance to see otters and dippers add to the appeal.

SEAL SHORE CAMPING AND TOURING SITE
Kildonan, Isle of Arran, page 286
In a truly magical location on the south coast of Arran with fabulous views across the water to Pladda Island and Ailsa Craig, this peaceful little site is set beside a sandy beach. Book early to bag a waterside pitch and expect to see seals and otters from your tent.

TYDDYN ISAF CARAVAN PARK
Dulas, Isle of Anglesey, page 292
A beautifully situated and very spacious family park on rising ground adjacent to a sandy beach, with magnificent views overlooking Lligwy Bay, best enjoyed from the restaurant terrace. A private footpath leads directly to the beach and there are two superb sea-view, Mediterranean-style beach huts.

RIVERSIDE CAMPING
Caernarfon, Gwynedd, page 299
Set in the grounds of a former garden centre and enjoying a superb location along the River Seiont, Riverside Camping certainly lives up to its name – open your tent or caravan door to the beautiful sight and sound of the Seiont from spacious waterside pitches. Fish in the river too, permits are available.

SKYSEA CAMPING & CARAVAN PARK
Port Eynon, Swansea, page 315
Set in an unrivalled location alongside the safe sandy beach of Port Eynon on the Gower Peninsula, this popular park is an ideal family holiday spot. Lush green sloping ground has been partially terraced to create excellent views of the beach, bay and surrounding cliffs.

RUSHIN HOUSE CARAVAN PARK
Belcoo, County Fermanagh, page 322
Occupying a scenic location overlooking Lough Macnean, this first-class park offers very generous, fully serviced pitches on a terrace overlooking the lough, a slipway providing boat access to the water and, of course, fishing; there is also an access path to the lake for less mobile visitors.

Sleningford Watermill Caravan & Camping Park, North Stainley

★★★★★ Platinum Parks

Platinum Parks are the very best sites in the UK, having achieved a 5-Star rating with a quality score of 95% and over.

ENGLAND

CAMBRIDGESHIRE
DODDINGTON
Fields End Water Caravan Park & Fishery

CORNWALL & ISLES OF SCILLY
BUDE
Wooda Farm Holiday Park
CARLYON BAY
Carlyon Bay Caravan & Camping Park
HOLYWELL BAY
Trevornick
NEWQUAY
Hendra Holiday Park
Treloy Touring Park
POLZEATH
Gunvenna Holiday Park
PORTHTOWAN
Porthtowan Tourist Park
PORTREATH
Landal Gwel an Mor
REDRUTH
Globe Vale Holiday Park
ST IVES
Ayr Holiday Park
Polmanter Touring Park
Trevalgan Touring Park
ST JUST-IN-ROSELAND
Trethem Mill Touring Park
WHITE CROSS
Piran Meadows Resort and Spa

CUMBRIA
AMBLESIDE
Skelwith Fold Caravan Park
KESWICK
Castlerigg Hall Caravan & Camping Park
WATERMILLOCK
The Quiet Site

DERBYSHIRE
ASHBOURNE
Rivendale Lodge Retreat

DEVON
AXMINSTER
Hawkchurch Resort & Spa
DAWLISH
Cofton Holidays
DREWSTEIGNTON
Woodland Springs Adult Touring Park
KINGSBRIDGE
Parkland Caravan and Camping Site
SAMPFORD PEVERELL
Minnows Touring Park
SIDMOUTH
Oakdown Holiday Park
SOUTH MOLTON
Riverside Caravan & Camping Park
TAVISTOCK
Woodovis Park

DORSET
BRIDPORT
Highlands End Holiday Park
POOLE
South Lytchett Manor Caravan & Camping Park
ST LEONARDS
Back of Beyond Touring Park
WAREHAM
Wareham Forest Tourist Park
WEYMOUTH
East Fleet Farm Touring Park

ISLE OF WIGHT
NEWBRIDGE
The Orchards Holiday Caravan Park
RYDE
Whitefield Forest Touring Park
WOOTTON BRIDGE
Woodside Bay Lodge Retreat

LANCASHIRE
CAPERNWRAY
Old Hall Caravan Park
GISBURN
Hedgerow Luxury Glamping

SILVERDALE
Silverdale Holiday Park

LEICESTERSHIRE
MELTON MOWBRAY
Eye Kettleby Lakes

LINCOLNSHIRE
CAISTOR
Caistor Lakes

NORFOLK
BARNEY
The Old Brick Kilns
CLIPPESBY
Clippesby Hall

NORTHUMBERLAND
BELFORD
South Meadows Caravan Park
BERWICK-UPON-TWEED
Ord House Country Park
HALTWHISTLE
Herding Hill Farm Touring & Camping Site
Herding Hill Farm, Glamping site

OXFORDSHIRE
HENLEY-ON-THAMES
Swiss Farm Touring & Camping
STANDLAKE
Lincoln Farm Park Oxfordshire

SHROPSHIRE
RUYTON-XI-TOWNS
Riverside Cabins

SOMERSET
BATH
Bath Mill Lodge Retreat
BISHOP SUTTON
Bath Chew Valley Caravan Park
BREAN
Warren Farm Holiday Centre
BRIDGETOWN
Exe Valley Caravan Site
CHEDDAR
Cheddar Woods Resort & Spa

GLASTONBURY
Old Oaks Touring & Glamping
WELLS
Wells Touring Park
WIVELISCOMBE
Waterrow Touring Park

SUSSEX, WEST
CHICHESTER
Concierge Camping
Concierge Glamping

YORKSHIRE, NORTH
ALLERSTON
Vale of Pickering Caravan Park
WYKEHAM
St Helens in the Park

CHANNEL ISLANDS
JERSEY
TRINITY
Durrell Wildlife Camp

SCOTLAND
FIFE
ST ANDREWS
Cairnsmill Holiday Park
Craigtoun Meadows Holiday Park

WALES
ANGLESEY, ISLE OF
DULAS
Tyddyn Isaf Caravan Park
MARIAN-GLAS
Home Farm Caravan Park

GWYNEDD
PWLLHELI
Hafan y Môr Holiday Park
TALYBONT
Islawrffordd Caravan Park

WREXHAM
EYTON
Plassey Holiday Park

★★★★★ Premier Parks

Premier Parks are among the top sites in the UK, having achieved either a 5 gold (pages 39–40) or 5 black (page 41) Star rating.

ENGLAND

CHESHIRE
CODDINGTON
Manor Wood Country Caravan Park

WHITEGATE
Lamb Cottage Caravan Park

CORNWALL & ISLES OF SCILLY
BUDE
Upper Lynstone Caravan Park

CHACEWATER
Killiwerris Touring Park

LOSTWITHIEL
Eden Valley Holiday Park

NEWQUAY
Monkey Tree Holiday Park

PENTEWAN
Heligan Caravan & Camping Park

PERRANPORTH
Perran Sands Holiday Park

SENNEN
Trevedra Farm Caravan & Camping Site

ST AUSTELL
River Valley Holiday Park

ST HILARY
Wayfarers Caravan & Camping Park

ST MERRYN
Atlantic Bays Holiday Park

WATERGATE BAY
Watergate Bay Touring Park

CUMBRIA
BEWALDETH
Keswick Reach Lodge Retreat

POOLEY BRIDGE
Hillcroft Park
Park Foot Holiday Park

SILLOTH
Stanwix Park Holiday Centre

WATERMILLOCK
The Quiet Site Glamping

WINDERMERE
Park Cliffe Camping & Caravan Estate

DEVON
BERRYNARBOR
Mill Park Touring Caravan & Camping Park

CLYST ST MARY
Crealy Theme Park & Resort

COMBE MARTIN
Newberry Valley Park

CROYDE
Bay View Farm Caravan & Camping Park

DARTMOUTH
Woodlands Grove Caravan & Camping Park

KINGSBRIDGE
Parkland Caravan and Camping Site

PAIGNTON
Beverley Park Caravan & Camping Park

SIDMOUTH
Salcombe Regis Caravan & Camping Park

TAVISTOCK
Harford Bridge Holiday Park

WOOLACOMBE
Golden Coast Holiday Park
Twitchen House Holiday Village

DORSET
BRIDPORT
Freshwater Beach Holiday Park

CHARMOUTH
Monkton Wyld Holiday Park

CHIDEOCK
Golden Cap Holiday Park

HOLDITCH
Mallinson's Woodland Retreat

POOLE
Rockley Park

SWANAGE
Ulwell Holiday Park

WEYMOUTH
Littlesea Holiday Park
Weymouth Bay Holiday Park

WOOL
Whitemead Caravan Park

KENT
ASHFORD
Broadhembury Caravan & Camping Park

MARDEN
Tanner Farm Touring Caravan & Camping Park

ROCHESTER
Kent Coast Leisure Park

LANCASHIRE
FAR ARNSIDE
Hollins Farm Holiday Park

SKELMERSDALE
The Secret Garden Glamping

LINCOLNSHIRE
WOODHALL SPA
Woodhall Country Park

NORFOLK
GREAT YARMOUTH
Seashore Holiday Park

HOPTON ON SEA
Hopton Holiday Village

HUNSTANTON
Searles Leisure Resort

NORTHAMPTONSHIRE
BULWICK
New Lodge Farm Caravan & Camping Site

NORTHUMBERLAND
BAMBURGH
Waren Caravan & Camping Park

BELLINGHAM
Bellingham Camping & Caravanning Club Site

BERWICK-UPON-TWEED
Berwick Holiday Park

RUTLAND
GREETHAM
In The Stix

Park Foot Holiday Park, Pooley Bridge

★★★★★ Premier Parks continued

SHROPSHIRE
LUDLOW
Westbrook Park

SHREWSBURY
Beaconsfield Holiday Park
Cartref Caravan & Camping
Love2Stay Shrewsbury
Oxon Hall Touring Park
Stoney Acres Luxury Holiday Park

SOMERSET
BREAN
Holiday Resort Unity
Northam Farm Holiday Park

SPARKFORD
Long Hazel Park

WATCHET
Doniford Bay Holiday Park

WESTON-SUPER-MARE
Country View Holiday Park

STAFFORDSHIRE
LONGNOR
Longnor Wood Holiday Park

SUFFOLK
DUNWICH
Haw Wood Farm Caravan Park

HOLLESLEY
Run Cottage Touring Park

LEISTON
Cakes & Ale

WOODBRIDGE
Moon & Sixpence

SUSSEX, WEST
PAGHAM
Church Farm Holiday Park

WILTSHIRE
SALISBURY
Coombe Touring Park

WORCESTERSHIRE
HONEYBOURNE
Ranch Caravan Park

YORKSHIRE, EAST RIDING OF
FLAMBOROUGH
Thornwick Bay Holiday Village

SPROATLEY
Burton Constable Holiday Park & Arboretum

YORKSHIRE, NORTH
ALNE
Alders Caravan Park

FILEY
Flower of May Holiday Park

HELMSLEY
Golden Square Caravan & Camping Park

HIGH BENTHAM
Riverside Caravan Park

OSMOTHERLEY
Cote Ghyll Caravan & Camping Park

YORK
York Caravan Park

YORKSHIRE, SOUTH
WALES BAR
Waleswood Caravan and Camping Park

SCOTLAND
ABERDEENSHIRE
HUNTLY
Huntly Castle Caravan Park

DUMFRIES & GALLOWAY
BRIGHOUSE BAY
Brighouse Bay Holiday Park

GATEHOUSE OF FLEET
Auchenlarie Holiday Park

LOTHIAN, EAST
DUNBAR
Thurston Manor Leisure Park

PERTH & KINROSS
BLAIR ATHOLL
Blair Castle Caravan Park

PERTH
Pathgreen Glamping

RENFREWSHIRE
BISHOPTON
The Paddocks Touring Park

SCOTTISH ISLANDS
KILMORY, ISLE OF ARRAN
Runach Arainn Glamping

WALES
CARMARTHENSHIRE
NEWCASTLE EMLYN
Cenarth Falls Resort Limited

CEREDIGION
NEW QUAY
Quay West Holiday Park

GWYNEDD
BARMOUTH
Trawsdir Touring Caravans & Camping Park

DINAS DINLLE
Dinlle Caravan Park

MONMOUTHSHIRE
LLANVAIR DISCOED
Penhein Glamping

PEMBROKESHIRE
ST DAVIDS
Caerfai Bay Caravan & Tent Park

POWYS
BRECON
Pencelli Castle Caravan & Camping Park

NORTHERN IRELAND
COUNTY ANTRIM
BUSHMILLS
Ballyness Caravan Park

Longnor Wood Holiday Park, Longnor

★★★★★ Premier Parks

ENGLAND

CORNWALL & ISLES OF SCILLY
HAYLE
Riviere Sands Holiday Park

LOOE
Tencreek Holiday Park

PADSTOW
The Retreats @ Padstow Holiday Park

ST AGNES
Beacon Cottage Farm Touring Park

TRURO
Cosawes Park

CUMBRIA
CARLISLE
Green Acres Caravan Park

FLOOKBURGH
Lakeland Leisure Park

KESWICK
Burns Farm Caravan, Camping & Glamping

KIRKBY LONSDALE
Woodclose Caravan Park

POOLEY BRIDGE
Waterfoot Park

ULVERSTON
Bardsea Leisure Park

DEVON
DAWLISH
Lady's Mile Holiday Park

KENNFORD
Kennford International Holiday Park

KINGSBRIDGE
Island Lodge Caravan & Camping Site

TAVISTOCK
Langstone Manor Camping & Caravan Park

DORSET
CHARMOUTH
Newlands Holidays

CHRISTCHURCH
Meadowbank Holidays

WEYMOUTH
Seaview Holiday Park

ESSEX
MERSEA ISLAND
Waldegraves Holiday Park

LANCASHIRE
BLACKPOOL
Marton Mere Holiday Village

BOLTON LE SANDS
Bay View Holiday Park

CARNFORTH
Marsh House Holiday Park

FLEETWOOD
Cala Gran Holiday Park

THORNTON
Waters Edge Country Park

LINCOLNSHIRE
BOSTON
Long Acres Touring Park

CAISTOR
Wolds View Country Park

CLEETHORPES
Cleethorpes Beach

MABLETHORPE
Golden Sands Holiday Park

SKEGNESS
Skegness Holiday Park

NORFOLK
BELTON
Rose Farm Touring & Camping Park

CAISTER-ON-SEA
Caister-on-Sea Holiday Park

DERSINGHAM
Pinecones Caravan and Camping

KING'S LYNN
King's Lynn Caravan and Camping Park

NORTH WALSHAM
Two Mills Touring Park

NORTHUMBERLAND
BERWICK-UPON-TWEED
Haggerston Castle Holiday Park

RUTLAND
GREETHAM
Rutland Caravan & Camping

SHROPSHIRE
BRIDGNORTH
Stanmore Hall Touring Park

TELFORD
Severn Gorge Park

SOMERSET
CASTLE CARY
Hadspen Glamping

SUSSEX, EAST
ST LEONARDS
Combe Haven Holiday Park

WARWICKSHIRE
HARBURY
Harbury Fields

WILTSHIRE
CHIPPENHAM
Plough Lane Touring Caravan Site

YORKSHIRE, EAST RIDING OF
BRANDESBURTON
Blue Rose Caravan & Country Park
Dacre Lakeside Park

SKIPSEA
Skirlington Leisure Park

YORKSHIRE, NORTH
HARROGATE
Ripley Caravan Park
Rudding Holiday Park

RIPON
Riverside Meadows Holiday Park

SHERIFF HUTTON
York Meadows Caravan Park

SUTTON-ON-THE-FOREST
Goosewood Holiday Park

THIRSK
Hillside Caravan Park

WHITBY
Ladycross Plantation Caravan Park

YORK
Flaxton Meadows

SCOTLAND

DUMFRIES & GALLOWAY
ECCLEFECHAN
Hoddom Castle Caravan Park

KIRKCUDBRIGHT
Seaward Holiday Park

LOTHIAN, EAST
LONGNIDDRY
Seton Sands Holiday Village

WALES

CONWY
LLANRWST
Bron Derw Touring Caravan Park

DENBIGHSHIRE
PRESTATYN
Presthaven Beach Holiday Park

GWYNEDD
BARMOUTH
Hendre Mynach Touring Caravan & Camping Park

PORTHMADOG
Greenacres Holiday Park

MONMOUTHSHIRE
USK
Pont Kemys Caravan & Camping Park

PEMBROKESHIRE
TENBY
Kiln Park Holiday Centre

POWYS
BUILTH WELLS
Fforest Fields Caravan & Camping Park

CHURCHSTOKE
Daisy Bank Caravan Park

LLANIDLOES
Red Kite Touring and Lodge Park

WREXHAM
OVERTON
The Trotting Mare Caravan Park

NORTHERN IRELAND

COUNTY ANTRIM
BALLYCASTLE
Causeway Coast Holiday Park

COUNTY FERMANAGH
BELCOO
Rushin House Caravan Park

AA Holiday Parks

These parks cater for all holiday needs. See page 12 for further information.

Freshwater Beach Holiday Park, Bridport

ENGLAND

CORNWALL & ISLES OF SCILLY

BUDE
Wooda Farm Holiday Park ★★★★★

HAYLE
Riviere Sands Holiday Park ★★★★★

LOOE
Tencreek Holiday Park ★★★★★

NEWQUAY
Hendra Holiday Park ★★★★★
Riverside Holiday Park ★★★★

PADSTOW
The Retreats @ Padstow Holiday Park ★★★★★

PERRANPORTH
Perran Sands Holiday Park ★★★★★

PORTREATH
Landal Gwel an Mor ★★★★★

WATERGATE BAY
Watergate Bay Touring Park ★★★★★

WHITE CROSS
Piran Meadows Resort and Spa ★★★★★

CUMBRIA

BEWALDETH
Keswick Reach Lodge Retreat ★★★★★

FLOOKBURGH
Lakeland Leisure Park ★★★★★

POOLEY BRIDGE
Hillcroft Park ★★★★★
Park Foot Holiday Park ★★★★★

SILLOTH
Solway Holiday Village ★★★★
Stanwix Park Holiday Centre ★★★★★

DERBYSHIRE

ASHBOURNE
Rivendale Lodge Retreat ★★★★

DEVON

AXMINSTER
Hawkchurch Resort & Spa ★★★★★

DAWLISH
Lady's Mile Holiday Park ★★★★

WOOLACOMBE
Golden Coast Holiday Park ★★★★★
Twitchen House Holiday Village ★★★★★

DORSET

BRIDPORT
Freshwater Beach Holiday Park ★★★★★

CHIDEOCK
Golden Cap Holiday Park ★★★★

POOLE
Rockley Park ★★★★★

SWANAGE
Ulwell Holiday Park ★★★★★

WEYMOUTH
Littlesea Holiday Park ★★★★★
Seaview Holiday Park ★★★★★
Weymouth Bay Holiday Park ★★★★★

ESSEX

MERSEA ISLAND
Waldegraves Holiday Park ★★★★★

ST OSYTH
The Orchards Holiday Park ★★★★

ISLE OF WIGHT

WOOTTON BRIDGE
Woodside Bay Lodge Retreat ★★★★★

KENT

ROCHESTER
Kent Coast Leisure Park ★★★★★

LANCASHIRE

BLACKPOOL
Marton Mere Holiday Village ★★★★★

FLEETWOOD
Cala Gran Holiday Park ★★★★★

LINCOLNSHIRE

BOSTON
Orchard Holiday Park ★★★★

CLEETHORPES
Cleethorpes Beach ★★★★★

MABLETHORPE
Golden Sands Holiday Park ★★★★★

SKEGNESS
Skegness Holiday Park ★★★★★

NORFOLK

BELTON
Wild Duck Holiday Park ★★★★

CAISTER-ON-SEA
Caister-on-Sea Holiday Park ★★★★★

GREAT YARMOUTH
Seashore Holiday Park ★★★★

HOPTON ON SEA
Hopton Holiday Village ★★★★★

HUNSTANTON
Searles Leisure Resort ★★★★★

NORTHUMBERLAND
BERWICK-UPON-TWEED
Berwick Holiday Park ★★★★
Haggerston Castle Holiday Park ★★★★★

SHROPSHIRE
SHREWSBURY
Beaconsfield Holiday Park ★★★★★

SOMERSET
BATH
Bath Mill Lodge Retreat ★★★★

BREAN
Holiday Resort Unity ★★★★
Warren Farm Holiday Centre ★★★★★

CHEDDAR
Cheddar Woods Resort & Spa ★★★★★

WATCHET
Doniford Bay Holiday Park ★★★★

SUSSEX, EAST
ST LEONARDS
Combe Haven Holiday Park ★★★★

SUSSEX, WEST
PAGHAM
Church Farm Holiday Park ★★★★

SELSEY
Warner Farm ★★★★

YORKSHIRE, EAST RIDING OF
BRANDESBURTON
Dacre Lakeside Park ★★★★★

FLAMBOROUGH
Thornwick Bay Holiday Village ★★★★★

SKIPSEA
Skirlington Leisure Park ★★★★★

YORKSHIRE, NORTH
FILEY
Blue Dolphin Holiday Park ★★★★
Flower of May Holiday Park ★★★★★
Orchard Farm Holiday Park ★★★★
Primrose Valley Holiday Park ★★★★
Reighton Sands Holiday Park ★★★★

PICKERING
Wayside Holiday Park ★★★★

RIPON
Riverside Meadows Holiday Park ★★★★★

SUTTON-ON-THE-FOREST
Goosewood Holiday Park ★★★★★

SCOTLAND
ANGUS
FOWLIS
Piperdam Leisure Resort ★★★★

DUMFRIES & GALLOWAY
GATEHOUSE OF FLEET
Auchenlarie Holiday Park ★★★★

LOTHIAN, EAST
LONGNIDDRY
Seton Sands Holiday Village ★★★★★

WALES
CEREDIGION
NEW QUAY
Quay West Holiday Park ★★★★★

CONWY
KINMEL BAY
Golden Sands Holiday Park ★★★★

DENBIGHSHIRE
PRESTATYN
Presthaven Beach Holiday Park ★★★★★

GWYNEDD
PORTHMADOG
Greenacres Holiday Park ★★★★★

PWLLHELI
Hafan y Môr Holiday Park ★★★★

TALYBONT
Barmouth Bay Holiday Park ★★★★

PEMBROKESHIRE
TENBY
Kiln Park Holiday Centre ★★★★★

SWANSEA
SWANSEA
Riverside Caravan Park ★★★★

NORTHERN IRELAND
COUNTY ANTRIM
BALLYCASTLE
Causeway Coast Holiday Park ★★★★★

Auchenlarie Holiday Park, Gatehouse of Fleet

Adults only – no children parks

The following parks are children-free sites with facilities just for adults.

ENGLAND

CAMBRIDGESHIRE
DODDINGTON
Fields End Water Caravan Park & Fishery ★★★★★

CHESHIRE
WHITEGATE
Lamb Cottage Caravan Park ★★★★★

CORNWALL & ISLES OF SCILLY
CHACEWATER
Chacewater Park ★★★★
Killiwerris Touring Park ★★★★★

LOSTWITHIEL
Eden Valley Holiday Park ★★★★★

ROSE
Higher Hendra Park ★★★

ST HILARY
Wayfarers Caravan & Camping Park ★★★★★

ST JUST-IN-ROSELAND
Trethem Mill Touring Park ★★★★★

TRURO
Cosawes Park ★★★★★

CUMBRIA
CARLISLE
Green Acres Caravan Park ★★★★★

MEALSGATE
Larches Caravan Park ★★★★

DEVON
BARNSTAPLE
Hallsdown Farm Touring Park ★★★★★

DREWSTEIGNTON
Woodland Springs Adult Touring Park ★★★★★

KINGSBRIDGE
Parkland Caravan and Camping Site ★★★★★

MODBURY
Moor View Touring Park ★★★★

TORQUAY
Widdicombe Farm Touring Park ★★★★★

DORSET
HOLDITCH
Mallinson's Woodland Retreat ★★★★★

ST LEONARDS
Back of Beyond Touring Park ★★★★★

GLOUCESTERSHIRE
CHELTENHAM
Briarfields Motel & Touring Park ★★★★

LANCASHIRE
GISBURN
Hedgerow Luxury Glamping ★★★★★

GREENHALGH
Charoland Farm Caravan Site ★★★★

LEICESTERSHIRE
MELTON MOWBRAY
Eye Kettleby Lakes ★★★★★

LINCOLNSHIRE
BOSTON
Long Acres Touring Park ★★★★★
Orchard Park ★★★★

CAISTOR
Caistor Lakes ★★★★★
Wolds View Country Park ★★★★★

NORFOLK
NORTH WALSHAM
Two Mills Touring Park ★★★★★

STANHOE
The Rickels Caravan & Camping Park Ltd ★★★

NORTHAMPTONSHIRE
BULWICK
New Lodge Farm Caravan & Camping Site ★★★★★

NOTTINGHAMSHIRE
SOUTHWELL
New Hall Farm Touring Park ★★★

SHROPSHIRE
SHREWSBURY
Beaconsfield Holiday Park ★★★★★
Cartref Caravan & Camping ★★★★★

TELFORD
Severn Gorge Park ★★★★

SOMERSET
BISHOP SUTTON
Bath Chew Valley Caravan Park ★★★★★

BRIDGETOWN
Exe Valley Caravan Site ★★★★★

GLASTONBURY
Old Oaks Touring & Glamping ★★★★★

SPARKFORD
Long Hazel Park ★★★★★

WELLS
Wells Touring Park ★★★★★

WIVELISCOMBE
Waterrow Touring Park ★★★★★

STAFFORDSHIRE
LONGNOR
Longnor Wood Holiday Park ★★★★★

SUFFOLK
HOLLESLEY
Run Cottage Touring Park ★★★★★

WILTSHIRE
CHIPPENHAM
Plough Lane Touring Caravan Site ★★★★★

YORKSHIRE, EAST RIDING OF
BRANDESBURTON
Blue Rose Caravan and Country Park ★★★★★

YORKSHIRE, NORTH
HARROGATE
Shaws Trailer Park QUALITY ASSESSED

HELMSLEY
Foxholme Springs Touring Park ★★★★

NABURN
Naburn Lock Caravan Park ★★★★★

YORK
Flaxton Meadows ★★★★★
Rawcliffe Manor Caravan Park ★★★★
York Caravan Park ★★★★★

WALES

MONMOUTHSHIRE
ABERGAVENNY
Wernddu Caravan Park ★★★

LLANVAIR DISCOED
Penhein Glamping ★★★★★

POWYS
CHURCHSTOKE
Daisy Bank Caravan Park ★★★★★

CRICKHOWELL
Riverside Caravan & Camping Park ★★★★

LLANIDLOES
Red Kite Touring and Lodge Park ★★★★★

WREXHAM
OVERTON
The Trotting Mare Caravan Park ★★★★★

Glamping sites

These campsites offer one or more types of glamping accommodation, i.e. wooden pods, tipis, yurts, bell tents, safari tents, shepherd's huts, geo domes and vintage caravans.

ENGLAND

BERKSHIRE
FINCHAMPSTEAD
California Chalet & Touring Park ★★★

CAMBRIDGESHIRE
DODDINGTON
Fields End Water Caravan Park & Fishery ★★★★★

CHESHIRE
DELAMERE
Fishpool Farm Caravan Park ★★★★
FRODSHAM
Lady Heyes Holiday Park ★★★★

CORNWALL & ISLES OF SCILLY
BODMIN
Mena Farm: Touring, Camping, Glamping ★★★★
BRYHER, ISLES OF SCILLY
Bryher Camp Site ★★★
BUDE
Willow Valley Holiday Park ★★★★
Wooda Farm Holiday Park ★★★★★
HAYLE
Atlantic Coast Holiday Park ★★★★
HOLYWELL BAY
Trevornick ★★★★★
KILKHAMPTON
Upper Tamar Lake ★★★
MAWGAN PORTH
Trevarrian Holiday Park ★★★★
NEWQUAY
Porth Beach Holiday Park ★★★★
Trenance Holiday Park ★★★★
PERRANPORTH
Perran Sands Holiday Park ★★★★★
Tollgate Farm Caravan & Camping Park ★★★★
POLZEATH
Gunvenna Holiday Park ★★★★★
PORTREATH
Tehidy Holiday Park ★★★★

PORTSCATHO
Trewince Farm Touring Park ★★★
RUTHERNBRIDGE
Ruthern Valley Holidays ★★★
ST JUST [NEAR LAND'S END]
Trevaylor Caravan & Camping Park ★★★
ST MARY'S, ISLES OF SCILLY
Garrison Campsite ★★★★
ST MERRYN
Tregavone Touring Park ★★★
TRURO
Summer Valley Touring Park ★★★★

CUMBRIA
AMBLESIDE
Skelwith Fold Caravan Park ★★★★★
CUMWHITTON
Cairndale Caravan Park ★★★
KESWICK
Burns Farm Caravan, Camping & Glamping ★★★★★
Castlerigg Hall Caravan & Camping Park ★★★★★
KIRKBY LONSDALE
New House Caravan Park ★★★★
Woodclose Caravan Park ★★★★★
NETHER WASDALE
Church Stile Farm & Holiday Park ★★★★
PATTERDALE
Sykeside Camping & Caravan Park ★★★
POOLEY BRIDGE
Waterfoot Caravan Park ★★★★★
SILLOTH
Stanwix Park Holiday Centre ★★★★★
WATERMILLOCK
The Quiet Site ★★★★★
The Quiet Site Glamping ★★★★★
Ullswater Holiday Park ★★★★

WINDERMERE
Park Cliffe Camping & Caravan Estate ★★★★★

DERBYSHIRE
BUXTON
Lime Tree Park ★★★★★
RIPLEY
Golden Valley Caravan & Camping Park ★★★★
ROSLISTON
Beehive Woodland Lakes ★★★★

DEVON
BERRYNARBOR
Mill Park Touring Caravan & Camping Park ★★★★★
CLAYHIDON
Kingsmead Centre Camping ★★★★
CLYST ST MARY
Crealy Theme Park & Resort ★★★★★
COMBE MARTIN
Newberry Valley Park ★★★★★
CROYDE
Bay View Farm Caravan & Camping Park ★★★★★
DAWLISH
Lady's Mile Holiday Park ★★★★★
DREWSTEIGNTON
Woodland Springs Adult Touring Park ★★★★★
KENTISBEARE
Forest Glade Holiday Park ★★★★
KINGSBRIDGE
Parkland Caravan and Camping Site ★★★★★
LYNTON
Lynmouth Holiday Retreat ★★★★
PAIGNTON
Whitehill Country Park ★★★★
SIDMOUTH
Oakdown Holiday Park ★★★★★

TAVISTOCK
Harford Bridge Holiday Park ★★★★★
Langstone Manor Camping & Caravan Park ★★★★★
Woodovis Park ★★★★★

DORSET
BRIDPORT
Highlands End Holiday Park ★★★★★
CHARMOUTH
Newlands Holidays ★★★★★
CHIDEOCK
Golden Cap Holiday Park ★★★★★
CORFE CASTLE
Woodyhyde Camp Site ★★★
FERNDOWN
St Leonards Farm Caravan & Camping Park ★★★★
HOLDITCH
Mallinson's Woodland Retreat ★★★★★
LYME REGIS
Shrubbery Touring Park ★★★★
POOLE
South Lytchett Manor Caravan & Camping Park ★★★★★
ST LEONARDS
Back of Beyond Touring Park ★★★★★
SWANAGE
Ulwell Holiday Park ★★★★★
WAREHAM
East Creech Farm Campsite ★★★
Ridge Farm Camping & Caravan Park ★★★
WEYMOUTH
Seaview Holiday Park ★★★★★

GLOUCESTERSHIRE
CHELTENHAM
Briarfields Motel & Touring Park ★★★★

Glamping sites *continued*

HERTFORDSHIRE
HODDESDON
Lee Valley Caravan Park, Dobbs Weir ★★★★

ISLE OF WIGHT
BRIGHSTONE
Grange Farm ★★★

KENT
ASHFORD
Broadhembury Caravan & Camping Park ★★★★★

MARDEN
Tanner Farm Touring Caravan & Camping Park ★★★★★

WHITSTABLE
Homing Park ★★★★

LANCASHIRE
BOLTON LE SANDS
Bay View Holiday Park ★★★★★

FAR ARNSIDE
Hollins Farm Holiday Park ★★★★★

GISBURN
Hedgerow Luxury Glamping ★★★★★

SILVERDALE
Silverdale Holiday Park ★★★★★

SKELMERSDALE
The Secret Garden Glamping ★★★★★

THORNTON
Waters Edge Country Park ★★★★★

LEICESTERSHIRE
MELTON MOWBRAY
Eye Kettleby Lakes ★★★★★

LINCOLNSHIRE
CAISTOR
Wolds View Country Park ★★★★★

LANGWORTH
Barlings Country Holiday Park ★★★★

SKEGNESS
Chapel Fields Holiday Park ★★★★

TATTERSHALL
Willow Holt Caravan Park ★★★★

WOODHALL SPA
Woodhall Country Park ★★★★★

LONDON
LONDON E4
Lee Valley Campsite, Sewardstone ★★★★

LONDON N9
Lee Valley Camping and Caravan Park, Edmonton ★★★★

NORFOLK
BELTON
Rose Farm Touring & Camping Park ★★★★★
Wild Duck Holiday Park ★★★★

CROMER
Forest Park ★★★★

HUNSTANTON
Searles Leisure Resort ★★★★★

KING'S LYNN
King's Lynn Caravan and Camping Park ★★★★★

NORTHAMPTONSHIRE
BULWICK
New Lodge Farm Caravan & Camping Site ★★★★★

NORTHUMBERLAND
BAMBURGH
Waren Caravan & Camping Park ★★★★★

BELFORD
South Meadows Caravan Park ★★★★★

BELLINGHAM
Bellingham Camping & Caravanning Club Site ★★★★★

BERWICK-UPON-TWEED
Ord House Country Park ★★★★★

HALTWHISTLE
Herding Hill Farm Touring & Camping Site ★★★★★
Herding Hill Farm, Glamping site ★★★★★

OXFORDSHIRE
FRINGFORD
Glebe Leisure ★★★

HENLEY-ON-THAMES
Swiss Farm Touring & Camping ★★★★★

RUTLAND
GREETHAM
In The Stix ★★★★★

SHROPSHIRE
RUYTON-XI-TOWNS
Riverside Cabins ★★★★★

SHREWSBURY
Cartref Caravan & Camping ★★★★★
Love2Stay Shrewsbury ★★★★★

SOMERSET
BISHOP SUTTON
Bath Chew Valley Caravan Park ★★★★★

BREAN
Holiday Resort Unity ★★★★★

CASTLE CARY
Hadspen Glamping ★★★★

COWSLIP GREEN
Brook Lodge Farm Camping & Caravan Park ★★★★

DULVERTON
Wimbleball Lake ★★★

GLASTONBURY
Old Oaks Touring & Glamping ★★★★★

MARTOCK
Southfork Caravan Park ★★★★

STAFFORDSHIRE
LONGNOR
Longnor Wood Holiday Park ★★★★★

SUFFOLK
HOLLESLEY
Run Cottage Touring Park ★★★★★

SUSSEX, WEST
BARNS GREEN
Sumners Ponds Fishery & Campsite ★★★★

CHICHESTER
Concierge Glamping ★★★★★

WILTSHIRE
BERWICK ST JAMES
Stonehenge Campsite & Glamping Pods ★★★★

LACOCK
Piccadilly Caravan Park ★★★

YORKSHIRE, EAST RIDING OF
SPROATLEY
Burton Constable Holiday Park & Arboretum ★★★★★

BRANDESBURTON
Dacre Lakeside Park ★★★★★

RUDSTON
Thorpe Hall Caravan & Camping Site ★★★★

YORKSHIRE, NORTH
ALLERSTON
Vale of Pickering Caravan Park ★★★★★

ALNE
Alders Caravan Park ★★★★★

ASKRIGG
Cherish Glamping ★★★★

CHOP GATE
Lordstones Country Park ★★★★

FILEY
Flower of May Holiday Park ★★★★★

HIGH BENTHAM
Wenningdale Escapes ★★★★

HUTTON-LE-HOLE
Hutton-le-Hole Caravan Park ★★★★

NORTHALLERTON
Otterington Park ★★★★

ROBIN HOOD'S BAY
Grouse Hill Caravan Park ★★★★

ROSEDALE ABBEY
Rosedale Abbey Caravan Park ★★★★

SCARBOROUGH
Killerby Old Hall Cottages & Caravan Site ★★★★

THIRSK
Hillside Caravan Park ★★★★★

WYKEHAM
St Helens in the Park ★★★★★

CHANNEL ISLANDS & ISLE OF MAN

GUERNSEY
ST SAMPSON
Le Vaugrat Camp Site ★★★

VALE
La Bailloterie Camping ★★★★

JERSEY
TRINITY
Durrell Wildlife Camp ★★★★★

ISLE OF MAN
KIRK MICHAEL
Glen Wyllin Campsite ★★★

SCOTLAND

ABERDEENSHIRE
MINTLAW
Aden Caravan and Camping ★★★

AYRSHIRE, SOUTH
BARRHILL
Barrhill Holiday Park ★★★★

DUMFRIES & GALLOWAY
BRIGHOUSE BAY
Brighouse Bay Holiday Park ★★★★★

ECCLEFECHAN
Hoddom Castle Caravan Park ★★★★★

KIRKCUDBRIGHT
Seaward Holiday Park ★★★★★

PALNACKIE
Kippford View Holiday Park ★★★★

SANDYHILLS
Sandyhills Bay Holiday Park ★★★★

STRANRAER
Aird Donald Caravan Park ★★★★

FIFE
ST ANDREWS
Cairnsmill Holiday Park ★★★★★
★★★★ Craigtoun Meadows Holiday Park

HIGHLAND
DUROR
Achindarroch Touring Park ★★★

FORT WILLIAM
Glen Nevis Caravan & Camping Park ★★★★

GLENCOE
Invercoe Caravan & Camping Park ★★★★

LANARKSHIRE, SOUTH
ABINGTON
Mount View Caravan Park ★★★

LOTHIAN, EAST
DUNBAR
Belhaven Bay Caravan & Camping Park ★★★★

LOTHIAN, WEST
LINLITHGOW
Beecraigs Caravan & Camping Site ★★★★

PERTH & KINROSS
BLAIR ATHOLL
Blair Castle Caravan Park ★★★★★

PERTH
Pathgreen Glamping ★★★★★

SCOTTISH ISLANDS
KILDONAN, ISLE OF ARRAN
Seal Shore Camping and Touring Site ★★★★

KILMORY, ISLE OF ARRAN
Runach Arainn Glamping ★★★★★

WALES

GWYNEDD
ABERSOCH
Bryn Bach Caravan & Camping Site ★★★★

BALA
Tyn Cornel Camping ★★★

BARMOUTH
Hendre Mynach Touring Caravan & Camping Park ★★★★★
Trawsdir Touring Caravans & Camping Park ★★★★★

CAERNARFON
Plas Gwyn Caravan & Camping Park ★★★★
Riverside Camping ★★★★

CRICCIETH
Eisteddfa ★★★★

DINAS DINLLE
Dinlle Caravan Park ★★★★★

MONMOUTHSHIRE
LLANVAIR DISCOED
Penhein Glamping ★★★★★

MONMOUTH
Rockfield Glamping ★★★★

PEMBROKESHIRE
FISHGUARD
Fishguard Bay Resort ★★★★

POWYS
BUILTH WELLS
Fforest Fields Caravan & Camping Park ★★★★★

CHURCHSTOKE
Daisy Bank Caravan Park ★★★★★

LLANDRINDOD WELLS
Disserth Caravan & Camping Park ★★★★

WREXHAM
EYTON
Plassey Holiday Park ★★★★★

Concierge Glamping, Chichester

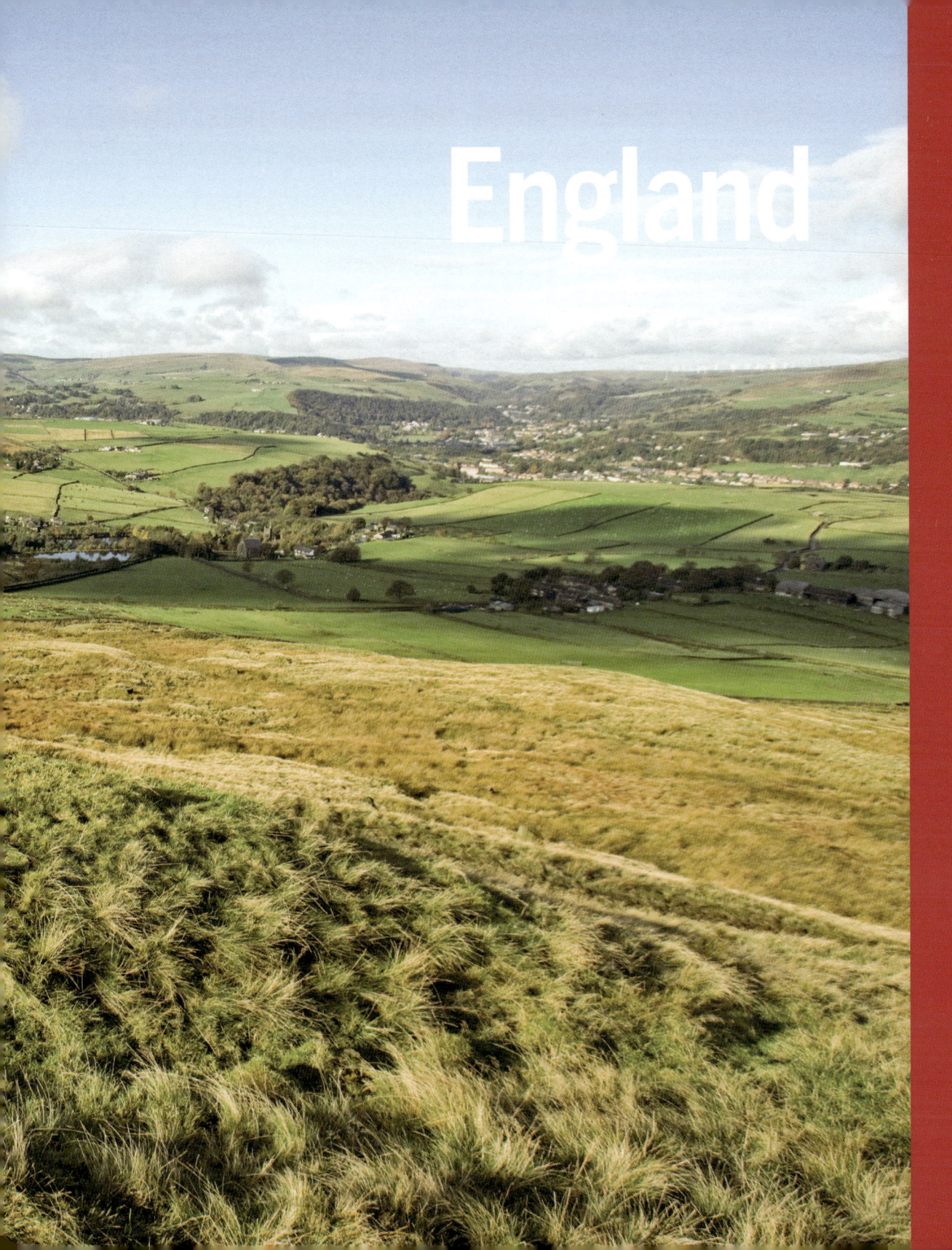
England

BERKSHIRE – CAMBRIDGESHIRE

BERKSHIRE

FINCHAMPSTEAD — Map 5 SU76

Places to visit

West Green House Gardens, HARTLEY WINTNEY, RG27 8JB, 01252 844611
www.westgreenhouse.co.uk

Museum of English Rural Life, READING, RG1 5EX, 0118 378 8660
merl.reading.ac.uk

Great for kids: The Look Out Discovery Centre, BRACKNELL, RG12 7QW, 01344 354200
www.bracknell-forest.gov.uk/leisure-services/look-out-discovery-centre

California Chalet & Touring Park
★★★   87%

tel: 0118 973 3928 & 07917 055444 **Nine Mile Ride RG40 4HU**
email: enquiries@californiapark.co.uk web: www.californiaholidaypark.co.uk
dir: *From A321 (south of Wokingham), right onto B3016 to Finchampstead. Follow Country Park signs on Nine Mile Ride.*

A simple, peaceful and well-located woodland site with secluded pitches among the trees, adjacent to the country park. The sparsely planted trees allow sunshine onto the pitches, and several occupy a prime position beside the lake with their own fishing area. The site has large hardstandings and the toilet block has quality vanity units and fully tiled showers.

Open: All year **Last arrival:** flexible **Last departure:** noon
Pitches: 🚐 🚙 ⛺ ; 44 hardstanding pitches
Leisure:
Facilities: 📶 WiFi
Services:
Within 3 miles:

Additional site information: 5.5 acre site. Cars can be parked by caravans and tents. Awnings permitted. No ground fires, no washing of caravans.
Glamping available: Wooden pods. **Changeover days:** Any day
Additional glamping information: Cars can be parked by units.

CAMBRIDGESHIRE

COMBERTON — Map 12 TL35

Places to visit

IWM Duxford, DUXFORD, CB22 4QR, 020 7091 3067
www.iwm.org.uk/visits/iwm-duxford

Chilford Hall Vineyard, LINTON, CB21 4LE, 01223 895600
www.chilfordhall.co.uk

Great for kids: Linton Zoo, LINTON, CB21 4NT, 01223 891308
www.lintonzoo.co.uk

Highfield Farm Touring Park
★★★★   95%

tel: 01223 262308 **Long Road CB23 7DG**
email: enquiries@highfieldfarmtouringpark.co.uk
web: www.highfieldfarmtouringpark.co.uk
dir: *M11 junction 12, A603 (Sandy). 0.5 mile, right onto B1046 to Comberton.*

Run by a very efficient and friendly family, this popular park is located on a well-sheltered hilltop, with spacious pitches including a cosy backpackers' and cyclists' area, and separate sections for couples and families. Around the family farm there is a one and a half mile marked walk that has stunning views.

Open: April to October **Last arrival:** 20.00 **Last departure:** 14.00
Pitches: 🚐 🚙 ⛺ ; 52 hardstanding pitches
Facilities:
Services:
Within 3 miles:

Additional site information: 8 acre site. Cars can be parked by caravans and tents. Awnings permitted. Maximum 2 dogs per pitch. Postbox.

PITCHES: 🚐 Caravans 🚙 Motorhomes ⛺ Tents 🏠 Glamping accommodation **LEISURE:** Indoor swimming pool Outdoor swimming pool Children's playground Kids' club Tennis court Games room Separate TV room golf course Pitch n putt Boats for hire Bikes for hire Cinema Entertainment Fishing Mini golf Watersports Gym Sports field Stables Spa

CAMBRIDGESHIRE 51 ENGLAND

DODDINGTON
Map 12 TL49

Places to visit

WWT Welney Wetland Centre, WELNEY, PE14 9TN, 01353 860711
www.wwt.org.uk/wetland-centres/welney

Flag Fen Archaeology Park, PETERBOROUGH, PE6 7QJ, 01733 864468
www.visitpeterborough.com/things-to-do/flag-fen-archaeological-park-p875681

Platinum Park

Fields End Water Caravan Park & Fishery
★★★★★

tel: 01354 740199 Benwick Road PE15 0TY
email: info@fieldsendfishing.co.uk web: www.fieldsendwater.co.uk
dir: *Exit A141, follow signs to Doddington. At clock tower in Doddington turn right into Benwick Road. Site 1.5 miles on right after sharp bends.*

This meticulously planned and well-executed park makes excellent use of its slightly elevated position in The Fens. The 80 fully serviced pitches, all with very generous hardstandings, are on smart terraces with sweeping views of the countryside. The toilet block contains several combined cubicle spaces. The new 'Camping Corner' comprises three astro turf tent pitches in a segregated section of The Paddock. There are shady walks through mature deciduous woodland adjacent to a large and appealingly landscaped fishing lake where there is also a really good lakeside café. A separate, well-designed area has 20 fully serviced pitches and four en suite camping pods around a lake. A footbridge across the lake links one side with the excellent facilities block which has fully serviced cubicles and underfloor heating.

Open: All year (restricted service: seasonal café) **Last arrival:** 20.00
Last departure: noon

Pitches: 🚐 🚗 ⛺ 🏠; 26 hardstanding pitches

Leisure: 🎣

Facilities: 🛁 ⊙ 🚿 ✳ ♿ 🛒 WiFi

Services: 🔌 🧺 🍴 🍺 ⬆ T

Within 3 miles: 🎣 ◎

Additional site information: 20 acre site. Adults only. 🐕 Cars can be parked by caravans and tents. Awnings permitted. No large groups.

Glamping available: 4 Glamping Pods. **Changeover days:** Any day

Additional glamping information: 3 pods are dog friendly, no bedding, crockery or cutlery supplied. Cars can be parked by units.

HEMINGFORD ABBOTS
Map 12 TL27

Places to visit

RSPB - Fen Drayton Lakes, SWAVESEY, CB24 4RB, 01954 233260
www.rspb.org.uk/reserves-and-events/reserves-a-z/fen-drayton-lakes

Houghton Mill, HOUGHTON, PE28 2AZ, 01480 301494
www.nationaltrust.org.uk/houghton-mill-and-waterclose-meadows

Great for kids: The Raptor Foundation, WOODHURST, PE28 3BT, 01487 741140
www.raptorfoundation.org.uk

Quiet Waters Caravan Park
★★★★ 80%

tel: 07729 630529 PE28 9AJ
email: contactus@quietwaterscaravanpark.co.uk
web: www.quietwaterscaravanpark.co.uk
dir: *From the new A14, follow A1307/St Ives signs.*

Quiet Waters is an attractive little site on the banks of the Great Ouse, and has been in the same family ownership for over 80 years. The A1307 is just a mile away, making this an ideal centre for touring Cambridgeshire. There are fishing opportunities, rowing boats for hire and many walks and cycling routes directly from the park. Holiday statics are available for hire.

Open: April to October **Last arrival:** 20.00 **Last departure:** noon

Pitches: 🚐 🚗; 20 hardstanding pitches; 20 seasonal pitches

Leisure: 🎣 ⛵

Facilities: 🛁 ⊙ 🚿 ✳ ♿ WiFi

Services: 🔌 🧺 🔒 ♻

Within 3 miles: 🎣 ◎ 🚲 🍴 🍺 🛒

Additional site information: 1 acre site. 🐕 Cars can be parked by caravans and tents. Awnings permitted. Dogs must be kept on leads at all times. No ground sheets. Boat mooring, fishing available.

Make your next UK holiday one to remember

Choose RatedTrips.com

FACILITIES: ⚡ Electric vehicle charging 🛁 Baths/Shower ⊙ Electric shaver sockets 🚿 Hairdryer ✳ Ice pack facility 👶 Baby facilities ♿ Disabled facilities 🛒 Shop on site or within 200yds 🍖 BBQ area 🌲 Picnic area WiFi WiFi 💻 Internet access **SERVICES:** 🔌 Electric hook-up 🧺 Launderette 🍺 Licensed bar 🛢 Calor Gas ♻ Campingaz T Toilet fluid 🍴 Café/Restaurant 🍟 Fast Food/Takeaway 🔋 Battery charging ⬆ Motorhome service point 💳 No credit or debit cards 🐕 Dogs permitted 🚫 No dogs

CAMBRIDGESHIRE

HUNTINGDON
Map 12 TL27

Places to visit

Ramsey Abbey Gatehouse, RAMSEY, PE26 1DH, 0344 800 1895
www.nationaltrust.org.uk/ramsey-abbey-gatehouse

RSPB - Fen Drayton Lakes, SWAVESEY, CB24 4RB, 01954 233260
www.rspb.org.uk/reserves-and-events/reserves-a-z/fen-drayton-lakes

Great for kids: The Raptor Foundation, WOODHURST, PE28 3BT, 01487 741140
www.raptorfoundation.org.uk

Huntingdon Boathaven & Caravan Park
★★★ 81%

tel: 01480 411977 **The Avenue, Godmanchester PE29 2AF**
email: info@huntingdonboathaven.co.uk **web:** www.huntingdonboathaven.co.uk
dir: *A14 junction 24, follow Godmanchester and Huntingdon signs onto B1044. Under A14, at mini-roundabout 2nd exit into Post Street. Just before A14 flyover bridge, left into site.*

The enthusiastic owners are gradually upgrading this well laid out site overlooking a boat marina and the River Ouse, set close to the A14 and within walking distance of Huntingdon town centre. The hardstanding area has been tidied up, trees cut back and seven gravel hardstandings have been created. The toilets are clean and well kept. A pretty area beside the marina has been created for tents, with wide views across the Ouse Valley. Boat hire is available and the park is open all year.

Open: All year (restricted service: Winter — open subject to weather conditions)
Last arrival: 21.00 **Last departure:** variable

Pitches: 🚐 🚙 ⛺ ; 18 hardstanding pitches; 12 seasonal pitches

Leisure: ✏ **Facilities:** 🏠 ☺ ☂ ✳ ♿ 🍴 WiFi

Services: 🍽 🧺 🔒 ⛽

Within 3 miles: 🚴 🎣 ⛳ 📅 💷

Additional site information: 2 acre site. 🐕 Cars can be parked by caravans. Awnings permitted. Dogs must be kept on leads at all times and owners must clear up after their dogs. Boat mooring and boat hire available.

WISBECH
Map 12 TF40

Places to visit

Peckover House & Garden, WISBECH, PE13 1JR, 01945 583463
www.nationaltrust.org.uk/peckover-house-and-garden

Great for kids: WWT Welney Wetland Centre, WELNEY, PE14 9TN, 01353 860711
www.wwt.org.uk/wetland-centres/welney

Little Ranch Leisure
★★★ 87%

tel: 01945 860066 **Begdale, Elm PE14 0AZ**
email: info@littleranchleisure.co.uk **web:** www.littleranchleisure.co.uk
dir: *From roundabout on A47 (southwest of Wisbech), take Redmoor Lane to Begdale.*

A friendly, family site set in an apple orchard, with 25 fully serviced pitches and a spacious toilet block with good facilities. The site overlooks two fishing lakes and pitches are available by the water; the famous horticultural auctions at Wisbech are nearby.

Open: All year

Pitches: 🚐 🚙 ⛺ ; 40 hardstanding pitches

Facilities: ☺ ☂ ✳ ♿

Services: 🍽 🗑 ⛽

Within 3 miles: 🎣 📅 💷

Additional site information: 10 acre site. 🐕 🚭 Cars can be parked by caravans and tents. Awnings permitted.

PITCHES: 🚐 Caravans 🚙 Motorhomes ⛺ Tents 🏕 Glamping accommodation **LEISURE:** 🏊 Indoor swimming pool 🏊 Outdoor swimming pool 🛝 Children's playground 🎈 Kids' club 🎾 Tennis court 🎮 Games room 📺 Separate TV room ⛳ golf course 🏌 Pitch n putt 🚤 Boats for hire 🚴 Bikes for hire 🎬 Cinema 🎵 Entertainment 🎣 Fishing ⛳ Mini golf 🏄 Watersports 💪 Gym ⚽ Sports field 🐎 Stables 💆 Spa

CHESHIRE 53 ENGLAND

CHESHIRE

CODDINGTON
Map 15 SJ45

Places to visit

Cholmondeley Castle Gardens, CHOLMONDELEY, SY14 8AH, 01829 720203
www.cholmondeleycastle.com

Hack Green Secret Nuclear Bunker, NANTWICH, CW5 8BL, 01270 629219
www.hackgreen.co.uk

Great for kids: Deva Roman Experience, CHESTER, CH1 1NL, 01244 343407
www.devaromancentre.co.uk

Chester Zoo, CHESTER, CH2 1EU, 01244 380280
www.chesterzoo.org

Premier Park

Manor Wood Country Caravan Park
★★★★★ 93%

tel: 01829 782990 & 07762 817787 **Manor Wood CH3 9EN**
email: info@manorwoodcaravans.co.uk **web:** www.cheshirecaravansites.co.uk
dir: *From A534 at Barton, turn opposite Cock O'Barton pub signed Coddington. Left in 100 yards. Site 0.5 mile on left.*

A secluded landscaped park in a tranquil country setting with extensive views towards the Welsh Hills across the Cheshire Plain. The park offers fully serviced pitches, a heated outdoor swimming pool and all-weather tennis courts. The generous pitch density provides optimum privacy and the superb amenity block has excellent decor, underfloor heating and smart modern facilities with very good privacy options. Wildlife is encouraged and there are two fishing lakes; country walks and nearby pubs are added attractions. There is also a stylish, combined reception, shop and café with patio overlooking the lake, and an on-site hairdressing salon.

Open: All year (restricted service: October to March – swimming pool closed)
Last arrival: 19.00 **Last departure:** 11.00

Pitches: 🚐 🚍 ▲; 38 hardstanding pitches; 30 seasonal pitches
Leisure: ⚓ ♨ 🎣 ⚽
Facilities: 🛁 ⊙ ✂ ♿ 🍳 WiFi 💻
Services: 🔌 🗑 ⚡ 🚽
Within 3 miles: 🎣 🛒

Additional site information: 8 acre site. 🚗 Awnings permitted. No noise after 23.00. Table tennis, pool table.

DELAMERE
Map 15 SJ56

Places to visit

Jodrell Bank Discovery Centre, JODRELL BANK, SK11 9DL, 01477 571766
www.jodrellbank.net

Little Moreton Hall, CONGLETON, CW12 4SD, 01260 272018
www.nationaltrust.org.uk/little-moreton-hall

Great for kids: Chester Zoo, CHESTER, CH2 1LH, 01244 380280
www.chesterzoo.org

Fishpool Farm Caravan Park
★★★★ 86%

tel: 01606 883970 & 07501 506583 **Fishpool Road CW8 2HP**
email: enquiries@fishpoolfarmcaravanpark.co.uk
web: www.fishpoolfarmcaravanpark.co.uk
dir: *From A49 (Tarporley to Cuddington road), onto A54 signed Chester. At Fishpool Inn left onto B5152 (Fishpool Road). Site on right.*

Located within easy reach of many notable attractions and a short walk from The Fishpool Inn, this constantly improving park provides well spaced, level pitches and a smart amenity block with good privacy options. A small clubhouse is open at busy times, there are many walking opportunities and children are encouraged to explore the adjacent natural woodland. A glamping village offers seven well-equipped pods with en suite facilities, a health and beauty pod and an adjacent private jacuzzi.

Open: 15 February to 15 January **Last arrival:** 19.00 **Last departure:** noon

Pitches: 🚐 🚍 ▲; 🛖 see prices below; 14 hardstanding pitches
Leisure: 🎣 🎱 ⚽
Facilities: 🛁 ⊙ ✂ ♿ 🍳 🪑 WiFi
Services: 🔌 🗑 ⚡
Within 3 miles: 🎣 🏌 ⛳ 🎯 🏊

Additional site information: 5.5 acre site. 🚗 Cars can be parked by caravans and tents. Awnings permitted. No noise after 23.00. Dog walks, play area.

Glamping available: Wooden pods from £80.

Additional glamping information: Jacuzzi available.

FRODSHAM
Map 15 SJ57

Places to visit
Lion Salt Works, MARSTON, CW9 6ES, 01606 275066
lionsaltworks.westcheshiremuseums.co.uk

Lady Heyes Holiday Park
★★★★ 91%

tel: 01928 788557 Kingsley Road WA6 6SU
email: enquiries@ladyheyespark.com web: www.ladyheyespark.com
dir: *M56 junction 12, follow Frodsham signs. At roundabout left, follow Frodsham signs into Clifton Road. At lights right onto A56. In Frodsham turn left into Fluin Lane signed Tarporley (A5152). At T-junction left onto B5152 (Kingsley Road). Site on left in approximately 1 mile.*

Peacefully situated in the heart of the Cheshire countryside, this long-established park enjoys the ideal location for a relaxing holiday experience. Surrounded by a wide range of mature trees, neat hedges, indigenous and cultivated plants, the pitch density is generous which creates good privacy; the touring pitches are fully serviced. There are many rentals on offer, from American RVs to stylish glamping pods with hot tubs. The amenity blocks have underfloor heating and modern fixtures. There are good on-site eating and drinking opportunities in addition to 14 retail outlets.

Open: All year
Pitches: 65 hardstanding pitches; 15 seasonal pitches
Leisure:
Facilities:
Services:
Within 3 miles:

Additional site information: 14 acre site. Cars can be parked by caravans and tents. Awnings permitted. Quiet time after 22.00 pm Children's playground, soft play centre, on-site bar and outdoor decking area

Glamping available: Pods, Stage Coaches, American RVs. **Changeover days:** Any Day

Additional glamping information: Family friendly accommodation. All units have private decking area and hot tubs. No dogs in glamping units. Cars can be parked by units.

NORTHWICH
Map 15 SJ67

Places to visit
Arley Hall & Gardens, NORTHWICH, CW9 6NA, 01565 777353
www.arleyhallandgardens.com

Lion Salt Works, MARSTON, CW9 6ES, 01606 275066
lionsaltworks.westcheshiremuseums.co.uk

Belmont Camping
★★★ 85%

tel: 01606 891235 & 07530 450019 **Belmont Hall, Great Budworth CW9 6JA**
email: info@belmontcamping.co.uk web: www.belmontcamping.co.uk
dir: *M56 junction 10, take A559 to Northwich. After 3 miles entrance at junction of A559 and Pole Lane (Note: for sat nav use post code CW9 6HX).*

Part of a small country estate in Great Budworth, under five miles from Northwich, a long meandering drive with a fine display of mature trees and fishing lakes is the approach to the peaceful touring and camping areas. Pitch density is generous to enhance privacy, and all caravan and motorhomes have either hardstandings and electric hook-ups or full services to include waste water disposal. Well-equipped toilet and shower facilities are located within a former indoor horse training arena.

Open: All year **Last arrival:** by prior arrangement **Last departure:** by prior arrangement
Pitches: 15 hardstanding pitches
Leisure:
Facilities:
Services:
Within 3 miles:

Additional site information: 1 acre site. Cars can be parked by caravans and tents. Awnings permitted. No noise after 23.00, children must be supervised, no campfires. Nature walk.

SIDDINGTON
Map 15 SJ87

Places to visit
Capesthorne Hall, CAPESTHORNE, SK11 9JY, 01625 861221
www.capesthorne.com

Gawsworth Hall, GAWSWORTH, SK11 9RN, 01260 223456
www.gawsworthhall.com

Great for kids: Jodrell Bank Discovery Centre, JODRELL BANK, SK11 9DL, 01477 571766
www.jodrellbank.net

Capesthorne Hall
★★★★ 88%

tel: 01625 861221 **Congleton Road SK11 9JY**
email: info@capesthorne.com web: www.capesthorne.com/caravan-park
dir: *Access to site from A34 between Congleton to Wilmslow. Phone site for detailed directions.*

Located within the grounds of the notable Jacobean Capesthorne Hall, this lush, all level site provides generously sized pitches, all with electricity and most with hardstandings. The Scandinavian-style amenity block has a smart, quality, modern interior and very good privacy levels. Guests also have the opportunity to visit the award-winning gardens on certain days and there are many extensive walking opportunities leading directly from the camping areas.

Open: 1 March to 31 October **Last arrival:** 22.00 **Last departure:** noon
Pitches: 30 hardstanding pitches
Facilities:
Services:
Within 3 miles:

Additional site information: 5 acre site. Cars can be parked by caravans. Awnings permitted. No motorised scooters or skateboards. Gas BBQs only. Touring area may close if large events take place (contact site for details). Access to Capesthorne Hall and Gardens – additional cost for Hall only.

CHESHIRE 55 ENGLAND

WHITEGATE
Map 15 SJ66

Places to visit

Beeston Castle, BEESTON, CW6 9TX, 01829 260464
www.english-heritage.org.uk/visit/places/beeston-castle-and-woodland-park

Chester Cathedral, CHESTER, CH1 2HU, 01244 324756
www.chestercathedral.com

Premier Park

Lamb Cottage Caravan Park
★★★★★ 93%

Best of British

tel: 01606 882302 **Dalefords Lane CW8 2BN**
email: info@lambcottage.co.uk web: www.lambcottage.co.uk
dir: *From A556 turn at Sandiway lights into Dalefords Lane, signed Winsford. Site 1 mile on right.*

Lamb Cottage Caravan Park is a secluded and attractively landscaped, adults-only park in a glorious location where the emphasis is on peace and relaxation. The serviced pitches are spacious with wide grass borders for sitting out and the high quality toilet block is spotlessly clean and immaculately maintained. It makes a good central base for exploring this area, with access to nearby woodland walks and cycle trails.

Open: All year **Last arrival:** 20.00 **Last departure:** noon

Pitches: 45 hardstanding pitches; 14 seasonal pitches

Facilities:

Services:

Within 3 miles:

Additional site information: 6 acre site. Adults only. Cars can be parked by caravans. Awnings permitted. No tents (except trailer tents), no commercial vehicles.

Cornwall & Isles of Scilly

It's not hard to see why thousands of tourists and holidaymakers flock to Cornwall every year. It has just about everything – wild moorland landscapes, glorious river valley scenery, picturesque villages and miles of breathtaking coastline. It has long been acknowledged as one of Britain's top holiday destinations.

Cornwall's southerly latitude and the influence of the Gulf Stream make the county the mildest and sunniest climate in Britain. It's not surprising therefore that one of its greatest and most popular pursuits is surfing. With more than 80 surfing spots, and plenty of sporting enthusiasts who make their way here to enjoy other similar coastal activities, such as wave-surfing, kite surfing and blokarting, the county is an internationally famous surfing hot spot. Blessed with wonderful surf beaches, Newquay is Cornwall's surfing capital. Nearby Watergate Bay is renowned for its glassy waves and Sennen, near Land's End, is where you might even get to surf with dolphins. Certainly the sea is strikingly blue here and the sands dazzlingly white.

A long-running TV series, filmed in a scenic location, is often a guaranteed way to boost tourism and that is certainly the case at Port Isaac on the north Cornwall coast. The village doubles as Portwenn in the drama *Doc Martin*, starring Martin Clunes as the irascible local GP. Much of Port Isaac has been used for location shooting over the years and it's quite common to bump into actors from the series at different points in the village when filming is taking place. Many films and TV series have been shot in Cornwall – including productions of Daphne du Maurier's *Jamaica Inn* and *Rebecca*, though the original version of the latter, made in 1940, was Alfred Hitchcock's first film in Hollywood and shot entirely in California.

In the book, the setting is a large house on the Cornish coast where the atmosphere is decidedly gothic. Daphne du Maurier modelled the house – which she called Manderley – and its location on the Menabilly estate, near Fowey. *Rebecca* was published in 1938 and five years later the writer made Menabilly her home.

The house is not open to the public, but it is possible to explore the setting for the story on foot, following a leafy path from the car park at Menabilly Barton Farm to Polridmouth Bay where there are two secluded and remote coves. A bird's eye view of the entire area is possible from the path to Gribben Head, though Menabilly, at the heart of the story, is hidden by trees, thus preserving the mystery of the book.

The Cornish coastline offers breathtakingly beautiful scenery. The north coast is open and exposed; the 735-ft High Cliff, between Boscastle and St Gennys, represents the highest sheer drop cliff in the county. The Lizard, at Cornwall's most southerly point, is a geological masterpiece of awesome cliffs, stacks and arches.

In recent years new or restored visitor attractions have helped to increase tourism in the region – Tim Smit has been the inspiration and driving force behind two of the county's most visited attractions. The Eden Project is famous for its giant geodesic domes housing exotic plants from different parts of the globe, while nearby the Lost Gardens of Heligan at Pentewan has impressive kitchen gardens and a wildlife hide.

Perhaps the last word on this magical corner of Britain should go to Daphne du Maurier. In her book *Vanishing Cornwall*, published in 1967, she wrote: 'A county known and loved in all its moods becomes woven into the pattern of life, something to be shared. As one who sought to know it long ago…in a quest for freedom, and later put down roots and found content, I have come a small way up the path. The beauty and the mystery beckon still.'

◁ *Shipwreck near Land's End*

CORNWALL & ISLES OF SCILLY

ASHTON
Map 2 SW62

Places to visit
Godolphin House, GODOLPHIN CROSS, TR13 9RE, 01736 763194
www.nationaltrust.org.uk/godolphin

Poldark Tin Mine and Gardens, TRENEAR, TR13 0ES, 01326 573173
www.poldarkmine.org.uk

Great for kids: Flambards, HELSTON, TR13 0QA, 01326 573404
www.flambards.co.uk

Boscrege Caravan & Camping Park
QUALITY ASSESSED

tel: 01736 762231 **TR13 9TG**
email: enquiries@caravanparkcornwall.com **web:** www.caravanparkcornwall.com
dir: *A394 from Helston signed Penzance. In Ashton (Lion and Lamb pub on right) right into Higher Lane, approximately 1.5 miles (thatched cottage on right) left at site sign. (Note: for recommended towing route contact the park).*

A quiet and bright little touring park divided into small paddocks with hedges, that offers plenty of open spaces for children to play in. There are no toilet or shower facilities. By an Area of Outstanding Natural Beauty at the foot of Tregonning Hill, this simple site makes an ideal base for touring the southern tip of Cornwall; Penzance, Land's End, St Ives and the beaches in between are all within easy reach.

Open: All year (restricted service: November to Easter – no caravans, motorhomes or tents) **Last arrival:** 22.00 **Last departure:** 11.00

Pitches: 🚐 🚙 ⛺; 10 seasonal pitches

Leisure: 🛝 ⚽

Facilities: 🏪 ⊙ 🚿 ❄ 🧺 🪑 WiFi

Services: 🔌 💧 🧺 🔒 💨 T

Within 3 miles: 🎣 🏌 U ◎ 🏊 ⛳ 🏪

Additional site information: 14 acre site. 🐾 Cars can be parked by caravans and tents. Awnings permitted. No fires, no noise after 23.00, no groups. Microwave and freezer available; fresh eggs available. Car hire can be arranged.

BLACKWATER
Map 2 SW74

Places to visit
Royal Cornwall Museum, TRURO, TR1 2SJ, 01872 272205
www.royalcornwallmuseum.org.uk

East Pool Mine, POOL, TR15 3NP, 01209 315027
www.nationaltrust.org.uk/east-pool-mine

Great for kids: National Maritime Museum Cornwall, FALMOUTH, TR11 3QY, 01326 313388
www.nmmc.co.uk

BLACKWATER
Map 2 SW74

Trevarth Holiday Park
★★★★ 88%

tel: 01872 560266 **TR4 8HR**
email: info@trevarth.co.uk **web:** www.trevarth.co.uk
dir: *Exit A30 at Chiverton roundabout onto B3277 signed St Agnes. At next roundabout follow Blackwater signs. Site on right in 200 metres.*

A neat, compact and well managed park with touring pitches (some fully serviced with upgraded electrics) laid out on attractive, well-screened high ground near to the A30 and A390. This pleasant little park is centrally located for touring, and is maintained to a very good standard. There is a large grassed area for children to play on which is away from all tents.

Open: April to October **Last arrival:** 21.30 **Last departure:** 11.30

Pitches: 🚐 🚙 ⛺; 21 hardstanding pitches; 12 grass pitches; 10 seasonal pitches

Leisure: 🛝 🔍

Facilities: 🏪 ⊙ 🚿 ❄ WiFi

Services: 🔌 💧 🧺 ⚡ 🔒 💨

Within 3 miles: 🏌 U 🏊 🏪

Additional site information: 4 acre site. 20 static caravans. 🐾 Cars can be parked by caravans and tents. Awnings permitted. No gazebos, no noise after 22.30.

CORNWALL & ISLES OF SCILLY — ENGLAND

BODMIN   Map 2 SX06

Places to visit

Restormel Castle, RESTORMEL, PL22 0EE, 01208 872687
www.english-heritage.org.uk/visit/places/restormel-castle

Lanhydrock, LANHYDROCK, PL30 4AB, 01208 265950
www.nationaltrust.org.uk/lanhydrock

Great for kids: Eden Project, ST AUSTELL, PL24 2SG, 01726 811972
www.edenproject.com

Mena Farm: Touring, Camping, Glamping
★★★★ 90%

tel: 01208 831845 **PL30 5HW**
email: enquiries@menafarm.co.uk **web:** www.menafarm.co.uk
dir: *Exit A30 onto A389 (north) signed Lanivet and Wadebridge. In 0.5 mile 1st right, pass under A30. 1st left signed Lostwithiel and Fowey. In 0.25 mile right at top of hill. 0.5 mile, 1st right. Entrance 100 yards on right.*

This grassy site is about four miles from The Eden Project and midway between the north and south Cornish coasts. Set in a secluded, elevated position with high hedges for shelter, it offers plenty of peace and quiet. There is a small coarse fishing lake on site, hardstanding pitches, a shop, electric vehicle charging points, and various glamping options are available for hire. The site is on the Saint's Way, and nearby is the neolithic hill fort of Helman Tor, the highest point on Bodmin Moor. Approximately one mile away is a fish and chip restaurant in Lanivet – and from this village, there is a bus service to Bodmin.

Open: All year **Last arrival:** 22.00 **Last departure:** noon
Pitches: see prices below; 4 hardstanding pitches
Leisure:
Facilities:
Services:
Within 3 miles:

Additional site information: 15 acre site. Cars can be parked by caravans and tents. Awnings permitted. No noise after 22.00. No dangerous dogs. No generators. Nature trails, bike service. Car hire can be arranged.

Glamping available: 3 bell tents from £70; 3 Lotus Belle tents from £80; 1 vintage caravan from £70. **Changeover days:** Any day

Additional glamping information: Bell tents are fully equipped including bedding (sleep 4). No dogs or pets. Cars can be parked by units.

BRYHER (ISLES OF SCILLY)   Map 2 SV81

Bryher Camp Site
★★★ 91%

tel: 01720 422068 **TR23 0PR**
email: relax@bryhercampsite.co.uk **web:** www.bryhercampsite.co.uk
dir: *Accessed from the mainland by ferry, plane or by boat from main island of St Mary's.*

Set on the smallest inhabited Scilly Isle with spectacular scenery and white beaches, this tent-only site is in a sheltered valley surrounded by hedges. Pitches are located in paddocks at the northern end of the island which is only a short walk from the quay. There is a good, modern toilet block, and plenty of peace and quiet. Although located in a very quiet area, the Fraggle Rock Bar and a well-equipped shop are within easy reach. There is easy boat access to all the other islands.

Open: Easter to 30 September
Pitches: see prices below
Facilities:
Services:
Within 3 miles:

Additional site information: 2.25 acre site. No pets.

Glamping available: Bell tents from £53. **Changeover days:** Saturdays (July and August); any day April to June and September to October

Additional glamping information: Minimum stay 3 nights. Bell tents include cutlery, crockery, utensils, pots, pans, kettle, cool box, camping stove, washing up equipment, 4 deck chairs, picnic bench, lantern and airbeds (double or single). Own bedding and towels required.

Make your next UK holiday one to remember

Choose RatedTrips.com

AA

FACILITIES: Electric vehicle charging · Baths/Shower · Electric shaver sockets · Hairdryer · Ice pack facility · Baby facilities · Disabled facilities · Shop on site or within 200yds · BBQ area · Picnic area · WiFi · Internet access **SERVICES:** Electric hook-up · Launderette · Licensed bar · Calor Gas · Campingaz · Toilet fluid · Café/Restaurant · Fast Food/Takeaway · Battery charging · Motorhome service point · No credit or debit cards · Dogs permitted · No dogs

ENGLAND 60 — CORNWALL & ISLES OF SCILLY

BUDE
Map 2 SS20

Places to visit
Penhallam Manor, WEEK ST MARY, EX22 6XW, 0370 333 1181
www.english-heritage.org.uk/visit/places/penhallam-manor

Platinum Park

Wooda Farm Holiday Park
★★★★★ HOLIDAY PARK

tel: 01288 352069 **Poughill EX23 9HJ**
email: stay@wooda.co.uk **web:** www.wooda.co.uk
dir: *From A39 at Stratton follow Poughill and brown site signs into Stamford Hill. Approximately 1 mile to site on right. Avoid Stone Hill, which is unsuitable for towing vehicles/motorhomes.*

Wooda Farm Holiday Park is an attractive site set on raised ground overlooking Bude Bay, with lovely sea views. The park is divided into paddocks by hedges and mature trees, and offers high quality facilities in the extensive and colourful gardens. A variety of activities is provided by way of the large sports hall and hard tennis court, and there's a super children's playground. There are holiday static caravans for hire. Gwelva Hills is a luxury collection of nine self-catering lodges tucked into the hillside with sweeping coastal views.

Wooda Farm Holiday Park

Open: Mid-March to mid-November (restricted service: mid-March to May and mid-September to mid-November)
Last arrival: 20.00 **Last departure:** 10.30

Pitches: from £34; from £34; from £22; see prices below; 80 hardstanding pitches

Leisure:
Facilities: WiFi
Services:
Within 3 miles:

Additional site information: 50 acre site. Restrictions on certain dog breeds. No skateboards, rollerblades or scooters. Woodland walks, nature trails, farmyard animals, wellness barn and art studio, cocktail bar, cycle trail, tennis court, badminton court, pitch n putt, table tennis, pool tables

Glamping available: Pitch with bathroom pod from £50, Eco lodges and holiday cottages. **Changeover days:** Friday and Monday

Additional glamping information: Short breaks available (Friday to Monday; Monday to Friday; Friday to Friday). Cars can be parked by units.

See advert below

WOODA CORNWALL
EST. 1975
5 Star Holiday Park in Bude with Sea Views
wooda.co.uk

PITCHES: Caravans • Motorhomes • Tents • Glamping accommodation **LEISURE:** Indoor swimming pool • Outdoor swimming pool • Children's playground • Kids' club • Tennis court • Games room • Separate TV room • Golf course • Pitch n putt • Boats for hire • Bikes for hire • Cinema • Entertainment • Fishing • Mini golf • Watersports • Gym • Sports field • Stables • Spa

CORNWALL & ISLES OF SCILLY   61   ENGLAND

Premier Park

Upper Lynstone Caravan Park
★★★★★ 90%

tel: 01288 352017 **Lynstone EX23 0LP**
email: reception@upperlynstone.co.uk **web:** www.upperlynstone.co.uk
dir: *From Bude follow Widemouth Bay signs. Site 0.75 mile south of Bude on coastal road (Vicarage Road becomes Lynstone Road) on right.*

There are extensive views over Bude to be enjoyed from this quiet, sheltered family-run park, a terraced grass site suitable for all units. There's a spotlessly clean and top quality toilet block, plus a children's playground, five hardstanding pitches, and a reception with a shop that sells basic food supplies and camping spares. Static caravans are available for holiday hire. A path leads directly to the coastal footpath with its stunning sea views, and the old Bude Canal is just a stroll away.

Open: 27 March to 3 October **Last arrival:** 21.00 **Last departure:** 10.00
Pitches: 🚐 🚚 ⛺; 8 hardstanding pitches
Leisure: 🛝
Facilities: 🏪 ☺ 🎀 ❄ ♿ 🪑 🪟 WiFi
Services: 🔌 🧺 🍽 🔒 ⛽ T
Within 3 miles: 🚶 ⚑ ⛳ ⊚ 🎣 ✈ 🍴

Additional site information: 6 acre site. 🐕 Cars can be parked by caravans and tents. Awnings permitted. No groups. Family bathroom.

Willow Valley Holiday Park
★★★★ 94%

tel: 01288 353104 **Bush EX23 9LB**
email: willowvalley@talk21.com **web:** www.willowvalley.co.uk
dir: *On A39, 0.5 mile north of junction with A3072 at Stratton.*

A small sheltered park in the Strat Valley with level grassy pitches and a stream running through it. All areas of this attractive park have been improved, including a smart toilet block, an excellent reception, and a summer shop housed in a converted horsebox. The park has direct access from the A39, and is only two miles from the sandy beaches at Bude. There are eight bell tents, each with a private decked area, and five lodges (three with hot tubs) for holiday hire.

Open: All year **Last arrival:** 21.00 **Last departure:** 11.00
Pitches: 🚐 🚚 ⛺ 🏠; 8 hardstanding pitches
Leisure: 🛝
Facilities: ☺ 🎀 ❄ ♿ 🪑 🪟 🪴 WiFi 💻
Services: 🔌 🧺 🍽 🛒 ⛽ T
Within 3 miles: 🚶 ⚑ ⛳ ⊚ 🎣 ✈

Additional site information: 11 acre site. 🐕 Cars can be parked by caravans and tents. Awnings permitted.
Glamping available: Bell tents
Additional glamping information: Bell tents have double beds, 2 air beds.

CAMELFORD   Map 2 SX18

Places to visit
Tintagel Castle, TINTAGEL, PL34 0HE, 01840 770328
www.english-heritage.org.uk/visit/places/tintagel-castle

Tintagel Old Post Office, TINTAGEL, PL34 0DB, 01840 770024
www.nationaltrust.org.uk/tintagel-old-post-office

Lakefield Caravan Park
★★★ 86%

tel: 01840 213279 **Lower Pendavey Farm PL32 9TX**
email: lakefieldequestriancentre@btconnect.com
web: www.lakefieldcornwall.com/camping-touring
dir: *From A39 in Camelford onto B3266, right at T-junction, site 1.5 miles on left.*

Set in a rural location, this friendly park is part of a specialist equestrian centre, and offers good quality services. All the facilities are immaculate and spotlessly clean. Riding lessons and hacks are always available, with a BHS qualified instructor. Newquay, Padstow and Bude are all easily accessed from this site.

Open: Easter or April to October **Last arrival:** 22.00 **Last departure:** 11.00
Pitches: 🚐 🚚 ⛺
Leisure: ⚽
Facilities: ☺ 🎀 ❄
Services: 🔌 🍽 🧺 🔒 ⛽ T
Within 3 miles: 🚶 ⚑ ⛳ 🎣

Additional site information: 5 acre site. 🐕 Cars can be parked by caravans and tents. Awnings permitted. On-site lake.

FACILITIES: 🔌 Electric vehicle charging 🛁 Baths/Shower ☺ Electric shaver sockets 🎀 Hairdryer ❄ Ice pack facility 🪑 Baby facilities ♿ Disabled facilities 🛒 Shop on site or within 200yds 🍖 BBQ area 🪑 Picnic area WiFi WiFi 🌐 Internet access   **SERVICES:** 🔌 Electric hook-up 🧺 Launderette 🍽 Licensed bar 🛢 Calor Gas ⛽ Campingaz T Toilet fluid ☕ Café/Restaurant 🍔 Fast Food/Takeaway 🔋 Battery charging ⛽ Motorhome service point 💳 No credit or debit cards 🐕 Dogs permitted 🚫 No dogs

ENGLAND 62 CORNWALL & ISLES OF SCILLY

CARLYON BAY
Map 2 SX05

Places to visit
The Shipwreck and Heritage Centre, ST AUSTELL, PL25 3NJ, 01726 69897
www.shipwreckcharlestown.co.uk

The Lost Gardens of Heligan, PENTEWAN, PL26 6EN, 01726 845100
www.heligan.com

Great for kids: Wheal Martyn, ST AUSTELL, PL26 8XG, 01726 850362
www.wheal-martyn.com

Eden Project, ST AUSTELL, PL24 2SG, 01726 811972
www.edenproject.com

Platinum Park

Carlyon Bay Caravan & Camping Park
★★★★★

tel: 01726 812735 **Cypress Avenue PL25 3RE**
email: holidays@carlyonbaycamping.co.uk web: www.carlyonbaycamping.co.uk
dir: *Exit A390 west of St Blazey, left onto A3092 for Par, right in 0.5 mile. Cypress Avenue to Carlyon Bay.*

Carlyon Bay Caravan & Camping Park is an attractive, secluded site set amongst a belt of trees with woodland in the background. The park is beautifully landscaped and offers quality toilet and shower facilities and plenty of on-site attractions, including a well-equipped games room, TV room and an inviting swimming pool. It is less than half a mile from a sandy beach and the Eden Project is approximately two miles away.

Carlyon Bay Caravan & Camping Park

Open: 17 April to 14 September (restricted service: Swimming pool closed until 24 May) **Last arrival:** 18.00 (low season) 19.00 (high season) **Last departure:** 11.00

Pitches: 🚐 🚍 ⛺; 15 fully serviced pitches, 12 hardstanding pitches. All pitches have electric hookup

Leisure: 🏊 ⛰ 🔍 📺 ⚽

Facilities: ☺ 🅿 ✳ ♿ 🛁 🚰 WiFi

Services: 🔌 🗑 🧺 💧 🔒 💨 🅣

Within 3 miles: 🚴 🎣 ⛳ 🎡 ⛵ 🚣 🚂

Additional site information: 30 acre site. 🐕 Cars can be parked by caravans and tents. Awnings permitted. No noise after 23.00, no hoverboards or motorised scooters (except invalid mobility scooters). Crazy golf.

See advert below

- Award winning Family run park.
- Located midway along the South Coast of Cornwall between Charlestown and Fowey.
- Set in over 30 acres of meadows and mature woodlands.
- 180 touring pitches (no static caravans).
- Footpath to large sandy beach.
- Free heated outdoor swimming pools.
- Free WiFi.
- Close to championship golf course.
- 2.5km from the Eden Project.

For enquiries: 01726 812735 • email: holidays@carlyonbaycamping.co.uk • Online bookings: www.carlyonbaycamping.co.uk

PITCHES: 🚐 Caravans 🚍 Motorhomes ⛺ Tents 🏕 Glamping accommodation   LEISURE: 🏊 Indoor swimming pool 🏊 Outdoor swimming pool
⛰ Children's playground 🧒 Kids' club 🎾 Tennis court 🔍 Games room 📺 Separate TV room ⛳ golf course ⛳ Pitch n putt ⛵ Boats for hire
🚴 Bikes for hire 🎬 Cinema 🎭 Entertainment 🎣 Fishing ⛳ Mini golf 🏄 Watersports 🏋 Gym ⚽ Sports field 🐴 Stables 💆 Spa

CORNWALL & ISLES OF SCILLY

CHACEWATER
Map 2 SW74

Places to visit
Royal Cornwall Museum, TRURO, TR1 2SJ, 01872 272205
www.royalcornwallmuseum.org.uk

Trelissick, TRELISSICK, TR3 6QL, 01872 862090
www.nationaltrust.org.uk/trelissick

Premier Park

Killiwerris Touring Park
★★★★★ 91%

tel: 01872 561356 & 07734 053593 **Penstraze TR4 8PF**
email: killiwerris@aol.com **web:** www.killiwerris.co.uk
dir: *Take A30 towards Penzance, at Chiverton Cross roundabout take 3rd exit signed St Agnes. At next mini roundabout take Blackwater exit, in 500 yards left into Kea Downs Road, park 1 mile on right.*

A small, adults-only, family-run touring park, just five miles from Truro and four miles from the coastal village of St Agnes, making it an ideal base for exploring west Cornwall. The owners have invested in the park, and made some great improvements — an excellent chemical disposal unit; a motorhome service point; a dog wash; and a walkway through the park to the village of Chacewater. The site has a sunny aspect yet is sheltered by mature trees giving it a very private feel. The facilities are of an exceptionally high standard and include a modern and smart amenity block. It is a peaceful spot in which to relax and get away from the crowds.

Open: All year **Last arrival:** 21.00 **Last departure:** 11.00
Pitches: ; 17 hardstanding pitches
Facilities:
Services:
Within 3 miles:
Additional site information: 2.2 acre site. Adults only. Cars can be parked by caravans. Awnings permitted. Car hire can be arranged.

Chacewater Park
★★★★ 86%

tel: 01209 820762 **Coxhill TR4 8LY**
email: chacewaterpark@hotmail.co.uk **web:** www.chacewaterpark.co.uk
dir: *From the A30 towards Redruth, take the A3047 signed Scorrier. At roundabout take left exit and at crossroads turn right onto the B3298 towards St Day. In one mile turn left at crossroads and in 0.75 mile at crossroads turn left. Park is next right.*

Surrounded by farmland in the heart of former tin mining country, Chacewater Park is an adults-only caravan touring park with picturesque views of old engine houses. It is ideally situated to explore the best of Cornwall and provides an intimate retreat for couples seeking a relaxing rural holiday. The park has two main touring areas and one is dog friendly. The hardstanding pitches are large with most being fully serviced. The two facility blocks are spotless and there is a well-stocked shop.

Open: 1 April to 30 September
Pitches:
Additional site information: 12 acre site. Adults only.

COVERACK
Map 2 SW71

Places to visit
Great for kids: Cornish Seal Sanctuary, GWEEK, TR12 6UG, 01326 221361
sealsanctuary.sealifetrust.org

Flambards, HELSTON, TR13 0QA, 01326 573404
www.flambards.co.uk

Little Trevothan Camping and Caravan Park
★★★★ 91%

tel: 01326 280260 **Trevothan, Coverack TR12 6SD**
email: holidays@littletrevothan.co.uk **web:** www.littletrevothan.co.uk
dir: *A394 to Helston (avoid turn for Gweek and Constantine – not suitable for towing or large vehicles). At 1st roundabout in Helston, left onto A394 towards Lizard. At 4th roundabout take 2nd exit towards Lizard on A3038. After RNAS Culdrose left at mini roundabout onto B3293 signed St Keverne (Coverack). Pass Goonhilly Earth Station, right just before Pace/Zoar garage (site signed here). 3rd left, site 300 yards on right.*

A secluded site, with excellent facilities, near the unspoilt fishing village of Coverack on the Lizard Peninsula, with a large recreation area, an adventure playground with nature trail, and smart amenity blocks with family rooms. Fire bowls and barbecues are available for hire. The nearby sandy beach has lots of rock pools for children to explore, and there are many walks starting from both the park and the village that offer stunning scenery.

Open: March to December (inclusive) - static caravans. March to October (inclusive) - touring and camping **Last arrival:** 19:00 (later arrivals by prior arrangement)
Last departure: 10.00 (Statics). 10.30 (Touring)
Pitches: ; 13 hardstanding pitches; 18 seasonal pitches
Leisure:
Facilities:
Services:
Within 3 miles:
Additional site information: 10.5 acre site. Cars can be parked by caravans and tents. Awnings permitted. Quiet time between 22.00–08.00. 5mph speed limit. Large playing field with adventure playground. Games Room.

CORNWALL & ISLES OF SCILLY

CRANTOCK (NEAR NEWQUAY) — Map 2 SW76

Places to visit
Trerice, TRERICE, TR8 4PG, 01637 875404
www.nationaltrust.org.uk/trerice

Treago Farm Caravan Site
★★★★ 90%

tel: 01637 830277 **TR8 5QS**
email: info@treagofarm.co.uk **web:** www.treagofarm.co.uk
dir: *From A3075 (west of Newquay) follow Crantock signs. Site signed beyond village.*

A grass site in open farmland in a south-facing sheltered valley with a fishing lake. This friendly family park has spotless toilet facilities, which include three excellent heated family rooms, a good shop and bar with takeaway food, and it has direct access to Crantock and Polly Joke beaches, National Trust land and many natural beauty spots.

Open: April to early October (restricted service: mid May, mid September to October – reduced hours in shop and bar) **Last arrival:** 22.00 **Last departure:** 18.00
Pitches: 🚐 🚗 ⛺
Leisure: 🎣 🎱
Facilities: 🏠 ☉ 🚿 ✳ 🚽 🍴 🪑
Services: 🔌 💧 🍳 🛒 🚯 🔒 🧴 🚾
Within 3 miles: 🎣 🏌 ⛳ ◎ 🚴 🚉

Additional site information: 5 acre site. 🐕 Cars can be parked by caravans and tents. Awnings permitted.

Quarryfield Holiday Park
★★★ 87%

tel: 01637 830338 **TR8 5RJ**
email: info@quarryfield.co.uk **web:** www.quarryfield.co.uk
dir: *From A3075 (Newquay to Redruth road) follow Crantock signs. Site signed.*

This park has a private path down to the dunes and golden sands of Crantock Beach, about 10 minutes away, and it is within easy reach of all that Newquay has to offer, particularly for families. The park has very modern facilities, and provides plenty of amenities including a great swimming pool.

Open: Easter to October **Last arrival:** 23.00 **Last departure:** 10.00
Pitches: 🚐 🚗 ⛺; 33 seasonal pitches
Leisure: 🎣 🎱 🎯
Facilities: 🏠 ☉ 🚿 ✳ ♿ 🚽 🍴 🪑 📶 💻
Services: 🔌 💧 🍳 🍽 🛒 🚯 🔒 🧴
Within 3 miles: 🎣 🏌 ⛳ ◎ 🚴 🚉

Additional site information: 10 acre site. 🐕 Cars can be parked by caravans and tents. Awnings permitted. No campfires, quiet after 22.30.

FALMOUTH — Map 2 SW83

Places to visit
Pendennis Castle, FALMOUTH, TR11 4LP, 01326 316594
www.english-heritage.org.uk/visit/places/pendennis-castle

Trebah Garden, MAWNAN SMITH, TR11 5JZ, 01326 252200
www.trebahgarden.co.uk

Great for kids: National Maritime Museum Cornwall, FALMOUTH, TR11 3QY, 01326 313388
www.nmmc.co.uk

Tregedna Farm Touring Caravan & Tent Park
★★★ 86%

tel: 01326 250529 **Maenporth TR11 5HL**
email: tregednafarmcamping@gmail.com **web:** www.tregednafarmholidays.co.uk
dir: *Take A39 from Truro to Falmouth. Turn right at Hill Head roundabout. Site 2.5 miles on right.*

Set in the picturesque Maen Valley, this gently-sloping, south-facing park is part of a 100-acre farm. It is surrounded by beautiful wooded countryside just minutes from the beach, and has spacious pitches and well-kept facilities.

Open: April to September **Last arrival:** 22.00 **Last departure:** 13.00
Pitches: 🚐 🚗 ⛺; 6 hardstanding pitches
Leisure: 🎯
Facilities: 🏠 ☉ ✳
Services: 🔌 💧
Within 3 miles: 🎣 ⛳ ◎ 🚴 🚉 🛒

Additional site information: 12 acre site. 🐕 🐾 Cars can be parked by caravans and tents. Awnings permitted. 1 dog only per pitch. No open fires. Boat storage.

HAYLE — Map 2 SW53

Places to visit
Tate St Ives, ST IVES, TR26 1TG, 01736 796226
www.tate.org.uk/visit/tate-st-ives

Barbara Hepworth Museum & Sculpture Garden, ST IVES, TR26 1AD, 01736 796226
www.tate.org.uk/visit/tate-st-ives/barbara-hepworth-museum-and-sculpture-garden

CORNWALL & ISLES OF SCILLY

HAYLE
Map 2 SW53

Premier Park

Riviere Sands Holiday Park
★★★★★ 88% HOLIDAY PARK

tel: 01736 752132 Riviere Towans TR27 5AX
email: rivieresands@haven.com web: www.haven.com/rivieresands
dir: *A30 towards Redruth. Follow signs into Hayle, straight on at double mini-roundabout. Turn right opposite petrol station signed Towans and beaches. Park 1 mile on right.*

Close to St Ives and with direct access to a safe, white-sand beach, Riviere Sands is an exciting holiday park with much to offer families. Children can enjoy the crazy golf, amusements, swimming pool complex, and the beach of course; the evening entertainment for adults is extensive and lively. There is a good range of holiday caravans and apartments for hire.

Open: 24 March to 30 October
Holiday Homes: Sleep 8, Bedrooms 2, Bathrooms 1, Toilets 1, Microwave, Freezer, TV, Sky/Freeview
Leisure:
Additional site information:

Atlantic Coast Holiday Park
★★★★ 86%

tel: 01736 752071 53 Upton Towns, Gwithian TR27 5BL
email: enquiries@atlanticcoastpark.co.uk web: www.atlanticcoastpark.co.uk
dir: *From A30 into Hayle, right at double roundabout. Site 1.5 miles on left.*

Fringed by the sand dunes of St Ives Bay and close to the golden sands of Gwithian Beach, the small, friendly touring area continues to improve year on year and offers fully serviced pitches, good toilet and shower facilities, a dog shower and a BBQ area. There's freshly baked bread, a takeaway and a bar next door. This park is ideally situated for visitors who enjoy the natural coastal beauty and attractions of south-west Cornwall. There is superb landscaping and planting, and campers have the use of facilities such as a kettle and microwave. Static caravans (some with hot tubs), 10 lodges, including a luxury Pod Lodge, and two shepherd's huts are available for holiday hire.

Open: 1 March to 2 January **Last arrival:** 20.00 **Last departure:** 11.00
Pitches: ; see prices below; 4 hardstanding pitches
Leisure:
Facilities:
Services:
Within 3 miles:
Additional site information: 4.5 acre site. Cars can be parked by caravans and tents. Awnings permitted. No commercial vehicles, gazebos or day tents. Freshly baked bread, croissants, pasties, newspapers available.
Glamping available: Shepherd's hut from £96. **Changeover days:** Any day (Saturday only high season)
Additional glamping information: Own private hot tub and decking area. Cars can be parked by units.

Treglisson Touring Park
★★★ 84%

tel: 01736 753141 Wheal Alfred Road TR27 5JT
email: treglisson@hotmail.co.uk web: www.treglisson.co.uk
dir: *From A30 (Camborne towards Penzance) take 4th exit at roundabout signed Hayle. Left at next mini-roundabout, follow site signs. Approximately 1.5 miles past golf course, site sign on left.*

A small, secluded site in a peaceful wooded meadow and a former apple and pear orchard. This quiet rural site has level grass pitches and a well-planned, modern toilet block, and is just two miles from the glorious beach at Hayle with its vast stretch of golden sand.

Open: Spring Bank Holiday to end September **Last arrival:** 20.00 **Last departure:** 11.00
Pitches: ; 6 hardstanding pitches
Leisure:
Facilities:
Services:
Within 3 miles:
Additional site information: 3 acre site. Cars can be parked by caravans and tents. Awnings permitted. Maximum 6 people per pitch, maximum tent size of 7 metres.

HELSTON
Map 2 SW62

Places to visit

Great for kids: Flambards, HELSTON, TR13 0QA, 01326 573404
www.flambards.co.uk

Cornish Seal Sanctuary, GWEEK, TR12 6UG, 01326 221361
sealsanctuary.sealifetrust.org

Polladras Holiday Park
★★★★ 94%

tel: 01736 762220 Carleen, Breage TR13 9NX
email: info@polladras.co.uk web: www.polladrasholidaypark.co.uk
dir: *From Helston take A394 then B3302 (Hayle Road) at Ward Garage, 2nd left to Carleen, site 2 miles on right.*

An attractive rural park with extensive views of surrounding fields, appealing to families who enjoy the countryside. The trees and shrubs are maturing, and help to divide the area into paddocks with spacious grassy pitches. The site has a dish washing area, a games room, a dog and nature walk, two fully serviced family rooms and WiFi.

Open: April to January **Last arrival:** 21.00 **Last departure:** 11.00
Pitches: ; 28 hardstanding pitches; 17 seasonal pitches
Leisure:
Facilities:
Services:
Within 3 miles:
Additional site information: 4 acre site. Cars can be parked by caravans and tents. Awnings permitted. No drones, hoverboards or camp fires. Caravan storage.

HELSTON continued

Skyburriowe Farm
★★★ 84%

tel: 01326 221646 **Garras TR12 6LR**
email: bkbenney@hotmail.co.uk **web:** www.skyburriowefarm.co.uk
dir: From Helston take A3083 to The Lizard. After Culdrose Naval Airbase continue straight on at roundabout, in 1 mile left at Skyburriowe Lane sign. In 0.5 mile right at Skyburriowe B&B/Campsite sign. Pass bungalow to farmhouse. Site on left.

A leafy, no-through road leads to this picturesque farm park in a rural location on the Lizard Peninsula. The toilet block offers excellent quality facilities, and most pitches have electric hook-ups. There are beautiful coves and beaches nearby, and for a great day out Flambards theme park is also close by. Under the supervision of the owner, children are permitted to watch his herd of Friesian cows being milked.

Open: April to October **Last arrival:** 22.00 **Last departure:** 11.00
Pitches: 🚐 🚙 ▲; 4 hardstanding pitches
Facilities: 🏠 ☉ ✳ ♿ WiFi 📺
Services: 🚿 🛒
Within 3 miles: ⚓ 🎣 ⛳ 🏊 🍴 🎰 🎲

Additional site information: 4 acre site. 🐕 Cars can be parked by caravans and tents. Awnings permitted. Quiet after 23.00. Fresh seasonal vegetables available.

HOLYWELL BAY — Map 2 SW75

Places to visit
Trerice, TRERICE, TR8 4PG, 01637 875404
www.nationaltrust.org.uk/trerice

AA HOLIDAY PARK OF THE YEAR 2024–25

Platinum Park

Trevornick
★★★★★

tel: 01637 830531 & 832905 **TR8 5PW**
email: bookings@trevornick.co.uk **web:** www.trevornick.co.uk
dir: 3 miles from Newquay exit A3075 towards Redruth. Follow Cubert and Holywell Bay signs.

Trevornick is a large seaside holiday complex with excellent facilities and amenities, including a pool complex with extra spa room, sun lounge area, children's splash pool and eating venues. There is plenty of entertainment including a children's club and an evening cabaret, adding up to a full holiday experience for all the family. A sandy beach is just a 15-minute footpath walk away. The park has 36 Euro tents for hire, plus luxury static caravans.

Open: 29 March to 30 October **Last arrival:** 21.00 **Last departure:** 10.00
Pitches: 🚐 🚙 ▲; 🏠 see prices below; 53 hardstanding pitches; 8 seasonal pitches
Leisure: 🏊 🎠 👶 🎾 🎱 🏓 ⛳ 🎯 ⚽ 🎡
Facilities: 🏠 ☉ 🚿 ✳ ♿ 🛒 WiFi
Services: 🚿 🛒 🍴 🎰 🛍 🎲 📺
Within 3 miles: 🎣 ⚓ 🏊 🍴

Additional site information: 20 acre site. 🐕 Cars can be parked by caravans and tents. Awnings permitted. Families and couples only. Arcade, dog walking field.
Glamping available: Euro tents from £150 for 3 nights. **Changeover days:** Saturday for ready-erected tents, Friday for luxury lodges
Additional glamping information: Ready-erected tents are fully equipped; some are dog friendly. Cars can be parked by ready-erected tents.

KENNACK SANDS — Map 2 SW71

Places to visit
Cornish Seal Sanctuary, GWEEK, TR12 6UG, 01326 221361
sealsanctuary.sealifetrust.org

Great for kids: Flambards, HELSTON, TR13 0QA, 01326 573404
www.flambards.co.uk

Silver Sands Holiday Park
★★★ 90%

tel: 01326 290631 **Gwendreath TR12 7LZ**
email: info@silversandsholidaypark.co.uk **web:** www.silversandsholidaypark.co.uk
dir: From Helston follow signs to St Keverne. After Goonhilly Satellite Station turn right at crossroads signed Kennack Sands, 1.5 miles, left at Gwendreath sign, site 1 mile. (Note: it is advisable to follow these directions not sat nav).

A small, family-owned park in a remote location, with individually screened pitches providing sheltered suntraps. The owners continue to upgrade the park, improving the landscaping, access roads and toilets; lovely floral displays greet you on arrival. A footpath through the woods leads to the beach and the local pub. One of the nearby beaches is the historic Mullion Cove, and for the children a short car ride will ensure a great day out at Flambards theme park.

Open: 21 March to 2 November **Last arrival:** 18.00 **Last departure:** 11.00
Pitches: 🚐 🚙 ▲
Leisure: 🎠 ⚽ ☉ **Facilities:** 🏠 ☉ 🚿 ✳ 🎰 🍴 🛒 WiFi
Services: 🚿 🛒 🛍 🎲 **Within 3 miles:** 🎣 ⚓ 🏊

Additional site information: 9 acre site. 🐕 Cars can be parked by caravans and tents (unless the ground is saturated). Awnings permitted. No noise after 22.00. Woodland walk to the beach. Car hire can be arranged.

KILKHAMPTON — Map 2 SS21

Places to visit
Bude Castle, BUDE, EX30 8LG
www.thecastlebude.co.uk

Upper Tamar Lake
★★★ 76%

tel: 01288 321712 **Upper Tamar Lake EX23 9SB**
email: info@swlakestrust.org.uk **web:** www.southwestlakes.co.uk
dir: From A39 at Kilkhampton onto B3254, left in 0.5 mile onto unclassified road, follow signs for approximately 4 miles to site.

A well-trimmed, slightly sloping site overlooking the lake and surrounding countryside, with several signed walks. The site benefits from the excellent facilities provided for the watersports centre and coarse anglers, with a rescue launch on the

CORNWALL & ISLES OF SCILLY

lake when the flags are flying. A good family site, with Bude's beaches and the surfing waves only eight miles away.

Open: April to October **Last arrival:** 17.00 **Last departure:** 11.00
Pitches: ; 2 hardstanding pitches
Leisure:
Facilities:
Services:
Within 3 miles:

Additional site information: 1 acre site. Cars can be parked by caravans and tents. Awnings permitted. No open fires, off-ground BBQs only. No swimming in lake. Canoeing, sailing, windsurfing, kayaking hire and launch, stand up paddle boarding.

Glamping available: Wooden pods.

Additional glamping information: Cars can be parked by units

LOOE
Map 2 SX25

Places to visit
Antony House, TORPOINT, PL11 2QA, 01752 812191
www.nationaltrust.org.uk/antony

Mount Edgcumbe House & Country Park, TORPOINT, PL10 1HZ, 01752 822236
www.mountedgcumbe.gov.uk

Great for kids: Wild Futures, LOOE, PL13 1NZ, 01503 262532
www.wildfutures.org

Premier Park

Tencreek Holiday Park
★★★★★ 86% HOLIDAY PARK

tel: 01503 262447 **Polperro Road PL13 2JR**
email: reception@tencreek.co.uk **web:** www.dolphinholidays.co.uk
dir: Take A387 1.25 miles from Looe. Site on left.

Occupying a lovely position with extensive countryside and sea views, this holiday park is in a rural spot but close to Looe and Polperro. There is a full family entertainment programme, with an indoor swimming pool, an adventure playground and an exciting children's club. The superb amenity blocks include several private family shower rooms with toilet and washbasin.

Open: All year **Last arrival:** 22.00 **Last departure:** 10.00
Pitches: ; 12 hardstanding pitches; 120 seasonal pitches
Leisure:
Facilities:
Services:
Within 3 miles:

Additional site information: 24 acre site. Families and couples only. Multi-sports pitch.

LOSTWITHIEL
Map 2 SX15

Places to visit
Restormel Castle, RESTORMEL, PL22 0EE, 01208 872687
www.english-heritage.org.uk/visit/places/restormel-castle

Lanhydrock, LANHYDROCK, PL30 4AB, 01208 265950
www.nationaltrust.org.uk/lanhydrock

Premier Park

Eden Valley Holiday Park
★★★★★ 91%

tel: 01208 872277 **PL30 5BU**
email: edenvalleyholidaypark@btconnect.com **web:** www.edenvalleyholidaypark.co.uk
dir: 1.5 miles southwest of Lostwithiel on A390 turn right at brown/white sign in 400 metres. (Note: it is advisable to follow these directions not sat nav).

Set in attractive paddocks with mature trees, this grassy, adults-only park is committed to conservation and wildlife preservation. The gradual upgrading of facilities continues, and both buildings and grounds, including the excellent, well-spaced pitches, are carefully maintained. This park is ideally located for visiting the Eden Project, the nearby golden beaches and sailing at Fowey. There are two self-catering lodges to rent.

Open: Easter or 1 April to October **Last arrival:** 20.00 (later arrivals by prior arrangement) **Last departure:** 11.00
Pitches: from £23; from £23; from £23; 40 hardstanding pitches; 25 seasonal pitches
Leisure:
Facilities:
Services:
Within 3 miles:

Additional site information: 12 acre site. Adults only. Cars can be parked by caravans and tents. Awnings permitted. Table football, pool, table tennis, football. Walks, wildlife conservation information room.

FACILITIES: Electric vehicle charging Baths/Shower Electric shaver sockets Hairdryer Ice pack facility Baby facilities Disabled facilities Shop on site or within 200yds BBQ area Picnic area WiFi Internet access **SERVICES:** Electric hook-up Launderette Licensed bar Calor Gas Campingaz Toilet fluid Café/Restaurant Fast Food/Takeaway Battery charging Motorhome service point No credit or debit cards Dogs permitted No dogs

CORNWALL & ISLES OF SCILLY

MAWGAN PORTH — Map 2 SW86

Places to visit

Prideaux Place, PADSTOW, PL28 8RP, 01841 532411
prideauxplace.co.uk

Goss Moor National Nature Reserve, CARNE, 01726 891096
www.gov.uk/government/publications/cornwalls-national-nature-reserves/cornwalls-nature-reserves

Trevarrian Holiday Park

★★★★ 91%

tel: 01637 860381 & 0845 225 5910 (Calls cost 7p per minute plus your phone company's access charge) **TR8 4AQ**
email: holiday@trevarrian.co.uk web: www.trevarrian.co.uk
dir: *From A39 at St Columb roundabout turn right onto A3059 towards Newquay. Fork right in approximately 2 miles for St Mawgan onto B3276. Turn right, site on left.*

Trevarrian Holiday Park is a well-established and well-run holiday park overlooking Mawgan Porth beach. It has a wide range of attractions including a free entertainment programme in peak season and a 10-pin bowling alley with licensed bar. Four glamping pods add to the holiday experience at the park. It is only a short drive to Newquay and approximately 20 minutes to Padstow.

Open: All year **Last arrival:** 22.00 **Last departure:** 11.00
Pitches: 🚐 🚌 ▲ 🏠; 10 hardstanding pitches
Leisure: ⛱ 🎣 ▢ 🎵 ⚽
Facilities: ⊙ 🚿 ✻ ♿ $ WiFi
Services: 🔌 🚽 🍽 🏢 🧺 ⬆ 🔒 ✂ T
Within 3 miles: 🚶 🐎 ∪ ◎ ⛴ 🎣 🗓

Additional site information: 7 acre site. 🚗 Cars can be parked by caravans and tents. Awnings permitted. No noise after midnight. Crazy golf.

NEWQUAY — Map 2 SW86

Places to visit

Blue Reef Aquarium, NEWQUAY, TR7 1DU, 01637 878134
www.bluereefaquarium.co.uk

Trerice, TRERICE, TR8 4PG, 01637 875404
www.nationaltrust.org.uk/trerice

Great for kids: Dairyland Farm Park, NEWQUAY, TR8 5AA, 01872 510246
dairylandfarmpark.com

Newquay Zoo, NEWQUAY, TR7 2LZ, 01637 873342
www.newquayzoo.org.uk

NEWQUAY — Map 2 SW86

Platinum Park

Hendra Holiday Park

★★★★★ **HOLIDAY PARK**

tel: 01637 875778 **TR8 4NY**
email: bookings@hendra-holidays.com web: www.hendra-holidays.com
dir: *A30 onto A392 signed Newquay. At Quintrell Downs over roundabout, signed Lane, site 0.5 mile on left.*

Hendra Holiday Park is a family-owned site nestled in the Cornish countryside. Just outside Newquay, Hendra has been family owned since 1972 so has over 50 years' experience of family holidays and knows how to make a holiday memorable. An award-winning park, Hendra is a top destination for bespoke holiday homes, as well as touring, camping and caravan holidays. The park is within easy access of Newquay's seven golden beaches, amazing local attractions, as well as a range of on-site activities and entertainment.

Open: 29 March to 4 November (restricted service: April to Spring Bank Holiday and September to October – outdoor pool closed) **Last arrival:** dusk **Last departure:** 10.00
Pitches: 🚐 🚌 ▲; 35 hardstanding pitches
Leisure: ⛱ ⛱ ⚡ 🎣 🔍 ▢ 🎵 🏓 ⚽
Facilities: 🏢 ⊙ 🚿 ✻ ♿ $ 🍽 🎪 WiFi 💻
Services: 🔌 🚽 🍽 🏢 🧺 ⬆ 🔒 ✂ T
Within 3 miles: 🚶 🐎 ∪ ◎ ⛴ 🎣 🗓

Additional site information: 80 acre site. 🚗 Families and couples only. Land train rides, skate and scooter park, indoor play centre.

Platinum Park

Treloy Touring Park

★★★★★

tel: 01637 872063 **TR8 4JN**
email: stay@treloy.co.uk web: www.treloy.co.uk
dir: *On A3059 (St Columb Major to Newquay road).*

Treloy is an attractive site with fine countryside views and within easy reach of resorts and beaches. The pitches are set in four paddocks with mainly level but some slightly sloping grassy areas. Maintenance and cleanliness are very high. There's a heated swimming pool and separate paddling pool surrounded by a paved patio area with tables, an excellent reception, shop and first aid room. The top class facilities feature 20 private washrooms, all with shower, toilet, washbasin, hand drier and bench, six parent and child rooms, baby bathroom and three dedicated family shower rooms. The site has lovely woodland trails and a wildlife pond, and also a small café/restaurant.

Open: 15 May to 30 September **Last arrival:** 20.00 **Last departure:** 10.00
Pitches: 🚐 🚌 ▲; 30 hardstanding pitches
Leisure: ⛱ ⚡ 🎣 🎵 ⚽
Facilities: 🏢 ⊙ 🚿 ✻ ♿ $ 🍽 🎪 🚻 WiFi 💻
Services: 🔌 🚽 🍽 🏢 🧺 ⬆ 🔒 ✂ T
Within 3 miles: 🚶 🐎 ∪ ◎ ⛴ 🎣 🗓

Additional site information: 23 acre site. 🚗 Cars can be parked by caravans and tents. Awnings permitted. No noise after 23.00. Concessionary green fees at Treloy Golf Club. Car hire can be arranged.

PITCHES: 🚐 Caravans 🚌 Motorhomes ▲ Tents 🏠 Glamping accommodation **LEISURE:** ⛱ Indoor swimming pool ⛱ Outdoor swimming pool ⚡ Children's playground 🎣 Kids' club 🎾 Tennis court 🔍 Games room ▢ Separate TV room 🏌 golf course 🏓 Pitch n putt ⛴ Boats for hire 🚲 Bikes for hire 🎬 Cinema 🎵 Entertainment 🎣 Fishing ◎ Mini golf ⛴ Watersports 💪 Gym ⚽ Sports field ∪ Stables ♨ Spa

Premier Park

Monkey Tree Holiday Park
★★★★★ 92%

tel: 01872 572032 Hendra Croft, Scotland Road TR8 5QR
email: enquiries@monkeytreeholidaypark.co.uk
web: www.monkeytreeholidaypark.co.uk
dir: *From M5 at Exeter take A30 to Redruth (ignore all signs for Newquay). At Carland Cross roundabout (with windmills on right) continue to follow signs for Perranporth. After 1 mile turn right at Boxheater junction onto B3285 signed Perranporth. After 0.5 mile turn right at crossroads into Scotland Road. After 1 mile, park on left.*

A large, well-managed holiday park situated on Cornwall's north coast close to Newquay and just minutes from Fistral Beach and Perranporth Beach – perfectly placed for surfing and great family days out and about. There's something for everyone here and the whole park is impressive, very neat and tidy, and over 500 pitches include standard, serviced, premium, super, super-deluxe and ultra-deluxe pitches, the latter having en suite facilities on the pitch. There are also five dedicated pitches for RVs and motorhomes over 24ft long, and 64 holiday homes for hire. Facilities include touring pitches with electric, eight well-maintained toilet blocks, an outdoor swimming pool complex, crazy golf, and a clubhouse with nightly entertainment in season.

Open: from 1st April **Last arrival:** 17.00 (later arrivals by prior arrangement) **Last departure:** 10.00
Pitches: 160 seasonal pitches
Leisure:
Facilities:
Services:
Within 3 miles:
Additional site information: 56 acre site. Cars can be parked by caravans and tents. Awnings permitted. Minimum noise between 23.00 and 07.00, 5mph speed limit, no groups or single-sex parties (family friendly campsite) Crazy golf, multisport area.

Trencreek Holiday Park
★★★★ 91%

tel: 01637 874210 Hillcrest, Higher Trencreek TR8 4NS
email: trencreek@btconnect.com web: www.trencreekholidaypark.co.uk
dir: *A392 to Quintrell Downs, right towards Newquay, left at 2 mini-roundabouts into Trevenson Road to site.*

An attractively landscaped park in the village of Trencreek, with modern toilet facilities of a very high standard. Two well-stocked fishing lakes, and evening entertainment in the licensed clubhouse, are extra draws. Located about two miles from Newquay with its beaches and surfing opportunities.

Open: Easter to September **Last arrival:** 22.00 **Last departure:** noon
Pitches: 8 hardstanding pitches
Leisure:
Facilities:
Services:
Within 3 miles:
Additional site information: 10 acre site. Cars can be parked by caravans and tents. Awnings permitted. Families and couples only.

Porth Beach Holiday Park
★★★★ 86%

tel: 01637 876531 Porth TR7 3NH
email: info@porthbeach.co.uk web: www.porthbeach.co.uk
dir: *From Newquay take A3058 towards St Columb Major. At roundabout left onto B3276 signed Padstow. Site on right.*

This attractive, popular park offers level, grassy pitches in neat and tidy surroundings. It is a well-run site set in meadowland in a glorious location adjacent to excellent sands of Porth Beach. The site offers two fully-equipped camping pods positioned on a raised terrace.

Open: March to November **Last arrival:** 18.00 **Last departure:** 10.00
Pitches: 19 hardstanding pitches
Facilities:
Services:
Within 3 miles:
Additional site information: 6 acre site. Cars can be parked by caravans and tents. Awnings permitted. Families and couples only.
Glamping available: Wooden pods. **Changeover days:** Any day
Additional glamping information: Wooden pods: 2 sets of single bunk beds, electricity, lighting and heating. Cars can be parked by units

See advert on page 70

NEWQUAY continued

Riverside Holiday Park
★★★★ 84% HOLIDAY PARK

tel: 01637 873617 **Gwills Lane TR8 4PE**
email: info@riversideholidaypark.co.uk **web:** www.riversideholidaypark.co.uk
dir: *A30 onto A392 signed Newquay. At Quintrell Downs at roundabout follow Lane sign. 2nd left in 0.5 mile onto unclassified road signed Gwills. Site in 400 yards.*

A sheltered valley beside a river in a quiet location is the idyllic setting for this lightly wooded park that caters for families and couples only; the site is well placed for exploring Newquay and Padstow. There is a lovely swimming pool. The site is close to the wide variety of attractions offered in Newquay. Self-catering lodges, cabins and static vans are available for hire.

Open: Easter to end October **Last arrival:** 22.00 **Last departure:** 10.00
Pitches: 🚐 🚍 ⛺
Leisure:
Facilities:
Services:
Within 3 miles:

Additional site information: 11 acre site. Cars can be parked by caravans and tents. Awnings permitted. Families and couples only.

Trenance Holiday Park
★★★★ 83%

tel: 01637 873447 **Edgcumbe Avenue TR7 2JY**
email: enquiries@trenanceholidaypark.co.uk **web:** www.trenanceholidaypark.co.uk
dir: *From Rejerrah on A3075 towards Newquay take A395 signed A392 and Newquay. At next roundabout right onto A3058 signed St Columb Minor. At double mini-roundabouts, right into Treninnick Hill. Site 1st right.*

A mainly static park popular with tenters, close to Newquay's vibrant nightlife. Set on high ground in an urban area of town, with cheerful owners and clean facilities; the site offers a motorhome service point. The local bus stops at the site entrance.

Open: 2 April to 26 September (restricted service: mid April to mid May – shop closed)
Last arrival: 22.00 **Last departure:** 10.00
Pitches: 🚐 🚍 ⛺ 🏕
Leisure:
Facilities:
Services:
Within 3 miles:

Additional site information: 12 acre site. Cars can be parked by caravans and tents. Awnings permitted. No pets, no noise after midnight.

Glamping available: Wooden pods. **Changeover days:** Any day

Additional glamping information: Wooden pods: electricity supplied, from £36. No drainage or water. No en suite toilets. Cars can be parked by units

Trebellan Park
★★★ 87%

tel: 01637 830522 **Cubert TR8 5PY**
email: enquiries@trebellan.co.uk **web:** www.trebellan.co.uk
dir: *South of Newquay from A392 onto A3075 towards Rejerrah. In approximately 4 miles, turn right signed Cubert. Left in 0.75 mile onto unclassified road.*

A terraced grassy rural park within a picturesque valley with views of Cubert Common, and adjacent to the Smuggler's Den, a 16th-century thatched inn. This park has a very inviting swimming pool and three well-stocked coarse fishing lakes.

Open: May to October **Last arrival:** 21.00 **Last departure:** 10.00
Pitches: 🚐 🚍 ⛺
Leisure:
Facilities:
Services:
Within 3 miles:

Additional site information: 8 acre site. Cars can be parked by caravans and tents. Awnings permitted. Families and couples only.

PorthBeach holiday park
Only 100m from the beach!
Caravans Touring Pods
Call: 01637 876531 or book online at www.porthbeach.co.uk
Porth, Newquay, Cornwall, TR7 3NH
follow us...

PITCHES: 🚐 Caravans 🚍 Motorhomes ⛺ Tents 🏕 Glamping accommodation **LEISURE:** Indoor swimming pool — Outdoor swimming pool — Children's playground — Kids' club — Tennis court — Games room — Separate TV room — golf course — Pitch n putt — Boats for hire — Bikes for hire — Cinema — Entertainment — Fishing — Mini golf — Watersports — Gym — Sports field — Stables — Spa

CORNWALL & ISLES OF SCILLY

PADSTOW
Map 2 SW97

Places to visit

Prideaux Place, PADSTOW, PL28 8RP, 01841 532411
prideauxplace.co.uk

The Shipwreck and Heritage Centre, ST AUSTELL, PL25 3NJ, 01726 69897
www.shipwreckcharlestown.co.uk

Great for kids: Eden Project, ST AUSTELL, PL24 2SG, 01726 811972
www.edenproject.com

Premier Park

The Retreats @ Padstow Holiday Park
★★★★★ 88% HOLIDAY PARK

tel: 01841 532289 **Cliffdowne PL28 8LB**
email: mail@padstowholidaypark.co.uk **web:** www.padstowholidaypark.co.uk
dir: *Exit A39 onto either A389 or B3274 to Padstow. Site signed 1.5 miles before Padstow.*

In an Area of Outstanding Natural Beauty and within a mile of the historic fishing village of Padstow (which can be reached via a footpath), this static-only park with one well-equipped unit for hire has seen huge investment in recent years and provides comfortable relaxing accommodation in a quiet and peaceful atmosphere. A superb building houses the reception, coffee lounge and an impressive 20-metre swimming pool. This is a quiet base that is convenient for the many attractions Cornwall has to offer.

Open: early February to early January
Holiday Homes: Sleep 4, Bedrooms 2, Bathrooms 1, Toilet 2, Two-ring burner, Microwave, Freezer, TV, Sky/Freeview, DVD player, WiFi
Leisure:
Within 3 miles:
Additional site information:

PENTEWAN
Map 2 SX04

Places to visit

The Lost Gardens of Heligan, PENTEWAN, PL26 6EN, 01726 845100
www.heligan.com

The Shipwreck and Heritage Centre, ST AUSTELL, PL25 3NJ, 01726 69897
www.shipwreckcharlestown.co.uk

Great for kids: Eden Project, ST AUSTELL, PL24 2SG, 01726 811972
www.edenproject.com

Premier Park

Heligan Caravan & Camping Park
★★★★★ 86%

tel: 01726 842714 & 844414 **PL26 6BT**
email: info@heligancampsite.com **web:** www.heligancampsite.com
dir: *From A390 take B3273 for Mevagissey at crossroads signed 'No caravans beyond this point'. Right onto unclassified road towards Gorran, site 0.75 mile on left.*

A pleasant, peaceful park adjacent to The Lost Gardens of Heligan, with views over St Austell Bay and well-maintained facilities, including superb quality toilet and shower facilities. Guests can also use the extensive amenities at the sister park, Pentewan Sands, and there's a footpath with direct access to The Lost Gardens of Heligan.

Open: 4 January to 17 November (restricted service: reception opening times: 09.00–11.00 and 17.00–18.00) **Last arrival:** 22.00 **Last departure:** 10.30
Pitches: 27 hardstanding pitches; 10 seasonal pitches
Leisure:
Facilities:
Services:
Within 3 miles:

Additional site information: 12 acre site. Cars can be parked by caravans and tents. Awnings permitted. Woodland walk and cycling trail.

PERRANPORTH
Map 2 SW75

Places to visit

Royal Cornwall Museum, TRURO, TR1 2SJ, 01872 272205
www.royalcornwallmuseum.org.uk

Trerice, TRERICE, TR8 4PG, 01637 875404
www.nationaltrust.org.uk/trerice

Great for kids: Blue Reef Aquarium, NEWQUAY, TR7 1DU, 01637 878134
www.bluereefaquarium.co.uk

Premier Park

Perran Sands Holiday Park
★★★★★ 91% HOLIDAY PARK

tel: 01872 573551 **TR6 0AQ**
email: perransands@haven.com **web:** www.haven.com/perransands
dir: *A30 onto B3285 towards Perranporth. Site on right before descent on hill into Perranporth.*

Perran Sands Holiday Park is situated amid 500 acres of protected dune grassland, and with a footpath through to the surf and three miles of golden sandy beach, this lively park is set in a large village-style complex. It offers a complete range of on-site facilities and entertainment for all the family, which makes it an extremely popular park. There are two top-of-the-range facility blocks. Safari tents, super tents, geo domes and yurts are available for hire.

Open: mid March to end October (restricted service: mid March to May and September to end October – some facilities may be reduced) **Last arrival:** 22.00 **Last departure:** 10.00
Pitches: see prices below; 28 hardstanding pitches
Leisure:
Facilities:
Services:
Within 3 miles:

Additional site information: 550 acre site. No commercial vehicles, no bookings by persons under 21 years unless a family booking. Maximum 2 dogs per booking, certain dog breeds banned.

Glamping available: Safari tents from £129; super tents from £99; yurts from £198; geo domes from £239. **Changeover days:** Monday, Friday, Saturdays

Additional glamping information: All glamping units: minimum stay 3 nights, kitchen, no sink.

FACILITIES: Electric vehicle charging · Baths/Shower · Electric shaver sockets · Hairdryer · Ice pack facility · Baby facilities · Disabled facilities · Shop on site or within 200yds · BBQ area · Picnic area · WiFi · Internet access **SERVICES:** Electric hook-up · Launderette · Licensed bar · Calor Gas · Campingaz · Toilet fluid · Café/Restaurant · Fast Food/Takeaway · Battery charging · Motorhome service point · No credit or debit cards · Dogs permitted · No dogs

PERRANPORTH continued

Tollgate Farm Caravan & Camping Park
★★★★ 90%

tel: 01872 572130 Budnick Hill TR6 0AD
email: enquiries@tollgatefarm.co.uk web: www.tollgatefarm.co.uk
dir: Exit A30 onto B3285 to Perranporth. Site on right 1.5 miles after Goonhavern.

A quiet site in a rural location with spectacular coastal views. Pitches are divided into four paddocks sheltered and screened by mature hedges, and there's a fully-equipped campers' kitchen. Children will enjoy the play equipment and pets' corner. The three miles of sand at Perran Bay are just a walk away through the sand dunes, or by car it is a three-quarter mile drive. There are five fully-serviced premium pitches (three grass and two hardstanding) as well as five camping pods for hire. There are also wardens on site.

Open: Easter to September **Last arrival:** 20.00 **Last departure:** 10.30
Pitches: see price below; 10 hardstanding pitches; 12 seasonal pitches
Leisure:
Facilities:
Services:
Within 3 miles:
Additional site information: 10 acre site. Cars can be parked by caravans and tents. Awnings permitted. No large groups. Car hire can be arranged.
Glamping available: Wooden pods
Additional glamping information: Wooden pods: minimum stay 2 nights (off-peak season), 3 nights (peak season). Sleep 4. From £55

POLPERRO — Map 2 SX25

Places to visit
Restormel Castle, RESTORMEL, PL22 0EE, 01208 872687
www.english-heritage.org.uk/visit/places/restormel-castle

Great for kids: Wild Futures, LOOE, PL13 1NZ, 01503 262532
www.wildfutures.org

Great Kellow Farm
★★★ 83%

tel: 01503 272387 PL13 2QL
email: enquiries@greatkellowfarm.co.uk web: www.greatkellowfarm.co.uk
dir: Sat nav and Google maps directions and approach from Polperro are not recommended. For tourers: from West Looe take A387 towards Polperro. Right onto B3359 signed Pelynt. In Pelynt left by church, follow Lansallos sign. Left at crossroads, 0.75 mile to staggered crossroads. Turn left, site sign visible. 0.5 mile, on right bend follow site sign, after 2 bends, site on left.

Set on a high-level grassy paddock with magnificent views across Polperro Bay, this tranquil and very friendly site is set on a working beef and sheep farm. The toilet and shower block offer excellent, clean facilities. It is ideally located for exploring the Cornish coast and countryside, nearby National Trust properties, and the fishing village of Polperro is only a 10-minute walk away. There is also a farm shop selling a good range of local produce, including beef and lamb reared on the farm.

Open: 1 April to 31 October (restricted service: 1 November to 3 January – seasonal pitches only) **Last arrival:** 21.00 (later arrival by arrangement). **Last departure:** 11.00
Pitches: ; 15 seasonal pitches
Facilities:
Services:
Within 3 miles:
Additional site information: 3 acre site. Cars can be parked by caravans and tents. Awnings permitted. No noise after 23.00. Dogs on leads at all times. 5mph speed limit.

POLZEATH — Map 2 SW97

Places to visit
Tintagel Castle, TINTAGEL, PL34 0HE, 01840 770328
www.english-heritage.org.uk/visit/places/tintagel-castle

Platinum Park

Gunvenna Holiday Park
★★★★★

tel: 01208 862405 St Minver PL27 6QN
email: gunvenna.bookings@gmail.com web: www.gunvenna.com
dir: From Wadebridge take B3314 (Port Isaac Road), Gunvenna is 4 miles from Wadebridge on right of B3314.

An attractive park with extensive rural views in a quiet country location, yet within three miles of Polzeath and Rock. This popular park is family owned and run, and provides top-notch facilities, including smart toilets and a welcoming reception cabin; an ideal position for touring north Cornwall. The park has excellent hardstanding pitches, maturing landscaping and a beautiful indoor swimming pool with a glass roof. A Scandinavian wooden glamping cabin, a holiday cottage and static caravans are for hire. The beach at Polzeath is very popular with the surfers and from Rock beach you can take the ferry across to Padstow.

Open: Easter to October **Last arrival:** 20.30 **Last departure:** 10.30
Pitches: see prices below; 33 hardstanding pitches; 18 seasonal pitches
Leisure:
Facilities:
Services:
Within 3 miles:
Additional site information: 10 acre site. Cars can be parked by caravans and tents. Awnings permitted. Children under 16 years must be accompanied by an adult in the swimming pool. Owners must clear up after their dogs and use the waste bins provided. Mobile pizza unit and mobile street kitchen.
Glamping available: Hobbit House £63–£69 **Changeover days:** Any day
Additional glamping information: Accommodates 2 adults and 2 children, non-smoking. Cars can be parked by units

CORNWALL & ISLES OF SCILLY 73 ENGLAND

Tristram Caravan & Camping Park
★★★ 93%
tel: 01208 862215 PL27 6TD
email: info@tristramcampsite.co.uk web: www.polzeathcamping.co.uk
dir: *From B3314 onto unclassified road signed Polzeath. Through village, up hill, site 2nd right.*

An ideal family site, positioned on a gently sloping cliff with grassy pitches and glorious sea views, which are best enjoyed from the terraced pitches, or over lunch or dinner at the excellent Cracking Crab café adjacent to the reception overlooking the beach. There is direct, gated access to the beach, where surfing is very popular, or a gentle paddle if you prefer! The local amenities of the village are only a few hundred yards away. Please note, this park no longer accepts tents.

Open: March to October (restricted service: mid September – reseeding the site)
Last arrival: 18.00 (low season) 19.00 high season **Last departure:** 11.00
Pitches: 🚐 🚗
Facilities: 🚿 ☉ 🎨 ✳ ♿ 🛒 🍖 WiFi
Services: 🔌 🔄 🍴 🧺 🔋 🔒 ⚡ T
Within 3 miles: 🏃 ⛳ ∪ ◎ 🚲 ⛵ 🏛
Additional site information: 3 acre site. 🚗 Cars can be parked by caravans. Awnings permitted with breathable groundsheet. No ball games, no disposable BBQs, no noise between 23.00–07.00.

Southwinds Caravan & Camping Park
★★★ 92%
tel: 01208 863267 & 862215 Polzeath Road PL27 6QU
email: info@southwindscamping.co.uk web: www.polzeathcamping.co.uk
dir: *Exit B3314 onto unclassified road signed Polzeath, site on right just past turn to New Polzeath.*

A peaceful site with beautiful sea and panoramic rural views, within walking distance of a golf complex, and just three quarters of a mile from beach and village. There are four spacious fields including one dedicated to family tents. Next door is the Beach Farm Café & Yard and a farm shop; camping accessories are available in the reception. Dogs are welcome here.

Open: May to September **Last arrival:** 20.00 **Last departure:** 10.30
Pitches: 🚐 🚗 ⛺
Facilities: 🚿 ☉ 🎨 ✳ ♿ WiFi
Services: 🔌 🔄 🍴 🧺 🔋 🔒 ⚡ T
Within 3 miles: 🏃 ⛳ ∪ ◎ 🚲 ⛵ 🏛 🎣
Additional site information: 16 acre site. 🚗 Cars can be parked by caravans and tents. Awnings and breathable groundsheets permitted. Families and couples only, no disposable BBQs, no noise 23.00–07.00. Families and couples only. Stepper Field open mid July to August (school holidays).

PORTHTOWAN
Map 2 SW64

Places to visit
Wheal Coates (NT), ST AGNES, TR5 0NT
www.nationaltrust.org.uk/visit/cornwall/wheal-coates

PORTHTOWAN
Map 2 SW64

Platinum Park

Porthtowan Tourist Park
★★★★★
tel: 01209 890256 Mile Hill TR4 8TY
email: admin@porthtowantouristpark.co.uk web: www.porthtowantouristpark.co.uk
dir: *From A30 at Redruth follow Portreath, B3300 and brown camping signs. On B3300 in approximately 2 miles turn right at T-junction, follow site sign. Site on left at top of hill.*

Porthtowan Tourist Park is a neat, level grassy site on high ground with plenty of shelter from mature trees and shrubs. Situated a mile from the Cornish surfing beach of Porthtowan, the site has grass pitches with easy access from the A30, an adventure play area, swings, a shop and games room. The park's modern facilities are maintained to a high standard and include a launderette, a washing-up area and a disablility-adapted toilet and shower block. The site also has a purpose-built games and meeting room with a good library where tourist information leaflets are available. A tearoom, adjacent to the campsite, serves takeaway meals during the peak season (limited opening hours at other times of the year) and barbeques are also allowed. Dogs are welcome on site. Winner of the AA Campsite of the Year 2023–24.

Open: 26 March to 30 September **Last arrival:** 19.00 **Last departure:** 11.00
Pitches: 🚐 🚗 ⛺; 14 hardstanding pitches
Leisure: 🎱 🎣 **Facilities:** 🚿 ☉ 🎨 ✳ ♿ 🛒 🍖 WiFi
Services: 🔌 🔄 🧺 🔋 ⚡ T **Within 3 miles:** 🏃 ⛳ ∪ ⛵ 🏛
Additional site information: 5 acre site. 🚗 Cars can be parked by caravans and tents. Awnings permitted. No bikes or skateboards during school summer holidays. Table tennis and pool table.

PORTREATH
Map 2 SW64

Places to visit
East Pool Mine, POOL, TR15 3NP, 01209 315027
www.nationaltrust.org.uk/east-pool-mine

Platinum Park

Landal Gwel an Mor
★★★★★ HOLIDAY PARK
tel: 01209 842354 Feadon Lane TR16 4PE
email: guestservices@landal.co.uk web: www.landal.co.uk/parks/gwel-an-mor

This Cornish holiday home complex is located close to the north coast resort of Portreath. There is a choice of accommodation comprising Scandinavian lodges, lakeside lodges, residence eco-lodges, Kinder lodges and accessible lodges. All have been tastefully appointed with designer decor, and most lodges have hot tubs. The activities on offer include golf, cycle hire, a gym, tennis, archery, swimming pool, spa, sauna, the Feadon Farm Wildlife Centre and Base Camp soft play area for children. The Terrace Restaurant serves a variety of dishes and meals can be delivered to your lodge.

FACILITIES: Electric vehicle charging · Baths/Shower · Electric shaver sockets · Hairdryer · Ice pack facility · Baby facilities · Disabled facilities · Shop on site or within 200yds · BBQ area · Picnic area · WiFi · Internet access **SERVICES:** Electric hook-up · Launderette · Licensed bar · Calor Gas · Campingaz · Toilet fluid · Café/Restaurant · Fast Food/Takeaway · Battery charging · Motorhome service point · No credit or debit cards · Dogs permitted · No dogs

CORNWALL & ISLES OF SCILLY

PORTREATH continued

Tehidy Holiday Park
★★★★ 92%

tel: 01209 216489 Harris Mill, Illogan TR16 4JQ
email: holiday@tehidy.co.uk web: www.tehidy.co.uk
dir: *Exit A30 at Redruth/Portreath junction onto A3047 to 1st roundabout. Left onto B3300. At junction straight over signed Tehidy Holiday Park. into next valley near bottom of hill on left.*

Minutes from beaches, cycle routes and central to all the main attractions in Cornwall, Tehidy Holiday Park is a clean, friendly and well kept park. Situated in an attractive wooded location in a quiet rural area, it's a great destination for both couples and families, offering a play area, games room, mostly level pitches on tiered ground with good privacy and seating, and bright, modern toilet facilities. Cottages, holiday caravans, camping/ touring and wigwam camping cabins are available for hire. Perfect for relaxing in the heart of Cornwall.

Tehidy Holiday Park

Open: All year (restricted service: November to March – shop and part of shower block closed) **Last arrival:** 20.00 **Last departure:** 10.00

Pitches: * from £22; from £22; from £20; 11 hardstanding pitches; 4 seasonal pitches

Leisure:

Facilities:

Services:

Within 3 miles:

Additional site information: 4.5 acre site. Cars can be parked by caravans and tents. Awnings permitted. No pets, quiet after 22.00. Pre-booking required for large motorhomes and caravans. Off licence, cooking shelter, trampoline.

Glamping available: Wooden wigwams. **Changeover days:** Any day except Sunday

Additional glamping information: Wooden wigwams (sleep maximum of 5) offer a cooking shelter, heating, fridge/freezer, microwave, kettle, TV and BBQ and picnic bench. Cars can be parked by units

See advert below

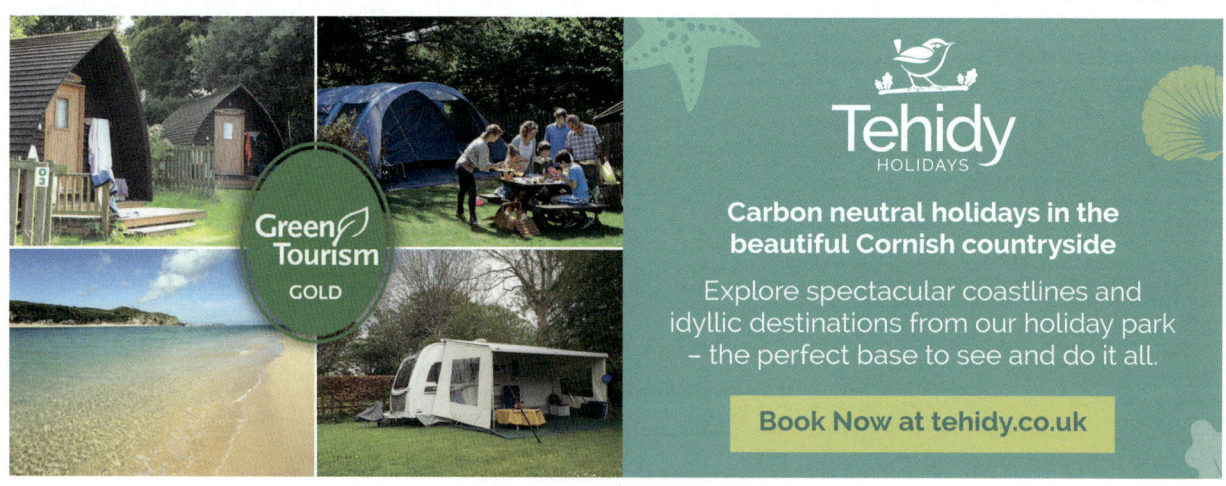

CORNWALL & ISLES OF SCILLY

PORTSCATHO
Map 2 SW83

Places to visit
St Mawes Castle, ST MAWES, TR2 5DE, 01326 270526
www.english-heritage.org.uk/visit/places/st-mawes-castle

Trelissick, TRELISSICK, TR3 6QL, 01872 862090
www.nationaltrust.org.uk/trelissick

Trewince Farm Touring Park
★★★ 86%

tel: 01872 580430 **TR2 5ET**
email: info@trewincefarm.co.uk web: www.trewincefarm.co.uk
dir: *From St Austell take A390 towards Truro. Left on B3287 to Tregony, follow signs to St Mawes. At Trewithian, turn left to St Anthony. Site 0.75 mile past church.*

A site on a working farm with spectacular sea views, three smart glamping pods and refurbished toilets and showers. There are many quiet golden sandy beaches close by, and boat launching facilities and mooring can be arranged at the nearby Percuil River Boatyard. The village of Portscatho, with shops, pubs and attractive harbour, is approximately one mile away.

Open: April to September **Last arrival:** 21.00 **Last departure:** 10.30

Pitches: 🚐 🚙 ⛺; 🛖 see prices below

Facilities: 🚿 ☉ 🪒 ❄ 🍖

Services: 🔌 🗑 🧺

Within 3 miles: ⚓ 🏄 ⛳ 🎣

Additional site information: 3 acre site. 🐕 🚗 Cars can be parked by caravans and tents. Awnings permitted.

Glamping available: Wooden pods from £45.

Additional glamping information: No dogs in pods or surrounding area. Cars can be parked by units

REDRUTH
Map 2 SW64

Places to visit
East Pool Mine, POOL, TR15 3NP, 01209 315027
www.nationaltrust.org.uk/east-pool-mine

Pendennis Castle, FALMOUTH, TR11 4LP, 01326 316594
www.english-heritage.org.uk/visit/places/pendennis-castle

Great for kids: National Maritime Museum Cornwall, FALMOUTH, TR11 3QY, 01326 313388
www.nmmc.co.uk

REDRUTH
Map 2 SW64

Platinum Park

Globe Vale Holiday Park
★★★★★

tel: 01209 891183 Radnor **TR16 4BH**
email: info@globevale.co.uk web: www.globevale.co.uk
dir: *From A30 at roundabout (northeast of Redruth) follow Portreath and B3300 signs. At next crossroads right into Radnor Road, follow brown site signs. In 0.5 mile turn left at site sign. Site 0.5 mile on left.*

A family owned and run park set in a quiet rural location yet close to some stunning beaches and coastline. The park's touring area has a range of pitches to suit all requirements, including a number of full facility hardstanding pitches, along with a high quality toilet block with privacy cubicles. There is also a stylish and comfortable lounge bar and conservatory serving an excellent selection of bar meals.

Open: All year (restricted service: January – March, October – December)
Last arrival: 20.00 **Last departure:** 10.00

Pitches: 🚐 🚙 ⛺; 57 hardstanding pitches; 10 seasonal pitches

Leisure: 🎱 ♠ ⚽ **Facilities:** 🚿 ❄ ♿ 🗑 📶

Services: 🔌 🗑 🍺 🍴 🚰 🧺 ⛽ 🔒 ♻ 🚽 **Within 3 miles:** ⛳ 🎣 🏪

Additional site information: 18 acre site. 🐕 🚗 Cars can be parked by caravans and tents. Awnings permitted. 5mph speed limit. Minimum noise after 22.00. Dogs must be kept on leads throughout the park. Shower block heated in winter.

See advert on page 76

REDRUTH continued

Lanyon Holiday Park
★★★★ 91%
tel: 01209 313474 Loscombe Lane, Four Lanes TR16 6LP
email: info@lanyonholidaypark.co.uk web: www.lanyonholidaypark.co.uk
dir: *Exit A30 signed Camborne and Pool onto A3047. Straight on at next two lights. Pass Tesco Extra on left. Right signed Four Lanes, over rail bridge. In Four Lanes right at staggered crossroads onto B2397, 2nd right at Pencoys Hall into Loscombe Lane. Site on left in approximately 400 metres.*

This is a small, friendly and rural park in an elevated position with fine views to distant St Ives Bay. It is a family-owned and -run park that continues to be upgraded in all areas; there is a smart toilet block with two family rooms, and larger pitches have been created. The park has a very inviting swimming pool. Stithians Reservoir for fishing, sailing and windsurfing is two miles away, and the site is close to a cycling trail. Two holiday cottages are available for hire.

Open: March to October (restricted service: March to Spring Bank Holiday and 1st weekend in September to October – bar and restaurant closed. March and October – pool closed) **Last arrival:** 21.00 **Last departure:** 11.00
Pitches: 5 seasonal pitches
Leisure:
Facilities:
Services:
Within 3 miles:
Additional site information: 14 acre site. Cars can be parked by caravans and tents. Awnings permitted. Families only, no commercial vehicles. Breakfast catering van during peak season school holidays.

Cambrose Touring Park
★★★ 82%
tel: 01209 890747 Portreath Road TR16 4HT
email: info@cambrosetouringpark.co.uk web: www.cambrosetouringpark.co.uk
dir: *A30 onto B3300 towards Portreath. Approximately 0.75 mile at 1st roundabout right onto B3300. Take unclassified road on right signed Porthtowan. Site 200 yards on left.*

Situated in a rural setting surrounded by trees and shrubs, this park is divided into grassy paddocks. It is about two miles from the harbour village of Portreath. The site has an excellent swimming pool with a sunbathing area.

Open: Easter to 31 October **Last arrival:** 22.00 **Last departure:** 11.30
Pitches: 6 seasonal pitches
Leisure:
Facilities:
Services:
Within 3 miles:
Additional site information: 6 acre site. Cars can be parked by caravans and tents. Awnings permitted. No noise after 23.30. Mini football pitch.

GLobe Vale caravan & camping holidays — open all year
www.globevale.co.uk e: info@globevale.co.uk t: 01209 891183
ONE OF THE TOP TEN SITES IN CORNWALL — AA PLATINUM AWARD WINNER

PITCHES: Caravans Motorhomes Tents Glamping accommodation **LEISURE:** Indoor swimming pool Outdoor swimming pool Children's playground Kids' club Tennis court Games room Separate TV room golf course Pitch n putt Boats for hire Bikes for hire Cinema Entertainment Fishing Mini golf Watersports Gym Sports field Stables Spa

CORNWALL & ISLES OF SCILLY

Stithians Lake Country Park
★★★ 80%

tel: 01209 860301 **Stithians Lake, Menherion TR16 6NW**
email: stithiansoa@swlakestrust.org.uk **web:** www.southwestlakes.co.uk
dir: *From Redruth take B3297 towards Helston. Follow brown tourist signs to Stithians Lake, entrance by Golden Lion Inn.*

This simple campsite is a two-acre field situated adjacent to the Watersports Centre, which forms part of a large activity complex beside Stithians Lake. The toilet and shower facilities at the centre include a family room and seven toilet/shower cubicles. The excellent waterside café also serves breakfasts. This is the perfect campsite for watersports enthusiasts.

Open: 3 April to 31 October **Last arrival:** anytime **Last departure:** 11.00

Pitches:
Leisure:
Facilities:
Services:
Within 3 miles:

Additional site information: 2.1 acre site. Cars can be parked by caravans and tents. Awnings permitted. No noise after midnight, no swimming in lake, charges apply to use equipment on lake.

ROSE — Map 2 SW75

Places to visit

Trerice, TRERICE, TR8 4PG, 01637 875404
www.nationaltrust.org.uk/trerice

Newquay Zoo, NEWQUAY, TR7 2LZ, 01637 873342
www.newquayzoo.org.uk

Higher Hendra Park
★★★ 81%

tel: 01872 571496 & 07932 572580 **Higher Hendra, Treamble TR4 9PS**
email: cowe43@btinternet.com **web:** www.higherhendraholidays.co.uk
dir: *From A30 between Carland Cross and Zelah Hill take B3285 signed Goonhavern and Perranporth. 0.5 mile turn right into Scotland Road signed Rejerrah. At T-junction right on A3075 signed Newquay. In 300 yards left signed Rejerrah. In approximately 0.75 mile site on right.*

Situated down quiet lanes close to Perranporth, this small adults-only touring park comprises just 10 very spacious pitches (8 hardstandings; 2 grass) set in a neat and well-landscaped semi-circle surrounding a paddock, all with electricity and stunning views across rolling fields to St Agnes Beacon. The good quality toilet and shower facilities are housed in a smart cabin. This is a very peaceful base – perfect for walking and visiting the nearby beaches.

Open: All year **Last departure:** 10.00

Pitches: ; 8 hardstanding pitches
Facilities:
Services:
Within 3 miles:

Additional site information: 2 acre site. Adults only. Cars can be parked by caravans. Awnings permitted. 5mph speed limit.

RUTHERNBRIDGE — Map 2 SX06

Places to visit

Prideaux Place, PADSTOW, PL28 8RP, 01841 532411
prideauxplace.co.uk

Cornwall's Regimental Museum, BODMIN, PL31 1EG, 01208 72810
www.cornwalls-regimentalmuseum.org

Great for kids: Pencarrow, BODMIN, PL30 3AG, 01208 841369
www.pencarrow.co.uk

Crealy Theme Park & Resort, CLYST ST MARY, EX5 1DR, 01395 233200
www.crealy.co.uk

Ruthern Valley Holidays
★★★ 88%

tel: 01208 831395 **PL30 5LU**
email: camping@ruthernvalley.com **web:** www.ruthernvalley.com
dir: *A389 through Bodmin, follow St Austell signs, then Lanivet signs. At top of hill right onto unclassified road signed Ruthernbridge. Follow signs.*

An attractive woodland site peacefully located in a small river valley west of Bodmin Moor. This away-from-it-all park is ideal for those wanting a quiet holiday, and the informal pitches are spread in four natural areas, with plenty of sheltered space. There are also 12 lodges, heated wooden wigwams, wooden pods, 'mega' pods and static holiday vans for hire.

Open: All year **Last arrival:** 20.30 **Last departure:** noon

Pitches: ; 2 hardstanding pitches
Leisure:
Facilities:
Services:
Within 3 miles:

Additional site information: 7.5 acre site. Cars can be parked by caravans and tents. Awnings permitted. No noise 22.30–07.00, no fires. Farm animals. Freshly baked bread and croissants.

Glamping available: 4 wooden wigwams; 3 wooden pods; 2 en suite mega pods.
Changeover days: Monday to Saturday

Additional glamping information: Cars can be parked by units

FACILITIES: Electric vehicle charging · Baths/Shower · Electric shaver sockets · Hairdryer · Ice pack facility · Baby facilities · Disabled facilities · Shop on site or within 200yds · BBQ area · Picnic area · WiFi · Internet access   SERVICES: Electric hook-up · Launderette · Licensed bar · Calor Gas · Campingaz · Toilet fluid · Café/Restaurant · Fast Food/Takeaway · Battery charging · Motorhome service point · No credit or debit cards · Dogs permitted · No dogs

ENGLAND — CORNWALL & ISLES OF SCILLY

ST AGNES — Map 2 SW75

Places to visit
Royal Cornwall Museum, TRURO, TR1 2SJ, 01872 272205
www.royalcornwallmuseum.org.uk

Trerice, TRERICE, TR8 4PG, 01637 875404
www.nationaltrust.org.uk/trerice

Premier Park

Beacon Cottage Farm Touring Park
★★★★★ 86%

tel: 01872 552347 & 07879 413862 **Beacon Drive TR5 0NU**
email: jane@beaconcottagefarmholidays.co.uk
web: www.beaconcottagefarmholidays.co.uk
dir: *From A30 at Threeburrows roundabout take B3277 to St Agnes, left into Goonvrea Road, right into Beacon Drive, follow brown sign to site.*

Beacon Cottage is a neat and compact site on a working farm, utilising a cottage and outhouses, an old orchard and adjoining walled paddock. The location on a headland looking north-east along the coast means stunning views towards St Ives, and the friendly family owners keep their site very well maintained.

Open: April to October **Last arrival:** 20.00 **Last departure:** noon
Pitches: 6 hardstanding pitches; 6 seasonal pitches
Leisure:
Facilities:
Services:
Within 3 miles:
Additional site information: 5 acre site. Cars can be parked by caravans and tents. Awnings permitted. No large groups, no noise after 22.00. Secure year-round caravan storage, dog exercise field.

Presingoll Farm Caravan & Camping Park
★★★★ 88%

tel: 01872 552333 **TR5 0PB**
email: pam@presingollfarm.co.uk web: www.presingollfarm.co.uk
dir: *From A30 at Chiverton roundabout take B3277 towards St Agnes. Site 3 miles on right.*

An attractive rural park adjoining farmland, with extensive views of the coast beyond. Family owned and run, with level grass pitches, and a modernised toilet block in smart converted farm buildings. There is also a campers' room with microwave, freezer, kettle and free coffee and tea, and a children's play area. This is an ideal base for touring the Newquay and St Ives areas.

Open: Easter and April to October (restricted service: 1 November – 1 April or Easter which ever is the earliest) **Last arrival:** 21.00 **Last departure:** 10.00
Pitches: 6 hardstanding pitches
Leisure:
Facilities:
Services:
Within 3 miles:
Additional site information: 5 acre site. Cars can be parked by caravans and tents. Awnings permitted. No large groups. Car hire can be arranged.

ST AUSTELL — Map 2 SX05

Places to visit
The Shipwreck and Heritage Centre, ST AUSTELL, PL25 3NJ, 01726 69897
www.shipwreckcharlestown.co.uk

Eden Project, ST AUSTELL, PL24 2SG, 01726 811972
www.edenproject.com

Great for kids: Wheal Martyn, ST AUSTELL, PL26 8XG, 01726 850362
www.wheal-martyn.com

PITCHES: Caravans Motorhomes Tents Glamping accommodation **LEISURE:** Indoor swimming pool Outdoor swimming pool Children's playground Kids' club Tennis court Games room Separate TV room golf course Pitch n putt Boats for hire Bikes for hire Cinema Entertainment Fishing Mini golf Watersports Gym Sports field Stables Spa

CORNWALL & ISLES OF SCILLY   79 ENGLAND

ST AUSTELL   Map 2 SX05

Premier Park

River Valley Holiday Park
★★★★★ 91%

tel: 01726 73533 **London Apprentice PL26 7AP**
email: mail@rivervalleyholidaypark.co.uk web: www.rivervalleyholidaypark.co.uk
dir: *Take B3273 from St Austell to London Apprentice. Site signed, direct access to site from B3273.*

A neat, well-maintained family-run park set in a pleasant river valley. The quality toilet block and attractively landscaped grounds make this a delightful base for a holiday. All pitches are hardstanding, mostly divided by low fencing and neatly trimmed hedges, and the park offers a good range of leisure facilities, including an inviting swimming pool, a games room, an internet room, and an excellent children's play area. There is direct access to river walks and an off-road cycle trail to the beach at Pentewan. The site is on the bus route to St Austell.

Open: April to end September **Last arrival:** 21.00 **Last departure:** 11.00
Pitches: ; 45 hardstanding pitches
Leisure:
Facilities:
Services:
Within 3 miles:
Additional site information: 2 acre site. Cars can be parked by caravans and tents. Awnings permitted.

Court Farm Campsite
★★★ 88%

tel: 01726 823684 & 07973 773681 **St Stephen PL26 7LE**
email: info@courtfarmcornwall.co.uk web: www.courtfarmcornwall.co.uk
dir: *Take A3058 towards St Austell, through St Stephen (pass Peugeot garage), right at St Stephen/Coombe Hay/Langreth/Industrial site sign. Site 400 yards on right.*

Set in a peaceful rural location, this large camping field offers plenty of space, and is handy for the Eden Project and the Lost Gardens of Heligan. The excellent amenity block provides very high standards. Star-gazing facilities at the Roseland Observatory (including astronomy lectures) are among the on-site attractions. It is a five-minute walk to a Co-op store, and also to the bus stop on the Newquay to St Austell route.

Open: May to September **Last arrival:** by dark **Last departure:** 11.00
Pitches: ; 5 hardstanding pitches
Leisure:
Facilities:
Services:
Within 3 miles:
Additional site information: 4 acre site. Cars can be parked by caravans and tents. Awnings permitted. No noise after dark.

ST BLAZEY GATE   MAP 2 SX05

Places to visit

Eden Project, ST AUSTELL, PL24 2SG, 01726 811972
www.edenproject.com

St Catherine's Castle, FOWEY, PL23 1JH, 0370 333 1181
www.english-heritage.org.uk/visit/places/st-catherines-castle

Great for kids: Wheal Martyn, ST AUSTELL, PL26 8XG, 01726 850362
www.wheal-martyn.com

Doubletrees Farm
★★★★ 86%

tel: 01726 812266 **Luxulyan Road PL24 2EH**
email: doubletreesfarm@gmail.com web: www.doubletreesfarm.co.uk
dir: *On A390 at Blazey Gate. Turn by Leek Seed Chapel, almost opposite petrol station. After approximately 300 yards turn right by public bench into site.*

A popular park with terraced pitches that offers superb sea and coastal views. It is close to beaches, and The Eden Project is only a 20-minute walk away. This site is very well maintained by the friendly owners and the facilities are spotlessly clean. There is a Chinese restaurant and a fish and chip shop just 300 yards away.

Open: All year **Last arrival:** 20.00 **Last departure:** 11.30
Pitches: ; 10 hardstanding pitches
Facilities:
Services:
Within 3 miles:
Additional site information: 1.57 acre site. Cars can be parked by caravans and tents. Awnings permitted. No noise after 22.30.

FACILITIES: Electric vehicle charging Baths/Shower Electric shaver sockets Hairdryer Ice pack facility Baby facilities Disabled facilities Shop on site or within 200yds BBQ area Picnic area WiFi Internet access **SERVICES:** Electric hook-up Launderette Licensed bar Calor Gas Campingaz Toilet fluid Café/Restaurant Fast Food/Takeaway Battery charging Motorhome service point No credit or debit cards Dogs permitted No dogs

CORNWALL & ISLES OF SCILLY

ST COLUMB MAJOR
Map 2 SW96

Places to visit
Prideaux Place, PADSTOW, PL28 8RP, 01841 532411
prideauxplace.co.uk

Cornwall's Regimental Museum, BODMIN, PL31 1EG, 01208 72810
www.cornwalls-regimentalmuseum.org

Great for kids: Pencarrow, BODMIN, PL30 3AG, 01208 841369
www.pencarrow.co.uk

Crealy Theme Park & Resort, CLYST ST MARY, EX5 1DR, 01395 233200
www.crealy.co.uk

Trewan Hall
★★★★ 88%

tel: 01637 880261 & 07900 677397 **TR9 6DB**
email: enquiries@trewan-hall.co.uk web: www.trewan-hall.co.uk
dir: *From A39 north of St Columb Major (do not enter town) turn left signed Talskiddy and St Eval. Site 1 mile on left.*

Trewan Hall lies at the centre of a Cornish estate amid 36 acres of wooded grounds. The site's extensive amenities include good toilet facilities, hook-ups and good security, plus a 25-metre swimming pool, and a free, live theatre in a stone barn throughout July and August. The campsite shop stocks everything from groceries to camping equipment. The site also has fine gardens, four acres of woodland for dog walking and a field available for ball games. St Columb is just a short walk away.

Open: 10 May to 9 September (restricted service: low season – shop opens for shorter hours) **Last arrival:** 20.00 **Last departure:** noon
Pitches: 🚐 🚙 ⛺
Leisure: 🏊 ≋ 🎢 🎵 ⚽
Facilities: 🚿 ☺ 🍴 ✳ ♿ 🛒 🪑 📶
Services: 🔌 🗑 🚰 🧺 🔒 ♻ 🅣
Within 3 miles: 🚴 ⛳ 🎱 ⛵ ✠

Additional site information: 14.27 acre site. 🐕 Cars can be parked by caravans and tents. Awnings permitted. Families and couples only, no cycling, no driving on fields from midnight to 08.00, no noise after 23.00. Library, billiard room, table tennis, pool table, woodland walk for dogs.

ST HILARY
Map 2 SW53

Places to visit
Godolphin, HELSTON, TR13 9RE, 01736 763194
www.nationaltrust.org.uk/visit/cornwall/godolphin

St Michael's Mount, MARAZION, TR17 0HS, 01736 887822

Premier Park

Wayfarers Caravan & Camping Park
★★★★★ 92%

tel: 01736 763326 Relubbus Lane, St Hilary **TR20 9EF**
email: jean@wayfarerspark.co.uk web: www.wayfarerspark.co.uk
dir: *Exit A30 onto A394 signed Helston. 2 miles, left at roundabout onto B3280 signed Goldsithney. Through Goldsithney. Site 1 mile on left on bend (Note: slow down at 1st brown sign; it is advisable to ignore sat nav as directions are not suitable if towing a caravan).*

Located in the centre of St Hilary, two and half miles from St Michael's Mount, Wayfarers is a quiet, sheltered park in a peaceful rural setting. It offers spacious, well-drained pitches and very well-maintained facilities, including an impressive toilet and shower block. The bistro serves breakfast daily and evening meals three nights a week.

Open: 3 March to 3 January **Last arrival:** 18.00 **Last departure:** 11.00
Pitches: 🚐 🚙 ⛺; 21 hardstanding pitches; 6 seasonal pitches
Leisure:
Facilities: 🚿 ☺ 🍴 ✳ ♿ 🪑 📶
Services: 🔌 🗑 🚰 🧺 🔒 ♻ 🅣
Within 3 miles: 🚴 ⛳ 🎱 ⛵ ✠

Additional site information: 4.8 acre site. Adults only. 🚫 Cars can be parked by caravans. Awnings permitted. No pets, flag/light poles or flags. Quiet from 23.00–7.00. Facilities for less able visitors, tourist information room, books and DVDs for sale. Car hire can be arranged.

ST IVES
Map 2 SW54

Places to visit
Barbara Hepworth Museum & Sculpture Garden, ST IVES, TR26 1AD, 01736 796226
www.tate.org.uk/visit/tate-st-ives/barbara-hepworth-museum-and-sculpture-garden

Tate St Ives, ST IVES, TR26 1TG, 01736 796226
www.tate.org.uk/visit/tate-st-ives

CORNWALL & ISLES OF SCILLY — ENGLAND

ST IVES
Map 2 SW54

Platinum Park

Ayr Holiday Park
★★★★★

tel: 01736 795855 **TR26 1EJ**
email: recept@ayrholidaypark.co.uk web: http://www.ayrholidaypark.co.uk
dir: *From A30 follow St Ives 'large vehicles' route via B3311 through Halsetown onto B3306. Site signed towards St Ives town centre.*

A well-established park on a cliff side overlooking St Ives Bay, Ayr Holiday Park has a heated toilet block that makes winter holidaying more appealing. There are stunning views from most pitches, and the town centre, harbour and beach are only half a mile away, with direct access to the coastal footpath. This makes an excellent base for surfing enthusiasts. A recent addition is the superb indoor pool with its stylish café/bar serving a range of meals throughout the day and evening, accompanied by the amazing view.

Open: All year **Last arrival:** 22.00 **Last departure:** 11.00
Pitches: 🚐 🚙 ⛺; 50 hardstanding pitches
Leisure:
Facilities:
Services:
Within 3 miles:

Additional site information: 6 acre site. Cars can be parked by caravans and tents. Awnings permitted. No disposable BBQs.

---

polmanter
ST IVES

AA PLATINUM CAMPSITE 2024

5* award-winning camping within walking distance of St Ives

Enjoy generous pitches along with an on-site bar and restaurant

Heated outdoor pool, indoor and outdoor play areas

Luxury self-catering apartments and hot tub cottages

Cornwall Tourism Awards 2022/23 GOLD
South West England Tourism Excellence Awards 2022/2023 BRONZE
AA Caravan & Camping ★★★★★ 2024
Tripadvisor Travellers' Choice Awards Best of the Best 2024

+44 (0)1736 795640   www.polmanter.com
Polmanter Touring Park, St Ives, Cornwall, TR26 3LX

FACILITIES: Electric vehicle charging · Baths/Shower · Electric shaver sockets · Hairdryer · Ice pack facility · Baby facilities · Disabled facilities · Shop on site or within 200yds · BBQ area · Picnic area · WiFi · Internet access **SERVICES:** Electric hook-up · Launderette · Licensed bar · Calor Gas · Campingaz · Toilet fluid · Café/Restaurant · Fast Food/Takeaway · Battery charging · Motorhome service point · No credit or debit cards · Dogs permitted · No dogs

ENGLAND 82 CORNWALL & ISLES OF SCILLY

ST IVES continued

Platinum Park

Polmanter Touring Park
★★★★★
tel: 01736 795640 **Halsetown TR26 3LX**
email: reception@polmanter.com **web:** www.polmanter.com
dir: *Signed from B3311 at Halsetown.*

A well-developed touring park on high ground, Polmanter is an excellent choice for family holidays – high quality is evident everywhere, from the immaculate, modern toilet blocks and the state-of-the-art dog wash/grooming facility, to the outdoor swimming pool and hard tennis courts. The pitches are individually marked and sited in meadows, and the tastefully landscaped park also offers a field with full-facility hardstanding pitches to accommodate larger caravans and motorhomes. The smart reception and shop building has two upstairs apartments available for hire. The fishing port of St Ives and the beaches are just a mile and a half away, and there is a convenient bus service in high season.

Open: 1 April to 31 October (restricted service: mid September to end of May – pool closed) **Last arrival:** 22.00 **Last departure:** 11.00
Pitches: 🚐 from £31.50; 🚙 from £31.50; ⛺ from £23.50; 88 hardstanding pitches
Leisure: ⚡ 🎿 🏊 🎯 ⚽ **Facilities:** 🏠 ☺ 🚿 ✳ ♿ 💲 WiFi 💻
Services: 🔌 🛁 🚽 🍽 🧺 🛒 🚮 🗑 🚻
Within 3 miles: 🎣 ⛳ 🏌 ◉ 🚴 🚤 🛶 🚌
Additional site information: 20 acre site. 🐕 Cars can be parked by caravans and tents. Awnings permitted. Family camping only, no skateboards, rollerblades or heelys. Putting green, tennis courts, treatment rooms, indoor soft play, shop on site. Grass tent pitch – non-electric; grass caravan/motorhome pitch – electric.

See advert on page 81

Platinum Park

Trevalgan Touring Park
★★★★★
tel: 01736 791892 **Trevalgan TR26 3BJ**
email: reception@trevalgantouringpark.co.uk **web:** www.trevalgantouringpark.co.uk
dir: *From A30 follow holiday route to St Ives. B3311 through Halsetown to B3306. Left towards Land's End. Site signed 0.5 mile on right.*

In an Area of Outstanding Natural Beauty and just two miles from St Ives, Trevalgan is an award-winning, luxury, five-star, family camping and touring park with stunning coastal and countryside views. Owned and run by Neil and Annette Osborne, the park is surrounded by open farmland, with gorse and heather-covered hills behind, and is within walking distance of the rugged and beautiful South West Coast Path. Sustainability is at the forefront of all they do, and the owners are passionate about sharing this beautiful place they call home. The pitches are spacious and allow for plenty of relaxation. A new addition is a fenced dog walking area.

Open: 28 April to 24 September **Last arrival:** 20.00 **Last departure:** 11.00
Pitches: 🚐 🚙 ⛺; 13 hardstanding pitches
Leisure: ⚡ 🎿 ⚽ **Facilities:** 🏠 ☺ 🚿 ✳ ♿ 💲 WiFi
Services: 🔌 🛁 🚽 🛒 🚮 🗑 **Within 3 miles:** 🎣 ⛳ ◉ 🚴 🚤 🛶 🚌
Additional site information: 9 acre site. 🐕 Cars can be parked by caravans and tents. Awnings permitted. Fresh bread, pastries, coffee, local produce available. Bus to St.Ives.

See advert opposite

PITCHES: 🚐 Caravans 🚙 Motorhomes ⛺ Tents 🏕 Glamping accommodation **LEISURE:** 🏊 Indoor swimming pool 🏊 Outdoor swimming pool ⚡ Children's playground 👋 Kids' club 🎾 Tennis court 🎱 Games room 📺 Separate TV room ⛳ golf course 🏌 Pitch n putt 🚤 Boats for hire 🚴 Bikes for hire 🎬 Cinema 🎵 Entertainment 🎣 Fishing ◉ Mini golf 🛶 Watersports 🏋 Gym ⚽ Sports field 🐎 Stables 💆 Spa

CORNWALL & ISLES OF SCILLY 83 ENGLAND

Higher Penderleath Caravan & Camping Park
★★★★ 81%
tel: 01736 798403 **Towednack TR26 3AF**
email: penderleath@gmail.com web: www.penderleath.co.uk
dir: *From A30 take A3074 towards St Ives. Left at 2nd mini-roundabout, approximately 3 miles to T-junction. Left, then immediately right. Next left.*

Set in a rugged rural location, this tranquil park has extensive views towards St Ives Bay and the north coast. Facilities are all housed in modernised granite barns, and include spotless toilets with fully serviced shower rooms. A beautiful part of Cornwall with many guests returning year after year to enjoy the spectacular coastline. The owners are welcoming and helpful. There is a bus service to St Ives, available in high season.

Open: All year **Last arrival:** 21.30 **Last departure:** 10.30
Pitches: 🚐 🚙 ⛺; 5 seasonal pitches
Leisure: 🎱 🎣
Facilities: 🏠 ⊙ 🚿 ♿ 💲 🍽
Services: 🔌 🧺 🍴 🍽 🔋 🛒 🔒 💧 T
Within 3 miles: 🎣 ⛳ U ◎ 🛒 🚉 🚌

Additional site information: 10 acre site. 🚗 Cars can be parked by caravans and tents. Awnings permitted. No campfires, no noise after 23.00. Dogs must be well behaved and on a fixed short lead.

ST JUST [NEAR LAND'S END] Map 2 SW3

Places to visit
Geevor Tin Mine, PENDEEN, TR19 7EW, 01736 788662 geevor.com
Carn Euny Ancient Village, SANCREED, TR20 8RB, 0370 333 1181
www.english-heritage.org.uk/visit/places/carn-euny-ancient-village

Roselands Caravan and Camping Park
★★★ 91%
tel: 01736 788571 & 07718 745065 **Dowran TR19 7RS**
email: info@roselands.co.uk web: www.roselands.co.uk
dir: *From A30 (Penzance bypass) onto A3071 for St Just. 5 miles, left at sign after tin mine chimney, follow signs to site.*

Roselands is a small, friendly park in a sheltered rural setting, an ideal location for a quiet family holiday. The owners continue to upgrade the park that includes installing three electric vehicle charging points. There is an indoor games room, children's playground and good toilet facilities.

Open: March to October **Last arrival:** 21.00 **Last departure:** 11.00
Pitches: 🚐 🚙 ⛺
Leisure: 🎱 🎣 **Facilities:** ⚡ 🏠 ⊙ 🚿 ❄ 💲 🍽 🪑 WiFi 💻
Services: 🔌 🧺 🍴 🔒 💧 T **Within 3 miles:** 🎣 ⛳ U 🛒

Additional site information: 4 acre site. 🚗 Cars can be parked by caravans and tents. Awnings permitted. Dog walks on moor adjacent to park.

TREVALGAN
TOURING PARK

5 star, award winning, luxury, family site in an Area of Outstanding Natural Beauty just 2 miles from St Ives

trevalgantouringpark.co.uk
01736 791 892
St Ives, Cornwall TR26 3BJ

FACILITIES: ⚡ Electric vehicle charging 🏠 Baths/Shower ⊙ Electric shaver sockets 🪮 Hairdryer ❄ Ice pack facility 🍼 Baby facilities ♿ Disabled facilities 💲 Shop on site or within 200yds 🍖 BBQ area 🪑 Picnic area WiFi WiFi 💻 Internet access **SERVICES:** 🔌 Electric hook-up 🧺 Launderette 🍴 Licensed bar 🛒 Calor Gas 🔥 Campingaz T Toilet fluid 🍽 Café/Restaurant 🍔 Fast Food/Takeaway 🔋 Battery charging ⛽ Motorhome service point 💳 No credit or debit cards 🐕 Dogs permitted 🚫 No dogs

CORNWALL & ISLES OF SCILLY

ST JUST (NEAR LAND'S END) continued

Trevaylor Caravan & Camping Park
★★★ 90%

tel: 01736 787016 Botallack TR19 7PU
email: trevaylor@cornishcamping.co.uk web: www.cornishcamping.co.uk
dir: On B3306 (St Just to St Ives road), site on right 0.75 mile from St Just.

Trevaylor is a sheltered grassy site in a peaceful location at the western tip of Cornwall. The dramatic coastline and pretty villages nearby are truly unspoilt. Clean, well-maintained facilities are offered, along with pitches that have electric hook-ups, two well-appointed bell tents for hire, and a shower block with heating. The regular bus service and the seasonal open-top bus to St Ives, Penzance, Land's End and Porthcurno both stop at the site entrance.

Open: Easter/April to October, Christmas and New Year **Last arrival:** 19.00 **Last departure:** 11.00
Pitches: see prices below; 11 hardstanding pitches
Leisure: **Facilities:** WiFi
Services: Within 3 miles:
Additional site information: 5 acre site. Cars can be parked by caravans and tents. Awnings permitted. 5 mph speed limit, Quiet after 22.30, no fires, dogs on leads at all times, no washing of caravans, motorhomes etc, breathable ground sheets only, no supermarket deliveries allowed.
Glamping available: 2 Bell tents from £75 **Changeover days:** Any day
Additional glamping information: No dogs permitted. Cars can be parked by units

ST JUST-IN-ROSELAND   Map 2 SW83

Places to visit

St Mawes Castle, ST MAWES, TR2 5DE, 01326 270526
www.english-heritage.org.uk/visit/places/st-mawes-castle

Trelissick, TRELISSICK, TR3 6QL, 01872 862090
www.nationaltrust.org.uk/trelissick

Platinum Park

Trethem Mill Touring Park
★★★★★

tel: 01872 580504 Trethem TR2 5JF
email: reception@trethem.com web: www.trethem.com
dir: From Tregony follow A3078 to St Mawes. After approximately 5 miles enter Trewithian. Continue for 2 miles, after dropping down a long hill follow the Caravan and Camping sign on right.

Family owned, Trethem Mill is a top-notch, adults-only park in a tranquil haven tucked away in a lovely rural setting on the Roseland Peninsula, close to beaches and St Mawes. It's a quality park in all areas, immaculately maintained and with good amenities including a shop, laundry, individual shower rooms and disabled facility, and spacious pitches separated by young trees and shrubs. There's a good choice of fully serviced, all-weather and grass pitches. A pizza van, serving excellent wood-fired pizzas, visits the site once a week. Year-on-year improvements, high standards and great attention to detail across the park ensures this remains one of Cornwall's top parks.

Open: 1 April to 9 October **Last arrival:** 19.00 **Last departure:** 11.00
Pitches: ; 67 hardstanding pitches
Facilities: WiFi
Services: Within 3 miles:
Additional site information: 12 acre site. Adults only. Cars can be parked by caravans and tents. Awnings permitted. 22.30 – 8.00 no noise. 5mph speed limit. Dogs must be kept on leads. Information area

ST MARY'S (ISLES OF SCILLY)   Map 2 SV91

Places to visit

Isles of Scilly Museum, ST MARY'S, TR21 0JT, 01720 422337
www.iosmuseum.org

Bant's Carn Burial Chamber and Halangy Down Ancient Village, ST MARY'S, TR21 0NS
www.english-heritage.org.uk/visit/places/bants-carn-burial-chamber-and-halangy-down-ancient-village

Garrison Campsite
★★★★ 87%

tel: 01720 422670 Tower Cottage, The Garrison TR21 0LS
email: info@garrisonholidays.com web: www.garrisonholidays.com
dir: 10 minutes' walk from quay to site.

Set on the top of an old fort with superb views, this park offers tent-only pitches in a choice of well-sheltered paddocks, including eight fully-equipped, ready-erected tents which are available for hire. There are good toilet and shower facilities, a nearby children's play area and a well-stocked shop at this attractive site, which is only 10 minutes from the town, the quay and the nearest beaches. There is easy access to the other islands via the direct boat service from the Hugh Town quay; the campsite owners will transport all luggage and camping equipment to and from the quay. Good food is available in the many hostelries in the main town.

Open: Easter to October **Last arrival:** 20.00 **Last departure:** 19.00
Pitches: ; see prices below
Facilities:
Services: Within 3 miles:
Additional site information: 9.5 acre site. Dogs by prior arrangement only. No cars on site, no open fires.
Glamping available: Ready-erected tents from £165.
Changeover days: Monday to Saturday
Additional glamping information: Ready-erected tents sleep 1-4 people, minimum stay 3 nights. No dogs allowed.

ST MERRYN (NEAR PADSTOW)   Map 2 SW87

Places to visit

Prideaux Place, PADSTOW, PL28 8RP, 01841 532411
prideauxplace.co.uk

Great for kids: Crealy Theme Park & Resort, CLYST ST MARY, EX5 1DR, 01395 233200
www.crealy.co.uk

PITCHES: Caravans Motorhomes Tents Glamping accommodation **LEISURE:** Indoor swimming pool Outdoor swimming pool Children's playground Kids' club Tennis court Games room Separate TV room golf course Pitch n putt Boats for hire Bikes for hire Cinema Entertainment Fishing Mini golf Watersports Gym Sports field Stables Spa

CORNWALL & ISLES OF SCILLY — ENGLAND

ST MERRYN (NEAR PADSTOW)   Map 2 SW87

Premier Park

Atlantic Bays Holiday Park
★★★★★   92%

tel: 01841 520855   PL28 8PY
email: info@atlanticbaysholidaypark.co.uk   web: www.atlanticbaysholidaypark.co.uk
dir: *From A30 southwest of Bodmin take exit signed Victoria and Roche, 1st exit at roundabout. At Trekenning roundabout 4th exit signed A39 and Wadebridge. At Winnards Perch roundabout left, B3274 signed Padstow. Left in 3 miles, follow signs.*

Atlantic Bays has a mix of hardstanding and grass pitches, a high quality toilet and shower block and a comfortable bar and restaurant. The park is set in a rural area yet is only two miles from the coast and beautiful sandy beaches, and within easy reach of the quaint fishing village of Padstow, and Newquay for fantastic surfing.

Open: March to 2 January **Last arrival:** 21.00 **Last departure:** noon
Pitches: 50 hardstanding pitches; 6 seasonal pitches
Leisure: **Facilities:**
Services: Within 3 miles:
Additional site information: 27 acre site. Cars can be parked by caravans and tents. Awnings permitted.

Carnevas Holiday Park
★★★★   90%

tel: 01841 520230   Carnevas Farm PL28 8PN
email: carnevascampsite@aol.com   web: www.carnevasholidaypark.com
dir: *From St Merryn on B3276 towards Porthcothan Bay. In approximately 2 miles turn right at site sign onto unclassified road opposite Tredrea Inn. Site 0.25 mile on right.*

A family-run park on a working farm, divided into four paddocks on slightly sloping grass. The toilets are central to all areas, and there is a small licensed bar serving meals. An ideal base for exploring the fishing town of Padstow or the surfing beach at Newquay.

Open: April to October (restricted service: April to end May and early September to end October – shop, bar and restaurant closed)
Pitches:
Leisure: **Facilities:**
Services: Within 3 miles:
Additional site information: 8 acre site. Cars can be parked by caravans and tents. Awnings permitted. No skateboards, no supermarket deliveries.

Tregavone Touring Park
★★★   88%

tel: 01841 520148 & 07812 841024   Tregavone Farm PL28 8JZ
email: info@tregavonefarm.co.uk   web: www.tregavonefarm.co.uk
dir: *From A389 towards Padstow, right after Little Petherick. In 1 mile just after Padstow Holiday Park turn left onto unclassified road signed Tregavone. Site on left in approximately 1 mile.*

Situated on a working farm with unspoilt country views, this spacious grassy park, run by friendly family owners, has seen investment which includes the addition of a quality shower block. Also, a new bar is now on site which also serves tasty woodfired pizzas. Tregavone Touring Park makes the ideal base for exploring the north Cornish coast and the seven nearby golden beaches with surfing areas, or for enjoying quiet country walks that lead from the park.

Open: March to October **Last arrival:** 22.00 **Last departure:** 10.00
Pitches: see prices below; 24 seasonal pitches
Leisure: **Facilities:**
Services: Within 3 miles:
Additional site information: 3 acre site. Cars can be parked by caravans and tents. Awnings permitted. Dogs must be kept on leads at all times. No noise after 23.00, BBQs and fire pits to be put on blocks. Fresh eggs and fresh bread available; forest school and yoga on site.

Glamping available: Bell tents from £30. **Changeover days:** Friday
Additional glamping information: Furnished with double beds, fridge, shared kitchen area with BBQ, gas stove, fire pit and picnic table. Under-shelter canvas for eating and drinking. Cars can be parked by units

SENNEN   Map 2 SW32

Places to visit
Carn Euny Ancient Village, SANCREED, TR20 8RB, 0370 333 1181
www.english-heritage.org.uk/visit/places/carn-euny-ancient-village

Chysauster Ancient Village, GULVAL, TR20 8XA, 07470 115475
www.english-heritage.org.uk/visit/places/chysauster-ancient-village

Great for kids: Geevor Tin Mine, PENDEEN, TR19 7EW, 01736 788662
www.geevor.com

Premier Park

Trevedra Farm Caravan & Camping Site
★★★★★   90%

tel: 01736 871818   Nr Sennen, Penzance TR19 7BE
email: campsite@trevedrafarm.co.uk   web: www.trevedrafarm.co.uk
dir: *Take A30 towards Land's End. After junction with B3306 turn right into farm lane. (Note: sat nav directs beyond site entrance to next lane which is unsuitable for caravans). www.what3words.com/bedding.etchings.connected*

A working farm, just a mile from Land's End, with sea views over Gwynver Beach to the Scilly Isles beyond. This popular campsite offers an excellent and well-appointed toilet block, some fully serviced hardstanding pitches, a well-stocked shop plus cooked breakfasts, Sunday roasts and evening meals are available from the food bar; takeaway is also available. The heated amenity block includes four separate bathrooms. There is direct access to the coastal footpath, and two beautiful beaches are just a short walk away.

Open: All year (restricted service: October limited shop/café hours. November to March no shop/café.) **Last arrival:** 19.00 (later arrivals by prior arrangement) **Last departure:** 10.30 (later by arrangement)
Pitches:
Leisure: **Facilities:**
Services: Within 3 miles:
Additional site information: 8 acre site. Cars can be parked by caravans and tents. Awnings permitted. No open fires, no noise 22.00–08.00. Fresh produce, newspapers, bread, milk, local meat available. Car hire can be arranged.

CORNWALL & ISLES OF SCILLY

SUMMERCOURT
Map 2 SW85

Places to visit
Trerice, TRERICE, TR8 4PG, 01637 875404
www.nationaltrust.org.uk/trerice

Blue Reef Aquarium, NEWQUAY, TR7 1DU, 01637 878134
www.bluereefaquarium.co.uk

Great for kids: Dairyland Farm Park, NEWQUAY, TR8 5AA, 01872 510246
dairylandfarmpark.com

Carvynick Holiday Park
★★★★ 91%

tel: 01872 510716 **TR8 5AF**
email: info@carvynick.co.uk **web:** www.carvynick.co.uk
dir: *Accessed from A3058.*

Set within the gardens of an attractive country estate, this spacious park is ideal for large RV-style motorhomes and provides full facility pitches on hardstandings. Amenities include an on-site pub where visitors can enjoy quality food and drink, with plenty of outdoor seating for sunny days. Dogs are very welcome on the park. Close to Newquay's beaches and just a 15 minute drive from Truro with its fine cathedral and shopping facilities.

Carvynick Holiday Park

Open: All year **Last arrival:** 16.00 (late arrivals possible) **Last departure:** 11.00
Pitches: ; 47 hardstanding pitches
Leisure:
Facilities: WiFi
Services:

Additional site information: 13 acre site. Cars can be parked by caravans. Awnings permitted. Dogs must be kept on leads.

See advert below

Relax & Unwind at *Carvynick Holiday Park*, a park nestled away in the Cornish Countryside near Summercourt.

Superbly presented fully-serviced touring pitches with hardstanding, water, electric and chemical/toilet waste outlet. Tent pitches with fabulous views. A pub on-site offers fine dining.

Carvynick is set in a perfect location with easy access to nearby Newquay, Padstow, St Austell, Bodmin and Truro. Open all year round.

Tel: 01872 510716
info@carvynick.co.uk • www.carvynick.co.uk

PITCHES: Caravans Motorhomes Tents Glamping accommodation **LEISURE:** Indoor swimming pool Outdoor swimming pool Children's playground Kids' club Tennis court Games room Separate TV room golf course Pitch n putt Boats for hire Bikes for hire Cinema Entertainment Fishing Mini golf Watersports Gym Sports field Stables Spa

CORNWALL & ISLES OF SCILLY

TRURO
Map 2 SW84

Places to visit

Royal Cornwall Museum, TRURO, TR1 2SJ, 01872 272205
www.royalcornwallmuseum.org.uk

Trelissick, TRELISSICK, TR3 6QL, 01872 862090
www.nationaltrust.org.uk/trelissick

Premier Park

Cosawes Park
★★★★★ 88%

tel: 01872 863724 Perranarworthal TR3 7QS
email: info@cosawes.com **web:** www.cosawes.co.uk
dir: *Exit A39 midway between Truro and Falmouth. Direct access at site sign after Perranarworthal.*

Cosawes is a small touring park, close to Perranarworthal, in a peaceful wooded valley, midway between Truro and Falmouth, with a two-acre touring area. There are spotless toilet facilities (with underfloor heating) that include two smart family rooms. Its stunning location is ideal for visiting the many nearby hamlets and villages close to the Carrick Roads, a stretch of tidal water, which is a centre for sailing and other boating activities. This is an adults only park.

Open: All year **Last arrival:** 21.00 **Last departure:** 10.00
Pitches: 30 hardstanding pitches; 15 seasonal pitches
Facilities: [icons]
Services: [icons] **Within 3 miles:** [icons]
Additional site information: 2 acre site. Adults only. Cars can be parked by caravans and tents. Awnings permitted. No skates, scooters, bicycles etc. Car hire can be arranged.

Summer Valley Touring Park
★★★★ 91%

tel: 07933 212643 Shortlanesend TR4 9DW
email: summervalleytruro@gmail.com **web:** www.summervalley.co.uk
dir: *From Truro take B3284 to Shortlanesend (approximately 3 miles). Through village, site on left.*

Summer Valley is situated in picturesque parkland with far-reaching views of farms and woodland. Facilities are well-maintained and there's plenty of local knowledge on hand. There's a smart reception, a shop selling local produce, as well as a modern amenity block. Pitch sizes are spacious, including 14 metre-wide grass super pitches and fully-serviced hardstanding pitches. A glamping pod and two hobbit houses are available plus there is free WiFi and a children's playground.

Open: 1 April to 30 September **Last arrival:** 20.00 **Last departure:** 10.30
Pitches: 6 hardstanding pitches
Leisure: [icons] **Facilities:** [icons]
Services: [icons] **Within 3 miles:** [icons]
Additional site information: 3 acre site. Cars can be parked by caravans and tents. Awnings permitted. No noise after 22.30. Mobile bar in peak season
Glamping available: Wooden pod and Family Hobbit Houses **Changeover days:** Any day
Additional glamping information: No smoking in pod. Cars can be parked by units

WADEBRIDGE
Map 2 SW97

Places to visit

Prideaux Place, PADSTOW, PL28 8RP, 01841 532411
prideauxplace.co.uk

Cornwall's Regimental Museum, BODMIN, PL31 1EG, 01208 72810
www.cornwalls-regimentalmuseum.org

Great for kids: Pencarrow, BODMIN, PL30 3AG, 01208 841369
www.pencarrow.co.uk

Crealy Theme Park & Resort, CLYST ST MARY, EX5 1DR, 01395 233200
www.crealy.co.uk

The Laurels Holiday Park
★★★★ 94%

tel: 01208 813341 & 07957 154578 Padstow Road, Whitecross PL27 7JQ
email: info@thelaurelsholidaypark.co.uk **web:** www.thelaurelsholidaypark.co.uk
dir: *A39 onto A389 signed Padstow, follow signs. Site entrance 1st right.*

A very smart and well-equipped park with individual pitches screened by hedges and young shrubs. The enclosed dog walk is of great benefit to pet owners, and the Camel (cycle) Trail and Padstow are not far away. This is an excellent base for visiting the Royal Cornwall Showground. Four holiday cottages and an unfurnished bell tent are also available.

Open: 1 April to 31 October **Last arrival:** 20.00 (or by dark if earlier) **Last departure:** 11.00
Pitches: 15 hardstanding pitches; 10 seasonal pitches
Leisure: [icons] **Facilities:** [icons]
Services: [icons]
Within 3 miles: [icons]
Additional site information: 2.2 acre site. Cars can be parked by caravans and tents. Awnings permitted. Family park, no group bookings, no commercial vehicles. Wet suit dunking bath and drying area.

Little Bodieve Holiday Park
★★★ 88%

tel: 01208 812323 Bodieve Road PL27 6EG
email: info@littlebodieve.co.uk **web:** www.littlebodieve.co.uk
dir: *From A39 roundabout on Wadebridge by-pass take B3314 signed Rock and Port Isaac, site 0.25 mile on right.*

Rurally located with pitches in three large grassy paddocks, this family park is close to the Camel Estuary. The licensed clubhouse provides bar meals, with an entertainment programme in high season, and there is a swimming pool with sun terrace. This makes a good base from which to visit the Royal Cornwall Showground.

Open: mid March to October (restricted service: early and late season – shop, pool and clubhouse closed) **Last arrival:** 21.00 **Last departure:** 11.00
Pitches: [icons]
Leisure: [icons] **Facilities:** [icons]
Services: [icons]
Within 3 miles: [icons]
Additional site information: 22 acre site. Cars can be parked by caravans and tents. Awnings permitted. Families and couples only. Crazy golf.

FACILITIES: Electric vehicle charging · Baths/Shower · Electric shaver sockets · Hairdryer · Ice pack facility · Baby facilities · Disabled facilities · Shop on site or within 200yds · BBQ area · Picnic area · WiFi · Internet access **SERVICES:** Electric hook-up · Launderette · Licensed bar · Calor Gas · Campingaz · Toilet fluid · Café/Restaurant · Fast Food/Takeaway · Battery charging · Motorhome service point · No credit or debit cards · Dogs permitted · No dogs

ENGLAND 88 CORNWALL & ISLES OF SCILLY

WATERGATE BAY
Map 2 SW86

Places to visit
Carnewas at Bedruthan, TRENANCE, PL27 7UW, 01637 860563
www.nationaltrust.org.uk/carnewas-at-bedruthan

Premier Park

Watergate Bay Touring Park
★★★★★ 93% HOLIDAY PARK

tel: 01637 860387 **Watergate Bay Touring Park, Tregurrian TR8 4AD**
email: email@watergatebaytouringpark.co.uk
web: www.watergatebaytouringpark.co.uk
dir: *From Bodmin on A30 follow Newquay airport signs. Continue past airport, left at T-junction, site 0.5 mile on right. (Note: for sat nav use TR8 4AE).*

Watergate Bay Touring Park

A well-established park above Watergate Bay, where acres of golden sand, rock pools and surf all contribute to making this a holidaymakers' paradise. The toilet facilities are appointed to a high standard and include top quality family/disabled rooms; there is a well-stocked shop and café, an inviting swimming pool, and a wide range of activities including tennis. There is regular entertainment in the clubhouse and outdoor facilities are tailored for all ages.

Open: March to November (restricted service: March to Spring Bank Holiday and September to October – restricted bar, café, shop and pool) **Last arrival:** 22.00
Last departure: noon

Pitches: 🚐 🚗 ▲; 35 hardstanding pitches
Leisure: 🏊 ⛱ ✋ 🎾 🎯 🎮 🎵 ⚽ **Facilities:** ☉ 🚿 ✳ ♿ 🛒 ☕ WiFi 💻
Services: 🔌 🗑 🍳 🍽 🏪 🧺 ⬇ 🔒 🧹 T **Within 3 miles:** 🚴 ⛳ ◎ 🏄
Additional site information: 30 acre site. 🐕
See advert below

Situated Only 1/2 Mile From Watergate Bay's Glorious Sand And Surf. 4 Miles From The Premier Resort Of Newquay.

Watergate Bay Touring Park

T: 01637 860387
F: 0871 661 7549

Tregurrian, Newquay, Cornwall TR8 4AD
email@watergatebaytouringpark.co.uk
www.watergatebaytouringpark.co.uk

FREE SHOWERS * LICENSED CLUBHOUSE * FREE ENTERTAINMENT
MINI SUPERMARKET * CAFE * GAMES ROOM * KIDS CLUB
COURTESY BEACHBUS * LAUNDERETTE * SKATE RAMPS
IN/OUTDOOR HEATED SWIMMING POOL * DOG EXERCISE FIELD

PITCHES: 🚐 Caravans 🚗 Motorhomes ▲ Tents 🏕 Glamping accommodation **LEISURE:** 🏊 Indoor swimming pool ⛱ Outdoor swimming pool 🛝 Children's playground 👶 Kids' club 🎾 Tennis court 🎮 Games room 📺 Separate TV room ⛳ golf course 🏌 Pitch n putt 🚣 Boats for hire 🚴 Bikes for hire 🎬 Cinema 🎵 Entertainment 🎣 Fishing ◎ Mini golf 🏄 Watersports 🏋 Gym ⚽ Sports field 🐎 Stables ♨ Spa

CORNWALL & ISLES OF SCILLY   89   ENGLAND

WHITE CROSS — Map 2 SW96

Places to visit
Trerice, TRERICE, TR8 4PG, 01637 875404
www.nationaltrust.org.uk/trerice

Great for kids: Dairyland Farm Park, NEWQUAY, TR8 5AA, 01872 510246
dairylandfarmpark.com

Platinum Park

Piran Meadows Resort and Spa
★★★★★ HOLIDAY PARK

tel: 01726 860415 **TR8 4LW**
email: enquiries@piranmeadows.co.uk **web:** www.piranmeadows.co.uk
dir: *From A30 take A392 toward Newquay. At crossroads in White Cross left, under rail bridge, site on right.*

A stunning development that provides excellent standards and facilities for couples and families. Generously spaced, superbly equipped lodges and static holiday homes are equipped with both practical and thoughtful extras and have unrivalled countryside views. The stylish main building, with a welcoming reception, is appointed with quality and comfort in mind, and the many facilities include a modern swimming pool and special areas and attractions for children. The 'Go Active Plus' sports programme has its own instructors, and the restaurant, with bar, has a spacious outdoor area for alfresco dining.

Open: All year
Holiday Homes: Sleep 8, Bedrooms 4, Bathrooms 3, Toilets 3, Two-ring burner, Dishwasher, Washing Machine, Microwave, Freezer, TV, Sky/Freeview, DVD player, WiFi, Linen included, Towels included, Electricity included, Gas included
Leisure:
Facilities:
Within 3 miles:
Additional site information:

WIDEMOUTH BAY — Map 2 SS20

Places to visit
Penhallam Manor, WEEK ST MARY, EX22 6XW, 0370 333 1181
www.english-heritage.org.uk/visit/places/penhallam-manor

Penhalt Farm Holiday Park
★★★ 85%

tel: 01288 361210 & 07970 521549 **EX23 0DG**
email: info@penhaltfarm.co.uk **web:** www.penhaltfarm.co.uk
dir: *From Bude on A39 take 2nd right to Widemouth Bay road, left at end by Widemouth Manor signed Millook onto coastal road. Site 0.75 mile on left.*

Splendid views of the sea and coast can be enjoyed from all pitches on this sloping but partly level site, set in a lovely rural area on a working farm. About one mile away is one of Cornwall's finest beaches which proves popular with all the family as well as surfers.

Open: Easter to October **Last arrival:** 21.00 **Last departure:** 11.00
Pitches: ; 12 hardstanding pitches
Leisure:
Facilities:
Services:
Within 3 miles:
Additional site information: 8 acre site. Cars can be parked by caravans and tents. Awnings permitted. No rollerblades, no noise after midnight. Pool table, netball, air hockey and table tennis.

Make your next UK holiday one to remember

Choose RatedTrips.com

Cumbria

Cumbria means the Lake District really – a rumpled, rugged landscape that is hard to beat for sheer natural beauty and grandeur. It is almost certainly England's best known and most scenic national park, famous for Lake Windermere, the country's largest lake, and Derwentwater, described as the 'Queen of the English Lakes.'

The Lake District is a region of Britain that leaves some visitors relaxed, others completely exhausted. The list of activities and places to visit is endless. The old adage 'always leave something to come back for' is certainly apt in this remote corner of the country.

This region has long been inextricably associated with poets, artists and writers. Not surprisingly, it was this beautiful countryside that inspired William Wordsworth, Samuel Taylor Coleridge, Arthur Ransome and Robert Southey. Born in the Cumbrian town of Cockermouth, Wordsworth and his sister Dorothy moved to Dove Cottage in Grasmere in 1799. Their annual rent was £5. The poet later moved to Rydal Mount in Ambleside, a family home with a 4-acre garden and a charming setting on the banks of Rydal Water. Today, both Dove Cottage and Rydal Mount are among the most visited of all the Lake District attractions. Another house with strong literary links is Hill Top, the 17th-century farmhouse home of Beatrix Potter who moved here in 1905. Located near Windermere, Hill Top and its surroundings sparked Potter's imagination and she painstakingly reproduced much of what she saw and cherished in her charming book illustrations. Tom Kitten, Samuel Whiskers and Jemima Puddleduck were all created here and the success of the 2006 film about Potter's life has introduced her extraordinary work to new audiences.

Walkers are spoilt for choice in Cumbria and the Lake District. The 70-mile Cumbria Way follows the valley floors rather than the mountain summits, while the 190-mile Coast to Coast has just about every kind of landscape and terrain imaginable. The route, pioneered by the well-known fell walker and writer Alfred Wainwright, cuts across the Lake District, the Yorkshire Dales and the North York Moors, spanning the width of England between St Bees on the Cumbrian west coast, and Robin Hood's Bay on the North Yorkshire and Cleveland Heritage Coast. The region is also popular with cyclists and there are a great many cycle hire outlets and plenty of routes available.

As with any popular scenic region of the country, the Lake District has an abundance of attractions but there are plenty of places within its boundaries and outside them where you can experience peace, tranquillity and a true sense of solitude. The southern half of Cumbria is often overlooked in favour of the more obvious attractions of the region. The Lune Valley, for example, remains as lovely as it was when Turner came here to paint. In the 19th century, writer John Ruskin described the view from 'The Brow', a walk running behind Kirkby Lonsdale's parish church, as 'one of the loveliest scenes in England.'

The Cumbrian coast is also one of the county's secret gems. Overlooking the Solway Firth and noted in the area for its wide cobbled streets and spacious green, the town of Silloth is one of the finest examples of a Victorian seaside resort in the north of England and yet outside Cumbria few people know its name. There are other historic towns along this coastline, including Whitehaven, Workington and Maryport. The Roman defences at Ravenglass are a reminder of the occupation, as is the Cumbrian section of Hadrian's Wall where it follows the county's northern coast. Well worth a visit is the ancient and historic city of Carlisle. Once a Roman camp – its wall still runs north of the city – it was captured during the Jacobean rising of 1745. The cathedral dates back to the early 12th century.

◁ Lake Windermere

CUMBRIA

AMBLESIDE
Map 18 NY30

Places to visit
The Armitt Museum & Library, AMBLESIDE, LA22 9BL, 015394 31212
www.armitt.com

Beatrix Potter Gallery, HAWKSHEAD, LA22 0NS, 015394 36355
www.nationaltrust.org.uk/beatrix-potter-gallery-and-hawkshead

AA CAMPSITE OF THE YEAR FOR ENGLAND & NORTH WEST REGION 2024–25

Platinum Park

Skelwith Fold Caravan Park
★★★★★

tel: 015394 32277 **LA22 0HY**
email: info@skelwith.com web: www.skelwith.com
dir: *From Ambleside on A593 towards Coniston, left at Clappersgate onto B5286 (Hawkshead road). Site 1 mile on right.*

Skelwith Fold is in a beautiful setting close to Lake Windermere, in the grounds of a former mansion. Touring areas are dotted in paddocks around the extensively wooded grounds, and the all-weather pitches are set close to the many facility buildings; the premium pitches are top quality. There are also five safari tents, superb en suite family Hideaway Pods and lodges for hire. Residents of all ages can enjoy the large nature trail, and the younger ones will love the excellent children's play area and astro turf five-a-side football pitch. The shop is well-stocked and sells an extensive range of groceries. There is a drying room, dishwasher, library and a private family bathroom.

Open: 1 March to 20 November **Last arrival:** dusk **Last departure:** noon
Pitches: 130 hardstanding pitches
Leisure:
Facilities:
Services:
Within 3 miles:
Additional site information: 130 acre site. Cars can be parked by caravans. Awnings permitted.
Glamping available: Safari tents, Hideaway Pods.
Additional glamping information: Safari tents from £467 (3 nights minimum), pods – see website for prices.

Hawkshead Hall Farm
★★★ 83%

tel: 015394 36221 **Hawkshead LA22 0NN**
email: enquiries@hawksheadhall-campsite.co.uk
web: www.hawksheadhall-campsite.co.uk
dir: *From Ambleside take A593 signed Coniston, then B5286 signed Hawkshead. Site signed on left just before Hawkshead. Or from Coniston take B5285 to T-junction. Left, then 1st right into site.*

Hawkshead Hall Farm is a small site that is situated on a working Lakeland farm in a perfect location for those looking for an active holiday in the heart of one of the most beautiful parts of the Lake District National Park. The campsite lies just 10 minutes away, by foot, from the small attractive village of Hawkshead; a path has been created to enable guests to walk safely off-road into the village to shop or explore. There are pitches for tourers, including 20 fully serviced hardstandings, and for tents. This busy site has very good amenities, with spotlessly clean, well-appointed toilets and a spacious, comfortable TV room, plus free WiFi.

Open: March to January **Last arrival:** 21.00 **Last departure:** noon
Pitches: 20 hardstanding pitches
Leisure:
Facilities: WiFi
Services:
Within 3 miles:
Additional site information: 3 acre site. Cars can be parked by caravans and tents. Awnings permitted. No noise 23.00–07.00. Dogs must be kept on a lead at all times.

BARROW-IN-FURNESS
Map 18 SD26

Places to visit
The Dock Museum, BARROW-IN-FURNESS, LA14 2PW, 01229 876400
www.dockmuseum.org.uk

Furness Abbey, BARROW-IN-FURNESS, LA13 0PJ, 01229 823420
www.english-heritage.org.uk/visit/places/furness-abbey

Great for kids: South Lakes Safari Zoo, LINDAL-IN-FURNESS, LA12 0LU, 01229 466086
www.southlakessafarizoo.com

PITCHES: Caravans · Motorhomes · Tents · Glamping accommodation **LEISURE:** Indoor swimming pool · Outdoor swimming pool · Children's playground · Kids' club · Tennis court · Games room · Separate TV room · golf course · Pitch n putt · Boats for hire · Bikes for hire · Cinema · Entertainment · Fishing · Mini golf · Watersports · Gym · Sports field · Stables · Spa

CUMBRIA   93   ENGLAND

BARROW-IN-FURNESS   Map 18 SD26

South End Caravan Park
★★★★ 86%

tel: 01229 472823 **Walney Island LA14 3YQ**
email: enquiries@secp.co.uk web: www.southendcaravanpark.co.uk
dir: *M6 junction 36, A590 to Barrow, follow signs for Walney Island. Cross bridge, turn left. Site 6 miles south.*

A friendly family-owned and run park next to the sea and close to a nature reserve, on the southern end of Walney Island. It offers an extensive range of quality amenities including an adult lounge, and high standards of cleanliness and maintenance.

Open: March to October (restricted service: March to Easter and October – pool closed)
Last arrival: 22.00 **Last departure:** noon

Pitches: ; 15 hardstanding pitches; 34 seasonal pitches

Leisure:

Facilities:

Services:

Within 3 miles:

Additional site information: 7 acre site. Cars can be parked by caravans. Awnings permitted. Bowling green, snooker table.

BEWALDETH   Map 18 NY23

Places to visit
Mirehouse, KESWICK, CA12 4QE, 017687 72287
www.mirehouse.co.uk

Wordsworth House and Garden, COCKERMOUTH, CA13 9RX, 01900 824805
www.nationaltrust.org.uk/wordsworth-house-and-garden

Great for kids: Lake District Wildlife Park, BASSENTHWAITE, CA12 4RD, 01768 776239
www.lakedistrictwildlifepark.co.uk

Premier Park

Keswick Reach Lodge Retreat
★★★★★ 93% HOLIDAY PARK

tel: 01768 776510 **Bewaldeth CA13 9SY**
email: reception@keswickreach.co.uk web: www.keswickreach.co.uk
dir: *Signed from A591, south of Bothel.*

Opened following significant investment and renovation by Darwin Escapes several years ago, with creative architecture and landscaping, this former campsite has been transformed into an award-winning and must-visit destination for lovers of wildlife and outdoor activities. An ornamental lake and areas that attract wildlife was created, and the only distractions are running water and birdsong. The activities centre houses a smart reception, shop, a stylish bar and brasserie, and a well-equipped spa with treatments, sauna, gym and hot tub. The one to four-bedroom lodges are very well spaced and angled to create optimum privacy as well as affording stunning views; some of the premier lodges feature private hot tubs. Keswick Reach is also very pet friendly offering pet packs on arrival and dog-washing facilities.

Open: All year **Last arrival:** 20.00 **Last departure:** 10:00

Holiday Homes: Sleep 8, Bedrooms 4, Bathrooms 2, Toilets 2, Two-ring burner, Dishwasher, Washing Machine, Tumble dryer, Microwave, Freezer, TV, DVD player, WiFi, Linen included, Towels included, Electricity included, Gas included, Woodburner

Changeover days: 4 night breaks Monday – Thursday, 3 night breaks Friday – Sunday

Leisure:

Facilities:

Additional site information:

BOWNESS-ON-WINDERMERE

See Windermere

FACILITIES: Electric vehicle charging Baths/Shower Electric shaver sockets Hairdryer Ice pack facility Baby facilities Disabled facilities Shop on site or within 200yds BBQ area Picnic area WiFi Internet access **SERVICES:** Electric hook-up Launderette Licensed bar Calor Gas Campingaz Toilet fluid Café/Restaurant Fast Food/Takeaway Battery charging Motorhome service point No credit or debit cards Dogs permitted No dogs

ENGLAND 94 CUMBRIA

CARLISLE — Map 18 NY35

Places to visit

Lanercost Priory, BRAMPTON, CA8 2HQ, 01697 73030
www.english-heritage.org.uk/visit/places/lanercost-priory

Tullie House Museum & Art Gallery Trust, CARLISLE, CA3 8TP, 01228 618718
www.tulliehouse.co.uk

Premier Park

Green Acres Caravan Park
★★★★★ 89%

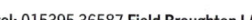

tel: 01228 675418 & 07720 343820 **High Knells, Houghton CA6 4JW**
email: info@greenacrescumbria.co.uk **web:** www.greenacrescumbria.co.uk
dir: M6 junction 44, A689 east towards Brampton for 1 mile. Left at Scaleby sign. Site 1 mile on left.

A beautiful adults-only touring park set in peaceful rural surroundings and close to M6, with distant views of the fells. The park is surrounded by mature trees and high hedges. Almost all the pitches are fully serviced, creating optimum comfort. This immaculately presented park is run by hands on, enthusiastic and friendly owners, who maintain high standards throughout. The park has a motorhome pressure-washer area, a choice of woodland or field dog walks and superb modern amenity blocks providing excellent privacy options for all. There is a sports hall which contains a badminton court, pool and table tennis tables, and essentials can be bought on-site from the well-stocked honesty shop.

Open: March to October **Last arrival:** 20.00 **Last departure:** 11:00
Pitches: 🚐 🚗; 35 hardstanding pitches; 17 seasonal pitches
Leisure: ⚽ ⚽
Facilities: 🚿 ☀ 🍴 ♿ 🚽 🪑 WiFi 💻
Services: 🚰 🗑 ⛽ 🛒
Within 3 miles: ⛳ 🛒

Additional site information: 3 acre site. Adults only. 🐕 Cars can be parked by caravans. Awnings permitted. No group bookings. Woodland walk (joins public footpath), sports hall, boules pitch, dog exercise field, car/caravan wash

CARTMEL — Map 18 SD37

Places to visit

Holker Hall & Gardens, HOLKER, LA11 7PL, 015395 58328
www.holker.co.uk

Hill Top, NEAR SAWREY, LA22 0LF, 015394 36269
www.nationaltrust.org.uk/hill-top

Great for kids: Lakes Aquarium, LAKESIDE, LA12 8AS, 015395 30153
www.lakesaquarium.co.uk

CARTMEL — Map 18 SD37

Greaves Farm Caravan Park
★★★ 85%

tel: 015395 36587 **Field Broughton LA11 6HR**
email: info@greavesfarmcaravanpark.co.uk **web:** www.greavesfarmcaravanpark.co.uk
dir: M6 junction 36, A590 signed Barrow. Approximately 1 mile before Newby Bridge, turn left at end of dual carriageway signed Cartmel and Holker. Site 2 miles on left just before church, or second right after church when approaching from the south.

A small family-owned park set in a peaceful rural area and close to a working farm. Motorhomes are either parked in a quiet paddock or on the main field, both with spacious hardstandings. There is lots of space for tents and caravans too here. This park is carefully maintained and offers electric pitches (6amp), and there is always a sparkle to the toilet facilities. Static holiday caravans are available for hire. (Note: sat nav (including Garmin Camper) directions should not be used for accessing this site; follow directions given here).

Open: March to end October **Last arrival:** 20.00 **Last departure:** noon
Pitches: 🚐 🚗 ⛺; 9 hardstanding pitches
Facilities: 🚿 ☀ 🍴 ❄
Services: 🚰 🛒
Within 3 miles: ⛳ 🚴 ⛵ 🎣 🛒

Additional site information: 3 acre site. 🐕 Cars can be parked by caravans and tents. Awnings permitted. Couples and families only. No open fires. Minimum noise after 22.30. Separate chalet for dishwashing, small freezer and fridge available.

CROOKLANDS — Map 18 SD58

Places to visit

Levens Hall, LEVENS, LA8 0PD, 015395 60321
www.levenshall.co.uk

RSPB Leighton Moss & Morecambe Bay Nature Reserve, SILVERDALE, LA5 0SW, 01524 701601
www.rspb.org.uk/reserves-and-events/reserves-a-z/leighton-moss

Waters Edge Caravan Park
★★★★ 84%

tel: 015395 67708 **LA7 7NN**
email: stay@watersedgecaravanpark.co.uk **web:** www.watersedgecaravanpark.co.uk
dir: M6 junction 36, A65 towards Kirkby Lonsdale, at 2nd roundabout follow signs for Crooklands and Endmoor. Site 1 mile on right at Crooklands garage, just after 40mph sign.

A truly lovely site bordered by streams and woodland. Despite being an oasis of calm, the site is just a short distance from the M6 and is ideal either as a stopover or for longer stays. There is a wonderful reception that shares space with a small shop, behind which is a comfortable bar. The pitches are excellent and very well maintained, as are the spotlessly clean toilets.

Open: March to 14 November (restricted service: bar open daily 9–6 & evenings Friday to Sunday) **Last arrival:** 22.00 **Last departure:** noon
Pitches: 🚐 🚗 ⛺; 26 hardstanding pitches; 10 seasonal pitches
Leisure: ⚽ 📺 **Facilities:** 🚿 ☀ 🍴 ❄ ♿ 🛒 🚽 🪑 WiFi 💻
Services: 🚰 🗑 🍴 ⛽ 🧺 📱 **Within 3 miles:** 🚴 ⛵

Additional site information: 3 acre site. 🐕 Cars can be parked by caravans and tents. Awnings permitted. No noise after midnight.

PITCHES: 🚐 Caravans 🚗 Motorhomes ⛺ Tents 🏕 Glamping accommodation **LEISURE:** 🏊 Indoor swimming pool 🏊 Outdoor swimming pool 🎠 Children's playground 🎨 Kids' club 🎾 Tennis court ⚽ Games room 📺 Separate TV room ⛳ golf course ⛳ Pitch n putt 🚣 Boats for hire 🚴 Bikes for hire 🎬 Cinema 🎵 Entertainment 🎣 Fishing ⛳ Mini golf 🏄 Watersports 🏋 Gym ⚽ Sports field 🐴 Stables 💆 Spa

CUMBRIA 95 ENGLAND

CUMWHITTON
Map 18 NY55

Places to visit
Lanercost Priory, BRAMPTON, CA8 2HQ, 01697 73030
www.english-heritage.org.uk/visit/places/lanercost-priory

Cairndale Caravan Park
★★★ 75%

tel: 01768 896020 **CA8 9BZ**
dir: *Exit A69 at Warwick Bridge on unclassified road through Great Corby to Cumwhitton, left at village sign, site 1 mile.*

A lovely grass site set in the tranquil Eden Valley with good views to distant hills. The all-weather touring pitches have electricity and are located close to the immaculately maintained toilet facilities. In addition to static hire caravans, four luxury glamping pods, located in a separate field and overlooking the lake, offer en suites and kitchen facilities plus the benefit of decking areas with picnic tables.

Open: March to October **Last arrival:** 22.00
Pitches: 🚐 🚗 🏠; 5 hardstanding pitches
Facilities: 🛖 ⊙ ✻
Services: 🔌 🔒
Within 3 miles: ⛳ 🎣 🚲

Additional site information: 2 acre site. 🐕 Cars can be parked by caravans. Awnings permitted.

Glamping available: Wooden pods

FLOOKBURGH
Map 18 SD37

Places to visit
Holker Hall & Gardens, HOLKER, LA11 7PL, 015395 58328
www.holker.co.uk

FLOOKBURGH
Map 18 SD37

Premier Park

Lakeland Leisure Park
★★★★★ 88% HOLIDAY PARK

tel: 015395 58556 Moor Lane **LA11 7LT**
email: lakeland@haven.com **web:** www.haven.com/lakeland
dir: *On B5277 pass Grange-over-Sands to Flookburgh. Left at village square, site in 1 mile.*

A leisure park with full range of activities and entertainment, making this flat, grassy site ideal for families. The touring area, which includes 24 fully-serviced pitches, is quietly situated away from the main amenities, but the swimming pools and evening entertainment are just a short stroll away. In addition to the stylish Lakeside Bay bar/bistro you will also find Cook's Fish & Chips, a Papa Johns and mini market. There is a host of activities including an adventure trail, climbing wall, aerial adventure activities, indoor swimming pool, arcade area, and a lake offering non-motorised water sports.

Open: mid March to end October (restricted service: mid March to May and September to October – reduced activities, outdoor pool closed) **Last arrival:** anytime **Last departure:** 10.00
Pitches: 🚐 🚗 ⛺; 24 hardstanding pitches
Leisure: 🏊 ⛵ 🎱 🎯 🎣 🎵 🎪 ⚽
Facilities: 🛖 ⊙ 🍽 ✻ ♿ 🛁 🍴 🪑 🐕 📶 🖥
Services: 🔌 🧺 🍺 🍴 🛒 🔒 T
Within 3 miles: 🎣 🎳 🎯 🚲

Additional site information: 105 acre site. 🐕 No commercial vehicles, no bookings by persons under 21 years unless a family booking. Maximum 2 dogs per booking, certain dog breeds banned.

HOLMROOK
Map 18 SD09

Places to visit
Great for kids: Ravenglass & Eskdale Railway, RAVENGLASS, CA18 1SW, 01229 717171
www.ravenglass-railway.co.uk

Seven Acres Caravan Park
★★★ 76%

tel: 01946 822777 **CA19 1YD**
email: reception@seacote.com **web:** www.sevenacrespark.co.uk
dir: *Site signed on A595 between Holmrook and Gosforth.*

This sheltered park is close to quiet west Cumbrian coastal villages and beaches, and also handy for Eskdale and Wasdale. There is a good choice of pitches, some are hedged bays for privacy and some have coastal views. There is a pleasant rewilding ethos here and the site is great for bird and wildlife spotting.

Open: All year **Last arrival:** 21.00 **Last departure:** 10.00
Pitches: 🚐 🚗 ⛺; 20 hardstanding pitches
Facilities: 🛖 ⊙ 🪑
Services: 🔌 🧺 **Within 3 miles:** ⛳ 🎣 🎳 🎯 💲

Additional site information: 7 acre site. 🐕 Cars can be parked by caravans and tents. Awnings permitted.

CUMBRIA

KESWICK
Map 18 NY22

Places to visit
The Derwent Pencil Museum, KESWICK, CA12 5NG, 01768 773626
www.derwentart.com/en-gb/c/about/company/derwent-pencil-museum

Honister Slate Mine, BORROWDALE, CA12 5XN, 01768 777230
www.honister.com

Great for kids: Mirehouse, KESWICK, CA12 4QE, 017687 72287
www.mirehouse.co.uk

Platinum Park

Castlerigg Hall Caravan & Camping Park
★★★★★

tel: 017687 74499 **Castlerigg Hall CA12 4TE**
email: info@castlerigg.co.uk **web:** www.castlerigg.co.uk
dir: *1.5 miles southeast of Keswick on A591, turn right at sign. Site 200 metres on right after Heights Hotel.*

Castlerigg Hall is situated in the heart of the Lake District with truly breathtaking views across Derwentwater to Catbells and other well-known Lakeland fells. This really is a superb location for anyone interested in exploring the area on foot, bike or by vehicle. As well as superb toilet blocks and pitches, there is a well-stocked shop and an excellent indoor campers' kitchen. In addition, there are pods and caravans for hire. Castlerigg is notable for the outstanding quality across all aspects of the operation.

Castlerigg Hall Caravan & Camping Park

Open: mid March to 7 November **Last arrival:** 21.00 **Last departure:** 11.30

Pitches: 🚐 🚗 ⛺ 🏠; 75 hardstanding pitches

Leisure: ⚽

Facilities: 🛍 ⊙ 🍳 ✳ ♿ 📷 📶

Services: 🔌 🚿 🧺 ⛽ 🚮 📱

Within 3 miles: 🚶 🎣 ⛳ 🏇 🛥 🚴 🚌

Additional site information: 8 acre site. 🚗 Cars can be parked by caravans and tents. Awnings permitted. Dogs must not be left unattended. No noise after 22.30. Campers' kitchen, sitting room, gallery.

Glamping available: Wooden pods.

Additional glamping information: Standard & Family Pods, Castle Pods (no pets permitted), Inspire Pods (no pets permitted) and Hex Pods. Maximum of 2 dogs permitted in Standard, Family and Hex Pods. Cars can be parked by units.

See advert below

Premier Park

Burns Farm Caravan, Camping & Glamping
★★★★★ 85%

tel: 017687 79225 Burns Farm, St Johns in the Vale CA12 4RR
email: linda@burns-farm.co.uk web: www.burns-farm.co.uk
dir: *Exit A66 signed Castlerigg Stone Circle, Youth Centre and Burns Farm. Site on right in 0.5 mile.*

Burns Farm Caravan, Camping & Glamping is situated in the heart of Cumbria and is a rural Lakeland site situated on a working farm surrounded by picturesque views. Its location, just three miles east of Keswick, makes it the perfect destination for nature lovers, walkers, cyclists and those seeking peace and quiet. The luxurious wooden cabins are a highlight here and offer the highest glamping quality and comfort; all are en suite and have private outside areas with bubbling hot tubs. Cosy bell tents are also available in a separate field. The campsite is more traditional and is divided into different sections with two non-electric tent fields (choice of dog-free or dog-friendly) and two additional sections with hardstanding, fully serviced caravan pitches. The shower block is modern, stylish and also offers seven private bathrooms (including two that are accessible). There are charging lockers for phones and bike batteries, and you will find three pubs in the village of Threlkeld, located only a mile away.

Open: All year **Last arrival:** 21.00 **Last departure:** noon
Pitches:

KIRKBY LONSDALE   Map 18 SD67

Places to visit
Sizergh, SIZERGH, LA8 8DZ, 015395 60951
www.nationaltrust.org.uk/sizergh

Premier Park

Woodclose Caravan Park
★★★★★ 90%

tel: 015242 71597 High Casterton LA6 2SE
email: info@woodclosepark.com web: www.woodclosepark.com
dir: *On A65, 0.25 mile after Kirkby Lonsdale towards Skipton, park on left.*

A peaceful, well-managed park set in idyllic countryside within the beautiful Lune Valley, and centrally located for exploring the Lakes and Dales. It is just a 10-minute walk from the market town of Kirkby Lonsdale and offers riverside and woodland walks for both families and dogs, and amenity blocks with fully serviced cubicles – one is allocated for the glamping pods and hive cabins. The generous hardstanding and fully serviced pitches are surrounded by mature trees and seasonal planting. Parts of the site are havens for wildlife and River Lune is nearby for fishing.

Open: March to January **Last arrival:** 21.00 (no arrivals before 13.00) **Last departure:** noon
Pitches: ; 20 hardstanding pitches; 22 seasonal pitches
Leisure:
Facilities:
Services:
Within 3 miles:

Additional site information: 9 acre site. Cars can be parked by caravans. Awnings permitted. Crock boxes for hire. One self catering flat.
Glamping available: 10 wooden pods, 2 hive cabins.
Additional glamping information: Minimum stay 3 night stay at weekends and 4 nights mid-week in peak periods. Variety of pods, some dog friendly, some fully en suite.

New House Caravan Park
★★★★ 83%

tel: 015242 71590 LA6 2HR
email: colinpreece9@aol.com web: newhousecaravanpark.co.uk
dir: *1 mile south-east of Kirkby Lonsdale on A65, turn right into site entrance 300 yards after Whoop Hall Inn.*

Colourful floral displays greet new arrivals, creating an excellent first impression at this former farm, which has been carefully changed to provide well-spaced pitches, with hardstandings sheltered by surrounding mature trees and shrubs. Three stylish, well spaced bell tents are available for those looking for a peaceful, rural glamping experience. This is an ideal base for exploring the Yorkshire Dales and the Lake District.

Open: All year **Last arrival:** 21.00 **Last departure:** noon
Pitches: ; 50 hardstanding pitches
Facilities:
Services: **Within 3 miles:**

Additional site information: 3 acre site. Cars can be parked by caravans. Awnings permitted. No cycling.
Glamping available: Bell tents
Additional glamping information: Bell tents sleep 4

MEALSGATE   Map 18 NY24

Places to visit
Wordsworth House and Garden, COCKERMOUTH, CA13 9RX, 01900 824805
www.nationaltrust.org.uk/wordsworth-house-and-garden

Larches Caravan Park
★★★★ 82%

tel: 016973 71379 CA7 1LQ
email: thelarches@hotmail.co.uk web: www.facebook.com/TheLarchesCaravanPark
dir: *On A595 (Carlisle to Cockermouth road).*

This over 18s-only park is set in wooded rural surroundings on the fringe of the Lake district National Park, close to Cockermouth and Bassenthwaite Lake. Touring units are spread out over two sections. Very much a friendly, family-run park offering good facilities, including a well-stocked shop that provides a very good range of camping and caravanning spares. Privacy and peace are the clear attractions for staying here.

Open: March to October (restricted service: in early and late season) **Last arrival:** 21.30 **Last departure:** noon
Pitches: ; 30 hardstanding pitches
Facilities:
Services: **Within 3 miles:**

Additional site information: 20 acre site. Adults only. Cars can be parked by caravans and tents. Awnings permitted.

CUMBRIA

NETHER WASDALE
Map 18 NY10

Places to visit

Ravenglass & Eskdale Railway, RAVENGLASS, CA18 1SW, 01229 717171
www.ravenglass-railway.co.uk

Hardknott Roman Fort, BOOT, CA19 1TH
www.english-heritage.org.uk/visit/places/hardknott-roman-fort

Church Stile Farm & Holiday Park
★★★★ 85%

tel: 01946 726252 **Church Stile** CA20 1ET
email: info@churchstile.com web: www.churchstile.com
dir: *M6 junction 36, (follow signs for Western Lakes) A590, A5092, A595 (towards Whitehaven). In Gosforth follow Nether Wasdale signs. Pass 2 pubs. Site immediately after church.*

A superb, secluded park surrounded by mature trees, hedging and Lakeland-stone walls in a peaceful valley setting. The combination of indigenous trees and summer wildflowers creates stunning displays to complement the beauty of the surrounding hills. A renowned farm shop, with a wide range of local produce, is situated in the stylish reception and café. The site offers static caravans, two shepherd's huts and wooden pods for hire, alongside spacious grassy areas for tents and a handful of excellent hardstanding motorhome pitches. Families and dogs are welcome here and are all well-catered for.

Open: March to 15 October **Last arrival:** 21.00 **Last departure:** 11.00
Pitches: 16 hardstanding pitches
Leisure:
Facilities:
Services:
Within 3 miles:

Additional site information: 10 acre site. Cars can be parked by tents. Awnings permitted. No noise after 23.00. Picnic tables, table tennis, woodland walk.
Glamping available: Shepherd's hut; bell tent; pods.
Changeover days: Friday, Saturday, Monday
Additional glamping information: Bell tent: minimum stay 2 nights (3 nights on bank holiday weekends). Pods: minimum stay 2 nights. Cars can be parked by units

PATTERDALE
Map 18 NY31

Places to visit

Aira Force and Ullswater, PENRITH, 017684 82067
www.nationaltrust.org.uk/aira-force-and-ullswater

Sykeside Camping & Caravan Park
★★★ 81%

tel: 017684 82239 **Brotherswater, Hartsop** CA11 0NZ
email: info@sykeside.co.uk web: www.sykeside.co.uk
dir: *From south: M6 at junction 36, A591 to Windermere. Right onto A592 towards Kirkstone Pass and Ullswater. Over pass, at The Brotherswater Inn on left, turn into pub car park to site behind the pub. From north: M6 junction 40, A66 towards Keswick. 0.25 mile left onto A592 to Ullswater, 6 miles towards Windermere and Kirkstone Pass. Site 2 miles after Patterdale on right.*

A campers' delight, this family-run park is situated at the foot of Kirkstone Pass, under the 2,000ft Hartsop Dodd in a spectacular area with breathtaking views. The park has mainly grass pitches and around 30 hardstandings, and for those campers without a tent there is bunkhouse accommodation, and three glamping pods for hire. The park attracts a wide variety of wildlife and the Brotherswater Inn serves breakfast and bar meals.

Open: All year (restricted service: October to Easter) **Last arrival:** 20.00
Last departure: noon
Pitches: 30 hardstanding pitches
Facilities:
Services:
Within 3 miles:

Additional site information: 10 acre site. Cars can be parked by caravans and tents. Awnings permitted. There will be no refund on campsite fees due to bad weather conditions. 3 night minimum stay on all Bank Holidays. No groups of larger than 6 adults. Quiet hours between 23.00 and 07.30. Small shop for provisions (Easter until October)
Glamping available: Wooden pods
Changeover days: Monday and Friday
Additional glamping information: Cars can be parked by units

Make your next UK holiday one to remember

Choose RatedTrips.com

AA

PITCHES: Caravans · Motorhomes · Tents · Glamping accommodation **LEISURE:** Indoor swimming pool · Outdoor swimming pool · Children's playground · Kids' club · Tennis court · Games room · Separate TV room · golf course · Pitch n putt · Boats for hire · Bikes for hire · Cinema · Entertainment · Fishing · Mini golf · Watersports · Gym · Sports field · Stables · Spa

CUMBRIA — ENGLAND

POOLEY BRIDGE
Map 18 NY42

Places to visit
Dalemain House & Gardens, DALEMAIN, CA11 0HB, 017684 86450
www.dalemain.com

Great for kids: Rheged, PENRITH, CA11 0DQ, 01768 868000
www.rheged.com

AA MOST IMPROVED CAMPSITE OF THE YEAR 2024–25

Premier Park

Park Foot Holiday Park
★★★★★ 94% HOLIDAY PARK

tel: 017684 86309 **Howtown Road CA10 2NA**
email: holidays@parkfootullswater.co.uk web: www.parkfootullswater.co.uk
dir: *M6 junction 40, A66 towards Keswick, then A592 to Ullswater. Turn left for Pooley Bridge, right at church, right at crossroads signed Howtown. Alternatively from Penrith take A6 to Shap, then B5320 to Pooley Bridge, turn left towards Howton, site 1 mile on left.*

Park Foot is located in a gorgeous area right beside Ullswater and the wonderful fells – it's perfect for those that wish to explore the many paths in the area and there is a lovely walk from the park's shorefront to picturesque Pooley Bridge from where the Ullswater steamer departs. You'll discover a range of excellent touring pitches for caravans, motorhomes and tents, with high quality amenities in each of the touring areas. Pony-trekking is possible from the site. Featuring a very well-stocked shop, TJ'S Restaurant and Bar and activities for all age groups, this park is a high quality family-owned holiday centre. The new Ninja Trail playground is popular with children of all ages.

Open: All year (restricted service: March to April and mid September to October – clubhouse open weekends only) **Last arrival:** 20.00 **Last departure:** 11.00

Pitches: 50 hardstanding pitches
Leisure:
Facilities:
Services:
Within 3 miles:

Additional site information: 40 acre site. Families and couples only. Boat launch, pony-trekking, table tennis, lakeside walk.

Premier Park

Hillcroft Park
★★★★★ 90% HOLIDAY PARK

tel: 017684 86363 **Roe Head Lane CA10 2LT**
email: info@hillcroftpark.co.uk web: www.hillcroftpark.co.uk

Hillcroft Park is a family-run site set in the beautiful Ullswater Valley in the north of the Lake District. It offers a range of hardstanding pitches, some fully serviced, and tents are also welcome in the dedicated grass areas. There is a modern amenity block with an arcade room, and private bathrooms are available to hire. The luxurious lodges have been thoughtfully equipped for a very comfortable stay. There is small shop selling essentials, and a van provides takeaway food during peak season.

Open: Mid February to early January **Last arrival:** 20.00 **Last departure:** 11.00

Additional site information: 55 acre site.

Premier Park

Waterfoot Caravan Park
★★★★★ 77%

tel: 017684 86302 **CA11 0JF**
email: bookings@waterfootpark.co.uk web: www.waterfootpark.co.uk
dir: *M6 junction 40, A66 for 1 mile, A592 for 4 miles, site on right before lake. (Note: do not leave A592 until site entrance; sat nav is not compatible).*

A quality touring park with fully serviced hardstanding pitches in a grassy glade in the wooded grounds of an elegant Georgian mansion, just a short distance from the shores of Ullswater. The lounge bar, with a separate family room, enjoys lake views and serves pizzas during the season. The Ullswater Way leads down to the lake and nearby Dalemain House & Gardens. Pooley Bridge is a 15-minute walk and Aira Force waterfall is close by. Wooden glamping pods and five self-catering cottages are available for hire. Please note that there is no access for caravans and motorhomes via Dacre; sat nav should not be used.

Open: March to November (S-Pod cabins, glamping pods and cottages March to January) **Last arrival:** 21.30 **Last departure:** noon

Pitches: 31 hardstanding pitches
Leisure:
Facilities:
Services:
Within 3 miles:

Additional site information: 22 acre site. Cars can be parked by caravans. Awnings permitted. No tents allowed. Coffee lounge, fish and chips mobile unit (peak season only), table tennis, badminton nets, pool table.

Glamping available: Glamping pods, S-pod cabins (please see website for minimum stays and check in/out information.) **Changeover days:** Any day

Additional glamping information: Minimum stay 2 night weekends, 4 nights Easter, 3 nights over Bank Holidays. Cars can be parked by units

CUMBRIA

SILLOTH
Map 18 NY15

Places to visit
RSPB Campfield Marsh, BOWNESS-ON-SOLWAY, CA7 5AG, 01697 351330
www.rspb.org.uk/reserves-and-events/reserves-a-z/campfield-marsh

---

Premier Park

Stanwix Park Holiday Centre
★★★★★ 92% HOLIDAY PARK

tel: 016973 32666 **Greenrow CA7 4HH**
email: enquiries@stanwix.com **web:** www.stanwix.com
dir: *1 mile southwest on B5300. From A596 (Wigton bypass) follow signs to Silloth on B5302. In Silloth follow signs to site, approximately 1 mile on B5300.*

A large and well-run family park within easy reach of the Lake District. Attractively laid out, with lots of amenities to ensure a lively holiday, including a 4-lane automatic 10-pin bowling alley, and a choice of indoor and outdoor swimming pools. There are excellent touring areas with four glamping pods and hardstanding pitches, all within a short walk of the main leisure complex, a campers' kitchen and clean, well-maintained toilet facilities.

Open: All year (restricted service: closed 25–26 December; November to February (except New Year) – no entertainment, shop closed) **Last arrival:** 21.00 **Last departure:** 11.00
Pitches: 🚐 🚗 ⛺; 🏠 see prices below; 95 hardstanding pitches; 28 seasonal pitches
Leisure:
Facilities:
Services:
Within 3 miles:

Additional site information: 26 acre site. Families only. Amusement arcade, bowling alley, leisure centre.
Glamping available: Wooden pods from £30. **Changeover days:** Any day
Additional glamping information: Wooden pods sleep 4. Pet friendly pods available. No charge for pets. Own camping equipment required. Cars can be parked by units

---

Hylton Caravan Park
★★★★ 88%

tel: 016973 32666 **Eden Street CA7 4AY**
email: enquiries@stanwix.com **web:** www.stanwix.com
dir: *On entering Silloth on B5302 follow signs for site, approximately 0.5 mile on left, at end of Eden Street.*

A smart, modern touring park with excellent toilet facilities including several bathrooms. This high quality park is a sister site to Stanwix Park, which is just a mile away and offers all the amenities of a holiday centre, which are available to Hylton tourers. Note: you need to check in at Stanwix Park.

Open: March to November **Last arrival:** 21.00 **Last departure:** 11.00
Pitches: 🚐 🚗 ⛺; 23 hardstanding pitches; 20 seasonal pitches **Leisure:**
Facilities: **Services:** 🔌 **Within 3 miles:**

Additional site information: 18 acre site. Cars can be parked by caravans and tents. Awnings permitted. Families only. Use of facilities at Stanwix Park Holiday Centre.

Solway Holiday Village
★★★★ 84% HOLIDAY PARK

tel: 016973 31236 **Skinburness Drive CA7 4QQ**
email: solway@cove.co.uk **web:** www.cove.co.uk/solway
dir: *Phone for directions.*

Solway Holiday village is ideally located minutes away from the beach of Silloth, which is a long-established holiday destination. This site will suit anyone looking for an action-packed adventure to more relaxing escapes, as it offers a wide range of indoor and outdoor activities, including a pottery studio, heated pool, axe-throwing court and so much more. Meals are served all day in the stylish Borders Bar and Restaurant, and there are also a fish and chip and pizza vans for takeaways. The grassed touring area is served by a modern amenity block with underfloor heating and good privacy options.

Open: March to 10 November **Last arrival:** 18.00 **Last departure:** 10.00
Pitches: 🚐 🚗 ⛺; 18 hardstanding pitches **Leisure:**
Facilities: **Services:**

Additional site information: 130 acre site. Dogs must be kept on leads at all times. Dog exercise area.

ULVERSTON
Map 18 SD27

Places to visit
The Dock Museum, BARROW-IN-FURNESS, LA14 2PW, 01229 876400
www.dockmuseum.org.uk

Furness Abbey, BARROW-IN-FURNESS, LA13 0PJ, 01229 823420
www.english-heritage.org.uk/visit/places/furness-abbey

Great for kids: South Lakes Safari Zoo, LINDAL-IN-FURNESS, LA12 0LU, 01229 466086
www.southlakessafarizoo.com

Premier Park

Bardsea Leisure Park
★★★★★ 89%

tel: 01229 584712 **Priory Road LA12 9QE**
email: reception@bardsealeisure.co.uk **web:** www.bardsealeisure.co.uk
dir: M6 junction 36, A590 towards Barrow. At Ulverston take A5087, site 1 mile on right.

Bardsea Leisure Park is set in a former quarry, which creates a quiet and very sheltered site; set on the southern edge of the town, it is convenient for both the coast and the Lake District. Many of the generously-sized pitches offer all-weather, fully serviced hardstandings. The site has a well-stocked caravan accessories shop and is also a caravan and motorhome dealer/service point. Please note, this site does not accept tents.

Open: All year **Last arrival:** 22.00 **Last departure:** noon
Pitches: 83 hardstanding pitches; 50 seasonal pitches
Leisure: **Facilities:**
Services: Within 3 miles:
Additional site information: 5 acre site. Cars can be parked by caravans. Awnings permitted. No noise after 22.30.

WATERMILLOCK
Map 18 NY42

Places to visit
Aira Force and Ullswater, PENRITH, 017684 82067
www.nationaltrust.org.uk/aira-force-and-ullswater

Dalemain House & Gardens, DALEMAIN, CA11 0HB, 017684 86450
www.dalemain.com

Platinum Park

The Quiet Site
★★★★★

tel: 07768 727016 **Ullswater CA11 0LS**
email: info@thequietsite.co.uk **web:** www.thequietsite.co.uk
dir: M6 junction 40, A66 signed Workington. At next roundabout left onto A592 signed Ullswater. 5 miles (Ullswater on left), turn right at Brackenrigg Inn signed Bennethead. Approximately 1.5 miles to site on right.

A wonderful sustainable park with breathtaking views across Ullswater, and only a short drive away from some of the best fell walking and attractions in the Lake District, including Aira Force, Lowther Castle and Helvellyn. Caravans, motorhomes and tents enjoy well-sized terraced pitches, and fantastic glamping options can be found at the top of the park, including the Glamping Burrows and Gingerbread Houses. This is a site justifiably proud of its green credentials, and very much ahead of the norm; the park is 90% self-sufficient as energy is powered through solar panels, a biomass boiler, a ground source heat pump and PV panels. Fast free WiFi is available throughout the park and residents also have access to a TV/meeting room. The 16th-century 'Quiet Bar' with its authentic, rustic decor is open all year around. 'The Quiet Bite' offers breakfast crêpes and bacon rolls, as well as an evening pizza takeaway service. A smart, well-equipped shower block has private, fully serviced cubicles. England and Overall Campsite of the Year 2023–24.

Open: All year (restricted service: low season – bar may close on weekdays)
Last arrival: 21.00 **Last departure:** noon (or 11.00 for pods)
Pitches: see prices below; 60 hardstanding pitches; 15 seasonal pitches
Leisure:
Facilities:
Services:
Within 3 miles:

Additional site information: 10 acre site. Cars can be parked by caravans and tents. Awnings permitted. Quiet from 22.00. Pool table, soft play area for toddlers, caravan storage. Car hire can be arranged.

Glamping available: Glamping Cabins, Gingerbread Houses, Glamping Burrow & Camping Pods
Changeover days: Any day

Additional glamping information: Minimum stay – 2 nights at weekends. Cars can be parked by units

Premier Park

The Quiet Site Glamping
★★★★★ 90% GLAMPING ONLY

tel: 01768 486337 **Ullswater CA11 0LS**
email: info@thequietsite.co.uk **web:** www.thequietsite.co.uk
dir: M6 junction 40, A66 signed Workington. At next roundabout left onto A592 signed Ullswater. 5 miles (Ullswater on left), turn right at Brackenrigg Inn signed Bennethead. Approximately 1.5 miles to site on right.

The aptly named Quiet Site is a top sustainable park where guests can savour the stunning views of Ullswater and surrounding fells. Located at the top of the park are fabulous glamping options – posh camping pods and cabins, unique Glamping Burrows (Hobbit Holes), and quirky Gingerbread Houses – all built by owner Daniel Holder and his on-site team. Virtually invisible within the gorgeous Lake District landscape, unless you know where to look, the Burrows are large underground living spaces with en suite shower rooms and amazing views over the Ullswater Valley; all are very secure, superbly insulated by soil and grass, and very energy efficient. Equally unusual are the Gingerbread Houses which are carbon positive spaces with photovoltaic (PV) panelled roofs, triple insulation and ground-source heating. They are surrounded by 'ginger' beech hedges. Guests staying in the Burrows or Gingerbread Houses are required to bring their own cutlery, plates and mugs, and bedding. There is a zero-waste shop, an authentic bar in a 16th-century barn, the Quiet Bite for breakfast bacon rolls and evening pizzas, and a smartly refurbished amenity block with excellent fully-serviced cubicles.

Open: All year

Glamping available: Glamping Cabins, Gingerbread Houses, Glamping Burrow & Camping Pods

ENGLAND 102 CUMBRIA

WATERMILLOCK continued

Ullswater Holiday Park
★★★★ 86%

tel: 017684 86666 **High Longthwaite CA11 0LR**
email: info@ullswaterholidaypark.co.uk web: www.ullswaterholidaypark.co.uk
dir: *M6 junction 40, A66 signed Workington. At next roundabout left onto A592 signed Ullswater. 5 miles. (Ullswater on left for 2 miles), turn right at phone box signed Longthwaite. Site 0.5 mile on right.*

A pleasant rural site with its own nearby boat launching and marine storage facility that makes it ideal for those who love sailing. The family-owned and run park enjoys fell and lake views, and there is a bar, The Daffodil Coffee Shop, arcade room, a splendid undercover picnic area for campers, and a shop on site. Many of the pitches are fully serviced and there are wooden cabins (some en suite) with barbecues. Please note that the Marine Park is one mile from the camping area.

Open: March to 14 November (restricted service: on-site bar open Wednesday to Sunday, 16.00 – 22.00) **Last arrival:** 21.00 **Last departure:** noon (camping and touring) 10:00 (statics, cottages and cabins) 11:00 (pods)

Pitches: * from £30; from £30; from £25.50; see prices below; 58 hardstanding pitches

Leisure:
Facilities:
Services:
Within 3 miles:

Additional site information: 12 acre site. Cars can be parked by caravans and tents. Awnings permitted. No open fires, no noise after 23.00. Boat launching and moorings in 1 mile.

Glamping available: Camping cabins from £48, Glamping pods from £100
Changeover days: Any day

Additional glamping information: Some cabins are dog friendly. Cars can be parked by units

---

WINDERMERE — Map 18 SD49

Places to visit

Holehird Gardens, WINDERMERE, LA23 1NP, 015394 46008
www.holehirdgardens.org.uk

Blackwell - The Arts & Crafts House, BOWNESS-ON-WINDERMERE, LA23 3JT, 015394 46139
www.lakelandarts.org.uk/blackwell

Great for kids: Brockhole on Windermere, WINDERMERE, LA23 1LJ, 015394 46601
www.brockhole.co.uk

WINDERMERE — Map 18 SD49

Premier Park

Park Cliffe Camping & Caravan Estate
★★★★★ 91%

tel: 015395 31344 **Birks Road, Tower Wood LA23 3PG**
email: info@parkcliffe.co.uk web: www.parkcliffe.co.uk
dir: *M6 junction 36, A590. Right at Newby Bridge onto A592. 3.6 miles right into site. (Note: due to difficult access from main road this is the only advised direction for approaching the site).*

Park Cliffe Camping & Caravan Estate is a lovely hillside park set in 25 secluded acres of fell land. The camping area is sloping and uneven in places but well drained and sheltered, and some pitches have spectacular views of Lake Windermere and the Langdales. The park offers a high level of customer care and is very well equipped for families (including family bathrooms) with breakfast, bar and the River Box which serves delicious takeaway food (seasonal hours apply). Wooden pods (including an en suite family unit), a shepherd's hut, holiday apartments and static holiday caravans for hire.

Open: Opening March to mid November (restricted service: food and drink facilities not available all season)
Last arrival: 22.00 (gates locked at 23.00)
Last departure: noon (camping/touring), 10.00 (rental)

Pitches: ; see prices below; 60 hardstanding pitches; 30 seasonal pitches

Leisure:
Facilities:
Services:
Within 3 miles:

Additional site information: 25 acre site. Cars can be parked by caravans. Awnings permitted. No noise 23.00–07.30. Off licence, bathrooms for hire. Takeaway food from 'The Riverbox' & breakfast restaurant, seasonal hours apply.

Glamping available: 20 wooden pods from £50 per night; 1 shepherd's hut from £82 per night. **Changeover days:** Varies depending on type of accommodation booked

Additional glamping information: Couples, Park Cliffe, Family and Family Comfort pods are dog friendly. Cars can be parked by units.

PITCHES: Caravans Motorhomes Tents Glamping accommodation **LEISURE:** Indoor swimming pool Outdoor swimming pool Children's playground Kids' club Tennis court Games room Separate TV room golf course Pitch n putt Boats for hire Bikes for hire Cinema Entertainment Fishing Mini golf Watersports Gym Sports field Stables Spa

DERBYSHIRE

ASHBOURNE
Map 10 SK14

Platinum Park

Rivendale Lodge Retreat
★★★★★ **HOLIDAY PARK**

tel: 01335 310441 Buxton Road, Alsop en le Dale DE6 1QU
web: www.darwinescapes.co.uk/rivendale-lodge-retreat

Rivendale Lodge Retreat is set in a former quarry, and there are lots of places to visit and things to do nearby, including the adjacent Tissington Trail. Natural landscaping includes a wide range of tree varieties as well as indigenous and cultivated pants; there's a large colony of great crested newts in addition to many bird species. The well-spaced lodges are beautifully equipped, with superb comfortable interiors and all have the benefit of generous decked areas; some also have hot tubs. Further facilities include a well-stocked, licensed shop, a stylish bistro and a bar that benefits from great countryside views.

Open: All year **Last departure:** 10.00
Additional site information: 37 acre site.

BAKEWELL
Map 16 SK26

Places to visit
Chatsworth, CHATSWORTH, DE45 1PP, 01246 565300
www.chatsworth.org

Greenhills Holiday Park
★★★★ 90%

tel: 01629 813052 & 813467 Crowhill Lane DE45 1PX
email: info@greenhillsholidaypark.co.uk web: www.greenhillsholidaypark.co.uk
dir: *1 mile northwest of Bakewell on A6. Signed before Ashford-in-the-Water, onto unclassified road on right.*

A well-established park set in lovely countryside within the Peak District National Park. Many pitches enjoy uninterrupted views, and there is easy access to all facilities, including the amenity block (a new washroom block was added for the 2024 season) and games room, not to mention the on-site pub and well-equipped children's play area and spacious football field. The park is very well situated for Bakewell, Chatsworth House and other local attractions.

Open: February to November (restricted service: February to April and October to November – bar and shop closed) **Last arrival:** 22.00 **Last departure:** noon

Pitches: 🚐 🚗 ▲; 85 hardstanding pitches; 50 seasonal pitches
Leisure: 🎱 ⚽
Facilities: 🚿 ⊙ ✂ ✳ ♿ 🛒 🍴 WiFi 💻
Services: 🔌 🧺 🍺 🍽 🛏 ⛽ 🔒 ♨ T **Within 3 miles:** 🚶 🎣 ⛳ ◎

Additional site information: 8 acre site. 🚗 Cars can be parked by caravans and tents. Awnings permitted.

BUXTON
Map 16 SK07

Places to visit
Poole's Cavern (Buxton Country Park), BUXTON, SK17 9DH, 01298 26978
www.poolescavern.co.uk

Great for kids: Go Ape Buxton, BUXTON, SK17 9DH, 01603 895500
www.goape.co.uk/locations/buxton

Beech Croft Farm Caravan and Camping Park
★★★★ 95%

tel: 01298 85330 Blackwell in the Peak SK17 9TQ
email: mail@beechcroftfarm.co.uk web: www.beechcroftfarm.co.uk
dir: *Exit A6 midway between Buxton and Bakewell. Site signed.*

Beech Croft Farm Caravan and Camping Park is a small, family run site with lovely Peak District views. There's a fine stone-built toilet block with ultra-modern fittings, underfloor heating and additional unisex facilities. The shop is fully stocked with camping essentials and an array of local produce plus a regular bakery delivery. Hardstanding caravan pitches, a campers' shelter and a super tarmac pathway leading from the camping field to the toilet block are all maintained to a high standard. All the tent pitches have electrical hook-up via a pre-payment card system. There's a boot, dog and bike wash. A stylish catering chalet, with alfresco seating provides breakfasts, coffee and cake and evening takeaway options. Daisies Coffee Shop proves very popular too. This makes an ideal site for those touring or walking in the Peak District.

Open: All year (restricted service: November to February – tents not accepted)
Last arrival: 18.00 (later arrivals by prior arrangement, no problem if discussed)
Last departure: noon

Pitches: * 🚐 from £29; 🚗 from £29; ▲ from £20; 30 hardstanding pitches
Leisure: 🎱 ⚽ **Facilities:** 🚿 ⊙ ✳ ♿ 🛒 WiFi 💻
Services: 🔌 🧺 🍽 ⛽ 🔒 ♨ T

Additional site information: 3 acre site. 🚗 Cars can be parked by caravans and tents. Awnings permitted. No noise after 22.00. No group bookings. 5mph speed limit. Microwave available.

BUXTON continued

Lime Tree Park
★★★★ 92%

tel: 01298 22988 Dukes Drive SK17 9RP
email: info@limetreeparkbuxton.com web: www.limetreeparkbuxton.com
dir: *1 mile south of Buxton, between A515 and A6.*

A very attractive and well-designed site, set on the side of a narrow valley in an elevated location, with separate, neatly landscaped areas for statics, tents, touring caravans, motorhomes and four glamping pods. Expect good attention to detail throughout the park and a stylish amenity block. Its backdrop of a magnificent old railway viaduct and views over Buxton and the surrounding hills, make this a sought-after destination which has easy access to the Peak District's many attractions.

Open: March to October **Last arrival:** 18.00 **Last departure:** noon
Pitches: 🚐 🚙 ⛺ 🛖; 22 hardstanding pitches
Leisure: ⛱ ⚽ 🎮
Facilities: 🚿 ⊙ ⚒ ✳ ♿ 🚮 WiFi 🖥
Services: 🔌 🗑 🛒 🔒 ∅ T
Within 3 miles: 🚴 ∪ ◎ 🏊

Additional site information: 10.5 acre site. 🚗 Cars can be parked by caravans and tents. Awnings permitted. No noise after 22.00, no fires.

Glamping available: Glamping pods.
Additional glamping information: Glamping pods from £49.

HARTINGTON Map 16 SK16

Places to visit

The Heights of Abraham, MATLOCK BATH, DE4 3NT, 01629 582365
www.heightsofabraham.com

Alton Towers Resort, ALTON, ST10 4DB, 01538 704096
www.altontowers.com

Bank House Farm
★★★★ 86%

tel: 01298 687333 Mill Lane, Hulme End SK17 0EX
email: bankhousecampsite@gmail.com web: www.bankhousefarmcamping.co.uk

Located in Staffordshire Moorlands side of the Peak District, this constantly improving family holiday destination is popular for those wishing for a back-to-nature experience in an Area of Outstanding Natural Beauty. Most pitches are level and very well spaced, with surrounding mature trees ensuring privacy. The amenity block has underfloor heating and contains very good facilities. The Manifold Inn, specialising in campers' breakfasts, is located opposite the park entrance. Great for families.

Open: 1 March to 31 October **Last arrival:** 20.00 **Last departure:** noon
Pitches: 🚐 🚙 ⛺; 40 hardstanding pitches
Facilities: 🚿 ⊙ ⚒ ✳ 🚮 WiFi
Services: 🔌 🗑 ⛽ 🔒 ∅ T

Additional site information: 15 acre site. 🚗 Cars can be parked by caravans and tents. Awnings permitted. No noise after 10.30. No groups Pizza van Friday nights

---

HOPE Map 16 SK18

Places to visit

Peveril Castle, CASTLETON, S33 8WQ, 01433 620613
www.english-heritage.org.uk/visit/places/peveril-castle

Speedwell Cavern, CASTLETON, S33 8WA, 01433 623018
www.speedwellcavern.co.uk

Pindale Farm Outdoor Centre
★★★ 83%

tel: 01433 620111 Pindale Road S33 6RN
email: info@pindalefarm.co.uk web: www.pindalefarm.co.uk
dir: *From A6187 in Hope follow Pindale sign between church and Woodroffe Arms. Site 1 mile on left.*

Set around a 13th-century farmhouse and a former lead mine pump house (now converted to a self-contained bunkhouse accommodating up to 60 people), this simple, off-the-beaten-track site is an ideal base for walking, climbing, caving and various outdoor pursuits. Around the farm are several deeply wooded areas available for pitching tents, and old stone buildings that have been converted to house modern toilet facilities. Super-fast WiFi is also available throughout the site for a small fee.

Open: March to October
Pitches: ⛺
Facilities: 🚿 ⊙ ✳ WiFi
Services: 🔌 🗑
Within 3 miles: ∪ 🏊

Additional site information: 4 acre site. 🚗 Cars can be parked by tents. Awnings permitted. No anti-social behaviour, noise must be kept to minimum after 21.00, no fires. Charge for WiFi.

DERBYSHIRE 105 ENGLAND

RIDDINGS
Map 16 SK45

Places to visit

Denby Pottery Village, DENBY, DE5 8NX, 01773 740799
www.denbypottery.com

Midland Railway Butterley, RIPLEY, DE5 3QZ, 01773 570140
www.midlandrailway-butterley.co.uk

Riddings Wood Holiday Park
★★★★ 86%

tel: 01773 605160 **Bullock Lane, Riddings DE55 4BP**
email: info@riddingswoodholidaypark.co.uk **web:** www.riddingswoodholidaypark.co.uk
dir: *M1 junction 27, A608 signed Heanor. Right onto B600 signed Alfreton and Selston. Left onto B6016 signed Jacksdale. Through Jacksdale towards Ridding. Site on right.*

Located close to both Derby and Nottingham, this site's layout can be described as a sloping amphitheatre. It is surrounded by the mature trees of Riddings Wood on all sides and has a fabulous panoramic view looking down towards Jacksdale. Beyond the sweeping driveway and security barrier, you'll find a smart chalet-style reception and a stylish amenity block with good privacy options. Picnic benches are scattered around the park for campers to use, and fully serviced pitches are available. Lodges, sleeping up to six people, are available for hire; exclusive use of a hot tub is included in the price. A local bus service runs every nine minutes from the site entrance to both Derby and Nottingham.

Open: All year **Last arrival:** 22.00 **Last departure:** 11.30
Pitches: ; 26 hardstanding pitches
Leisure: **Facilities:**
Services: **Within 3 miles:**

Additional site information: 11.5 acre site. Cars can be parked by caravans and tents. Awnings permitted. Children must be accompanied by an adult at all times. Rubbish must be placed in designated areas. No noise after 22.00. Dogs must be kept on leads at all times.

RIPLEY
Map 16 SK35

Places to visit

Midland Railway Butterley, RIPLEY, DE5 3QZ, 01773 570140
www.midlandrailway-butterley.co.uk

Denby Pottery Village, DENBY, DE5 8NX, 01773 740799
www.denbypottery.com

Golden Valley Caravan & Camping Park
★★★★ 87%

tel: 01773 513881 **Coach Road DE55 4ES**
email: enquiries@goldenvalleycaravanpark.co.uk
web: www.goldenvalleycaravanpark.co.uk
dir: *M1 junction 26, A610 to Codnor. Right at lights. Right into Alfreton Road. In 1 mile left into Coach Road, park on left. (Note: it is advisable to ignore sat nav for last few miles and follow these directions).*

This superbly landscaped park is set within 30 acres of woodland in the Amber Valley. The fully serviced pitches are set out in informal groups in clearings amongst the trees. The park has a cosy bar and bistro with a dining room and upstairs event space, plus an outside patio, a fully-stocked fishing lake, an innovative and well-equipped play area and fully-equipped fitness suite. There is also a wildlife pond and a nature trail; camping pods are available for hire.

Open: All year (restricted service: low season – bar and café open, children's activities at weekends only) **Last arrival:** 20.00 (call if any later) **Last departure:** noon
Pitches: ; see prices below; 45 hardstanding pitches; 12 seasonal pitches
Leisure:
Facilities:
Services:
Within 3 miles:

Additional site information: 30 acre site. Cars can be parked by caravans and tents. Awnings permitted. No vehicles on grass, no open fires or disposable BBQs, no noise after 22.30. Zip slide, tractor train, log flume ride, bouncy castle, paddle boats, crazy golf, segways (high season only).

Glamping available: Wooden pod, wooden barrel pod from £50.

Additional glamping information: Wooden pod sleeps 2, wooden barrel pod sleeps 4. No dogs, no smoking, no fires. Own sleeping equipment and camping accessories required.

ROSLISTON
Map 10 SK21

Places to visit

Ashby-de-la-Zouch Castle, ASHBY-DE-LA-ZOUCH, LE65 1BR, 01530 413343
www.english-heritage.org.uk/visit/places/ashby-de-la-zouch-castle

Great for kids: Conkers, MOIRA, DE12 6GA, 01283 216633
www.visitconkers.com

Beehive Woodland Lakes
★★★★ 86%

tel: 01283 763981 **DE12 8HZ**
email: info@beehivefarm-woodlandlakes.co.uk
web: www.beehivefarm-woodlandlakes.co.uk
dir: *From A444 in Castle Gresley into Mount Pleasant Road. Follow Rosliston signs for 3.5 miles through Linton. Left at T-junction signed Beehive Farms.*

A small, informal and continually developing caravan area secluded away from an extensive woodland park in the heart of the National Forest National Park. The toilet facilities include four family rooms. Young children will enjoy the playground, whilst anglers can pass many a happy hour fishing at the park's three lakes. There are also five camping pods available to hire. The park is also licenced for weddings in the nearby 'Hidden Hive'.

Open: All year **Last arrival:** 19.00 (17.00 in low season) **Last departure:** noon
Pitches: ; see prices below; 46 hardstanding pitches; 18 seasonal pitches
Leisure:
Facilities:
Services:
Within 3 miles:

Additional site information: 2.5 acre site. Cars can be parked by caravans and tents. Awnings permitted. Gas BBQs only, no generators, no unaccompanied groups of young people. Takeaway food delivered to site.

Glamping available: Wooden pods from £40.

Additional glamping information: Wooden pods sleep 4 (suitable for families). No pets. Cars can be parked by units

Devon

With magnificent coastlines, two historic cities and the world-famous Dartmoor National Park, Devon sums up all that is best about the British landscape. For centuries it has been a fashionable and much loved holiday destination – especially south Devon's glorious English Riviera.

When the crime writer Agatha Christie was born in Torquay on Devon's glorious south coast, the town was a popular seaside resort. It was 1890, the start of Queen Victoria's last decade as monarch, and Torquay was a fashionable destination for all sorts of people; those looking for a permanent home by the sea as well as holidaymakers in search of long hours of sunshine and a mild climate. In many ways, Torquay remains much the same today and its impressive setting still evokes a sense of its Victorian heyday. A local steam train attraction adds to the atmosphere; you can travel from Paignton to Dartmouth, alighting on the way at the small station at Churston, just as Hercule Poirot does in Christie's 1930s detective novel *The ABC Murders*. The Queen of Crime herself used this station when she had a summer home nearby. The house, Greenway, overlooks a glorious sweep of the River Dart and is now managed as a popular visitor attraction by the National Trust.

Close to the English Riviera lies Dartmoor, one of the south-west's most spectacular landscapes. The contrast between the traditional attractions of the coast and this expanse of bleak, brooding moorland could not be greater. The National Park, which contains Dartmoor, covers 365 square miles and includes many fascinating geological features – isolated granite tors and two summits exceeding 2,000 feet among them. Dartmoor's waterfalls, including the tumbling Whitelady Waterfall at Lydford Gorge, can be seen in full spate even in the depths of winter. Everywhere you venture on Dartmoor, there are stone circles, burial chambers and mysterious clues to the distant past. The place oozes antiquity. Sir Arthur Conan Doyle set his classic Sherlock Holmes story *The Hound of the Baskervilles* on Dartmoor, and Agatha Christie stayed at a local hotel for two weeks at the height of the First World War in order to finish writing her first detective novel *The Mysterious Affair at Styles*, first published in 1920.

Not surprisingly, Dartmoor equates with walking and the opportunities are enormous. For something really adventurous, try the Two Moors Way. This long-distance route begins at Ivybridge and crosses the National Park to enter neighbouring Exmoor, which straddles the Devon/Somerset border. At Lynton and Lynmouth the trail connects with the South West Coast Path, which takes walkers on a breathtaking journey to explore north Devon's gloriously rugged coastline, renowned for its extraordinary collection of peaks and outcrops. Cycling in the two National Parks is also extremely popular and there is a good choice of off-road routes taking you to the heart of Dartmoor and Exmoor.

Devon's towns and cities offer a pleasing but stimulating alternative to the rigours of the countryside. There are scores of small market towns in the region – for example there is Tavistock with its popular farmers' market, one of many in the county. Plymouth lies in Devon's south-west corner and is a striking city and naval port. Much of its transformation over the years is a reminder of the devastation it suffered, together with Exeter, during the Second World War. The city places particular emphasis, of course, on the Spanish Armada and the voyage of the Pilgrim Fathers to America.

On the theme of sailing, Devon is synonymous with this most invigorating of boating activities. Salcombe, on the county's south coast, is a sailing playground. Situated on a tree-fringed estuary beneath lush rolling hills, the town thrives on boats – it hosts the week-long Salcombe Regatta in August. It's even suitable for swimming, with several sandy beaches and sheltered bays.

◁ *Combe Martin Beach, Exmoor National Park*

DEVON

ASHBURTON Map 3 SX77

Places to visit

Compton Castle, COMPTON, TQ3 1TA, 01803 661906
www.nationaltrust.org.uk/compton-castle

Parkers Farm Holiday Park

★★★★ 89%

tel: 01364 654869 **Higher Mead Farm TQ13 7LJ**
email: parkersfarm@btconnect.com **web:** www.parkersfarmholidays.co.uk
dir: *From Exeter on A38, 2nd left after Plymouth (29 miles) sign, signed Woodland and Denbury. From Plymouth on A38 take A383 Newton Abbot exit, turn right across bridge, rejoin A38, then as above.*

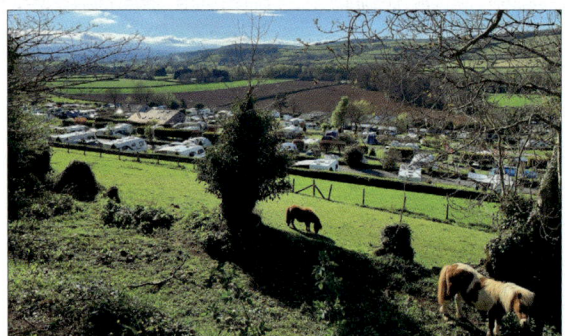

Parkers Farm is a well-developed site terraced into rising ground with stunning views across rolling countryside to the Dartmoor tors. Part of a working farm, this park offers spacious grassy pitches and 12 excellent fully serviced hardstanding pitches, which make the most of the fine views. It is beautifully maintained and has good quality toilet facilities, a popular games room and a bar/restaurant that serves excellent meals. Large family rooms with two shower cubicles, a large sink and a toilet are especially appreciated by families with small children. There are farm walks and tractor rides during high summer, when all the family can meet and feed the various animals.

Open: 30 March to 31 October (restricted service: low season – bar and restaurant open at weekends only) **Last arrival:** 22.00 **Last departure:** 10.00 (Touring) 9:00 (Static)

Pitches: ; 20 hardstanding pitches

Leisure:

Facilities: WiFi

Services:

Within 3 miles:

Additional site information: 25 acre site. Cars can be parked by caravans and tents. Awnings permitted. Large field available for dog walking.

River Dart Country Park

★★★★ 89%

tel: 01364 652511 **Holne Park TQ13 7NP**
email: info@riverdart.co.uk **web:** www.riverdart.co.uk
dir: *M5 junction 31, A38 towards Plymouth. In Ashburton at Peartree junction follow brown site signs. Site 1 mile on left. (Note: Peartree junction is 2nd exit at Ashburton; do not exit at Linhay junction as narrow roads are unsuitable for caravans).*

Set in 90 acres of magnificent parkland that was once part of a Victorian estate, with many specimen and exotic trees, this peaceful, hidden-away touring park occupies several camping areas, all served with good quality toilet facilities. In spring the park is a blaze of colour from the many azaleas and rhododendrons. There are numerous outdoor activities for all ages including abseiling, caving and canoeing, plus high quality, well-maintained facilities. The open moorland of Dartmoor is only a few minutes away.

Open: April to September (restricted service: Low and mid season – reduced opening hours at shop and café bar) **Last arrival:** 20.00 **Last departure:** 10.30

Pitches: ; 34 hardstanding pitches

Leisure:

Facilities: WiFi

Services: **Within 3 miles:**

Additional site information: 90 acre site. Cars can be parked by caravans and tents. Awnings permitted. Dogs must be kept on leads at all times. Adventure Playground, Dare Devil activities, cycle track.

AXMINSTER Map 4 SY29

Places to visit

Axe Valley Wildlife Park, AXMINSTER, EX13 7RA, 01297 34472
www.axevalleypark.co.uk

Axminster Heritage Museum, AXMINSTER, EX13 5AH, 01297 34386
www.axminsterheritage.org

Platinum Park

Hawkchurch Resort & Spa

★★★★★ HOLIDAY PARK

tel: 01297 678402 **Hawkchurch EX13 5UL**
email: reception@hawkchurchresort.co.uk **web:** www.hawkchurchresort.co.uk
dir: *From A35 between Axminster and Charmouth take B3165 signed Crewkerne. Left signed Hawkchurch.*

This superb lodge park is located in lovely countryside near Axminster and the Jurassic Coast and enjoys views over the Axe Valley. The luxury lodges are fully equipped and there are excellent leisure facilities – including the Ezina Spa offering a wide range of luxury treatments, plus a spa pool and gym. In addition, there is a good restaurant, The Beeches, as well as an alfresco eating and drinking area.

Open: All year

Holiday Homes: Sleep 8, Two-ring burner, Dishwasher, Washing Machine, Tumble dryer, Microwave, Freezer, TV, Sky/Freeview, DVD player, WiFi, Linen included, Towels included, Electricity included, Gas included

Leisure:

Additional site information:

PITCHES: Caravans Motorhomes Tents Glamping accommodation **LEISURE:** Indoor swimming pool Outdoor swimming pool Children's playground Kids' club Tennis court Games room Separate TV room golf course Pitch n putt Boats for hire Bikes for hire Cinema Entertainment Fishing Mini golf Watersports Gym Sports field Stables Spa

Andrewshayes Holiday Park
★★★★ 91%

tel: 01404 831225 Dalwood EX13 7DY
email: info@andrewshayes.co.uk **web:** www.andrewshayes.co.uk
dir: *3 miles from Axminster towards Honiton on A35, right at Taunton Cross signed Dalwood and Stockland. Site 150 metres on right.*

Andrewshayes Holiday Park is an attractive park within easy reach of Lyme Regis, Charmouth, Seaton and Sidmouth in an ideal touring location. This popular family run park has a lovely free swimming pool, a cosy bar and restaurant, play areas for children and modern toilet facilities. There are also luxury holiday homes for hire and to purchase. The site is dog friendly with its own woodland walk.

Open: 28 March to 3 November (restricted service: off-peak season–bar and restaurant reduced hours) **Last arrival:** 20.00 **Last departure:** 10.30

Pitches: * from £37; from £37; from £37; 130 hardstanding pitches; 105 seasonal pitches

Leisure:
Facilities:
Services:
Within 3 miles:

Additional site information: 12 acre site. Cars can be parked by caravans and tents. Awnings permitted. Children under 16 must be supervised by an adult in the pool. Table tennis, woodland walk. Bar and restaurant seasonal.

BARNSTAPLE
Map 3 SS53

Places to visit

Exmoor Zoo, BLACKMOOR GATE, EX31 4SG, 01598 763352
www.exmoorzoo.co.uk

Arlington Court and the National Trust Carriage Museum, ARLINGTON, EX31 4LP, 01271 850296
www.nationaltrust.org.uk/arlington-court-and-the-national-trust-carriage-museum

---

Hallsdown Farm Touring Park
★★★★ 88%

tel: 01271 850847 Hallsdown Farm, Arlington EX31 4SW
email: andrew.mather@yahoo.co.uk **web:** www.hallsdownfarm.co.uk
dir: *A361 (signed South Molton-Barnstaple) to A399 (signed Blackmoorgate). Approximately 1 mile after junction with B3358 turn left signed Loxhore, campsite on right.*

Located on a working farm, Hallsdown Farm Touring Park, a small and very peaceful adults-only park, is tucked in a glorious part of north Devon, yet is close to Barnstaple, Exmoor and the dramatic north Devon coast. There are four toilet/shower cubicles, all kept spotlessly clean, as well as a dish-wash area and laundry room. 10 hardstanding, premium pitches each have a toilet, shower and washbasin in their own cabin. Campers can expect good access from the main road, neat grass, shelter from surrounding trees and hedges, and CCTV security.

Open: 15 March to 31 October **Last arrival:** 20.00 (Later arrivals by prior arrangement) **Last departure:** 11.00

Pitches: * from £24; from £24; 20 hardstanding pitches; 10 seasonal pitches

Facilities:
Services:
Within 3 miles:

Additional site information: 2.5 acre site. Adults only. Cars can be parked by caravans. Awnings permitted.

Make your next UK holiday one to remember

Choose RatedTrips.com

AA

BERRYNARBOR
Map 3 SS54

Places to visit
Great for kids: Watermouth Castle & Family Theme Park, ILFRACOMBE, EX34 9SL, 01271 867474
www.watermouthcastle.com

Combe Martin Wildlife & Dinosaur Park, COMBE MARTIN, EX34 0NG, 01271 882486
cmwdp.co.uk

Premier Park

Mill Park Touring Caravan & Camping Park
★★★★★ 93%

tel: 01271 882647 Mill Lane EX34 9SH
email: enquiries@millpark.com web: www.millpark.com
dir: M5 junction 27, A361 towards Barnstaple. Right onto A399 towards Combe Martin. At Sawmills Inn take turn opposite Berrynarbor sign.

Under enthusiastic ownership, this well managed park is set in an attractive wooded valley with a stream that runs into a lake where coarse fishing is available. There is a quiet bar and restaurant with a family room, a very pleasant camping meadow, an excellent children's play area, and clean and tidy toilet facilities. The park now has 100% fully serviced pitches. The site has lakeside wooden pods (cocoons), wooden pods (glampods) and Lotus Belle tents for hire. It is located two miles from Combe Martin and Ilfracombe and just a stroll across the road from the small harbour at Watermouth.

Open: March to October **Last arrival:** 21.00 **Last departure:** 10.00
Pitches: see prices below; 42 hardstanding pitches; 60 seasonal pitches
Leisure:
Facilities:
Services:
Within 3 miles:

Additional site information: 30 acre site. Cars can be parked by caravans and tents. Awnings permitted. No open fires, no groundsheets/footprints under tents. Fresh coffee and croissants available everyday. Family bathroom, accessible wetroom.

Glamping available: Lotus Belle tents from £50; wooden pods from £40

Additional glamping information: Lotus Belle tents: no dogs allowed. Lotus Belle tents, wooden cocoons and wooden pods offer fridge, heater, kettle, light, electricity, BBQ and picnic table. Cars can be parked by units

See advert opposite

BIDEFORD
Map 3 SS42

Places to visit
Tapeley Park Gardens, BIDEFORD EX39 4NT, 01271 860897
www.historichouses.org/house/tapeley-park/visit

Northam Burrows Country Park, Sandymere Rd, Northam, BIDEFORD EX39 1XS
www.visitdevon.co.uk/listing/northam-burrows-country-park/252353301

Great for kids: The Big Sheep Farm & Theme Park, Abbotsham, BIDEFORD EX39 5AP, 01237 472366
www.thebigsheep.co.uk

North Devon Maritime Museum, 5 Odun Rd, Appledore, BIDEFORD EX39 1PT, 01237 422064
www.northdevonmaritimemuseum.co.uk

Adventure Camping
★★★ 80%

tel: 01237 880028 Ultimate Adventure EX39 5AP
email: centre.nd@inspiring-learning.com

This 'ultimate adventure' campsite is located in rolling North Devon countryside close to the town of Bideford and the surfing beach of Westward Ho! Accommodation comprises family camping, eco-lodges and two dormitory-style hostels. The level grassy camping area caters for tents, motorhomes and caravans with electric hook up on offer, and there's a small shop selling essentials and a café serving breakfast, lunch and evening meals. Activities include an assault course, archery, climbing walls, kayaking, surfing, and bikes can be hired on site.

Open: End of March to start of November **Last arrival:** 22:00 **Last departure:** 10:00
Additional site information: 35 acre site.

BRAUNTON
Map 3 SS43

Places to visit
Marwood Hill Gardens, BARNSTAPLE, EX31 4EA, 01271 342528
www.marwoodhillgarden.co.uk

Great for kids: Combe Martin Wildlife & Dinosaur Park, COMBE MARTIN, EX34 0NG, 01271 882486
cmwdp.co.uk

DEVON 111 ENGLAND

BRAUNTON Map 3 SS43

Lobb Fields Caravan & Camping Park
★★★★ 87%

tel: 01271 812090 **Saunton Road EX33 1HG**
email: info@lobbfields.com **web:** lobbfields.com
dir: *At crossroads in Braunton take B3231 towards Saunton and Croyde. Park is signed on right approximately 1 mile from centre of Braunton.*

Located between Braunton and the miles of golden sands at Saunton, Lobb Fields Caravan & Camping Park, a bright, tree-lined park with gently-sloping grass pitches, is dog-friendly and offers 180 pitches in two areas. Seasonal pitches and caravan storage are available. Apart from relaxing and taking in the views in this UNESCO World Biosphere area, there's plenty of surfing and cycling to be enjoyed with the 30-mile Tarka Trail cycle route nearby.

Open: All year **Last arrival:** 22.00 **Last departure:** 10.30

Pitches: * from £16; from £16; from £12; 20 hardstanding pitches; 21 seasonal pitches

Leisure: **Facilities:** **Services:** **Within 3 miles:**

Additional site information: 14 acre site. Cars can be parked by caravans and tents. Awnings permitted. No under 18s unless accompanied by an adult, no fires, no noise after 23.00. Glamping hire and surf boards and wet suits for hire, wet suit washing areas. Dog wash areas.

BRIDESTOWE Map 3 SX58

Places to visit
Lydford Castle and Saxon Town, LYDFORD, EX20 4BH, 0370 333 1181
www.english-heritage.org.uk/visit/places/lydford-castle-and-saxon-town

Museum of Dartmoor Life, OKEHAMPTON, EX20 1HQ, 01837 52295
www.dartmoorlife.org.uk

Bridestowe Caravan Park
★★★ 78%

tel: 01837 861261 **EX20 4ER**
email: ali.young53@btinternet.com **web:** www.glebe-park.co.uk
dir: *Exit A30 at A386 and Sourton Cross junction, follow B3278 signed Bridestowe, left in 3 miles. In village centre, left onto unclassified road for 0.5 mile.*

A small, well-established park in a rural setting close to Dartmoor National Park. This mainly static park has a small, peaceful touring space, and there are many activities to enjoy in the area including fishing and riding. Part of the National Cycle Route 27 (the Devon Coast to Coast) passes close to this park.

Open: March to December **Last arrival:** 22.30 **Last departure:** noon

Pitches: ; 3 hardstanding pitches **Leisure:** **Facilities:**
Services: **Additional site information:** 1 acre site. Cars can be parked by caravans and tents. Awnings permitted.

Away from the crowds but near to the fun...
...at peaceful Mill Park Caravan and Camping Park
Berrynarbor, nr Ilfracombe, North Devon EX34 9SH

Mill Park is a sheltered caravan and camping site set around a sparkling 1.5 acre fishing lake just back from the main seaside holiday resorts of North Devon. Set in an attractive wooded valley; it is perfectly situated for beaches, coastal activities and attractions, plus adjacent to stunning coastal walks and the breathtaking beauty of Exmoor.
   Mill Park offers fully serviced hard standing pitches, as well as good sized level grassed pitches with electrical hook-ups, insulated modern shower blocks, laundry room and camping supplies. There is an onsite pub and a well stocked shop which both specialise in local foods and drinks plus a family room. An attractive flat grassed area for camping, a number of glamping options and a dog exercise field are also available.

Call 01271 882647 | www.millpark.com | enquiries@millpark.com

FACILITIES: Electric vehicle charging Baths/Shower Electric shaver sockets Hairdryer Ice pack facility Baby facilities Disabled facilities Shop on site or within 200yds BBQ area Picnic area WiFi Internet access **SERVICES:** Electric hook-up Launderette Licensed bar Calor Gas Campingaz Toilet fluid Café/Restaurant Fast Food/Takeaway Battery charging Motorhome service point No credit or debit cards Dogs permitted No dogs

BROADWOODWIDGER Map 3 SX48

Places to visit

Lydford Gorge, LYDFORD, EX20 4BH, 01822 820320
www.nationaltrust.org.uk/lydford-gorge

Launceston Steam Railway, LAUNCESTON, PL15 8DA, 01566 775665
www.launcestonsr.co.uk

Roadford Lake
★★★ 82%

tel: 01409 211507 **Lower Goodacre PL16 0JL**
email: info@swlakestrust.co.uk web: www.southwestlakes.co.uk
dir: *Exit A30 between Okehampton and Launceston at Roadford Lake signs, cross dam wall, site 0.25 mile on right.*

Located right at the edge of Devon's largest inland water, this popular rural park is well screened by mature trees and shrubs. There is an excellent watersports school for sailing, windsurfing, rowing and kayaking, with hire and day launch facilities. This is an ideal location for brown trout fly fishing.

Open: 12 February to 31 October **Last arrival:** late arrivals by prior arrangement **Last departure:** 11.00

Pitches: 🚐 🚙 ⛺; 13 hardstanding pitches

Leisure:

Facilities:

Services:

Within 3 miles:

Additional site information: 3 acre site. Cars can be parked by caravans and tents. Awnings permitted. Off-ground BBQs only, no open fires. Climbing wall, archery, high ropes, watersports.

BUCKFASTLEIGH Map 3 SX76

Places to visit

Buckfast Abbey, BUCKFASTLEIGH, TQ11 0EE, 01364 645500
www.buckfast.org.uk

Great for kids: Dartmoor Otter Sanctuary and Buckfast Butterfly Farm, BUCKFASTLEIGH, TQ11 0DZ, 01364 642916
www.ottersandbutterflies.co.uk

Beara Farm Caravan & Camping Site
Quality Assessed

tel: 01364 642234 **Colston Road TQ11 0LW**
email: info@bearafarm.co.uk web: bearafarm.co.uk
dir: *From Exeter take Buckfastleigh exit at Dart Bridge, follow South Devon Steam Railway and Butterfly Farm signs. 200 metres after South Devon Steam Railway entrance take 1st left into Old Totnes Road, 0.5 mile, right at red brick cottages signed Beara Farm. Approximately 1 mile to site.*

A very good farm park, with clean unisex facilities, run by very keen and friendly owners. Close to the River Dart and the Dart Valley Steam Railway line and within easy reach of the sea and the moors, this site has a well-trimmed camping field that offers peace and quiet. Please note that the approach to the site is narrow, with passing places, and care needs to be taken.

Open: All year **Last arrival:** 21.00 **Last departure:** anytime

Pitches: 🚐 🚙 ⛺; 1 hardstanding pitch

Facilities:

Services:

Within 3 miles:

Additional site information: 3.63 acre site. Cars can be parked by caravans and tents. Awnings permitted. No noise after 22.30. Access to River Dart.

CLAYHIDON Map 4 ST11

Places to visit

Coldharbour Mill Working Wool Museum, UFFCULME, EX15 3EE, 01884 840960
www.coldharbourmill.org.uk

Kingsmead Centre Camping
★★★★ 83%

tel: 01823 421630 **EX15 3TR**
email: contact@kingsmeadcentre.com web: www.kingsmeadcentre.com
dir: *M5 junction 26 onto A38 signed Wellington, continue southbound. Turn left signed Ford Street, continue until crossroads at top of hill and turn left. Follow signs for Kingsmead Centre. From A303 at Eagle Cross junction follow signs for Wellington. Continue to T-junction, turn right (pass The Holman Clavel pub on left). After 3 miles, turn left signed Kingsmead Centre.*

Located in the middle of a forest, this well-maintained site offers two good, clean toilet blocks and caters for everyone, with a good mix of pitches for tents, caravans and motorhomes, plus the added attraction of a yurt, a Lotus Belle tent and a bell tent for hire. There are two fishing lakes on the site.

Open: All year (restricted service: end August to Easter – hardstandings and statics only) **Last arrival:** 21.00 **Last departure:** 11.00

Pitches: 🚐 🚙 ⛺ 🏕; 7 hardstanding pitches

Leisure:

Facilities:

Services:

Within 3 miles:

Additional site information: 7 acre site. Cars can be parked by caravans and tents. Awnings permitted. No amplified music; no noise after 21.00 (Monday to Friday) or after 22.00 (Saturday to Sunday). Firepits available for hire.

Glamping available: 1 Lotus Belle tent; 1 bell tent; 1 yurt. **Changeover days:** Any day

Additional glamping information: 2 nights minimum stay. Available between Easter and end of September. Cars can be parked by units

CLYST ST MARY Map 3 SX99

Places to visit

Exeter Cathedral, EXETER, EX1 1HS, 01392 255573
www.exeter-cathedral.org.uk

Exeter's Underground Passages, EXETER, EX1 1GA, 01392 665887
www.exeter.gov.uk/passages

Great for kids: The World of Country Life, EXMOUTH, EX8 5BY, 01395 274533
www.worldofcountrylife.co.uk

DEVON 113 ENGLAND

CLYST ST MARY   Map 3 SX99

Premier Park

Crealy Theme Park & Resort
★★★★★ 91%

tel: 01395 234888 Sidmouth Road EX5 1DR
email: fun@crealy.co.uk web: www.crealy.co.uk
dir: *M5 junction 30, A3052 signed Exmouth. At roundabout take A3052 signed Seaton. Follow brown Crealy Theme Park & Resort signs. Turn right.*

A quality park with excellent toilet facilities, spacious, fully serviced pitches and good security, situated adjacent to the popular Crealy Theme Park; free or discounted entry is available for all campers. Pre-erected luxury safari cabins are for hire, and also in the Camelot Village there are medieval-style pavilion tents for a real glamping holiday. In addition, there are 37 spacious lodges with hot tubs for all the family to enjoy. For children, there is a unique 'own pony' and 'character breakfast' experience, plus there's a multi-use games area and adventure golf. There is a clubhouse with bar and restaurant, located next to reception. Free WiFi is available and free kennel accommodation is offered on request. The park is within a short drive of Exeter and the seaside attractions at Sidmouth.

Open: All year **Last arrival:** 20.00 **Last departure:** 10.00
Pitches: 🚐 🚗 ⛺ 🏠; 29 hardstanding pitches
Leisure: 🎯 🎱 ⚽
Facilities: 🏪 📡 ❄ ♿ $ 🚻 WiFi 💻
Services: 🔌 🧺 🍽 🍴 🍞 🔒 🛢 T

Within 3 miles: ♿ 🎣 ◎
Additional site information: 14.65 acre site. 🅿 Cars can be parked by caravans and tents. Awnings permitted. Underfloor heating in bathrooms. Crealy Theme Park within walking distance.
Glamping available: Safari cabins, medieval pavillions.
Changeover days: Monday and Friday
Additional glamping information: Maximum occupancy 8 persons. Cars can be parked by units

COMBE MARTIN   Map 3 SS54

Places to visit
Arlington Court and the National Trust Carriage Museum, ARLINGTON, EX31 4LP, 01271 850296
www.nationaltrust.org.uk/arlington-court-and-the-national-trust-carriage-museum

Great for kids: Combe Martin Wildlife & Dinosaur Park, COMBE MARTIN, EX34 0NG, 01271 882486
cmwdp.co.uk

Premier Park

Newberry Valley Park
★★★★★ 91%

tel: 01271 882334 Woodlands EX34 0AT
email: relax@newberryvaleypark.co.uk web: www.newberryvalleypark.co.uk
dir: *M5 junction 27, A361 towards Barnstaple. Right at North Aller roundabout onto A399, through Combe Martin to sea. Left into site.*

A family owned and run touring park on the edge of Combe Martin, with all its amenities just a five-minute walk away. The park is set in a wooded valley with its own coarse fishing lake and has a stunning toilet block with underfloor heating and excellent unisex privacy cubicles. There is a wooden pod, named Lily, and a shepherd's hut, named Rose, located in a quite spot and available to hire. The safe beaches of Newberry and Combe Martin are reached by a short footpath opposite the park entrance, where the South West Coast Path passes.

Open: 17 March to 28 October (restricted service: low season – office hours limited)
Last arrival: variable (last arrival time is dusk in winter) **Last departure:** 11.00
Pitches: 🚐 🚗 ⛺; 🏠 see prices below; 40 hardstanding pitches; 18 seasonal pitches
Leisure: 🎯 🎣
Facilities: 🏪 ☉ 📡 ❄ ♿ $ 🚻 🚻 WiFi
Services: 🔌 🧺 🍽 🛢 T
Within 3 miles: ♿ ⛳ 🏊 ⛴

Additional site information: 20 acre site. 🅿 Cars can be parked by caravans and tents. Awnings permitted. No camp fires. Kitchen preparation area, fridge and microwave available; fresh bread and butchery delivery. Car hire can be arranged.
Glamping available: Wooden hut from £34; shepherd's hut from £44.
Changeover days: Any day
Additional glamping information: Cars can be parked by units

ENGLAND 114 DEVON

CROYDE — Map 3 SS43

Places to visit
Marwood Hill Gardens, BARNSTAPLE, EX31 4EA, 01271 342528
www.marwoodhillgarden.co.uk

Great for kids: Watermouth Castle & Family Theme Park, ILFRACOMBE, EX34 9SL, 01271 867474
www.watermouthcastle.com

Premier Park

Bay View Farm Caravan & Camping Park
★★★★★ 90%

tel: 01271 890501 **EX33 1PN**
email: info@bayviewfarm.co.uk **web:** www.bayviewfarm.co.uk
dir: *M5 junction 27, A361, through Barnstaple to Braunton, left onto B3231. Site at entrance to Croyde.*

A very busy and popular park close to surfing beaches and rock pools, with a public footpath leading directly to the sea. Set in a stunning location with views out over the Atlantic to Lundy Island, it is just a short stroll from Croyde. The two elite pods and the shepherd's huts at the top of the park make the most of the sea views. The facilities are clean and well maintained; a family bathroom is available. There is a fish and chip shop on site. Please note that dogs are not permitted.

Open: March to October **Last arrival:** 21.30 **Last departure:** 11.00
Pitches: 🚐 🚙 ⛺ 🏠; 40 hardstanding pitches; 15 seasonal pitches
Leisure: 🛝
Facilities: 🏠 ☉ 🚿 ❄ ♿ 💈 📶
Services: 🔌 🗑 🚰 🔒 🚮 📞
Within 3 miles: 🚴 🚶 ⛳ 🎣

Additional site information: 10 acre site. 🚫 Cars can be parked by caravans and tents. Awnings permitted. No noise after midnight. Fresh produce available in high season.

Glamping available: Wooden pods.
Additional glamping information: Cars can be parked by units

CULLOMPTON

See Kentisbeare

DARTMOUTH — Map 3 SX85

Places to visit
Dartmouth Castle, DARTMOUTH, TQ6 0JN, 01803 834445
www.english-heritage.org.uk/visit/places/dartmouth-castle

DARTMOUTH — Map 3 SX85

Premier Park

Woodlands Grove Caravan & Camping Park
★★★★★ 93%

tel: 01803 712598 **Blackawton TQ9 7DQ**
email: holiday@woodlandsgrove.com **web:** www.woodlandsgrove.com
dir: *From Dartmouth take A3122, 4 miles. Or from A38 take A385 to Totnes. Then A381 towards Salcombe, after Halwell take A3122 towards Dartmouth, site signed (brown tourist signs).*

A quality caravan and tent park with smart toilet facilities (including excellent family rooms), spacious pitches, including decent hardstandings and good attention to detail throughout, all set in an extensive woodland environment with a terraced grass camping area. Free entry to the adjoining Woodlands Theme Park makes an excellent package holiday for families, but also good for adults travelling without children who are perhaps seeking a low season break. Please check with the site with reference to their minimum stay policy. There is a bus stop at the entrance.

Open: End of March to 31 October **Last arrival:** 21.30 **Last departure:** 11.00
Pitches: 🚐 🚙 ⛺; 129 hardstanding pitches
Leisure: 🛝 🎱 🎮 🎵 🏓 **Facilities:** 🏠 ☉ 🚿 ❄ ♿ 💈 🍴 📶
Services: 🔌 🗑 🍽 🚰 🧺 ↕ 🔒 🚮 📞
Within 3 miles: 🚴 ⛳

Additional site information: 16 acre site. 🐕 Cars can be parked by caravans and tents. Awnings permitted. No open fires, fire pits or chimeneas, quiet 22.30–08.00. Falconry centre, woodland walk, mini-golf, zoo-farm, dog kennels, free entry into Woodlands Family Theme Park.

DEVON — ENGLAND

DAWLISH
Map 3 SX97

Places to visit
Powderham Castle, POWDERHAM, EX6 8JQ, 01626 890243
www.powderham.co.uk

Platinum Park

Cofton Holidays
★★★★★

tel: 01626 890111 & 0800 085 8649 Starcross EX6 8RP
email: info@coftonholidays.co.uk web: www.coftonholidays.co.uk
dir: *On A379 (Exeter to Dawlish road), 3 miles from Dawlish.*

An attractive, family-orientated holiday park set in 80 acres of landscaped grounds in a beautiful rural location close to Dawlish. Most of the spacious hardstanding touring or grass camping pitches overlook either the swimming pool complex or the coarse fishing lakes and woodlands. Excellent purpose-built toilet blocks offer smart modern facilities, and the on-site pub serves drinks, meals and snacks for all the family, and a mini market caters for most shopping needs. In addition to outside and indoor pools, there's a beauty room, several children's play areas, a high ropes course, and scenic walking and cycling trails. There are fully serviced pitches and the 12 lodges, all with hot tubs, located high above the park.

Open: All year Last arrival: 20.00 Last departure: 11.00
Pitches: 60 hardstanding pitches; 110 seasonal pitches

Leisure:
Facilities:
Services:
Within 3 miles:

Additional site information: 80 acre site. Cars can be parked by caravans and tents. Awnings permitted. Soft play area, sauna and steam room, bowlingo.

Premier Park

Lady's Mile Holiday Park
★★★★★ 89% HOLIDAY PARK

tel: 01626 863411 EX7 0LX
email: info@ladysmile.co.uk web: www.ladysmile.co.uk
dir: *1 mile north of Dawlish on A379.*

A family owned and run touring park with a wide variety of pitches, including some that are fully serviced. There are plenty of activities for everyone, including two swimming pools with waterslides, a children's splash pool, a well-equipped gym, a sauna in the main season, a large adventure playground, extensive restaurant facilities, and a bar with entertainment in high season. Facilities are kept very clean, and the surrounding beaches are easily accessed. Holiday homes and high quality safari tents are also available.

Open: All year Last arrival: 20.00 Last departure: 11.00
Pitches: ; 100 hardstanding pitches; 200 seasonal pitches
Leisure:
Facilities:
Services:
Within 3 miles:

Additional site information: 60 acre site. Cars can be parked by caravans and tents. Awnings permitted. No noise after 23.00. Bowling alley.

Glamping available: Safari tents. **Changeover days:** Friday, Saturday, Monday

Additional glamping information: Safari tents have a king-size four-poster bed and hot tub. Cars can be parked by units.

FACILITIES: Electric vehicle charging · Baths/Shower · Electric shaver sockets · Hairdryer · Ice pack facility · Baby facilities · Disabled facilities · Shop on site or within 200yds · BBQ area · Picnic area · WiFi · Internet access **SERVICES:** Electric hook-up · Launderette · Licensed bar · Calor Gas · Campingaz · Toilet fluid · Café/Restaurant · Fast Food/Takeaway · Battery charging · Motorhome service point · No credit or debit cards · Dogs permitted · No dogs

ENGLAND 116 DEVON

DREWSTEIGNTON   Map 3 SX79

Places to visit

Castle Drogo, DREWSTEIGNTON, EX6 6PB, 01647 433306
www.nationaltrust.org.uk/castle-drogo

Finch Foundry, STICKLEPATH, EX20 2NW, 01837 840046
www.nationaltrust.org.uk/finch-foundry

Platinum Park

Woodland Springs Adult Touring Park
★★★★★

tel: 01647 231648 **Venton EX6 6PG**
email: enquiries@woodlandsprings.co.uk **web:** woodlandsprings.co.uk
dir: Exit A30 at Whiddon Down junction onto A382 towards Moretonhampstead. Site 1.5 miles on left.

Woodland Springs is an attractive and very well managed adults-only touring park in a rural area within Dartmoor National Park. This site, surrounded by woodland and farmland and featuring a wildflower meadow, is very peaceful. Guests can expect high levels of customer care. There is an impressive reception/shop building, spacious hardstanding pitches for larger units, an excellent motorhome service point and a dog shower. The toilet block offers superb facilities, including four fully serviced cubicles, some suitable for disabled visitors. There are two glamping pods for hire.

Open: All year **Last arrival:** 20.00 **Last departure:** 11.00
Pitches: see prices below; 50 hardstanding pitches; 20 seasonal pitches
Facilities:
Services:
Within 3 miles:

Additional site information: 6 acre site. Adults only. Cars can be parked by caravans and tents. Awnings permitted. No fires, no noise 23.00–08.00. Day kennels, freezer, coffee vending machine.

Glamping available: Wooden pods from £45.

Additional glamping information: Maximum 2 adults. No cooking inside pod. Cars can be parked by units

EAST WORLINGTON   Map 3 SS71

Places to visit

Knightshayes, KNIGHTSHAYES, EX16 7RQ, 01884 254665
www.nationaltrust.org.uk/knightshayes

Yeatheridge Farm Caravan Park
★★★★ 92%

tel: 01884 860330 **EX17 4TN**
email: info@yeatheridge.co.uk **web:** www.yeatheridge.co.uk
dir: M5 junction 27, A361, at 1st roundabout at Tiverton take B3137 for 9 miles towards Witheridge. Fork left 1 mile after Nomansland onto B3042. Site on left in 3.5 miles. (Note: do not enter East Worlington).

The scenic approach down the long farm drive and the arrival at the attractive reception building, which combines with the bar/restaurant, toilets and swimming pool, sets the scene for a relaxing holiday in the glorious mid-Devon countryside. The park offers superb on-site facilities, including a large children's play area, immaculate and well maintained toilets, plus there is an indoor swimming pool, sauna and a good information and games room. Guests can expect a friendly atmosphere and high levels of customer care from the hands-on owners. Two fishing lakes are also available.

Open: 15 March to 1st weekend in October **Last arrival:** 22.00 **Last departure:** 10.00
Pitches: ; 11 hardstanding pitches
Leisure:
Facilities:
Services:
Within 3 miles:

Additional site information: 12 acre site. Cars can be parked by caravans and tents. Awnings permitted. Quiet after 22.30.

Make your next UK holiday one to remember

Choose RatedTrips.com

AA

PITCHES: Caravans Motorhomes Tents Glamping accommodation LEISURE: Indoor swimming pool Outdoor swimming pool Children's playground Kids' club Tennis court Games room Separate TV room golf course Pitch n putt Boats for hire Bikes for hire Cinema Entertainment Fishing Mini golf Watersports Gym Sports field Stables Spa

DEVON 117 ENGLAND

HOLSWORTHY
Map 3 SS30

Places to visit

Dartington Crystal, GREAT TORRINGTON, EX38 7AN, 01805 626242
www.visitdartington.co.uk

RHS Garden Rosemoor, GREAT TORRINGTON, EX38 8PH, 01805 624067
www.rhs.org.uk/rosemoor

Great for kids: The Milky Way Adventure Park, CLOVELLY, EX39 5RY, 01237 431255
www.themilkyway.co.uk

Headon Farm Caravan Site & Storage
★★★ 93%

tel: 01409 254477 **Headon Farm, Hollacombe EX22 6NN**
email: reader@headonfarm.co.uk **web:** www.headonfarm.co.uk
dir: *From Holsworthy A388 signed Launceston. 0.5 mile, at hill brow left into Staddon Road. 1 mile (follow site signs) turn right signed Ashwater. 0.5 mile, left at hill brow. Site in 25 yards.*

Set on a working farm in a quiet rural location. All pitches have extensive views of the Devon countryside, yet the park is only two and a half miles from the market town of Holsworthy, and within easy reach of roads to the coast and beaches of north Cornwall.

Open: All year **Last arrival:** 19.00 **Last departure:** noon
Pitches: 🚐 🚙 ⛺; 11 hardstanding pitches
Leisure: ⚽
Facilities: 🏠 ☉ ✳ 🍴 🎪 WiFi 💻
Services: 🔌 🧺
Within 3 miles: ⚓ ✎ ∪ ≋ 🛒

Additional site information: 2 acre site. 🚗 Cars can be parked by caravans and tents. Awnings permitted. Breathable groundsheets only. Caravan and motorhome storage (outside or undercover). Car hire can be arranged.

Noteworthy Farm Caravan and Campsite
★★★ 83%

tel: 01409 253731 & 07811 000071 **Bude Road EX22 7JB**
email: enquiries@noteworthy-devon.co.uk **web:** www.noteworthy-devon.co.uk
dir: *On A3072 between Holsworthy and Bude. 3 miles from Holsworthy on right.*

This campsite is owned by a friendly young couple with their own children. There are good views from the quiet rural location, and simple toilet facilities. There is now a café on site serving breakfasts and lunches. The local bus stops outside the gate on request.

Open: All year **Last departure:** 11.00
Pitches: 🚐 🚙 ⛺; 3 hardstanding pitches
Leisure: ✎
Facilities: 🏠 ☉ ✳
Services: 🔌 🛒
Within 3 miles: ⚓ ∪ ≋ 🛒

Additional site information: 5 acre site. 🚗 🐕 Cars can be parked by caravans and tents. Awnings permitted. No open fires, no noise after 22.30. Dog grooming available.

ILFRACOMBE
Map 3 SS54

Places to visit

Arlington Court and the National Trust Carriage Museum, ARLINGTON, EX31 4LP, 01271 850296
www.nationaltrust.org.uk/arlington-court-and-the-national-trust-carriage-museum

Exmoor Zoo, BLACKMOOR GATE, EX31 4SG, 01598 763352
www.exmoorzoo.co.uk

Great for kids: Watermouth Castle & Family Theme Park, ILFRACOMBE, EX34 9SL, 01271 867474
www.watermouthcastle.com

Sunnymead Farm Camping & Touring Site
★★★★ 85%

tel: 01271 879845 & 07826 184874 **Sunnymead Farm, Mortehoe Road EX34 8NZ**
email: info@sunnymead-farm.co.uk **web:** www.sunnymead-farm.co.uk
dir: *From the A361 at Mullacott Cross roundabout, take B3343 signed Woolacombe. Site approximately 1 mile on right, just after Veterinary Hospital; opposite High Ways House (guest house).*

Peace and tranquillity abound at Sunnymead Farm Camping & Touring Site that's set in the beautiful north Devon countryside close to breathtaking coastal walks and within easy reach of Ilfracombe and Woolacombe. 30 grass pitches are set around a well mown and tended paddock, most have electric hook-up and some enjoy superb sea views. Expect spotlessly clean toilet facilities and a traditional camping atmosphere.

Open: Easter to October (restricted service: low season – reduced hours at reception/shop) **Last arrival:** 18.30 (Later contactless check-in available if pre arranged)
Last departure: 11.00 (Camping) 10.00 (Statics)
Pitches: * 🚐 from £25; 🚙 from £25; ⛺ from £25; 6 hardstanding pitches; 12 seasonal pitches
Leisure: 🏕
Facilities: 🏠 ☉ ✳ ♿ 🛒 WiFi
Services: 🔌 🧺 🚽
Within 3 miles: ⚓ ✎ ∪ ◎ ≋ ⚲ 🛒 🛍

Additional site information: 3 acre site. 🚗 Cars can be parked by caravans and tents. Awnings permitted. Kids' play area. Wetsuit washing area. bus stop at entrance, direct access to lovely countryside walks

---

FACILITIES: ⚡ Electric vehicle charging 🛁 Baths/Shower ☉ Electric shaver sockets ✎ Hairdryer ✳ Ice pack facility 🍴 Baby facilities ♿ Disabled facilities 🛒 Shop on site or within 200yds 🎪 BBQ area 🍽 Picnic area WiFi WiFi 💻 Internet access **SERVICES:** 🔌 Electric hook-up 🧺 Launderette 🍷 Licensed bar 🔥 Calor Gas ⛽ Campingaz 🚽 Toilet fluid ☕ Café/Restaurant 🍔 Fast Food/Takeaway 🔋 Battery charging 🚐 Motorhome service point 💳 No credit or debit cards 🐕 Dogs permitted 🚫🐕 No dogs

KENNFORD
Map 3 SX98

Places to visit
Canonteign Falls, CHUDLEIGH, EX6 7RH, 01647 252434
www.canonteignfalls.co.uk

Custom House Visitor Centre, EXETER, EX2 4AN, 01392 271611
exeter.gov.uk/leisure-and-culture/our-attractions/custom-house-visitor-centre

Great for kids: Crealy Theme Park & Resort, CLYST ST MARY, EX5 1DR, 01395 233200
www.crealy.co.uk

Premier Park

Kennford International Holiday Park
★★★★★ 88%

tel: 01392 833046 **EX6 7YN**
email: ian@kennfordinternational.com web: www.kennfordinternational.co.uk
dir: *At end of M5 take A38, site signed at Kennford slip road.*

Screened from the A38 by trees and shrubs, this park offers pitches divided by hedging for privacy. A high quality toilet block complements the park's facilities. A good, centrally-located base for exploring the coast and touring the countryside of Devon, and Exeter is easily accessible via buses that stop nearby.

Open: All year **Last arrival:** 21.00 (winter – check with site for arrival times) **Last departure:** 11.00

Pitches: 🚐 🚙 ⛺ ; 9 hardstanding pitches

Leisure: 🛝

Facilities: 🚻 ☉ ♿ WiFi

Services: 🔌 🗑 🧺 ⬇ T

Within 3 miles: ⚓ 🎾 🏇 ⛳ 🎬 🛍

Additional site information: 15 acre site. 🚗 Cars can be parked by caravans and tents. Awnings permitted.

KENTISBEARE
Map 3 ST00

Places to visit
Killerton, KILLERTON, EX5 3LE, 01392 881345
www.nationaltrust.org.uk/killerton

Custom House Visitor Centre, EXETER, EX2 4AN, 01392 271611
exeter.gov.uk/leisure-and-culture/our-attractions/custom-house-visitor-centre

Great for kids: Diggerland, CULLOMPTON, EX15 2PE, 01634 711711
www.diggerland.com

Forest Glade Holiday Park
★★★★ 89%

tel: 01404 841381 **Near Kentisbeare EX15 2DT**
email: enquiries@forest-glade.co.uk web: www.forest-glade.co.uk
dir: *Tent traffic: from A373 turn left past Keepers Cottage Inn (2.5 miles east of M5 junction 28). (Note: due to narrow roads, touring caravans and larger motorhomes must approach from Honiton direction. Phone site for access details).*

A quiet, attractive park in a forest clearing with well-kept gardens and beech hedge screening. One of the main attractions is the site's immediate proximity to the forest which offers magnificent hillside walks with surprising views over the valleys. There's an undercover heated swimming pool, a good children's play area and large games room; camping pods are available for hire. Please note, that because the roads are narrow around the site, it is best to phone the site for suitable route details.

Open: mid March to mid November **Last arrival:** 21.00 **Last departure:** noon

Pitches: 🚐 🚙 ⛺ 🏠 ; 40 hardstanding pitches; 28 seasonal pitches

Leisure: 🏊 🛝 🎾 ⚽

Facilities: 🚻 ☉ 🍳 ❄ ♿ 💷 🍴 🛒 WiFi

Services: 🔌 🗑 🧺 🧴 ⬇ 🔒 ♻ T

Within 3 miles: 🎾 🏇

Additional site information: 26 acre site. 🚗 Cars can be parked by caravans and tents. Awnings permitted. Families and couples only. Adventure and soft play areas, paddling pool, ball games area, badminton lawn, forest walks.

Glamping available: Wooden pods. **Changeover days:** Any day

Additional glamping information: Wooden pods: no dogs permitted. Cars can be parked by units

KINGSBRIDGE
Map 3 SX74

Places to visit
Kingsbridge Cookworthy Museum, KINGSBRIDGE, TQ7 1AW, 01548 853235
www.kingsbridgemuseum.org.uk

Overbeck's Garden, SALCOMBE, TQ8 8LW, 01548 842893
www.nationaltrust.org.uk/overbecks-garden

KINGSBRIDGE

Map 3 SX74

Platinum Park

Parkland Caravan and Camping Site
★★★★★

tel: 01548 852723 & 07968 222008 **Sorley Green Cross TQ7 4AF**
email: enquiries@parklandsite.co.uk web: www.parklandsite.co.uk
dir: A38 South, then A384 to Totnes, A381 towards Kingsbridge. 12 miles, at Stumpy Post Cross roundabout turn right, 1 mile. Site 200 yards on left after Sorley Green Cross. Please use these directions if you are towing.

Parkland Caravan and Camping Site

Open: All year **Last arrival:** 19.00 (later arrivals by prior arrangement) **Last departure:** 11.30

Pitches: * from £35; from £35; from £35; see prices below; 30 hardstanding pitches; 25 seasonal pitches

Leisure:

Facilities:

Services:

Within 3 miles:

Additional site information: 3 acre site. Adults only. Cars can be parked by caravans and tents. Awnings permitted. No camp fires/disposable BBQ's. No noise from 22.00 to 09.00. Barrier access. Campers' kitchen with fridge/freezer, microwave, hot plate, mini oven, kettle, toaster. Guest lounge with sofas, dining area, large screen TV. Complimentary tea and coffee, lending library. Short term caravan storage facility. Car hire can be arranged.

Glamping available: Shepherd's hut from £75; small cabin from £75; Glamping pods from £65 - all accommodation maximum two guests **Changeover days:** Any day

Additional glamping information: Adults only, all linen provided, TV, microwave, kettle, toaster, utensils/crockery, patio. Most options with private washrooms. Minimum 2 night stay. No pets. Cars can be parked by units

See advert below

Expect a high level of customer care at this adults-only, family-run park set in the glorious South Hams countryside; it has panoramic views over Salcombe and the rolling countryside towards Dartmoor. The immaculately maintained grounds offer generous grass pitches and hardstanding super pitches, along with a larger, deluxe option with private facilities. There's a well-appointed shepherd's hut, with stunning views across Salcombe estuary, and smart, en suite glamping pods and a cosy cabin for hire. The on-site licensed shop sells local seasonal produce, everyday provisions and camping supplies. The facilities feature quality, individual washrooms with large showers and baths, along with a fully-fitted disabled suite. You can also relax in a cosy guest lounge which includes a dining area and workstation. A bus stop at the site entrance offers easy access to the local towns of Kingsbridge, Salcombe, Totnes and Dartmouth.

PARKLAND
especially for grown ups

Five Star Touring, Camping and Glamping in the heart of the South Hams

Open All Year
Adults Only
Private Facilities
Onsite Shop
Guest Lounge
Seasonal Pitches
Bus Stop

Kingsbridge, Nr Salcombe, South Devon TQ7 4AF
01548 852723 • 07968 222008 • www.parklandsite.co.uk • enquiries@parklandsite.co.uk

---

FACILITIES: Electric vehicle charging Baths/Shower Electric shaver sockets Hairdryer Ice pack facility Baby facilities Disabled facilities Shop on site or within 200yds BBQ area Picnic area WiFi Internet access **SERVICES:** Electric hook-up Launderette Licensed bar Calor Gas Campingaz Toilet fluid Café/Restaurant Fast Food/Takeaway Battery charging Motorhome service point No credit or debit cards Dogs permitted No dogs

ENGLAND 120 DEVON

KINGSBRIDGE *continued*

Premier Park

Island Lodge Caravan & Camping Site
★★★★★ 88%

tel: 01548 852956 & 07968 222007 **Stumpy Post Cross TQ7 4BL**
email: enquiries@islandlodgesite.co.uk
web: www.islandlodgesite.co.uk
dir: *Take A381 from Totnes towards Kingsbridge. In 12 miles, at roundabout (Stumpy Post Cross) right, 300 metres left into lane, site signed. 200 metres on left.*

Island Lodge is a small, peaceful and well established park, with extensive views over the South Hams. The site has a security barrier, low level lighting around the park, good hardstanding pitches and a motorhome service point. The immaculate toilet facilities are of good quality. A scenic 40-minute walk will take you into Kingsbridge, and there are several dog-friendly beaches nearby, as well as a newly created dog walking area within easy access of the park.

Open: All year (restricted service: November to March) **Last arrival:** 19.00 **Last departure:** 11.30
Pitches: * from £35; from £35; from £35; 4 hardstanding pitches; 24 seasonal pitches
Leisure: **Facilities:** **Services:** Within 3 miles:
Additional site information: 2 acre site. Cars can be parked by caravans and tents. Awnings permitted. No generators. No disposable barbecues. Play area open 09.00–21.00. Electronic security barrier closed overnight. Only 2 dogs per pitch. Restrictions on certain dog breeds. 24-hour CCTV, fridge/freezer, secure caravan and boat storage park. Dog shower/dog exercise area. Local brewery with off licence 200 yards from site. Car hire can be arranged.

LYNTON Map 3 SS74

Places to visit
Arlington Court and the National Trust Carriage Museum, ARLINGTON, EX31 4LP, 01271 850296
www.nationaltrust.org.uk/arlington-court

Great for kids: Exmoor Zoo, BLACKMOOR GATE, EX31 4SG, 01598 763352
www.exmoorzoo.co.uk

Lynmouth Holiday Retreat
★★★★ 90%

tel: 01598 753349 **Manor Farm EX35 6LD**
email: Lynmouth@coastandcountryparks.co.uk
web: coastandcountryparks.co.uk/lynmouth-holiday-retreat
dir: *On A39 from Barbrook towards Hillsford Bridge. Approximately 0.5 mile to site on left.*

On top of the cliffs overlooking the Bristol Channel, Lynmouth Holiday Retreat is a peaceful, well-maintained park in the Exmoor National Park, close to both Lynton and Lynmouth. In addition to the stunning views and good reception shop, there are a wide selection of super serviced, serviced and electric pitches, both grass and hardstanding, as well as glamping pods, geodomes, safari tents, static caravans, and luxury lodges with hot tubs. There is also a modern amenities block, with both private and family bathrooms and a dishwasher, plus a dog shower and dog exercise area. Pitches can be selected from either those in a hidden hedged area or those with panoramic views over the coast. Local walks accessible from the Retreat include Lynton, Lynmouth, Watersmeet, Valley of the Rocks and the South West Coast Path.

Open: March to November **Last arrival:** 19.00 **Last departure:** noon
Pitches: * from £26; from £18; from £18 ; 15 hardstanding pitches
Facilities: **Services:** Within 3 miles:
Additional site information: 5 acre site. Cars can be parked by caravans and tents. Awnings permitted. Groups by prior arrangement only. Parent and baby room. Access to local walks from the Retreat.
Glamping available: Wooden pods, geodomes and safari tents.
Additional glamping information: Pet friendly units. Cars can be parked by units. No gazebos or open fires. Early arrival and late departure can be arranged subject to availability. Dog shower and excercise area. Maximum 2 dogs per pitch. Private bathrooms available to hire. 24 hour CCTV. Reception shop selling gifts, essentials and baked goods.

MODBURY
Map 3 SX65

Places to visit

Kingsbridge Cookworthy Museum, KINGSBRIDGE, TQ7 1AW, 01548 853235
www.kingsbridgemuseum.org.uk

Overbeck's Garden, SALCOMBE, TQ8 8LW, 01548 842893
www.nationaltrust.org.uk/overbecks-garden

Moor View Touring Park
★★★★ 85%

tel: 01548 821485 **California Cross PL21 0SG**
email: sharon@mcfarlandhomes.co.uk **web:** moorviewtouringpark.co.uk

Moor View Touring Park is an adults-only family run park tucked away in rural Devon countryside close to the glorious South Hams coast. The first impressions are of peace and quiet with just the sound of birds, and the excellent choice of pitches includes very large, fully serviced hardstanding pitches; all enjoy far-reaching moorland views. The park is dog friendly, offering the personal touch with no extra charges for dogs, and an extensive, fenced and secure dog walking field. The toilet/shower facilities are clean, modern and well maintained. Guests can use the comfortable lounge area and there's free WiFi across the park. A shop, garage, and a pub serving good meals are nearby.

Open: All year **Last arrival:** 18.00 **Last departure:** 10.00

Additional site information: Adults only.

Pennymoor Camping & Caravan Park
★★★ 90%

tel: 01548 830542 **Modbury, Nr Salcombe PL21 0SB**
email: enquiries@pennymoor-camping.co.uk **web:** www.pennymoor-camping.co.uk
dir: From A38 at Wrangaton Cross take A3121 signed Ermington. At 1st roundabout take 3rd exit signed South Brent (A3121). After Ugborough and Ermington at roundabout take 1st exit onto A379 signed Kingsbridge and Modbury. Left at Harraton Cross. Site signed here. Site on left. Other routes are not recommended.

Owned and run by the same family since 1935, this well-established, rural and lovingly tended park is tucked away in the South Hams; it is close to glorious beaches and has good views over rolling countryside to Dartmoor in the distance. On part level, part gently sloping grass, Pennymoor is an ideal base for exploring south Devon and offers everything for a relaxing and peaceful family stay, with spotless, well-maintained toilets, a fully-equipped children's play area, a well-stocked shop and popular café, laundrette, dedicated dog-walking areas; site-wide WiFi and a relaxing atmosphere.

Open: 15 March to 15 November (camping/touring caravans). 15 March to 15 January (holiday caravan rental) (restricted service: 15 March to mid May — only one toilet and shower block open) **Last arrival:** 20.00 (later arrival times by prior arrangement) **Last departure:** 11.00 (touring); 10.00 (holiday caravans)

Pitches: 🚐 🚗 ⛺; 7 hardstanding pitches; 14 seasonal pitches

Leisure: 🎯

Facilities: 🏠 ⊙ ☂ ✻ ♿ 🅂 🐕 WiFi

Services: 🔌 🗑 🍽 🏨 🛁 ⛽ 🌿 T

Within 3 miles: ↓

Additional site information: 12.5 acre site. 🚗 Cars can be parked by caravans and tents. Awnings permitted. No skateboards or scooters, Children's park to be cleared by 22.00, no noise after 23.00. Defibrilator onsite; Table tennis; Flo Gas; Holiday caravans for hire and for sale

MORTEHOE
Map 3 SS44

Places to visit

Marwood Hill Gardens, BARNSTAPLE, EX31 4EA, 01271 342528
www.marwoodhillgarden.co.uk

Great for kids: Watermouth Castle & Family Theme Park, ILFRACOMBE, EX34 9SL, 01271 867474
www.watermouthcastle.com

North Morte Farm Caravan & Camping Park
★★★★ 92%

tel: 01271 870381 **North Morte Road EX34 7EG**
email: info@northmortefarm.co.uk **web:** www.northmortefarm.co.uk
dir: From B3343 into Mortehoe, right at post office. Site 500 yards on left.

Set in spectacular coastal countryside close to National Trust land and 500 yards from the South west Coast Path. This attractive park is very well run and maintained by friendly family owners, and the quaint village of Mortehoe with its cafés, shops and pubs, is just a five-minute walk away.

Open: 27 March to 31 October **Last arrival:** 21.00 **Last departure:** noon

Pitches: 🚐 🚗 ⛺; 25 hardstanding pitches; 13 seasonal pitches

Leisure: 🎯

Facilities: 🏠 ⊙ ☂ ✻ ♿ 🅂 🐕 WiFi

Services: 🔌 🗑 🏨 🛁 ⛽ 🌿 T

Within 3 miles: ↓ 🎣 ⛳ ◎ 日

Additional site information: 22 acre site. 🚗 Cars can be parked by caravans and tents. Awnings permitted. No large groups.

ENGLAND 122 DEVON

PAIGNTON
Map 3 SX86

Places to visit
Dartmouth Steam Railway & River Boat Company, PAIGNTON, TQ4 6AF, 01803 555872
www.dartmouthrailriver.co.uk

Kents Cavern, TORQUAY, TQ1 2JF, 01803 215136
www.kents-cavern.co.uk

Great for kids: Paignton Zoo, PAIGNTON, TQ4 7EU, 01803 697500
www.paigntonzoo.org.uk

Premier Park

Beverley Park Caravan & Camping Park
★★★★★ 90%

tel: 01803 843887 **Goodrington Road TQ4 7JE**
email: info@beverley-holidays.co.uk **web:** www.beverley-holidays.co.uk
dir: *On A380, A3022, 2 miles south of Paignton left into Goodrington Road. Beverley Park on right.*

A high quality family-run park with extensive views of the bay and plenty of on-site amenities. The park boasts indoor and outdoor heated swimming pools, plus good bars and restaurants. The toilet facilities are modern and very clean and include excellent fully serviced family rooms. The park complex is attractively laid out with the touring areas divided into nicely screened sections.

Open: All year **Last arrival:** 21.00 **Last departure:** 10.00
Pitches: ; 49 hardstanding pitches
Leisure:
Facilities:
Services:
Within 3 miles:

Additional site information: 12 acre site. Cars can be parked by caravans and tents. Awnings permitted. Hot tub, sauna, steam room, gym, play area, soft play, crazy golf.

Whitehill Country Park
★★★★ 91%

tel: 01803 782338 **Stoke Road TQ4 7PF**
email: info@whitehill-park.co.uk **web:** www.whitehill-park.co.uk
dir: *A385 through Totnes towards Paignton. Turn right by Parkers Arms into Stoke Road towards Stoke Gabriel. Site on left in approximately 1.5 miles.*

A family-owned and run park set in rolling countryside, with many scenic beaches just a short drive away. This extensive country park covers 40 acres with woodland walks and nature trails, and has an excellent outdoor swimming pool with splash pad and poolside spa, an indoor swimming pool complex, a café, a bar and restaurant plus summer entertainment. There is also a fully equipped gym with an impressive array of equipment. The park offers ideal facilities, including luxury caravans, lodges and camping pods (dog-friendly accommodation is available) for a memorable holiday.

Open: Late March to end of October **Last arrival:** 21.00 **Last departure:** 10.00
Pitches: ; 30 hardstanding pitches; 40 seasonal pitches
Leisure:
Facilities:
Services:
Within 3 miles:

Additional site information: 40 acre site. Cars can be parked by caravans and tents. Awnings permitted. Letter box trail, craft room, table tennis, soft play area, woodland walking trails, poolside spa and splash pad. Picnic area. Freshly baked bread available.

Glamping available: 6 wooden pods. **Changeover days:** Any day

Additional glamping information: Wooden pods offer fold-out beds, heating, lighting, plug socket and outdoor furniture.

PITCHES: Caravans Motorhomes Tents Glamping accommodation **LEISURE:** Indoor swimming pool Outdoor swimming pool Children's playground Kids' club Tennis court Games room Separate TV room golf course Pitch n putt Boats for hire Bikes for hire Cinema Entertainment Fishing Mini golf Watersports Gym Sports field Stables Spa

PLYMOUTH
Map 3 SX45

Places to visit
Saltram, PLYMPTON, PL7 1UH, 01752 333500
www.nationaltrust.org.uk/saltram

Riverside Caravan Park
★★★★ 87%

tel: 01752 344122 Leigham Manor Drive PL6 8LL
email: office@riversidecaravanpark.com web: www.riversidecaravanpark.com
dir: *From A38 at Marsh Mills roundabout, follow signs for Plympton (B3416) and brown 'Riverside' signs. At lights left into Riverside Road signed 'Riverside'. 400 metres, right into Leigham Manor Drive (River Plym on right) to site on right.*

A well-groomed site on the outskirts of Plymouth on the banks of the River Plym, in a surprisingly peaceful location surrounded by woodland. The toilet facilities are appointed to a very good standard, and include private cubicles, plus there's a good games room, a heated outdoor swimming pool, and bar/restaurant serving food. This park is an ideal stopover for the ferries to France and Spain, and makes an excellent base for touring Dartmoor and the coast. The local bus stop is just a 10-minute walk from the site.

Open: All year (restricted service: October to Easter – bar, restaurant, takeaway and pool closed) **Last arrival:** 22.00 **Last departure:** 11.00

Pitches: ; 63 hardstanding pitches

Leisure:

Facilities:

Services:

Within 3 miles:

Additional site information: 11 acre site. Cars can be parked by caravans and tents. Awnings permitted.

SALCOMBE
Map 3 SX73

Places to visit
Overbeck's Garden, SALCOMBE, TQ8 8LW, 01548 842893
www.nationaltrust.org.uk/overbecks-garden

Kingsbridge Cookworthy Museum, KINGSBRIDGE, TQ7 1AW, 01548 853235
www.kingsbridgemuseum.org.uk

Karrageen Caravan & Camping Park
★★★★ 86%

tel: 01548 561230 Bolberry, Malborough TQ7 3EN
email: phil@karrageen.co.uk web: www.karrageen.co.uk
dir: *At Malborough on A381, sharp right through village, in 0.6 mile right again, 0.9 mile, site on right.*

A small friendly, family-run park with secluded hidden dells for tents and terraced grass pitches giving extensive sea and country views. There is a well-stocked shop and an excellent toilet block that has two cubicled units – one suitable for families and for less able visitors. This park is just one mile from the beach and the pretty hamlet of Hope Cove and is a really peaceful site from which to explore the South Hams coast.

Open: 26 March to 19 September **Last arrival:** 21.00 **Last departure:** 11.30

Pitches:

Facilities:

Services:

Within 3 miles:

Additional site information: 7.5 acre site. Cars can be parked by caravans and tents. Awnings permitted. Noise to be kept to a minimum after 22.00. Freshly baked bread and croissants available. BACS payments accepted.

Make your next UK holiday one to remember

Choose RatedTrips.com

AA

FACILITIES: Electric vehicle charging · Baths/Shower · Electric shaver sockets · Hairdryer · Ice pack facility · Baby facilities · Disabled facilities · Shop on site or within 200yds · BBQ area · Picnic area · WiFi · Internet access **SERVICES:** Electric hook-up · Launderette · Licensed bar · Calor Gas · Campingaz · Toilet fluid · Café/Restaurant · Fast Food/Takeaway · Battery charging · Motorhome service point · No credit or debit cards · Dogs permitted · No dogs

SALCOMBE continued

Higher Rew Caravan & Camping Park
★★★★ 84%

tel: 01548 842681 Higher Rew, Malborough TQ7 3BW
email: enquiries@higherrew.co.uk web: www.higherrew.co.uk
dir: A381 to Malborough. Right at Townsend Cross, follow signs to Soar. 1 mile, left at Rew Cross, 0.5 mile, site on right.

A long-established park in a remote location within sight of the sea. The spacious, open touring field has some tiered pitches in the sloping grass, and there are lovely countryside or sea views from every pitch. The friendly family owners are continually improving the facilities; they have added a family bathroom, outside hot showers, and a covered children's play area.

Open: Easter to October **Last arrival:** 22.00 **Last departure:** noon
Pitches: 🚐 🚙 ⛺
Leisure: /Ⱥ\ ≋ ⚲
Facilities: ⊙ ℱ ✼ 🛒 WiFi 🖥
Services: 🔌 🗑 🚰 🧺 🛢 ⌀ T
Within 3 miles: ℘ ⛳ ≋

Additional site information: 5 acre site. 🐕 🚗 Cars can be parked by caravans and tents. Awnings permitted. Minimum noise after 23.00. Play barn with table tennis. Freshly baked bread and croissants available in high season.

Bolberry House Farm Caravan & Camping Park
★★★★ 83%

tel: 01548 561251 Bolberry TQ7 3DY
email: enquiries@bolberryhousefarm.com web: www.bolberryhousefarm.com
dir: Note: do not use sat nav. Follow A381 around Kingsbridge to Salcombe. At Malborough turn sharp right follow Bolberry and Soar sign. Follow road through village, past church, keeping to left signed Bolberry and Soar. In 0.6 mile turn right, follow brown sign for Bolberry House Farm. Site signed in 0.5 mile.

A very popular park, close to the fishing village of Hope Cove and to Salcombe, in a peaceful setting on a coastal farm with sea views, fine cliff walks and nearby beaches. Customers are assured of a warm welcome. The spacious pitches are set in six acres of well-maintained grounds with views across the valley towards the sea. There is a smart toilet block. A mobile fish and chip van calls weekly in high season, and there's a super dog-walking area in a large adjacent meadow.

Open: Easter to October **Last arrival:** 20.00 **Last departure:** noon
Pitches: 🚐 🚙 ⛺; 7 hardstanding pitches; 10 seasonal pitches
Facilities: 🛁 ⊙ ℱ ✼ 🛒 WiFi
Services: 🔌 🗑 🧺 T

Within 3 miles: ≋ ℘ ◎ ≋ ⛳ 🎯

Additional site information: 6 acre site. 🐕 🚗 Cars can be parked by caravans and tents. Awnings permitted. Minimum noise 22.00–08.30. Dogs must not be left unattended. Shop on site (high season only).

SAMPFORD PEVERELL
Map 3 ST01

Places to visit
Tiverton Castle, TIVERTON, EX16 6RP, 01884 253200
www.tivertoncastle.com

Tiverton Museum of Mid Devon Life, TIVERTON, EX16 6PJ, 01884 256295
www.tivertonmuseum.org.uk

Great for kids: Diggerland, CULLOMPTON, EX15 2PE, 01634 711711
www.diggerland.com

Platinum Park

Minnows Touring Park
★★★★★

tel: 01884 821770 Holbrook Lane EX16 7EN
email: admin@minnowstouringpark.co.uk web: www.minnowstouringpark.co.uk
dir: M5 junction 27, A361 signed Tiverton and Barnstaple. In 600 yards take 1st slip road, right over bridge, site ahead.

Minnows Touring Park is a small, well-sheltered park, peacefully located amidst fields and mature trees. All pitches are hardstanding with some large enough for American RVs; fully serviced pitches are also available. The toilet facilities are of a high quality in keeping with the rest of the park, and there is a good laundry and tourist information room. The park has direct gated access to the canal towpath; a brisk 20-minute walk leads to a choice of pubs and a farm shop, and the bus stop is 15 minutes away.

Open: 3 March to 27 October **Last arrival:** 20.00 (earliest arrival 13.00)
Last departure: noon
Pitches: 🚐 🚙 ⛺; 59 hardstanding pitches
Facilities: 🛁 ⊙ ℱ ✼ ♿ 🛒 🪑 WiFi
Services: 🔌 🗑 🧺 ⛽ 🛢 T
Within 3 miles: ⛳ ℘ ≋

Additional site information: 5.5 acre site. 🐕 🚗 Cars can be parked by caravans. Awnings permitted. No cycling, no groundsheets on grass. Children aged 14 years and over accepted. Caravan storage, fishing and boating permits available. Car hire can be arranged.

DEVON ENGLAND

SIDMOUTH
Map 3 SY18

Places to visit
The Old Bakery Branscombe, BRANSCOMBE, EX12 3DB, 01752 346585
www.nationaltrust.org.uk/branscombe

Otterton Mill, OTTERTON, EX9 7HG, 01395 568521
www.ottertonmill.com

Great for kids: Pecorama, BEER, EX12 3NA, 01297 21542
www.pecorama.co.uk

Platinum Park

Oakdown Holiday Park
★★★★★

tel: 01297 680387 Gatedown Lane, Weston EX10 0PT
email: enquiries@oakdown.co.uk **web:** www.oakdown.co.uk
dir: Exit A3052, 2.5 miles east of junction with A375.

A quality, friendly, well-maintained park with good landscaping and plenty of maturing trees that make it well screened from the A3052. Pitches are grouped in groves surrounded by shrubs, with a 50-pitch development replete with an upmarket toilet block. The park has excellent facilities including a spacious reception building, a 9-hole par 3 golf course, a dog-wash facility, and a good shop and café. There are four-berth wooden pods and a toilet cabin for the pods, and two shepherd's huts for hire. The park's conservation areas, with their natural flora and fauna, offer attractive walks, and there is a hide by the Victorian reed bed for both casual and dedicated birdwatchers.

Open: March to November **Last arrival:** 22.00 **Last departure:** 10.30
Pitches: from £19.50; from £19.50; from £19.50; see prices below; 90 hardstanding pitches; 35 seasonal pitches
Leisure:
Facilities:
Services:
Within 3 miles:

Additional site information: 16 acre site. Cars can be parked by caravans and tents. Awnings permitted. No bikes, skateboards, drones or kite flying. Microwave available, field trail to donkey sanctuary.

Glamping available: Wooden pods from £69; shepherd's huts from £97.
Changeover days: Any day
Additional glamping information: Shepherd's huts: Linen supplied, TV and microwave. Patio area with table and chairs. Cars can be parked by units

Premier Park

Salcombe Regis Caravan & Camping Park
★★★★★ 92%

tel: 01395 514303 Salcombe Regis EX10 0JH
email: contact@salcombe-regis.co.uk **web:** www.salcombe-regis.co.uk
dir: A375 to Sidford onto A3052 towards Lyme Regis, 1 mile, turn right at brown Salcombe Regis/campsite sign. From Lyme Regis towards Sidford on A3052 turn left after Donkey Sanctuary (Note: it is advisable to follow brown tourist signs not sat nav).

Set in quiet countryside with glorious views, this spacious park has well-maintained facilities, including an impressive, spacious and modern reception building, where guests will also find a good shop and excellent toilet facilities. The park offers a good mix of grass and hardstanding pitches and a footpath runs from the park to the coastal path and the beach. There is a self-catering holiday cottage for hire. This is a perfect location for visiting Sidmouth, Lyme Regis and the coastal area of south-east Devon.

Open: Easter to end October **Last arrival:** 20.15 **Last departure:** noon
Pitches: ; 40 hardstanding pitches; 30 seasonal pitches
Leisure:
Facilities:
Services:
Within 3 miles:

Additional site information: 16 acre site. Cars can be parked by caravans and tents. Awnings permitted. Quiet at 22.00, no noise from 23.00. No open fires, no drones or remote controlled planes or helicopters. Putting green, table tennis, goal posts, badminton. Croissants baked to order. Car hire can be arranged.

DEVON

SOUTH MOLTON
Map 3 SS72

Places to visit
Quince Honey Farm, SOUTH MOLTON, EX36 3RD, 01769 572401
www.quincehoneyfarm.co.uk

Cobbaton Combat Collection, CHITTLEHAMPTON, EX37 9RZ, 01769 540740
www.cobbatoncombat.co.uk

Great for kids: Exmoor Zoo, BLACKMOOR GATE, EX31 4SG, 01598 763352
www.exmoorzoo.co.uk

Platinum Park

Riverside Caravan & Camping Park
★★★★★

tel: 01769 579269 Marsh Lane, North Molton Road EX36 3HQ
email: relax@exmoorriverside.co.uk **web:** www.exmoorriverside.co.uk
dir: *M5 junction 27, A631 towards Barnstaple. Site signed 1 mile before South Molton on right. (Note: as we went to press construction work was continuing between Portmore roundabout and Borners Bridge).*

A family-run park set alongside the River Mole and in 70 acres of landscaped parkland with 10 acres of woodland trails. This is an ideal base for exploring Exmoor, as well as north Devon's golden beaches. It offers 78 premium, fully-serviced pitches for RVs, motorhomes, caravans and campervans, 40 jumbo grass pitches with electricity for tents, a large camping field and rally field, an award-winning shower block, the Country Club restaurant and bar, family entertainment, caravan storage and a collection service. Nine stylish apartments are available above the bar/restaurant. There is a public footpath linking the park to South Molton and the local bus stops at park entrance.

Riverside Caravan & Camping Park

Open: All year **Last arrival:** 19.00 (summer 21.00) **Last departure:** 10.00
Pitches: 54 hardstanding pitches
Leisure:
Facilities:
Services:
Within 3 miles:

Additional site information: 70 acre site. Cars can be parked by caravans and tents. Awnings permitted. Quiet after 23.00. Woodland and valley walks. AWS approved workshop and service engineer. Family friendly luxury lodges available and en suite rooms and statics are dog friendly.

See advert below

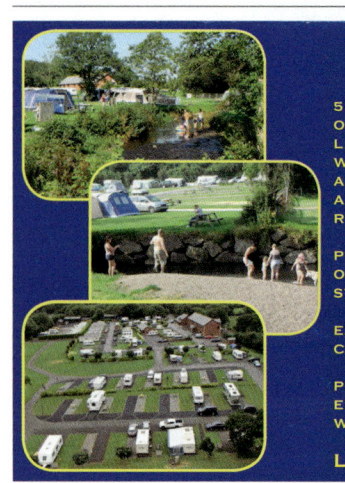

RIVERSIDE CARAVAN AND CAMPING PARK
SOUTH MOLTON, NORTH DEVON

5 STAR FAMILY PET FRIENDLY PARK, OPEN ALL YEAR, OFFERING 5 STAR AWARD WINNING FACILITIES, SET IN 70 ACRES OF LANDSCAPED PARKLANDS WITH 10 ACRES OF MATURE WOODLAND WALKS AND SPECIMEN CARP LAKES, ON THE GATEWAY TO EXMOOR AND THE GOLDEN COASTLINE OF NORTH DEVON, CARAVAN STORAGE AND COLLECTION SERVICE AVAILABLE, CHILDREN'S PLAY AREA, RESTAURANT, BAR AND ENTERTAINMENT.

PREMIUM PITCHES, JUMBO PTICHES, LAKESIDE, RIVERSIDE, WOODSIDE, OPEN FIELD PITCHES, RALLY FIELD AVAILABLE, LUXURIOUS MODERN STATICS, ALL ACCOMMODATION IS PET FRIENDLY.

EASY ACCESS OFF THE A361 FOR RV'S, MOTORHOMES, CARAVANS, CAMPERVANS & TENTS.

PHONE TODAY ON 01769 579269
EMAIL: RELAX@EXMOORRIVERSIDE.CO.UK
WEB: WWW.EXMOORRIVERSIDE.CO.UK

LUXURIOUS ENSUITE ROOMS

   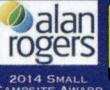 

STOKE GABRIEL   Map 3 SX85

Places to visit

Berry Pomeroy Castle, TOTNES, TQ9 6NJ, 01803 866618
www.english-heritage.org.uk/visit/places/berry-pomeroy-castle

Totnes Museum, TOTNES, TQ9 5RU, 01803 863821
www.totnesmuseum.org

Great for kids: Paignton Zoo, PAIGNTON, TQ4 7EU, 01803 697500
www.paigntonzoo.org.uk

Higher Well Farm Holiday Park
★★★★   86%

tel: 01803 782289 **Waddeton Road TQ9 6RN**
email: info@higherwellfarmholidaypark.co.uk
web: www.higherwellfarmholidaypark.co.uk
dir: *From Exeter A380 to Paignton, turn right onto A385 for Totnes, in 0.5 mile left for Stoke Gabriel, follow signs.*

Set in a peacefully rural area just four miles from Paignton, Higher Well Farm is on the outskirts of the picturesque village of Stoke Gabriel. There's a toilet block, with some en suite facilities, and tourers are sited in an open field with very good views.

Open: One week before Easter to end of October **Last arrival:** 18.00 (later arrivals by prior arrangement) **Last departure:** 10.00

Pitches: 3 hardstanding pitches; 30 seasonal pitches

Facilities:

Services:

Within 3 miles:

Additional site information: 10 acre site. Cars can be parked by caravans and tents. Awnings permitted. No commercial vehicles. Pets must not be left unattended in caravans, motorhomes or tents.

TAVISTOCK   Map 3 SX47

Places to visit

Morwellham Quay, MORWELLHAM, PL19 8JL, 01822 832766
www.morwellham-quay.co.uk

TAVISTOCK   Map 3 SX47

AA CAMPSITE OF THE YEAR FOR SOUTH WEST ENGLAND 2024–25

Platinum Park

Woodovis Park
★★★★★

tel: 01822 832968 **Gulworthy PL19 8NY**
email: info@woodovis.com **web:** www.woodovis.com
dir: *A390 from Tavistock signed Callington and Gunnislake. At hill top right at roundabout signed Lamerton and Chipshop. Site 1 mile on left.*

A well-kept park in a remote woodland setting on the edge of the Tamar Valley. Peacefully located at the end of a private, half-mile, tree-lined drive, it offers superb on-site facilities and high levels of customer care from the owners. The toilets are immaculate and well maintained, plus there is an indoor swimming pool, sauna, well-stocked shop, good information and games rooms, and a campers' kitchen with pizza oven, all creating a friendly atmosphere. The onsite 'Snack Shack' serves a variety of foods to enjoy – from tasty snacks to complete meals. Facilities include electric bike hire and a charging point for electric cars. 2-berth and 4-berth wooden pods are available for hire. There is a real commitment to sustainability here and solar panels have been installed, producing enough power for the whole park.

Open: 14 March to 2 November **Last arrival:** 20.00 **Last departure:** 11.00

Pitches: see prices below; 28 hardstanding pitches; 8 seasonal pitches

Leisure:

Facilities:

Services:

Within 3 miles:

Additional site information: 14.5 acre site. Cars can be parked by caravans and tents. Awnings permitted. No open fires. Pétanque court, outdoor table tennis, archery, water-walking, infrared therapy cabin, hot tub, circus skills workshops and story telling (in school holidays). Wifi available across the site.

Glamping available: Wooden pods from £54. **Changeover days:** Any day

Additional glamping information: Wooden pods: 1 night stay not possible for Fridays or Saturdays. Cars can be parked by units

TAVISTOCK continued

Premier Park

Harford Bridge Holiday Park
★★★★★ 91%

tel: 01822 810349 Peter Tavy PL19 9LS
email: stay@harfordbridge.co.uk web: harfordbridge.co.uk
dir: *A386 from Tavistock towards Okehampton, 2 miles, right signed Peter Tavy, site 200 yards on right.*

This beautiful, spacious and well-equipped park is set beside the River Tavy in the Dartmoor National Park. Pitches are located beside the river and around copses. An adventure playground and games room keep children entertained, and there is a free tennis court. Studio lodges (Escape Pods) and a lovely, authentic shepherd's hut, complete with fridge and woodburner, are available to let, or for something different, why not try one of the new tipis.

Open: 14 March to 15 November (camping and touring); self-catering accomodation available all year. **Last arrival:** 18.00 **Last departure:** noon
Pitches: 20 hardstanding pitches; 10 seasonal pitches
Leisure:
Facilities:
Services:
Within 3 miles:

Additional site information: 16 acre site. Cars can be parked by caravans and tents. Awnings permitted. Baguettes, croissants, snacks, sweets, cold drinks, ices and grocery basics available. Expedition groups and rallies welcome by prior arrangement.
Glamping available: Shepherd's hut; studio lodges (Escape Pods) – sleeps 2 and 4; tipi – sleeps 4.
Changeover days: Saturday
Additional glamping information: No smoking or vaping in holiday accommodation. Shepherd's hut and 2 person studio lodges are adult only. Cars can be parked by units

Premier Park

Langstone Manor Camping & Caravan Park
★★★★★ 85%

tel: 01822 613371 Moortown PL19 9JZ
email: jane@langstonemanor.co.uk web: www.langstonemanor.co.uk
dir: *Take B3357 from Tavistock to Princetown. Approximately 1.5 miles turn right at crossroads, follow signs. Over bridge, cattle grid, up hill, left at sign, left again to park (Note: do not follow sat nav).*

A secluded and very peaceful site set in the well-maintained grounds of a manor house in Dartmoor National Park. Many attractive mature trees provide screening within the park, yet the west-facing terraced pitches on the main park enjoy the superb summer sunsets. There are excellent toilet facilities plus a popular lounge bar offering a very good menu of reasonably priced evening meals. Plenty of activities and places of interest can be found within the surrounding moorland. Dogs are accepted and there are 12 camping pods and six mega pods for hire.

Open: mid March to 30 October (restricted service: bar and restaurant seasonal opening times) **Last arrival:** 20.00 **Last departure:** 11.00
Pitches: see prices below; 18 hardstanding pitches
Leisure:
Facilities:
Services:
Within 3 miles:

Additional site information: 6.5 acre site. Cars can be parked by caravans and tents. Awnings permitted. Cycle shed. Baguettes, croissants etc available. Car hire can be arranged.
Glamping available: Wooden pods from £77; mega pods from £110.
Changeover days: Any day
Additional glamping information: Cars can be parked by units

TORQUAY
Map 3 SX96

Places to visit
Torre Abbey, TORQUAY, TQ2 5JE, 01803 293593
www.torre-abbey.org.uk

Bygones, TORQUAY, TQ1 4PR, 01803 326108
www.bygones.co.uk

Widdicombe Farm Touring Park
★★★★ 92%

tel: 01803 558325 The Ring Road (A380), Marldon TQ3 1ST
email: liz@widdicombefarm.co.uk web: www.widdicombefarm.co.uk
dir: *On A380, midway between Torquay and Paignton.*

A friendly family-run park on a working farm with good quality facilities, extensive views and easy access as there are no narrow roads. The level pitches are terraced to take advantage of the views towards the coast and Dartmoor. This is the only adult touring park within Torquay, and is also handy for Paignton and Brixham. There's a bus service from the park to the local shopping centre and Torquay's harbour. It has a purpose-built reception facility, complete with well-stocked shop, a restaurant and a bar with entertainment from Easter to the end of September. Club

WiFi is available throughout the park and The Nippy Chippy van calls regularly.

Open: mid March to mid October **Last arrival:** 20.00 **Last departure:** 11.00
Pitches: 🚐 🚗 ⛺; 180 hardstanding pitches; 20 seasonal pitches
Leisure: ♪
Facilities: ☺ ℱ ✻ ♿ 🛁 🍴 WiFi 💻
Services: 🔌 🗑 🍽 🍱 🚿 🧺 ⬇ 🧼 ⊤
Within 3 miles: ↯ ℘ ◎ ≋ ✚ 🚌

Additional site information: 12 acre site. Adults only. 🐾 Cars can be parked by caravans and tents. Awnings permitted. No groups. Mini bus service

---

WOOLACOMBE	Map 3 SS44

Places to visit
Great for kids: Combe Martin Wildlife & Dinosaur Park, COMBE MARTIN, EX34 0NG, 01271 882486
cmwdp.co.uk

Premier Park

Twitchen House Holiday Village
★★★★★ 92% HOLIDAY PARK

tel: 01271 872302 Mortehoe Station Road, Mortehoe EX34 7ES
email: goodtimes@woolacombe.com web: www.woolacombe.co.uk
dir: *M5 junction 27, A361 to Ilfracombe. From Mullacott Cross roundabout take B3343 (Woolacombe road) to Turnpike Cross junction. Take right fork, site 1.5 miles on left.*

A very attractive, seaside park with excellent leisure facilities, all-weather activities and entertainment. The touring area features many fully serviced pitches and 80 that are available for tents; they have either sea views or a woodland countryside outlook. There are super pitches with TV aerial, water, drainage, electricity and a night light. The shower rooms have underfloor heating and individual cubicles, plus there's a sauna, steam room, launderette, washing up area and chemical disposal facilities. The site offers a range of entertainment options with a show lounge, indoor soft play area, a cinema, pottery painting studio and many all-weather activities including indoor and outdoor heated pools with water slides and toddler water play areas, bush craft classes, ten pin bowling, climbing wall, bungee trampoline and adventure golf course. Visitors can also use the amenities at the other villages owned by Woolacombe Bay Holiday Parks and all in walking distance to a big sandy beach.

Open: 26 March to 1 November (restricted service: mid March to mid May and September to October – outdoor pool closed) **Last arrival:** midnight **Last departure:** 10.00
Pitches: 🚐 🚗 ⛺; 110 hardstanding pitches
Leisure: 🏊 🏊 ⛰ 👋 ♣ 🎱 🎵 ℘ 🏓 ⚽
Facilities: 🏪 ☺ ℱ ✻ ♿ 🛁 🍴 🎠 WiFi 💻
Services: 🔌 🗑 🍽 🍱 🚿 🧺 ⬇ 🧼 ⊤
Within 3 miles: ↯ ∪ ◎ ≋ ✚ 🚌

Additional site information: 45 acre site. 🐾 Indoor waterslides, woodland walk, adventure golf, amusement arcade, climbing wall, cinema. The beach bus takes guests to the beach or to sister parks.

Premier Park

Golden Coast Holiday Park
★★★★★ 91% HOLIDAY PARK

tel: 01271 872000 Station Road EX34 7HW
web: www.verdantleisure.co.uk/golden-coast
dir: *M5 junction 27, A361 to Ilfracombe. At Mullacott roundabout 1st exit to Woolacombe.*

A seaside holiday village, set beside a three-mile sandy beach, that offers excellent leisure facilities. There is a neat touring area with a unisex toilet block that has underfloor heating and individual cubicles – all maintained to a high standard; the super pitches have water, drainage, electricity, TV aerial and night light. There are apartments and lodges for hire, an outdoor swimming pool complex and a bowling alley. The sports complex features a high ropes course, climbing wall, surfing simulator, adventure golf and much more; there are over 40 free activities available to try.

Open: February to November (restricted service: February to May and mid September to November – outdoor pool closed) **Last arrival:** midnight **Last departure:** 10.00
Pitches: 🚐 🚗 ⛺; 89 hardstanding pitches
Leisure: 🏊 🏊 ⛰ 👋 ♣ 🎱 🎵 ℘ 🏓 🎠 ⚽
Facilities: 🏪 ☺ ℱ ✻ ♿ 🛁 🍴 🎠 WiFi 💻
Services: 🔌 🗑 🍽 🍱 🚿 🧺 ⬇ 🧼 ⊤
Within 3 miles: ↯ ∪ ◎ ≋ ✚ 🚌

Additional site information: 10 acre site. 🐾 Dogs only in pet accommodation. No pets allowed on caravan, motorhome or tent pitches. Playzone, three kids' clubs, high ropes course, surfing simulator, adventure golf, amusement arcade and climbing wall.

Easewell Farm Holiday Village
★★★★ 88%

tel: 01271 872302 Mortehoe Station Road, Mortehoe EX34 7EH
email: goodtimes@woolacombe.com web: www.woolacombe.co.uk
dir: *M5 junction 27, A361 to Ilfracombe. At Mullacott roundabout 1st exit to Woolacombe. Follow Mortehoe signs.*

A peaceful cliff-top park with superb views that offers full facility pitches for caravans and motorhomes – there are super pitches with TV aerial, water, drainage, electricity and a night light. The shower rooms have individual cubicles plus there's a washing up area, launderette and chemical disposal facilities. The park offers a traditional campsite experience in a rural setting and also has a professional sea view 9-hole (18 tee) par 33 golf course and direct access to the South West Coast Path which runs through the grounds. There is an indoor heated pool with a toddler pool, outdoor adventure play area, convenience store and a sports bar plus you can use the facilities and activities at the other nearby villages owned by Woolacombe Bay Holiday Parks. There is also a bus that connects them all and goes to the beach.

Open: mid March to 2 November (restricted service: at Easter) **Last arrival:** 22.00 **Last departure:** 10.00
Pitches: 🚐 🚗 ⛺; 186 hardstanding pitches; 130 seasonal pitches
Leisure: 🏊 ⛰ 👋 ♣ ♪
Facilities: 🏪 ☺ ℱ ✻ ♿ 🛁 🍴 🎠 WiFi 💻
Services: 🔌 🗑 🍽 🍱 🚿 🧺 🧼 ⊤
Within 3 miles: ℘ ∪ ◎ ≋ ✚ 🚌

Additional site information: 17 acre site. 🐾 Cars can be parked by caravans and tents. Awnings permitted. Toddlers' pool, amusement arcade, pool table, indoor bowls, darts and outdoor adventure play area. Seasonal pitches and storage available.

Dorset

Dorset means rugged varied coastlines and high chalk downlands with more than a hint of Thomas Hardy, its most famous son. Squeezed in among the cliffs and set amid some of Britain's most beautiful scenery is a chain of picturesque villages and seaside towns.

Along the coast you'll find the Lulworth Ranges, which run from Kimmeridge Bay in the east to Lulworth Cove in the west. Walking is the most obvious and rewarding recreational activity here, but the British Army firing ranges mean that access to this glorious landscape is restricted. This is Britain's Jurassic Coast, a UNESCO World Heritage Site and Area of Outstanding Natural Beauty, noted for its layers of shale and numerous fossils embedded in the rock. Among the best-known natural landmarks on this stretch of the Dorset coast is Durdle Door, a rocky arch that has been shaped and sculpted to perfection by the elements. The whole area has the unmistakable stamp of prehistory. The landscape and coastal views may be spectacular but the up-and-down nature of the walking here is often physically demanding.

This designated coastline stretches from Swanage and the Isle of Purbeck to east Devon, offering miles of breathtaking scenery. Beyond the seaside town of Weymouth is Chesil Beach, a long shingle reef running for 10 miles between Portland and Abbotsbury. The beach is covered by a vast wall of shingle left by centuries of dramatic weather-induced activity along the Devon and Dorset coast. Beyond Bridport and West Bay, where the hugely successful TV series *Broadchurch* was filmed, lies quaint Lyme Regis, with its sturdy breakwater, known as The Cobb. It's the sort of place where Georgian houses and pretty cottages jostle with historic pubs and independently run shops. With its blend of architectural styles and old world charm, Lyme Regis looks very much like a film set. Perhaps that is why film producers chose this setting as a location for the making of *The French Lieutenant's Woman* in 1981. Jeremy Irons and Meryl Streep starred in the film, based on the novel by John Fowles.

Away from Dorset's magical coastline lies a landscape with a very different character and atmosphere, but one that is no less appealing. Here, winding, hedge-lined country lanes lead beneath lush, green hilltops to snug, sleepy villages hidden from view and the wider world. The main roads lead to the country towns of Sherborne, Blandford Forum, Wareham and Shaftesbury and in September these routes fill with even more traffic as the county prepares to host the annual Great Dorset Steam Fair. This famous event draws many visitors who come to admire the various vintage and classic vehicles on display. The same month is also set aside for the two-day County Show, an eagerly anticipated annual fixture.

Inland there are further links with literature. Dorset is justifiably proud of the achievements of Thomas Hardy, and much of the county is immortalised in his writing. He was born at Higher Bockhampton, near Dorchester, and this quaint old cob-and-thatch cottage was where the writer lived until he was 34. As a child, Hardy spent much of his time here reading and writing poems about the countryside. The cottage contains the desk where he wrote *Far from the Madding Crowd*. In later years Hardy lived at Max Gate on the edge of Dorchester and here he was visited by many distinguished writers of the day, including Rudyard Kipling and Virginia Woolf. Even the Prince of Wales called on him one day in 1923. Both homes are now in the care of the National Trust.

One of Thomas Hardy's great friends was T. E. (Thomas Edward) Lawrence, better known as Lawrence of Arabia, who lived nearby in a modest cottage known as Clouds Hill. The cottage, also managed by the National Trust, was Lawrence's secluded retreat from the world, where he could read and play music.

◁ *Lyme Regis*

DORSET

BLANDFORD FORUM — Map 4 ST80

Places to visit

Kingston Lacy, WIMBORNE, BH21 4EA, 01202 883402
www.nationaltrust.org.uk/kingston-lacy

Old Wardour Castle, TISBURY, SP3 6RR, 01747 870487
www.english-heritage.org.uk/visit/places/old-wardour-castle

Great for kids: Monkey World, WOOL, BH20 6HH, 01929 462537
monkeyworld.org

The Inside Park
★★★★ 89%

tel: 01258 453719 **Down House Estate DT11 9AD**
email: mail@theinsidepark.co.uk **web:** www.theinsidepark.co.uk
dir: *From Blandford Forum follow Winterborne Stickland signs. Site in 1.5 miles.*

An attractive, well-sheltered and quiet park, half a mile along a country lane in a wooded valley, yet close to Blandford Forum. The spacious pitches are divided by mature trees and shrubs, and the amenities are housed in an 18th-century coach house and stables. There are some lovely woodland walks within the park, an excellent fenced play area for children and a dog-free area; four dog kennels are available for daily hire. This site makes the perfect base for anyone visiting the Blandford Steam Fair in August, and there are over six miles of private waymarked farm walks for guests to enjoy.

Open: Easter to October **Last arrival:** 22.00 **Last departure:** noon
Pitches:
Leisure:
Facilities:
Services:
Within 3 miles:

Additional site information: 12 acre site. Cars can be parked by caravans and tents. Awnings permitted. Kennels (charges apply).

BRIDPORT — Map 4 SY49

Places to visit

Dorset Museum, DORCHESTER, DT1 1XA, 01305 756827
www.dorsetmuseum.org

Abbotsbury Subtropical Gardens, ABBOTSBURY, DT3 4LA, 01305 871387
www.abbotsburyswannery.co.uk

Great for kids: Abbotsbury Swannery, ABBOTSBURY, DT3 4JG, 01305 871858
www.abbotsburyswannery.co.uk

Platinum Park

Highlands End Holiday Park
★★★★★

tel: 01308 422139 & 426947 **Eype DT6 6AR**
email: holidays@wdlh.co.uk **web:** www.wdlh.co.uk
dir: *1 mile west of Bridport on A35, follow signs for Eype. Site signed.*

A well-screened site with magnificent cliff-top views over the Channel and the Dorset coast, adjacent to National Trust land and overlooking Lyme Bay. The pitches are mostly sheltered by hedging and are well spaced on hardstandings. The excellent facilities include a stylish bar and restaurant, indoor pool, leisure centre and The Cowshed Café, a very good coffee shop with a stunning view, and a soft-play area for children. There is a mixture of statics and tourers, but the tourers enjoy the best cliff-top positions, including gravel hardstanding pitches overlooking Lyme Bay. Ten luxury lodges and wooden pods, that sleep four, are available for hire.

Open: March to November **Last arrival:** 22.00 **Last departure:** 11.00
Pitches: ; 45 hardstanding pitches
Leisure:
Facilities:
Services:
Within 3 miles:

Additional site information: 9 acre site. Cars can be parked by caravans and tents. Awnings permitted. Steam room, sauna, pitch and putt.

Glamping available: Wooden pods. **Changeover days:** Monday, Friday, Saturday (Saturday only in peak season)

Additional glamping information: Cars can be parked by units

Make your next UK holiday one to remember

Choose RatedTrips.com

AA

PITCHES: Caravans   Motorhomes   Tents   Glamping accommodation   **LEISURE:** Indoor swimming pool   Outdoor swimming pool   Children's playground   Kids' club   Tennis court   Games room   Separate TV room   golf course   Pitch n putt   Boats for hire   Bikes for hire   Cinema   Entertainment   Fishing   Mini golf   Watersports   Gym   Sports field   Stables   Spa

DORSET 133 ENGLAND

Premier Park

Freshwater Beach Holiday Park
★★★★★ 92% **HOLIDAY PARK**

tel: 01308 897317 **Burton Bradstock DT6 4PT**
email: office@freshwaterbeach.co.uk web: www.freshwaterbeach.co.uk
dir: *Take B3157 from Bridport towards Burton Bradstock. Site 1.5 miles from Crown Inn roundabout on right.*

A family holiday park sheltered by a sand bank and enjoying its own private beach. The park offers a wide variety of leisure and entertainment programmes for all the family, plus the Jurassic Fun Centre with indoor pool, gym, 6-lane bowling alley, restaurant and bar is excellent. There is an adults-only Sunset Lounge Bar and Cellar function room. The park is well placed at one end of the Weymouth to Bridport coastal area with spectacular views of Chesil Beach. There are three immaculate toilet blocks with excellent private rooms.

Open: mid March to mid November **Last arrival:** 22.00 **Last departure:** 10.00
Pitches: 25 hardstanding pitches
Leisure:
Facilities:
Services:
Within 3 miles:
Additional site information: 40 acre site. Most credit cards accepted. Families and couples only. Large TV, kids' club in high season and bank holidays, ten-pin bowling alley.

See advert on page 134

CERNE ABBAS
Map 4 ST60

Places to visit
Athelhampton House, ATHELHAMPTON, DT2 7LG, 01305 848363
www.athelhampton.com

Hardy's Cottage, DORCHESTER, DT2 8QJ, 01305 262366
www.nationaltrust.org.uk/hardys-cottage

Great for kids: Maiden Castle, DORCHESTER, DT2 9PP, 0370 333 1181
www.english-heritage.org.uk/visit/places/maiden-castle

Giants Head Caravan & Camping Park
★★★ 82%

tel: 01300 341242 & 07970 277730
Giants Head Farm House, Old Sherborne Road DT2 7TR
email: holidays@giantshead.co.uk web: www.giantshead.co.uk
dir: *From Dorchester to Cerne Abbas avoiding bypass, at Top O'Town roundabout take A352 (Sherborne road), in 500 yards right fork at BP (Loder's) garage and Lidl store.*

A pleasant, though rather basic, park set in Dorset downlands near the Cerne Giant (the famous landmark figure cut into the chalk) and with stunning views. There are smart toilet and shower blocks which are kept very clean. This is a good stopover site especially for tenters and backpackers on The Ridgeway National Trail; the site also offers 'Treasure Trail' routes for Dorset. Holiday chalets are available to let.

Open: Easter to October **Last arrival:** 20.00 (later by prior arrangement)
Last departure: noon
Pitches:
Facilities:
Services:
Within 3 miles:

Additional site information: 4 acre site. Cars can be parked by caravans and tents. Awnings permitted. Dogs must be on leads at all times. Owners must clean up after their pets – bins provided. Ice cream on site at busy times.

FACILITIES: Electric vehicle charging Baths/Shower Electric shaver sockets Hairdryer Ice pack facility Baby facilities Disabled facilities Shop on site or within 200yds BBQ area Picnic area WiFi Internet access **SERVICES:** Electric hook-up Launderette Licensed bar Calor Gas Campingaz Toilet fluid Café/Restaurant Fast Food/Takeaway Battery charging Motorhome service point No credit or debit cards Dogs permitted No dogs

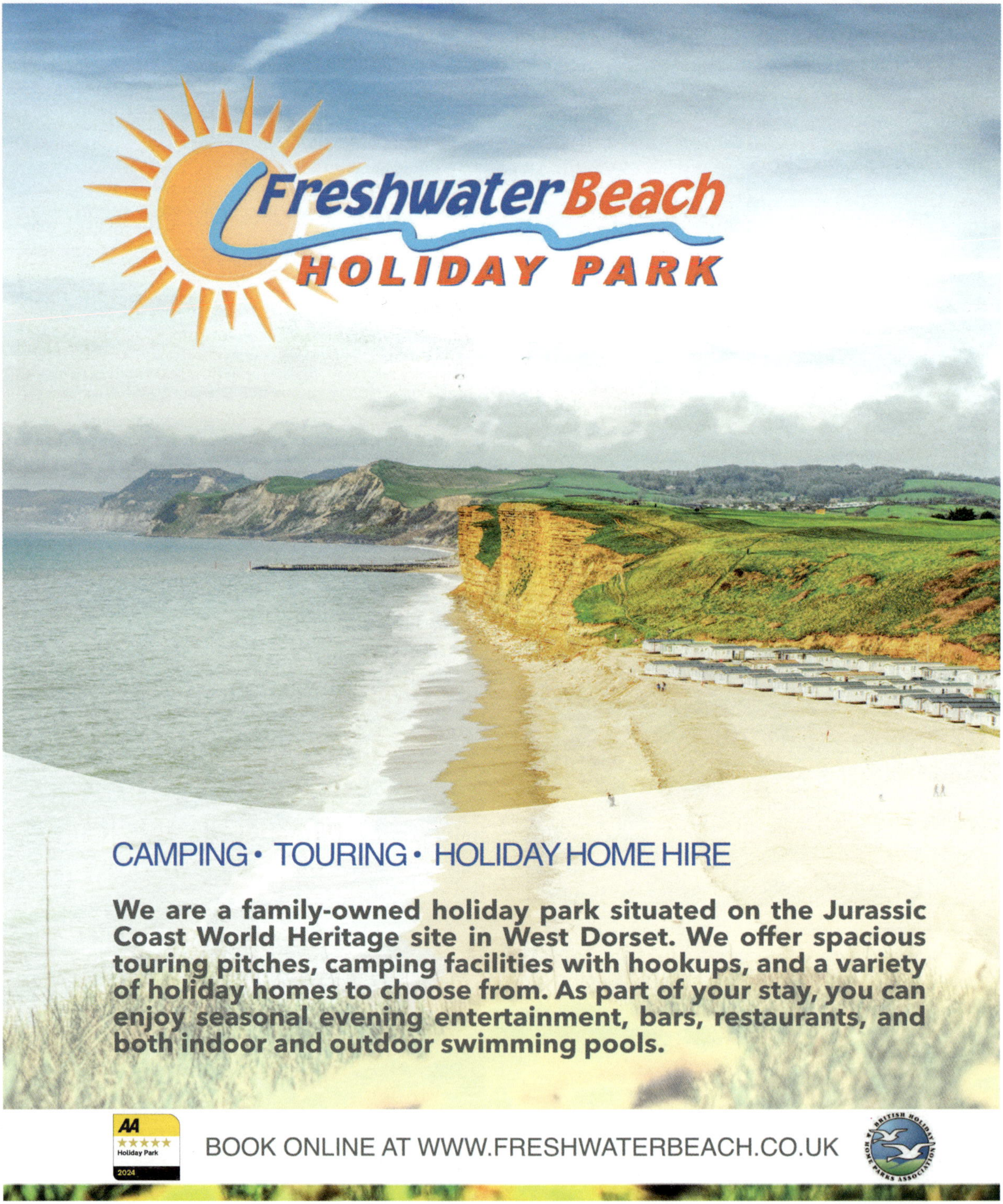
Freshwater Beach
HOLIDAY PARK
CAMPING • TOURING • HOLIDAY HOME HIRE
We are a family-owned holiday park situated on the Jurassic Coast World Heritage site in West Dorset. We offer spacious touring pitches, camping facilities with hookups, and a variety of holiday homes to choose from. As part of your stay, you can enjoy seasonal evening entertainment, bars, restaurants, and both indoor and outdoor swimming pools.
AA
Holiday Park
2024
BOOK ONLINE AT WWW.FRESHWATERBEACH.CO.UK
BRITISH HOLIDAY HOME PARKS ASSOCIATION

PITCHES: Caravans Motorhomes Tents Glamping accommodation **LEISURE:** Indoor swimming pool Outdoor swimming pool Children's playground Kids' club Tennis court Games room Separate TV room golf course Pitch n putt Boats for hire Bikes for hire Cinema Entertainment Fishing Mini golf Watersports Gym Sports field Stables Spa

DORSET 135 ENGLAND

CHARMOUTH
Map 4 SY39

Places to visit
Forde Abbey, THORNCOMBE, TA20 4LU, 01460 221290
www.fordeabbey.co.uk

Great for kids: Abbotsbury Swannery, ABBOTSBURY, DT3 4JG, 01305 871858
abbotsbury-tourism.co.uk/swannery

Premier Park

Monkton Wyld Holiday Park
★★★★★ 93%

tel: 01297 631131 Scott's Lane DT6 6DB
email: stay@monktonwyld.co.uk web: www.monktonwyld.co.uk

A large park, affiliated to the Camping & Caravanning Club, set in glorious, rolling Dorset countryside and just three miles to the beaches of Lyme Regis and Charmouth. Expect first-class facilities, including immaculate toilet/shower blocks, spacious pitches, including 42 fully serviced hardstanding pitches, backing onto hedges or banks for shelter, and a wealth of useful info, from local walks to the best pubs in the area, in the information room. The conservation areas of the park feature wild meadows and bug hotels. This is a peaceful park close to the popular Dorset coast.

Monkton Wyld Holiday Park

Open: early February to early November

Additional site information: 2 secure caravan storage areas. Dedicated dog exercise area and doggy wash. Super fast WiFi and shop on site.

See advert below

Gold Winning Holiday Park
Nr Charmouth, West Dorset
monktonwyld.co.uk
01297 631131

FACILITIES: Electric vehicle charging · Baths/Shower · Electric shaver sockets · Hairdryer · Ice pack facility · Baby facilities · Disabled facilities · Shop on site or within 200yds · BBQ area · Picnic area · WiFi · Internet access **SERVICES:** Electric hook-up · Launderette · Licensed bar · Calor Gas · Campingaz · Toilet fluid · Café/Restaurant · Fast Food/Takeaway · Battery charging · Motorhome service point · No credit or debit cards · Dogs permitted · No dogs

CHARMOUTH continued

Premier Park

Newlands Holidays
★★★★★ 88%
tel: 01297 560259 DT6 6RB
email: enq@newlandsholidays.co.uk web: www.newlandsholidays.co.uk
dir: *6.4 miles west of Bridport on A35.*

A very smart site with excellent touring facilities, set close to the sea in 23 acres of landscaped grounds in hilly Dorset countryside with fine views. Level and very spacious pitches are available. During the high season, the park offers occasional entertainment and children's daytime activities, and boasts a clubhouse, an indoor swimming pool and an outdoor pool, toddler splash zone, and sauna/gym facilities. Lodges, apartments and motel rooms are available, plus there are four camping pods for hire.

Open: 3 March to 2 November **Last arrival:** 21.00 **Last departure:** 10.00
Pitches: 72 hardstanding pitches; 40 seasonal pitches
Leisure:
Facilities:
Services:
Within 3 miles:

Additional site information: 23 acre site. Cars can be parked by caravans and tents. Awnings permitted. Kids' club during school holidays, freshly baked bread available. On-site nature trail. Car hire can be arranged.
Glamping available: Wooden pods. **Changeover days:** Any day
Additional glamping information: Cars can be parked by units

Manor Farm Holiday Centre
★★★★ 87%
tel: 01297 560226 DT6 6QL
email: enquiries@manorfarmholidaycentre.co.uk
web: www.manorfarmholidaycentre.co.uk
dir: *From east: A35 into Charmouth, site 0.75 mile on right.*

Set just a short walk from the safe sand and shingle beach at Charmouth, this popular family park offers a good range of facilities. There is an indoor-outdoor swimming pool plus café, a fully-equipped gym and sauna. Children certainly enjoy the activity area and the park also offers a lively programme of events in the extensive bar and entertainment complex. In addition, there are 16 luxury cottages available for hire and smart lodges for sale.

Open: All year (restricted service: mid March to end October – statics only)
Last arrival: 20.00 **Last departure:** 10.00
Pitches: 80 hardstanding pitches; 100 seasonal pitches
Leisure:
Facilities:
Services:
Within 3 miles:

Additional site information: 30 acre site. Cars can be parked by caravans and tents. Awnings permitted. No skateboards. 5mph speed limit, gates locked at night, depending on time of year.

CHIDEOCK   Map 4 SY49

Places to visit
Mapperton, BEAMINSTER, DT8 3NR, 01308 862645
mapperton.com

Premier Park

Golden Cap Holiday Park
★★★★★ 90% HOLIDAY PARK
tel: 01308 422139 & 426947 Seatown DT6 6JX
email: holidays@wdlh.co.uk web: www.wdlh.co.uk
dir: *On A35, in Chideock follow Seatown signs, site signed.*

A grassy site, overlooking the sea and beach and surrounded by National Trust parkland. This uniquely placed park slopes down to the sea, although pitches are generally level. A slight dip hides the view of the beach from the back of the park, but this area benefits from having trees, scrub and meadows, unlike the barer areas closer to the sea which do have a spectacular outlook. There is a smart toilet and shower block, plus there's a shop, café and takeaway. Luxury lodges, with outstanding views, and different types of glamping accommodation are available, including impressive Premier Pods. This makes an ideal base for touring Dorset and Devon. Lake fishing is possible (a licence can be obtained locally).

Open: March to November **Last arrival:** 22.00 **Last departure:** 11.00
Pitches: 24 hardstanding pitches
Leisure:
Facilities:
Services:
Within 3 miles:

Additional site information: 11 acre site. Cars can be parked by caravans and tents. Awnings permitted.
Glamping available: Wooden pods; safari tents; Lotus Belle tents.
Changeover days: Monday, Friday, Saturday (Saturday only in peak)
Additional glamping information: Cars can be parked by units

PITCHES: Caravans Motorhomes Tents Glamping accommodation LEISURE: Indoor swimming pool Outdoor swimming pool Children's playground Kids' club Tennis court Games room Separate TV room golf course Pitch n putt Boats for hire Bikes for hire Cinema Entertainment Fishing Mini golf Watersports Gym Sports field Stables Spa

DORSET — ENGLAND

CHRISTCHURCH Map 5 SZ19

Places to visit

Red House Museum & Gardens, CHRISTCHURCH, BH23 1BU, 01202 482860
www.hampshireculture.org.uk/red-house-museum-and-gardens

Great for kids: Oceanarium, BOURNEMOUTH, BH2 5AA, 01202 311993
www.oceanarium.co.uk

Premier Park

Meadowbank Holidays
★★★★★ 88%

tel: 01202 483597 Stour Way BH23 2PQ
email: enquiries@meadowbankholidays.co.uk web: www.meadowbank-holidays.co.uk
dir: *A31 onto A338 towards Bournemouth. 5 miles, left towards Christchurch on B3073. Right at 1st roundabout into St Catherine's Way, becomes River Way. 3rd right into Stour Way to site.*

A very smart park on the banks of the River Stour, with a colourful display of hanging baskets and flower-filled tubs placed around the superb reception area. The toilet block is excellent and offers modern, stylish facilities. There's a choice of pitch sizes including luxury, fully serviced ones. There is also an excellent play area, a cycle storage facility, a good shop on site and coarse fishing. Statics are available for hire. The park is well located in a peaceful area and very convenient for visiting nearby Christchurch, the south coast and the New Forest.

Open: March to October **Last arrival:** 21.00 **Last departure:** noon
Pitches: 22 hardstanding pitches
Leisure:
Facilities:
Services:
Within 3 miles:

Additional site information: 2 acre site. Cars can be parked by caravans. Awnings permitted. No pets. Table tennis, riverside walk. Car hire can be arranged.

CORFE CASTLE Map 4 SY98

Places to visit

Brownsea Island, BROWNSEA ISLAND, BH13 7EE, 01202 707744
www.nationaltrust.org.uk/brownsea-island

Corfe Castle, CORFE CASTLE, BH20 5EZ, 01929 481294
www.nationaltrust.org.uk/corfe-castle

Great for kids: Swanage Railway, SWANAGE, BH19 1HB, 01929 425800
www.swanagerailway.co.uk

Norden Farm Touring Caravan and Camping Site
★★★★ 86%

tel: 01929 480098 Norden Farm BH20 5DS
email: info@nordenfarm.com web: www.nordenfarm.com
dir: *On A351 from Wareham towards Swanage, on right.*

This delightful farm site offers traditional camping but with excellent toilet and shower facilities. It is a very dog-friendly site and is ideally suited for those who want a peaceful, rural getaway or enjoy country pursuits. There are four level grass fields, three with electric hook-up and an additional six-acre free pitching field for tents and VW camper vans in peak season. A well-stocked farm shop sell groceries, fresh produce and camping essentials. Its location is very close to Corfe Castle, so it's convenient for visiting the Isle of Purbeck and Swanage (the Swanage Railway now runs seasonal trains from Swanage through to Wareham). There is a holiday cottage and Norden House (exclusive use) for hire.

Open: March to October (weather depending) **Last arrival:** 18:00 **Last departure:** 11.00 (late departures sometimes available, must be arranged with reception beforehand)
Pitches:
Leisure:
Facilities:
Services:
Within 3 miles:

Additional site information: 14 acre site. Cars can be parked by caravans and tents. Awnings permitted. Strict 5mph speed limit on site, no noise after 23.00. Fresh bakery deliveries daily, hot showers, washroom for dogs, footpaths to local attractions, on-site food vans.

Make your next UK holiday one to remember

Choose RatedTrips.com

AA

FACILITIES: Electric vehicle charging · Baths/Shower · Electric shaver sockets · Hairdryer · Ice pack facility · Baby facilities · Disabled facilities · Shop on site or within 200yds · BBQ area · Picnic area · WiFi · Internet access SERVICES: Electric hook-up · Launderette · Licensed bar · Calor Gas · Campingaz · Toilet fluid · Café/Restaurant · Fast Food/Takeaway · Battery charging · Motorhome service point · No credit or debit cards · Dogs permitted · No dogs

CORFE CASTLE continued

Woodyhyde Camp Site
★★★ 86%

tel: 01929 480274 **Valley Road BH20 5HT**
email: camp@woodyhyde.co.uk web: www.woodyhyde.co.uk
dir: *From Corfe Castle towards Swanage on A351, site approximately 1 mile on right.*

A large grassy campsite in a sheltered location for tents and motorhomes only, divided into three paddocks – one is dog free. This site offers traditional camping in a great location between Corfe Castle and Swanage, and the Swanage steam railway that runs past the site adds interest for campers. There is a well-stocked shop on site, a modern toilet and shower block, and there's a regular bus service that stops near the site entrance. Electric hook-ups and some hardstandings are available and glamping accommodation is offered, consisting of five yurts and two shepherd's huts.

Woodyhyde Camp Site

Open: March to October **Last departure:** noon
Pitches: ; 25 hardstanding pitches
Facilities: WiFi
Services:
Within 3 miles:

Additional site information: 13 acre site. Cars can be parked by tents. Awnings permitted. No noise after 23.00, no open fires.
Glamping available: 2 shepherd's huts; 5 yurts.

See advert below

WOODYHYDE

Woodyhyde Campsite, Valley Road, Corfe Castle, Isle of Purbeck, Dorset, BH20 5HT
Tel: 01929 480274   Email: camp@woodyhyde.co.uk

Woodyhyde campsite is situated in the heart of the stunning Purbeck countryside. Set in 13 acres of beautiful open countryside, within an Area of Outstanding Natural Beauty. We are just 20 minutes walk to the stunning ruins of Corfe Castle and a short distance from the seaside town of Swanage. The location of our campsite makes it suitable for all types of holidays or weekends away.

Book now at
www.woodyhyde.co.uk

PITCHES: Caravans Motorhomes Tents Glamping accommodation **LEISURE:** Indoor swimming pool Outdoor swimming pool Children's playground Kids' club Tennis court Games room Separate TV room golf course Pitch n putt Boats for hire Bikes for hire Cinema Entertainment Fishing Mini golf Watersports Gym Sports field Stables Spa

DORSET 139 ENGLAND

FERNDOWN
Map 5 SU00

Places to visit
Kingston Lacy, WIMBORNE, BH21 4EA, 01202 883402
www.nationaltrust.org.uk/kingston-lacy

Great for kids: Oceanarium, BOURNEMOUTH, BH2 5AA, 01202 311993
www.oceanarium.co.uk

St Leonards Farm Caravan & Camping Park

★★★★ 85%

tel: 01202 872637 **Ringwood Road, West Moors BH22 0AQ**
email: enquiries_stleonards@yahoo.co.uk **web:** www.stleonardsfarmpark.com
dir: *From Ringwood on A31 (dual carriageway) towards Ferndown, exit left into slip road at site sign. From Wimborne Minster on A31 at roundabout (junction of A31 & A347) follow signs for Ringwood (A31) (pass Texaco garage on left) to next roundabout. 3rd exit (ie double back towards Ferndown) exit at slip road for site.*

A private road accessed from the A31 leads to this well-screened park divided into paddocks that have spacious pitches. The site has an excellent, secure children's soft-play area and an indoor play barn. There is a toilet and shower block with excellent family/disabled rooms, and a late arrival point with electricity and water. Two shepherd's huts and bell tents, complete with a fully-equipped utility cabin, are available for hire. The park is also well located for visiting nearby Bournemouth and the New Forest National Park.

St Leonards Farm Caravan & Camping Park

Open: February to November **Last arrival:** late arrivals by prior arrangement
Last departure: noon

Pitches: 15 hardstanding pitches; 30 seasonal pitches

Leisure:

Facilities:

Services:

Within 3 miles:

Additional site information: 12 acre site. Cars can be parked by caravans and tents. Awnings permitted. No large groups, no noise after 23.00, no disposable BBQs, no gazebos, no commercial vehicles.

Glamping available: Shepherd's huts, bell tents.
Additional glamping information: Cars can be parked by units

See advert below

FACILITIES: Electric vehicle charging, Baths/Shower, Electric shaver sockets, Hairdryer, Ice pack facility, Baby facilities, Disabled facilities, Shop on site or within 200yds, BBQ area, Picnic area, WiFi, Internet access **SERVICES:** Electric hook-up, Launderette, Licensed bar, Calor Gas, Campingaz, Toilet fluid, Café/Restaurant, Fast Food/Takeaway, Battery charging, Motorhome service point, No credit or debit cards, Dogs permitted, No dogs

ENGLAND — 140 DORSET

HOLDITCH — Map 4 ST30

Places to visit

Forde Abbey, THORNCOMBE, TA20 4LU, 01460 220231
www.fordeabbey.co.uk

Premier Park

Mallinson's Woodland Retreat
★★★★★ 90% GLAMPING ONLY

tel: Woodland Workshop, Yonder Hill TA20 4NL
email: enquiries@mallinson.co.uk **web:** mallinson.co.uk
dir: *From A358 between Axminster and Chard, in Tytherleigh into Broom Lane signed Holditch (becomes Holditch Lane). Through Holditch, after Manor Farm, after sharp left bend, car park on left in 200 yards. (Note: it is advisable not to use sat nav).*

Mallinson's Woodland Retreat offers a unique holiday adventure in peaceful and beautiful surroundings. If you have a desire to experience a different type of holiday, then this adults-only site could fit the bill. Choose from three spectacular treehouses — Woodsman, the ship-themed Dazzle, or Pinwheel, a glass-topped living space in the tree canopy. Woodsman (featured on *George Clarke's Amazing Spaces* on Channel 4 and winner of several design awards) is a stunning tree house — there's a double bed, toilet and shower facilities, including a copper bath, a wood-burning stove, and a decked area with table and chairs, hammock, pizza oven and even an open-air shower. There is a spiral staircase to an upper level, which has a sauna and a hot tub — you can even get to the forest floor via a slide! The retreat also has a communal kitchen and eating area, and woodland craft courses are also available. Although hidden away in the hamlet of Holditch, it is close to Axminster, Lyme Regis and the Jurassic Coast.

Open: All year **Arrival:** From 16.00 **Last departure:** 10.00
Facilities:
Within 3 miles:

Accommodation available: Bell tent from £130; tipi from £155; yurts from £155; treehouses from £495.

Changeover days: Monday, Wednesday, Friday

Additional site information: 14 acre site. Adults only. No pets. No noise. Private wood fired pizza oven and sauna yurt

LYME REGIS — Map 4 SY39

Places to visit

Shute Barton, SHUTE, EX13 7PT, 01752 346585
www.nationaltrust.org.uk/shute-barton

Great for kids: Pecorama, BEER, EX12 3NA, 01297 21542
www.pecorama.co.uk

Shrubbery Touring Park
★★★★ 92%

tel: 01297 442227 **Rousdon DT7 3XW**
email: info@shrubberypark.co.uk **web:** www.shrubberypark.co.uk
dir: *3 miles west of Lyme Regis on A3052 (coast road).*

Mature trees enclose this peaceful park, which has distant views of the lovely countryside. The modern facilities are well kept and include well designed family rooms, the hardstanding pitches are spacious, and there is plenty of space for children to play in the grounds. There is a small area set aside for adults only and there are two camping pods for hire. Well located for visiting Lyme Regis, Sidmouth and Seaton, the park is right on the Jurassic Coast bus route, which is popular with visitors to this area.

Open: April to October **Last arrival:** 21.00 **Last departure:** 11.00
Pitches: ; 40 hardstanding pitches; 12 seasonal pitches
Leisure:
Facilities:
Services:
Within 3 miles:

Additional site information: 10 acre site. Cars can be parked by caravans and tents. Awnings permitted. No groups (except rallies), no motor scooters, roller skates or skateboards. Crazy golf.

Glamping available: 2 wooden pods.

Additional glamping information: Cars can be parked by units

POOLE — Map 4 SZ09

Places to visit

Brownsea Island, BROWNSEA ISLAND, BH13 7EE, 01202 707744
www.nationaltrust.org.uk/brownsea-island

Poole Museum, POOLE, BH15 1BW, 01202 128 888
www.poolemuseum.org.uk

Great for kids: Oceanarium, BOURNEMOUTH, BH2 5AA, 01202 311993
www.oceanarium.co.uk

DORSET 141 ENGLAND

POOLE
Map 4 SZ09

Platinum Park

South Lytchett Manor Caravan & Camping Park
★★★★★

tel: 01202 622577 Dorchester Road, Lytchett Minster BH16 6JB
email: info@southlytchettmanor.co.uk web: www.southlytchettmanor.co.uk
dir: Exit A35 onto B3067, 1 mile east of Lytchett Minster, 600 yards on right after village.

Year-on-year improvements are made by the passionate, hands-on owners at South Lytchett in order to exceed guest expectations – there's a very popular café, six glamping pods, 21 hardstanding pitches, and posh mobile toilet units in the touring and camping fields. Situated in the grounds of a historic manor house, the site has modern facilities that are spotless and well maintained. There's a TV hook-up on every pitch and free WiFi across the park. A warm and friendly welcome awaits at this lovely site which is well located for visiting Poole and Bournemouth; the Jurassic X53 bus route (Exeter to Poole) has a stop just outside the park. Four stylishly furnished and well-equipped Romany caravans, replete with double bed and two singles plus kitchen and fridge, are available for hire. There are also seven top-notch shepherd's huts with luxury interiors and underfloor heating.

Open: March to 2 January **Last arrival:** 21.00 **Last departure:** 11.00
Pitches: ; see prices below; 90 hardstanding pitches
Leisure:
Facilities:
Services:
Within 3 miles:

Additional site information: 22 acre site. Cars can be parked by caravans and tents. Awnings permitted. No camp fires or Chinese lanterns. No noise after 22.30. Table tennis, football nets. Bread and croissants available. Café and takeaway food in high season. Car hire can be arranged.

Glamping available: 6 glamping pods, 7 shepherd's huts and 4 Romany caravans from £65.

Additional glamping information: Some units are dog friendly. Please advise site in advance of any allergies. Cars can be parked by units

Premier Park

Rockley Park
★★★★★ 94% HOLIDAY PARK

tel: 0800 197 2075 & 01202 679293 Hamworthy BH15 4LZ
email: rockleypark@haven.com web: www.haven.com/rockleypark
dir: M27 junction 1, A31 to Poole centre, then follow signs to site.

A complete holiday experience, including a wide range of day and night entertainment, and plenty of sports and leisure activities, notably watersports. There is also mooring and launching from the park. A great base for all the family, set in a good location for exploring Poole and Bournemouth, offering something for all ages, and there are a wide choice of quality eating outlets.

Open: March to 2 January **Last arrival:** any time **Last departure:** 10.00
Holiday Homes: Sleep 8, Bedrooms 3, Bathrooms 2, Toilets 2, Two-ring burner, Dishwasher, Microwave, Freezer, TV, Sky/Freeview, DVD player, WiFi, Towels included, Electricity included, Gas included
Prices: Low season from £121 High season from £499
Changeover days: Fridays, Saturdays, Mondays
Leisure:
Facilities:
Within 3 miles:

Additional site information: The facilities provided in the holiday homes may differ depending on the grade. Most dog breeds accepted (please check when booking). Dogs must be kept on leads at all times.

PORTESHAM
Map 4 SY68

Places to visit
Tutankhamun Exhibition, DORCHESTER, DT1 1UW, 01305 269571
www.tutankhamun-exhibition.co.uk

Maiden Castle, DORCHESTER, DT2 9PP, 0370 333 1181
www.english-heritage.org.uk/visit/places/maiden-castle

Great for kids: Teddy Bear Museum, DORCHESTER, DT1 1JU, 01305 2660401
www.teddybearmuseum.co.uk

Portessham Dairy Farm Campsite
★★★★ 86%

tel: 01305 871297 DT3 4HG
email: info@porteshamdairyfarm.co.uk web: www.porteshamdairyfarm.co.uk
dir: From Dorchester take A35 towards Bridport. In 5 miles left at Winterbourne Abbas, follow Portesham signs. Through village, left at Kings Arms pub, site 350 yards on right.

Located at the edge of the picturesque village of Portesham close to the Dorset coast, this family-run, level park is part of a small working farm in a quiet rural location. Fully serviced and seasonal pitches are available and there's a smart entrance and reception building. There is an excellent pub and a country store just a short walk from the site, and a bus stops outside the park. This quiet site is close to Abbotsbury Swannery and well situated for visiting many areas of the west Dorset coast.

Open: All year **Last arrival:** 21.00 **Last departure:** 11.00
Pitches: ; 70 hardstanding pitches; 60 seasonal pitches
Leisure:
Facilities:
Services:
Within 3 miles:

Additional site information: 8 acre site. Cars can be parked by caravans and tents. Awnings permitted. No commercial vehicles, groups accepted by prior arrangement only, no camp fires, minimum noise after 22.00. Caravan storage.

FACILITIES: Electric vehicle charging Baths/Shower Electric shaver sockets Hairdryer Ice pack service Baby facilities Disabled facilities Shop on site or within 200yds BBQ area Picnic area WiFi Internet access **SERVICES:** Electric hook-up Launderette Licensed bar Calor Gas Campingaz Toilet fluid Café/Restaurant Fast Food/Takeaway Battery charging Motorhome service point No credit or debit cards Dogs permitted No dogs

ENGLAND — 142 DORSET

PUNCKNOWLE
Map 4 SY58

Places to visit
Hardy's Cottage, DORCHESTER, DT2 8QJ, 01305 262366
www.nationaltrust.org.uk/hardys-cottage

Abbotsbury Swannery, ABBOTSBURY, DT3 4JG, 01305 871858
abbotsbury-tourism.co.uk/swannery

Great for kids: Dinosaur Museum, DORCHESTER, DT1 1EW, 01305 269880
www.thedinosaurmuseum.com

Home Farm Caravan and Campsite
★★★ 83%

tel: 01308 897258 **Home Farm, Rectory Lane DT2 9BW**
web: www.caravanandcampingwestdorset.co.uk
dir: *From Dorchester towards Bridport on A35, left at start of dual carriageway, at hill bottom right to Litton Cheney. Through village, 2nd left to Puncknowle (Hazel Lane). Left at T-junction, left at phone box. Site 150 metres on right. Caravan route: approach via A35 Bridport, then Swyre on B3157, continue to Swyre Lane and Rectory Lane.*

This quiet site, hidden away on the edge of a little hamlet, has good facilities and is an excellent place to camp; hardstanding pitches are available. It offers sweeping views of the Dorset countryside from most pitches, and is just five miles from Abbotsbury, and one and a half miles from the South West Coast Path. This is a really good base from which to tour this attractive area. There is an excellent pub in the village, just a short walk from the campsite.

Open: April to 6 October **Last arrival:** 20.00 (arrivals until 21.00 by prior arrangement only) **Last departure:** noon
Pitches: ; 2 hardstanding pitches; 14 seasonal pitches
Facilities:
Services:
Within 3 miles:

Additional site information: 6.5 acre site. Cars can be parked by caravans and tents. Awnings permitted. No cats, no wood-burning fires, skateboards, rollerblades, motorised toys, drones or loud music. Dogs must be kept on leads at all times. Calor Gas exchange.

ST LEONARDS
Map 5 SU10

Places to visit
Rockbourne Roman Villa, ROCKBOURNE, SP6 3PG, 01725 518541
www.hampshireculturaltrust.org.uk/rockbourne-roman-villa

Red House Museum & Gardens, CHRISTCHURCH, BH23 1BU, 01202 482860
www.hampshireculture.org.uk/red-house-museum-and-gardens

Platinum Park

Back of Beyond Touring Park
★★★★★

tel: 01202 876968 **234 Ringwood Road BH24 2SB**
email: info@backofbeyondtouringpark.co.uk
web: www.backofbeyondtouringpark.co.uk
dir: *From north and east: M3 junction 13 follow signs onto M27 westbound, onto A31 (signed Ringwood) to St Leonards, pass St Leonard's Hotel, at next roundabout U-turn into lane immediately left. Site at end of lane. From west: on A31 pass Texaco garage and Woodman Inn, immediately left to site.*

This lovely adults-only park, a member of the Tranquil Parks group, is set in 30 acres of woodland and offers plenty of pleasant walks. Visitors are sure to receive a warm welcome from the owners and their team. In addition to good caravan and motorhome pitches, including premium fully serviced pitches, there are some excellent areas for tents. The site has a fishing lake and a picnic area, and the whole area is a haven for wildlife. The facilities are well appointed and very clean. There is Monty's Bar with an attractive alfresco seating area, plus fish and chip and pizza nights as well as BBQ evenings, and guests will find an excellent shop stocked with local produce. A secluded and separate glamping area offers camping pods, a yurt, two shepherd's huts, and cabins for hire – all have their own spacious decking areas.

Open: March to October **Last arrival:** 19.00 **Last departure:** 11.00
Pitches: ; see prices below; 34 seasonal pitches
Leisure:
Facilities:
Services:
Within 3 miles:

Additional site information: 30 acre site. Adults only. Cars can be parked by caravans and tents. Awnings permitted. No commercial vehicles, no groups, no noise after 22.30. Visiting food vans, coffee and tea available, morning bakery. Licensed to sell alcohol. Car hire can be arranged.

Glamping available: Pods (furnished) from £45; yurt (furnished) from £45; lodges (furnished) from £45; shepherd's huts (furnished) from £45.
Changeover days: Any day

Additional glamping information: Dogs allowed in lodges and shepherd's huts. Woodburner in yurt and shepherd's huts. Cars can be parked by units

---

PITCHES: Caravans Motorhomes Tents Glamping accommodation **LEISURE:** Indoor swimming pool Outdoor swimming pool Children's playground Kids' club Tennis court Games room Separate TV room golf course Pitch n putt Boats for hire Bikes for hire Cinema Entertainment Fishing Mini golf Watersports Gym Sports field Stables Spa

DORSET 143 ENGLAND

SIXPENNY HANDLEY
Map 4 ST91

Places to visit
Larmer Tree Gardens, TOLLARD ROYAL, SP5 5PT, 01725 516971
www.larmertree.co.uk

Shaftesbury Abbey Museum & Garden, SHAFTESBURY, SP7 8JR, 01747 852910
www.shaftesburyabbey.org.uk

Great for kids: Moors Valley Country Park and Forest, RINGWOOD, BH24 2ET, 01425 470721
moors-valley.co.uk

Church Farm Caravan & Camping Park
★★★★ 75%
tel: 01725 552563 & 07766 677525 The Bungalow, Church Farm SP5 5ND
email: churchfarmcandcpark@yahoo.co.uk **web:** www.churchfarmcandcpark.com
dir: *1 mile south of Handley Hill roundabout. Exit for Sixpenny Handley, right by school, site 300 yards by church.*

A spacious park located within the Cranborne Chase Area of Outstanding Natural Beauty which has been awarded Dark Sky status; the site is split into several camping areas including one for adults only. There is a facility block with private facilities, a café and restaurant, and a function room, Hanlega's. The pretty village of Sixpenny Handley, with all its amenities, is just 200 yards away, and the site is well positioned for visiting the Great Dorset Steam Fair, the New Forest National Park, Bournemouth, Poole and Stonehenge.

Open: All year (restricted service: November to March – 10 vans maximum)
Last arrival: 21.00 **Last departure:** 11.00

Pitches: 🚐 🚛 ▲; 4 hardstanding pitches; 5 seasonal pitches
Facilities: 🛁 ⊙ ✻ ♿ 🎪 WiFi 💻
Services: 🔌 🔋 🍽 🍴 🧺 🧳 ⛽ 🚿 T
Within 3 miles: ⚓ 🛒

Additional site information: 10 acre site. 🐕 Cars can be parked by caravans and tents. Awnings permitted. Quiet after 23.00. Use of fridge freezer and microwave.

SWANAGE
Map 5 SZ07

Places to visit
Corfe Castle, CORFE CASTLE, BH20 5EZ, 01929 477060
www.nationaltrust.org.uk/corfe-castle

Brownsea Island, BROWNSEA ISLAND, BH13 7EE, 01202 707744
www.nationaltrust.org.uk/brownsea-island

Great for kids: Swanage Railway, SWANAGE, BH19 1HB, 01929 425800
www.swanagerailway.co.uk

Premier Park

Ulwell Holiday Park
★★★★★ 91% HOLIDAY PARK
tel: 01929 422823 Ulwell Cottage, Ulwell BH19 3DG
email: enq@ulwellholidaypark.co.uk **web:** www.ulwellholidaypark.co.uk
dir: *From Bournemouth via Sandbanks chain ferry onto B3351 towards Swanage. Through Studland, fork left follow Swanage signs. Site on right. Or from Wareham on A351 to Swanage, left on seafront towards Studland (Shore Road becomes Ulwell Road). Approximately 2 miles, left at campsite sign.*

Sitting under the Purbeck Hills and surrounded by scenic walks, this park is only two miles from the beach. It is family-run and caters well for families and couples, and offers a toilet and shower block complete with good family rooms (heated in winter), all appointed to a high standard. There are fully serviced pitches and a good indoor swimming pool; the village inn offers a good range of meals. There is a camping pod for hire and, suitable for a couple, a stylish self-contained S-pod with a decking area.

Open: March to 7 January (restricted service: Easter to 31 October – shop has variable opening times) **Last arrival:** 22.00 **Last departure:** 11.00

Pitches: 🚐 🚛 ▲; 🏠 see prices below; 23 hardstanding pitches
Leisure: 🏊 ▲ ⚽
Facilities: 🛁 ⊙ 🔥 ✻ ♿ 🛒 🎪 WiFi 💻
Services: 🔌 🔋 🍽 🍴 🧳 ⛽ 🚿
Within 3 miles: ⚓ 🏌 ⛳ ∪ ◎ 🛒 ✈ 日

Additional site information: 13 acre site. 🐕 Cars can be parked by caravans and tents. Awnings permitted. No bonfires or fireworks.

Glamping available: Wooden pods, cabin (S-pod); from £35
Changeover days: Variable

Additional glamping information: Linen only supplied if requested. Cars can be parked by units

---

FACILITIES: 🔌 Electric vehicle charging 🛁 Baths/Shower ⊙ Electric shaver sockets 🔥 Hairdryer ✻ Ice pack facility 👶 Baby facilities ♿ Disabled facilities 🛒 Shop on site or within 200yds 🍖 BBQ area 🎪 Picnic area WiFi WiFi 💻 Internet access **SERVICES:** 🔌 Electric hook-up 🔋 Launderette 🍽 Licensed bar 🥫 Calor Gas ⛽ Campingaz T Toilet fluid 🍴 Café/Restaurant 🍟 Fast Food/Takeaway 🔋 Battery charging ⛽ Motorhome service point ∅ No credit or debit cards 🐕 Dogs permitted ⊘ No dogs

SWANAGE continued

Acton Field Camping Site
★★★ 82%

tel: 01929 424184 Acton Field, Langton Matravers BH19 3HS
email: enquiries@actonfieldcampsite.co.uk web: www.actonfieldcampsite.co.uk
dir: *From A351 right after Corfe Castle onto B3069 to Langton Matravers, 2nd right after village (bridleway sign).*

This informal campsite, bordered by farmland on the outskirts of Langton Matravers, offers good toilet facilities. There are superb views of the Purbeck Hills and towards the Isle of Wight, and a footpath leads to the coastal path. The site occupies what was once a stone quarry so rock pegs may be required. Its location and views make it a wonderful place to camp.

Open: Early May Bank Holiday weekend, Spring Bank Holiday weekend, early July to end August (organised groups from Easter to end October) **Last arrival:** 17.00 **Last departure:** noon
Pitches: 🚐 🚙 ⛺
Facilities: ☺ ✻
Services: 🛒 🚻
Within 3 miles: ⚓ ✎ ⟳ ⚲ ⚵ ⚶ ▤ 🏛

Additional site information: 7 acre site. 🐕 Cars can be parked by caravans and tents. Awnings permitted. No open or wood fires, no noise after 23.00. Mobile grocer calls during school summer holidays, phone charger on site.

THREE LEGGED CROSS Map 5 SU00

Places to visit
Moors Valley Country Park and Forest, RINGWOOD, BH24 2ET, 01425 470721
moors-valley.co.uk

Woolsbridge Manor Farm Caravan Park
★★★★ 88%

tel: 01202 826369 **BH21 6RA**
email: woolsbridge@btconnect.com web: www.woolsbridgemanorcaravanpark.co.uk
dir: *From Ringwood take A31 towards Ferndown. Approximately 1 mile, follow signs for Three Legged Cross and Horton. Site 2 miles on right.*

A small farm site with spacious pitches on a level field. This quiet site is an excellent central base for touring the New Forest National Park, Salisbury and the south coast, and is close to Moors Valley Country Park for outdoor family activities. The facilities are good and very clean and there are excellent family rooms available.

Open: March to October **Last arrival:** 20.00 **Last departure:** 10.30
Pitches: 🚐 🚙 ⛺
Leisure: 🎯 ✎
Facilities: 🚿 ☺ 🚽 ✻ ♿ 🛒 ☕ 📶
Services: 🛒 🚻 🧺 🔒 ⛽ 📞
Within 3 miles: ⚓ ⟳

Additional site information: 6.75 acre site. 🐕 Cars can be parked by caravans and tents. Awnings permitted. Car hire can be arranged.

See advert opposite

WAREHAM

Map 4 SY98

Places to visit

Brownsea Island, BROWNSEA ISLAND, BH13 7EE, 01202 707744
www.nationaltrust.org.uk/brownsea-island

Platinum Park

Wareham Forest Tourist Park
★★★★★

tel: 01929 551393 **North Trigon BH20 7NZ**
email: holiday@warehamforest.co.uk web: www.warehamforest.co.uk
dir: *From A35 between Bere Regis and Lytchett Minster follow Wareham sign into Sugar Hill. Site on left.*

A woodland park within the tranquil Wareham Forest, with its many walks and proximity to Poole, Dorchester and the Purbeck coast. Two luxury blocks, with combined washbasin and toilets for total privacy, are maintained to a high standard of cleanliness. A heated outdoor swimming pool, off licence, shop and games room add to the enjoyment of a stay on this top quality park. There is a bike wash and a separate dog wash with hot water. Year-on-year investment ensures optimum privacy within touring areas coupled with excellent security, which includes barriers and CCTV. Its location and high standards make this one of the leading parks in the country.

Wareham Forest Tourist Park

Open: All year (restricted service: limited services available in off-peak season)
Last arrival: 21.00 **Last departure:** 11.00

Pitches: ; 70 hardstanding pitches; 70 seasonal pitches

Leisure:

Facilities:

Services:

Within 3 miles:

Additional site information: 55 acre site. Cars can be parked by caravans and tents. Awnings permitted. Families and couples only, no group bookings. Table tennis. Fresh bread and croissants available in high season.

See advert on page 146

 Woolsbridge Manor Farm TOURING PARK

woolsbridgemanorcaravanpark.co.uk
Call us: 01202 826369 | Email: enquiries@woolsbridge.co.uk

An award-winning, popular touring campsite, within a family-run organic working farm on the Dorset-Hampshire border. The emphasis is on the park being a quiet, relaxed atmosphere, with all amenities close at hand.

Ideal for visiting Moors Valley Country Park, accessed directly from the campsite via pathways, or exploring the New Forest National Park, beaches and historic towns, heritage sites, leisure and entertainment places nearby.

WAREHAM continued

Birchwood Tourist Park
★★★★   88%

tel: 01929 554763 **Bere Road, Coldharbour BH20 7PA**
email: birchwoodtouristpark@hotmail.com web: www.birchwoodtouristpark.co.uk
dir: *From Poole (A351) or Dorchester (A352) on north side of railway line at Wareham, follow Bere Regis signs. 2nd park after 2.25 miles.*

Set in 50 acres of parkland located within Wareham Forest, this site offers direct access to areas that are ideal for walking, mountain biking and horse and pony riding. This is a spacious open park, ideal for families, with plenty of room for young people to play games, including football, and there is a small pool for children and a games room. There is also a dog shower. The modern facilities are in two central locations and are very clean. The site has a good security barrier system and CCTV. The park is only a short drive from Bournemouth and Swanage.

Open: All year **Last arrival:** 21.00 **Last departure:** 11.00 (until 16.00 – fee applies)

Pitches: 30 hardstanding pitches; 75 seasonal pitches

Leisure:

Facilities:

Services: Within 3 miles:

Additional site information: 25 acre site. Cars can be parked by caravans and tents. Awnings permitted. For families, couples and singles, small groups by arrangement only. Dogs to be kept on short leads. Quiet 22.00 – 07.00. Barrier closed to vehicles overnight. No camp fires. Minimum number of nights applies over Bank Holidays. Shop for basic groceries and camping equipment in reception. Paddling pool (end May to end August), table tennis, swings, play area.

East Creech Farm Campsite
★★★   87%

tel: 01929 480519 **East Creech Farm, East Creech BH20 5AP**
email: farmhouse@eastcreechfarm.co.uk web: www.eastcreechfarm.co.uk
dir: *From Wareham on A351 south towards Swanage. On bypass at 3rd roundabout take Furzebrook/Blue Pool Road exit, site approximately 2 miles on right.*

This grassy park is set in a peaceful location beneath the Purbeck Hills, with extensive views towards Poole and Brownsea Island. The park boasts bright, clean toilet facilities, a woodland play area, a farm shop selling milk, eggs and bread, and a children's play area. There are also four coarse fishing lakes teeming with fish. A good tearoom, The Cake House Tea Room, adjacent to the site, is open in the main season. The park is close to Norden Station on the Swanage to Norden steam railway line, and is well located for visiting Corfe Castle, Swanage and the Purbeck coast.

Open: April to October **Last arrival:** 20.00 **Last departure:** noon

Pitches: see prices below

Leisure:

Facilities:

Services:

Within 3 miles:

Additional site information: 4 acre site. Cars can be parked by caravans and tents. Awnings permitted. No camp fires, no loud noise.

Glamping available: 2 wooden pods from £65.

Additional glamping information: Minimum 2 nights stay. No pets. No smoking. No stag/hen parties. Cars can be parked by units

Ridge Farm Camping & Caravan Park
★★★ 86%

tel: 01929 556444 **Barnhill Road, Ridge BH20 5BG**
email: enquiries@ridgefarm.co.uk **web:** www.ridgefarm.co.uk
dir: *From Wareham take B3075 towards Corfe Castle, cross river, into Stoborough, left to Ridge. Follow site signs for 1.5 miles.*

Ridge Farm is a quiet rural park, next to a working farm and surrounded by trees and bushes. This away-from-it-all park is ideal for touring this part of Dorset, and is especially good for birdwatchers, walkers and cyclists. Nearby are the Arne Nature Reserve, the Blue Pool and Corfe Castle. There are good supermarkets and shops in nearby Wareham.

Open: April to 29 September **Last arrival:** 21.00 **Last departure:** noon
Pitches: 🚐 🚗 Å; 🏠 see prices below; 2 hardstanding pitches; 20 seasonal pitches
Facilities:
Services:
Within 3 miles:

Additional site information: 3.47 acre site. Cars can be parked by caravans and tents. Awnings permitted. Dogs accepted by prior arrangement. On site shop, fresh bakery items and freshly ground coffee.

Glamping available: Bell tent from £70 **Changeover days:** Any day
Additional glamping information: No dogs in bell tents. Cars can be parked by units

---

WEYMOUTH
Map 4 SY67

Places to visit
RSPB Nature Reserve Radipole Lake, WEYMOUTH, DT4 7TZ, 01305 778313
www.rspb.org.uk/reserves-and-events/reserves-a-z/radipole-lake

Portland Castle, PORTLAND, DT5 1AZ, 01305 820539
www.english-heritage.org.uk/visit/places/portland-castle

Great for kids: Sea Life Weymouth, WEYMOUTH, DT4 7SX, 01305 761070
www.visitsealife.com/weymouth

Platinum Park

East Fleet Farm Touring Park
★★★★★

tel: 01305 785768 **Chickerell DT3 4DW**
email: enquiries@eastfleet.co.uk **web:** www.eastfleet.co.uk
dir: *On B3157 (Weymouth to Bridport road), 3 miles from Weymouth.*

This site is set on a working organic farm and has a unique location on the shores of the Fleet Lagoon, overlooking Chesil Beach and the sea, with direct access to the South West Coast Path. There is a wide variety of pitches, including hardstandings and fully serviced pitches, and the largest family tents can be accommodated. This park offers excellent toilet and shower facilities with family rooms. There are good play facilities for children, including an excellent fenced play area for younger ones and a separate play barn with table tennis and other activities. The Old Barn has a tasteful bar and lovely patio area where customers are welcome to take their own food, or order locally and have the food delivered to the bar. In addition, there is 'Festival Food', an area for pizzas and fish and chips, which is very popular with guests. The park is well positioned for visiting Weymouth and Portland, as well as other local attractions, such as the Abbotsbury Swannery and the Abbotsbury Subtropical Gardens. There is a fine drive along the coast road from East Fleet to Bridport with spectacular views of Chesil Beach.

Open: 16 March to end October **Last arrival:** 18.00 **Last departure:** 10.30
Pitches: 🚐 🚗 Å; 90 hardstanding pitches; 5 seasonal pitches
Leisure:
Facilities:
Services:
Within 3 miles:

Additional site information: 21 acre site. Cars can be parked by caravans and tents. Awnings permitted. Camping and caravan accessories shop. Car hire can be arranged.

Premier Park

Weymouth Bay Holiday Park
★★★★★ 93% **HOLIDAY PARK**

tel: 01305 832271 **Preston DT3 6BQ**
email: weymouthbay@haven.com **web:** www.haven.com/weymouthbay
dir: *From A35 towards Dorchester take A354 signed Weymouth. Follow Preston signs onto A353. At Chalbury roundabout 1st left into Preston Road. Park on right.*

This well-located holiday park, just a short drive away from Weymouth beach, offers the complete holiday experience for the whole family. It has excellent indoor and outdoor pools complete with a Lazy River attraction. There is a good choice of eating outlets as well as a full entertainment programme, and an excellent range of sporting activities for all ages. Although a large holiday park, it is of exceptional quality and very well cared for, and guests can expect top customer service throughout their stay. The holiday homes are well appointed throughout. The park is conveniently placed for visiting Portland Bill, Lulworth Cove and Chesil Beach.

Open: mid March to October

Holiday Homes: Sleep 8, Bedrooms 2, Bathrooms 1, Toilets 1, Microwave, Freezer, TV, Sky/Freeview, DVD player, WiFi, Linen included, Towels included, Electricity included

Leisure:
Facilities:
Within 3 miles:

Additional site information: The facilities provided in the holiday homes may differ depending on the grade. Most dog breeds accepted (please check when booking). Dogs must be kept on leads at all times. Papa John's®, high chairs for hire, entertainment and sports area.

WEYMOUTH continued

Premier Park

Littlesea Holiday Park
★★★★★ 91% HOLIDAY PARK
tel: 01305 774414 Lynch Lane DT4 9DT
email: littlesea@haven.com web: www.haven.com/littlesea
dir: *A35 onto A354 signed Weymouth. Right at 1st roundabout, 3rd exit at 2nd roundabout towards Chickerell. Left into Lynch Lane after lights. Site at far end of road.*

Just three miles from Weymouth with its lovely beaches and many attractions, Littlesea has a cheerful family atmosphere and fantastic facilities. Indoor and outdoor entertainment and activities are on offer for all the family, and the toilet facilities on the touring park are modern and spotlessly clean as well as being nice and warm. The touring section of this holiday complex is at the far end of the site adjacent to the South West Coast Path in a perfect location. An excellent base for visiting the many attractions close to Weymouth and Portland.

Open: end March to end October (restricted service: end March to May and September to end October – facilities may be reduced) **Last arrival:** 20.30 **Last departure:** 10.00
Pitches: 🚐 🚗 ▲; 17 hardstanding pitches
Leisure: 🏊 ♨ ⛹ 👐 🎯 🎵 ⚽
Facilities: 🏠 ☺ 🚿 ✳ ♿ 🚽 🍽 🪑 🐕 WiFi
Services: ⚡ 🚰 🗑 🍴 🛒 🔒 🚰 ⓣ
Within 3 miles: ⛳ 🎣 ⛵ ◎ 🛒 🚲 🎡

Additional site information: 100 acre site. 🐕 No commercial vehicles, no bookings by persons under 21 years unless a family booking, no boats. Maximum 2 dogs per booking, certain dog breeds banned. Bakery, Starbucks, Papa John's®, fish and chips, adventure golf. Touring hardstandings – pea gravel topped.

Premier Park

Seaview Holiday Park
★★★★★ 88% HOLIDAY PARK
tel: 01305 832271 Preston DT3 6DZ
email: seaview@haven.com web: www.haven.com/parks/dorset/seaview
dir: *A354 to Weymouth, follow signs for Preston and Wareham onto A353. Site 3 miles on right just after Weymouth Bay Holiday Park.*

A fun-packed holiday park especially suited to families and for all ages, with plenty of activities and entertainment during the day or evening. Guests can use the facilities offered at the sister park, Weymouth Bay Holiday Park, which can be reached via a walkway from Seaview Holiday Park. There is a touring section for caravans, motorhomes and tents, the upper area having all fully serviced pitches, whilst the lower section is mainly for tents. There are also six fully-equipped safari tents in this area for anyone wishing to try a glamping experience.

Open: Mid March to end October (restricted service: Mid March to May and September to end October – some facilities may be reduced) **Last arrival:** Midnight **Last departure:** 10.00
Pitches: 🚐 🚗 ▲; 🏕 see prices below; 35 hardstanding pitches
Leisure: 🏊 ♨ ⛹ 👐 🎵 ⚽
Facilities: 🏠 ☺ 🚿 ♿ 🚽 🍽 🪑 WiFi
Services: ⚡ 🍴 🛒
Within 3 miles: ⛳ 🎣 ⛵ 🚲 🎡 ◎

Additional site information: 20 acre site. 🐕 No commercial vehicles, no bookings by persons under 21 years unless a family booking. Maximum 2 dogs per booking, certain dog breeds banned.

Glamping available: Safari tents from £125 (price for 3 nights).
Changeover days: Fridays and Mondays

Additional glamping information: Safari tents: minimum stay 3 nights. Kitchen equipment included.

Bagwell Farm Touring Park
★★★★ 93%
tel: 01305 782575 Knights in the Bottom, Chickerell DT3 4EA
email: aa@bagwellfarm.co.uk web: www.bagwellfarm.co.uk
dir: *From A354 follow signs for Weymouth town centre, then B3157 to Chickerell and Abbotsbury, 1 mile after Chickerell turn left into site 500 yards after Victoria Inn.*

This well located park is set in a small valley with access to the South West Coast Path and is very convenient for visiting Weymouth and Portland. It has excellent facilities including a good shop, pets' corner, children's play area plus the Red Barn bar and grill. A good range of hardstandings is available, including numerous super pitches which are very spacious and can take the longest units. This is an excellent place to stay at any time of the year.

Open: All year (restricted service: winter – bar closed) **Last arrival:** 21.00 **Last departure:** 11.00
Pitches: 🚐 🚗 ▲; 40 hardstanding pitches; 70 seasonal pitches
Leisure: ⛹
Facilities: 🏠 ☺ 🚿 ✳ ♿ 🚽 🍽 🪑 🐕 WiFi 💻
Services: ⚡ 🚰 🗑 🍴 🛒 🚰 🔒 ⓣ

Additional site information: 14 acre site. 🐕 Cars can be parked by caravans and tents. Awnings permitted. Families and couples only, no noise after 23.00. Wet suit shower, campers' shelter, dog wash. Car hire can be arranged.

Pebble Bank Caravan Park
★★★★ 91%

tel: 01305 774844 **Camp Road, Wyke Regis DT4 9HF**
email: info@pebblebank.co.uk **web:** www.pebblebank.co.uk
dir: *A354 to Weymouth, B3155 signed Portland. At lights into Wyke Road signed Wyke Regis. Straight on at roundabout, 1st left into Camp Road. Site on left. Or from Portesham take B3157 signed Weymouth. Right onto B3156 (Lanehouse Rocks Road). Right into Camp Road.*

This site, although only one and a half miles from Weymouth, is in a peaceful location overlooking Chesil Beach and The Fleet, and is an excellent place to stay. The bar and restaurant has an alfresco decking area and enjoys fabulous views. The toilet and shower block is very modern and spotlessly clean and there are 12 hardstandings available. The park is adjacent to the South West Coast Path, making it a good base for walkers.

Open: Easter to mid October (restricted service: bar open in high season and at weekends only) **Last arrival:** 18.00 **Last departure:** 11.00

Pitches: 🚐 🚗 ⛺
Leisure: 🎱
Facilities: 🛁 ☉ 🪒 ❄ ♿ 📶
Services: 🔌 🔄 🍽 🎂 🔒
Within 3 miles: ⚓ 🎣 ⛳ ◎ 🚣 🚴 🚌

Additional site information: 4 acre site. 🐕 Cars can be parked by caravans and tents. Awnings permitted.

West Fleet Holiday Farm
★★★ 92%

tel: 01305 782218 **Fleet DT3 4EF**
email: aa@westfleetholidays.co.uk **web:** www.westfleetholidays.co.uk
dir: *From Weymouth take B3157 towards Abbotsbury for 3 miles. Past Chickerell turn left at mini roundabout to Fleet, site 1 mile on right.*

A spacious farm site with both level and sloping pitches divided into paddocks and screened by hedges. This site has good views of the Dorset countryside, and is a relaxing place for a family holiday, particularly suited to tents, especially family-sized tents, and small motorhomes or campervans. The Barn Clubhouse has a bar, restaurant and entertainment area. There is an excellent and very popular outdoor swimming pool, which is great for families, and modern toilet facilities. WiFi is also available.

Open: Easter to September (restricted service: mid and low season – clubhouse closed; low season – pool closed) **Last arrival:** 19.00 **Last departure:** 11.00 (late departures available low and high season)

Pitches: 🚐 🚗 ⛺
Leisure: 🏊 🎱 🎵 ⚽
Facilities: 🛁 ☉ 🪒 ❄ ♿ 🛒 📶
Services: 🔌 🔄 🍽 🎂 🍔 🔋 ♻ 🚽
Within 3 miles: ⚓

Additional site information: 12 acre site. 🐕 Cars can be parked by caravans and tents. Awnings permitted. Non-family groups by arrangement only. Dogs restricted to certain areas. Site suitable for tents, campervans, motorhomes and caravans.

Rosewall Camping
★★★ 91%

tel: 01305 832248 **East Farm Dairy, Osmington Mills DT3 6HA**
email: holidays@weymouthcamping.com **web:** www.weymouthcamping.com
dir: *Take A353 towards Weymouth. At Osmington Mills sign (opposite garage) turn left, 0.25 mile, site on 1st right.*

This well-positioned sloping tent site, just a few miles to the east of Weymouth, is adjacent to the South West Coast Path and affords great sea views from virtually every pitch. There are excellent toilet and shower facilities including a block at the bottom of the campsite. There is a well-stocked shop and for those that like horse riding or are thinking of learning how to ride, there is Rosewall Equestrian Centre near the site entrance. This is a great place to bring a tent and makes a good base for exploring this area.

Open: Easter to October (restricted service: April to May and September to October – shop opening times vary) **Last arrival:** 22.00 **Last departure:** 11.00

Pitches: 🚗 ⛺
Leisure: 🎱 🎣
Facilities: 🛁 ☉ ❄ ♿ 🛒
Services: 🔄 🎂 🔒 ♻
Within 3 miles: 🚣 🚴 🚌

Additional site information: 13 acre site. 🐕 Cars can be parked by tents. Awnings permitted. Families and couples only, no noise after 23.00. Riding stables and coarse fishing.

Sea Barn Farm Camping Park
★★★ 85%

tel: 01305 782218 **Sea Barn Farm, Fleet Road, DT3 4ED**
email: aa@seabarnfarm.co.uk **web:** www.seabarnfarm.co.uk
dir: *From Weymouth take B3157 towards Abbotsbury for 3 miles. Past Chickerell turn left at mini-roundabout into Fleet Road, site 1 mile on left.*

This site is set high on the Dorset coast and has spectacular views over Chesil Beach, The Fleet and Lyme Bay, and it is also on the South West Coast Path. The pitches are sheltered by hedging, and there is an excellent toilet facility block, a motorhome service point, and plenty of space for outdoor games. This site is suitable for tents, small motorhomes, campervans and caravans.

Open: 15 March to early October **Last arrival:** 19.00 **Last departure:** 11.00 (Late departures available in low and mid season)

Pitches: 🚐 🚗 ⛺
Leisure: 🎱
Facilities: 🛁 ☉ 🪒 ❄ ♿ 🛒 📶
Services: 🔌 🔄 🚽 🔒 ♻
Within 3 miles: ⚓ 🎣 🚴 🚌

Additional site information: 12 acre site. 🐕 Cars can be parked by caravans and tents. Awnings permitted. Non-family groups by prior arrangement only. Dogs must be kept on leads at all times. No noise after 23.00. Gates locked at 23.00. Use of West Fleet facilities including outdoor pool, bar and restaurant (open in high season – dates on request).

FACILITIES: Electric vehicle charging · Baths/Shower · Electric shaver sockets · Hairdryer · Ice pack facility · Baby facilities · Disabled facilities · Shop on site or within 200yds · BBQ area · Picnic area · WiFi · Internet access **SERVICES:** Electric hook-up · Launderette · Licensed bar · Calor Gas · Campingaz · Toilet fluid · Café/Restaurant · Fast Food/Takeaway · Battery charging · Motorhome service point · No credit or debit cards · Dogs permitted · No dogs

DORSET–COUNTY DURHAM

WOOL
Map 4 SY88

Places to visit
Lulworth Castle & Park, LULWORTH, BH20 5QS, 01929 400352
www.lulworth.com/visit/places-to-visit/castle-and-park

Great for kids: Monkey World, WOOL, BH20 6HH, 01929 462537
monkeyworld.org

Premier Park

Whitemead Caravan Park
★★★★★ 90%

tel: 01929 462241 **East Burton Road BH20 6HG**
email: book@whitemeadcaravanpark.co.uk **web:** www.whitemeadcaravanpark.co.uk
dir: *From A352 (opposite petrol station) in Wool into East Burton Road signed East Burton. Site on right.*

This quality park situated in the village of Wool is well placed for visiting the many attractions of the area and also has the advantage of a train station within walking distance – a great alternative to driving and easy for visiting Poole or Weymouth. The facilities are excellent and spotlessly clean. There is a good shop selling basic provisions, wine and camping accessories. The site is also close to Bovington Tank Museum.

Open: 14 March to 31 October **Last arrival:** 18.00 (later arrivals by prior arrangement) **Last departure:** 10.30

Pitches: 🚐 🚙 ⛺; 10 hardstanding pitches; 40 grass pitches
Leisure: ⛰ 🎣
Facilities: 🏠 ⊙ 🚿 ✻ ♿ 🛒 🍽 📶
Services: 🔌 🗑 ♨ 🔒 🛢 📞
Within 3 miles: ⚓ ⛳

Additional site information: 5.5 acre site. 🐕 Cars can be parked by caravans and tents. Awnings permitted. No pit fires, no ball games. River walks, bridle path.

COUNTY DURHAM

BARNARD CASTLE
Map 19 NZ01

Places to visit
Barnard Castle, BARNARD CASTLE, DL12 8PR, 01833 638212
www.english-heritage.org.uk/visit/places/barnard-castle

The Bowes Museum, BARNARD CASTLE, DL12 8NP, 01833 690606
thebowesmuseum.org.uk

Pecknell Farm Caravan Park
★★★ 83%

tel: 01833 638357 **Lartington DL12 9DF**
web: www.pecknell.co.uk
dir: *1.5 miles from Barnard Castle. From A66 take B6277. Site on right 1.5 miles from junction with A67.*

Pecknell Farm Caravan Park is a family-run site set on a working farm, in beautiful rural meadowland, with spacious, marked pitches on level ground. There is a choice of grass or gravel hardstanding pitches, and some are equipped with electric hook-ups. The amenity block is heated and has four comfortable shower cubicles. There are many walking opportunities that start directly from this friendly site. Please note tents are not permitted here.

Open: April to October **Last arrival:** 20.00 **Last departure:** noon
Pitches: 🚐 🚙; 5 hardstanding pitches
Facilities: 🏠 ⊙ 🚿
Services: 🔌 🛢
Within 3 miles: ⚓ ⛳ 🎣 🏊 🏪 🍴 🛒

Additional site information: 1.5 acre site. 🐕 Cars can be parked by caravans. Awnings permitted. No noise after 22.30. Maximum of 2 dogs.

ESSEX

MERSEA ISLAND
Map 7 TM01

Places to visit

Layer Marney Tower, LAYER MARNEY, CO5 9US, 01206 330784
www.layermarneytower.co.uk

Premier Park

Waldegraves Holiday Park
★★★★★ 88% HOLIDAY PARK

tel: 01206 382898 & 381195 **CO5 8SE**
email: holidays@waldegraves.co.uk **web:** www.waldegraves.co.uk
dir: B1025 to Mersea Island. Cross Strood Channel via the causeway, take left fork to East Mersea. Take 2nd right and follow cream and brown Tourist Board signs to Waldegraves. What 3 Words ///prickly.teadrop.rift

A spacious and pleasant site located between farmland and its own private beach on the Blackwater Estuary. There are well-maintained standard grass pitches and a limited selection of hardstanding and serviced pitches — some have hedges that offer a greater level of privacy; the pitches are flat and spacious. There are excellent facilities including the restaurant, bar, shop, coarse fishing lakes, entertainment, a boat slipway, a heated outdoor swimming pool and WiFi.

Open: March to November (touring); 15 February to 15 January (static)
Last arrival: 22.00 **Last departure:** 13.00 (touring); 10.00 (static)
Pitches: 🚐 🚙 🛆; 26 hardstanding pitches; 100 seasonal pitches
Leisure: ♨ ♠ 🐟 ● ♪ 🎵 🎱 🐾 ⚽
Facilities: 🏪 ☉ 🅿 ✳ ♿ 🛁 🍳 🪑 🐕 WiFi 🖥
Services: 🔌 🗑 🍽 🍴 🚮 🧺 ⛽ 🚿 T
Within 3 miles: ⛳ ◉ 🏊 ♒

Additional site information: 25 acre site. 🐕 No groups of under 21s, 10mph speed limit, minimum noise after 23.00, no noise after midnight. Boating lake, slipway, driving range, crazy golf, foot golf, family games room, family entertainment. Car hire can be arranged.

Fen Farm Caravan Site
★★★★ 86%

tel: 01206 383275 **Moore Lane, East Mersea CO5 8FE**
email: havefun@fenfarm.co.uk **web:** www.fenfarm.co.uk
dir: B1025 from Colchester to Mersea Island, left signed East Mersea. 1st right after Dog and Pheasant pub into Moore Lane. (Note: road is tidal, please check tide times).

The first tents were pitched at Fen Farm in 1923 and over the years the farm gave way entirely to becoming a caravan park. Enjoying an enviable location beside the Blackwater Estuary, it has unique atmosphere with a mixture of meadow, woodland and marine shore, and varied wildlife to match each environment. There are two excellent solar-heated toilet blocks, which include three family rooms and privacy cubicles, with the newest block constructed in the local style of black clapboard and a red tile roof. There is a woodland dog walk and two well-equipped play areas, as well as a dog friendly beach and pub close by; crabbing in the beach pools is also a popular pastime. The site also offers an electric car charger.

Open: mid March to end October **Last arrival:** dusk
Pitches: 🚐 🚙 🛆; 80 seasonal pitches (plus 40 'bookable' pitches)
Leisure: ♨ ⚽
Facilities: 🔌 🏪 ☉ 🅿 ✳ ♿ 🛁 WiFi
Services: 🔌 🗑 🧺 🚿 ⛽ T
Within 3 miles: 🏊 ◉

Additional site information: 25 acre site. 🐕 Cars can be parked by caravans and tents. Awnings permitted. No open fires, no noise after 23.00. Electric car charger.

Make your next UK holiday one to remember

Choose RatedTrips.com

ENGLAND — ESSEX–GLOUCESTERSHIRE

ST OSYTH
Map 7 TM11

Places to visit

Beth Chatto Gardens, COLCHESTER, CO7 7DB, 01206 822007
www.bethchatto.co.uk

Colne Estuary National Nature Reserve, BRIGHTLINGSEA, 0300 060 3900
www.essexwt.org.uk/nature-reserves/colne-point

Great for kids: Colchester Zoo, COLCHESTER, CO3 0SL, 01206 331292
www.colchester-zoo.com

The Orchards Holiday Park
★★★★ 88% HOLIDAY PARK

tel: 01255 820651 **CO16 8LJ**
email: theorchards@haven.com **web:** www.haven.com/theorchards
dir: *From Clacton-on-Sea take B1027 towards Colchester. Left after petrol station, straight on at crossroads in St Osyth. Follow signs to Point Clear. Park in 3 miles.*

The Orchards offers good touring facilities with a centrally heated toilet block which includes a laundry, play area and two very spacious family rooms. The touring pitches are generously sized. There's also direct access to all the leisure, entertainment and dining outlets available on this large popular holiday park on the Essex coast.

Open: end March to end October (restricted service: end March to May and September to October – some facilities may be reduced) **Last arrival:** anytime **Last departure:** 10.00

Pitches: 🚐 🚙 ⛺
Leisure: (icons)
Facilities: (icons) WiFi
Services: (icons)
Within 3 miles: (icons)

Additional site information: 140 acre site. No commercial vehicles, no bookings by persons under 21 years unless a family booking. Maximum of 2 dogs per booking, certain dog breeds banned.

GLOUCESTERSHIRE

BERKELEY
Map 4 ST69

Places to visit

WWT Slimbridge Wetland Centre, SLIMBRIDGE, GL2 7BT, 01453 891900
www.wwt.org.uk/slimbridge

Dr Jenner's House, Museum and Garden, BERKELEY, GL13 9BN, 01453 810631
jennermuseum.com

Great for kids: Berkeley Castle, BERKELEY, GL13 9BQ, 01453 810303
www.berkeley-castle.com

Hogsdown Farm Caravan & Camping Park
★★★ 80%

tel: 01453 810224 **Hogsdown Farm, Lower Wick GL11 6DD**
web: www.hogsdownfarm.co.uk
dir: *M5 junction 14 (Falfield), A38 towards Gloucester. Through Stone and Woodford. After Newport turn right signed Lower Wick.*

A pleasant site with good toilet facilities, located between Bristol and Gloucester. It is well positioned for visiting Berkeley Castle and the Cotswolds, and makes an excellent overnight stop when travelling to or from the West Country.

Open: All year **Last arrival:** 21.00 **Last departure:** 16.00

Pitches: 🚐 🚙 ⛺; 12 hardstanding pitches
Leisure: (icon)
Facilities: (icons)
Services: (icons)
Within 3 miles: (icons)

Additional site information: 5 acre site. Cars can be parked by caravans and tents. Awnings permitted. No skateboards or bikes.

PITCHES: 🚐 Caravans 🚙 Motorhomes ⛺ Tents Glamping accommodation   **LEISURE:** Indoor swimming pool Outdoor swimming pool Children's playground Kids' club Tennis court Games room Separate TV room golf course Pitch n putt Boats for hire Bikes for hire Cinema Entertainment Fishing Mini golf Watersports Gym Sports field Stables Spa

GLOUCESTERSHIRE 153 ENGLAND

CHELTENHAM
Map 10 SO92

Places to visit
Holst Victorian House, CHELTENHAM, GL52 2AY, 01242 524846
holstvictorianhouse.org.uk

Sudeley Castle & Gardens, WINCHCOMBE, GL54 5JD, 01242 604244
sudeleycastle.co.uk

Briarfields Motel & Touring Park
★★★★ 91%

tel: 01242 235324 Gloucester Road GL51 0SX
email: reception@briarfields.net web: www.briarfields.net
dir: *M5 junction 11, A40 towards Cheltenham. At roundabout left onto B4063, site 200 metres on left.*

This is a well-designed, level, adults-only park, with a motel, where the facilities are modern and very clean. The amenity block has been fully upgraded and there's a real commitment towards sustainability across the park. It is well-positioned between Cheltenham and Gloucester, with easy access to the Cotswolds. And, being close to the M5, it makes a perfect overnight stopping point.

Open: All year **Last arrival:** 20.00 **Last departure:** 11.00
Pitches: 🚐 🚙 ⛺ 🏕 see prices below; 72 hardstanding pitches
Facilities: 🏠 ⊙ 🔥 ✳ ♿ 💲 🛒 WiFi
Services: 🔌 🧺 ⛽
Within 3 miles: ⛳ 🎣 ⛷ 🚴 🏇

Additional site information: 5 acre site. Adults only. 🚗 Cars can be parked by caravans and tents. Awnings permitted. No noise 22.00–08.00. Car hire can be arranged.

Glamping available: Pods from £50 per night.

Additional glamping information: Pods sleep two and include double or twin beds, electric sockets, USB sockets, fridge, microwave, kettle, table and chairs. Outdoor picnic area. Arrivals from 13.00, departures by 11.00. Cars can be parked by units

CIRENCESTER
Map 5 SP00

Places to visit
New Brewery Arts, CIRENCESTER, GL7 1JH, 01285 657181
www.newbreweryarts.org.uk

Corinium Museum, CIRENCESTER, GL7 2BX, 01285 655611
coriniummuseum.org

Mayfield Park
★★★★ 91%

tel: 01285 831301 & 07483 327535 Cheltenham Road GL7 7BH
email: enquiries@mayfieldpark.co.uk web: www.mayfieldpark.co.uk
dir: *In Cirencester at roundabout junction of A429 and A417, take A417 signed Cheltenham and A435. Right onto A435 signed Cheltenham, follow brown camping signs, pass golf course, site on left.*

A much improved and gently sloping park on the edge of the Cotswolds that offers level pitches and a warm welcome. Popular with couples and families, it has a reception area, a small shop selling essentials and offers well-appointed, fully serviced hardstanding pitches and caravans for hire. There is also a children's play area and dog exercising space. This lovely park makes an ideal base for exploring the Cotswolds and its many attractions, and for walking the nearby Monarch's Way and the Cotswold Way long-distance paths.

Open: All year
Pitches: 🚐 🚙 ⛺; 25 hardstanding pitches; 21 seasonal pitches
Leisure: 🎱 ⚽
Facilities: 🏠 ⊙ 🔥 ✳ ♿ 💲 🛒 WiFi 💻
Services: 🔌 🧺 🛒 ⛽ ♻ T
Within 3 miles: ⛳

Additional site information: 13 acre site. 🚗 Cars can be parked by caravans and tents. Awnings permitted. No bikes, scooters or skateboards, no noise after 23.00, minimum 3 nights stay for bank holidays.

SLIMBRIDGE
Map 4 SO70

Places to visit
WWT Slimbridge Wetland Centre, SLIMBRIDGE, GL2 7BT, 01453 891900
www.wwt.org.uk/wetland-centres/slimbridge

Great for kids: Berkeley Castle, BERKELEY, GL13 9BQ, 01453 810303
www.berkeley-castle.com

Tudor Caravan & Camping
★★★★ 88%

tel: 01453 890483 Shepherds Patch GL2 7BP
email: aa@tudorcaravanpark.co.uk web: www.tudorcaravanpark.com
dir: *M5 junctions 13 and 14, follow WWT Slimbridge Wetland Centre signs. Site at rear of Tudor Arms pub.*

Tudor Caravan & Camping park benefits from one of the best locations in the county, situated right alongside the Sharpness to Gloucester canal and just a short walk from the famous Wildfowl & Wetlands Trust at Slimbridge. The site has two areas, one for adults only, and a more open area with a facility block. There are both grass and gravel pitches complete with electric hook-ups. Being beside the canal, there are excellent walks plus the National Cycle Network route 41 can be accessed from the site. There is a pub and restaurant adjacent to the site.

Open: All year **Last arrival:** 20.00 **Last departure:** 11.00
Pitches: * 🚐 from £21; 🚙 from £21; ⛺ from £21; 48 hardstanding pitches; 4 seasonal pitches
Leisure: 🎣
Facilities: 🏠 ⊙ 🔥 ✳ ♿ 💲 🛒 🍴 WiFi 💻
Services: 🔌 🧺 🍽 🍴 🛒 ⛽ ♻ T
Within 3 miles: 🚴 🎣 🏇

Additional site information: 8 acre site. 🚗 Cars can be parked by caravans and tents. Awnings permitted. Debit cards accepted (no credit cards).

GREATER MANCHESTER

LITTLEBOROUGH   Map 16 SD91

Places to visit

Standedge Tunnel and Visitor Centre, MARSDEN, HD7 6NQ, 01484 844298
www.canalrivertrust.org.uk/places-to-visit/standedge-tunnel-and-visitor-centre

Hollingworth Lake Caravan Park
★★★ 75%

tel: 01706 378661 Round House Farm, Rakewood Road OL15 0AT
email: info@hollingworthlakecaravanpark.com **web:** hollingworthlakecaravanpark.com
dir: *From Littleborough or Milnrow (M62 junction 21), follow Hollingworth Lake Country Park signs to Fishermans Inn and The Wine Press. Take 'No Through Road' to Rakewood, then 2nd right.*

A popular park adjacent to Hollingworth Lake, at the foot of the Pennines, within easy reach of many local attractions. Backpackers walking the Pennine Way are welcome at this family-run park, and there are also large rally fields.

Open: All year **Last arrival:** 20.00 **Last departure:** noon
Pitches: 🚐 🚙 ⛺; 25 hardstanding pitches
Leisure: ⚽
Facilities: 🏠 ☺ ✻ ♿ 🛒 🍴
Services: 🔌 🚽 🧺 💧 🔒 ♻ 📞
Within 3 miles: 🎣 🚲 ⌔ ✈

Additional site information: 5 acre site. 🐕 Cars can be parked by caravans and tents. Awnings permitted. Family groups only. Maximum of 1 dog per pitch. Pony trekking.

HAMPSHIRE

BRANSGORE   Map 5 SZ19

Places to visit

Sammy Miller Museum, NEW MILTON, BH25 5SZ, 01425 620777
sammymiller.co.uk

Red House Museum & Gardens, CHRISTCHURCH, BH23 1BU, 01202 482860
www.hampshireculture.org.uk/red-house-museum-and-gardens

Great for kids: Moors Valley Country Park and Forest, RINGWOOD, BH24 2ET, 01425 470721
www.moors-valley.co.uk

Harrow Wood Farm Caravan Park
★★★★ 86%

tel: 01425 672487 Harrow Wood Farm, Poplar Lane BH23 8JE
email: harrowwood@caravan-sites.co.uk **web:** www.caravan-sites.co.uk
dir: *From Ringwood take B3347 towards Christchurch. At Sopley, left for Bransgore, to T-junction. Turn right. Straight on at crossroads. Left in 400 yards (just after garage) into Poplar Lane.*

A well laid-out, well-drained and spacious site in a pleasant rural position adjoining woodland and fields. Facilities are well appointed and very clean. Free on-site coarse fishing is available at this peaceful park. Well located for visiting Christchurch, the New Forest National Park and the south coast.

Open: March to early January **Last arrival:** 22.00 **Last departure:** noon
Pitches: 🚐 🚙 ⛺; 60 hardstanding pitches
Leisure: 🎣
Facilities: 🏠 ☺ 🍴 ✻ ♿ WiFi
Services: 🔌 🚽 🧺 💧 🔒
Within 3 miles: 🛒

Additional site information: 6 acre site. 🐕 Cars can be parked by caravans and tents. Awnings permitted. No open fires.

PITCHES: 🚐 Caravans 🚙 Motorhomes ⛺ Tents 🏠 Glamping accommodation **LEISURE:** Indoor swimming pool Outdoor swimming pool Children's playground Kids' club Tennis court Games room Separate TV room golf course Pitch n putt Boats for hire Bikes for hire Cinema Entertainment Fishing Mini golf Watersports Gym Sports field Stables Spa

HAMPSHIRE—HERTFORDSHIRE   ENGLAND

WARSASH   Map 5 SU40

Places to visit

Explosion Museum of Naval Firepower, GOSPORT, PO12 4LE, 023 9283 9766
www.nmrn.org.uk/visit-us/explosion-museum-naval-firepower

Portchester Castle, PORTCHESTER, PO16 9QW, 02392 378291
www.english-heritage.org.uk/visit/places/portchester-castle

Great for kids: Blue Reef Aquarium, PORTSMOUTH, PO5 3PB, 023 9287 5222
www.bluereefaquarium.co.uk/portsmouth

Dibles Park
★★★★   90%

tel: 01489 575132 **SO31 9SA**
email: dibles.park@btconnect.com **web:** www.diblespark.co.uk
dir: M27 junction, onto A3024 signed Southampton. At roundabout 1st left onto A27 signed Park Gate. 2.9 miles to roundabout with Esso garage on right. Take 3rd exit into Brook Lane signed Warsash. Straight on at 4 mini roundabouts. Park is 500 yards on left as road dips. (Note: sat nav not recommended as it can lead to a dead end). What 3 Words ////eased.bikes.ocean

Dibles Park is a small peaceful touring park adjacent to a private residential park. The facilities are excellent and spotlessly clean, and the spacious pitches are hardstanding with electric and can take the largest RVs. A warm welcome awaits visitors to this well-managed park, which is conveniently located for the Hamble, the Solent and is very well positioned for an overnight stay if heading for the cross-channel ferry port at Portsmouth, about 14 miles away. WiFi is available. It is close to local amenities and the park offers many excellent walks around the area.

Open: All year **Last arrival:** Late arrivals welcome **Last departure:** 11.00 (unless a pre-booked late stay)

Pitches: * from £29; from £29; 11 hardstanding pitches

Facilities:

Services:

Within 3 miles:

Additional site information: 0.75 acre site. Cars can be parked by caravans. Awnings permitted. No noise after 23.00, no children's ball games, no cycling, no scooters. No dog walking on site.

HERTFORDSHIRE

HODDESDON   Map 6 TL30

Places to visit

RSPB Rye Meads, STANSTEAD ABBOTTS, SG12 8JS, 01992 708383
www.rspb.org.uk/reserves-and-events/reserves-a-z/rye-meads

Lee Valley Caravan Park, Dobbs Weir
★★★★   81%

tel: 03000 030 619 **Charlton Meadows, Essex Road EN11 0AS**
email: dobbsweircampsite@leevalleypark.org.uk **web:** leevalleypark.org.uk/en/content/cms/where-to-stay-and-short-breaks/dobbs-weir-caravan-park
dir: From A10 follow Hoddesdon signs, at 2nd roundabout left signed Dobbs Weir. At next roundabout take 3rd exit. 1 mile to site on right.

This site provides much needed camping facilities close to London. Situated on level ground beside the River Lee, the park has a modernised toilet block with good facilities, a large timber chalet housing the reception and shop, and an extremely innovative motorhome service point. Wooden wigwams, family safari tents and luxury lodges are available to hire. On-site fishing is available and there's free WiFi.

Open: March to January **Last arrival:** 20.00 **Last departure:** 11.00 (late departures by prior arrangement)

Pitches: ; see prices below; 21 hardstanding pitches

Leisure:

Facilities:

Services:

Within 3 miles:

Additional site information: 11 acre site. Cars can be parked by caravans and tents. Awnings permitted. No commercial vehicles. Under 18s must be accompanied by an adult. Fire pit hire. Fresh produce in shop.

Glamping available: Wooden wigwams from £75; safari tents from £105.

Additional glamping information: Safari tents have cooking galleys. Cars can be parked by units.

Isle of Wight

There is a timeless quality to the Isle of Wight. For many it embodies the spirit and atmosphere of English seaside holidays over the years, and being an island, it has a unique and highly distinctive identity. Small and intimate – it's just 23 miles by 13 miles – it's a great place to get away-from-it-all, and with its mild climate, long hours of sunshine and colourful architecture, it has something of a continental flavour.

The Isle of Wight is probably most famous for the world's premier sailing regatta. Cowes Week, which takes place at the height of summer, is a key annual fixture in the country's sporting calendar, with the regatta drawing more than 1,000 boats and around 100,000 spectators. It is a hugely colourful event attracting Olympic veterans, weekend sailors and top names from the worlds of sport and the media. Various spectator boats offer good views of the action, but for something less hectic and more sedate, take to the island's 65-mile Coast Path, which offers a continual, unfolding backdrop of magnificent coastal scenery and natural beauty. The sea is seen at numerous points along the route and during Cowes Week, you get constant views of the energetic sailing activity. The regatta is held in the first week of August.

The Isle of Wight Coast Path is a good way to explore the island's varied coastline at any time of the year. Even in the depths of winter, the weather conditions are often favourable for walking. Much of the trail in the southern half of the island represents a relatively undemanding walk over majestic chalk downs. Beyond Freshwater Bay the coast is largely uninhabited with a palpable air of isolation. It is on this stretch that walkers can appreciate how the elements have shaped and weathered the island over many centuries. Away from the coast an intricate network of paths offers the chance to discover a rich assortment of charming villages, hidden valleys and country houses. In all, the Isle of Wight has more than 500 miles of public rights of way and over half the island is acknowledged as an Area of Outstanding Natural Beauty. There is an annual walking festival in May and a weekend walking festival in October. Cycling is also extremely popular here, with the Round the Island Cycle Route attracting many enthusiasts. The route runs for 49 miles and there are starting points at Yarmouth, Cowes and Ryde.

Away from walking and cycling, the Isle of Wight offers numerous attractions and activities. You could plan a week's itinerary on the island and not set foot on the beach. The island's history is a fascinating and crucial aspect of its story. It was long considered as a convenient stepping stone for the French in their plan to invade the mainland, and various fortifications – including Fort Victoria and Yarmouth Castle – reflect its key strategic role in the defence of our coastline. Carisbrooke Castle at Newport – the island's capital – is where Charles I was held before his execution in 1649.

The Isle of Wight has been a fashionable destination for the rich and famous over the years, and members of royalty made their home here. Queen Victoria and Prince Albert boosted tourism hugely when they chose the island as the setting for their summer home, Osborne House, which is now open to the public. Elsewhere, there are echoes of the Isle of Wight's fascinating literary links. Charles Dickens is said to have written six chapters of *David Copperfield* in the village of Bonchurch, near Ventnor, and the Victorian Poet Laureate Alfred Lord Tennyson lived at Faringford House, near Freshwater Bay. He claimed that the air on the coast here was worth 'sixpence a pint.'

◁ *Bembridge*

ISLE OF WIGHT

BRIGHSTONE   Map 5 SZ48

Places to visit

Mottistone Gardens, MOTTISTONE, PO30 4ED, 01983 741302
www.nationaltrust.org.uk/mottistone-gardens-and-estate

Grange Farm
★★★★ 79%

tel: 01983 740296 Grange Chine PO30 4DA
email: grangefarmholidays@gmail.com **web:** www.grangefarmholidays.com
dir: *From Freshwater Bay take A3055 towards Ventnor, 5 miles (pass Isle of Wight Pearl). Site in approximately 0.5 mile on right.*

This family-run site is set in a stunning location on the south-west coast of the island in Brighstone Bay. The range of facilities is very good. For children there is an imaginative play area and a wide range of animals to see including llamas, goats and a donkey. This site is right on the coastal path and ideally located for those who like walking and cycling. There are camping pods for hire plus static homes on a lower level by the beach.

Open: March to October **Last arrival:** noon **Last departure:** noon
Pitches: 8 hardstanding pitches
Facilities:
Services:
Within 3 miles:

Additional site information: 8 acre site. Cars can be parked by caravans and tents. Awnings permitted. No fires. Bakery.
Glamping available: Wooden pods.

FRESHWATER   Map 5 SZ38

Places to visit

Yarmouth Castle, YARMOUTH, PO41 0PB, 01983 760444
www.english-heritage.org.uk/visit/places/yarmouth-castle

Dimbola Museum & Galleries, FRESHWATER, PO40 9QE, 01983 756814
www.dimbola.co.uk

Great for kids: The Needles Park, ALUM BAY, PO39 0JD, 01983 752401
www.theneedles.co.uk

Heathfield Farm Camping
★★★★ 90%

tel: 01983 407822 Heathfield Road PO40 9SH
email: web@heathfieldcamping.co.uk **web:** www.heathfieldcamping.co.uk
dir: *2 miles west from Yarmouth ferry port on A3054, left to Heathfield Road, entrance 200 yards on right.*

Heathfield Farm Camping is a well located park in the far west of the island, perfect for visiting the Needles, Freshwater, Totland and Tennyson Down. There are large grass pitches offering plenty of space, and the facilities are modern, well appointed and very clean. There is also a good backpackers' area with picnic tables, and a good children's play area. The local town of Freshwater has an excellent supermarket and good range of shops. The closest ferry point is at Yarmouth but the site is easily reached from all ferry ports.

Open: May to September **Last arrival:** 1900 **Last departure:** 11.00
Pitches:
Leisure:
Facilities:
Services:
Within 3 miles:

Additional site information: 10 acre site. Cars can be parked by caravans and tents. Awnings permitted. Car hire can be arranged.

ISLE OF WIGHT 159 ENGLAND

NEWBRIDGE　　　　　　　　　　　　　Map 5 SZ48

Places to visit
Newtown Old Town Hall, NEWTOWN, PO30 4PA, 01983 531785
www.nationaltrust.org.uk/newtown-national-nature-reserve-and-old-town-hall

Great for kids: Yarmouth Castle, YARMOUTH, PO41 0PB, 01983 760444
www.english-heritage.org.uk/visit/places/yarmouth-castle

Platinum Park

The Orchards Holiday Caravan Park
★★★★★

tel: 01983 531331 & 531350 **Main Road PO41 0TS**
email: info@orchardsholidaypark.co.uk **web:** www.info@orchardsholidaypark.co.uk
dir: *A3054 from Yarmouth, right in 3 miles at Horse & Groom Inn. Follow signs to Newbridge. Entrance opposite post office. Or from Newport, 6 miles, via B3401.*

A really excellent, well-managed park set in a peaceful village location amid downs and meadowland, with glorious down land views. The pitches are terraced and offer a good provision of hardstandings, including those that are water serviced. There is a high quality facility centre offering really good, spacious showers and family rooms, plus there is access for less able visitors to all site facilities including disabled toilets. The park has indoor and outdoor swimming pools, a takeaway and licensed shop. Static homes are available for hire and sale and 'ferry plus stay' packages are on offer. The site is just 10 minutes from the Wightlink ferry terminal in Yarmouth and there are buses that stop at the site entrance every hour.

Open: 31 March to 30 October (restricted service: March to late May and mid/late September to October – outdoor pool closed) **Last arrival:** 23.00
Last departure: 11.00
Pitches: 52 hardstanding pitches
Leisure:
Facilities:
Services:
Within 3 miles:

Additional site information: 15 acre site. Cars can be parked by caravans and tents. Awnings permitted. No cycling. No noise after midnight. Table tennis room. Fin2Fit mermaid experience. Poolside coffee shop. Pool room. Arcade. Play areas. Football. Live music on Tuesday evenings. Car hire can be arranged.

RYDE　　　　　　　　　　　　　　　Map 5 SZ59

Places to visit
Nunwell House & Gardens, BRADING, PO36 0JQ, 01983 407240
www.nunwellhouse.co.uk

Bembridge Windmill, BEMBRIDGE, PO35 5SQ, 01983 873945
www.nationaltrust.org.uk/bembridge-windmill

Great for kids: Robin Hill Country Park, ARRETON, PO30 2NU, 01983 527352
www.robin-hill.com

RYDE　　　　　　　　　　　　　　　Map 5 SZ59

Platinum Park

Whitefield Forest Touring Park
★★★★★

tel: 01983 617069 **Brading Road PO33 1QJ**
email: pat&louise@whitefieldforest.co.uk **web:** www.whitefieldforest.co.uk
dir: *From Ryde follow A3055 towards Brading, after Tesco roundabout site in 0.5 mile on left.*

Whitefield Forest Touring Park is beautifully laid out in the Whitefield Forest, and offers a wide variety of pitches, including 45 fully serviced pitches. The site is conveniently located on a bus route. It offers excellent, modern facilities which are kept spotlessly clean. The park takes great care to retain the natural beauty of the forest and is a haven for wildlife; red squirrels can be spotted throughout the park. Two luxury lodges are available to book all year round and special rates for the ferry are available when booking either touring and camping or the lodges. Bookings can now be made online as well as over the phone.

Open: 4 April to 6 October **Last arrival:** 21.00 **Last departure:** 11.00
Pitches: * from £11.75; from £11.75; from £11; 45 hardstanding pitches
Leisure:
Facilities:
Services:
Within 3 miles:

Additional site information: 23 acre site. Cars can be parked by caravans and tents. Awnings permitted.

FACILITIES: Electric vehicle charging　Baths/Shower　Electric shaver sockets　Hairdryer　Ice pack facility　Baby facilities　Disabled facilities　Shop on site or within 200yds　BBQ area　Picnic area　WiFi　Internet access　**SERVICES:** Electric hook-up　Launderette　Licensed bar　Calor Gas　Campingaz　Toilet fluid　Café/Restaurant　Fast Food/Takeaway　Battery charging　Motorhome service point　No credit or debit cards　Dogs permitted　No dogs

ENGLAND — 160 — ISLE OF WIGHT

SHANKLIN
Map 5 SZ58

Places to visit
Shanklin Chine, SHANKLIN, PO37 6BW, 01983 866432
www.shanklinchine.co.uk

Ventnor Botanic Garden, VENTNOR, PO38 1UL, 01983 855397
www.botanic.co.uk

Great for kids: Dinosaur Isle, SANDOWN, PO36 8QA, 01983 404344
www.dinosaurisle.com

Ninham Country Holidays
★★★★ 93%

tel: 01983 864243 Ninham Farm, Ninham PO36 9PJ
email: office@ninham-holidays.co.uk **web:** www.ninham-holidays.co.uk
dir: Signed from A3056 (Newport to Sandown road).

Enjoying a beautiful woodland and arable farmland setting with fine country views, this delightful, spacious park is well-maintained and offers a good pitch layout. Ninham Country Holidays has a firm emphasis on sustainable tourism and being 'nature friendly'. Close by are the sea and good beaches. It has an excellent toilet and shower block; there is also a heated outdoor pool, a games room and a very good children's play area. Willow Brook, next to the reception is a separate camping area open only from July to September. This is a great place for families and is close to Shanklin and Sandown.

Open: May to September **Last arrival:** 20.00 **Last departure:** 10.00
Pitches:
Leisure:

Facilities:
Services:
Within 3 miles:

Additional site information: 10 acre site. Cars can be parked by caravans and tents. Awnings permitted. Recycling obligatory. No groups bookings. Families and couples only

WOOTTON BRIDGE
Map 5 SZ59

Places to visit
Osborne House, EAST COWES, PO32 6JX, 01983 200022
www.english-heritage.org.uk/visit/places/osborne

Carisbrooke Castle, CARISBROOKE, PO30 1XY, 01983 522107
www.english-heritage.org.uk/visit/places/carisbrooke-castle

Great for kids: Robin Hill Country Park, ARRETON, PO30 2NU, 01983 527352
www.robin-hill.com

Platinum Park

Woodside Bay Lodge Retreat
★★★★★ **HOLIDAY PARK**

tel: 01983 885220 **Lower Woodside Road PO33 4JT**
email: reception@woodside-bay.co.uk
web: www.darwinescapes.co.uk/woodside-bay-lodge-retreat
dir: From A3054 between Ryde and Newport, turn right into New Road, becomes Lower Woodside Road.

This luxury park is located on the north-east shore of the Isle of Wight near Wootton Bridge – the setting is absolutely fabulous and the sloping terrain offers lovely views over the Solent. The restaurant and its position on the park is ideal, and if the weather's good you can enjoy your meal or drinks on a covered veranda along with the views. There is a gym plus an alfresco eating area, The Braai. Accommodation offered is a variety of luxury fully-equipped lodges sleeping 4, 6 or 8 plus two spectacular tree houses that sleep two. Follow brown signs or the site information for directions.

Open: All year
Holiday Homes: Two-ring burner, Dishwasher, Washing Machine, Tumble dryer, Microwave, Freezer, TV, Sky/Freeview, DVD player, WiFi, Linen included, Towels included, Electricity included, Gas included
Leisure:
Facilities: WiFi
Within 3 miles:
Additional site information:

Kite Hill Farm Caravan & Camping Park
★★★ 86%
tel: 01983 883261 **Firestone Copse Road PO33 4LE**
email: welcome@kitehillfarm.co.uk web: www.kitehillfarm.co.uk
dir: *Signed from A3054 at Wootton Bridge, between Ryde and Newport.*

This traditional park, on a gently sloping field, is tucked away behind the owners' farm, just a short walk from the village and attractive river estuary. The facilities are of a good standard and very clean. This park provides a pleasant, relaxing atmosphere for a stay on the island and is well located for visiting Cowes and the many attractions on this part of the island. Rallies are welcome here.

Open: Late March to late October **Last arrival:** 18.00 **Last departure:** noon. Booking advised

Pitches: 🚐 🚗 ⛺

Leisure: 🎱

Facilities: 🚿 ⊙ ✳ ♿

Services: 🔌 🧺 🧴 🪵 🍃

Within 3 miles: 🎣 ⛳ U ◎ 🚴 ⛷ 📅 🏪

Additional site information: 12.5 acre site. 🐾 Cars can be parked by caravans and tents. Awnings permitted. Owners must clean up after their pets.

KENT

ASHFORD
Map 7 TR04

Places to visit
Kent & East Sussex Railway, TENTERDEN, TN30 6HE, 01580 765155
www.kesr.org.uk

Great for kids: Port Lympne Wild Animal Park, LYMPNE, CT21 4LR, 01303 264647
www.aspinallfoundation.org/port-lympne

Premier Park

Broadhembury Caravan & Camping Park
★★★★★ 92%

tel: 01233 620859 Steeds Lane, Kingsnorth TN26 1NQ
email: info@broadhembury.co.uk web: www.broadhembury.co.uk
dir: *M20 junction 10, A2070 towards Brenzett. Straight on at 1st roundabout. Left at 2nd roundabout (ignore fork left). Straight on at next roundabout. Left at 2nd crossroads in village.*

Broadhembury Caravan & Camping Park is a well-run and well-maintained small family park surrounded by open pasture; it is neatly landscaped with pitches sheltered by mature hedges. In the family area, there is a well-equipped campers' kitchen adjacent to the spotless, upgraded toilet facilities, bespoke wooden cabins for hire, and children will love the play areas, games room and football pitch. The adults-only area, close to the excellent reception building, includes popular fully serviced hardstanding pitches; this area has its own first-class, solar heated toilet block, and two well-equipped belle tents for hire.

Open: All year **Last arrival:** 7pm or within 1 hour of nightfall, if earlier. Later arrivals by prior arrangement only. **Last departure:** 12-noon (Touirng), 10.00am (Glamping & holiday homes). Later departures by prior arrangment only.

Pitches: from £26; from £26; from £26; 20 hardstanding pitches
Leisure:
Facilities:
Services:
Within 3 miles:

Additional site information: 10 acre site. Cars can be parked by caravans and tents. Awnings permitted. No noise after 22.00. Bakery, table tennis, pool, skittle alley and air hockey.

Glamping available: 5 bespoke luxury pods **Changeover days:** Any day
Additional glamping information: Bespoke luxury pods: minimum stay 2 nights. Double bed & 2 single beds. Fully equipped. Bed linen can be hired. BBQ and picnic table. Cars can be parked by units.

LEYSDOWN-ON-SEA
Map 7 TR07

Places to visit
RSPB Capel Fleet Raptor Viewpoint, LEYSDOWN-ON-SEA, ME12 4BG
01634 222480
rspb.org.uk/reserves-and-events/reserves-a-z/capel-fleet

Priory Hill
★★★ 75%

tel: 01795 510267 Wing Road ME12 4QT
email: touringpark@prioryhill.co.uk web: www.prioryhill.co.uk
dir: *M2 junction 5, A249 signed Sheerness, then A2500 to Eastchurch, then B2231 to Leysdown, follow brown tourist signs.*

A small well-maintained touring area on an established family-run holiday park close to the sea, with views of the north Kent coast. Amenities include a clubhouse and a swimming pool. The pitch price includes membership of the clubhouse with live entertainment, and use of the indoor swimming pool.

Open: March to October **Last arrival:** 18.00 **Last departure:** noon
Pitches:
Leisure:
Facilities:
Services:
Within 3 miles:

Additional site information: 1.5 acre site. Cars can be parked by caravans and tents. Awnings permitted. Cakes and fresh coffee available. Fresh bread and pastries baked daily.

KENT

MARDEN
Map 6 TQ74

Places to visit

Scotney Castle, LAMBERHURST, TN3 8JN, 01892 893820
www.nationaltrust.org.uk/scotney-castle

Premier Park

Tanner Farm Touring Caravan & Camping Park

★★★★★ 91%

tel: 01622 832399 Tanner Farm, Goudhurst Road TN12 9ND
email: enquiries@tannerfarmpark.co.uk web: www.tannerfarmpark.co.uk
dir: From A21 or A229 onto B2079. Midway between Marden and Goudhurst.

At the heart of a 150-acre Wealden farm, this extensive, long-established touring park is peacefully tucked away down a quiet farm drive deep in unspoilt Kent countryside, yet close to Sissinghurst Castle and within easy reach of London (Marden station is three miles away). Perfect for families, as it has two excellent play areas, a football field and a recreation/wet weather room (with TV). It offers quality toilet blocks with privacy cubicles, a good shop, spacious hardstandings (12 fully serviced), and high levels of security and customer care. There is a camping meadow with 20 pitches (all with water and electric), and luxury yurts are planned in the adjoining woodland. Dogs are welcome and there are some excellent walks leading directly from the park. Two camping pods are available for hire.

Open: All year (restricted service: winter months – no tents accepted)
Last arrival: 20.00 **Last departure:** noon

Pitches: 34 hardstanding pitches; 13 seasonal pitches

Leisure:

Facilities:

Services:

Within 3 miles:

Additional site information: 15 acre site. Cars can be parked by caravans and tents. Awnings permitted. No groups, 1 car per pitch, no commercial vehicles. Recreation room with table football and TV. Woodland walks.

Glamping available: Wooden pods.

Additional glamping information: Wooden pods sleep 2. Minimum stay 2 nights Friday to Sunday. Cars can be parked by units

ROCHESTER
Map 6 TQ76

Places to visit

Guildhall Museum, ROCHESTER, ME1 1PY, 01634 332900
www.medway.gov.uk/info/200182/arts_and_heritage/316/historic_places_in_medway

Upnor Castle, UPNOR, ME2 4XG, 01634 718742
www.english-heritage.org.uk/visit/places/upnor-castle

Great for kids: Diggerland, STROOD, ME2 2NU, 0871 227 7007 (calls cost 10p per minute plus your phone company's access charge)
www.diggerland.com/days-out-in-kent-diggerland

Premier Park

Kent Coast Leisure Park
★★★★★ 93% HOLIDAY PARK

tel: 01634 270785 Allhallows-on-Sea ME3 9QD
web: www.haven.com/parks/kent/kent-coast
dir: M25 junction 2, A2 signed Rochester, A289 signed Gillingham. A228 signed Grain. Follow site signs.

Located in a peaceful country park setting beside the Thames estuary close to Rochester, just an hour's drive from London, Allhallows is a popular static-only holiday park. It offers a wide range of sporting and leisure activities for all the family, including swimming pools, tennis courts, a 9-hole golf course, a fishing lake and fencing. Children will love the kids' club and play area, while there is a restaurant and bar with evening entertainment for adults. Recent developments include the Adventure Village and the Marina bar and stage venue.

Open: March to October **Last arrival:** 24-hour check in **Last departure:** 10.00

Holiday Homes: Sleep 8, Bedrooms 2, Bathrooms 1, Toilets 1, Two-ring burner, Dishwasher, Microwave, Freezer, TV, Sky/Freeview, DVD player, WiFi, Linen included, Electricity included, Gas included

Leisure:

Facilities:

Within 3 miles:

Additional site information: 188 acre site. The facilities provided in the holiday homes may differ depending on the grade. Most dog breeds accepted (please check when booking). Dogs must be kept on leads at all times. Towels and garden furniture available for hire.

Make your next UK holiday one to remember

Choose RatedTrips.com

AA

FACILITIES: Electric vehicle charging | Baths/Shower | Electric shaver sockets | Hairdryer | Ice pack facility | Baby facilities | Disabled facilities | Shop on site or within 200yds | BBQ area | Picnic area | WiFi | Internet access **SERVICES:** Electric hook-up | Launderette | Licensed bar | Calor Gas | Campingaz | Toilet fluid | Café/Restaurant | Fast Food/Takeaway | Battery charging | Motorhome service point | No credit or debit cards | Dogs permitted | No dogs

KENT—LANCASHIRE

WHITSTABLE — Map 7 TR16

Places to visit
Westgate Towers Museum & Viewpoint, CANTERBURY, CT1 2BZ, 01227 808755
www.onepoundlane.co.uk/westgate-towers

Great for kids: Druidstone Park, CANTERBURY, CT2 9JR, 01227 765168
www.druidstone.net

Homing Park
★★★★ 87%

tel: 01227 771777 Church Lane, Seasalter CT5 4BU
email: info@homingpark.co.uk **web:** www.homingpark.co.uk
dir: Exit A299 for Whitstable and Canterbury, left at brown camping-caravan sign into Church Lane. Site entrance has 2 large flag poles.

A small touring park close to Seasalter Beach and Whitstable, which is famous for its oysters. All pitches are generously sized and fully serviced, and most are separated by hedging and shrubs. A clubhouse and swimming pool are available on site with a small cost for the use of the swimming pool. Wooden camping pods, for four or six people, are available for hire; their design of outwardly sloping walls adds to the internal space.

Open: Easter to October **Last arrival:** 20.00 **Last departure:** 11.00

Pitches: 🚐 🚙 ⛺; 🛖 see prices below

Leisure: 🏊 ⛹ 🎾

Facilities: 🚿 ☺ 🅿 ✳ ♿ WiFi

Services: 🔌 🗑 🚽 🍽 🛒

Within 3 miles: 🎣 🚴 ⛴ 🏪

Additional site information: 12.6 acre site. 🚗 Cars can be parked by caravans and tents. Awnings permitted. No commercial vehicles, no tents larger than 8 berths or 5 metres wide, no unaccompanied minors, no cycles or scooters.

Glamping available: Wooden pods from £35. **Changeover days:** Any day

Additional glamping information: Minimum stay 2 nights (3 nights at bank holiday weekends). Cars can be parked by units

LANCASHIRE

BLACKPOOL — Map 18 SD33

Places to visit
Madame Tussauds Blackpool, BLACKPOOL, FY1 5AA, www.madametussauds.com/blackpool

Great for kids: Blackpool Zoo, BLACKPOOL, FY3 8PP, 01253 830830
www.blackpoolzoo.org.uk

Premier Park

Marton Mere Holiday Village
★★★★★ 87% HOLIDAY PARK

tel: 01253 767544 Mythop Road FY4 4XN
web: www.haven.com/martonmere
dir: M55 junction 4, A583 towards Blackpool. Right at Clifton Arms lights into Mythop Road. Site 150 yards on left.

A very attractive holiday park in an unusual setting on the edge of the mere, with plenty of birdlife to be spotted. The site has a stylish Mediterranean seaside-themed Boathouse Restaurant and the on-site entertainment is tailored for all ages, and includes a superb show bar. There's a regular bus service into Blackpool for those who want to explore further afield. The separate touring area is well equipped with hardstandings and electric pitches.

Open: mid March to end October (restricted service: March to end May and September to October – reduced facilities, splash zone closed) **Last arrival:** 22.00 **Last departure:** 10.00

Pitches: 🚐 🚙; 82 hardstanding pitches

Leisure: 🏊 ⛹ 👋 🎵

Facilities: 🚿 ☺ 🅿 ✳ ♿ 🏪 🍴 WiFi 💻

Services: 🔌 🗑 🚽 🍽 🛒 🔒 🧺

Within 3 miles: 🎣 🚴 ⛳ 🎯 ⛴ 🏌 ♨ 📅

Additional site information: 30 acre site. 🚗 No commercial vehicles, no bookings by persons under 21 years unless a family booking. Maximum of 2 dogs per booking, certain dog breeds banned. 24-hour on-site team.

BOLTON-LE-SANDS — Map 18 SD46

Places to visit
Lancaster Maritime Museum, LANCASTER, LA1 1RB, 01524 382264
www.lancaster.gov.uk/sport-and-leisure/museums/maritime-museum

Lancaster City Museum, LANCASTER, LA1 1HT, 01524 64637
www.lancaster.gov.uk/sport-and-leisure/museums/city-museum

Great for kids: Lancaster Castle, LANCASTER, LA1 1YJ, 01524 64998
www.lancastercastle.com

LANCASHIRE 165 ENGLAND

BOLTON-LE-SANDS
Map 18 SD46

Premier Park

Bay View Holiday Park
★★★★★ 88%

tel: 01524 732854 & 701508 **LA5 9TN**
email: info@holgates.co.uk web: www.holgates.co.uk
dir: *M6 junction 25, A6 through Carnforth to Bolton-le-Sands. Site on right.*

A high quality, family-oriented seaside destination with fully serviced, all-weather pitches, many of which have views of Morecambe Bay and the Cumbrian hills. In addition to the superb amenity block, just one of the park's many facilities is a stylish bar/restaurant featuring local produce and providing a dog-friendly area, an arcade room, and an outdoor playing area. There is a wide range of activities and attractions on offer within a few miles. Two luxury en suite pods (one dog-friendly) are available to hire. This makes a good choice for a family holiday by the sea.

Bay View Holiday Park

Open: All year (restricted service: at quieter times – restaurant and bar reduced hours)
Last arrival: 20.00 **Last departure:** noon
Pitches: 25 hardstanding pitches; 127 seasonal pitches
Leisure:
Facilities:
Services:
Within 3 miles:

Additional site information: 40 acre site. Cars can be parked by caravans and tents. Awnings permitted. No noise after 23.00. Car hire can be arranged.

Glamping available: 2 en suite pods (1 is dog friendly).
Changeover days: Monday, Friday and Saturday

Additional glamping information: Wooden pods (sleep 2 adults and 3 small children) offer light, heater, electrical sockets and pull-out bed/sofa.

See advert below

FACILITIES: Electric vehicle charging Baths/Shower Electric shaver sockets Hairdryer Ice pack facility Baby facilities Disabled facilities Shop on site or within 200yds BBQ area Picnic area WiFi Internet access **SERVICES:** Electric hook-up Launderette Licensed bar Calor Gas Campingaz Toilet fluid Café/Restaurant Fast Food/Takeaway Battery charging Motorhome service point No credit or debit cards Dogs permitted No dogs

ENGLAND — 166 LANCASHIRE

BOLTON-LE-SANDS *continued*

Red Bank Farm
★★★ 84%

tel: 01524 823196 **LA5 8JR**
email: mark.archer@hotmail.co.uk web: www.redbankfarm.co.uk
dir: *From Morecambe take A5015 towards Carnforth. After Hest Bank left into Pastures Lane (follow brown site sign). Over rail bridge, right (follow site sign). At T-junction left into The Shore to site at end.*

The gently sloping grassy field with mature hedges at Red Bank Farm is right on the seashore and set beside a RSPB reserve. This farm site has smart toilet facilities, a superb view across Morecambe Bay to the distant Lake District hills and is popular with tenters. The delightful Archers Café, with a timbered alfresco eating, serves a good range of cooked food, including home-reared marsh lamb dishes.

Open: March to mid December **Last arrival:** 22.00
Pitches: **Facilities:** **Within 3 miles:**
Services:
Additional site information: 3 acre site. Cars can be parked by tents. Awnings permitted. No noise after 22.30. Pets' corner.

CAPERNWRAY Map 18 SD57

Places to visit
Leighton Hall, CARNFORTH, LA5 9ST, 01524 734474
www.leightonhall.co.uk

RSPB Leighton Moss & Morecambe Bay Nature Reserve, SILVERDALE, LA5 0SW, 01524 701601
www.rspb.org.uk/reserves-and-events/reserves-a-z/leighton-moss

---

Platinum Park

Old Hall Caravan Park
★★★★★

tel: 01524 733276 **LA6 1AD**
email: hello@oldhallcaravanpark.co.uk web: www.oldhallcaravanpark.co.uk
dir: *M6 junction 35, A601(M) follow signs for Over Kellet, at T-junction left onto B6254. In Over Kellet left at village green signed Capernwray. Site 1.5 miles on right.*

Old Hall Caravan Park is a lovely secluded park set in a clearing among trees, at the end of a half-mile-long drive. This peaceful park is home to a wide variety of wildlife, and there are marked walks in the woods. The reception and administration block is at the edge of the touring areas. All pitches are fully serviced and the stylish amenity block contains superb combined shower, toilet and washbasin rooms with excellent fixtures and fittings. The facilities are well maintained by the friendly owners, and booking is advisable. Please note, on bank holidays a minimum stay of three nights is required.

Open: 1 March to 1 December (restricted service: December to March — seasonal tourers can stay longer by prior arrangement) **Last arrival:** 20:00
Last departure: 12 noon
Pitches: * from £36; from £36; 38 hardstanding pitches; 30 seasonal pitches
Leisure: **Facilities:**
Services: **Within 3 miles:**
Additional site information: 3 acre site. Cars can be parked by caravans. Awnings permitted. No skateboards, scooters, rollerblades or roller boots. Woodland walk, information room.

CARNFORTH Map 18 SD47

Places to visit
Warton Old Rectory, Main Street, Warton, Carnforth, Lancashire, LA5 9PH, www.english-heritage.org.uk/visit/places/warton-old-rectory

Leighton Hall, Carnforth, Lancashire, LA5 9ST, 01524 734474
www.leightonhall.co.uk

Premier Park

Marsh House Holiday Park
★★★★★ 86%

tel: 01524 732854 & 701508 **Marsh House Farm LA5 9JA**
email: marshhouse@holgates.co.uk web: www.holgates.co.uk/our-parks/marsh-house

Situated close to the Lancashire/Cumbria border on the outskirts of Carnforth, a picturesque market town, the park is a welcoming holiday destination for seasonal touring and static holiday home ownership. All pitches are fully serviced and a stylish amenity block provides excellent privacy options. A choice of restaurants, shops and supermarkets is located nearby in Carnforth, Bolton-le-Sands and the historic city of Lancaster. Further afield, you will find the Lake District, Kendal and Forest of Bowland, ideal for days of endless exploring.

Open: All year (restricted service: touring March to November only)
Facilities: **Services:**
Additional site information: 10 acre site. Cars can be parked by caravans. Awnings permitted.

See advert opposite

LANCASHIRE 167 ENGLAND

COCKERHAM
Map 18 SD45

Places to visit
Lancaster Cathedral, LANCASTER, LA1 3BT, 01524 384820
www.lancastercathedral.org.uk

Moss Wood Caravan Park
★★★★ 91%

tel: 01524 791041 **Crimbles Lane LA2 0ES**
email: info@mosswood.co.uk web: www.mosswood.co.uk
dir: *M6 junction 33, A6, approximately 4 miles to site. From Cockerham take west A588. Left into Crimbles Lane to site.*

A tree-lined grassy park with sheltered, level pitches, located on peaceful Cockerham Moss. A spacious, air-conditioned, licensed shop at the entrance stocks a variety of local produce including cheeses, smoked bacon and ales. The modern amenity block provides excellent standards and good privacy with cubicled washing units, plus there's a launderette. Two private lakes are also available for coarse fishing enthusiasts.

Open: March to October **Last arrival:** 20.00 **Last departure:** 16.00

Pitches: ; 31 hardstanding pitches; 12 seasonal pitches

Leisure:

Facilities: WiFi

Services:

Within 3 miles:

Additional site information: 25 acre site. Cars can be parked by caravans. Awnings permitted. Woodland walks, fishing lake, nature trail.

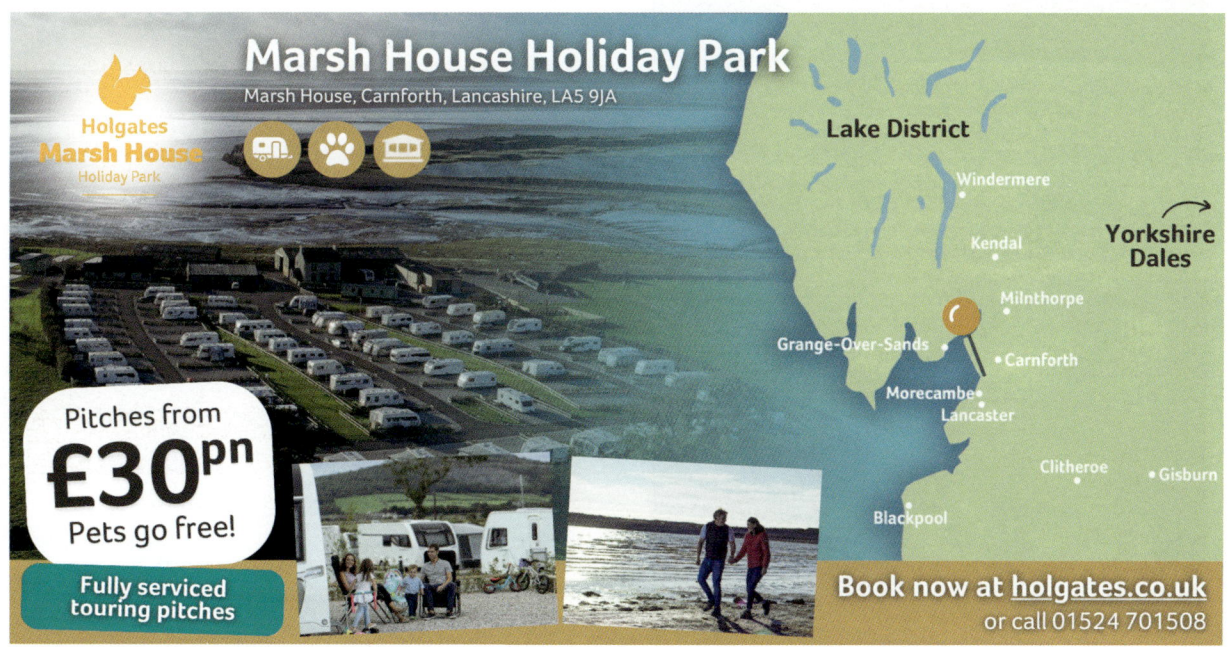

FACILITIES: Electric vehicle charging Baths/Shower Electric shaver sockets Hairdryer Ice pack facility Baby facilities Disabled facilities Shop on site or within 200yds BBQ area Picnic area WiFi Internet access **SERVICES:** Electric hook-up Launderette Licensed bar Calor Gas Campingaz Toilet fluid Café/Restaurant Fast Food/Takeaway Battery charging Motorhome service point No credit or debit cards Dogs permitted No dogs

ENGLAND 168 LANCASHIRE

FAR ARNSIDE
Map 18 SD47

Places to visit
Rufford Old Hall, RUFFORD, L40 1SG, 01704 821254
www.nationaltrust.org.uk/rufford-old-hall

RSPB Leighton Moss & Morecambe Bay Nature Reserve, SILVERDALE, LA5 0SW, 01524 701601
www.rspb.org.uk/reserves-and-events/reserves-a-z/leighton-moss

Premier Park

Hollins Farm Holiday Park
★★★★★ 91%

tel: 01524 701767 & 701508 **LA5 0SL**
email: reception@holgates.co.uk web: www.holgates.co.uk
dir: *M6 junction 35, A601 (Carnforth). Left in 1 mile at roundabout to Carnforth. Right in 1 mile at lights signed Silverdale. Left in 1 mile into Sands Lane, signed Silverdale. 2.4 miles over auto-crossing, 0.3 mile to T-junction. Right, follow signs to site, in approximately 3 miles take 2nd left after passing Holgates.*

Hollins Farm is a long-established park that continues to be upgraded by the owners. There are fully serviced hardstanding pitches for tourers and fully serviced tent pitches; the excellent amenity block provides very good facilities and privacy options. It has a traditional family camping feel and offers high standard facilities; most pitches have views towards Morecambe Bay or fields, and WiFi is available throughout the park. A mini glamping village with quality pods is located in a carefully hedge-screened area and leisure and recreation facilities are available at nearby sister park Silverdale. The park is open all year.

Open: All year **Last arrival:** 20.00 **Last departure:** noon
Pitches: 🚐 🚍 ⛺; 🛖 see prices below; 5 hardstanding pitches; 38 seasonal pitches
Leisure: 🛝 ⚽ 🎮
Facilities: 🚿 ⊙ ✳ ♿ 🍳 WiFi
Services: 🚰 🗑 ⬇ 🔒 ⛽ T
Within 3 miles: ↯ ⌕ ∪ ◎ ≈ 🛒

Additional site information: 30 acre site. 🐕 Cars can be parked by caravans and tents. Awnings permitted. No unaccompanied children, no fire pits or chimeneas, no gazebos, no commercial vehicles at reception after unloading, no noise after 22.30.
Glamping available: Wooden pods from £90.
Additional glamping information: Wooden pods offer sofa bed and heater.

See advert opposite

FLEETWOOD
Map 18 SD34

Places to visit
Blackpool Zoo, BLACKPOOL, FY3 8PP, 01253 830830
www.blackpoolzoo.org.uk

Premier Park

Cala Gran Holiday Park
★★★★★ 86% HOLIDAY PARK

tel: 01253 872555 **Fleetwood Road FY7 8JY**
web: www.haven.com/parks/blackpool/cala-gran
dir: *M55 junction 3, A585 signed Fleetwood. At 4th roundabout (Nautical College on left) take 3rd exit. Park 250 yards on left.*

Cala Gran is a lively holiday park close to Blackpool with a range of quality holiday caravans. The park is all about fun, and the entertainment includes live music, comedy shows and resident DJs, while for children there are swimming pools and a SplashZone, a pick and paint room, climbing wall, and also a sports range for supervised archery and fencing.

Open: mid March to 30 October

Holiday Homes: Sleep 8, Bedrooms 2, Bathrooms 1, Toilet 1, Microwave, Freezer, TV, Sky/Freeview
Leisure: 🏊 🛝 ⚽ 🎾 🎵 🐕
Facilities: 🛒 🍴 WiFi 💻
Within 3 miles: ↯ ◎ 日

Additional site information: 🐕 The facilities provided in the holiday homes may differ depending on the grade. Most dog breeds accepted (please check when booking). Dogs must be kept on leads at all times. All-weather sports court.

PITCHES: 🚐 Caravans 🚍 Motorhomes ⛺ Tents 🛖 Glamping accommodation **LEISURE:** 🏊 Indoor swimming pool 🏊 Outdoor swimming pool 🛝 Children's playground 👦 Kids' club 🎾 Tennis court ⚽ Games room 📺 Separate TV room ⛳ golf course 🏌 Pitch n putt 🚣 Boats for hire 🚲 Bikes for hire 🎬 Cinema 🎵 Entertainment 🎣 Fishing ⛳ Mini golf 🏄 Watersports 🏋 Gym ⚽ Sports field ∪ Stables ♨ Spa

LANCASHIRE 169 ENGLAND

GARSTANG
Map 18 SD44

Places to visit
Lancaster Maritime Museum, LANCASTER, LA1 1RB, 01524 382264
www.lancaster.gov.uk/sport-and-leisure/museums/maritime-museum

Lancaster City Museum, LANCASTER, LA1 1HT, 01524 64637
www.lancaster.gov.uk/sport-and-leisure/museums/city-museum

Great for kids: Lancaster Castle, LANCASTER, LA1 1YJ, 01524 64998
www.lancastercastle.com

Bridge House Marina & Caravan Park
★★★★ 91%

tel: 01995 603207 Nateby Crossing Lane, Nateby PR3 0JJ
email: info@bridgehousemarina.co.uk web: www.bridgehousemarina.co.uk
dir: *Exit A6 at pub and Knott End sign, immediately right into Nateby Crossing Lane, over canal bridge to site on left.*

A family-run site set in the attractive countryside by the Lancaster Canal. You will drive through an extensive boatyard to arrive at this carefully landscaped park. It has excellent hardstanding pitches, some of which are fully serviced, a motorhome service point and a superb modern amenity block offering excellent quality and privacy. Four-legged friends are also welcomed; there is a separate dog washroom and a fenced dog exercise area. Drinks and food can be ordered from the café next to reception. Do not miss the modern games room, fishing pond and the children's tower play area.

Open: March to 4 January **Last arrival:** 22.00 **Last departure:** 13.00

Pitches: 42 hardstanding pitches; 20 seasonal pitches

Leisure:

Facilities:

Services:

Within 3 miles:

Additional site information: 4 acre site. Cars can be parked by caravans. Awnings permitted.

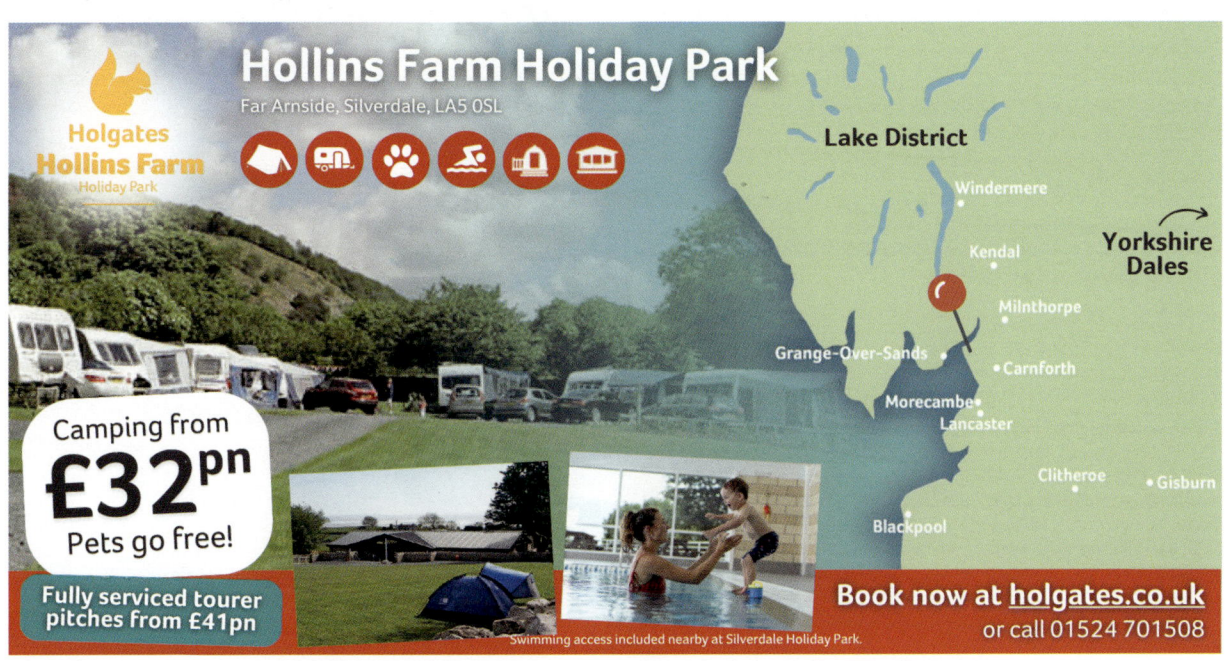

GISBURN
Map 18 SD84

Places to visit
Sawley Abbey, CLITHEROE, BB7 4NH, 0370 333 1181
www.english-heritage.org.uk/visit/places/sawley-abbey

Platinum Park

Hedgerow Luxury Glamping
★★★★★ GLAMPING ONLY

tel: 07828 311422 Knott Lane, Newsholme BB7 4JF
email: info@hedgerowluxuryglamping.com web: www.hedgerowluxuryglamping.com
dir: *M65 junction 13, A682, 8 miles to Gisburn. Right onto A59 (Main Street). At roundabout 1st exit onto A682 for 2 miles. Right into Knott Lane, site 2 miles on left. Using postcode BB7 4JF on sat nav takes you to Knott Lane. What 3 Words: ///giggles.geology.situates.*

Hedgerow Luxury Glamping is an adult-only site located on a dairy farm, surrounded by fields, meadows, and hedgerows (of course). The pods are very private and offer high levels of comfort with all the equipment needed for a relaxing stay. They all have dishwashers and private bathrooms, and some even have dressing rooms and saunas. The beds are sumptuous, and you can also relax in the individual hot tubs or enjoy an evening beside the fire. There's also a communal kitchen and a cosy 'firepit cabin' for community gatherings. The 'honesty shop' offers a range of essentials as well as homemade and local produce. Guests are also welcome to collect eggs from 'Cluckingham Palace' for their breakfasts every morning. The adjacent fields are home to alpacas and a couple of Highland cattle.

Open: All year **Last arrival:** 21.00 (later arrivals via codepad) **Last departure:** 10.00
Facilities:
Within 3 miles:
Accommodation available: 1.5 acre site. 2 adults per pod. Scandinavian fire den.
Changeover days: Monday, Thursday, Friday
Additional site information: 1.5 acre site. Adults only. Scandinavian fire den. No pets. Linen and towels supplied. All pods are en suite and have underfloor heating, king-size bed, dishwasher, hob, microwave, coffee machine, BBQ, fire pit, and private patio. Cars can be parked by units

GREENHALGH
Map 18 SD43

Charoland Farm Caravan Site
★★★★ 85%

tel: 07876 196434 & 01253 836595 Greenhalgh Lane, Greenhalgh PR4 3HL
email: enquiries@charolandfarm.co.uk web: www.charolandfarm.co.uk
dir: *Exit M55 junction 3 onto A585 signed Fleetwood. Left into Greenhalgh Lane.*

A hedge-screened, adults-only and dog-friendly touring park based on an award-winning beef cattle and sheep farm. It is ideally located for touring the plentiful Fylde Coast attractions and close to many shops and restaurants. All pitches have hardstandings, electric hook up and water supply and are surrounded by attractive shrubs and flowers; cosy BBQ/picnic area with a small raised pond is also provided by the caring owners Walter and Jane. Please note that there is no laundry facility at this park.

Open: 1 March to 31 October **Last arrival:** 20.00 **Last departure:** 11.00
Pitches: ; 10 hardstanding pitches
Facilities:
Services:
Within 3 miles:
Additional site information: 0.5 acre site. Adults only. Cars can be parked by caravans. Awnings permitted. No commercial vehicles or vans. No fifth wheel caravans. Pets by prior arrangement.

LANCASTER
Map 18 SD46

Places to visit
Lancaster Maritime Museum, LANCASTER, LA1 1RB, 01524 382264
www.lancaster.gov.uk/sport-and-leisure/museums/maritime-museum

Lancaster City Museum, LANCASTER, LA1 1HT, 01524 64637
www.lancaster.gov.uk/sport-and-leisure/museums/city-museum

Great for kids: Lancaster Castle, LANCASTER, LA1 1YJ, 01524 64998
www.lancastercastle.com

New Parkside Farm Caravan Park
★★★ 83%

tel: 015247 70723 Denny Beck, Caton Road LA2 9HH
email: enquiries@newparksidefarm.co.uk web: www.newparksidefarm.co.uk
dir: *M6 junction 34, A683 towards Caton and Kirkby Lonsdale. Site 1 mile on right.*

With easy access from the M6, this very pleasant and peaceful rural park is set in an Area of Outstanding Natural Beauty in the Lune Valley, near to the historic city of Lancaster and the beautiful Trough of Bowland. This is a friendly, family-run park and part of a working farm and has a smart amenity block. Pitches (a mixture of hardstanding and grass) are generously sized with views over the surrounding hills.

Open: March to October **Last arrival:** 20.00 **Last departure:** 16.00
Pitches: ; 40 hardstanding pitches
Facilities:
Services:
Within 3 miles:
Additional site information: 4 acre site. Cars can be parked by caravans and tents. Awnings permitted. No football.

LANCASHIRE 171 ENGLAND

LYTHAM ST ANNES
Map 18 SD32

Places to visit

Blackpool Zoo, BLACKPOOL, FY3 8PP, 01253 830830
www.blackpoolzoo.org.uk

Lytham Hall, LYTHAM, FY8 4TQ, 01253 736652 www.lythamhall.org.uk

Great for kids: Blackpool Pleasure Beach, BLACKPOOL, FY4 1EZ
0333 003 2212 www.blackpoolpleasurebeach.com

Eastham Hall Holiday Park
★★★★ 89%

tel: 01253 737907 Saltcotes Road FY8 4LS
email: info@easthamhall.co.uk web: www.easthamhall.co.uk
dir: M55 junction 3 towards Lytham. At 4th roundabout straight ahead onto B5259. Through Wrea Green and Moss Side. Park 1 mile after level crossing on the left.

A large family-run park close to the coast in a tranquil rural setting, surrounded by trees and mature shrubs. Many pitches have been updated this year, most are fully serviced. The amenity blocks offer very good comfort levels and are well looked after throughout the day. A superb all-weather, rustic-style children's activity park ensures good family memories will be made, and there is also a fenced dog field and a nature trail. Lytham's attractions and restaurants are just a few minutes' drive away. Please note, this site does not accept tents.

Eastham Hall Holiday Park

Open: 1 March to 30 November **Last arrival:** 20.00 **Last departure:** noon
Pitches: 27 hardstanding pitches; 86 seasonal pitches
Leisure: **Facilities:** WiFi
Services: Within 3 miles:
Additional site information: 30 acre site. Cars can be parked by caravans. Awnings permitted. Dogs must be kept on leads at all times. No tents, no noise after 23.00, 10mph speed limit. Football field, dog exercise area, wildlife walk. Local produce, newspapers available. 27 night-touring pitches.

FACILITIES: Electric vehicle charging Baths/Shower Electric shaver sockets Hairdryer Ice pack facility Baby facilities Disabled facilities Shop on site or within 200yds BBQ area Picnic area WiFi Internet access **SERVICES:** Electric hook-up Launderette Licensed bar Calor Gas Campingaz Toilet fluid Café/Restaurant Fast Food/Takeaway Battery charging Motorhome service point No credit or debit cards Dogs permitted No dogs

ENGLAND 172 LANCASHIRE

SILVERDALE
Map 18 SD47

Places to visit
Leighton Hall, CARNFORTH, LA5 9ST, 01524 734474
www.leightonhall.co.uk

Great for kids: RSPB Leighton Moss & Morecambe Bay Nature Reserve, SILVERDALE, LA5 0SW, 01524 701601
www.rspb.org.uk/reserves-and-events/reserves-a-z/leighton-moss

Platinum Park

Silverdale Holiday Park
★★★★★

tel: 01524 701508 Middlebarrow Plain, Cove Road LA5 0SH
email: reception@holgates.co.uk web: www.holgates.co.uk/our-parks/silverdale
dir: M6 junction 35, A601(M) follow Kirkby Lonsdale (B6254) signs. At T-junction right to Carnforth. In Carnforth centre at crossroads, straight on (Silverdale). 1 mile, left into Sands Lane (Silverdale). 2.4 miles, over automatic level crossing. Right at T-junction, follow Holgates sign. 1 mile left, 0.5 mile right into Cove Road, 0.7 mile to site.

Silverdale is a superb family holiday destination, enveloped in wooded countryside and overlooking Morecambe Bay. All areas of the park are maintained in excellent condition with mature trees, shrubs and seasonal flowers; creating a peaceful and relaxing atmosphere. The pitch density is generous and the spotlessly clean amenity blocks are conveniently located. There is a choice of two superb indoor swimming pools, a well-stocked, licensed shop, a stylish bar and restaurant, bowling alley with amusements, toddlers' soft play area and a state-of-the-art gym. Free WiFi is available throughout the park. Luxury en suite glamping is also available.

Open: All year **Last arrival:** 20.00 **Last departure:** noon
Pitches: see prices below; 80 hardstanding pitches; 2 seasonal pitches
Leisure:
Facilities:
Services:
Within 3 miles:

Additional site information: 100 acre site. Cars can be parked by caravans and tents. Awnings permitted. No unaccompanied children, no gazebos, no fire pits or chimeneas, no noise after 22.30. Sauna, spa pool, steam room, bowling alley, ice cream parlour, indoor play area. Freshly baked bread.

Glamping available: Wooden pods from £46.

See advert on page 171

SKELMERSDALE
Map 15 SD40

Places to visit
Knowsley Safari, PRESCOT, L34 4AN, 0151 430 9009
www.knowsleysafariexperience.co.uk

Premier Park

The Secret Garden Glamping
★★★★★ 93% GLAMPING ONLY

tel: 07732 812409 Mole Hall, Holland Moss WN8 9PZ
email: thesecretgardenglamping@outlook.com
web: www.thesecretgardenglamping.uk

The Secret Garden Glamping is set in four acres of land, with idyllic views and private 2.5-acre woodland. Don't be surprised if you're visited by wild deer in the morning as you wake up to a new day in this unique environment. Lovingly created within a mature woodland with arboretum-standard tree varieties, these units are sure to amaze with their creative attention to detail. The luxurious pods and yurt have been located in woodland where no trees were felled, and the decking is moulded around the tree trunks. The interiors are equipped with quality fixtures and fittings and all units are individually themed. The units are well spaced apart and each includes a screened hot tub for total privacy plus log burners, fire pits and barbecues. Each unit comfortably accommodates a family of four.

Open: All year **Last departure:** 10.00
Leisure:
Facilities:
Within 3 miles:

Accommodation available: 3 pods, 1 yurt and 1 lodge
Changeover days: Any Day
Additional site information: Hot tubs, saunas, smart TVs. Cars can be parked by units

---

PITCHES: Caravans Motorhomes Tents Glamping accommodation **LEISURE:** Indoor swimming pool Outdoor swimming pool Children's playground Kids' club Tennis court Games room Separate TV room golf course Pitch n putt Boats for hire Bikes for hire Cinema Entertainment Fishing Mini golf Watersports Gym Sports field Stables Spa

LANCASHIRE–LEICESTERSHIRE 173 ENGLAND

THORNTON
Map 18 SD34

Places to visit
Blackpool Zoo, BLACKPOOL, FY3 8PP, 01253 830830
www.blackpoolzoo.org.uk

Premier Park

Waters Edge Country Park
★★★★★ 86%

tel: 01253 823632 River Road, Stanah FY5 5LR
web: www.ukleisureparks.co.uk/parks/waters-edge-country-park
dir: *Exit A585 at roundabout onto B5412 to Little Thornton. Right at mini-roundabout after school into Stanah Road, over 2nd mini-roundabout, leading to River Road.*

A quality park quietly located adjacent to the River Wyre and The Wyre Estuary Country Park, conveniently placed for the attractions of Blackpool which is only seven miles away. It offers well spaced hardstanding seasonal pitches and residential statics. The excellent amenity block provides very good privacy options and there is an outdoor play area for children. Please note: the park no longer offers touring pitches.

Open: March to mid November (restricted service: March and early November – shop closed) **Last arrival:** 20.00 **Last departure:** noon
Pitches: see prices below; 40 hardstanding seasonal pitches; 12 seasonal pitches
Leisure:
Facilities:
Services:
Within 3 miles:

Additional site information: 10 acre site. Cars can be parked by caravans. Awnings permitted. No commercial vehicles. Maximum of 3 dogs (chargeable) per unit. No gazebos or shade sails, complete quiet after midnight.

Glamping available: Wooden pods from £45. **Changeover days:** Any day

Additional glamping information: Wooden pods: minimum advanced booking 2 nights (3 for bank holidays). Arrival 15.00, depart noon. Standard pods sleep 3; family pods sleep 4. Own bedding and other equipment required. No smoking/vaping, no pets, no unaccompanied teenagers. Cars can be parked by units

LEICESTERSHIRE

MELTON MOWBRAY
Map 11 SK71

Places to visit
Melton Carnegie Museum, MELTON MOWBRAY, LE13 1RB, 0116 305 3860
www.meltonmuseum.org

Platinum Park

Eye Kettleby Lakes
★★★★★

tel: 01664 565900 Eye Kettleby LE14 2TN
email: info@eyekettlebylakes.com web: www.eyekettlebylakes.com
dir: *A607 from Melton Mowbray towards Leicester for approximately 2 miles. Left signed Great Dalby and Eye Kettleby Lakes. Site 1 mile on left.*

A haven for lovers of coarse fishing and walking, this long-established leisure destination, located in the hamlet of Eye Kettleby, provides very high standards. There are eight fishing lakes as well as designated walking areas and accommodation located in lodges, a glamping forest and touring fields. Touring pitches are fully serviced and divided by mature hedges to provide optimum privacy. The top-notch amenity blocks provide excellent standards in respect of fittings and privacy. The spacious reception chalet also contains a well-stocked shop selling local produce, and the large Scandinavian log building houses a café and shop where regular evening entertainment is provided. The owners have a real commitment towards sustainability and environmentally friendly practices, with an on-site wind turbine and over 300 solar panels working in conjunction to generate electricity for the site.

Open: All year **Last arrival:** 22.00 **Last departure:** noon
Pitches: see prices below; 130 hardstanding pitches
Leisure:
Facilities:
Services:
Within 3 miles:

Additional site information: 150 acre site. Adults only. Cars can be parked by caravans and tents. Awnings permitted. Cycle routes, coarse/specimen fishing.

Glamping available: Wooden pods from £62.50. **Changeover days:** Any day (July to August – arrive Monday to Thursday; 3-day mini breaks Friday to Sunday).

Additional glamping information: Wooden pods have an en suite bathroom.

Make your next UK holiday one to remember

Choose RatedTrips.com

AA

FACILITIES: Electric vehicle charging | Baths/Shower | Electric shaver sockets | Hairdryer | Ice pack facility | Baby facilities | Disabled facilities | Shop on site or within 200yds | BBQ area | Picnic area | WiFi | Internet access **SERVICES:** Electric hook-up | Launderette | Licensed bar | Calor Gas | Campingaz | Toilet fluid | Café/Restaurant | Fast Food/Takeaway | Battery charging | Motorhome service point | No credit or debit cards | Dogs permitted | No dogs

ENGLAND — LINCOLNSHIRE

LINCOLNSHIRE

ANCASTER
Map 11 SK94

Places to visit

Belton House Park & Gardens, BELTON, NG32 2LS, 01476 566116
www.nationaltrust.org.uk/belton-house

Woodland Waters
★★★★ 85%

tel: 01400 230888 **Willoughby Road NG32 3RT**
email: info@woodlandwaters.co.uk web: www.woodlandwaters.co.uk
dir: *On A153 west of junction with B6403.*

On an impressive estate, with a wide variety of mature trees and five beautifully landscaped fishing lakes, this popular holiday destination provides lodges including Wood View lodges and level touring areas with smart modern amenity blocks. A pub and clubhouse, with restaurant, are additional benefits.

Open: All year **Last arrival:** 20.00 **Last departure:** noon
Pitches: 🚐 🚍; 20 hardstanding pitches
Leisure: ⚲ 🎣 ✏ **Facilities:** ⊙ 🛉 ♿ 🚿 🛒 🪑 📶
Services: 🔌 🗑 🍴 🍽 ♨ 🔑 ♻ **Within 3 miles:** 🎣 🐕

Additional site information: 72 acre site. 🐕 Cars can be parked by caravans and tents. Awnings permitted. No noise after 23.00.

BOSTON
Map 12 TF34

Places to visit

Battle of Britain Memorial Flight Visitor Centre, CONINGSBY, LN4 4SY,
01522 782040 www.lincolnshire.gov.uk/bbmf

Tattershall Castle, TATTERSHALL, LN4 4LR, 01526 342543
www.nationaltrust.org.uk/tattershall-castle

Premier Park

Long Acres Touring Park
★★★★★ 83%

Best of British

tel: 01205 871555 **Station Road, Old Leake PE22 9RF**
email: info@long-acres.co.uk web: www.long-acres.co.uk
dir: *From A16 take B1184 at Sibsey (by church); approximately 1 mile at T-junction turn left. 1.5 miles, after level crossing take next right into Station Road. Park entrance approximately 0.5 mile on left.*

Long Acres Touring Park is a small, peaceful, rural and adults-only park, in an attractive setting within easy reach of Boston, Spalding and Skegness. An ideal space to relax in tranquil surroundings. Excellent shelter is provided by the high, mature boundary hedging, and there is a fenced field to walk dogs. The park has a smart toilet block which is very clean and has an appealing interior with modern fittings and an indoor dishwashing room. There is also a very practical motor service point and a separate laundry room. A holiday cottage is available to let.

Open: 1 March to 1 December **Last arrival:** 19.00 **Last departure:** 11.00
Pitches: * 🚐 from £26; 🚍 from £26; ⛺ from £26; 40 hardstanding pitches
Facilities: 🛁 🏠 ⊙ 🛉 ✻ ♿ 📶 **Services:** 🔌 🗑 ♻
Within 3 miles: ✏ 🛒 **Additional site information:** 3 acre site. Adults only. 🐕 Cars can be parked by caravans and tents. Awnings permitted.

Orchard Park
★★★★ 86% **HOLIDAY PARK**

tel: 01205 290328 **Frampton Lane, Hubbert's Bridge PE20 3QU**
email: info@orchardpark.co.uk web: www.orchardpark.co.uk
dir: *On B1192 between A52 (Boston to Grantham) and A1121 (Boston to Sleaford).*

Ideally located for exploring the unique Fenlands, this family-run park has two lakes – one for fishing and the other set aside for conservation. There is a cosy licensed bar adjacent to the reception, and PJ's Café is open for meals and drinks during the day. The touring and static pitches are separated over two distinct fields. The tourers' park is for adults-only and there is a choice of grass or hardstanding pitches.

Open: All year (restricted service: December to February – bar closed) **Last arrival:** 20.00 **Last departure:** 16.00
Pitches: 🚐 🚍 ⛺; 15 hardstanding pitches
Leisure: 🎣 🎵 ✏ ⚽
Facilities: 🏠 ⊙ 🛉 ✻ ♿ 🚿 🛒 🪑 📶 🖥
Services: 🔌 🗑 🍴 🍽 ♨ 🔑 🛡 ♻ 📺
Within 3 miles: 🎣 🐕 ◎

Additional site information: 51 acre site. Adults only. 🐕 Cars can be parked by caravans and tents. Awnings permitted. No washing lines. Dogs must be kept on a lead at all times.

PITCHES: 🚐 Caravans 🚍 Motorhomes ⛺ Tents 🏕 Glamping accommodation **LEISURE:** 🏊 Indoor swimming pool 🏊 Outdoor swimming pool ⚲ Children's playground 👶 Kids' club 🎾 Tennis court 🎮 Games room 📺 Separate TV room ⛳ golf course ⛳ Pitch n putt 🚤 Boats for hire 🚴 Bikes for hire 🎬 Cinema 🎵 Entertainment 🎣 Fishing ◎ Mini golf 🏄 Watersports 💪 Gym ⚽ Sports field 🐎 Stables ♨ Spa

LINCOLNSHIRE 175 ENGLAND

CAISTOR Map 17 TA10

Places to visit
Gainsthorpe Medieval Village, KIRTON-IN-LINDSEY, DN21 4JH
www.english-heritage.org.uk/visit/places/gainsthorpe-medieval-village

Platinum Park

Caistor Lakes
★★★★★

tel: 01472 859626 **99a Brigg Road LN7 6RX**
email: info@caistorlakes.co.uk web: www.caistorlakes.co.uk
dir: *From Caistor bypass follow Immingham and Humber Bridge signs onto A1173. 1st left signed Brigg (A1084) into Grimsby Road (becomes High Street, then Brigg Road). Site on left.*

This is a stunning seven-acre park that was developed beside three fishing lakes and is reserved for adults only. The owners have created a very impressive park with excellent landscaping, 28 double wide hardstanding pitches and 16 luxurious lakeside lodges equipped with jacuzzi hot tubs, WiFi and air-conditioning. Some of the lodges are pet-friendly and all have private decking overlooking the lakes. The modern amenity block is well appointed with top-notch toilets and showers. The first-class facilities include a professionally run reception, as well as The Ugly Duckling Restaurant, which is open seven days a week. A shop is also available on site, selling fishing supplies and essentials. Ideal for fishing enthusiasts.

Open: All year **Last arrival:** 17.30 **Last departure:** noon (Touring) 10.00 (Lodges)
Pitches: ; 28 hardstanding pitches
Leisure:
Facilities:
Services:
Within 3 miles:

Additional site information: 7 acre site. Adults only. Cars can be parked by caravans. Awnings permitted. No swimming in lakes, gates are locked at 22.00.

Premier Park

Wolds View Country Park
★★★★★ 85%

tel: 01472 851099 **115 Brigg Road LN7 6RX**
email: woldsviewcaistor@gmail.com web: www.woldsviewcountrypark.co.uk
dir: *From A46, at Caistor, follow Brigg and A1084 signs. 1st left signed Brigg and Caistor. Through Caistor, continue on A1084. Approximately 1 mile, site on left.*

Wolds View Country Park is an adult-only site set in the Lincolnshire Wolds with wide access, stoned roads and hedging throughout. The facilities block is a modern purpose-designed building, notably equipped with underfloor heated washrooms and with full wheelchair access. At one end is a stylish café serving breakfasts, light lunches and afternoon teas. Heated outdoor taps are available across the park, as well as professional washer/dryers. The reception is centrally located and essential goods can be bought on site. A high hedge screened pod village is also a feature here, with interiors that have heating, a double bed, TV, fridge and microwave.

Open: All year **Last arrival:** 20.00 (18.00 weekdays) **Last departure:** 13.00
Pitches: ; see prices below; 20 hardstanding pitches
Facilities:
Services:
Within 3 miles:

Additional site information: 4.5 acre site. Adults only. Cars can be parked by caravans and tents. Awnings permitted. No groups. No noise after 23.00.
Glamping available: Wooden pod from £55. **Changeover days:** Any day
Additional glamping information: Wooden pod: minimum stay 2 nights. King-size bed, TV, toaster, microwave, tea and coffee making facilities, oil radiator, 2 chairs, outdoor patio set. Own bedding required. Cars can be parked by units

CLEETHORPES Map 17 TA30

Places to visit
Fishing Heritage Centre, GRIMSBY, DN31 1UZ, 01472 323345
www.fishingheritage.com

Premier Park

Cleethorpes Beach
★★★★★ 86% HOLIDAY PARK

tel: 01472 813395 **DN35 0PW**
email: thorpepark@haven.com
web: www.haven.com/parks/lincolnshire/cleethorpes-beach
dir: *From A180 at Cleethorpes take unclassified road signed 'Humberstone and Holiday Park'.*

A large static site, adjacent to the beach, with touring facilities including fully serviced pitches and hardstandings. This holiday park offers excellent recreational and leisure activities including an indoor pool, archery range, climbing wall, lake coarse fishing and a 9-hole golf course. There is also an Adventure Village that offers bungee trampoline, aerial adventures, crazy golf, bike hire and more. The Carousel bar and restaurant with its unique fairground theme is popular, along with several very good takeaway food options such as Burger King® and Papa John's®. A recent addition is the Sports Bar and its many TVs. Dogs are welcome and can enjoy the obstacle course at the 'Bark Yard'.

Open: mid March to end October (restricted service: mid March to May and September to end October – some facilities may be reduced) **Last arrival:** anytime **Last departure:** 10.00
Pitches: ; 81 hardstanding pitches
Leisure:
Facilities:
Services:
Within 3 miles:

Additional site information: 300 acre site. No commercial vehicles, no bookings by persons under 21 years unless a family booking. Maximum 2 dogs per booking, certain dog breeds banned.

LANGWORTH
Map 17 TF07

Places to visit
The Collection: Art & Archaeology in Lincolnshire, LINCOLN, LN2 1LP, 01522 782040
www.lincolnmuseum.com

Lincoln Cathedral, LINCOLN, LN2 1PX, 01522 561600
lincolncathedral.com

Barlings Country Holiday Park
★★★★ 85%

tel: 01522 753200 & 07931 227673 **Barlings Lane LN3 5DF**
email: info@barlingscountrypark.co.uk web: www.barlingscountrypark.co.uk
dir: *From Lincoln take A158 towards Horncastle. In Langworth right into Barlings Lane signed Barlings and Reepham.*

Set in rural Lincolnshire and only a short car journey from Lincoln, this idyllic 26-acre site offers both seasonal and touring pitches, positioned around four lakes. The park is well landscaped, with beautifully mown grass, trimmed shrubs and plenty of trees. The octagon retreat is the largest lodge available with its four bedrooms, and is equipped with a hot tub. The wooden reception chalet and two amenity blocks are spotlessly clean; one is modern and the other has well-maintained, older-style toilet facilities, including family rooms. This site is ideal for a relaxing break and fishing is possible from purpose-built jetties on two of the lakes.

Open: All year **Last arrival:** 18.00 (late arrivals can be arranged) **Last departure:** noon
Pitches: 43 hardstanding pitches; 40 seasonal pitches
Leisure:
Facilities:
Services:
Within 3 miles:

Additional site information: 26 acre site. Cars can be parked by caravans and tents. Awnings permitted. No music after 22.00, quiet 23.00–08.00. Mobile shop Friday 11–11.30 only, ice cream van (summer).
Glamping available: 2 small cabins. **Changeover days:** Any day
Additional glamping information: Small cabins offer hot tubs. Cars can be parked by units

MABLETHORPE
Map 17 TF58

Places to visit
Great for kids: Skegness Natureland Seal Sanctuary, SKEGNESS, PE25 1DB, 01754 764345
www.skegnessnatureland.co.uk

Premier Park

Golden Sands Holiday Park
★★★★★ 84% HOLIDAY PARK

tel: 01507 477871 **Quebec Road LN12 1QJ**
email: goldensands@haven.com web: www.haven.com/goldensands
dir: *From centre of Mablethorpe left into Quebec Road (seafront road). Site on left.*

A large, well-equipped seaside holiday park with many all-weather attractions and eating options, including the stylish Quayside Bar and Restaurant and a Burger King® takeaway outlet. The large touring area is serviced by two amenity blocks and is close to the mini market and laundry. Just across the road is The Mablethorpe Seal Sanctuary and Wildlife Centre. On site, enjoy the 'Adventure Village', outdoor play area, two swimming pools, live shows, fishing lakes, karts, segways, bikes, and plenty more activities.

Open: mid March to end October **Last arrival:** anytime **Last departure:** 10.00
Pitches: 20 hardstanding pitches
Leisure:
Facilities:
Services:
Within 3 miles:

Additional site information: 23 acre site. No commercial vehicles, no bookings by persons under 21 years unless a family booking. Maximum 2 dogs per booking, certain dog breeds banned. Mini bowling alley, snooker and pool, amusement arcade.

Kirkstead Holiday Park
★★★★ 78%

tel: 01507 441483 **North Road, Trusthorpe LN12 2QD**
email: kirksteadholidaypark@outlook.com web: www.kirkstead.co.uk
dir: *From Mablethorpe town centre take A52 south towards Sutton-on-Sea. 1 mile, sharp right by phone box into North Road. Site signed in 300 yards.*

Kirkstead Holiday Park is a well-established family-run park catering for all age groups. Ideally located just a few minutes' walk from Trusthorpe and the sandy beaches of Mablethorpe. The main touring area, which is serviced by good quality toilet facilities, offers a choice of serviced, hardstanding and grass pitches. In addition to a shop, there is a clubhouse that serves meals through the day, both inside and in the beer garden. There is plenty of space for ball games, as well as two outdoor play areas, a children's room and a snooker room.

Open: March to November **Last arrival:** 21.00 **Last departure:** 11.00
Pitches: 3 hardstanding pitches; 30 seasonal pitches
Leisure: **Facilities:**
Services:
Within 3 miles:

Additional site information: 12 acre site. Cars can be parked by caravans and tents. Awnings permitted. No dogs in tents.

SKEGNESS
Map 17 TF56

Places to visit
Skegness Natureland Seal Sanctuary, SKEGNESS, PE25 1DB, 01754 764345
www.skegnessnatureland.co.uk

Premier Park

Skegness Holiday Park
★★★★★ 84% HOLIDAY PARK

tel: 01754 762097 **Richmond Drive PE25 3TQ**
web: www.haven.com/parks/lincolnshire/skegness-holiday-park

A multi-million pound transformation means that Skegness Holiday Park is an ideal base for a family holiday on the beautiful Lincolnshire coast. There's a state-of-the-art entertainment complex, a restaurant, plenty of takeaway options, lots of exciting activities and an attractive central piazza.

Open: March to November

LINCOLNSHIRE 177 ENGLAND

Chapel Fields Holiday Park
★★★★ 86%

tel: 01754 879600 Trunch Lane, Chapel St Leonards PE24 5UA
email: info@chapel-fields.co.uk web: www.chapel-fields.co.uk

Chapel Fields Holiday Park is situated on the outskirts of Chapel St Leonards, minutes away from many attractions, activities and theme parks. There are four well-stocked fishing lakes on site with carp, catfish and pike, and a fishing shop. All touring pitches are fully serviced and hardstanding. There are also six modern pods/cabins with waterside views and beds for six people. Breakfast, lunch and dinner are served in 'The Den' café, and there's a brand new playing area for children. Dogs, on leads are welcome, and there's a dedicated dog walking area in the park.

Open: **Last arrival:** 17.00 **Last departure:** 10.00
Pitches:

Eastview Caravan Park
★★★★ 81%

tel: 01754 875324 Trunch Lane, Chapel St Leonards PE24 5UA
email: enquiries@eastviewcaravans.co.uk web: www.eastviewcaravans.co.uk
dir: A52 from Skegness to Chapel St Leonards. Turn left into Trunch Lane. 2nd caravan park on left.

Set in 15 acres and only a short walk from one of Lincolnshire's finest beaches, Eastview Caravan Park is neat and tidy and a good all-round campsite. It has beautifully mown grass, well-trimmed shrubbery and spotlessly clean and practical toilet facilities. The park has many seasonal pitches, as well as 62 pitches that can accommodate touring caravans, motorhomes, trailer tents and tents. There is a children's playground, a dog wash area and a shop. The park is well secured and even has a security patrol at night. It is well placed for exploring both the coast and the countryside, especially the beautiful Lincolnshire Wolds.

Open: March to October **Last arrival:** 17.00 (Friday 20.00) **Last departure:** 10.30 (later departures until 17.00 – fee applies).
Pitches: ; 56 hardstanding pitches; 116 seasonal pitches
Facilities:
Services:
Within 3 miles:

Additional site information: 15 acre site. Cars can be parked by caravans and tents. Awnings permitted. No motorised scooters, BB guns or kites. Maximum 2 dogs per pitch. BBQs to be at least 1 foot off ground, quiet after 22.30. Dog wash.

TATTERSHALL — Map 17 TF25

Places to visit

Tattershall Castle, TATTERSHALL, LN4 4LR, 01526 342543
www.nationaltrust.org.uk/tattershall-castle

Willow Holt Caravan Park
★★★★ 82%

tel: 07919003254 Lodge Road LN4 4JS
email: sales@willowholt.co.uk web: willowholt.co.uk

Willow Holt Caravan Park welcomes caravans, tents and motorhomes, and is set around two fishing and boating lakes. There's also a glamping pod which can sleep up to five people. The park is both child and dog friendly and there's a great kids' play area, and an aqua park on the main lake – the resident ducks and geese often walk around the grounds. The Boat House Diner has a well-stocked bar and serves home-cooked meals on weekends and everyday during the summer. There's a modern shower block with underfloor heating.

Open: 15 March to 31 October **Last arrival:** 20.30 **Last departure:** noon
Pitches: ; 2 hardstanding pitches; 45 seasonal pitches
Additional site information: 25 acre site.
Glamping available: 1 wooden pod

WOODHALL SPA — Map 17 TF16

Places to visit

Tattershall Castle, TATTERSHALL, LN4 4LR, 01526 342543
www.nationaltrust.org.uk/tattershall-castle

Battle of Britain Memorial Flight Visitor Centre, CONINGSBY, LN4 4SY, 01522 782040
www.lincolnshire.gov.uk/bbmf

Premier Park

Woodhall Country Park
★★★★★ 93%

tel: 01526 353710 Stixwould Road LN10 6UJ
email: info@woodhallcountrypark.co.uk web: www.woodhallcountrypark.co.uk
dir: In Woodhall Spa at roundabout in High Street take Stixwould Road. 1 mile, site on right, just before Village Limits pub.

A peaceful and attractive touring park situated in a woodland area, and just a short walk from the village of Woodhall Spa. This is an ideal countryside retreat for campers who wish to get away from a hectic lifestyle. Well organised and well laid out, the park offers fishing lakes, three well-appointed log cabin amenity blocks and high levels of customer care. A choice of grass, hardstanding, serviced and fully serviced pitches is offered. Glamping pods and splendid luxury lodges are also available for hire. There's a strong ethos towards sustainability and a bio-mass boiler provides all the heating and hot water to the amenity blocks. This is a family-friendly park with a play area, several walks and trails, bike rental, a food prep room and a small shop.

Open: March to November **Last arrival:** 20.00 **Last departure:** noon
Pitches: ; see prices below; 98 hardstanding pitches
Leisure:
Facilities:
Services:
Within 3 miles:

Additional site information: 80 acre site. Cars can be parked by caravans and tents. Awnings permitted. No fires, Chinese lanterns or fireworks, no noise between 23.00–07.00. BBQs must be off ground. Walking and cycling trail, food preparation room including worktops, fridge/freezer, kettle, sinks and microwave available. Herb garden.

Glamping available: Wooden pods from £40; cabins from £40.
Changeover days: Any day

Additional glamping information: Minimum stay 2 nights; check-in from 15.00, check-out by 11.00. Cabins have their own kitchenette and shower/toilet. Cabins allow dogs. No dogs in wooden pods. Bedding and towel packs available for hire. Cars can be parked by units

---

FACILITIES: Electric vehicle charging Baths/Shower Electric shaver sockets Hairdryer Ice pack facility Baby facilities Disabled facilities Shop on site or within 200yds BBQ area Picnic area WiFi Internet access **SERVICES:** Electric hook-up Launderette Licensed bar Calor Gas Campingaz Toilet fluid Café/Restaurant Fast Food/Takeaway Battery charging Motorhome service point No credit or debit cards Dogs permitted No dogs

WOODHALL SPA continued

Petwood Caravan Park
★★★★ 90%

tel: 01526 354799 Off Stixwould Road LN10 6QH
email: info@petwoodcaravanpark.co.uk web: www.petwoodcaravanpark.com
dir: *From Lincoln take A15 towards Sleaford. Left onto B1188 signed Woodhall Spa. In approximately 7.5 miles at Metheringham left onto B1189 (signed Billinghay). 3.7 miles, left onto B1191 (Woodhall Spa). In approximately 6 miles at roundabout in Woodhall Spa, 1st exit into Stixwould Road. In 0.3 mile left into Jubilee Park, follow site signs.*

Covering seven immaculate acres of beautifully manicured grounds, Petwood Caravan Park is a peaceful, hidden gem located in the heart of the picturesque village of Woodhall Spa. There are 98 pitches, each equipped with electric hook-ups and fresh water taps; the majority have spacious hardstanding space, but many grass pitches are also available. There is a modern reception area where the helpful wardens can be found, and where DVDs, books and games can be borrowed. There are also two excellent heated toilet blocks, each containing a spotlessly maintained baby-changing area, an accessible room, Elsan point, laundry and dishwashing area. Four-legged friends are welcomed and there is a dedicated, fenced walking area. Children can play ball games in the large fenced field. Note: tents are no longer accepted at the park.

Open: 25 March to 13 October **Last arrival:** 20.00 **Last departure:** noon
Pitches: 58 hardstanding pitches; 20 seasonal pitches
Facilities:
Services:
Within 3 miles:

Additional site information: 7 acre site. Cars can be parked by caravans and tents. Awnings permitted. No rollerblades, skateboards, hoverboards or segways. No noise after 22.00.

LONDON

LONDON E4
Map 6 TQ39

Places to visit
Waltham Abbey Gatehouse & Bridge, WALTHAM ABBEY, EN9 1XQ, www.english-heritage.org.uk/visit/places/waltham-abbey-gatehouse-and-bridge

Lee Valley Campsite, Sewardstone
★★★★ 81%

tel: 03000 030 623 Sewardstone Road, Chingford E4 7RA
email: sewardstonecampsite@leevalleypark.org.uk
web: www.visitleevalley.org.uk/wheretostay
dir: *M25 junction 26, A112. Site signed.*

Overlooking King George's Reservoir and close to Epping Forest, this popular and very peaceful park features very good, modern facilities and excellent hardstanding pitches including nine that are able to accommodate larger motorhomes. This impressive park is maintained to a high standard and there is glamping accommodation (2-berth cocoons and 4-berth small cabins) in a separate shady glade. A bus calls at the site hourly to take passengers to the nearest tube station, and Enfield is easily accessible.

Open: March to January **Last arrival:** 20.00 **Last departure:** 11.00 (late departures by prior arrangement)
Pitches: 65 hardstanding pitches
Leisure:
Facilities:
Services:
Within 3 miles:

Additional site information: 12 acre site. Cars can be parked by caravans and tents. Awnings permitted. Under 18s must be accompanied by an adult, no commercial vehicles. Fresh produce, bike hire, fire pit.

Glamping available: Wooden pods.

Additional glamping information: 2 and 4 berth wooden pods. Cars can be parked by units

MERSEYSIDE 179 ENGLAND

LONDON N9
Map 6 TQ39

Places to visit
Queen Elizabeth's Hunting Lodge, LONDON, E4 7QH, 020 7332 1911
www.cityoflondon.gov.uk/things-to-do/green-spaces/epping-forest

Lee Valley Camping and Caravan Park, Edmonton

★★★★ 81%

tel: 03000 030 625 **Meridian Way N9 0AR**
email: edmontoncampsite@vibrantpartnerships.co.uk
web: www.visitleevalley.org.uk/wheretostay
dir: M25 junction 25, A10 south, 1st left onto A1055, approximately 5 miles to Leisure Complex. From A406 (North Circular), north on A1010, left after 0.25 mile, right into Pickets Lock Lane.

A pleasant, open site within easy reach of London yet peacefully located close to two large reservoirs. There are excellent gravel access roads to the camping field, good signage and lighting and smart toilets. The site has the advantage of being next to an 18-hole golf course and a multi-screen cinema. There are also camping pods (cocoons), ready-erected tents and small timber cabins for hire. A convenient bus stop provides a direct service to central London.

Open: All year **Last arrival:** 20.00 **Last departure:** 11.00 (late departures by prior arrangement)
Pitches: 54 hardstanding pitches
Leisure:
Facilities:
Services:
Within 3 miles:
Additional site information: 7 acre site. Cars can be parked by caravans and tents. Awnings permitted. Under 18s must be accompanied by an adult. Foot golf. Fresh produce available.
Glamping available: Wooden pods (cocoons and cabins).
Additional glamping information: Cars can be parked by units

MERSEYSIDE

SOUTHPORT
Map 15 SD31

Places to visit
RSPB Marshside, SOUTHPORT, PR9 9PJ, 01704 211690
www.rspb.org.uk/reserves-and-events/reserves-a-z/marshside

British Lawnmower Museum, SOUTHPORT, PR8 5AJ, 01704 501336
www.lawnmowerworld.co.uk

Great for kids: Dunes Splash World, SOUTHPORT, PR8 1RX, 01704 537160
www.splashworldsouthport.com

Willowbank Holiday Home & Touring Park

★★★★ 88%

tel: 01704 571566 **Coastal Road, Ainsdale PR8 3ST**
email: enquiries@willowbankcp.co.uk **web:** www.willowbankcp.co.uk
dir: From A565 between Formby and Ainsdale exit at Woodvale lights onto coast road, site 150 metres on left. From north: M6 junction 31, A59 towards Preston, A565, through Southport and Ainsdale, right at Woodvale lights.

Ideally located five miles from the centre of Southport and within walking distance of a National Trust nature reserve and Sefton Coast (an SSSI), this consistently improving park is set in peaceful woodlands. Expect mature trees, shrubs and colourful, seasonal flowers surrounding the neat pitches, and modern amenity blocks. The park is well secured and there is space for car parking at every plot. There is also a dog walking path around the park, and a children's playground.

Open: 14 February to 31 January **Last arrival:** 20.30 **Last departure:** noon
Pitches: 61 hardstanding pitches
Leisure:
Facilities:
Services:
Within 3 miles:
Additional site information: 8 acre site. Awnings permitted. Cannot accommodate continental door entry units, no commercial vehicles, only towing car can park by caravan. No dangerous dog breeds, maximum of 2 dogs, no cats. Cycling trail.

Make your next UK holiday one to remember

Choose RatedTrips.com

AA

FACILITIES: Electric vehicle charging · Baths/Shower · Electric shaver sockets · Hairdryer · Ice pack facility · Baby facilities · Disabled facilities · Shop on site or within 200yds · BBQ area · Picnic area · WiFi · Internet access **SERVICES:** Electric hook-up · Launderette · Licensed bar · Calor Gas · Campingaz · Toilet fluid · Café/Restaurant · Fast Food/Takeaway · Battery charging · Motorhome service point · No credit or debit cards · Dogs permitted · No dogs

Norfolk

Think of Norfolk, and the theme of water – in particular the Norfolk Broads, a complex network of mostly navigable rivers and man-made waterways – usually springs to mind. This delightfully unspoiled region attracts thousands of visitors every year, as does the North Norfolk Coast, designated an Area of Outstanding Natural Beauty and probably the finest of its kind in Europe.

'A long way from anywhere' and 'a remote corner of England that has been able to hold on to its traditions and ancient secrets,' are two of the apt descriptions that apply to this spacious corner of the country that still seems a separate entity, as if it is strangely detached from the rest of the country. The coastline here represents a world of lonely beaches, vast salt marshes and extensive sand dunes stretching to the far horizon. It remains essentially unchanged, a stark reminder of how this area has long been vulnerable to attack and enemy invasion.

The highly successful thriller writer Jack Higgins chose this theme as the subject of his hugely popular adventure yarn *The Eagle has Landed*, published in 1975. The book, about a wartime Nazi plot to kidnap and assassinate Winston Churchill while he is spending the weekend at a country house near the sea in this part of East Anglia, vividly conveys the strange, unsettling atmosphere of the North Norfolk Coast.

Walking is the best way to gain a flavour of that atmosphere and visit the story's memorable setting. The 93-mile Peddars Way and North Norfolk Coast Path is one of Britain's most popular national trails. Made up of two paths strung together to form one continuous route, the trail begins near Thetford on the Suffolk/Norfolk border and follows ancient tracks and sections of Roman road before reaching the coast near Hunstanton. Cycling is another popular pastime in this region and in places you can combine it with a local train ride. One option, for example, is to cycle beside the Bure Valley Railway on a 9-mile trail running from Aylsham to Wroxham, returning to the start by train. There is also the North Norfolk Coast Cycleway between King's Lynn and Cromer, among other routes.

Norfolk prides itself on its wealth of historic houses, the most famous being Sandringham, where the royal family traditionally spend Christmas. The Grade II-listed house, which is surrounded by 20,000 acres, has been the private home of five generations of monarchs since 1862. 'Dear old Sandringham, the place I love better than anywhere in the world,' wrote King George V. The house and gardens are open to visitors. Among the other great houses in the region are Holkham Hall – the magnificent Palladian home of the Earls of Leicester – and the National Trust properties of Blickling Hall and Felbrigg Hall.

Many of Norfolk's towns have a particular charm and a strong sense of community. The quiet market towns of Fakenham and Swaffham are prime examples, and there is also Thetford, with its popular museum focusing on the iconic TV comedy series *Dad's Army*. Much of the filming for this cherished BBC production took place in the town and in nearby Thetford Forest. On the coast, you'll find a string of quaint villages and small towns. Wells-next-the-Sea is a popular destination for many visitors to Norfolk, as is Blakeney, renowned for its mudflats and medieval parish church, dedicated to the patron saint of seafarers, standing guard over the village and the estuary of the River Glaven. With its iconic pier, a key feature of coastal towns, Cromer is a classic example of a good old fashioned seaside resort where rather grand Victorian hotels look out to sea. Together with Sheringham, Cromer hosts a Crab and Lobster Festival in May.

◁ *Thetford Forest*

NORFOLK

BARNEY
Map 13 TF93

Places to visit

Baconsthorpe Castle, BACONSTHORPE, NR25 6LL,
www.english-heritage.org.uk/visit/places/baconsthorpe-castle

Holkham Hall, HOLKHAM, NR23 1AB, 01328 710227
www.holkham.co.uk

Great for kids: Roarr! Dinosaur Adventure, LENWADE, NR9 5JW, 01603 876310
www.roarrdinosauradventure.co.uk

Platform Park

The Old Brick Kilns
★★★★★

tel: 01328 878205 **Little Barney Lane NR21 0NL**
email: enquiries@old-brick-kilns.co.uk **web:** www.old-brick-kilns.co.uk
dir: *From A148 (Fakenham to Cromer road) follow brown tourist signs to Barney, left into Little Barney Lane. Site at end of lane.*

This award-winning, secluded and peaceful park is approached via a quiet, leafy country lane. The park is on two levels with its own boating and fishing pool and many mature trees. Excellent, well-planned and beautifully appointed toilet facilities include a smart washroom block and two first class, fully-serviced cubicles, and there is a short dog walk around the site. In Barney's Restaurant & Bar, takeaway food (eat in or out) is available on selected nights of the week. The shop sells local produce, freshly baked bread and newspapers. There's also a games room and a secluded bird hide overlooking feeders. Please note, due to a narrow access road, no arrivals are accepted until after 1.30pm. There are also four self-catering holiday cottages and B&B available.

Open: 15 March to 2 January (restricted service: Easter to September — bar food and takeaway available on selected nights only) **Last arrival:** 21.00 **Last departure:** 11.00
Pitches: 🚐 🚙 ⛺; 65 hardstanding pitches; 7 seasonal pitches
Leisure: 🎠 🎣 📺 ✏️
Facilities: 🚿 ☺ ⚑ ❄ ♿ 🧺 🍴 🎪 🐕 📶 💻
Services: ⛽ 🗑 🧼 🍴 🛒 🧊 ⬇ 🔒 ♻ Ⓣ

Additional site information: 12.73 acre site. 🐕 Cars can be parked by caravans and tents. Awnings permitted. No gazebos. Outdoor draughts, chess and family games. Freshly baked bread available.

BELTON
Map 13 TG40

Places to visit

Burgh Castle, BURGH CASTLE, NR31 9QB, 0370 333 1181
www.english-heritage.org.uk/visit/places/burgh-castle

Premier Park

Rose Farm Touring & Camping Park
★★★★★ 80%

tel: 01493 738292 **Stepshort NR31 9JS**
email: office@rosefarmtouringpark.com **web:** www.rosefarmtouringpark.com
dir: *From A143 follow signs to Belton. In Belton, from mini-roundabout on New Road into Stepshort, site on right.*

A former railway line is the setting for this very peaceful, beautifully presented site which enjoys rural views. It is landscaped with many flower and herb beds. The toilet facilities are spotlessly clean and include a smart, fully serviced cabin in the tent field at the far end of the park. There is a modern reception building and security barrier, and the customer care here is exceptional.

Open: All year **Last arrival:** 21.00 **Last departure:** 14.00
Pitches: 🚐 🚙 ⛺ 🏕; 26 hardstanding pitches; 60 seasonal pitches
Leisure: 🎣 📺
Facilities: 🚿 ☺ ⚑ ❄ ♿ 💻
Services: ⛽ 🗑 🔒 ♻
Within 3 miles: 🚴 🎯 ⛳ ◎ 🎣 🛒

Additional site information: 10 acre site. 🐕 Cars can be parked by caravans and tents. Awnings permitted. No dog fouling, dogs must be kept on leads.

Glamping available: Cabins (summerhouses).

Additional glamping information: Summerhouses: cabin for daily, weekly, or seasonal hire (includes fridge, TV, microwave, wardrobe, bunk beds, sofa bed, toaster, kettle). Cars can be parked by units

---

Make your next UK holiday one to remember

Choose RatedTrips.com

PITCHES: 🚐 Caravans 🚙 Motorhomes ⛺ Tents 🏕 Glamping accommodation **LEISURE:** 🏊 Indoor swimming pool 🏊 Outdoor swimming pool 🎠 Children's playground 🧒 Kids' club 🎾 Tennis court 🎮 Games room 📺 Separate TV room ⛳ golf course 🏌 Pitch n putt ⛵ Boats for hire 🚲 Bikes for hire 🎬 Cinema 🎭 Entertainment 🎣 Fishing ⛳ Mini golf 🏄 Watersports 💪 Gym ⚽ Sports field ♞ Stables ♨ Spa

NORFOLK 183 ENGLAND

Wild Duck Holiday Park
★★★★ 87% HOLIDAY PARK

tel: 01493 780268 **Howards Common NR31 9NE**
email: wildduck@haven.com web: www.haven.com/wildduck
dir: *A47 to Great Yarmouth, 3rd exit at Asda roundabout, straight on at next 2 roundabouts. Left onto A143 signed Beccles. Right at lights, 2 miles to dual carriageway, right at roundabout signed Belton. Straight on at mini-roundabout. Right at T-junction, left at next T-junction. Park 200 yards on right.*

This is a holiday complex with plenty to do for all ages both indoors and out. Located in woodland, it's a level grassy park with well laid-out facilities and good quality static caravans set in peaceful, well landscaped glades. Clubs for children and teenagers, sporting activities and evening shows all add to the fun of a stay here.

Open: 16 March to 5 November (restricted service: mid March to May and September to early November – some facilities may be reduced) **Last arrival:** 21.00 **Last departure:** 10.00
Pitches: see prices below
Leisure:
Facilities:
Services:
Within 3 miles:

Additional site information: 97 acre site. No commercial vehicles, no bookings by persons under 21 years unless a family booking. Maximum 2 dogs per booking, certain dog breeds banned.
Glamping available: Safari tents from £119. **Changeover days:** Mondays, Fridays
Additional glamping information: Safari tents: minimum stay 3 nights.

BURNHAM DEEPDALE   Map 13 TF84X

Places to visit
Brancaster Estate (NT), BRANCASTER STAITHE, PE31 8BW, 01263 740241
www.nationaltrust.org.uk/brancaster-estate

RSPB Nature Reserve Titchwell Marsh, TITCHWELL, PE31 8BB, 01485 210579
www.rspb.org.uk/reserves-and-events/reserves-a-z/titchwell-marsh

Great for kids: Wells & Walsingham Light Railway, WELLS-NEXT-THE-SEA, NR23 1QB, 01328 711630
www.wwlr.co.uk

Deepdale Camping & Rooms
★★★★ 90%

tel: 01485 210256 **Deepdale Farm PE31 8DD**
email: stay@deepdalebackpackers.co.uk web: www.deepdalecamping.co.uk
dir: *On south side of A149 (coast road), opposite church, between Hunstanton and Wells-next-the-Sea.*

Within the heart of this notable tourist destination, near craft and food shops, a petrol station and visitor centre, which are all part of the Deepdale Estate, this park is a must for lovers of peace and tranquillity. The touring areas, spread over six distinctive fields, offer generous pitch sizes, including hammock pitches, and most are equipped with electric hook-ups. There are also five fully serviced pitches capable of accommodating RVs. Three separate amenity blocks provide superb decor, fixtures and fittings and have excellent privacy options, including 18 fully serviced cubicles. The site is located a short stroll from the coastal path.

Open: All year **Last arrival:** 21.00 **Last departure:** 11.00
Pitches: 7 hardstanding pitches
Leisure:
Facilities:
Services:
Within 3 miles:

Additional site information: 8 acre site. Cars can be parked by tents. Awnings permitted. Quiet policy after 22.00. See website for terms and conditions. Visitor information centre.

CAISTER-ON-SEA   Map 13 TG51

Places to visit
Caister Roman Fort, CAISTER-ON-SEA, NR30 5RN, 0370 333 1181
www.english-heritage.org.uk/visit/places/caister-roman-fort

Thrigby Hall Wildlife Gardens, FILBY, NR29 3DR, 01493 369477
www.thrigbyhall.com

Premier Park

Caister-on-Sea Holiday Park
★★★★★ 88% HOLIDAY PARK

tel: 01493 728931 **Ormesby Road NR30 5NH**
email: caister@haven.com web: www.haven.com/caister
dir: *A1064 signed Caister-on-Sea. At roundabout 2nd exit onto A149, at next roundabout 1st exit onto Caister bypass, at 3rd roundabout 3rd exit to Caister-on-Sea. Park on left.*

An all-action holiday park located beside the beach north of the resort of Great Yarmouth, yet close to the attractions of the Norfolk Broads. The former touring field has been beautifully landscaped, creating a very spacious static area (Reedham) with top quality caravans, parking areas, tree planting and extra privacy. Customer care is of an extremely high standard.

Open: mid March to end October **Last arrival:** anytime **Last departure:** 10.00
Pitches: 49 seasonal pitches
Leisure:
Facilities:
Services:
Within 3 miles:

Additional site information: 138 acre site. Maximum 2 dogs per booking, certain dog breeds not accepted. No tents, no commercial vehicles, no bookings by persons under 21 years unless a family booking.

FACILITIES: Electric vehicle charging · Baths/Shower · Electric shaver sockets · Hairdryer · Ice pack facility · Baby facilities · Disabled facilities · Shop on site or within 200yds · BBQ area · Picnic area · WiFi · Internet access **SERVICES:** Electric hook-up · Launderette · Licensed bar · Calor Gas · Campingaz · Toilet fluid · Café/Restaurant · Fast Food/Takeaway · Battery charging · Motorhome service point · No credit or debit cards · Dogs permitted · No dogs

CLIPPESBY
Map 13 TG41

Places to visit
Fairhaven Woodland & Water Garden, SOUTH WALSHAM, NR13 6DZ, 01603 270449
www.fairhavengarden.co.uk

Caister Roman Fort, CAISTER-ON-SEA, NR30 5RN, 0370 333 1181
www.english-heritage.org.uk/visit/places/caister-roman-fort

Platinum Park

Clippesby Hall
★★★★★

tel: 01493 367800 Hall Lane NR29 3BL
email: holidays@clippesby.com web: www.clippesbyhall.com
dir: *From A47 follow tourist signs for The Broads. At Acle roundabout take A1064, in 2 miles left onto B1152, 0.5 mile left opposite village sign, site 400 yards on right.*

Clippesby Hall is a lovely country house estate with secluded pitches hidden among the trees or in sheltered sunny glades – guests can expect spacious pitches and good privacy. The toilet facilities, appointed to a very good standard, provide a wide choice of cubicles. The fabulous 'Basecamp' amenity area is complete with a reception, a stylish bar and café area, a superb alfresco terrace for summer eating and drinking, and a well-stocked mini-market. Excellent all-weather pitches are available as the park is open all year. There are pine lodges, cottages and a shepherd's hut for holiday lets.

Open: All year (restricted service: November to March – coffee shop, bar and restaurant opening times vary) **Last arrival:** 17.30 **Last departure:** 11.00

Pitches: 🚐 🚌 ▲; 41 hardstanding pitches

Leisure: ⛺ ⚽ 🎣 🏓 ♫ ⛳ ⚽

Facilities: 🏠 ☉ ℉ ❄ ♿ 👗 🍴 💺 📶 🖥

Services: 🔌 🚽 🍳 🍽 🧺 ⛽ ⬆ 🔒 ♻ T

Within 3 miles: 🎣 🎯 ⛪ ◎ ⛴ ⛳

Additional site information: 30 acre site. 🐕 Cars can be parked by caravans and tents. Awnings permitted. No groups, no noise after 23.00, no camp fires. Table tennis, cycle trail.

See advert opposite

CROMER
Map 13 TG24

Places to visit
RNLI Henry Blogg Museum, CROMER, NR27 9ET, 01263 511294
rnli.org/find-my-nearest/museums/henry-blogg-museum

Felbrigg Hall, FELBRIGG, NR11 8PR, 01263 837444
www.nationaltrust.org.uk/felbrigg-hall-gardens-and-estate

Forest Park
★★★★ 85%

tel: 01263 513290 Northrepps Road NR27 0JR
email: info@forest-park.co.uk web: www.forest-park.co.uk
dir: *A140 from Norwich, left at T-junction signed Cromer, right signed Northrepps, right then immediately left, left at T-junction, site on right.*

Surrounded by forest, this gently sloping park offers a wide choice of pitches. Visitors have the use of a heated indoor swimming pool, a large clubhouse which provides entertainment, and shop with a small café. For a glamping experience there are 12 en suite Wigwam® cabins that have running water, microwave, toaster, a two-ring hob and small fridge.

Open: 15 March to 15 January **Last arrival:** 21.00 **Last departure:** 11.00

Pitches: 🚐 🚌 ▲ 🛖; 5 hardstanding pitches

Leisure: 🏊 ⛺ ♫

Facilities: 🏠 ☉ ℉ ❄ ♿ 👗 🍴 📶

Services: 🔌 🚽 🍳 🍽 🧺 ⛽ ⬆ 🔒 ♻ T

Within 3 miles: 🎣 🎯 ◎ ⛴ ⛳ 🚌

Additional site information: 100 acre site. 🐕 Cars can be parked by caravans and tents. Awnings permitted. Freshly baked bread and croissants available. Woodland walk.

Glamping available: Wooden cabins. **Changeover days:** Any day

Additional glamping information: Wooden cabins: very short walk to dedicated car park.

Manor Farm Caravan & Camping Site
★★★★ 84%

tel: 01263 512858 East Runton NR27 9PR
email: stay@manorfarmcampsite.co.uk web: www.manorfarmcaravansite.co.uk
dir: *1 mile west of Cromer, exit A148 or A149 (recommended towing route) at Manor Farm sign.*

A well-established family-run site on a working farm enjoying panoramic sea views. There are good, modern facilities across the site, including several smart toilet blocks that include quality family rooms and privacy cubicles, plus two good play areas and a large expanse of grass for games as the park is very popular with families. All amenity blocks are appointed to a good standard. Care must be taken when approaching the site, which is along a 0.5 mile farm track; if required, please ask for directions from reception, housed in a smart brick-and-flint barn.

Open: Easter to September **Last arrival:** 20.30 **Last departure:** noon

Pitches:

Leisure:

Facilities:

Services:

Within 3 miles:

Additional site information: 17 acre site. Cars can be parked by caravans and tents. Awnings permitted. No groups, no noise after 23.00. 1 dog-free field available.

DERSINGHAM   Map 12 TF63

Places to visit

Sandringham House & Gardens, Sandringham Estate, Norfolk, PE35 6EN, 01485 544 112   www.sandringhamestate.co.uk

Dersingham Bog National Nature Reserve, King's Lynn, Norfolk, PE31 6HA, 0845 600 3078   www.visiteastofengland.com/attraction_activity/dersingham-bog-national-nature-reserve

Great for kids: Snettisham Park, Bircham Road, Snettisham, King's Lynn, Norfolk, PE31 7NG, 01485 542425   www.snettishampark.co.uk

DERSINGHAM   Map 12 TF63

Premier Park

Pinecones Caravan and Camping

★★★★★ 88%

tel: 01485 544224 **A149 Bypass PE31 6WL**
email: martin.bennett@pinecones.co.uk **web:** www.pinecones.co.uk

Created from a former council picnic area by the Bennett family, Pinecones is a very popular touring park, well located just off the Dersingham bypass between King's Lynn and Hunstanton, close to Sandringham, bird reserves, and vast sandy beaches. There are tent pitches, three camping pods, large fully serviced hardstanding pitches, picnic huts or pergolas and two smart wooden cabins with excellent fully-serviced cubicles. Ben's Bar, a smart area serving a wide range of food and drinks, was added for 2024. Dogs are very welcome, with good facilities provided.

Open: All year **Last arrival:** 21.00 **Last departure:** 11.00
Additional site information: 10 acre site.

www.clippesbyhall.com
01493 367800

FACILITIES: Electric vehicle charging Baths/Shower Electric shaver sockets Hairdryer Ice pack facility Baby facilities Disabled facilities Shop on site or within 200yds BBQ area Picnic area WiFi Internet access **SERVICES:** Electric hook-up Launderette Licensed bar Calor Gas Campingaz Toilet fluid Café/Restaurant Fast Food/Takeaway Battery charging Motorhome service point No credit or debit cards Dogs permitted No dogs

DOWNHAM MARKET
Map 12 TF60

Places to visit

WWT Welney Wetland Centre, WELNEY, PE14 9TN, 01353 860711
www.wwt.org.uk/wetland-centres/welney

Oxburgh Hall, OXBOROUGH, PE33 9PS, 01366 328258
www.nationaltrust.org.uk/oxburgh-hall

Lakeside Caravan Park & Fisheries
★★★★ 84%

tel: 01366 383491 & 387074 **Sluice Road, Denver PE38 0EG**
email: richesflorido@aol.com **web:** www.lakesidedenver.co.uk
dir: *Exit A10 towards Denver, follow signs to Denver Windmill, site on right.*

A peaceful park set around five pretty fishing lakes with several well maintained grassy touring areas which are sheltered by mature trees and hedging. Facilities on site include a shop selling essentials and fishing tackle and bait, a hairdresser, laundry room and a children's play area. Electric hook-up pitches are available and rallies are welcome. Two electric car charging points were added in 2024.

Open: All year (restricted service: October to March depending on weather)
Last arrival: 21.00 (other times by prior arrangement) **Last departure:** 10.30 (unless pre-arranged for a late departure)
Pitches: 🚐 🚙 🛆; 10 hardstanding pitches; 50 seasonal pitches
Leisure: **Facilities:**
Services: Within 3 miles:

Additional site information: 30 acre site. 🐕 Cars can be parked by caravans and tents. Awnings permitted. No noise after 22.00. Fishing tackle and bait, caravan accessories, caravan storage, gas, hairdresser, newspapers, bread and milk available.

FAKENHAM
Map 13 TF92

Places to visit

Houghton Hall & Gardens, HOUGHTON, PE31 6UE, 01485 528569
www.houghtonhall.com

Great for kids: Penthorpe Natural Park, FAKENHAM, NR21 0LN, 01328 851465
www.pensthorpe.com

Norfolk Coast Caravan & Camping at Fakenham Racecourse
★★★★ 83%

tel: 01328 862388 **Fakenham Racecourse, Fakenham NR21 7NY**
email: caravan@fakenhamracecourse.co.uk
web: www.racecoursecampsite.co.uk
dir: *From B1146, south of Fakenham follow brown Racecourse signs (with tent and caravan symbols) leads to site entrance.*

A very well laid-out site set around the racecourse in a peaceful rural location, yet only a few minutes from Fakenham; a riverside path leads to the town centre. Tourers move to the centre of the course on race days, and enjoy free racing, and there's a wide range of sporting activities, including golf, at the Sports Club next door. Spacious hardstanding and grass pitches (with electric hook ups) are located across several paddocks close to the course and grandstands. Smart, modern, well refurbished toilet facilities include fully serviced cubicles. The site is a short drive from stunning beaches and historic houses and estates like Holkham Hall and Sandringham.

Open: All year **Last arrival:** 21.00 (earliest arrival 13.00) **Last departure:** 11.00
Pitches: 🚐 🚙 🛆; 25 hardstanding pitches; 22 seasonal pitches
Leisure:
Facilities:
Services:
Within 3 miles:

Additional site information: 11.4 acre site. 🐕 Cars can be parked by caravans and tents. Awnings permitted. Maximum 2 dogs per pitch. Dog walking, games field, horse racing (October to June), golf, tennis, squash, indoor bowls, free WiFi.

GREAT YARMOUTH
Map 13 TG50

Places to visit

Time and Tide Museum of Great Yarmouth Life, GREAT YARMOUTH, NR30 3BX, 01493 743930
www.museums.norfolk.gov.uk/time-tide

Great for kids: Sea Life Great Yarmouth, GREAT YARMOUTH, NR30 3AH, 01493 330631
www.visitsealife.com/great-yarmouth

Premier Park

Seashore Holiday Park
★★★★★ 90% HOLIDAY PARK

tel: 01493 851131 **North Denes NR30 4HG**
email: seashore@haven.com **web:** www.haven.com/seashore
dir: A149 from Great Yarmouth to Caister. Right at 2nd lights signed seafront and racecourse. Continue to sea, turn left. Park on left.

Bordered by sand dunes and with direct access to a sandy beach, Seashore Holiday Park is located in Great Yarmouth with easy access to the peaceful Norfolk Broads. Facilities include excellent water activities, a smart swimming pool, bike hire for children, the Coast House Bar and Grill, with the adjoining Cakery, and lively evening entertainment for adults. There is a good range of holiday homes for hire to suit both couples and families.

Open: mid March to end October

Holiday Homes: Sleep 8, Bedrooms 3, Bathrooms 1, Toilet 1, Two-ring burner, Microwave, Freezer, TV, Sky/Freeview, WiFi

Changeover days: Friday, Monday

Leisure:

Facilities:

Within 3 miles:

Additional site information: The facilities provided in the holiday homes may differ depending on the grade. Most dog breeds accepted (please check when booking). Dogs must be kept on leads at all times.

Ormesby Grange Tents & Touring
★★★★ 80%

tel: 01493 730306 & 730023 **Yarmouth Road, Ormesby St Margaret NR29 3QG**
email: info@grangetouring.co.uk **web:** www.grangetouring.co.uk
dir: From A149, 3 miles north of Great Yarmouth. Site at junction of A149 and B1159, signed.

A mature, family owned park located just one mile from the sea and within easy reach of both coastal attractions and the Norfolk Broads. The level pitches have WiFi and electric hook-ups and include hardstanding pitches. The toilet facilities include three spacious family rooms, and there's an electric car charging point.

Open: Easter to October **Last arrival:** 21.00 **Last departure:** 14.00

Pitches: ; 7 hardstanding pitches; 2 seasonal pitches

Leisure:

Facilities:

Services:

Within 3 miles:

Additional site information: 3.5 acre site. Cars can be parked by caravans and tents. Awnings permitted. No football, no open fires. Table tennis, bar/restaurant adjoining. Electric vehicle charging unit.

HOPTON ON SEA
Map 13 TM59

Places to visit

St Olave's Priory, ST OLAVES, NR31 9HE, 0370 333 1181
www.english-heritage.org.uk/visit/places/st-olaves-priory

Premier Park

Hopton Holiday Village
★★★★★ 94% HOLIDAY PARK

tel: 01502 730214 **NR31 9BW**
email: hopton@haven.com **web:** www.haven.com/hopton
dir: Site signed from A47 between Great Yarmouth and Lowestoft.

Located between Lowestoft and Great Yarmouth, close to beaches and the town attractions, this lively holiday park offers excellent sport activities, including a 9-hole golf course and tennis coaching, plus popular evening entertainment in the form of shows, music and dancing. A wide range of quality holiday homes is available for hire.

Open: mid March to 30 October

Holiday Homes: Sleep 8, Bedrooms 2, Bathrooms 1, Toilet 1, Microwave, Freezer, TV, Sky/Freeview

Prices: Low season from £79

Changeover days: Monday, Friday, Saturday

Leisure:

Facilities:

Within 3 miles:

Additional site information: The facilities provided in the holiday homes may differ depending on the grade. Most dog breeds accepted (please check when booking). Dogs must be kept on leads at all times.

ENGLAND 188 NORFOLK

HUNSTANTON
Map 12 TF64

Places to visit
Lynn Museum, KING'S LYNN, PE30 1NL, 01553 775001
www.museums.norfolk.gov.uk/lynn-museum

Norfolk Lavender, HEACHAM, PE31 7JE, 01485 570384
www.norfolk-lavender.co.uk

Great for kids: Hunstanton Sea Life Sanctuary, HUNSTANTON, PE36 5BH, 01485 533576
www.visitsealife.com/hunstanton

Premier Park

Searles Leisure Resort
★★★★★ 93% **HOLIDAY PARK**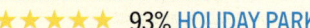

tel: 01485 534211 **South Beach Road PE36 5BB**
email: bookings@searles.co.uk web: www.searles.co.uk
dir: *A149 from King's Lynn to Hunstanton. At roundabout follow signs for South Beach. Straight on at 2nd roundabout. Site on left.*

A large seaside holiday complex with well managed facilities, adjacent to the sea and beach. The well-equipped touring areas have a range of serviced pitches offering good levels of privacy, as well as modern heated toilet blocks. Food options range from casual takeaways to more formal restaurant dining, and the site also has an on-site supermarket for essentials. The wide range of indoor and outdoor activities includes swimming pools and a full entertainment programme for all ages.

Open: All year
Pitches: 🚐 🚗 ⛺; 🏕 see prices below; 91 hardstanding pitches
Leisure:
Facilities:
Services:
Within 3 miles:

Additional site information: 50 acre site. 🐕 Restrictions on certain dog breeds (contact site for details).
Glamping available: Wooden pods from £32.
Additional glamping information: Cars can be parked by units

KING'S LYNN
Map 12 TF62

Places to visit
Bircham Windmill, GREAT BIRCHAM, PE31 6SJ, 01485 578393
www.birchamwindmill.co.uk

Castle Rising Castle, CASTLE RISING, PE31 6AH, 01553 631330
www.english-heritage.org.uk/visit/places/castle-rising-castle

Premier Park

King's Lynn Caravan and Camping Park
★★★★★ 87%

tel: 01553 840004 **New Road, North Runcton PE33 0RA**
email: klcc@btconnect.com web: www.kl-cc.co.uk
dir: *From King's Lynn take A47 signed Swaffham and Norwich, in 1.5 miles turn right signed North Runcton. Site 100 yards on left.*

Set in approximately 9 acres of parkland, this developing camping park is situated on the edge of North Runcton, just a few miles south of the historic town of King's Lynn. The three very extensive touring fields are equipped with 150 electric hook-ups and one field is reserved for rallies. There is an eco-friendly toilet block which is powered by solar panels and an air-source heat pump which also recycles rainwater – this in itself proves of great interest to visitors. There are high quality camping pods and 15 superb pine lodges for hire.

Open: All year **Last arrival:** flexible **Last departure:** flexible
Pitches: 🚐 🚗 ⛺ 🏕; 12 hardstanding pitches; 54 seasonal pitches
Leisure:
Facilities:
Services:
Within 3 miles:

Additional site information: 9 acre site. 🐕 Cars can be parked by caravans and tents. Awnings permitted. No skateboards or fires.
Glamping available: Wooden pods. **Changeover days:** Any day
Additional glamping information: No smoking in wooden pods, no dogs in wooden pods.

NORFOLK 189 ENGLAND

NORTH WALSHAM
Map 13 TG23

Places to visit

Blickling Estate, BLICKLING, NR11 6NF, 01263 738030
www.nationaltrust.org.uk/blickling-estate

Mannington Gardens, SAXTHORPE, NR11 7BB, 01263 584175
www.manningtongardens.co.uk

Premier Park

Two Mills Touring Park
★★★★★ 88%

tel: 01692 405829 **Yarmouth Road NR28 9NA**
email: enquiries@twomills.co.uk web: www.twomills.co.uk
dir: *In North Walsham at lights on A149 follow Norwich sign into Norwich Road. At mini-roundabout, right into Grammar School Road. At mini-roundabout (Lidl supermarket opposite) right into Yarmouth Road. Site on left in approximately 1 mile (after police station and hospital).*

An intimate, beautifully presented park set in superb countryside in a peaceful, rural spot, which is also convenient for touring. The 'Top Acre' section features fully serviced pitches with panoramic views over the site, an immaculate toilet block and good planting, plus the layout of pitches and facilities is excellent. A cabin-style building houses a fully-equipped disabled room. The very friendly owners keep the park in immaculate condition. Please note, this park is for adults only.

Open: March to 3 January **Last arrival:** 18.00 **Last departure:** noon

Pitches: 🚐 🚗 ⛺; 81 hardstanding pitches; 30 seasonal pitches

Facilities: 🛁 ☉ ℉ ✳ ♿ 🛒 🎪 WiFi 💻

Services: 🔌 🧺 🍽 ⚡ 🔒 ⚙ [T]

Within 3 miles: ✎

Additional site information: 8 acre site. Adults only. 🐕 Cars can be parked by caravans and tents. Awnings permitted. Maximum 2 dogs per pitch. Library, DVDs, tea and coffee facilities.

SCRATBY
Map 13 TG51

Places to visit

Time and Tide Museum of Great Yarmouth Life, GREAT YARMOUTH, NR30 3BX, 01493 743930
www.museums.norfolk.gov.uk/time-tide

Great for kids: Caister Roman Fort, CAISTER-ON-SEA, NR30 5RN, 0370 333 1181
www.english-heritage.org.uk/visit/places/caister-roman-fort

Scratby Hall Caravan Park
★★★★ 87%

tel: 01493 730283 **NR29 3SR**
email: scratbyhall@aol.com web: www.scratbyhall.co.uk
dir: *5 miles north of Great Yarmouth. Exit A149 onto B1159, site signed.*

A beautifully maintained park situated on former gardens and farmland with high wall or hedge surroundings to improve privacy and wind resistance. The well-spaced lush grass pitches include many with full services, and the amenity block includes unisex shower, toilet and washbasin rooms. The park also benefits from a well-stocked shop, and a popular children's play area.

Open: Easter to end September (restricted service: Easter to 3rd week July and September – shop hours reduced outside peak season) **Last arrival:** 21.00 **Last departure:** noon

Pitches: 🚐 🚗 ⛺

Leisure: 🎪

Facilities: 🛁 ☉ ℉ ✳ ♿ 🛒 WiFi

Services: 🔌 🧺 🍽 🔒 ⚙ [T]

Within 3 miles: ⚓ ✎ ☺ ✈

Additional site information: 5 acre site. 🐕 Cars can be parked by caravans and tents. Awnings permitted. No commercial vehicles, no noise after 23.00. Food preparation room, family/privacy bathroom.

FACILITIES: ⚡ Electric vehicle charging 🛁 Baths/Shower ☉ Electric shaver sockets ℉ Hairdryer ✳ Ice pack facility 🍼 Baby facilities ♿ Disabled facilities 🛒 Shop on site or within 200yds 🔥 BBQ area 🎪 Picnic area WiFi WiFi 💻 Internet access **SERVICES:** 🔌 Electric hook-up 🧺 Launderette 🍽 Licensed bar ⚡ Calor Gas ⚙ Campingaz [T] Toilet fluid 🍴 Café/Restaurant 🍔 Fast Food/Takeaway 🔋 Battery charging ⚡ Motorhome service point ⊘ No credit or debit cards 🐕 Dogs permitted 🚫 No dogs

ENGLAND — NORFOLK–NORTHAMPTONSHIRE

STANHOE
Map 13 TF83

Places to visit

Norfolk Lavender, HEACHAM, PE31 7JE, 01485 570384
www.norfolk-lavender.co.uk

Walsingham Abbey Grounds & Shirehall Museum, LITTLE WALSINGHAM, NR22 6BP, 01328 820510
www.walsinghamvillage.org

The Rickels Caravan & Camping Park Ltd
★★★ 87%

tel: 01485 518671 **Bircham Road, Stanhoe PE31 8PU**
email: info@therickels.co.uk **web:** www.therickels.co.uk
dir: *Take A149 (south of King's Lynn) signed Cromer (and A148). Right at roundabout onto A148 signed Fakenham and Cromer. Left on B1153 signed Flitcham and Great Bircham. In Great Bircham right onto B1155 signed Stanhoe. At crossroads (junction with B1454) straight across (Stanhoe). Site on left.*

Set in three acres of grassland, with sweeping country views, this adults-only park has a pleasant, relaxing atmosphere. The meticulously maintained grounds and facilities are part of the attraction, and the slightly sloping land has some level areas and sheltering for tents. The electronic security gate has key pad access.

Open: All year **Last arrival:** 20.00 **Last departure:** 11.00 (unless by prior arrangement)
Pitches: 🚐 🚍 ⛺
Leisure: 🖵
Facilities: 🚻 ⊙ ✻ WiFi
Services: 🔌 🗑 🧺 🔒 ⌀
Within 3 miles: 🛒

Additional site information: 3 acre site. Adults only. 🐕 Cars can be parked by caravans and tents. Awnings permitted. No groundsheets. Payment by cash or card on arrival.

NORTHAMPTONSHIRE

BULWICK
Map 11 SP99

Places to visit

Kirby Hall, DEENE, NN17 3EN, 01536 203230
www.english-heritage.org.uk/visit/places/kirby-hall

Deene Park, DEENE, NN17 3EW, 01780 450278
www.deenepark.com

Premier Park

New Lodge Farm Caravan & Camping Site
★★★★★ 90%

tel: 01780 450493 **New Lodge Farm NN17 3DU**
email: shop@newlodgefarm.com **web:** www.newlodgefarm.com
dir: *On A43 between Corby (5 miles) and Stamford (8 miles) turn right at Laxton and Harringworth junction. Site signed.*

Simon and Sarah Singlehurst have worked hard to create this beautiful adults-only site on their working farm in rural Northamptonshire. The result is impressive – large, fully serviced and level pitches (26 with hardstandings), all with views over the farm and rolling countryside. The heated toilet and amenity block is located in a beautifully restored stone barn, as is the site reception. There's an award-winning farm shop that sells home-reared meats, bread, cakes and locally grown fruit and vegetables. Attached to the shop is a cosy café and a stylish vaulted, canvas covered alfresco space is located opposite – in both areas breakfasts, lunches and afternoon teas are served. Nobbies Nook is a landscaped riverside chill-out area. The site is situated in the heart of Rockingham Forest, making this a good base for visiting Stamford, Oundle and Uppingham.

Open: 13 March to 31 October **Last arrival:** 20.00 **Last departure:** noon
Pitches: 🚐 🚍 ⛺; 🏠 see prices below; 26 hardstanding pitches; 10 seasonal pitches
Facilities: 🚻 ⊙ 🛁 ✻ ♿ 🚿 🧺 🪑 WiFi 💻
Services: 🔌 🗑 🍴 🍽 🧺 🛒 ⬇ 🔒 ⌀ 🅃
Within 3 miles: 🎣 🕳 ⛳

Additional site information: 4 acre site. Adults only. 🐕 Cars can be parked by caravans and tents. Awnings permitted. No noise after 23.00. Farm shop and butchery. Car hire can be arranged.

Glamping available: 2 wooden pods from £70.

Additional glamping information: Sleep 2. No dogs permitted. Wet room includes toilet, shower and basin. Guests to supply own towels and bedding.

NORTHUMBERLAND 191 ENGLAND

NORTHUMBERLAND

BAMBURGH
Map 21 NU13

Places to visit

Chillingham Wild Cattle Park, CHILLINGHAM, NE66 5NP, 01668 215250
www.chillinghamwildcattle.com

Bamburgh Castle, BAMBURGH, NE69 7DF, 01668 214208
www.bamburghcastle.com

Great for kids: Alnwick Castle, ALNWICK, NE66 1NG, 01665 511100
www.alnwickcastle.com

Premier Park

Waren Caravan & Camping Park
★★★★★ 92%

tel: 01668 214366 & 214224 Waren Mill NE70 7EE
email: waren@meadowhead.co.uk **web:** www.meadowhead.co.uk/parks/waren
dir: 2 miles east of town. From A1 onto B1342 signed Bamburgh. Take unclassified road past Waren Mill, signed Budle.

An especially attractive, family- and dog-friendly park sheltered within the grassy embankments of a former quarry and with truly stunning sea views over the beautiful Budle Bay. As well as a footpath leading to the sandy beach there are excellent walking and cycling opportunities in the surrounding area. The park offers first class facilities – fully serviced pitches, an on-site restaurant serving good breakfasts and smart toilet and shower blocks which include several family bathrooms. The site also has a wetlands area, an Airstream pizza takeaway operation, and outside gym equipment that make the most of the stunning views. There are also wooden wigwams for hire.

Open: March to October (restricted service: March to Spring Bank Holiday and October – splash pool closed) **Last arrival:** 20.00 **Last departure:** noon

Pitches: see prices below; 41 hardstanding pitches

Leisure:

Facilities:

Services:

Within 3 miles:

Additional site information: 4 acre site. Cars can be parked by caravans and tents. Awnings permitted. No noise after 23.00. 100 acres of private heathland. Fire pits for hire, BBQ hut for hire, freshly baked bread available. Car hire can be arranged.

Glamping available: Wooden wigwams from £15.50. **Changeover days:** Any day

Additional glamping information: Wooden wigwams sleep 5. Cars can be parked by units

Glororum Caravan Park
★★★★ 91%

tel: 01670 860256 Glororum Farm NE69 7AW
email: enquiries@northumbrianleisure.co.uk
web: www.northumbrianleisure.co.uk/our-parks/glororum
dir: Exit A1 at junction with B1341 (Purdy's Lodge). In 3.5 miles left onto unclassified road. Site 300 yards on left.

Glororum Caravan Park continues to go from strength to strength following serious investment in the amenities and the infrastructure across the park. Pleasantly situated in open countryside, the park offers good views of Bamburgh Castle. A popular holiday destination where tourers have their own separate area – 43 excellent, well-spaced, fully serviced pitches have a lush grass area in addition to the hardstanding. This field also has a top notch purpose-built amenity block with a smartly clad interior and modern, efficient fittings. Children will love the play area and skateboard park.

Open: March to end November **Last arrival:** 18.00 **Last departure:** noon

Pitches: ; 43 hardstanding pitches; 30 seasonal pitches

Leisure:

Facilities:

Services:

Within 3 miles:

Additional site information: 6 acre site. Cars can be parked by caravans. Awnings permitted. No commercial vehicles, no noise after 23.00.

ENGLAND 192 NORTHUMBERLAND

BELFORD Map 21 NU13

Places to visit

Bamburgh Castle, BAMBURGH, NE69 7DF, 01668 214208
www.bamburghcastle.com

Lindisfarne Castle, HOLY ISLAND (LINDISFARNE), TD15 2SH, 01289 389244
www.nationaltrust.org.uk/lindisfarne-castle

Great for kids: Alnwick Castle, ALNWICK, NE66 1NG, 01665 511100
www.alnwickcastle.com

Platinum Park

South Meadows Caravan Park
★★★★★

tel: 01668 213326 **South Road NE70 7DP**
email: info@southmeadows.co.uk **web:** www.southmeadows.co.uk
dir: *From A1 between Alnwick and Berwick-upon-Tweed take B6349 towards Belford, at right bend site signed, turn left, site on right.*

An excellent, justifiably very popular site that is ideally situated to exploit the many beaches and attractions of the nearby Northumbrian coast. It is set in open countryside with generous, very well laid out pitches set amongst attractive beech hedging. There is a great adventure playground for children of all ages, two very good dog walks on site – one through bluebell woods, and a first-class toilet block. Ongoing investment in the park continues to impress.

Open: All year **Last departure:** 16.00
Pitches: 🚐 🚗 ⛺; 🛖 see prices below; 57 hardstanding pitches; 65 seasonal pitches
Leisure: 🛝 ⚽
Facilities: 🚿 ☉ ⛾ ✻ ♿ 🗄 🍴 🛒 WiFi
Services: 🔌 🗑 🧺 ⬆ 🔒 🧼 📺
Within 3 miles: 🎣 ⛳

Additional site information: 50 acre site. 🐕 Cars can be parked by caravans and tents. Awnings permitted. Minimum noise after 23.00, under 12s must be supervised in toilet blocks. Woodland walk, football and recreation field.

Glamping available: 5 wooden pods from £65 per night.

Additional glamping information: Pods sleep up to 4 adults or 2/3 adults + 2/3 children. 5 people maximum per pod. Must bring own bedding. 1 dog allowed per pod. Cars can be parked by units

BELLINGHAM Map 21 NY88

Places to visit

Wallington, CAMBO, NE61 4AR, 01670 773600
www.nationaltrust.org.uk/wallington

Premier Park

Bellingham Camping & Caravanning Club Site
★★★★★ 90%

tel: 01434 220175 & 024 7647 5426 **Brown Rigg NE48 2JY**
email: bellingham.site@campingandcaravanningclub.co.uk
web: www.campingandcaravanningclub.co.uk/bellingham
dir: *From A69 take A6079 north to Chollerford and B6320 to Bellingham. Pass Forestry Commission land, site 0.5 mile south of Bellingham.*

A beautiful and peaceful campsite set in the glorious Northumberland National Park. It is exceptionally well managed by the enthusiastic owners who offer high levels of customer care, maintenance and cleanliness. The excellent toilet facilities are spotlessly clean, and there are family washrooms, a recreation room, a campers' kitchen, a drying room, and star-gazing equipment for customers to use. There are four camping pods for hire. This is a perfect base for exploring an undiscovered part of England, and it is handily placed for visiting the beautiful Northumberland coast.

Open: March to 4 January **Last arrival:** 20.00 **Last departure:** noon
Pitches: 🚐 🚗 ⛺; 🛖 see prices below; 42 hardstanding pitches
Leisure: 🛝 ⚽ 🎱
Facilities: 🚿 ☉ ⛾ ✻ ♿ 🗄 🍴 WiFi 💻
Services: 🔌 🗑 🧺 ⬆ 🔒 🧼 📺
Within 3 miles: 🎣 ⛳

Additional site information: 5 acre site. 🐕 Cars can be parked by caravans and tents. Awnings permitted. Site gates closed and quiet time from 23.00–07.00. BBQs allowed. No open fires. Only septic tank soft (green) toilet fluids accepted. Communal modern fitted kitchen, centrally heated indoor social space, drying room.

Glamping available: Wooden pods from £45.

NORTHUMBERLAND 193 ENGLAND

BERWICK-UPON-TWEED
Map 21 NT95

Places to visit

Berwick-upon-Tweed Barracks, BERWICK-UPON-TWEED, TD15 1DF, 01289 304493
www.english-heritage.org.uk/visit/places/berwick-upon-tweed-barracks-and-main-guard

Platinum Park

Ord House Country Park
★★★★★

tel: 01289 305288 East Ord TD15 2NS
email: ordhouse@maguires.org.uk
web: www.maguirescountryparks.co.uk/parks/ord-house
dir: *From A1 (Berwick bypass), or from A698, at roundabout (south of River Tweed) follow East Ord sign, then brown site signs.*

Set within the grounds of 18th-century Ord House, this very well-run park takes great pride in the quality of its landscaping and in the siting and spacing of touring pitches, some of which are fully serviced. The toilet blocks are truly superb. Youngsters are well catered for with a fantastic adventure playground, mini golf and a football field. A broad range of meals is available in Maguires Bar & Grill where there is also a soft toy play area for children and a relaxing adults-only bar. There is also a fenced dog walking trail that goes around the park.

Open: All year **Last arrival:** 23.00 **Last departure:** noon
Pitches: 🚐 🚙 ▲; 🏠 see prices below; 46 hardstanding pitches; 30 seasonal pitches
Leisure: /▲\ ⚽
Facilities: 🚿 ⊙ 🎣 ✻ ♿ 🛒 🍴 WiFi
Services: 🔌 🔥 🍺 🍽 🚮 ♨ 🔒 ♻
Within 3 miles: ⛴ 🎣 ◎ ✈ 🎯

Additional site information: 42 acre site. 🐕 Cars can be parked by caravans and tents. Awnings permitted. No noise after 22.30. Crazy golf, table tennis, football field, soft play area, woodland walk.
Glamping available: Wooden wishbone lodges from £48.
Additional glamping information: Wishbone lodges include bunk beds, camp beds, electricity and heating. No group bookings. Cars can be parked by units

Premier Park

Berwick Holiday Park
★★★★★ 91% HOLIDAY PARK

tel: 01289 307113 Magdalene Fields TD15 1NE
web: www.haven.com/berwick
dir: *From A1 follow Berwick-upon-Tweed signs. At Morrisons/McDonalds roundabout take 2nd exit. At mini roundabout straight on, into North Road (pass Shell garage on left). At next mini-roundabout 1st exit into Northumberland Avenue. Park at end.*

A very friendly, welcoming static-only holiday park with excellent entertainment and leisure facilities for all ages, and with direct access to the beach on the edge of Berwick. Exciting family activities and entertainment include indoor and outdoor swimming pools, the FunWorks Amusement Centre, Nature Rockz and a multi-sports court. Everything here is of a high standard – the holiday homes, the landscaping and the facilities – customer feedback on their holiday experience is very positive. Close to the stunning Northumberland coast for invigorating walks, dramatic castles and glorious sandy beaches.

Open: mid March to 30 October **Last departure:** 10.00
Holiday Homes: Sleep 8, Bedrooms 3, Bathrooms 1, Toilets 2, Microwave, Freezer, TV, Sky/Freeview, DVD player, Linen included, Electricity included, Gas included
Changeover days: Monday, Friday and Saturday
Leisure: 🏊 🏊 🎱 🎯 🎵
Facilities: ♿ 🛒 WiFi
Within 3 miles: ⛴

Additional site information: 🐕 The facilities provided in the holiday homes may differ depending on the grade. Most dog breeds accepted (please check when booking). Dogs must be kept on leads at all times.

Premier Park

Haggerston Castle Holiday Park
★★★★★ 83% HOLIDAY PARK

tel: 01289 381333 Beal TD15 2PA
web: www.haven.com/parks/northumberland/haggerston-castle
dir: *On A1, 7 miles south of Berwick-upon-Tweed, site signed.*

A large holiday centre along with a touring park, offering comprehensive holiday activities. The entertainment complex contains amusements for the whole family, and there are several bars, an adventure playground, boating on the lake, a children's club, a 9-hole golf course, tennis courts, and various eating outlets. Please note that this site does not accept tents.

Open: mid March to end October (restricted service: mid March to May and September to October – some facilities may be reduced) **Last arrival:** anytime **Last departure:** 10.00
Pitches: 🚐 🚙; 140 hardstanding pitches
Leisure: 🏊 /▲\ 🏌 🎱 🎣 🎵 🎯 🎯
Facilities: 🚿 ⊙ 🎣 ✻ ♿ 🛒 🍴 ➡ WiFi 💻
Services: 🔌 🔥 🍺 🍽 🚮 ♨ 🔒 T
Within 3 miles: ⛳ ◎ ✈

Additional site information: 100 acre site. 🐕 No commercial vehicles, no bookings by persons under 21 years unless a family booking. Maximum 2 dogs per booking, certain dog breeds banned.

FACILITIES: 🔌 Electric vehicle charging 🛁 Baths/Shower ⊙ Electric shaver sockets 🎣 Hairdryer ✻ Ice pack facility 👶 Baby facilities ♿ Disabled facilities 🛒 Shop on site or within 200yds 🍖 BBQ area 🍴 Picnic area WiFi WiFi 🖥 Internet access **SERVICES:** 🔌 Electric hook-up 🔥 Launderette 🍺 Licensed bar 🛢 Calor Gas ⛽ Campingaz T Toilet fluid 🍽 Café/Restaurant 🚮 Fast Food/Takeaway 🔋 Battery charging ♨ Motorhome service point 🚫 No credit or debit cards 🐕 Dogs permitted 🚫 No dogs

HALTWHISTLE   Map 21 NY76

Places to visit
Corbridge Roman Town – Hadrian's Wall, CORBRIDGE, NE45 5NT, 01434 632349
www.english-heritage.org.uk/visit/places/corbridge-roman-town-hadrians-wall

Chesters Roman Fort, WALWICK, NE46 4EU, 01434 681379
www.english-heritage.org.uk/visit/places/chesters-roman-fort-and-museum-hadrians-wall

Platinum Park

Herding Hill Farm Touring & Camping Site
★★★★★

tel: 01434 320175 Shield Hill NE49 9NW
email: bookings@herdinghillfarm.co.uk web: www.herdinghillfarm.co.uk
dir: *A69 to Haltwhistle. Follow the brown campsite signs. If towing a caravan – from west: exit A69 at Greenhead onto B6318. Follow brown campsite signs, right at Milecastle Inn; from east: exit A69 at Corbridge onto A68 north, left onto B6318 towards Chollerford. Follow brown campsite signs, left at Milecastle Inn.*

In an idyllic rural location with dark skies and gorgeous sunsets, above Haltwhistle and very close to Hadrian's Wall, this beautifully developed dog-friendly campsite is geared to families and offers a mix of accommodation. Amenities include excellent grass tent pitches, spacious, serviced hardstandings, a 6-berth lodge, family-friendly wigwam cabins (some with toilets and hot tubs), and a luxury glamping area exclusively for adults. The upmarket amenity block is ultra-modern – with accessible family bathroom, private bathrooms (with baths in the ladies), a private unisex sauna for hire, laundry, underfloor heating, and an indoor campers' kitchen. There is a small, licensed shop selling local produce, children's playground and ball field, BBQ hut for hire, animal petting farm, and a scenic dog walk and enclosed exercise field. Additional facilities include fire pits and BBQs for hire (breakfast and BBQ packs are available to purchase), croc boxes, linen, stargazing kits, and free WiFi. Pizzas are available on Friday evenings in season. Ideal for exploring Hadrian's Wall – the AD122 Hadrian's Wall bus stops at the campsite entrance.

Open: All year **Last arrival:** 20.00 (late arrivals with prior arrangement) **Last departure:** noon
Pitches: ; see prices below; 13 hardstanding touring pitches and 10 grass tent pitches
Leisure:
Facilities:
Services:
Within 3 miles:

Additional site information: 4.86 acre site. Cars can be parked by caravans and tents. Awnings permitted. No noise after 22.30. Private unisex sauna for hire. BBQ hut for hire; takeaway pizza Friday evenings in season. BBQ and breakfast meat packs available. Dog walk and enclosed excercise field. Animal petting farm (children can help at feeding times).

Glamping available: Wigwam cabins from £50; En suite Castle Pods with hot tubs from £115 **Changeover days:** Any day

Additional glamping information: Cars can be parked by Wigwam units; Castle Pod car park is a short walk.

Platinum Park

Herding Hill Farm, Glamping site
★★★★★   GLAMPING ONLY

tel: 01434 320175 Shield Hill NE49 9NW
email: bookings@herdinghillfarm.co.uk web: www.herdinghillfarm.co.uk
dir: *A69 to Haltwhistle. Follow the brown campsite signs. If towing a caravan – from west: exit A69 at Greenhead onto B6318. Follow brown campsite signs, right at Milecastle Inn; from east: exit A69 at Corbridge onto A68 north, left onto B6318 towards Chollerford. Follow brown campsite signs, left at Milecastle Inn.*

Located above the town of Haltwhistle and very close to Hadrian's Wall, this developing glamping site is ideally suited for walkers, ramblers and historians alike. Separate from the touring area at the bottom of the site on a rolling hillside, each unit offers wonderful panoramic views and dark Northumberland skies. All the huts (Wigwam® cabins) have electric heating and some also boast their own hot tubs; the luxury Castle Pods all have their own hot tubs and smart, enhanced facilities taking glamping to whole new level.

Open: All year **Last arrival:** 20.00 **Last departure:** 10.00
Leisure:
Facilities:
Within 3 miles:

Accommodation available: Wigwam cabins from £50; Wigwam cabins with hot tub from £100; Luxury en suite Castle Pods with hot tubs from £115

Changeover days: Any day

Additional site information: 4.86 acre site. No noise after 22.30. No electronic noise at any time. Unisex sauna for exclusive hire. Takeaway pizza Fridays in season. BBQ meat and breakfast packs available. Dog walk and enclosed exercise area. Cars can be parked by Wigwam units; Castle Pod car park is a short walk.

NORTHUMBERLAND—NOTTINGHAMSHIRE ENGLAND

HEXHAM
Map 21 NY96

Places to visit

Vindolanda (Chesterholm), BARDON MILL, NE47 7JN, 01434 344277
www.vindolanda.com

Temple of Mithras (Hadrian's Wall), CARRAWBROUGH, NE46 4DB, 0370 333 1181
www.english-heritage.org.uk/visit/places/temple-of-mithras-carrawburgh-hadrians-wall

Great for kids: Housesteads Roman Fort, HOUSESTEADS, NE47 6NN, 01434 344363
www.english-heritage.org.uk/visit/places/housesteads-roman-fort-hadrians-wall

Hexham Racecourse Caravan Site
★★★ 80%

tel: 01434 606847 & 606881 Hexham Racecourse NE46 2JP
email: caravansite@hexham-racecourse.co.uk
web: www.hexham-racecourse.co.uk/page/accommodation/caravan-camping-site
dir: *From Hexham take B6305 signed Allendale and Alston. Left in 3 miles signed to racecourse. Site 1.5 miles on right.*

A part-level and part-sloping grassy site, Hexham Racecourse Caravan Site offers commanding views from its elevated position, overlooking the Northumberland and Hexham Moors. You can watch the racing from your own pitch and discounted raceday tickets are available. Hadrian's Wall is nearby.

Open: May to mid-October **Last arrival:** 20.00 **Last departure:** noon
Pitches: 🚐 🚚 ⛺; 20 seasonal pitches
Leisure: 🎱
Facilities: 🚿 ☺ 🎨 ✳ 🍴 WiFi
Services: 🔌 🗑 🔒 ♻
Within 3 miles: ↧ 🎣 ◎ 🚴 🚌 🛍

Additional site information: 4 acre site. 🐕 Cars can be parked by caravans and tents. Awnings permitted. No noise after 23.00.

NOTTINGHAMSHIRE

CHURCH LANEHAM
Map 17 SK87

Places to visit

Newark Air Museum, NEWARK-ON-TRENT, NG24 2NY, 01636 707170
www.newarkairmuseum.org

Doddington Hall, LINCOLN, LN6 4RU, 01522 694308
www.doddingtonhall.com

Trentfield Farm
★★★ 86%

tel: 01777 651 DN22 0NJ
email: bookings@trentfield.co.uk web: www.trentfield.co.uk
dir: *A1 onto A57 towards Lincoln for 6 miles. Left signed Laneham, 1.5 miles, through Laneham and Church Laneham (pass Ferryboat pub on left). Site 300 yards on right.*

A delightfully rural and level grass park tucked away on the banks of the River Trent. The park has its own river frontage with free coarse fishing available to park residents. There are excellent walking opportunities in the area, and the neat touring areas are enhanced by large displays of pretty seasonal flowers. The facilities block is modern, hygienic and offers very good privacy options with two family rooms.

Open: Easter to November **Last arrival:** 20.00 **Last departure:** noon
Pitches: 🚐 🚚 ⛺; 20 seasonal pitches
Facilities: 🚿 ☺ 🎨 ✳ ♿ 🍴 WiFi
Services: 🔌 🗑 🔒 ♻
Within 3 miles: ↧ 🎣 🛍

Additional site information: 34 acre site. 🐕 Cars can be parked by caravans and tents. Awnings permitted. No open fires or fire pits. 24-hour mini shop.

Make your next UK holiday one to remember

Choose RatedTrips.com

AA

FACILITIES: ⚡ Electric vehicle charging 🛁 Baths/Shower ☺ Electric shaver sockets 🎨 Hairdryer ✳ Ice pack facility 🍼 Baby facilities ♿ Disabled facilities 🛍 Shop on site or within 200yds 🔥 BBQ area 🍴 Picnic area WiFi WiFi 💻 Internet access **SERVICES:** 🔌 Electric hook-up 🗑 Launderette 🍺 Licensed bar 🔒 Calor Gas ♻ Campingaz 🚽 Toilet fluid 🍽 Café/Restaurant 🍔 Fast Food/Takeaway 🔋 Battery charging ⬇ Motorhome service point 🚫 No credit or debit cards 🐕 Dogs permitted 🚷 No dogs

NOTTINGHAMSHIRE—OXFORDSHIRE

MANSFIELD — Map 16 SK56

Places to visit

Sherwood Forest National Nature Reserve, EDWINSTOWE, NG21 9RN, 01623 677321
www.visitsherwood.co.uk

Tall Trees Touring Park
★★★ 79%

tel: 01623 626503 **Old Mill Lane, Forest Town NG19 0JP**
email: info@talltreestouringpark.co.uk web: www.talltreestouringpark.co.uk
dir: *A60 from Mansfield towards Worksop. In 1 mile turn right at lights into Old Mill Lane. Site in approximately 0.5 mile on left.*

A pleasant park situated just on the outskirts of Mansfield and within easy walking distance of shops and restaurants. It is surrounded on three sides by trees and shrubs, and securely set at the back of the residential park. This site has a practical amenity block, a fishing lake to the rear of the site and an extra grassed area to give more space for caravans and tents.

Open: All year **Last arrival:** anytime **Last departure:** 11.00

Pitches: 🚐 🚙 ⛺; 12 hardstanding pitches; 15 seasonal pitches

Leisure: 🛝 🎣 ⚽

Facilities: 🚿 ☉ 🅿 ✱ ♿ 🍴 WiFi

Services: 🔌 🗑

Within 3 miles: 🚶 U 🏇 🎬 🛒

Additional site information: 10 acre site. 🚗 Cars can be parked by caravans and tents. Awnings permitted. No noise after 22.00.

SOUTHWELL — Map 17 SK65

Places to visit

The Workhouse, SOUTHWELL, NG25 0PT, 01636 817260
www.nationaltrust.org.uk/the-workhouse-southwell

SOUTHWELL — Map 17 SK65

New Hall Farm Touring Park
★★★ 84%

tel: 01623 883041 **New Hall Farm, Newhall Lane NG22 8BS**
email: enquiries@newhallfarm.co.uk web: www.newhallfarm.co.uk
dir: *From roundabout on A617 (east of Rainworth) take A614 signed Nottingham. At next roundabout left signed Farnsfield. Through Farnsfield and Edingley. At top of hill right into Newhall Lane. 0.5 mile, site on right. Or from Kirklington on A617 into Southwell Road follow signs to Edlington. At top of hill right into Newhall Lane. 0.5 mile, site on right.*

New Hall Farm is ideally suited for the discerning adult visitor. Sited on the most attractive area of the farm near mature oak, ash and beech trees, there are outstanding views in all directions. A log cabin viewing gantry offers a place to relax and take in the spectacular scenery. It's just three miles from Southwell and a short drive to Newark and Sherwood Forest.

Open: March to October **Last arrival:** 21.00 **Last departure:** noon

Pitches: 🚐 🚙 ⛺; 10 hardstanding pitches; 10 seasonal pitches

Facilities: 🚿 ☉ ✱ 🍴

Services: 🔌 🗑 🧺

Within 3 miles: 🚶 🎣 U 🛒

Additional site information: 2.5 acre site. Adults only. 🚗 🐕 Cars can be parked by caravans and tents. Awnings permitted. Quiet after 22.00. Dogs must be kept on leads around the park. Owners must clear up after their dogs. Walking trail, cycling trail, viewing gantry, ice cream for sale on site.

OXFORDSHIRE

BANBURY — Map 11 SP44

Places to visit

Banbury Museum, BANBURY, OX16 2PQ, 01295 236165
www.banburymuseum.org

Great for kids: Deddington Castle, DEDDINGTON, OX15 0TP, 0370 333 1181
www.english-heritage.org.uk/visit/places/deddington-castle

Barnstones Caravan & Camping Site
★★★★ 84%

tel: 01295 750289 **Great Bourton OX17 1QU**
web: www.barnstonescaravanpark.co.uk
dir: *Take A423 from Banbury signed Southam. In 3 miles turn right signed Great Bourton and Cropredy, site 100 yards on right.*

A popular, family-run site with plenty of hardstandings, some fully serviced pitches, practical washrooms and excellent rally facilities. Campers can expect to receive a warm welcome from the friendly family owners at this excellent value park. The site is well positioned for stopovers or for visiting nearby Banbury.

Open: All year **Last arrival:** by arrangement **Last departure:** by arrangement

Pitches: 🚐 🚙 ⛺; 44 hardstanding pitches

Leisure: 🛝 ⚽

Facilities: 🚿 ☉ ✱ ♿ 🚻 🍴 WiFi

Services: 🔌 🗑 🧺 🛒 💩 🚰

Within 3 miles: 🚶 🎣 U ⛳ 🏊 🏇 🎬 🛒

Additional site information: 3 acre site. 🚗 🐕 Cars can be parked by caravans and tents. Awnings permitted. No rollerblades. No noise after midnight.

OXFORDSHIRE 197 ENGLAND

FRINGFORD
Map 11 SP62

Places to visit
Rousham House, ROUSHAM, OX25 4QX, 01869 347110
www.rousham.org

Stowe House, STOWE, MK18 5EH, 01280 818002
www.stowe.co.uk

Great for kids: Buckinghamshire Railway Centre, QUAINTON, HP22 4BY, 01296 655120
www.bucksrailcentre.org

Glebe Leisure
★★★ 81%

tel: 01869 277800 **Stratton Lane OX27 8RJ**
email: ann.herring@btinternet.com web: www.glebeleisure.co.uk
dir: *M40 junction 10, A43 (signed Northampton). At next roundabout take B4100 signed Bicester. 2nd right onto unclassified road signed Hethe and Stoke Lyne. Follow brown site signs.*

Glebe Leisure is a small, peaceful park in a good countryside location just a few miles from Bicester and the M40, making it an ideal overnight stopover site. It is also very popular with fishing enthusiasts due to the well-stocked lake, and with keen shoppers wishing to spend time at the Bicester Village shopping outlet, three miles away. The park comprises two well-tended fields – one with hardstandings and four camping pods, the other with neat, grassy pitches; shepherd's huts are available too. The wash blocks (including a shower block in the rally field), offer clean, well-maintained facilities and there's a good motorhome service point.

Open: All year (restricted service: site closes at 19.00) **Last arrival:** March to September 19.00; October to February 18.00 **Last departure:** anytime (subject to request)
Pitches: see prices below; 15 hardstanding pitches
Leisure:
Facilities: WiFi
Services:
Within 3 miles:

Additional site information: 5 acre site. Cars can be parked by caravans and tents. Awnings permitted. No noise or taxis after 23.00, no unaccompanied children in toilet block or around lakes. Dog walks.
Glamping available: Wooden pods from £39 and £49 per night; shepherd's hut from £75.
Changeover days: Any day
Additional glamping information: Cars can be parked by units

HENLEY-ON-THAMES
Map 5 SU78

Places to visit
Greys Court, HENLEY-ON-THAMES, RG9 4PG, 01491 628529
www.nationaltrust.org.uk/greys-court

Great for kids: River & Rowing Museum, HENLEY-ON-THAMES, RG9 1BF, 01491 415600
www.rrm.co.uk

HENLEY-ON-THAMES
Map 5 SU78

Platinum Park

Swiss Farm Touring & Camping
★★★★★

tel: 01491 573419 **Marlow Road RG9 2HY**
email: info@swissfarmhenley.co.uk web: www.swissfarmhenley.co.uk
dir: *From Henley-on-Thames take A4155 towards Marlow. 1st left after rugby club.*

Swiss Farm Touring & Camping enjoys an excellent location within easy walking distance of the town and is perfect for those visiting Windsor, London, Oxford, or the Henley Regatta (but booking is essential at that time). Pitches are very spacious; most are fully serviced. A fabulous, licensed café serves coffee, breakfasts, light lunches and special evening menus. A sail awning covers the patio seating, and the excellent outdoor swimming pool is open during the summer. There are lakeside cedar cabins, luxury shepherd's huts and static holiday caravans for hire, and a well-stocked shop sells quality local food items.

Open: 14 February to November (restricted service: March to May and October to November – pool closed) **Last arrival:** 21.00 **Last departure:** noon
Pitches: see prices below; 100 hardstanding pitches
Leisure: **Facilities:** WiFi
Services: **Within 3 miles:**

Additional site information: 6 acre site. Cars can be parked by caravans and tents. Awnings permitted. No groups. No dogs during spring half term and summer holidays.
Glamping available: Wooden pods from £85. Lodges from £270 for 3 nights.
Changeover days: Friday and Monday

See advert on page 198

FACILITIES: Electric vehicle charging · Baths/Shower · Electric shaver sockets · Hairdryer · Ice pack facility · Baby facilities · Disabled facilities · Shop on site or within 200yds · BBQ area · Picnic area · WiFi · Internet access **SERVICES:** Electric hook-up · Launderette · Licensed bar · Calor Gas · Campingaz · Toilet fluid · Café/Restaurant · Fast Food/Takeaway · Battery charging · Motorhome service point · No credit or debit cards · Dogs permitted · No dogs

OXFORDSHIRE

STANDLAKE
Map 5 SP30

Places to visit

Buscot Park, BUSCOT, SN7 8BU, 01367 240786
www.buscot-park.com

Harcourt Arboretum, OXFORD, OX44 9PX, 01865 610300
www.obga.ox.ac.uk/visit-arboretum

Great for kids: Cotswold Wildlife Park and Gardens, BURFORD, OX18 4JP, 01993 823006
www.cotswoldwildlifepark.co.uk

Platinum Park

Lincoln Farm Park Oxfordshire
★★★★★

tel: 01865 300239 **High Street OX29 7RH**
email: info@lincolnfarmpark.co.uk web: www.lincolnfarmpark.co.uk
dir: *Exit A415 between Abingdon and Witney (5 miles south-east of Witney). Follow brown campsite sign in Standlake.*

This attractively landscaped family-run park, located in a quiet village near the River Thames, offers a truly excellent camping or caravanning experience. There are top class facilities throughout the park and through the combination of sound investment by the owner and passionate, caring managers, the park has seen significant improvements. It has excellent leisure facilities in the Standlake Leisure Centre complete with two pools plus a gym and sauna, and there's a spa/massage facility. This is the perfect base for visiting the many attractions in Oxfordshire and the Cotswolds. A warm welcome is assured from the friendly staff.

Open: February to November **Last arrival:** 20.00 **Last departure:** noon

Pitches: 🚐 🚗 ⛺; 75 hardstanding pitches

Leisure: 🏊 ♨ 🎣 🏐 🎯

Facilities: 🚻 ⊙ 🚿 ✳ ♿ 💲 🍴 📶

Services: 💧 🗑 🧺 🧳 🔒 ⛽ 📺

Within 3 miles: 👟 🎣 🏇 ⛵ 🏊

Additional site information: 9 acre site. 🐕 Cars can be parked by caravans and tents. Awnings permitted. No noise after 22.00. Information/reading room, games.

Swiss Farm
TOURING & CAMPING
FAMILY OWNED SINCE 1946

Touring · Camping · Glamping Holiday Caravan Hire · Café · Pool · Fishing

www.swissfarmhenley.co.uk
01491 573419

RUTLAND

GREETHAM Map 11 SK91

Places to visit

Rutland County Museum & Visitor Centre, OAKHAM, LE15 6HW, 01572 758440
www.rutlandcountymuseum.org.uk

Oakham Castle, OAKHAM, LE15 6DR, 01572 757578
www.oakhamcastle.org

Premier Park

In The Stix
★★★★★ 93% GLAMPING ONLY

tel: 07958 378971 **Brook Farm, Wood Lane LE15 7SN**
email: hello@inthestix.co.uk

Set in a private valley in the heart of the tranquil Rutland countryside, In The Stix is a very special glamping destination. Each of the six bespoke geodesic domes sleeps up to six guests, and they have been designed and furnished to a very high standard with the ultimate comfort and relaxation in mind; spacious and very smart living/sleeping spaces also have an additional mezzanine level. The wood-fired hot-tubs, fully-equipped kitchens, superb indoor and outdoor dining spaces (complete with Kamado Grill) really enhance the overall experience. The positioning of each dome has been thoughtfully considered to allow privacy, but for some socialising with other guests if you wish. Additional facilities include a sauna, 'Smoke 'n Stix', an impressive communal dining/event space, a communal fire-pit, a children's play area, and food hampers (breakfast and BBQ) to order.

Open: **Last arrival:** 19.00 **Last departure:** 10.30
Accommodation available: Domes
Additional site information: 13 acre site.

Premier Park

Rutland Caravan & Camping
★★★★★ 88%

tel: 01572 813520 **Park Lane LE15 7FN**
email: info@rutlandcaravanandcamping.co.uk
web: www.rutlandcaravanandcamping.co.uk
dir: From A1 onto B668 towards Greetham. Before Greetham turn right at crossroads, left to site.

This pretty caravan park, built to a high specification and surrounded by well-planted banks, continues to improve year after year due to the enthusiasm and vision of its owner. The site has a swimming pool, fully serviced pitches and luxury lodges. From the spacious reception and café to the innovative play area, everything is of a very high standard. This spacious, grassy site is close to the Viking Way and other footpath networks, and is well situated for visiting Rutland Water and the many picturesque villages in the area.

Open: All year **Last arrival:** 20.00
Pitches: 65 hardstanding pitches; 20 seasonal pitches
Leisure: **Facilities:**
Services: Within 3 miles:
Additional site information: 5 acre site. Cars can be parked by caravans and tents. Awnings permitted. No noise after 23.00. Dog shower.

SHROPSHIRE

BRIDGNORTH Map 10 SO79

Places to visit

Benthall Hall, BENTHALL, TF12 5RX, 01952 882159
www.nationaltrust.org.uk/benthall-hall

Great for kids: Dudmaston Estate, QUATT, WV15 6QN, 01746 780866
www.nationaltrust.org.uk/dudmaston

Premier Park

Stanmore Hall Touring Park
★★★★★ 88%

tel: 01746 761761 **Stourbridge Road WV15 6DT**
email: stanmore@morris-leisure.co.uk **web:** www.morris-leisure.co.uk/touring-caravan-sites/stanmore-hall-touring-park
dir: *Stanmore Hall Touring Park is located on the A458 Stourbridge Road, a short distance from Bridgnorth.*

Stanmore Hall Touring Park is an excellent park in peaceful surroundings offering outstanding facilities. The pitches, many fully serviced (with Freeview TV), are arranged around the lake close to Stanmore Hall. Arboretum standard trees include some magnificent Californian Redwoods and an oak that is nearly 700 years old. The site is handy for visiting Ironbridge, the Severn Valley Railway and the attractive market town of Bridgnorth. Free WiFi is available throughout all areas.

Open: All year **Last arrival:** 20.00 (late arrival pitches available) **Last departure:** noon
Pitches: 68 hardstanding pitches; 12 seasonal pitches
Leisure:
Facilities:
Services:
Within 3 miles:
Additional site information: 12.5 acre site. Cars can be parked by caravans and tents. Awnings permitted. Adult only section. Dog walk.

SHROPSHIRE

LUDLOW   Map 10 SO57

Places to visit
Ludlow Castle, LUDLOW, SY8 1AY, 01584 873355
www.ludlowcastle.com

Berrington Hall, near LEOMINSTER, HR6 0DW, 01568 615721
www.nationaltrust.org.uk/visit/worcestershire-herefordshire/berrington-hall

Premier Park

Westbrook Park
★★★★★ 91%

tel: 01584 711280 Little Hereford SY8 4AU
email: info@westbrookpark.co.uk web: www.westbrookpark.co.uk
dir: *A49 onto A456 signed Kidderminster/Tenbury. Continue to Little Hereford, turn right into Lynch Lane, signed Leysters. Take next left, park on left.*

Peacefully located along the banks of the River Teme and with the benefit of half a mile of private fishing, this long-established park is ideally placed for visiting nearby Tenbury Wells and historic Ludlow, with its fine reputation for historical architecture and quality food suppliers. Surrounded by high hedging, each spacious pitch has an all-weather hardstanding and is equipped with water, electric supply and grey waste drainage. The presentation of the grounds is noteworthy, with manicured grass, both indigenous and cultivated plants and pretty displays of seasonal flowers, all combine to create a colourful and relaxing atmosphere.

Open: 1 March to 30 November **Last arrival:** 21.00 **Last departure:** 11.00
Pitches: 🚐 🚙 ⛺; 53 hardstanding pitches; 10 seasonal pitches
Leisure: ⚽ 🎣 **Facilities:** 🚻 ☉ 🍴 ✻ ♿ 🛒 📶
Services: 🔌 🚮 ⛽ 🔒 📞 **Within 3 miles:** ⛳ 🎬 🍴

Additional site information: 5 acre site. 🚗 Cars can be parked by caravans and tents. Awnings permitted. No cycling, scooters or skateboards. New bike ride area available at the playground

LYNEAL   Map 15 SJ43

Places to visit
Old Oswestry Hill Fort, OSWESTRY, 0370 333 1181
www.english-heritage.org.uk/visit/places/old-oswestry-hillfort

Great for kids: Hawkstone Historic Park & Follies, WESTON-UNDER-REDCASTLE, SY4 5JY, 01948 841777 www.hawkstoneparkfollies.co.uk

LYNEAL   Map 15 SJ43

Fernwood Caravan Park
★★★★ 88%

tel: 01948 710221 SY12 0QF
email: enquiries@fernwoodpark.co.uk web: www.fernwoodpark.co.uk
dir: *From A495 in Welshampton take B5063, over canal bridge, turn right, follow signs.*

A peaceful park set in wooded countryside, with a screened, tree-lined touring area and coarse fishing lake. The approach to the park passes colourful shrubs and flower beds, and part of the static area is tastefully arranged around a children's play area. There is a small child-free touring area for those wanting complete relaxation, and the park has 40 acres of woodland where there are many walks to enjoy.

Open: March to November (restricted service: March and November – shop closed)
Last arrival: 21.00 **Last departure:** 17.00
Pitches: 🚐 🚙; 8 hardstanding pitches; 30 seasonal pitches
Leisure: ⚽ 🎣 **Facilities:** 🚻 ☉ 🍴 ✻ ♿ 🛒
Services: 🔌 🚮 ⛽ 🔒 📞
Within 3 miles: ⛳

Additional site information: 26 acre site. 🚗 Cars can be parked by caravans. Awnings permitted. No noise after 23.00. Guest WiFi available by site office.

RUYTON-XI-TOWNS   Map 15 SJ32

Places to visit
Old Oswestry Hill Fort, OSWESTRY, 0370 333 1181
www.english-heritage.org.uk/visit/places/old-oswestry-hillfort

Great for kids: Hawkstone Historic Park & Follies, WESTON-UNDER-REDCASTLE, SY4 5JY, 01948 841777
www.hawkstoneparkfollies.co.uk

Platinum Park

Riverside Cabins
★★★★★   GLAMPING ONLY

tel: 01939 260495 Weirbridge Cottage, Stanwardine Lane SY4 1HY
email: contact@riverside-cabins.co.uk web: www.riverside-cabins.co.uk

Located within a peaceful area of beautiful countryside, this relaxing park is an ideal base for exploring historic Oswestry, Shrewsbury and mid-Wales. Set in 10-acre grounds which include a former sandstone quarry and spacious and lush grassed areas. Both indigenous and cultivated plants and mature trees of an arboretum quality combine to create an atmosphere of tranquillity. The River Perry also borders the park and with peace assured, the only distractions are the welcome ones of running water and birdsong. The cedar cabins are very well spaced to create optimum privacy, and all have the benefit of hot tubs; the interiors are luxuriously appointed with underfloor heating and quality furnishings and fixtures. A large bell tent is available for group activities such as meditation and yoga, plus there are free-to-use paddle boards, kayaks and electric bikes. Dogs are welcome.

SHROPSHIRE 201 ENGLAND

SHREWSBURY
Map 15 SJ41

Places to visit
Attingham Park Estate Town Walls (NT), SHREWSBURY, SY1 1TN, 01743 708162
www.nationaltrust.org.uk/attingham-park-estate-town-walls-tower

Great for kids: Wroxeter Roman City, WROXETER, SY5 6PH, 01743 761330
www.english-heritage.org.uk/visit/places/wroxeter-roman-city

Premier Park

Beaconsfield Holiday Park
★★★★★ 93% HOLIDAY PARK

tel: 01939 210370 & 210399 Battlefield SY4 4BE
email: mail@beaconsfieldholidaypark.co.uk web: www.beaconsfieldholidaypark.co.uk
dir: At Hadnall, 1.5 miles northeast of Shrewsbury. Follow sign for Astley from A49.

A purpose-built, adults-only (21 years and over) family-run park on farmland in open countryside. This pleasant park offers quality in every area, including superior toilets, heated indoor swimming pool and attractive landscaping. Coarse fishing is available on the park's own lakes. The Croft restaurant and bar is open Tuesday to Sunday. Three different styles of luxury lodges are available for hire. Free WiFi is also available.

Beaconsfield Holiday Park

Open: All year **Last arrival:** 19.00 **Last departure:** 11.00
Pitches: ; 50 hardstanding pitches; 10 seasonal pitches
Leisure:
Facilities:
Services:
Within 3 miles:
Additional site information: 16 acre site. Adults only.

See advert below

speak to us 01939 210370 email us mail@beaconsfieldholidaypark.co.uk
Beaconsfield Holiday Park | Upper Battlefield | Shrewsbury | Shropshire | SY4 4BE

FACILITIES: Electric vehicle charging Baths/Shower Electric shaver sockets Hairdryer Ice pack facility Baby facilities Disabled facilities Shop on site or within 200yds BBQ area Picnic area WiFi Internet access **SERVICES:** Electric hook-up Launderette Licensed bar Calor Gas Campingaz Toilet fluid Café/Restaurant Fast Food/Takeaway Battery charging Motorhome service point No credit or debit cards Dogs permitted No dogs

SHROPSHIRE

SHREWSBURY continued

Premier Park

Cartref Caravan & Camping
★★★★★ 93%

tel: 01743 821688 & 07803 907061 **Cartref, Ford Heath SY5 9GD**
email: info@cartrefcaravansite.co.uk web: www.cartrefcaravansite.co.uk
dir: *From north: A5 from Oswestry. Exit off A5 onto A458 to Welshpool, in village of Ford turn left after petrol station (brown sign). 2nd right, campsite on left. From south: exit A5 onto B4386, approximately 2 miles turn right (brown sign), take 2nd left.*

Located in the peaceful hamlet of Ford Heath, less than five miles from Shrewsbury, this carefully designed adults-only holiday destination is ideal for caravans and motorhomes. Pitches, all fully serviced, are enclosed by mature hedges and colourful shrubs to create optimum privacy. A vintage caravan with a converted horsebox housing the en suite facilities creates that unique glamping experience. In addition to a well-equipped amenity block, a rustic-themed bar provides a wide range of wines, spirits and local ales, there's a takeaway service, and the well-stocked shop offers the best local produce. Additional features include a safe meadow area for dog walking and a wildlife pond carefully planted to attract a variety of birds and animals including the great crested newt.

Open: 6 March to 1 November **Last arrival:** 21.00 **Last departure:** 11.00 (later by prior arrangement)

Pitches: 🚐 🚍 ⛺; 🏠 see prices below; 31 hardstanding pitches; 13 seasonal pitches

Leisure: 🛝

Facilities: 🏠 ☺ ⛽ ✻ ♿ 🛁 🛒 🚿 WiFi

Services: 🔌 🔄 🚽 🍴 🚻 🧺 ⬆ 🔒 T

Within 3 miles: 🎣

Additional site information: 7.7 acre site. Adults only. 🐕 Cars can be parked by caravans and tents. Awnings permitted. No ball games or cycling. Strict no noise policy between 23.00–8.00. Fresh baked bread to order, breakfast baps and fresh baked pizza on Friday and Saturday evenings. Local information available. Local walk details available. Car hire can be arranged.

Glamping available: Vintage caravan from £100 per night (includes continental breakfast). **Changeover days:** Any day

Additional glamping information: Sleeps 2. Includes coffee machine, combination microwave and fridge. Wet room in converted horse box. No dogs or BBQs. Cars can be parked by units

Premier Park

Love2Stay Shrewsbury
★★★★★ 93%

tel: 01743 583124 **Emstrey SY5 6QS**
email: info@love2stay.co.uk web: www.love2stay.co.uk/Shrewsbury

Love2Stay Shrewsbury is a unique hospitality destination set on 24 acres of grounds. A combination of excellent fully serviced touring pitches, some with the availability of fully furnished stylish awnings, and a variety of unique glamping units, all with good alfresco areas and hot tubs. Adjacent to the glamping units, barbecue and pizza ovens are provided for communal gatherings, and a well-equipped gym with spa treatments is also available. A wild water swimming pool and a heated paddling pool with adjacent beach are further attractions, and an on-site cinema has twice daily film shows. Stylish public areas include an excellent reception with information area and a fully licensed bistro.

Open: All year **Last arrival:** 20.00 **Last departure:** 12.30

Pitches: 🚐 🚍 🏠

Additional site information: 24 acre site.

Premier Park

Stoney Acres Luxury Holiday Park
★★★★★ 93%

tel: 01743 213362 **Main Road, Dorrington SY5 7ED**
email: admin@stoneyacres.co.uk web: www.stoneyacres.co.uk

Stoney Acres is located on the edge of Dorrington village within easy reach of Shrewsbury and Ludlow. It's a purpose-built, adults-only park surrounded by honey stone walls and a river. All of the well spaced pitches are equipped with twin 16Amp electric supply, hardstandings, water supply and neat grassed areas. The modern amenity block provides spacious modern cubicles with high quality fixtures and fittings including monsoon showers. An adjacent quality holiday home park is also a feature.

Open: All year **Last arrival:** 21.00 **Last departure:** 12.00

Additional site information: 6 acre site.

Premier Park

Oxon Hall Touring Park
★★★★★ 91%

tel: 01743 340868 **Welshpool Road SY3 5FB**
email: oxon@morris-leisure.co.uk web: www.morris-leisure.co.uk
dir: *Exit A5 (ring road) at junction with A458. Site shares entrance with Oxon Park and Ride.*

A delightful park with quality facilities, including a top-notch toilet block and a choice of grass and fully serviced pitches. The adults-only section proves very popular, and there is an inviting patio area next to reception and the shop, overlooking a small lake. The site is ideally located for a visit to Shrewsbury and a regular bus service is available a short walk from the park entrance.

Open: All year **Last arrival:** 20.00 **Last departure:** noon

Pitches: 🚐 🚍 ⛺; 72 hardstanding pitches; 12 seasonal pitches

Leisure: 🛝

Facilities: 🏠 ☺ ⛽ ♿ 🛁 🚿 WiFi 💻

Services: 🔌 🔄 ⬆ 🔒 🧺 T

Within 3 miles: ⛳ 🎣 ♘ 🚌

Additional site information: 15 acre site. 🐕 Cars can be parked by caravans and tents. Awnings permitted. Maximum of 2 dogs per pitch. No children in adults-only area.

PITCHES: 🚐 Caravans 🚍 Motorhomes ⛺ Tents 🏠 Glamping accommodation **LEISURE:** 🏊 Indoor swimming pool 🏊 Outdoor swimming pool 🛝 Children's playground 👶 Kids' club 🎾 Tennis court 🎱 Games room 📺 Separate TV room ⛳ golf course ⛳ Pitch n putt ⛵ Boats for hire 🚲 Bikes for hire 🎬 Cinema 🎵 Entertainment 🎣 Fishing ⛳ Mini golf 🏄 Watersports 🏋 Gym 🏆 Sports field ♘ Stables 💆 Spa

Sunnyside Farm Caravan Park & Fishery
★★★★ 93%

tel: 01939 211704 **Sunnyside Farm, Astley Lane SY4 4BJ**
email: info@sunnyside-park.co.uk **web:** www.sunnyside-park.co.uk

Located on the outskirts of Shrewsbury, this park provides excellent facilities for both touring caravan and motorhome visitors with spacious and fully serviced pitches. Touring pitches benefit from stunning views of the lake and the surrounding countryside, and stylish amenity blocks are equipped with quality fixtures and fittings. Landscaping is particularly impressive with a balance of indigenous and cultivated plants creating year round colour and interest.

Open: 2 February to 2 January **Last arrival:** 19.00 **Last departure:** 11.00

Additional site information: 10 acre site.

Walnut Cottage Holiday Park
★★★★ 77%

tel: 07812 606787 **Milward Rise, Kenley SY5 6NS**
email: waynemilwardl@outlook.com **web:** www.camping-much-wenlock.co.uk/home

Walnut Cottage Holiday Park is located in the peaceful hamlet of Henley within easy travelling distance of Shrewsbury and Ludlow, this rural park enjoys fine views of the surrounding countryside. The pitches are well spaced and an ornamental, old fashioned garage with antique car, motor bike and cycles is featured in addition to a screened children's play park. A small shop sells essentials and a warm welcome is assured.

Open: All year **Last arrival:** 19.00 **Last departure:** 11.00

Pitches: ▲; 16 hardstanding pitches

Leisure:

Facilities:

Services:

Within 3 miles:

Additional site information: 3 acre site. Cars can be parked by caravans. Awnings permitted.

TELFORD — Map 10 SJ60

Places to visit

Lilleshall Abbey, LILLESHALL, TF10 9HW
www.english-heritage.org.uk/visit/places/lilleshall-abbey

Great for kids: Ironbridge Gorge Museums, IRONBRIDGE, TF8 7DQ, 01952 433424
www.ironbridge.org.uk

TELFORD — Map 10 SJ60

Premier Park

Severn Gorge Park
★★★★★ 81%

tel: 01952 684789 **Bridgnorth Road, Tweedale TF7 4JB**
email: info@severngorgepark.co.uk **web:** www.severngorgepark.co.uk
dir: *South of Telford take A442 towards Bridgnorth. Onto A4169 signed Telford Town Centre. Right at Cuckoo Oak roundabout into Bridgnorth Road (follow site signs). Site on right.*

A very pleasant wooded site in the heart of Telford, it is well screened and well maintained. The sanitary facilities are fresh and immaculate, and landscaping of the grounds is carefully managed. Although the touring section is small, this is a really delightful park to stay at, and it is also well positioned for visiting nearby Ironbridge and its museums. The Telford bus stops at the end of the drive.

Open: All year **Last arrival:** 20.00 by prior arrangement **Last departure:** noon

Pitches: 12 hardstanding pitches

Facilities:

Services:

Within 3 miles:

Additional site information: 6 acre site. Adults only. Cars can be parked by caravans. Awnings permitted. Well behaved dogs only.

WENTNOR — Map 15 SO39

Places to visit

Montgomery Castle, MONTGOMERY, SY15 6HN, 01443 336000
cadw.gov.wales/visit/places-to-visit/montgomery-castle

Great for kids: Shropshire Hills Discovery Centre, CRAVEN ARMS, SY7 9RS, 01588 676060
www.shropshirehillsdiscoverycentre.co.uk

The Green Caravan Park
★★★ 81%

tel: 01588 650605 **SY9 5EF**
email: lin@greencaravanpark.co.uk **web:** www.greencaravanpark.co.uk
dir: *1 mile northeast of Bishop's Castle on A489. Right at brown tourist sign.*

A river, with fishing available, runs though The Green which is also adjacent to a village pub. This family run park is in a peaceful setting within easy reach of Shrewsbury and Ludlow. The site is family oriented with good facilities. The grassy pitches are mostly level and some firm hardstandings are available.

Open: Easter to October **Last arrival:** 19.30 (later arrivals by prior arrangement) **Last departure:** noon (fee charged for late departures)

Pitches: ▲; 6 hardstanding pitches; 42 seasonal pitches

Leisure:

Facilities:

Services:

Additional site information: 15 acre site. Cars can be parked by caravans and tents. Awnings permitted. No open fires, quiet from 23.00–08.00, dogs must be kept on leads at all times except in exercise area. Car hire can be arranged.

FACILITIES: Electric vehicle charging · Baths/Shower · Electric shaver sockets · Hairdryer · Ice pack facility · Baby facilities · Disabled facilities · Shop on site or within 200yds · BBQ area · Picnic area · WiFi · Internet access **SERVICES:** Electric hook-up · Launderette · Licensed bar · Calor Gas · Campingaz · Toilet fluid · Café/Restaurant · Fast Food/Takeaway · Battery charging · Motorhome service point · No credit or debit cards · Dogs permitted · No dogs

Somerset

Somerset means 'summer pastures' – appropriate given that so much of this county remains rural and unspoiled. Ever popular areas to visit are the limestone and red sandstone Mendips Hills rising to over 1,000 feet, and by complete contrast, to the south and southwest, the flat landscape of the Somerset Levels.

At the heart of Somerset lies the city of Wells, one of the smallest in the country and surely one of the finest. The jewel in the city's crown is its splendid cathedral, with a magnificent Gothic interior; adorned with sculptures, the West Front is a masterpiece of medieval craftsmanship. Nearby are Vicar's Close, a delightful street of 14th-century houses, and the Bishop's Palace, which is 13th century and moated.

Radiating from Wells are numerous paths and tracks, offering walkers the chance to escape the noise and bustle of the city and discover Somerset's rural delights. Deep within the county are the Mendip Hills, 25 miles long by 5 miles wide, that have a distinctive character and identity.

One of Somerset's more adventurous routes, and a long-term favourite with walkers, is the West Mendip Way, running for 50 miles between the coast and the town of Frome. The starting point at Uphill is spectacular – a ruined hilltop church overlooking the coast near the classic seaside resort of Weston-super-Mare. The town's famous pier replaces a previous structure destroyed by fire in 2008. Weston and Minehead, which lie on the edge of Exmoor National Park, are two traditional, much-loved holiday destinations on this stretch of coastline.

From Uphill, the West Mendip Way makes for Cheddar Caves and Gorge where stunning geological formations attract countless visitors who are left with a lasting impression of unique natural beauty. For almost a mile the gorge's limestone cliffs rise vertically above the road, in places giving Cheddar a somewhat sinister and oppressive air. Beyond Cheddar the trail heads for Wells. The choice of walks in Somerset is impressive, as is the range of cycle routes.

Descend to the Somerset Levels, an evocative lowland landscape that was the setting for the Battle of Sedgemoor in 1685. In the depths of winter this is a desolate place and famously prone to extensive flooding. There is also a palpable sense of the distant past among these fields and scattered communities. It is claimed that Alfred the Great retreated here after his defeat by the Danes.

One of Somerset's most famous features is the ancient, enigmatic Glastonbury Tor. Steeped in early Christian and Arthurian legend, the Isle of Avalon is one of a number of 'islands' rising above the Somerset Levels. This was once the site of the largest and richest monastery in medieval England and it is claimed that in this setting, Joseph of Arimathea founded the first Christian church in the country. Today, near this spot, modern-day pilgrims come for worship of a very different kind – Glastonbury's legendary festival attracts big names from the world of music and large crowds who brave the elements to support them.

Away from the flat country are the Quantocks, once the haunt of poets. Samuel Taylor Coleridge wrote *The Ancient Mariner* while living in the area and William Wordsworth and his sister Dorothy visited on occasion and often accompanied their friend Coleridge on his country rambles among these hills. The Quantocks are noted for their gentle slopes, heather-covered moorland expanses and red deer. From the summit, the Bristol Channel is visible where it meets the Severn Estuary. So much of this hilly landscape has a timeless quality about it and large areas have hardly changed since Coleridge and William and Dorothy Wordsworth explored it on foot around the end of the 18th century.

◁ *Selworthy Beacon, Exmoor National Park*

SOMERSET

BATH
Map 4 ST76

Places to visit

Herschel Museum of Astronomy, BATH, BA1 2BL, 01225 446865
www.herschelmuseum.org.uk

Sally Lunn's Historic Eating House & Museum, BATH, BA1 1NX, 01225 461634
www.sallylunns.co.uk

Great for kids: Roman Baths & Pump Room, BATH, BA1 1LZ, 01225 477785
www.romanbaths.co.uk

Platinum Park

Bath Mill Lodge Retreat
★★★★★ HOLIDAY PARK

tel: 01225 333909 Newton Road BA2 9JF
email: reception@bathmill.co.uk web: www.bathmill.co.uk
dir: *From A36 from Bath towards Bristol at roundabout into Pennyquick Road signed Newton St Loe (Globe Inn on right). In 1 mile left into Newton Road. 1st left to park.*

Bath Mill offers very high quality lodge accommodation in a beautifully landscaped park close to Bath. The lodges are fully equipped to a very high standard and are available with two, three or four bedrooms, plus there are 'Studio Lodges', suitable for a couple, with king-size bed, sofa, a well-appointed bathroom and kitchen. There is an excellent bar and bistro and a well-equipped gym. It's a peaceful location that makes a perfect base for visiting Bath, Bristol and the Mendip Hills.

Open: All year

Holiday Homes: Sleep 8, Bedrooms 4, Two-ring burners, Dishwasher, Washing Machine, Microwave, Freezer, TV, Sky/Freeview, WiFi, Linen included, Towels included, Electricity included, Gas included

Changeover days: Monday, Friday and Saturday

Leisure: **Facilities:**
Within 3 miles: **Additional site information:**

BISHOP SUTTON
Map 4 ST55

Places to visit

Wookey Hole Caves & Papermill, WOOKEY HOLE, BA5 1BB, 01749 672243
www.wookey.co.uk

Roman Baths & Pump Room, BATH, BA1 1LZ, 01225 477785
www.romanbaths.co.uk

Platinum Park

Bath Chew Valley Caravan Park
★★★★★

tel: 01275 332127 Ham Lane BS39 5TY
email: enquiries@bathchewvalley.co.uk web: www.bathchewvalley.co.uk
dir: *From A4 towards Bath take A39 towards Weston-super-Mare. Right onto A368. 6 miles, right opposite The Red Lion into Ham Lane, site 250 metres on left.*

Bath Chew Valley Caravan Park, a peaceful adults-only park, can be described as 'a park in a garden', with caravan pitches set amidst lawns, shrubs and trees.

There are excellent private facilities – rooms with showers, washbasins and toilets – all spotlessly clean and well maintained. There is a good woodland walk on the park, and two stylish fully-equipped lodges are available for hire. WiFi is available throughout the site and there is a free internet workstation. This site is well situated for visiting Bath, Bristol, Wells, Cheddar and Wookey Hole, and for walking in the Mendip Hills. Chew Valley Lake, noted for its top quality fishing, is close by.

Open: All year **Last arrival:** 19.00 **Last departure:** 11.00

Pitches: * from £30; from £30; from £30 ; 45 hardstanding pitches; 4 seasonal pitches

Facilities:
Services: Within 3 miles:

Additional site information: 4.5 acre site. Adults only. Awnings permitted. Shop, pub/restaurant 200 metres from site. Car hire can be arranged.

Glamping available: 1 luxury contemporary lodge and 1 luxury cedar lodge.
Changeover days: Any day

Additional glamping information: Both lodges fully equipped. No dogs.

BREAN
Map 4 ST25

Places to visit

King John's Hunting Lodge, AXBRIDGE, BS26 2AP, 01934 732012
www.kingjohnshuntinglodge.co.uk

Weston Museum, WESTON-SUPER-MARE, BS23 1PR, 01934 621028
www.westonmuseum.org

Great for kids: The Helicopter Museum, WESTON-SUPER-MARE, BS24 8PP, 01934 635227
helimuseum.com

Platinum Park

Warren Farm Holiday Centre
★★★★★ HOLIDAY PARK

tel: 01278 751227 TA8 2RP
email: info@warrenfarm.co.uk web: www.warrenfarm.co.uk
dir: *Exit M5 junction 22 onto B3140 past Burnham-on-Sea to Berrow and Brean. Park on coastal road in Brean, 1 mile past Brean Leisure Park on right.*

A large family-run holiday park just a short walk from the beach and divided up into several fields (pet-friendly and pet-free), each with its own designated facilities. The pitches are spacious and level, with both grass pitches and hardstandings available, as well as luxury en suite super pitches. There are good panoramic views of the Mendip Hills and Brean Down. Perfect for couples and families; there is an indoor play barn (arcade and soft play), outdoor playgrounds, pets corner, fishing lake and farm walk. The park has its own Beachcomber bar, restaurant and entertainment area.

Open: April to October **Last arrival:** 20.00 **Last departure:** 11.00

Pitches: ; 165 hardstanding pitches; 500 seasonal pitches

Leisure:
Facilities:
Services: Within 3 miles:

Additional site information: 100 acre site. No vans or commercial vehicles. Arcade, play areas, fishing lake, farm walk, clubhouse, entertainment.

PITCHES:  Caravans Motorhomes Tents Glamping accommodation **LEISURE:** Indoor swimming pool Outdoor swimming pool Children's playground Kids' club Tennis court Games room Separate TV room golf course Pitch n putt Boats for hire Bikes for hire Cinema Entertainment Fishing Mini golf Watersports Gym Sports field Stables Spa

Premier Park

Holiday Resort Unity
★★★★★ 93% HOLIDAY PARK

tel: 01278 751235 Coast Road, Brean Sands TA8 2RB
email: admin@hru.co.uk web: www.hru.co.uk
dir: M5 junction 22, B3140 through Burnham-on-Sea, through Berrow to Brean. Site on left just before Brean Leisure Park.

This is an excellent, family-run holiday park offering very good touring facilities plus a wide range of family-oriented activities including bowling, RJ's entertainment club and the Brean Country Club. There's plenty of eating outlets – The Tavern, RJ's, an American-themed diner, the beach-themed Bucket & Spade (especially suitable for smaller children), cafés and takeaway options. Brean Splash Waterpark is situated directly opposite this touring park – a discounted entry price is available. Wooden camping pods and fully equipped safari tents are also available for hire. The park also holds 'themed' weekends and rallies are also welcome.

Open: February to November **Last arrival:** 21.00 **Last departure:** 10.00 (later departures – charges apply)

Pitches: see prices below; 158 hardstanding pitches; 168 seasonal pitches

Leisure:
Facilities: WiFi
Services:
Within 3 miles:

Additional site information: 200 acre site. Family parties of 3 or more must be over 21 years (young persons' policy applies). Arcade. Soft play. Dog walk.

Glamping available: Safari tents from £45; wooden pods from £35.
Changeover days: contact site for details

Additional glamping information: Safari tents: sleep 4. Wooden pods: sleep 2 adults and 2 children. Some units have own kitchen. Cars can be parked by units

Northam Farm Holiday Park
BREAN SANDS, SOMERSET

Treat yourself!

www.northamfarm.co.uk
Tel: 01278 751244 stay@northamfarm.co.uk

HOLIDAYS FOR TOURING CARAVANS, MOTORHOMES AND TENTS

ENGLAND 208 SOMERSET

BREAN *continued*

Premier Park

Northam Farm Holiday Park
★★★★★ 93%

tel: 01278 751244 **TA8 2SE**
email: stay@northamfarm.co.uk **web:** www.northamfarm.co.uk
dir: *M5 junction 22, B3140 to Burnham-on-Sea and Brean. Park on right 0.5 mile after Brean Leisure Park.*

An attractive site that's just a short walk from the sea and a long sandy beach. The park has lots of children's play areas and a top quality fishing lake on site. The facilities on this park are excellent and include 20 hardstandings and a bar/café/takeaway complex. The park has a main caravan dealership plus full workshop and repair facility.

Open: March to October (restricted service: March and October – reduced hours for shop, café and takeaway) **Last arrival:** 20.00 **Last departure:** 10.30
Pitches: 🚐 🚙 ⛺; 300 hardstanding pitches; 300 seasonal pitches
Leisure: 🛝 🎵 🎯 ⚽
Facilities: 🏪 ☕ 🚿 ❄ ♿ 🧺 🍴 🛒 WiFi
Services: 🔌 💧 🚰 🍽 🏪 🛁 ⬆ 🔒 ♻ T
Within 3 miles: ⚓ ◎ 🚌

Additional site information: 30 acre site. 🐕 Cars can be parked by caravans and tents. Awnings permitted. Families and couples only, no commercial vehicles. Indoor swimming, bike hire, gym within 3 miles. Car hire can be arranged.

See advert on page 207

BRIDGETOWN Map 3 SS93

Places to visit
Dunster Castle, DUNSTER, TA24 6SL, 01643 821314
www.nationaltrust.org.uk/dunster-castle-and-watermill

Cleeve Abbey, WASHFORD, TA23 0PS, 01984 640377
www.english-heritage.org.uk/visit/places/cleeve-abbey

Platinum Park

Exe Valley Caravan Site
★★★★★

tel: 01643 851432 Exe Valley Caravan Site, Week Lane **TA22 9JL**
email: info@exevalleycamping.co.uk **web:** www.exevalleycamping.co.uk
dir: *From south: M5 junction 27, A361 signed Tiverton. 7 miles, right at roundabout signed Bampton. Left at Exeter Inn roundabout, 2 miles, take A396. Through Exebridge to Bridgetown, left after Badgers Holt Inn, site on right. (NB for sat nav use TA22 9JN).*

Set in the Exmoor National Park, Exe Valley Caravan Site, an adults-only park, occupies an enchanting, peaceful spot in a wooded valley alongside the River Exe. There is free fly-fishing, an abundance of wildlife and excellent walks leading directly from the park to the surrounding woodlands and moor. The site has good, spotlessly clean facilities, and every pitch is fully serviced with WiFi, EHU, TV hook-up, water and drainage. Well placed for visiting Dunster Castle, the picturesque villages of Selworthy and Porlock, and the dramatic Valley of the Rocks on the north Devon coast.

Open: 14 March to 13 October **Last arrival:** 21.00 **Last departure:** 11.00
Pitches: 🚐 from £20; 🚙 from £20; ⛺ from £20; 18 hardstanding pitches; 1 seasonal pitch
Leisure: 🎣
Facilities: 🏪 ☕ 🚿 ❄ ♿ 🧺 🍴 🛒 WiFi 💻
Services: 🔌 💧 🚰 ⬆ 🔒 ♻ T
Within 3 miles: ⚓ 🚶 🚌

Additional site information: 4 acre site. Adults only. 🐕 Cars can be parked by caravans and tents. Awnings permitted. 17th-century mill, TV sockets and cables, dog wash, free WiFi and TV system.

PITCHES: 🚐 Caravans 🚙 Motorhomes ⛺ Tents 🏕 Glamping accommodation **LEISURE:** 🏊 Indoor swimming pool 🏊 Outdoor swimming pool 🛝 Children's playground 👦 Kids' club 🎾 Tennis court 🎱 Games room 📺 Separate TV room ⛳ golf course 🏌 Pitch n putt 🚣 Boats for hire 🚴 Bikes for hire 🎬 Cinema 🎵 Entertainment 🎣 Fishing ⛳ Mini golf 🏄 Watersports 💪 Gym ⚽ Sports field 🐴 Stables 💆 Spa

SOMERSET 209 ENGLAND

CASTLE CARY
Map 4 ST63

AA GLAMPING SITE OF THE YEAR 2024–25

Premier Park

Hadspen Glamping
★★★★★ 87% GLAMPING ONLY

tel: 07730 355645 **Lime Kiln Lane BA7 7NX**
email: hello@hadspenglamping.co.uk **web:** www.hadspenglamping.co.uk
dir: *A359 into Lime Kiln Lane. Hadspen Glamping in 400 yards on right.*
What3Words: ///retrieves.cheerily.swam

'Disconnect with city life, reconnect with nature and unwind in luxury' sums up the ethos of this idyllic, get-away haven deep in the Somerset countryside close to Castle Cary. Set on a hillside with stunning views, the three beautifully furnished, off-grid canvas eco-lodges are individually designed and decorated in a unique style – Horscombe sleeps up to four; Lime Kiln up to five; Grisway up to seven. All have a very stylish open-plan living area, fully-equipped kitchen, en suite shower room, and a veranda with outdoor seating and a barbecue. Horscombe Lodge has an outdoor copper bath hot tub, while Lime Kiln Lodge and Grisway Lodge have wood-fired hot tubs. There's excellent food (breakfast/picnic) and drinks hampers, sourced from local farm shops, which can be pre-booked when finalising your stay. Next door (just a 5-minute walk away) is the award-winning Newt, set in the grounds of Hadspen House, with its garden café, farm shop and magnificent gardens (membership required). Pick-ups and drop-offs from Castle Cary Station (2.8 miles) can be arranged. Please note there is no mains gas or electricity, and no WiFi access.

Open: 1 April – 31 October **Last arrival:** 21:00 (later arrivals by prior arrangement) **Last departure:** 10:30
Leisure:
Facilities:
Within 3 miles:
Accommodation available: 3 safari tents from £140
Changeover days: Monday and Friday
Additional site information: 1 acre site.
See advert on page 210

CHEDDAR
Map 4 ST45

Places to visit
Cheddar Gorge (NT), CHEDDAR, 01278 751874
www.nationaltrust.org.uk/cheddar-gorge

Glastonbury Abbey, GLASTONBURY, BA6 9EL, 01458 832267
www.glastonburyabbey.com

Great for kids: Wookey Hole Caves & Papermill, WOOKEY HOLE, BA5 1BB, 01749 672243
www.wookey.co.uk

Platinum Park

Cheddar Woods Resort & Spa
★★★★★ **HOLIDAY PARK**

tel: 01934 742610 **Axbridge Road BS27 3DB**
email: enquiries@cheddarwoods.co.uk
web: www.darwinescapes.co.uk/parks/cheddar-woods-resort-spa
dir: *From M5 junction 22 follow signs for 'Cheddar Gorge & Caves' (8 miles). Site midway between Cheddar and Axbridge on A371.*

Situated in the beautiful Mendip Hills, Cheddar Woods is the perfect place to relax and unwind, and this state-of-the-art park is an ideal location for family holidays. Both large and smaller lodges are available for hire, all offering top quality accommodation. There are excellent leisure facilities including a gym, spa and swimming pool plus a 'Go Active' programme, and a pizza bar. In addition, there is a very tasteful bar and good restaurant. The park is just outside the village of Cheddar with its famous caves and is well positioned for visiting Wells, Weston-super-Mare and many other attractions of the area. It should be noted this is a lodge-only park.

Open: All year **Last arrival:** midnight **Last departure:** 10.00
Holiday Homes: Sleep 8, Bedrooms 4, Bathrooms 2, Toilets 2, Two-ring burner, Dishwasher, Washing Machine, Tumble dryer, Microwave, Freezer, TV, Sky/Freeview, DVD player, WiFi, Linen included, Towels included, Electricity included, Gas included, Woodburner
Prices: Low season from £130. High season from £2500. Weekly from £600
Leisure:
Facilities:
Within 3 miles:
Additional site information:

COWSLIP GREEN
Map 4 ST46

Places to visit
Clevedon Court, CLEVEDON, BS21 6QU, 01275 872257
www.nationaltrust.org.uk/clevedon-court

Bristol Museum & Art Gallery, BRISTOL, BS8 1RL, 0117 922 3571
www.bristolmuseums.org.uk/bristol-museum-and-art-gallery

Brook Lodge Farm Camping & Caravan Park
★★★★ 93%

tel: 01934 862311 & 07538 055859 Cowslip Green, Redhill BS40 5RB
email: info@brooklodgefarm.com web: www.brooklodgefarm.com
dir: *M5 junction 22, A38 to Churchill. Site 4 miles on right opposite Holiday Inn. Or M5 junction 18, follow Bristol Airport signs. From A38 towards Bridgwater (airport on right). Site 3 miles on left at bottom of hill.*

A naturally sheltered country touring park sitting in a valley of the Mendip Hills, surrounded by trees and a historic walled garden. A friendly welcome is always assured by the family owners who are particularly keen on preserving the site's environment and have won a green tourism award. This park is particularly well placed for visiting the Bristol Balloon Festival, held in August, plus the many country walks in the area. There is a separate and very popular glamping area with bell tents and a toilet/shower block with outside decking. There is a motorhome service point and laundry room, and the woodland walk leads to a bus stop and farm shop.

Open: March to October **Last arrival:** 20.00 **Last departure:** 11.30
Pitches: 🚐 🚙 ⛺; 🏕; see prices below; 5 hardstanding pitches; 5 seasonal pitches
Leisure: 🎱
Facilities: 🏠 ⊙ ☕ ✳ ♿ 🚿 🚻 🪑 WiFi 💻
Services: 🔌 🗑 🧺 T
Within 3 miles: 🚶 🎣

Additional site information: 5 acre site. 🐕 Cars can be parked by caravans and tents. Awnings permitted. Dogs by prior arrangement only. Car hire can be arranged.

Glamping available: Bell tents from £150 (minimum 2 night stay); Shepherd's hut from £100 per night

Additional glamping information: No pets, no stag parties. Cars can be parked by units

DULVERTON
Map 3 SS92

Places to visit
Knightshayes, KNIGHTSHAYES, EX16 7RQ, 01884 254665
www.nationaltrust.org.uk/knightshayes

Great for kids: Tiverton Castle, TIVERTON, EX16 6RP, 01884 253200
www.tivertoncastle.com

DULVERTON
Map 3 SS92

Wimbleball Lake
★★★ 88%

tel: 01398 371460 & 371116 **Brompton Regis TA22 9NU**
email: wimbleball@swlakestrust.org.uk **web:** www.swlakestrust.org.uk
dir: *From A396 (Tiverton to Minehead road) take B3222 signed Dulverton Services, follow signs to Wimbleball Lake. Ignore 1st entry (fishing), take 2nd entry signed tea room and camping. (Note: care needed due to narrow roads).*

A grassy site overlooking Wimbleball Lake, set high up on Exmoor National Park. The camping area, which is adjacent to the visitor centre and café, has electric hook-ups, two hardstandings and good toilet/shower facilities; it's a quiet and peaceful setting with good views of the lake, which is nationally renowned for its trout fishing; boats can be hired with advance notice. There are two camping pods, three Lotus Belle tents and a cabin for hire.

Open: March to October **Last arrival:** 22.00 **Last departure:** 11.00
Pitches: see prices below; 2 hardstanding pitches
Leisure:
Facilities:
Services:
Within 3 miles:

Additional site information: 1.25 acre site. Cars can be parked by caravans and tents. Awnings permitted. No open fires, off-ground BBQs only, no swimming in lake. Dogs must be kept on leads at all times and are not permitted in the lake. Watersports and activity centre, birdwatching, cycling, lakeside walks and bushcraft.

Glamping available: 2 wooden pods; 3 Lotus Belle tents. From £35 (minimum two nights).

Additional glamping information: Cars can be parked by units

EXFORD
Map 3 SS83

Places to visit
Dunster Castle, DUNSTER, TA24 6SL, 01643 821314
www.nationaltrust.org.uk/dunster-castle-and-watermill

West Somerset Railway, MINEHEAD, TA24 5BG, 01643 704996
www.west-somerset-railway.co.uk

Great for kids: Exmoor Zoological Park, BLACKMOOR GATE, EX31 4SG, 01598 763352
www.exmoorzoo.co.uk

Westermill Farm Holidays Ltd
★★★ 89%

tel: 01643 831238 & 07970 594808 **Westermill Farm TA24 7NJ**
email: info@westermill.com **web:** www.westermill.com
dir: *In Exford follow Porlock sign. Left in 0.25 mile, left to Westermill, sign on tree. Fork left. (Note: this is the only recommended route).*

Westermill Farm is an idyllic site for those seeking peace and quiet – it is in a sheltered valley in the heart of Exmoor and has won many awards for conservation. Highly recommended for traditional camping, although there are a few hardstandings. There's 15 acres of mown meadows beside the River Exe – one field has fire pits set up ready for a campfire which proves popular with families and friends for a get-together. There are four waymarked walks over the 500-acre working farm and two miles of shallow water of the River Exe to bathe or fish in (not coarse fishing). Self-catering accommodation is also available. An ideal base for exploring the open moorland, wooded valleys and spectacular coastal scenery of Exmoor, or just simply for relaxing and escaping the hum drum of everyday life. Please note, this site should only be approached from Exford (other routes are difficult).

Open: March to October **Last arrival:** 20:00
Pitches: 4 hardstanding pitches
Leisure:
Facilities:
Services:

Additional site information: 12 acre site. Cars can be parked by caravans and tents. Awnings permitted. No noise after 23:00. Well behaved dogs accepted. 5mph speed limit. Children must be supervised at all times. 500-acre working hill farm.

FROME
Map 4 ST74

Places to visit
Stourhead, STOURHEAD, BA12 6QD, 01747 841152
www.nationaltrust.org.uk/stourhead

Nunney Castle, NUNNEY, BA11 4LW, 0370 333 1181
www.english-heritage.org.uk/visit/places/nunney-castle

Great for kids: Longleat, LONGLEAT, BA12 7NW, 01985 844400
www.longleat.co.uk

Seven Acres Caravan & Camping Site
★★★ 82%

tel: 01373 464222 **Seven Acres, West Woodlands BA11 5EQ**
dir: *From roundabout on A361 (Frome bypass) onto B3092 towards Maiden Bradley, 0.75 mile to site.*

A level meadowland site beside the shallow River Frome, with a bridge across to an adjacent field, and plenty of scope for families. The facilities are spotless. Set on the edge of the Longleat Estate with its stately home, wildlife safari park and many other attractions.

Open: March to October
Pitches: 16 hardstanding pitches
Facilities:
Services:
Within 3 miles:

Additional site information: 3 acre site. Cars can be parked by caravans and tents. Awnings permitted.

GLASTONBURY
Map 4 ST53

Places to visit
Lytes Cary Manor, KINGSDON, TA11 7HU, 01458 224471
www.nationaltrust.org.uk/lytes-cary-manor

Fleet Air Arm Museum, YEOVILTON, BA22 8HT, 01935 840565
www.fleetairarm.com

Great for kids: Haynes International Motor Museum, SPARKFORD, BA22 7LH, 01963 440804
www.haynesmotormuseum.com

GLASTONBURY Map 4 ST53

AA SUSTAINABLE PARK OF THE YEAR 2024–25

Platinum Park

Old Oaks Touring & Glamping
★★★★★

tel: 01458 831437 Wick Farm, Wick BA6 8JS
email: info@theoldoaks.co.uk **web:** www.theoldoaks.co.uk
dir: *M5 junction 23, A39 to Glastonbury. After Street take A39 towards Wells. At 3rd roundabout follow Wick and Brindham signs. Site 1.5 miles on right. (Note: it is advisable not to use sat nav for last part of journey).*

Old Oaks is an exceptional, adults-only park offering larger-than-average landscaped pitches (standard, super and premier), impeccably maintained grounds and wonderful views. The perfect 'get away from it all' spot where you can enjoy walking, cycling, fishing and touring or simply relaxing amid the abundant wildlife. The top-class facilities include a well-stocked shop selling locally-sourced produce, cakes and gifts, two smart shower blocks with excellent wet rooms, free WiFi, free walking and cycling maps, a half-acre fishing lake, dog walk, dog field with swimming pond and even a hot doggy shower. Glamping comprises six 2-person, heated wooden glamping cabins, two shepherd's huts and four mini lodges, all beautifully equipped to a high standard. Three of the glamping units have private hot tubs.

Open: March to mid November **Last arrival:** 18.30 **Last departure:** noon (touring), 10.30 (glamping)

Pitches: 🚐 🚗 ▲; 🏠 see prices below; 88 hardstanding pitches

Leisure: ▫ ✏ **Facilities:** 🏠 ☺ ⛲ ✱ ♿ 🅢 WiFi 💻

Services: 🔌 🔄 🧺 🚰 ⛽ 🔒 ♻ T

Additional site information: 15 acre site. Adults only. 🚗 Cars can be parked by caravans and tents. Awnings permitted. No groups, no noise after 22.00. Hot food 7 nights a week, breakfast available 6 mornings, TV & pool room, off licence, local produce boxes, dog owners' information pack, dog walk, dog shower, camper clean machine, fishing pond, woodland walk. Car hire can be arranged.

Glamping available: Wooden pods from £75; shepherd's hut from £113; shepherd's hut with hot tub from £131; mini cedar lodges from £131; mini cedar lodges with hot tub from £149. **Changeover days:** Any day for pods, Mon & Fri for lodges/huts

Additional glamping information: Glamping pods have fire pit, picnic bench, seating, decking, kettle, toaster, king size bed. Shepherd's huts have fire pit, picnic bench, outdoor seating, sun loungers, kitchenette, private shower and toilet. Cars can be parked by units

Isle of Avalon Touring Caravan Park
★★★★ 90%

tel: 01458 833618 Godney Road BA6 9AF
email: candicehatwell@hotmail.co.uk **web:** www.avalontouringpark.co.uk
dir: *M5 junction 23, A39 to outskirts of Glastonbury, 2nd exit signed Wells at B&Q roundabout, straight on at next roundabout, 1st exit at next roundabout (B3151), site 200 yards on right.*

A popular site, on the south side of this historic town, and within easy walking distance of the centre. It is a level park, with a separate tent field, that offers a quiet environment. It makes an ideal spot from which to explore the many local attractions that include Glastonbury Tor, Wells, Wookey Hole and Clarks Village. Approved caravan storage is available.

Open: All year **Last arrival:** 21.00 **Last departure:** 11.00

Pitches: 🚐 🚗 ▲; 70 hardstanding pitches

Facilities: ☺ ⛲ ✱ ♿ 🅢 🚿 🪑 WiFi 💻

Services: 🔌 🔄 🧺 🚰 ⛽ 🔒 ♻ T

Within 3 miles: ✏ ⛳ 🎿

Additional site information: 8 acre site. 🚗 Cars can be parked by caravans and tents. Awnings permitted. No ball games.

MARTOCK Map 4 ST41

Places to visit
Montacute House, MONTACUTE, TA15 6XP, 01935 823289
www.nationaltrust.org.uk/montacute-house

Great for kids: Fleet Air Arm Museum, YEOVILTON, BA22 8HT, 01935 840565
www.fleetairarm.com

Southfork Caravan Park
★★★★ 88%

tel: 01935 825661 Parrett Works TA12 6AE
email: info@southforkcaravans.co.uk **web:** www.southforkcaravans.co.uk
dir: *From A303: approximately 2 miles after Cargate roundabout exit left A303, over flyover, signed A356 Martock. At junction left, then after sharp bend, next right. Site approximately 1 mile on right. M25 junction 25: follow A358 signed Yeovil. At roundabout junction of A303/A358, 1st exit signed Andover/London. Follow A303, to junction then left to Martock.*

A neat, level mainly grass park in a quiet rural area on the Somerset Levels, just outside the pretty village of Martock. Some excellent, spacious hardstandings are available. The facilities are always spotless and the whole site is well cared for. There's a superb café and deli with a tempting menu, either to eat in or takeaway. The park is unique in that it also has a fully approved caravan repair and servicing centre. There are also static caravans, a camping pod and a lodge available for hire. Caravan storage is also possible. The good walking options nearby include the long-distance Parrett Trail.

Open: All year **Last arrival:** 22.30 **Last departure:** noon

Pitches: 🚐 🚗 ▲; 🏠 see prices below; 5 hardstanding pitches

Facilities: 🏠 ☺ ⛲ ✱ 🅢 WiFi 💻

Services: 🔌 🔄 🍽 🧺 🔒 ♻ T

Within 3 miles: 🎣 ✏

Additional site information: 2 acre site. Cars can be parked by caravans and tents. Awnings permitted. No loud noise after 22.30. Dogs must be kept on short leads at all times.

Glamping available: Wooden pod from £35. **Changeover days:** Any day

Additional glamping information: 12 volt supply only, double beds, picnic table outside. Cars can be parked by units

PORLOCK   Map 3 SS84

Places to visit

West Somerset Railway, MINEHEAD, TA24 5BG, 01643 704996
www.west-somerset-railway.co.uk

Dunster Castle, DUNSTER, TA24 6SL, 01643 821314
www.nationaltrust.org.uk/dunster-castle-and-watermill

Great for kids: Tropiquaria Zoo, WASHFORD, TA23 0QB, 01984 640688
www.tropiquaria.co.uk

Burrowhayes Farm Caravan & Camping Site & Riding Stables
★★★★ 95%

tel: 01643 862463 **West Luccombe TA24 8HT**
email: info@burrowhayes.co.uk **web:** www.burrowhayes.co.uk
dir: A39 from Minehead towards Porlock for 5 miles. Left at Red Post to Horner and West Luccombe, site 0.25 mile on right, immediately before humpback bridge.

A delightful site on the edge of Exmoor that slopes gently down to Horner Water. The farm buildings have been converted into riding stables from where escorted rides onto the moors can be taken; the excellent toilet facilities are housed in timber-clad buildings. Hardstandings are available – some are fully serviced and many of the hook-ups have TV points. There is a popular, well-stocked shop and many countryside walks can be accessed directly from the site.

Open: 15 March to 31 October (restricted service: before Easter – caravan hire and riding not available) **Last arrival:** 22.00 **Last departure:** 11.00

Pitches: ; 16 hardstanding pitches

Facilities:

Services:

Within 3 miles:

Additional site information: 8 acre site. Cars can be parked by caravans and tents. Awnings permitted. Croissants and baguettes can be ordered.

PRIDDY   Map 4 ST55

Places to visit

Glastonbury Abbey, GLASTONBURY, BA6 9EL, 01458 832267
www.glastonburyabbey.com

The Helicopter Museum, WESTON-SUPER-MARE, BS24 8PP, 01934 635227
helimuseum.com

Great for kids: Wookey Hole Caves & Papermill, WOOKEY HOLE, BA5 1BB, 01749 672243
www.wookey.co.uk

Cheddar Mendip Heights Camping & Caravanning Club Site
★★★★ 91%

tel: 01749 870241 & 024 7647 5426 **Townsend, Priddy BA5 3BP**
email: cheddar.site@campingandcaravanningclub.co.uk
web: www.campingandcaravanningclub.co.uk/cheddar
dir: From A39 take B3135 to Cheddar. Left in 4.5 miles. Site 200 yards on right, signed.

A gently sloping site set high on the Mendip Hills and surrounded by trees. This excellent campsite offers really good facilities, including top notch family rooms and private cubicles which are spotlessly maintained. Fresh bread is baked daily and, along with pastries, can be ordered each morning from the well-stocked shop. The site is well positioned for visiting local attractions such as Cheddar, Wookey Hole, Wells and Glastonbury, and is popular with walkers. Self-catering caravans are available for hire.

Open: Mid March to end of November **Last arrival:** 20.00 **Last departure:** noon

Pitches: ; 41 hardstanding pitches

Leisure:

Facilities:

Services:

Within 3 miles:

Additional site information: 4.5 acre site. Cars can be parked by caravans and tents. Awnings permitted. Site gates closed 23.00–07.00. No fires, BBQs must be raised off the ground. Dogs must be on leads at all times. Quiet after 23.00. Freshly baked bread and pastries, local preserves, bacon, sausages, beer, cider and cheese available at site shop. Car hire can be arranged.

FACILITIES: Electric vehicle charging · Baths/Shower · Electric shaver sockets · Hairdryer · Ice pack facility · Baby facilities · Disabled facilities · Shop on site or within 200yds · BBQ area · Picnic area · WiFi · Internet access   **SERVICES:** Electric hook-up · Launderette · Licensed bar · Calor Gas · Campingaz · Toilet fluid · Café/Restaurant · Fast Food/Takeaway · Battery charging · Motorhome service point · No credit or debit cards · Dogs permitted · No dogs

ENGLAND 214 SOMERSET

SPARKFORD
MAP 4 ST62

Places to visit
Lytes Cary Manor, KINGSDON, TA11 7HU, 01458 224471
www.nationaltrust.org.uk/lytes-cary-manor

Haynes International Motor Museum, SPARKFORD, BA22 7LH, 01963 440804
www.haynesmotormuseum.com

Premier Park

Long Hazel Park
★★★★★ 90%

tel: 01963 440002 **High Street BA22 7JH**
email: longhazelpark@hotmail.com web: www.longhazelpark.co.uk
dir: *400 yards from Hazlegrove Roundabout on A303/A359 at Sparkford. Proceed into village along High Street, entrance sign on left just past 40mph sign.*

A very neat, adults-only park next to the village inn in the high street. This attractive park is run by friendly owners to a very good standard. Some of the spacious hardstanding pitches are fully serviced. There are two luxury holiday lodges on site for hire, each sleeping up to four adults, with one adapted for wheelchair use. The site is close to the Haynes International Motor Museum, the Fleet Air Arm Museum, the Hauser & Wirth Art Gallery in Bruton, and several National Trust properties and gardens.

Open: All year **Last arrival:** 22.00 (by prior arrangement) **Last departure:** 11.00 (touring). £5 fee payable for departure by 18.00

Pitches: 🚐 🚙 ⛺; 27 hardstanding pitches
Facilities: 🏠 ☺ ♒ ✴ ♿ 🪑 WiFi
Services: 🅿 🔳 🏢 🧰 ⚙ ⚡
Within 3 miles: ♨ ✒ ∪ ⊚ 🅟

Additional site information: 3.5 acre site. Adults only. 🐕 🚗 Cars can be parked by caravans and tents. Awnings permitted. 16 amp electric hook-ups servicing all pitches; 10 fully serviced touring pitches

TAUNTON
Map 4 ST22

Places to visit
Hestercombe Gardens, TAUNTON, TA2 8LG, 01823 413923
www.hestercombe.com

Barrington Court, BARRINGTON, TA19 0NQ, 01460 241938
www.nationaltrust.org.uk/barrington-court

TAUNTON
Map 4 ST22

Cornish Farm Touring Park
★★★★ 92%

tel: 01823 327746 **Shoreditch TA3 7BS**
email: info@cornishfarm.com web: www.cornishfarm.com
dir: *M5 junction 25, take A358 towards Taunton. From dual carriageway take 1st left at traffic lights following signs for Racecourse and Corfe. 3rd left into Ilminster Road (following Corfe signs). Right at roundabout onto Blackbrook Road, left at next roundabout onto Chestnut Drive. Right at T-junction following campsite brown sign, 1st left into Killams Drive, 2nd left into Killams Avenue. Continue along Killams Avenue and over the motorway bridge. Site on left, access via 2nd entrance with large sign for Cornish Farm Touring Park and Van Bitz.*

This smart park provides really top quality facilities throughout, including an updated amenity block and enhanced security (CNPR barrier). Only two miles from Taunton, it is set in open countryside and is a very convenient base for visiting the many attractions of the area such as Clarks Village, Glastonbury, Cheddar Gorge, north Somerset and Devon coastlines, and Exmoor. It also makes an excellent base for watching county cricket at the nearby Somerset County Ground.

Open: All year **Last arrival:** anytime **Last departure:** 11.30 (later times can be arranged with the warden subject to a surcharge if not already booked)

Pitches: 🚐 🚙 ⛺; 25 hardstanding pitches
Facilities: 🏠 ☺ ♒ ♿ 🪑 WiFi 💻
Services: 🅿 🔳 ⚙ 🔒 🅣 **Within 3 miles:** ♨ ✒ ∪ ⊚ 🍴 🅟

Additional site information: 3.5 acre site. 🐕 🚗 Cars can be parked by caravans and tents. Awnings permitted.

PITCHES: 🚐 Caravans 🚙 Motorhomes ⛺ Tents 🏕 Glamping accommodation **LEISURE:** 🏊 Indoor swimming pool 🌊 Outdoor swimming pool 🛝 Children's playground 🎈 Kids' club 🎾 Tennis court 🎱 Games room 📺 Separate TV room ⛳ golf course 🏌 Pitch n putt 🚣 Boats for hire 🚴 Bikes for hire 🎬 Cinema 🎭 Entertainment 🎣 Fishing ⛳ Mini golf 🏄 Watersports 🏋 Gym ⚽ Sports field ♘ Stables 💆 Spa

SOMERSET 215 ENGLAND

Ashe Farm Camping & Caravan Site
★★★★ 87%

tel: 01823 443764 & 07891 989482 **Thornfalcon TA3 5NW**
email: info@ashefarm.co.uk **web:** www.ashefarm.co.uk
dir: M5 junction 25, A358, east for 2.5 miles. Right at Nags Head pub. Site 0.25 mile on right.

A well-screened site surrounded by mature trees and shrubs, with two large touring fields. The modern, facilities block includes toilets and showers plus a separate laundry room. This site is not far from the bustling market town of Taunton, and is handy for both south and north coasts; it also makes a good stopover for people travelling on the nearby M5.

Open: 1 April to 30 October **Last arrival:** 22.00 **Last departure:** noon
Pitches: 🚐 🚙 ⛺; 11 hardstanding pitches
Leisure: ⛱ ♨
Facilities: 🛁 ☉ ✂ ❄ ♿
Services: 🔌 🗄
Within 3 miles: ⛳ 🎣 ♘ ◎ 🚌 🏪

Additional site information: 7 acre site. 🐕 🚗 Cars can be parked by caravans and tents. Awnings permitted. No camp fires, no noise after 22.00.

WATCHET
Map 3 ST04

Places to visit

West Somerset Railway, MINEHEAD, TA24 5BG, 01643 704996
www.west-somerset-railway.co.uk

Dunster Castle, DUNSTER, TA24 6SL, 01643 821314
www.nationaltrust.org.uk/dunster-castle-and-watermill

Great for kids: Tropiquaria Zoo, WASHFORD, TA23 0QB, 01984 640688
www.tropiquaria.co.uk

Premier Park

Doniford Bay Holiday Park
★★★★★ 94% **HOLIDAY PARK**

tel: 01984 632423 **TA23 0TJ**
email: donifordbay@haven.com **web:** www.haven.com/donifordbay
dir: M5 junction 23, A38 towards Bridgwater, A39 towards Minehead. 15 miles, at West Quantoxhead, right after St Audries garage. Park 1 mile on right.

This well-appointed holiday park, adjacent to a shingle and sand beach, offers a wide range of activities for the whole family. The holiday homes are spacious and well presented and there is plenty to keep children (of all ages) interested, including great indoor and outdoor pools, a multi-sports centre, slides and archery. The park has good eating outlets including a nice café/restaurant. Being close to the Exmoor National Park, it offers visitors the chance to seek out some of the best scenery in the county.

Open: mid March to end October **Last departure:** 10.00
Holiday Homes: Sleep 8, Bedrooms 2, Bathrooms 1, Toilet 1, Microwave, Freezer, TV, Sky/Freeview
Leisure: 🏊 ♨ ⛱ 👶 ♨ 🎾
Facilities: 📶 WiFi 💻

Additional site information: 🐕 Most dog breeds accepted (please check when booking). Dogs must be kept on leads at all times.

WELLS
Map 4 ST54

Places to visit

Glastonbury Abbey, GLASTONBURY, BA6 9EL, 01458 832267
www.glastonburyabbey.com

The Bishop's Palace, WELLS, BA5 2PD, 01749 988111
www.bishopspalace.org.uk

Platinum Park

Wells Touring Park
★★★★★

tel: 01749 676869 **Haybridge BA5 1AJ**
email: info@wellstouringpark.co.uk **web:** www.wellstouringpark.co.uk
dir: On A371 between Wells and Westbury-sub-Mendip.

This well established, adults-only holiday park has first-class toilet facilities and many hardstandings, some of which are fully serviced. It is a restful park set in countryside on the outskirts of Wells, and is within easy walking distance of the city centre, with its spectacular cathedral and Bishop's Palace. Cheddar Gorge, Bath, Bristol, Weston-super-Mare, Wookey Hole and Glastonbury are all within easy driving distance. The site has a function room, The Lounge, which has free WiFi and an excellent coffee shop, plus a really good doggy shower. Holiday cottages are available for hire and luxury lodges for sale.

Open: All year **Last arrival:** 20.00 **Last departure:** noon
Pitches: 🚐 🚙; 54 hardstanding pitches; 10 seasonal pitches
Leisure: 🎱 🎯
Facilities: 🛁 ☉ ✂ ❄ ♿ 🗄 🍼 🎪 WiFi 💻
Services: 🔌 🗄 🍺 🍴 🚿 🔋 ⛽ 🔒 ♻ T
Within 3 miles: ⛳ 🎣 ♘ ◎ 🚌

Additional site information: 7.5 acre site. Adults only. 🐕 🚗 Cars can be parked by caravans. Awnings permitted. No tents. Pétanque. Car hire can be arranged.

FACILITIES: ⚡ Electric vehicle charging 🛁 Baths/Shower ☉ Electric shaver sockets ✂ Hairdryer ❄ Ice pack facility 🍼 Baby facilities ♿ Disabled facilities 🗄 Shop on site or within 200yds 🍖 BBQ area 🧺 Picnic area WiFi WiFi 💻 Internet access **SERVICES:** 🔌 Electric hook-up 🗄 Launderette 🍺 Licensed bar 🔥 Calor Gas ♻ Campingaz T Toilet fluid 🍴 Café/Restaurant 🍔 Fast Food/Takeaway 🔋 Battery charging 🚿 Motorhome service point 🚫 No credit or debit cards 🐕 Dogs permitted 🚫 No dogs

SOMERSET

WESTON-SUPER-MARE Map 4 ST36

Places to visit

Weston Museum, WESTON-SUPER-MARE, BS23 1PR, 01934 621028
www.westonmuseum.org

Great for kids: The Helicopter Museum, WESTON-SUPER-MARE, BS24 8PP, 01934 635227
helimuseum.com

Premier Park

Country View Holiday Park
★★★★★ 90%

tel: 01934 627595 **Sand Road, Sand Bay BS22 9UJ**
email: info@cvhp.co.uk **web:** www.cvhp.co.uk
dir: M5 junction 21, A370 towards Weston-super-Mare. Immediately into left lane, follow Kewstoke and Sand Bay signs. Straight over 3 roundabouts onto Lower Norton Lane. At Sand Bay right into Sand Road, site on right.

A pleasant open site in a rural area a few hundred yards from Sandy Bay and the beach. The park is also well placed for energetic walks along the coast at either end of the beach and is only a short drive away from Weston-super-Mare. There is a touring section for tents, caravans and motorhomes with a toilet and shower block. There are hardstanding pitches plus grass pitches, all with electricity. The facilities are excellent and well maintained, including a nice outdoor swimming pool and small, tasteful bar. There is also a separate seasonal touring section with its own facility block.

Open: March to January **Last arrival:** 20.00 **Last departure:** noon
Pitches: 🚐 🚍 ▲; 150 hardstanding pitches; 90 seasonal pitches
Leisure: ≋ ● ♪ ☺
Facilities: 🏠 ☉ ⌕ ✲ ♿ ㅠ WiFi 🖥
Services: 🚐 🛢 🍴 T
Within 3 miles: ⌕ ⌕ U ◎ ≋ ⚓ 日 ⓢ

Additional site information: 20 acre site. 🐕 Cars can be parked by caravans and tents. Awnings permitted.

WINSFORD Map 3 SS93

Places to visit

Dunster Castle, DUNSTER, TA24 6SL, 01643 821314
www.nationaltrust.org.uk/dunster-castle-and-watermill

Cleeve Abbey, WASHFORD, TA23 0PS, 01984 640377
www.english-heritage.org.uk/visit/places/cleeve-abbey

Great for kids: Tropiquaria Zoo, WASHFORD, TA23 0QB, 01984 640688
www.tropiquaria.co.uk

Halse Farm Caravan & Camping Park
★★★★ 86%

tel: 01643 851259 **TA24 7JL**
email: info@halsefarm.co.uk **web:** www.halsefarm.co.uk
dir: Signed from A396 at Bridgetown. In Winsford turn left, bear left past pub. 1 mile up hill, entrance on left immediately after cattle grid.

Halse Farm is a peaceful little site on Exmoor overlooking a wooded valley with glorious views. This moorland site is quite remote, so it's a good base for exploring the Exmoor National Park, while Minehead, Porlock and Lynton are only a short drive away. There are good, modern toilet facilities which are kept immaculately clean.

Open: mid-April to 31 October **Last arrival:** 22.00 **Last departure:** 11.00
Pitches: 🚐 🚍 ▲
Leisure: /⚑
Facilities: 🏠 ☉ ⌕ ✲ ♿ WiFi
Services: 🚐 🛢 🔒 ⌀
Within 3 miles: ⌕ U ⓢ

Additional site information: 3 acre site. 🐕 Cars can be parked by caravans and tents. Awnings permitted.

SOMERSET—STAFFORDSHIRE 217 ENGLAND

WIVELISCOMBE
Map 3 ST02

Places to visit
Cleeve Abbey, WASHFORD, TA23 0PS, 01984 640377
www.english-heritage.org.uk/visit/places/cleeve-abbey

Hestercombe Gardens, TAUNTON, TA2 8LG, 01823 413923
www.hestercombe.com

Platinum Park

Waterrow Touring Park
★★★★★

tel: 01984 623464 **Bouchers Farm**, Waterrow TA4 2AZ
email: info@waterrowpark.co.uk web: www.waterrowpark.co.uk
dir: *M5 junction 25, A358 signed Minehead (bypassing Taunton), B3227 through Wiveliscombe. Site in 3 miles at Waterrow, 0.25 mile past Rock Inn.*

Under pro-active ownership, this really delightful park for adults has spotless facilities, plenty of spacious hardstandings, including fully serviced pitches and a motorhome service point. The River Tone runs along a valley beneath the park, accessed by steps to a nature area created by the owners, where fly-fishing is permitted. Watercolour painting workshops and other activities are available, and the local pub is a short walk away. There is also a bus stop just outside the site.

Open: All year **Last arrival:** 19.00 **Last departure:** 11.30
Pitches: 🚐 🚚 ⛺; 30 hardstanding pitches; 12 seasonal pitches
Facilities: ⊙ ☂ ✻ ♿ ☕ WiFi 💻
Services: 🔌 🛢 🗑 🔋 🛒 🔒 T
Within 3 miles: 🎣 🛒

Additional site information: 8 acre site. Adults only. 🐕 Cars can be parked by caravans and tents. Awnings permitted. No gazebos. Maximum 3 dogs per unit. Caravan storage.

STAFFORDSHIRE

LONGNOR
Map 16 SK06

Places to visit
Chatsworth, BAKEWELL, DE45 1PP
www.chatsworth.org

Poole's Cavern (Buxton Country Park), BUXTON, SK17 9DH, 01298 26978
poolescavern.co.uk

Haddon Hall, HADDON HALL, DE45 1LA, 01629 812855
www.haddonhall.co.uk

LONGNOR
Map 16 SK06

AA CAMPSITE OF THE YEAR FOR HEART OF ENGLAND 2024–25

Premier Park

Longnor Wood Holiday Park
★★★★★ 92%

tel: 01298 83648 **Newtown** SK17 0NG
email: info@longnorwood.co.uk web: www.longnorwood.co.uk
dir: *From A53 follow Longnor sign. Site signed from village, 1.25 miles.*

Enjoying a secluded setting in the heart of the Peak District National Park, Longnor Wood is a spacious adults-only park. Surrounded by rolling countryside and sheltered by woodland it offers a warm welcome from a dedicated team. Under-cover dishwashing and a campers' kitchen are available and there's a new gym, a sauna for private hire and games room. Takeaway pizzas are available Saturday evenings and breakfast rolls on Sunday mornings. There's a 4-acre dog walk, enclosed exercise field and a hot water dog wash for the family friend, while the reception building contains a small, licensed shop that promotes local produce. An EV charging point and free WiFi are available. Luxury hot tub lodges, en suite glamping pods and caravan holiday homes with hot tub are also available for hire.

Open: February to January **Last arrival:** 17.00 (later arrivals by prior arrangement) **Last departure:** noon
Pitches: 🚐 🚚 ⛺; 🏠 see prices below; 47 hardstanding pitches; 23 seasonal pitches; 4 hardstanding tent pitches
Leisure: 🎱 🎯
Facilities: ⚡ 🛁 ⊙ ☂ ✻ 🛒 ☕ WiFi
Services: 🔌 🛢 T 🍺 🛒
Within 3 miles: ⛳ 🛒

Additional site information: 10.5 acre site. Adults only. 🐕 Cars can be parked by caravans and tents. Awnings permitted. No fires, no noise after 23.00.
Glamping available: 2 pods from £90. **Changeover days:** Any time
Additional glamping information: Pods: en suite bathroom, underfloor heating, double bed and linen, fully equipped kitchen unit, TV/DVD, large external deck, outside furniture. Car parking a short distance from the units.

FACILITIES: ⚡ Electric vehicle charging 🛁 Baths/Shower ⊙ Electric shaver sockets ☂ Hairdryer ✻ Ice pack facility 🍼 Baby facilities ♿ Disabled facilities 🛒 Shop on site or within 200yds 🍖 BBQ area ☕ Picnic area WiFi WiFi 💻 Internet access **SERVICES:** 🔌 Electric hook-up 🛢 Launderette 🍺 Licensed bar 🔒 Calor Gas ⊘ Campingaz T Toilet fluid 🍽 Café/Restaurant 🍔 Fast Food/Takeaway 🔋 Battery charging 🛒 Motorhome service point ⊘ No credit or debit cards 🐕 Dogs permitted 🚫 No dogs

Suffolk

Suffolk is Constable country, where the county's crumbling, time-ravaged coastline spreads itself under wide skies to convey a wonderful sense of remoteness and solitude. Highly evocative and atmospheric, this is where rivers wind lazily to the sea and notorious 18th-century smugglers hid from the excise men.

It was the artist John Constable who was responsible for raising the region's profile in the 18th century. Constable immortalised these expansive flatlands in his paintings and today the marketing brochures and websites usually refer to the area as Constable Country. Situated on the River Stour at Flatford, Constable's mill is now a major tourist attraction in the area but a close look at the surroundings confirms rural Suffolk is little changed since the family lived here. Constable himself maintained that the Suffolk countryside 'made me a painter and I am grateful.'

Facing the European mainland and with easy access by the various rivers, the county's open, often bleak, landscape made Suffolk vulnerable in early times to attack from waves of invaders. In the Middle Ages, however, it prospered under the wool merchants: it was their wealth that built the great churches which dominate the countryside.

Walking is one of Suffolk's most popular recreational activities. It may be flat but the county has much to discover on foot – not least the isolated Heritage Coast, which can be accessed via the Suffolk Coast Path. Running along the edge of the shore, between Felixstowe and Lowestoft, the trail is a fascinating blend of ecology and military history. Near its southerly start, the path passes close to one of the National Trust's most unusual acquisitions – Orford Ness. Acquired by the Trust in 1993, and officially opened in 1995, this spectacular stretch of coastline had previously been closed to the public since 1915 when the Royal Flying Corps chose Orford Ness as the setting for military research. These days, it is a Site of Special Scientific Interest, recognised in particular for its rare shingle habitats. Visitors to Orford Ness cross the River Ore by National Trust ferry from Orford Quay.

Beyond Orford, the Suffolk Coast Path parts company with the North Sea, albeit briefly, to visit Aldeburgh. Nearby are Snape Maltings, renowned internationally as the home of the Aldeburgh Festival that takes place in June. Benjamin Britten lived at Snape and wrote *Peter Grimes* here. The Suffolk coast is where both the sea and the natural landscape have influenced generations of writers, artists and musicians. An annual literary festival is staged at Aldeburgh on the first weekend in March.

Back on the Suffolk coast, the trail makes for Southwold, with its distinctive, white-walled lighthouse standing sentinel above the town and its colourful beach huts and attractive pier that feature on many a promotional brochure. The final section of the walk is one of the most spectacular, with low, sandy cliffs, several shallow Suffolk broads and the occasional church tower peeping through the trees. Much of Suffolk's coastal heathland is protected as a designated Area of Outstanding Natural Beauty and shelters several rare creatures including the adder, the heath butterfly and the nightjar.

In addition to walking, there is a good choice of cycling routes. There is the Heart of Suffolk Cycle Route, which extends for 78 miles, while the National Byway, a 4,000-mile cycle route around Britain takes in part of Suffolk and is a very enjoyable way to explore the county.

For something less demanding, visit some of Suffolk's best-known towns. Bury St Edmunds, Sudbury and Ipswich feature prominently on the tourist trail, while Lavenham, Kersey and Debenham are a reminder of the county's important role in the wool industry and the vast wealth it yielded the wool merchants. In these charming old towns look out for streets of handsome, period buildings and picturesque, timber-framed houses.

◁ *Dunwich coast*

SUFFOLK

BUNGAY — Map 13 TM38

Places to visit
Norfolk & Suffolk Aviation Museum, FLIXTON, NR35 1NZ, 01986 896644
www.aviationmuseum.net

Outney Meadow Caravan Park
★★★ 80%

tel: 01986 892338 Outney Meadow NR35 1HG
email: c.r.hancy@ukgateway.net web: www.outneymeadow.co.uk
dir: *In Bungay, site signed from roundabout junction of A143 and A144.*

Three pleasant grassy areas close to the River Waveney, with screened grass pitches, plus a few hardstandings. The central toilet block offers modern facilities and is open at all times. The views from the riverside across the wide flood plain could be straight out of a Constable painting. Canoeing and boating, coarse fishing and cycling are all available here.

Open: March to October **Last arrival:** 21.00 **Last departure:** 16.00
Pitches: ; 7 hardstanding pitches; 15 seasonal pitches
Facilities:
Services:
Within 3 miles:

Additional site information: 6 acre site. Cars can be parked by caravans and tents. Awnings permitted. Boat and canoe.

DUNWICH — Map 13 TM47

Places to visit
RSPB Nature Reserve Minsmere, WESTLETON, IP17 3BY, 01728 648281
www.rspb.org.uk/reserves-and-events/reserves-a-z/minsmere

DUNWICH — Map 13 TM47

Premier Park

Haw Wood Farm Caravan Park
★★★★★ 93%

tel: 01502 359550 Hinton IP17 3QT
email: info@hawwoodfarm.co.uk web: www.hawwoodfarm.co.uk
dir: *Exit A12, 1.5 miles north of Darsham level crossing at Two Magpies bakers. Site 0.5 mile on right.*

An unpretentious, family-orientated park divided up by hedgerows and with three smaller camping meadows. The amenity block is appointed to a very high standard – it includes an excellent reception with café, a good play area and exceptional toilet and shower facilities. With a keen attention to detail and high levels of customer care assured, the visitor experience is constantly improving.

Open: March to 14 January **Last arrival:** 21.00 **Last departure:** 11.00
Pitches: ; 19 hardstanding pitches; 9 seasonal pitches
Leisure:
Facilities:
Services:
Within 3 miles:

Additional site information: 15 acre site. Cars can be parked by caravans and tents. Awnings permitted. No noise after 22.00. 19 fully serviced hardstanding pitches, fresh bread and pastries available. Dog meadow and Woodland walk, books and board games, table tennis. Beach and forest nearby.

SUFFOLK 221 ENGLAND

FELIXSTOWE
Map 13 TM33

Places to visit
Ipswich Museum, IPSWICH, IP1 3QH, 01473 433551
ipswich.cimuseums.org.uk/visit/ipswich-museum

Christchurch Mansion, IPSWICH, IP4 2BE, 01473 433554
ipswich.cimuseums.org.uk/visit/christchurch-mansion

Peewit Caravan Park
★★★★ 81%

tel: 01394 284511 **Walton Avenue IP11 2HB**
email: enquiries@peewitcaravanpark.co.uk **web:** www.peewitcaravanpark.co.uk
dir: *A14 junction 62, follow sign for town centre. Site 100 metres on left.*

A grass touring area fringed by trees, with well-maintained grounds and a colourful floral display. This handy urban site is not overlooked by houses, and new toilet and shower facilities housed in well converted shipping containers were added in 2024. A function room has a TV and library. The beach is a few minutes away by car.

Open: April (or Easter if earlier) to October **Last arrival:** 21.00 **Last departure:** 11.00 (later departures possible)

Pitches: 🚐 🚙 ▲; 4 hardstanding pitches

Leisure: 🎱

Facilities: 🛁 ⊙ 🗡 ✳ ♿ 📶

Services: 🔌 🌀 🔒

Within 3 miles: ↯ ✎ ◎ ⚓ 🍴 🚻

Additional site information: 13 acre site. 🐕 Cars can be parked by caravans and tents. Awnings permitted. 5mph speed restriction on site, only foam footballs permitted. Dogs must be kept on leads. Boules area, bowling green, small play area. Car hire can be arranged.

HOLLESLEY
Map 13 TM34

Places to visit
Woodbridge Tide Mill, WOODBRIDGE, IP12 1BY, 01394 388202
woodbridgetidemill.org.uk

Sutton Hoo, WOODBRIDGE, IP12 3DJ, 01394 389700
www.nationaltrust.org.uk/sutton-hoo

Premier Park

Run Cottage Touring Park
★★★★★ 90%

tel: 01394 411309 **Alderton Road IP12 3RQ**
email: info@runcottage.co.uk **web:** www.runcottage.co.uk
dir: *From A12 (Ipswich to Saxmundham road) onto A1152 at Melton. 1.5 miles, right at roundabout onto B1083. 0.75 mile, left to Hollesley. In Hollesley right into The Street, through village, down hill, over bridge, site 100 yards on left.*

Located in the peaceful village of Hollesley on the Suffolk coast, this landscaped, adults-only park is set behind the owners' house. The generously sized pitches, which include six super pitches, are serviced by a well-appointed and immaculately maintained toilet block which includes two fully serviced cubicles. Another landscaped field offers 22 extra pitches, each with an electric hook-up and TV point, 12 hardstanding pitches and a smart washroom block. Two camping pods and electric bikes are available for hire. This site is handy for the National Trust's Sutton Hoo, and also by travelling a little further north, the coastal centre and beach at Dunwich Heath, and the RSPB bird reserve at Minsmere.

Open: March to January **Last arrival:** 20.00 **Last departure:** 11.00

Pitches: 🚐 🚙 🏠 see prices below; 45 hardstanding pitches

Facilities: 🛁 ⊙ 🗡 ✳ ♿ 🍴 📶

Services: 🔌 🌀 🧺 🅣

Within 3 miles: ↯ ✎ ♘ 🍴

Additional site information: 4.25 acre site. Adults only. 🐕 Cars can be parked by caravans and tents. Awnings permitted. No groundsheets. Satellite TV point on some pitches, touring hardstandings serviced from £31 per night.

Glamping available: Wooden pods from £60. **Changeover days:** Any day

Additional glamping information: Wooden pods: minimum stay 2 nights in summer. Microwave, toaster, tea and coffee, BBQ stand, bedding included. Cars can be parked by units

---

FACILITIES: 🗲 Electric vehicle charging 🛁 Baths/Shower ⊙ Electric shaver sockets 🗡 Hairdryer ✳ Ice pack facility 👶 Baby facilities ♿ Disabled facilities 🏪 Shop on site or within 200yds 🍴 BBQ area 🪑 Picnic area 📶 WiFi 💻 Internet access **SERVICES:** 🔌 Electric hook-up 🌀 Launderette 🍺 Licensed bar 🔥 Calor Gas 🚐 Campingaz 🅣 Toilet fluid 🍽 Café/Restaurant 🍔 Fast Food/Takeaway 🔋 Battery charging ⛽ Motorhome service point 💳 No credit or debit cards 🐕 Dogs permitted 🚫 No dogs

ENGLAND — 222 SUFFOLK

LEISTON
Map 13 TM46

Places to visit
Long Shop Museum, LEISTON, IP16 4ES, 01728 832189
www.longshopmuseum.co.uk

Leiston Abbey, LEISTON, IP16 4TD, 0370 333 1181
www.english-heritage.org.uk/visit/places/leiston-abbey

Great for kids: Easton Farm Park, EASTON, IP13 0EQ, 01728 746475
www.eastonfarmpark.co.uk

Premier Park

Cakes & Ale
★★★★★ 90%

tel: 01728 831655 **Abbey Lane, Theberton IP16 4TE**
email: reception@cakesandale.co.uk **web:** www.cakesandale.co.uk
dir: *From Saxmundham east on B1119. 3 miles, follow minor road over level crossing, turn right, in 0.5 mile straight on at crossroads, entrance 0.5 mile on left.*

A large, well spread out and beautifully maintained site on a former World War II airfield that has many trees and bushes. The spacious touring area includes plenty of hardstandings and 55 super pitches, and there is a good bar. There is a high-quality, solar-powered toilet block containing four fully serviced family rooms, seven cubicled toilet and washbasin rooms, dishwashing facilities, laundry and underfloor heating.

Open: April to end October (restricted service: low season – club, shop and reception reduced opening hours) **Last arrival:** 19.00 **Last departure:** 13.00
Pitches: 55 hardstanding pitches
Leisure:
Facilities: WiFi
Services:
Within 3 miles:

Additional site information: 45 acre site. Cars can be parked by caravans and tents. Awnings permitted. No group bookings, no noise between 21.00–08.00. Golf practice range, football pitch, boules, table tennis.

MOON & SIXPENCE
Near Woodbridge, Suffolk

Secluded, serviced, tourer and motorhome sites with some hardstandings. Good choice of caravan holiday homes for sale; owner occupiers only. Superb, tranquil, landscaped 85 acres parkland & 100 acres of woodland. 9 hole compact golf course, 3 hard tennis courts, volleyball, basketball. Sandy beach, woods. Dog walks, cycle trails. Attractive lounge, bar, restaurant and shop. Located in unspoilt Coastal Suffolk. Close to Woodbridge & River Deben.

AA 5 STAR GOLD AWARD PREMIER PARK

Moon & Sixpence, Waldringfield, Woodbridge, IP12 4PP   www.moonandsixpence.co.uk
Tel: 01473 736650   **e-mail:** info@moonandsixpence.co.uk

PITCHES: Caravans Motorhomes Tents Glamping accommodation **LEISURE:** Indoor swimming pool Outdoor swimming pool Children's playground Kids' club Tennis court Games room Separate TV room golf course Pitch n putt Boats for hire Bikes for hire Cinema Entertainment Fishing Mini golf Watersports Gym Sports field Stables Spa

SUFFOLK 223 ENGLAND

SAXMUNDHAM
Map 13 TM36

Places to visit
Long Shop Museum, LEISTON, IP16 4ES, 01728 832189
www.longshopmuseum.co.uk

Leiston Abbey, LEISTON, IP16 4TD, 0370 333 1181
www.english-heritage.org.uk/visit/places/leiston-abbey

Great for kids: RSPB Nature Reserve Minsmere, WESTLETON, IP17 3BY, 01728 648121
www.rspb.org.uk/reserves-and-events/reserves-a-z/minsmere

Marsh Farm Caravan Site
★★★ 91%

tel: 01728 602168 Sternfield IP17 1HW
web: www.marshfarm-caravansite.co.uk
dir: *A12 onto A1094 (Aldeburgh road), at Snape crossroads left signed Sternfield, follow signs to site.*

A very pretty site overlooking reed-fringed lakes which offer excellent coarse fishing. The facilities are very well maintained and include a basic but fully equipped facility block with showers. The park truly is a peaceful haven, but no tents are allowed.

Open: February to November (weather dependent) **Last arrival:** 21.00 **Last departure:** 14.00

Pitches: 🚐 🚙

Leisure:

Facilities: 🏠 ❄ 🍳 🧺 🍴

Services: 🔌 🛏

Within 3 miles: ⛳ ♘ 🏛

Additional site information: 30 acre site. 🐕 Cars can be parked by caravans. Awnings permitted. Campers must report to reception on arrival. Site closed when freezing temperatures are forecast. Only 1 car per caravan on site. No tents accepted.

WOODBRIDGE
Map 13 TM24

Places to visit
Sutton Hoo, WOODBRIDGE, IP12 3DJ, 01394 389700
www.nationaltrust.org.uk/sutton-hoo

Orford Castle, ORFORD, IP12 2ND, 01394 450472
www.english-heritage.org.uk/visit/places/orford-castle

Great for kids: Easton Farm Park, EASTON, IP13 0EQ, 01728 746475
www.eastonfarmpark.co.uk

WOODBRIDGE
Map 13 TM24

Premier Park

Moon & Sixpence
★★★★★ 92%

tel: 01473 736650 Newbourn Road, Waldringfield IP12 4PP
email: info@moonandsixpence.co.uk **web:** www.moonandsixpence.co.uk
dir: *From roundabout on A12 (east of Ipswich) follow brown Moon & Sixpence signs (Waldringfield). In 1.5 miles left at crossroads, follow signs.*

A well-planned site in a parkland setting, with touring caravans and motorhomes, occupying a sheltered valley position around an attractive lake with a sandy beach. Toilet facilities are housed in a smart Norwegian log cabin with laundry and dishwashing areas. Leisure facilities include tennis courts, outdoor table tennis, woodland walks and trails, outdoor play area and a compact 9-hole golf course. The park has an adult-only area, and a strict 'no groups and no noise after 9pm' policy. All pitches are fully serviced with 6-amp electric hook-up included. Please note, tents are not accepted.

Open: April to October (restricted service: low season – reduced opening hours at club, shop and reception) **Last arrival:** 20.00 **Last departure:** noon

Pitches: 🚐 🚙; 6 hardstanding pitches

Leisure: 🎯 🏊 ♣ ⛳ **Facilities:** 🏠 ⊙ 🚿 ❄ 🍳 🧺 📶 💻

Services: 🔌 🧺 🍺 🍽 🏪 🛏 ⛽ 💧 **Within 3 miles:** ⛳ 🎣 🏛

Additional site information: 5 acre site. 🐕 Cars can be parked by caravans. Awnings permitted. No tents. No group bookings or commercial vehicles, quiet from 21.00–08.00. 10-acre sports area, 110-acre woods, lake and sandy beaches.

See advert opposite

FACILITIES: ⚡ Electric vehicle charging 🛁 Baths/Shower ⊙ Electric shaver sockets 🪮 Hairdryer ❄ Ice pack facility 👶 Baby facilities ♿ Disabled facilities 🏪 Shop on site or within 200yds 🍴 BBQ area 🌳 Picnic area 📶 WiFi 💻 Internet access **SERVICES:** 🔌 Electric hook-up 🧺 Launderette 🍺 Licensed bar ⛽ Calor Gas 🔥 Campingaz 🚽 Toilet fluid 🍽 Café/Restaurant 🍔 Fast Food/Takeaway 🔋 Battery charging ⛽ Motorhome service point 💳 No credit or debit cards 🐕 Dogs permitted 🚫 No dogs

Sussex

East and West Sussex are adjoining counties packed with interest. This is a land of stately homes and castles, miles of breezy chalk cliffs overlooking the English Channel, pretty rivers, picturesque villages and links to our glorious past. Since 2010 it has been the home of Britain's newest national park – the South Downs

Mention Sussex to many people and images of the South Downs immediately spring to mind – 'vast, smooth, shaven, serene,' as the writer Virginia Woolf described them. She and her husband lived at Monk's House in the village of Rodmell, near Lewes, and today, her modest home is managed by the National Trust and open to the public.

Close by, on the downs, is Charleston Farmhouse where Woolf's sister, the artist Vanessa Bell, lived a bohemian life as part of the renowned Bloomsbury group, whose members were mainly notable writers, artists and thinkers. Rudyard Kipling resided at Bateman's, near Burwash, and described the house as 'a good and peaceable place,' after moving there in 1902. 'We have loved it ever since our first sight of it,' he wrote later. Bateman's is also in the care of the National Trust, as is Uppark House at South Harting, near Petersfield. The writer H. G. Wells stayed at Uppark as a boy while his mother was employed there as housekeeper. Away to the east, inland from Hastings, lies Great Dixter, an ancient house in a magical garden. This was the home of the pioneering gardening writer Christopher Lloyd and today both Great Dixter and its garden are open to visitors.

There are a great many historic landmarks within Sussex, but probably the most famous is the battlefield where William, Duke of Normandy defeated Harold and his Saxon army to become William the Conqueror of England. By visiting Battle, near Hastings, you can, with a little imagination, picture the bloody events that led to his defeat. Before the Battle of Hastings, William vowed that if God gave him victory that day, he would build an abbey on the site of the battle at Senlac Field. This he did, with the high altar set up on the spot where Harold died. The abbey was enlarged and improved over the years and today is maintained by English Heritage.

In terms of walking in Sussex, this county is spoilt for choice. Studying the map reveals a multitude of routes – many of them to be found within the boundaries of the South Downs National Park – and an assortment of scenic long-distance trails leading towards distant horizons; all of them offer a perfect way to get to the heart of 'Sussex by the sea,' as it has long been known. The Monarch's Way, one of the region's most popular trails, broadly follows Charles II's escape route in 1651, while the most famous of them, the South Downs Way, follows hill paths and cliff-top tracks all the way from Winchester to Eastbourne. As well as a good range of walks, Sussex offers exhilarating cycle rides through the High Weald, along the South Downs Way and via coastal routes between Worthing and Rye. There is also the Forest Way through East Grinstead to Groombridge. If you enjoy cycling with the salty tang of the sea for company, try the ride between Chichester and West Wittering. You can vary the return journey by taking the Itchenor ferry to Bosham.

Sussex is renowned for its many pretty towns, of course. There is Arundel, littered with period buildings and dominated by the castle, the family home of the Duke of Norfolk, that dates back nearly 1,000 years. Midhurst, Lewes, Rye and Uckfield also have their charms, while the cities of Chichester and Brighton offer countless museums and fascinating landmarks. Brighton's best-known and grandest feature is surely the Royal Pavilion, created as the seaside palace of the Prince Regent (later George IV). The town's genteel Regency terraces and graceful crescents reflect his influence on Brighton. Often referred to as 'London by the sea,' the city has long enjoyed a colourful reputation and has been used as a location in many high profile and highly successful films, including *Brighton Rock* and *Quadrophenia*.

◁ *Beachy Head*

ENGLAND 226 EAST SUSSEX

EAST SUSSEX

BATTLE
Map 7 TQ71

Places to visit

1066 Battle of Hastings, Abbey and Battlefield, BATTLE, TN33 0AE, 0370 333 1181
www.english-heritage.org.uk/visit/places/1066-battle-of-hastings-abbey-and-battlefield

Great for kids: The Observatory Science Centre, HERSTMONCEUX, BN27 1RN, 01323 832731
www.the-observatory.org

Senlac Wood
★★★ 85%

tel: 01424 773969 Catsfield Road, Catsfield TN33 9LN
email: enquiries@senlacwood.co.uk **web:** www.senlacwood.co.uk
dir: *A271 from Battle onto B2204 signed Bexhill. Site on left.*

A woodland site with many secluded hardstanding bays and two peaceful grassy glades for tents. The toilet facilities are clean, tidy and well maintained. This campsite is ideal for anyone looking for seclusion and shade, and it is well placed for visiting nearby Battle and the south coast beaches.

Open: March to October **Last arrival:** 22.00 **Last departure:** noon

Pitches: 🚐 🚗 ⛺; 16 hardstanding pitches

Leisure: 🎱

Facilities: 🏪 ☉ 🚿 ❄ 🚽 WiFi

Services: 🚙 🚛

Within 3 miles: ⛳ 🎣 ↻

Additional site information: 20 acre site. 🐕 Cars can be parked by caravans and tents. Awnings permitted. No camp fires, no noise after 23.00. Caravan storage.

HASTINGS & ST LEONARDS
Map 7 TQ80

Places to visit

Shipwreck Museum, HASTINGS, TN34 3DW, 01424 437452
shipwreckmuseum.co.uk

Great for kids: Blue Reef Aquarium, HASTINGS, TN34 3DW, 01424 718776
hastingsaquarium.co.uk

Premier Park

Combe Haven Holiday Park
★★★★★ 88% HOLIDAY PARK

tel: 01424 427891 Harley Shute Road, St Leonards-on-Sea TN38 8BZ
email: combehaven@haven.com **web:** www.haven.com/combehaven
dir: *A21 towards Hastings. In Hastings take A259 towards Bexhill. Park signed on right.*

Close to a beach and the resort attractions of Hastings and the south coast, this holiday park occupies a sloping valley site and has been designed with families in mind. Activities include a pirates' adventure playground, heated indoor and outdoor swimming pools and a wealth of sports and outdoor activities – zip wire, archery, climbing and target shooting. Adults can enjoy the Mash & Barrel bar/eatery and nightly live entertainment in season.

Open: mid March to October

Holiday Homes: Sleep 8, Bedrooms 3, Bathrooms 1, Toilet 1, Microwave, Freezer, TV, Sky/Freeview

Leisure: 🏊 🏊 🎱 🚴

Additional site information: 🐕 The facilities provided in the holiday homes may differ depending on the grade. Most dog breeds accepted (please check when booking). Dogs must be kept on leads at all times.

PITCHES: 🚐 Caravans 🚗 Motorhomes ⛺ Tents 🏕 Glamping accommodation **LEISURE:** 🏊 Indoor swimming pool 🏊 Outdoor swimming pool 🎠 Children's playground 🧒 Kids' club 🎾 Tennis court 🎱 Games room 🎮 Separate TV room ⛳ golf course 🏌 Pitch n putt ⛵ Boats for hire 🚴 Bikes for hire 🎬 Cinema 🎵 Entertainment 🎣 Fishing ⛳ Mini golf 🏄 Watersports 🏋 Gym ⚽ Sports field 🐎 Stables 💆 Spa

WEST SUSSEX 227 ENGLAND

WEST SUSSEX

ARUNDEL — MAP 6 TQ00

Places to visit

Arundel Castle, ARUNDEL, BN18 9AB, 01903 882173
www.arundelcastle.org

Harbour Park, LITTLEHAMPTON, BN17 5LH, 01903 721200
www.harbourpark.com

Great for kids: Harbour Park, LITTLEHAMPTON, BN17 5LL, 01903 721200
www.harbourpark.com

Ship & Anchor Marina
★★★ 80%

tel: 01243 551262 **Station Road, Ford BN18 0BJ**
email: enquiries@shipandanchormarina.co.uk
dir: *From A27 at Arundel take road south signed Ford. Site 2 miles on left after level crossing.*

Well located just south of Arundel and the South Downs, this small, traditional and neatly maintained campsite has dated, but spotlessly clean toilet facilities, a secluded tent area, and enjoys a pleasant position beside the Ship & Anchor pub and the tidal River Arun. There are good walks from the site to Arundel and the coast. River fishing is also possible.

Open: March to October **Last arrival:** 21.00 **Last departure:** noon

Pitches: 🚐 🚗 ⛺; 11 hardstanding pitches; 40 seasonal pitches

Leisure: 🎯

Facilities: 🏠 ☺ ᛦ ✳ ♿ 💲

Services: 🔌 🍽 🍴 🧺 🔋 🛢 🚽

Within 3 miles: 🚶 🎣 🍺 ⓜ 🚣 ✈ 🚉

Additional site information: 12 acre site. 🐕 🚗 Cars can be parked by caravans and tents. Awnings permitted. No music audible to others, no visitors, no ball games. Pub on site, river walk.

BARNS GREEN — Map 6 TQ12

Places to visit

Parham House & Gardens, PULBOROUGH, RH20 4HS, 01903 742021
www.parhaminsussex.co.uk

Great for kids: Bignor Roman Villa, BIGNOR, RH20 1PH, 01798 869259
www.bignorromanvilla.co.uk

Sumners Ponds Fishery & Campsite
★★★★ 92%

tel: 01403 732539 **Chapel Road RH13 0PR**
email: bookings@sumnersponds.co.uk **web:** www.sumnersponds.co.uk
dir: *From A272 at Coolham crossroads, north towards Barns Green. In 1.5 miles take 1st left at small crossroads. 1 mile, over level crossing. Site on left just after right bend.*

Dedication to provide high quality camping continues at this working farm set in attractive surroundings on the edge of the quiet village of Barns Green. There are three touring areas — one continues to develop and includes extra hardstandings, and another, which has a stunning modern toilet block, has excellent pitches on the banks of one of the well-stocked fishing lakes. For a glamping holiday there are wooden pods, impressive, fully-equipped safari tents, lodges, shepherd's huts. The Bell tents and two luxury cabins all enjoy a fabulous lakeside setting. A secluded family-only field (with hook-ups and fire pits) is located close to woodland and a lake. There are many cycle paths and two dog-walking fields on site and the woodland walk has direct access to miles of footpaths. The excellent Café by the Lake has alfresco seating on a waterside pontoon and serves meals from breakfast onwards. Horsham and Brighton are within easy reach.

Open: All year **Last arrival:** 20.00 **Last departure:** noon

Pitches: 🚐 🚗 ⛺; 🏠 see prices below; 45 hardstanding pitches

Leisure: 🎯 ✏

Facilities: 🏠 ☺ ᛦ ✳ ♿ 💲 🅿 📶

Services: 🔌 🧺 🍽 🍴 🧺 🛢 🚽

Within 3 miles: 🚶 ⓜ ✈

Additional site information: 100 acre site. 🐕 🚗 Cars can be parked by caravans and tents. Awnings permitted. 1 car per pitch. Well behaved dogs. No noise after 22.30. Fishing lakes, footpaths.

Glamping available: 6 sleeping pods from £36; 4 shepherd's huts from £100; safari tents from £255.

Additional glamping information: Sleeping pods: minimum stay 1 night (2 nights at weekends, school holidays), 3 nights at bank holiday weekends; Shepherd's huts: minimum stay 2 nights (3 at weekends; 4 nights at Easter weekend); Safari tents minimum stay 3 nights Friday to Monday (4 nights Monday to Friday; 7 nights Friday to Friday or Monday to Monday) All units — electricity; no smoking. Shepherd's huts and safari tents — log burners; no dogs. Sleeping pods — electric heater. Cars can be parked by units

WEST SUSSEX

CHICHESTER
Map 5 SU80

Places to visit
Pallant House Gallery, CHICHESTER, PO19 1TJ, 01243 774557
pallant.org.uk

Chichester Cathedral, CHICHESTER, PO19 1PX, 01243 782595
www.chichestercathedral.org.uk

AA CAMPSITE OF THE YEAR FOR SOUTH EAST ENGLAND 2024–25

Platinum Park

Concierge Camping
★★★★★

Best of British

tel: 01243 573118 Ratham Estate, Ratham Lane PO18 8DL
email: service@conciergecamping.co.uk web: www.conciergecamping.co.uk
dir: *From A27 onto A259 to Bosham. In Bosham at roundabout into Station Road. Over railway line, over A27. At T-junction left onto B2146 signed West Ashling. 1st left into Ratham Lane.*

Concierge Camping is a multi award-winning park. It is a first-class, small park for 37 units offering large, fully serviced pitches suitable for American RVs, and the attention to detail throughout is very impressive. Everything is high spec, from very spacious pitches and the reception, complete with a shop that sells local produce, coffee, drinks, late-arrival hampers, a smart covered rear terrace with excellent food offerings (Notso & Notdough, a twist on Asian and Japanese street food), to the state-of-the-art amenity block. Here, you'll find ultra-efficient rain showers, stylish washbasins and showers with temperature controls, piped radio and Ratham Estate toiletries plus an excellent room for families or disabled guests. Gladiator pitches have a mini-safari tent living space, replete with wood-fired oven, Smart TV, Nespresso machine, dining table and bench seating. Ten unique Emperor pitches were added in 2024 for the ultimate 'Concierge' experience. Set in an adjoining meadow, each pitch has a stunning day-living cabin with en suite bathroom, a stylish, fully-fitted kitchen with log-burning cooker, and spacious dining areas inside and outside on a decked area. A tranquil wooded area next to the stream has been cleared to create a natural, shady outside 'lounge area' – a real treat for guests. Close to Chichester (cathedral and harbour), excellent beaches, the South Downs National Park and the Goodwood Estate.

Concierge Camping

Open: All year **Last arrival:** 18.00 (earliest arrival 13.00, later arrival times by prior arrangement) **Last departure:** 11.00

Pitches: 🚐 🚙; hardstanding pitches

Facilities: 🏪 ☉ ⌕ ♿ 🚿 ♨ 🍴 📶 💻

Services: 🔌 🗑 ♻ 🍽 🧺 ⛽ 🅃

Within 3 miles: 🎣 ⛳ ∪ 🎿 🎒

Additional site information: 4 acre site. 🐕 Cars can be parked by caravans. Awnings permitted. No bookings accepted by under 18 years. No noise after 23.00.

See advert opposite

Make your next UK holiday one to remember

Choose RatedTrips.com

AA

PITCHES: 🚐 Caravans 🚙 Motorhomes ⛺ Tents 🏕 Glamping accommodation **LEISURE:** 🏊 Indoor swimming pool 🏊 Outdoor swimming pool 🛝 Children's playground 🎪 Kids' club 🎾 Tennis court 🎱 Games room 📺 Separate TV room ⛳ golf course 🏌 Pitch n putt 🚤 Boats for hire 🚲 Bikes for hire 🎬 Cinema 🎵 Entertainment 🎣 Fishing ⛳ Mini golf 🏄 Watersports 🏋 Gym ⚽ Sports field ∪ Stables ♨ Spa

Platinum Park

Concierge Glamping
★★★★★ GLAMPING ONLY

tel: 01243 573118 Ratham Estate, Ratham Lane PO18 8DL
email: service@conciergecamping.co.uk web: www.conciergecamping.co.uk
dir: *From A27 onto A259 to Bosham. In Bosham at roundabout into Station Road. Over railway line, over A27. At T-junction left onto B2146 signed West Ashling. 1st left into Ratham Lane.*

Quality and attention to detail are very evident at Guy and Tracey Hodgkin's Concierge Glamping park near Chichester. They offer four stunning safari lodges, idyllically situated beside a babbling chalk stream. These impressive 'lodges' are made from wood and top-quality canvas – they ooze style and comfort, with a range cooker, dishwasher, fridge-freezer, TV, underfloor heating and a Nespresso machine in the fully-fitted kitchen, a smart en suite shower room (complete with piped radio), and two good-size bedrooms; the twin-bedded room is situated at the top of a wooden staircase. Each lodge has a large veranda with stylish seating, picnic bench and barbecue, that overlooks the stream. Mature laurel hedging ensures each lodge offers excellent privacy from the camping park.

Open: All year **Last arrival:** 18.00 **Last departure:** 10.00
Facilities:
Within 3 miles:
Accommodation available: Safari Lodges from £435.
Changeover days: Monday and Friday
Additional site information: 4 acre site. Booking advisable. Large inside and alfresco areas, bar and coffee shop. Minimum stay 3 nights.

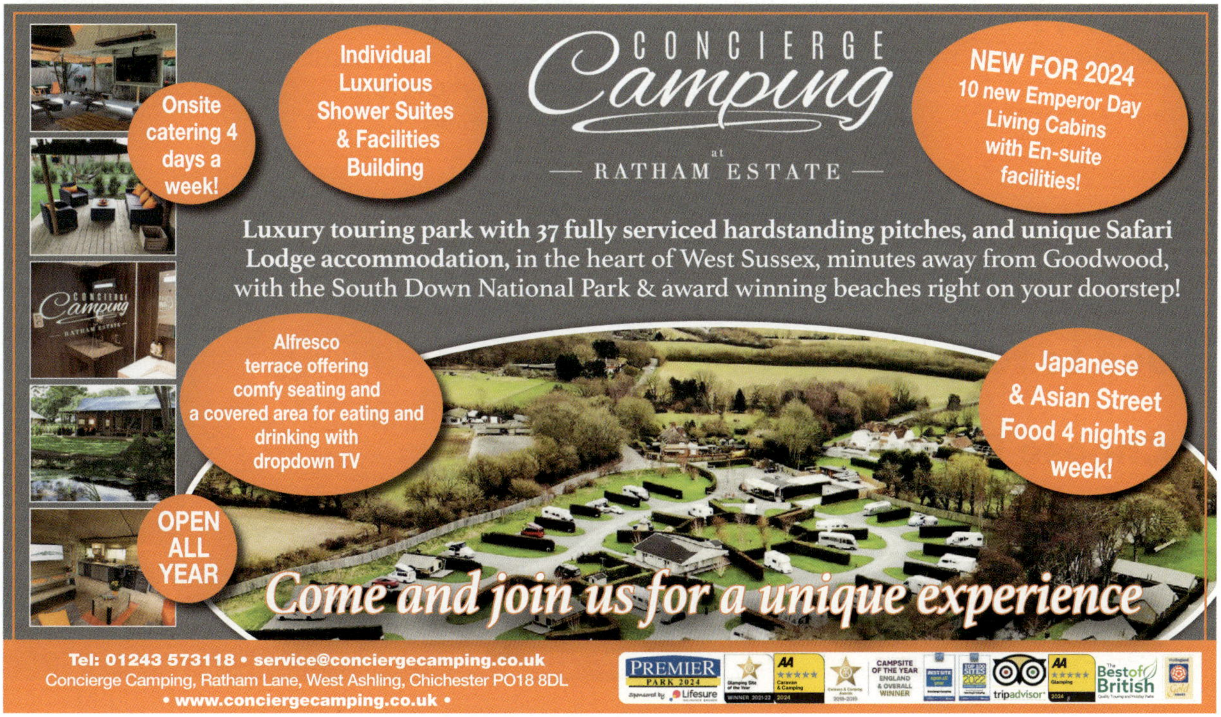

CONCIERGE Camping at RATHAM ESTATE

- Onsite catering 4 days a week!
- Individual Luxurious Shower Suites & Facilities Building
- NEW FOR 2024 — 10 new Emperor Day Living Cabins with En-suite facilities!
- Alfresco terrace offering comfy seating and a covered area for eating and drinking with dropdown TV
- Japanese & Asian Street Food 4 nights a week!
- OPEN ALL YEAR

Luxury touring park with 37 fully serviced hardstanding pitches, and unique Safari Lodge accommodation, in the heart of West Sussex, minutes away from Goodwood, with the South Down National Park & award winning beaches right on your doorstep!

Come and join us for a unique experience

Tel: 01243 573118 • service@conciergecamping.co.uk
Concierge Camping, Ratham Lane, West Ashling, Chichester PO18 8DL
• www.conciergecamping.co.uk •

WEST SUSSEX

PAGHAM
Map 6 SZ89

Places to visit
RSPB Pagham Harbour LNR, SIDLESHAM, PO20 7NE, 01243 641508
www.rspb.org.uk/reserves-and-events/reserves-a-z/pagham-harbour-local-nature-reserve

Premier Park

Church Farm Holiday Park
★★★★★ 94% HOLIDAY PARK

tel: 01243 262635 Church Lane PO21 4NR
email: churchfarm@haven.com web: www.haven.com/parks/sussex/church-farm
dir: *At roundabout on A27 (south of Chichester) take B2145 signed Hunston and Selsey. At mini-roundabout take 1st left signed North Mundham, Pagham and Bognor Regis. Site in approximately 3 miles.*

Close to Portsmouth, Chichester and south coast beaches, this relaxing and fun-packed holiday park is located on the edge of Pagham Harbour Nature Reserve. On-site activities include golf on the 9-hole course, tennis coaching, shopping, kids' play areas, excellent indoor and outdoor swimming pools, a pool-side bar and pizzeria, and a Show Bar for evening entertainment. There is a range of holiday caravans and lodges for hire.

Open: 15 March to 31 October
Holiday Homes: Sleep 8, Bedrooms 2, Bathrooms 1, Toilet 1, Microwave, Freezer, TV, Sky/Freeview
Leisure:
Additional site information:

SELSEY
Map 5 SZ89

Places to visit
RSPB Pagham Harbour LNR, SIDLESHAM, PO20 7NE, 01243 641508
www.rspb.org.uk/reserves-and-events/reserves-a-z/pagham-harbour-local-nature-reserve

Fishbourne Roman Palace, FISHBOURNE, PO19 3QR, 01243 785859
sussexpast.co.uk/attraction/fishbourne-roman-palace

Warner Farm
★★★★ 84% HOLIDAY PARK

tel: 01243 604499 & 979501 Warner Lane, Selsey PO20 9EL
web: www.cove.co.uk/sealbayresort/camping-touring
dir: *From B2145 in Selsey turn right into School Lane, follow signs.*

A well-screened touring site that adjoins the three static parks under the same ownership. A courtesy bus runs around the complex to the entertainment areas and supermarkets. The park backs onto open grassland and offers modern toilet facilities and an excellent children's play area, and the leisure facilities with bar, amusements and bowling alley, and swimming pool/sauna complex are also accessible to tourers. Guests can also use the top-quality leisure complex with swimming pool and restaurants on neighbouring White Horse Park.

Open: March to January **Last arrival:** 19.00 (off peak 17.00) **Last departure:** 10.00
Pitches: ; 60 hardstanding pitches; 25 seasonal pitches
Leisure:
Facilities:
Services:
Within 3 miles:
Additional site information: 10 acre site.

Make your next UK holiday one to remember

Choose RatedTrips.com

AA

WARWICKSHIRE—WILTSHIRE   ENGLAND

WARWICKSHIRE

HARBURY   Map 11 SP35

Places to visit
Warwick Castle, WARWICK, CV34 4QU, 01926 406610
www.warwick-castle.com

Farnborough Hall, FARNBOROUGH, OX17 1DU, 01295 690002
www.nationaltrust.org.uk/farnborough-hall

Great for kids: British Motor Museum, GAYDON, CV35 0BJ, 01926 641188
www.britishmotormuseum.co.uk

Premier Park

Harbury Fields
★★★★★ 86%

tel: 01926 612457 Harbury Fields Farm CV33 9JN
email: info@harburyfields.co.uk web: www.harburyfields.co.uk
dir: *M40 junction 12, B4451 (signed Kineton and Gaydon). 0.75 mile, right signed Lightborne. 4 miles, right at roundabout onto B4455 (signed Harbury). 3rd right by petrol station, site in 700 yards by two cottages.*

This peaceful park is in a farm setting with lovely countryside views. All pitches are hardstanding and fully serviced, the reception is housed in an attractive wooden chalet, and the facility block has fully serviced cubicles. The park is well positioned for visiting Warwick and Royal Leamington Spa as well as NEC Birmingham and Stoneleigh Park. Stratford is just 10 miles away, and Upton House (NT) and Compton Verney Art Gallery and Park are nearby.

Open: February to 1 December **Last arrival:** 20.00 **Last departure:** noon
Pitches: ; 59 hardstanding pitches
Facilities:
Services: Within 3 miles:
Additional site information: 6 acre site. Cars can be parked by caravans. Awnings permitted. No traffic noise midnight to 07.30.

WOLVEY   Map 11 SP48

Places to visit
Arbury Estate, NUNEATON, CV10 7PZ, 01676 540529
arburyestate.co.uk

Lunt Roman Fort, COVENTRY, CV8 3AJ, 024 7623 7522
www.luntromanfort.org

Great for kids: Coventry Transport Museum, COVENTRY, CV1 1JD, 024 7623 4270   www.transport-museum.com

Wolvey Villa Farm Caravan & Camping Park
★★★ 80%

tel: 01455 220493 LE10 3HF
email: wolveycaravanpark@outlook.com web: www.wolveycaravanpark.com
dir: *M6 junction 2, B4065 follow Wolvey signs. Or M69 junction 1 and follow Wolvey signs.*

A level grass site, surrounded by trees and shrubs, on the border of Warwickshire and Leicestershire. This quiet country site has its own popular fishing lake, and is convenient for visiting Coventry and Leicester. In addition, there are enclosures with goats, horses and donkeys for the enjoyment of all. There are limited pitches available between October and March and the park closes from November to February.

Open: 1 March to 31 October **Last arrival:** 22.00 **Last departure:** noon
Pitches: ; 24 hardstanding pitches
Leisure: **Facilities:**
Services: Within 3 miles:
Additional site information: 7 acre site. Cars can be parked by caravans and tents. Awnings permitted. No noise after 23.00. No fire pits, no twin axle vehicles. Putting green.

WILTSHIRE

BERWICK ST JAMES   Map 5 SU03

Places to visit
Stonehenge, STONEHENGE, SP4 7DE, 0370 333 1181
www.english-heritage.org.uk/visit/places/stonehenge

Stonehenge Campsite & Glamping Pods
★★★★ 86%

tel: 07786 734732 & 01722 792750 SP3 4TQ
email: stay@stonehengecampsite.co.uk web: www.stonehengecampsite.co.uk
dir: *From Stonehenge Visitor Centre take A303 west, 2 miles. Through Winterbourne Stoke. Left onto B3083 towards Berwick St James. Site on left in 0.5 mile.*

This small campsite is split into three areas and has good, modern toilets and showers including a laundry facility. The lower end of the site has hardstandings for caravans and motorhomes plus eight glamping pods, including Bustopia that sleeps four adults and two children, and a yurt. The middle field is for tents, both for families and individuals, whilst the top area is for larger groups who can enjoy some of their holiday time sitting around open fires or fire pits. The site is close to Stonehenge and Longleat; there are plenty of excellent walks from the campsite and two good pubs nearby.

Open: All year **Last arrival:** 20.00 **Last departure:** 10.45
Pitches: * from £30; from £30; from £20 ; 12 hardstanding pitches
Facilities:
Services: Within 3 miles:
Additional site information: 4 acre site. Cars can be parked by caravans and tents. Awnings permitted. No noise 22.00–08.00, no music at any time, cashless site. Camp fire and mobile fire pits, WiFi on request.

Additional glamping information: No dogs allowed in glamping pods.

FACILITIES: Electric vehicle charging   Baths/Shower   Electric shaver sockets   Hairdryer   Ice pack facility   Baby facilities   Disabled facilities   Shop on site or within 200yds   BBQ area   Picnic area   WiFi   Internet access   **SERVICES:** Electric hook-up   Launderette   Licensed bar   Calor Gas   Campingaz   Toilet fluid   Café/Restaurant   Fast Food/Takeaway   Battery charging   Motorhome service point   No credit or debit cards   Dogs permitted   No dogs

ENGLAND 232 WILTSHIRE

CHIPPENHAM Map 4 ST97

Places to visit
Lacock Abbey, Fox Talbot Museum and Village, LACOCK, SN15 2LG, 01249 730459
www.nationaltrust.org.uk/lacock-abbey-fox-talbot-museum-and-village

Corsham Court, CORSHAM, SN13 0BZ, 01249 712214
www.corsham-court.co.uk

Premier Park

Plough Lane Touring Caravan Site
★★★★★ 89%

tel: 01249 750146 Plough Lane SN15 5PS
email: enquiries@ploughlane.co.uk **web:** www.ploughlane.co.uk
dir: *Exit A350 north of Chippenham.*

Plough Lane is a family run, adults-only caravan site with a reputation for high standards. Located just 25 minutes from Bath and ideally sited for exploring the southern Cotswolds, Wiltshire and Bristol. The 52 pitches are set in beautifully laid out grounds with mature shrub beds separating the site into bays. All pitches are 50% hardstanding and 50% grass and are easily accessible, and have an electric hook-up and access to free WiFi.

Open: April to October
Additional site information: Adults only.

COOMBE BISSETT Map 5 SU12

Places to visit
Breamore House & Countryside Museum, BREAMORE, SP6 2DF, 01725 512858
www.breamorehouse.com

Summerlands Caravan Park
★★★ 88%

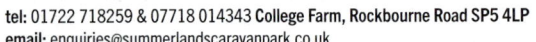

tel: 01722 718259 & 07718 014343 College Farm, Rockbourne Road SP5 4LP
email: enquiries@summerlandscaravanpark.co.uk
web: www.summerlandscaravanpark.co.uk
dir: *Signed from junction of A354 and Rockbourne Road. Approximately 6 miles south of Salisbury.*

Approached via a long private drive and situated well off the beaten track within Cranborne Chase, yet close to Salisbury, this small, family-run park offers peace and quiet and superb views across rolling countryside. Twenty level grass pitches are located in a neat meadow and the well-maintained toilet and shower facilities are kept spotlessly clean. Dogs are welcome and there's plenty of space for children to play.

Open: April to October **Last arrival:** 21.00 **Last departure:** noon
Pitches: 🚐 🚌 ⛺
Facilities: 🏠 ☉ 🚿 ✲ ♿
Services: 🔌 🍴 ⬇
Within 3 miles: 💲
Additional site information: 3.3 acre site. Cars can be parked by caravans and tents. Awnings permitted. No noise after 23.00. Vehicle access restrictions 23.00–07.00.

LACOCK Map 4 ST96

Places to visit
Lacock Abbey, Fox Talbot Museum and Village, LACOCK, SN15 2LG, 01249 730459
www.nationaltrust.org.uk/lacock-abbey-fox-talbot-museum-and-village

Corsham Court, CORSHAM, SN13 0BZ, 01249 712214
www.corsham-court.co.uk

Piccadilly Caravan Park
★★★★ 88%

tel: 01249 263164 Folly Lane West SN15 2LP
email: info@piccadillylacock.co.uk **web:** www.piccadillylacock.co.uk
dir: *4 miles south of Chippenham just past Lacock. Exit A350 signed Gastard. Site 300 yards on left.*

A peaceful, beautifully laid-out park, close to the National Trust village of Lacock and Lacock Abbey, that has been family run for 40 years. Both the facilities and the grounds are neatly maintained; very good hedge screening for privacy; and there's a new, high quality children's play area. A section of the park has been developed to provide spacious pitches especially for tents and luxury glamping bell tents, where guests will find not only cosy beds but also homemade biscuits, and marshmallows for toasting.

Open: Easter and April to October **Last arrival:** 20.00 **Last departure:** noon
Pitches: 🚐 🚌 ⛺ 🏕; 12 hardstanding pitches
Leisure: 🎠 ⚽
Facilities: 🏠 ☉ 🚿 ✲ WiFi
Services: 🔌 🍴 ⬇ 🔒 ⊘
Within 3 miles: 🎣 ⛳ ♻ 🚌 💲
Additional site information: 2.5 acre site. Cars can be parked by caravans and tents. Awnings permitted. No excessive noise.
Glamping available: 2 fully furnished bell tents (one sleeps 4, one sleeps 2). Emperor bell tent (unfurnished) sleeps 6–8.

SALISBURY Map 5 SU12

Places to visit
The Salisbury Museum, SALISBURY, SP1 2EN, 01722 332151
salisburymuseum.org.uk

Salisbury Cathedral, SALISBURY, SP1 2EJ, 01722 555120
www.salisburycathedral.org.uk

PITCHES: 🚐 Caravans 🚌 Motorhomes ⛺ Tents 🏕 Glamping accommodation **LEISURE:** 🏊 Indoor swimming pool 🏊 Outdoor swimming pool 🎠 Children's playground Kids' club 🎾 Tennis court Games room Separate TV room ⛳ golf course Pitch n putt Boats for hire Bikes for hire Cinema Entertainment Fishing Mini golf Watersports Gym Sports field Stables Spa

WILTSHIRE—WORCESTERSHIRE 233 ENGLAND

SALISBURY
Map 5 SU12

Premier Park

Coombe Touring Park
★★★★★ 93%

tel: 01722 328451 **Race Plain, Netherhampton SP2 8PN**
email: enquiries@coombecaravanpark.co.uk web: www.coombecaravanpark.co.uk
dir: *From Salisbury take A345 towards Blandford. Onto A3094 then follow Stratford Tony and site signs. After racecourse turn left. 700 yards to site on right. Or from A36 (west of Salisbury) onto A3094 (signed Bournemouth), at Netherhampton Corner follow Stratford Tony and racecourse signs. After racecourse turn left. 700 yards to site on right.*

A very neat and attractive site adjacent to the racecourse with views over the downs. The park is well landscaped with shrubs and maturing trees, and the very colourful beds are stocked from the owner's own greenhouse. This is a lovely, quiet and peaceful park to stay on with an excellent toilet and shower block, plus a fully-equipped function room with a kitchen that makes for a welcome campers' retreat. The well stocked shop offers daily baked bread and all the essentials which is a bonus. Improvements to security and six hardstanding pitches are new additions. There are four static homes available for hire.

Open: All year **Last arrival:** 21.00 (April to October) 20.00 (October to April)
Last departure: noon (touring) 11.00 (static)
Pitches: 🚐 🚙 ⛺; 6 hardstanding pitches
Leisure: 🎱 📺 **Facilities:** 🛁 ☉ 🪒 ❄ ♿ 💈 🍴 🪑
Services: 🔌 🧺 🍽 ⬇ 🍃 🚽 **Within 3 miles:** ⚓ ⛳ 🚌

Additional site information: 8 acre site. 🐕 Cars can be parked by caravans and tents. Awnings permitted. No open fires, no mini motorbikes, no drones, no noise between 23.00–07.00. Table tennis, campers' kitchen, children's bathroom.

WORCESTERSHIRE

HONEYBOURNE
Map 10 SP14

Places to visit
Kiftsgate Court Garden, MICKLETON, GL55 6LN, 01386 438777
www.kiftsgate.co.uk

Hidcote Manor Garden, MICKLETON, GL55 6LR, 01386 438333
www.nationaltrust.org.uk/hidcote

Great for kids: Anne Hathaway's Cottage, SHOTTERY, CV37 9HH, 01789 338532
www.shakespeare.org.uk/visit/anne-hathaways-cottage

Premier Park

Ranch Caravan Park
★★★★★ 94%

tel: 01386 830744 **Station Road WR11 7PR**
email: enquiries@ranch.co.uk web: www.ranch.co.uk
dir: *From village crossroads towards Bidford, site 400 metres on left.*

An attractive, well-run and improving park set amidst farmland in the Vale of Evesham and landscaped with trees and bushes. Tourers have their own excellent facilities in two locations, and the use of an outdoor heated swimming pool in peak season. The facilities block really does have the wow factor, with underfloor heating to the laundry, wash-up area and the showers and toilets, which include family/accessible, fully serviced cubicles. Two superb children's play areas are geared to provide entertainment for all ages, and alfresco areas are provided at the licenced club. There are lodges and a 3-bedroom cottage for hire. Please note that this site does not accept tents.

Open: March to November (restricted service: March to May and September to November – swimming pool closed, shorter club hours) **Last arrival:** 20.00
Last departure: noon
Pitches: 🚐 🚙; 23 seasonal pitches
Leisure: 🏊 🎣 🎱 📺 🎵 ⚽
Facilities: 🛁 ☉ 🪒 ❄ ♿ 💈 💻
Services: 🔌 🧺 🍽 🍴 🛒 ⬇ 🚽 🍃 📞
Within 3 miles: ⚓ ⛳ 🚌

Additional site information: 12 acre site. 🐕 Cars can be parked by caravans. Awnings permitted. No unaccompanied minors. 46 touring pitches. Car hire can be arranged.

Yorkshire

There is nowhere in the British Isles quite like Yorkshire. With such scenic and cultural diversity, it is almost a country within a country. For sheer scale, size and grandeur, there is nowhere to beat it. Much of it in the spectacular Pennines, Yorkshire is a land of glorious moors, gentle dales, ruined abbeys and picturesque market towns.

'My Yorkshire, a land of pure air, rocky streams and hidden waterfalls,' was how the celebrated vet Alf Wight described his adopted home. Wight was born in Sunderland but moved to the North Yorkshire market town of Thirsk soon after the outbreak of the Second World War. He fell in love with the place and in later years his affection for the beauty, spirit and character of this great county translated to the printed page when Wight, writing under the name of James Herriot, wrote eight best-selling volumes of memoirs about the life of a Yorkshire vet, which spawned films and TV series. Today, thousands of visitors from near and far travel to the landscape he loved so dearly to see it all for themselves. His veterinary practice, and original home, in Thirsk is open to the public.

Not surprisingly, walking features prominently on the list of things to do in Yorkshire. There are countless footpaths and bridleways to explore and miles of long-distance trails across vast open moorland and through tranquil meandering valleys. The 81-mile Dales Way is a perfect way to discover the magnificent scenery of Wharfedale, Ribblesdale and Dentdale, while the Calderdale Way offers a fascinating insight into the Pennine heartland of industrial West Yorkshire. Most famous of all the region's longer routes is surely the Pennine Way, which opened over 50 years ago in April 1965. Its inception was the most important achievement in the history of the Ramblers' Association, marking Britain's first national long-distance footpath.

The Pennine Way was the brainchild of Tom Stephenson, one-time secretary of the Association but his vision for a trail for everyone was a long time in the planning. Landowners regularly thwarted his attempts to make the landscape accessible to walkers and there were countless prosecutions for trespassing 'I could never understand how anyone could own a mountain,' Stephenson wrote. 'Surely it was there for everybody.'

One of the more surprising features to be found on the route of the Pennine Way is the ruined house known as Top Withins. This is thought to be the inspiration for *Wuthering Heights*, the Earnshaw home in Emily Brontë's stirring novel of the same name. The Brontë sisters knew the area well, and their home, now the Brontë Parsonage Museum, lies just a few miles from the ruins in the village of Haworth. The parsonage draws thousands of visitors every year; its atmospheric setting amid bleak moorland and gritstone houses vividly captures the spirit of this uniquely talented trio of writers.

An easier, more comfortable way of exploring much of Yorkshire's scenic landscape is by train. A ride on the famous Settle to Carlisle railway represents one of the region's most memorable train journeys. For a while during the late 1980s the future of this line was in serious doubt, when it seemed British Rail might close it because of soaring maintenance costs. Thanks to Michael Portillo, a noted railway enthusiast who was Secretary of State for Transport at the time, the line was saved. Essentially, the Settle to Carlisle railway is a lifeline for commuters and the people of the more remote communities of the western Dales, but it is also an extremely popular tourist attraction. Carriages are regularly filled with summer visitors in search of stunning scenery and they are not disappointed. Elsewhere in Yorkshire, a very different train recalls a very different age. In the National Railway Museum at York you'll find countless locomotives, including a replica of Stephenson's Rocket and the much-loved *Flying Scotsman*.

◁ *Lower Wharfedale*

ENGLAND 236 EAST RIDING OF YORKSHIRE

EAST RIDING OF YORKSHIRE

BRANDESBURTON — Map 17 TA14

Places to visit

Beverley Guildhall, BEVERLEY, HU17 9XX, 01482 392783
www.eastridingmuseums.co.uk/find-a-museum/?entry=beverley_guildhall

Burton Constable Hall, SPROATLEY, HU11 4LN, 01964 562400
www.burtonconstable.com

Premier Park

Dacre Lakeside Park
★★★★★ 87% HOLIDAY PARK

tel: 0800 180 4556 & 01964 543704 YO25 8RT
email: dacrepark@btconnect.com web: www.dacrepark.co.uk
dir: *From A165 (bypass) midway between Beverley and Hornsea, follow Brandesburton and brown site sign.*

An expanding holiday park which has not finished evolving. It offers an array of luxurious lodges and camping pods are also available for hire. The large lake at the centre of this site adds to the peaceful setting and is very popular with water sports enthusiasts. There are a few touring and seasonal pitches for caravanning near the water, as well as a camping field nearer reception. The stylish Bert's Pizzeria & Gelato serves a wide range of food and drinks. The six-acre lake is used for kayaking, paddle boarding and fishing, and adventure golf or foot golf activities can also be booked. There is also a beauty salon on site.

Open: March to October **Last arrival:** 21.00 **Last departure:** noon
Pitches: see prices below; 2 hardstanding pitches; 107 seasonal pitches
Leisure:
Facilities:
Services:
Within 3 miles:

Additional site information: 8 acre site. No noise 23.00–08.00, no craft with engines permitted on lake.

Glamping available: Wooden pods from £45.

Premier Park

Blue Rose Caravan and Country Park
★★★★★ 80%

tel: 01964 543366 & 07504 026839 Star Carr Lane YO25 8RU
email: info@bluerosepark.com web: www.bluerosepark.com
dir: *From A165 at roundabout into New Road, signed Brandesburton, which becomes Star Carr Lane. In approximately 1 mile, site on left.*

High standards of customer care are assured at this neat and well-maintained adults-only site that is well placed for visiting Hornsea and the Yorkshire coastline. The park is within walking distance of Brandesburton and offers an idyllic stopover for caravanners wanting a peaceful break in the countryside.

Open: All year **Last arrival:** 20.00 **Last departure:** noon
Pitches: ; 59 hardstanding pitches; 35 seasonal pitches
Facilities: WiFi
Services:
Within 3 miles:

Additional site information: 113 acre site. Adults only. Cars can be parked by caravans. Awnings permitted.

BRIDLINGTON — Map 17 TA16

Places to visit

Sewerby Hall and Gardens, BRIDLINGTON, YO15 1EA, 01262 673769
www.sewerbyhall.co.uk

RSPB Bempton Cliffs, BEMPTON, YO15 1JF, 01262 422212
www.rspb.org.uk/reserves-and-events/reserves-a-z/bempton-cliffs

Great for kids: Burton Agnes Hall, BURTON AGNES, YO25 4NB, 01262 490324
www.burtonagnes.com

Fir Tree Caravan Park
★★★★ 83%

tel: 01262 676442 Jewison Lane, Sewerby YO16 6YG
email: info@flowerofmay.com web: www.flowerofmay.com
dir: *1.5 miles from centre of Bridlington. Left onto B1255 at Marton Corner. Site 600 yards on left.*

Fir Tree Caravan Park is a large, mainly static park that has a well laid out touring area with its own facilities. It has an excellent swimming pool complex with an adjacent conservatory bar. There is also a family bar, games room and outdoor children's play area. Please note, this park only offers seasonal touring pitches.

Open: March to October (restricted service: early and late season – bar and entertainment restrictions)
Pitches: ; 45 hardstanding pitches; 45 seasonal pitches
Leisure:
Facilities: WiFi
Services:
Within 3 miles:

Additional site information: 22 acre site. Cars can be parked by caravans. Awnings permitted. No noise after midnight. Dogs accepted by prior arrangement only. Football area and dog walking area.

PITCHES: Caravans Motorhomes Tents Glamping accommodation **LEISURE:** Indoor swimming pool Outdoor swimming pool Children's playground Kids' club Tennis court Games room Separate TV room golf course Pitch n putt Boats for hire Bikes for hire Cinema Entertainment Fishing Mini golf Watersports Gym Sports field Stables Spa

EAST RIDING OF YORKSHIRE

FLAMBOROUGH
Map 17 TA27

Places to visit
RSPB Bempton Cliffs, BEMPTON, YO15 1JF, 01262 422212
www.rspb.org.uk/reserves-and-events/reserves-a-z/bempton-cliffs

Premier Park

Thornwick Bay Holiday Village
★★★★★ 89% HOLIDAY PARK

tel: 01262 850369 **North Marine Road YO15 1AU**
email: thornwickbay@haven.com web: www.haven.com/parks/yorkshire/thornwick-bay
dir: *From Flamborough take B1255 (Tower Street) signed North Landing. Site entrance on left in approximately 1 mile.*

A large holiday village close to the beach with a superb range of attractions. These include indoor swimming pools, lake fishing, a sports zone, paddle boarding, kayaking, a Nerf Adventure and much more. Eating options are many – the stylish Lighthouse Bar & Grill, Sports Bar, Chopsticks, Cook's Fish & Chips and seasonal food vans. The large cliff-top touring and camping areas are mainly level and grassed; there are a few hardstandings and fully serviced pitches plus two smart amenity blocks, one with family rooms.

Open: mid March to end October **Last arrival:** 22.00 **Last departure:** 10.00
Pitches: 57 hardstanding pitches
Leisure:
Facilities:
Services:
Within 3 miles:

Additional site information: 4 acre site. No commercial vehicles, no bookings by person under 21 years unless a family booking. 2 dogs per booking, certain dog breeds banned. Bakery, fishing lake, sports and nature activities, nature trails. Car hire can be arranged.

RUDSTON
Map 17 TA06

Places to visit
Sewerby Hall and Gardens, BRIDLINGTON, YO15 1EA, 01262 673769
www.sewerbyhall.co.uk

Thorpe Hall Caravan & Camping Site
★★★★ 85%

tel: 01262 420393 **Thorpe Hall Caravan Site YO25 4JE**
email: info@thorpehall.co.uk web: www.thorpehall.co.uk
dir: *From Bridlington take B1253 west for 5 miles.*

Thorpe Hall Caravan & Camping Site is a delightful, peaceful small park within the walled gardens of Thorpe Hall yet within a few miles of the bustling seaside resort of Bridlington. The site offers a games field and its own coarse fishery. There are numerous walks locally.

Open: 1 March to 31 October **Last arrival:** 20.00 (later arrivals by prior arrangement only) **Last departure:** 11.30
Pitches: * from £23; from £23; from £23
Leisure:

Facilities:
Services:

Additional site information: 4.5 acre site. Cars can be parked by caravans and tents. Awnings permitted. 10mph speed limit, ball games/kite flying in games field only, no noise 23.00–08.00. Dogs on lead at all times on site (dangerous breeds not allowed). No gazebos/day shelters/kitchen tents/pup tents unless booking a separate pitch. No fire pits. Games Field. Dog Walk Area. Fishing Lake (tariff and rules apply)

Glamping available: Bell Tents: minimum of 2 nights, adults only, no pets
Changeover days: Monday, Wednesday and Fridays

Additional glamping information: Linen supplied, furnished

SKIPSEA
Map 17 TA15

Places to visit
Hornsea Museum, HORNSEA, HU18 1AB, 01964 533443
www.hornseamuseum.co.uk

Sewerby Hall and Gardens, BRIDLINGTON, YO15 1EA, 01262 673769
www.sewerbyhall.co.uk

Premier Park

Skirlington Leisure Park
★★★★★ 89% HOLIDAY PARK

tel: 01262 468213 & 468466 **YO25 8SY**
email: info@skirlington.com web: www.skirlington.com
dir: *From M62 towards Beverley then Hornsea. Between Skipsea and Hornsea on B1242.*

A large well-run seaside park close to the beach in partly-sloping meadowland, with a fine variety of indigenous trees and plants which are supplemented by a large display of colourful seasonal flowers. The park has five toilet blocks, a well-stocked mini market, a fish and chip shop and coffee lounge. A wide range of indoor and outdoor attractions include a swimming pool, amusement arcade, 10-pin bowling alley and occasional entertainment in the clubhouse.

Open: March to October (restricted service: diner and some facilities open from Friday to Sunday only (except school holidays and bank holidays)) **Last arrival:** 20.00 **Last departure:** 11.00
Pitches: ; 15 hardstanding pitches; 180 seasonal pitches
Leisure:
Facilities:
Services:
Within 3 miles:

Additional site information: 140 acre site. No noise after 22.00. Putting green, fishing lake, arcade, mini bowling alley, Sunday market.

EAST RIDING OF YORKSHIRE—NORTH YORKSHIRE

SPROATLEY
Map 17 TA13

Places to visit
Burton Constable Hall, SPROATLEY, HU11 4LN, 01964 562400
www.burtonconstable.com

Streetlife Museum Hull, KINGSTON UPON HULL, HU1 1PS, 01482 300300
www.hcandl.co.uk/museums-and-galleries/streetlife-museum/streetlife-museum

Great for kids: The Deep, KINGSTON UPON HULL, HU1 4DP, 01482 381000
www.thedeep.co.uk

Premier Park

Burton Constable Holiday Park & Arboretum
★★★★★ 88%

tel: 01964 562508 **Old Lodges HU11 4LJ**
email: info@burtonconstable.co.uk **web:** www.burtonconstableholidaypark.co.uk
dir: A165 onto B1238 to Sproatley. Follow Park Road alongside the Constable Arms for approximately 500 yards, follow signs to holiday park ahead. For sat nav use HU11 4PG.

Within the extensive estate of Burton Constable Hall, this large and secluded holiday destination provides a wide range of attractions including fishing and boating on the two 10-acre lakes. The Woodland Store offers local produce and takeaway breakfasts and pizzas and there's a licensed bar with a designated family room. The grounds are immaculately maintained and generous pitch density offers good privacy. Nine pods (two with en suite facilities), static caravans and lodges are available for hire.

Open: March to beginning of November (touring) (restricted service: November to mid February) **Last arrival:** 18.00 (later by prior arrangement) **Last departure:** 11.00
Pitches: see prices below; 26 hardstanding pitches; 14 seasonal pitches
Leisure:
Facilities:
Services:
Within 3 miles:
Additional site information: 90 acre site. Cars can be parked by caravans and tents. Awnings permitted. No fires, skateboards or rollerblades. Snooker, table tennis, woodland walks, cycling, toddlers' play area, night security warden. Beer garden and events at Lakeside bar.
Glamping available: Wooden pods from £40. **Changeover days:** Any day
Additional glamping information: Deluxe pods with shower, toilet, washbasin and kitchen are available, sleep 5. Cars can be parked by units

NORTH YORKSHIRE

ACASTER MALBIS
Map 16 SE54

Places to visit
National Railway Museum, YORK, YO26 4XJ, 033 0058 0058
www.railwaymuseum.org.uk

York Minster, YORK, YO1 7HH, 01904 557200
yorkminster.org

Great for kids: Jorvik Viking Centre, YORK, YO1 9WT, 01904 615505
www.jorvikvikingcentre.co.uk

Moor End Farm
★★★ 79%

tel: 01904 706727 & 07860 405872 **YO23 2UQ**
email: dawnhhall@hotmail.co.uk **web:** www.moor-end-farm.co.uk
dir: At junction of A64 and A1237 at Copmanthorpe follow Acaster Malbis signs. In Copmanthorpe left into Station Road signed Acaster Malbis. In approximately 1.8 miles site on left.

A very pleasant farm site with modernised facilities including a heated family/disabled shower room. The site has 12 touring pitches and seven static caravans. A river boat pickup to York is 150 yards from the site entrance, and the village inn and restaurant are a short stroll away. A very convenient site for visiting York Racecourse. Dogs are accepted.

Open: Easter or April to October **Last arrival:** 22.00 **Last departure:** noon
Pitches:
Facilities:
Services:
Within 3 miles:
Additional site information: 1 acre site. Cars can be parked by caravans and tents. Awnings permitted. BACS payments accepted. Fridge, freezer and microwave available.

NORTH YORKSHIRE 239 ENGLAND

ALLERSTON
Map 19 SE88

Places to visit

Scarborough Castle, SCARBOROUGH, YO11 1HY, 01723 372451
www.english-heritage.org.uk/visit/places/scarborough-castle

Pickering Castle, PICKERING, YO18 7AX, 01751 474989
www.english-heritage.org.uk/visit/places/pickering-castle

Great for kids: Flamingo Land Resort, KIRBY MISPERTON, YO17 6UX, 0800 408 8840
www.flamingoland.co.uk

Platinum Park

Vale of Pickering Caravan Park
★★★★★

tel: 01723 859280 **Carr House Farm YO18 7PQ**
email: info@valeofpickering.co.uk web: www.valeofpickering.co.uk
dir: On B1415, 1.75 miles from A170 (Pickering to Scarborough road).

A well-maintained and spacious family park with excellent facilities, including immaculate modern toilet facilities. A beautifully designed extension to the toilet block houses five family bathrooms and an accessible wet room. Children will enjoy the brand new play area, or the large ball sports field. There is a well-stocked shop and the café serves pizza two nights a week during the holidays. Tastefully furnished pods and bell tents are also available for a glamping experience. The park is set in open countryside bounded by hedges with manicured grassland and stunning seasonal floral displays. Handy for the North Yorkshire Moors and the attractions of Scarborough.

Vale of Pickering Caravan Park

Open: 1 March to 2 January **Last arrival:** 19.00 (later arrivals by prior arrangement) **Last departure:** 11.30

Pitches: 🚐 🚙 ⛺ ; 🛖 see prices below; 100 hardstanding pitches; 70 seasonal pitches

Leisure: ⚽ ❂ **Facilities:** 🚻 ☉ ♿ ✼ ♿ 🛒 ♨ ⌂ ⛌ WiFi

Services: 💧 🗑 🍴 🧺 ⚡ 🔒 🅃 **Within 3 miles:** ⛳ ✂ ◉

Additional site information: 13 acre site. 🐕 Cars can be parked by caravans and tents. Awnings permitted. No open fires or Chinese lanterns, no noise after 23.00. Microwave available.

Glamping available: Bell tents from £80.

Additional glamping information: No pets. Cars can be parked by units

See advert below

Carr House Farm, Allerston, Pickering, North Yorkshire, YO18 7PQ
01723 859 280
info@valeofpickering.co.uk

FACILITIES: 🔌 Electric vehicle charging 🛁 Baths/Shower ☉ Electric shaver sockets 💨 Hairdryer ✼ Ice pack facility 👶 Baby facilities ♿ Disabled facilities 🛒 Shop on site or within 200yds 🍖 BBQ area 🍽 Picnic area WiFi WiFi 💻 Internet access **SERVICES:** ⚡ Electric hook-up 🧺 Launderette 🍺 Licensed bar 🔥 Calor Gas ⛽ Campingaz 🚽 Toilet fluid 🍴 Café/Restaurant 🍔 Fast Food/Takeaway 🔋 Battery charging ⛽ Motorhome service point ⊘ No credit or debit cards 🐕 Dogs permitted ⊘ No dogs

ENGLAND 240 NORTH YORKSHIRE

ALNE
Map 19 SE46

Places to visit
Beningbrough Hall, Gallery and Gardens, BENINGBROUGH, YO30 1DD, 01904 472027
www.nationaltrust.org.uk/beningbrough-hall-gallery-and-gardens

Sutton Park, SUTTON-ON-THE-FOREST, YO61 1DP, 01347 810249
www.sutton-park.co.uk

Great for kids: National Railway Museum, YORK, YO26 4XJ, 033 0058 0058
www.railwaymuseum.org.uk

Premier Park

Alders Caravan Park
★★★★★ 92%

tel: 01347 838722 **Home Farm YO61 1RY**
email: enquiries@homefarmalne.co.uk **web:** www.alderscaravanpark.co.uk
dir: *From A19 exit at Alne sign, in 1.5 miles left at T-junction, 0.5 mile site on left in village centre.*

A tastefully developed park on a working farm with screened pitches laid out in horseshoe-shaped areas. This well-designed park offers excellent toilet facilities including a bathroom and fully-serviced washing and toilet cubicles. A woodland area is a pleasant place to walk. A summer house with comfortable seating is located at the edge of the village cricket grounds. Wooden pods are generously spaced in a separate enclosed area and a large, covered communal area for eating and relaxation is also provided. A welcoming reception and stylish café with alfresco area are located at entrance to park.

Open: March to October **Last arrival:** 21.00 **Last departure:** 14.00
Pitches: see prices below; 6 hardstanding pitches; 71 seasonal pitches
Facilities:
Services:
Within 3 miles:
Additional site information: 12 acre site. Cars can be parked by caravans and tents. Awnings permitted. Maximum 2 dogs per pitch. Summer house. Farm produce for sale. Woodland walk, cricket club, Sustrans cycle track route 65. Car hire can be arranged.
Glamping available: Wooden pods from £40. **Changeover days:** Any day
Additional glamping information: No dogs in pods. Parking 20 metres from pods.

ASKRIGG
Map 18 SD99

Places to visit
Bolton Castle, near LEYBURN, DL8 4ET, 01969 623981
boltoncastle.co.uk

Cherish Glamping
★★★★ 92% GLAMPING ONLY

tel: 01969 650932 **West Shaw Cote Farm, Low Abbotside DL8 3JH**
email: contact@cherishglamping.co.uk **web:** www.cherishglamping.co.uk
dir: *From east: take A684 to Bainbridge. After crossing river bear right. Right signed Askrigg. Left onto Long Shaw signed Hardraw. Site entrance on right. From west: From Hawes centre follow one-way system onto A684. Left signed Hardraw. Right signed Askrigg onto Long Shaw. Site on left.*

Cherish Glamping is a small dog- and family-friendly site situated in the heart of Upper Wensleydale, surrounded by picturesque views of the dales, and on a working farm. There are seven beautifully decorated yurts, each with its own private wet room, custom-made wooden bed, hot-tub, wood stove, coffee machine, mini-fridge, power sockets and Denby crockery set. Breakfasts can be delivered to your door in the morning and if you don't wish to use the barbecue, evening meals and packed lunches can also be pre-ordered. There is a small, but well-equipped outdoor spa overlooking the valley, and WiFi is available throughout the site. This is a charming owner-run park with much to offer.

Open: 1 April – 30 October **Last arrival:** 20:00 (later by prior arrangement)
Last departure: 10.00
Leisure:
Facilities:
Within 3 miles:
Accommodation available: Yurts
Changeover days: Any day
Additional site information: 27 acre site. Minimum noise after 21:00. Food delivered to yurts. Spa area for hire. Torch and bath robe recommended.

Make your next UK holiday one to remember

Choose RatedTrips.com

AA

NORTH YORKSHIRE 241 ENGLAND

CHOP GATE
MAP 19 SE59

Places to visit

Mount Grace Priory, OSMOTHERLEY, DL6 3JG, 01609 883494
www.english-heritage.org.uk/visit/places/mount-grace-priory

Captain Cook Schoolroom Museum, GREAT AYTON, TS9 6NB
captaincookschoolroommuseum.co.uk

Lordstones Country Park
★★★★ 86%

tel: 01642 778482 Carlton Bank TS9 7JH
email: info@lordstones.com web: www.lordstones.com
dir: *From A172 between Stokesley and Osmotherley follow signs to Carlton-in-Cleveland. Through Carlton-in-Cleveland to Lordstones entrance.*

Situated in the North York Moors National Park and commanding one of the highest spots in the county, Lordstones has glorious views that extend over 40 miles. It is a privately-owned country park that has been developed to become a distinctive camping venue. There is a selection of grass pitches for tents, some luxurious jumbo wooden glamping pods (each with a wood-burning stove), and four round houses with both heating and electricity. The site has a neat, purpose-built amenity building. Beltie Bar & Grill offers a range of steaks and other appealing dishes, while hot drinks can be enjoyed in the Lordstones café, and estate produce can be purchased at the farm shop. The Cleveland Way national trail and the coast-to-coast walk pass close to the site.

Open: All year **Last arrival:** 17.00 **Last departure:** 11.00
Pitches:
Facilities:
Services:

Additional site information: 150 acre site. Cars can be parked by tents. Awnings permitted.

Glamping available: Wooden pods, timber roundhouses.
Changeover days: Monday, Friday

CONSTABLE BURTON
Map 19 SE19

Places to visit

Middleham Castle, MIDDLEHAM, DL8 4QG, 01969 623899
www.english-heritage.org.uk/visit/places/middleham-castle

Great for kids: Bedale Museum, BEDALE, DL8 1AA, 01677 427516
bedale-tc.gov.uk/bedale-museum

Constable Burton Hall Caravan Park
★★★★ 84%

tel: 01677 450428 DL8 5LJ
email: caravanpark@constableburton.com web: www.cbcaravanpark.co.uk
dir: *From Leyburn on A684 towards Bedale, approximately 3 miles to site on left.*

This pretty site in the former deer park of the adjoining Constable Burton Hall, is screened from the road by park walls and surrounded by mature trees in a quiet rural location. The laundry is housed in a converted 18th-century deer barn and there's a pub and restaurant opposite. Seasonal pitches are available. Please note that this site does not accept tents.

Open: April to October **Last arrival:** 20.00 **Last departure:** noon
Pitches:
Facilities:
Services:
Within 3 miles:

Additional site information: 10 acre site. Cars can be parked by caravans. Awnings permitted. No commercial vehicles, no ball games plus no children's play area. Family shower room.

FILEY
Map 17 TA18

Places to visit

Scarborough Castle, SCARBOROUGH, YO11 1HY, 01723 372451
www.english-heritage.org.uk/visit/places/scarborough-castle

Great for kids: Sea Life Scarborough, SCARBOROUGH, YO12 6RP, 01723 373414
www.visitsealife.com/scarborough

Premier Park

Flower of May Holiday Park
★★★★★ 92% HOLIDAY PARK

tel: 01723 584311 Lebberston Cliff YO11 3NU
email: info@flowerofmay.com web: www.flowerofmay.com
dir: *Take A165 from Scarborough towards Filey. Site signed.*

Flower of May is a well-run family holiday park situated on the east coast between Scarborough and Filey. This large, landscaped park offers a full range of recreational activities, including an indoor swimming pool, outdoor and indoor playgrounds and other sports facilities. There is also a bar and entertainment complex area, a fish and chip shop and a well-stocked supermarket. Grass and hardstanding pitches are available – all are on level ground and arranged in avenues screened by shrubs. There are 4 and 5-berth wooden camping pods, each with a decking area. You can also enjoy the 'Scarborough Fair' museum with its collection of restored fairground attractions, including rides, organs and vintage cars.

Open: Easter to October (restricted service: early and late season – reduced opening hours in café, shop and bars) **Last arrival:** dusk **Last departure:** noon
Pitches: see prices below; 250 hardstanding pitches; 200 seasonal pitches
Leisure:
Facilities:
Services:
Within 3 miles:

Additional site information: 13 acre site. No noise after midnight. 1 dog per pitch by prior arrangement only. Squash, basketball court, skate park, table tennis.

Glamping available: Wooden pods: 4 berth from £48; 5 berth from £55.
Changeover days: Any day

Additional glamping information: Wooden pods: (sleep 4 or 5) minimum stay 2 nights (3 nights at bank holidays and in school holidays). Microwave, kettle, beds with mattresses, sockets, lighting and decking area included. Cars can be parked by units

---

FACILITIES: Electric vehicle charging · Baths/Shower · Electric shaver sockets · Hairdryer · Ice pack facility · Baby facilities · Disabled facilities · Shop on site or within 200yds · BBQ area · Picnic area · WiFi · Internet access **SERVICES:** Electric hook-up · Launderette · Licensed bar · Calor Gas · Campingaz · Toilet fluid · Café/Restaurant · Fast Food/Takeaway · Battery charging · Motorhome service point · No credit or debit cards · Dogs permitted · No dogs

FILEY continued

Orchard Farm Holiday Park
★★★★ 92% HOLIDAY PARK

tel: 01723 891582 Stonegate, Hunmanby YO14 0PU
email: reception@orchardfarmholidayvillage.co.uk
web: www.orchardfarmholidaypark.com
dir: *A165 from Scarborough towards Bridlington. Turn right signed Hunmanby, site on right just after rail bridge.*

Orchard Farm Holiday Park is a family-friendly park situated close to the seaside towns of Scarborough, Filey, Bridlington and Cayton Bay. The pitches are well-surfaced and all are equipped with electric hook-ups. Many of the statics are positioned around peaceful lakes. There is a well-stocked fishing lake and bar on-site, as well as a modern amenity block, games room, arcade room, and a fenced play area. Essentials can be purchased from the shop at reception.

Open: March to October (restricted service: off-peak season — some facilities reduced) **Last arrival:** 23.00 **Last departure:** 11.00

Pitches: 🚐 🚍 🛆; 48 hardstanding pitches

Leisure: 🏊 🛝 🎱 🎮 🎵 ✏️

Facilities: 🚿 ☉ ℉ ✳ ♿ 🍽 🥘 WiFi 💻

Services: 🔌 🗑 🍴 🧺 T

Within 3 miles: ⛳ ◎ 🏄

Additional site information: 14 acre site. 🚗 Cars can be parked by caravans and tents. Awnings permitted. No scooters, skateboards or similar.

Crows Nest Caravan Park
★★★★ 91%

tel: 01723 582206 Gristhorpe YO14 9PS
email: enquiries@crowsnestcaravanpark.com web: www.crowsnestcaravanpark.com
dir: *5 miles south of Scarborough and 2 miles north of Filey. On seaward side of A165, signed from roundabout, near petrol station.*

A family-friendly park situated on the beautiful Yorkshire coast with excellent panoramic views. This large and mainly static park offers lively entertainment and two bars. There is also an indoor swimming pool and large outdoor playground. There is a small touring area close to the attractions, but the main touring and camping section is at the top of the park overlooking the sea; this area is equipped with some excellent fully serviced pitches and an amenity block. Dogs are welcome and there is a dedicated park for them too.

Open: March to October **Last departure:** noon

Pitches: 🚐 🚍 🛆; 50 hardstanding pitches

Leisure: 🏊 🛝 🎱 🎵 ⚽

Facilities: 🚿 ☉ ℉ ✳ ♿ 🍽 🛒 WiFi 💻

Services: 🔌 🗑 🍴 🛒 ⛽ 🛢 🌿 T

Within 3 miles: ⛳ ✏ U ◎ 🏄

Additional site information: 20 acre site. 🚗 Cars can be parked by caravans and tents. Awnings permitted. Dog park. Prices based on 1 car and 4 adults.

Primrose Valley Holiday Park
★★★★ 91% HOLIDAY PARK

tel: 01723 513771 YO14 9RF
email: primrosevalley@haven.com web: www.haven.com/primrosevalley
dir: *Signed from A165 (Scarborough to Bridlington road), 3 miles south of Filey.*

A large, all-action holiday centre with a wide range of sports and leisure activities to suit everyone, from morning until late in the evening. The touring area is completely separate from the main park and has its own high quality amenity block. All touring pitches are fully serviced hardstandings with grassed awning strips. The lakeside development near the touring area provides a dine-in and takeaway bistro, as well as watersport activities. In the main complex, there's a large arcade zone, an entertainment bar, a J D Wetherspoons pub and other food outlets, including a 'Slim Chickens' fast-food restaurant. A swimming pool is also available and the sea is nearby.

Open: mid March to end October **Last arrival:** anytime **Last departure:** 10.00

Pitches: 🚐 🚍; 34 hardstanding pitches

Leisure: 🏊 🏊 🛝 🎱 🎮 🎵 ✏ ✏️

Facilities: 🚿 ℉ ♿ 🍽 🥘 🛒 WiFi 💻

Services: 🔌 🗑 🍴 🍽 ⛽ 🛢 🌿

Within 3 miles: ⛳ ◎ 🏄

Additional site information: 160 acre site. 🚗 No commercial vehicles, no bookings by persons under 21 years unless a family booking. Maximum 2 dogs per booking, certain dog breeds banned.

Reighton Sands Holiday Park
★★★★ 86% HOLIDAY PARK

tel: 01723 890476 Reighton Gap YO14 9SH
email: reightonsands@haven.com web: www.haven.com/reightonsands
dir: *On A165, 5 miles south of Filey at Reighton Gap, signed.*

A large, lively holiday centre with a wide range of entertainment and all-weather leisure facilities (including an indoor play area). There is direct access to a long sandy beach, which is accessible on foot or via a small train. Although tents are not accepted, there are good all-weather pitches with panoramic sea views. The site is particularly geared towards families with younger children. Meals are served throughout the day in the Hawkwood Restaurant and and there is also a Papa John's pizza van. They offer a range of live entertainment shows throughout the season and there is also a 9-hole golf course at the top of the park.

Open: mid March to end October (restricted service: mid March to May and September to end October — some facilities may be reduced) **Last arrival:** 22.00 **Last departure:** 10.00

Pitches: 🚐 🚍; 47 hardstanding pitches

Leisure: 🏊 🏊 🛝 🛝 🎱 ⛳ 🎵

Facilities: 🚿 ☉ ℉ ♿ 🍽 🥘 🛒 WiFi

Services: 🔌 🗑 🍴 🍽 ⛽ 🛢

Within 3 miles: ✏ U ◎ 🎢

Additional site information: 229 acre site. 🚗 No commercial vehicles, no bookings by persons under 21 years unless a family booking. Maximum 2 dogs per booking, certain dog breeds banned.

NORTH YORKSHIRE 243 ENGLAND

Blue Dolphin Holiday Park
★★★★ 82% HOLIDAY PARK

tel: 01723 515155 Gristhorpe Bay YO14 9PU
web: www.haven.com/bluedolphin
dir: On A165, 2 miles north of Filey.

There are great cliff-top views to be enjoyed from this fun-filled holiday centre with an extensive and separate touring area. The emphasis is on non-stop entertainment, with organised sports and clubs, all-weather leisure facilities in the SportsDrome, including a climbing wall and roller disco, plus heated swimming pools (with multi-slide), and plenty of well-planned amusements. Pitches are mainly on level or gently-sloping grass plus there are some fully serviced hardstandings. There's also a fishing lake and the beach is just two miles away.

Open: mid March to end October **Last arrival:** midnight **Last departure:** 10.00
Leisure:
Facilities:
Services:
Within 3 miles:

Additional site information: 85 acre site. No commercial vehicles, no bookings by persons under 21 years unless a family booking. Maximum 2 dogs per booking, certain dog breeds banned.

Filey Brigg Touring Caravan & Country Park
★★★ 86%

tel: 01723 513852 & 512512 North Cliff YO14 9ET
email: fileybriggcaravanpark.gov.uk web: www.fileybriggcaravanpark.co.uk
dir: A165 from Scarborough to Filey. Left onto A1039, at roundabout into Church Cliff Drive, to site.

A municipal park overlooking Filey Brigg with splendid views along the coast and set in a country park – the beach is just a short walk away, as is the resort of Filey. There is a choice of hardstanding or grass pitches and 50 are 'all-weather'. Most pitches are equipped with electric hook-ups, with the exception of the tent camping field. There are two good amenity blocks with a covered dishwashing area, and a motorhome service point. A well-stocked shop, café and an excellent children's playground are adjacent to the touring areas.

Open: end February to 2 January **Last arrival:** 18.00 **Last departure:** noon
Pitches: ; 82 hardstanding pitches
Leisure:
Facilities:
Services:
Within 3 miles:

Additional site information: 9 acre site. Cars can be parked by caravans and tents. Awnings permitted. No ball games.

HARROGATE
Map 19 SE35

Places to visit
RHS Garden Harlow Carr, HARROGATE, HG3 1QB, 01423 565418
www.rhs.org.uk/gardens/harlow-carr

The Royal Pump Room Museum, HARROGATE, HG1 2RY, 01423 556188
www.harrogate.gov.uk/royal-pump-room-museum

Great for kids: Brimham Rocks, BRIMHAM, HG3 4DW, 01423 780688
www.nationaltrust.org.uk/brimham-rocks

Premier Park

Ripley Caravan Park
★★★★★ 87%

tel: 01423 770050 Knaresborough Road, Ripley HG3 3AU
email: info@ripleycaravanpark.com web: www.ripleycaravanpark.com
dir: 3 miles north of Harrogate on A61. Right at roundabout onto B6165 signed Knaresborough. Site 300 yards left.

A well-run rural site set in attractive meadowland which has been landscaped with mature tree plantings. The resident owners lovingly maintain the facilities and there is a heated swimming pool with sauna, a games room and an information lounge. A bus calls every 15 minutes which gives easy access to Ripon and Leeds, and a cycleway/walkway leads from the site directly to Harrogate which is approximately three miles away. A former tractor shed has been tastefully converted into a two bedroom holiday home cottage, available for hire.

Open: 2nd week March to 31 October **Last arrival:** 21.00 **Last departure:** noon
Pitches: ; 60 hardstanding pitches; 75 seasonal pitches
Leisure:
Facilities:
Services:
Within 3 miles:

Additional site information: 24 acre site. Cars can be parked by caravans and tents. Awnings permitted. Family camping only. No open fires, off-ground BBQs only, no skateboards or rollerblades. No motorised scooters. No noise after 22.00. Football, volleyball, table tennis, pool table.

NORTH YORKSHIRE

HARROGATE continued

Premier Park

Rudding Holiday Park
★★★★★ 86%

tel: 01423 870439 Follifoot HG3 1JH
email: holiday-park@ruddingpark.com web: www.ruddingholidaypark.co.uk
dir: *From A1 take A59 to A658 signed Bradford. 4.5 miles, right and follow signs.*

A spacious site set in the beautiful mature parkland of Rudding Park. The setting has been tastefully enhanced with beautiful shrubbery and dry-stone walls. There is a choice of grass or hardstanding pitches. A separate area houses super pitches where all services are supplied, including picnic benches. The two amenity blocks offer very good comfort levels. An 18-hole golf course, 6-hole short course, driving range, golf academy, destination spa, heated outdoor swimming pool, playground, the Deer House Family Pub and a children's play area complete the picture.

Open: March to January **Last arrival:** 22.00 **Last departure:** 11.00
Pitches: 🚐 🚍 ▲; 20 hardstanding pitches; 50 seasonal pitches
Leisure:
Facilities:
Services:
Within 3 miles:

Additional site information: 50 acre site. Cars can be parked by caravans. Awnings permitted. Under 18s must be accompanied by an adult. Car hire can be arranged.

Harrogate Caravan Park
★★★★ 85%

tel: 01423 546145 Great Yorkshire Showground HG2 8NZ
email: info@harrogatecaravanpark.co.uk web: www.harrogatecaravanpark.co.uk
dir: *A1(M) junction 47, A59 to Harrogate. A658, then A661. At Sainsbury's lights turn left into Railway Road.*

Located on the perimeter of the Yorkshire Showground and owned by the Yorkshire Agricultural Society, this very peaceful park offers easy main road access and is popular at weekends and during the days of the shows. The site has a high standard amenity block (including a dog wash), extensive tree planting and smart, gravelled hardstanding pitches. There is a direct walkway to the adjacent Fodders farmers' market and café. This is a good base for visiting Harrogate and the Yorkshire Dales.

Open: early March to early November **Last arrival:** 20.00 **Last departure:** 11.00
Pitches: 🚐 🚍 ▲; 57 hardstanding pitches
Leisure:
Facilities:
Services:
Within 3 miles:

Additional site information: 3.56 acre site. Cars can be parked by caravans and tents. Awnings permitted. No fires/fire pits. Shop and café adjacent, supermarket at end of road.

High Moor Farm Park
★★★★ 85%

tel: 01423 563637 Skipton Road HG3 2LT
email: highmoorfarmpark@btconnect.com web: www.highmoorfarmpark.co.uk
dir: *4 miles west of Harrogate on A59 towards Skipton.*

A family site with very good facilities, set beside a small wood and surrounded by thorn hedges. The pitches are located in meadowland and fields, and one area is fully serviced. A large heated indoor swimming pool, games room, licensed bar and outdoor children play area are also available on site. Please note that this park does not accept tents.

Open: Easter or April to October **Last arrival:** 21.00 **Last departure:** 15.00
Pitches: 🚐 🚍; 51 hardstanding pitches; 57 seasonal pitches
Leisure:
Facilities:
Services:
Within 3 miles:

Additional site information: 15 acre site. Cars can be parked by caravans. Awnings permitted. No noise after midnight, no electric scooters, hover or skateboards.

NORTH YORKSHIRE 245 ENGLAND

Shaws Trailer Park
QUALITY ASSESSED
tel: 01423 884432 **5 Main Street, (Knaresborough Road) HG2 7NE**
web: edan.io/shaws-trailer-park
dir: *On A59, 1 mile from town centre. Site 0.5 mile southwest of Starbeck railway crossing.*

A long-established site just a mile from the centre of Harrogate. The all-weather pitches are arranged around a carefully kept grass area, and the toilets are basic but functional. The entrance is on the bus route to Harrogate. Nearby attractions include fishing, golf, horse riding, walks and hikes, among many others.

Open: All year **Last arrival:** 20.00 **Last departure:** 14.00
Pitches: ; 29 hardstanding pitches
Facilities:
Services:
Within 3 miles:

Additional site information: 11 acre site. Adults only. Cars can be parked by caravans and tents. Awnings permitted.

HELMSLEY   Map 19 SE68
Places to visit

Duncombe Park, HELMSLEY, YO62 5EB, 01439 770213
www.duncombepark.com

Helmsley Castle, HELMSLEY, YO62 5AB, 01439 770442
www.english-heritage.org.uk/visit/places/helmsley-castle

Great for kids: Flamingo Land Resort, KIRBY MISPERTON, YO17 6UX, 0800 408 8840
www.flamingoland.co.uk

Premier Park
Golden Square Caravan & Camping Park
★★★★★ 91%
tel: 01439 788269 **Oswaldkirk YO62 5YQ**
email: reception@goldensquarecaravanpark.com
web: www.goldensquarecaravanpark.com
dir: *From York take B1363 to Oswaldkirk. Left onto B1257, 2nd left onto unclassified road signed Ampleforth, site 0.5 mile on right. Or A19 from Thirsk towards York. Left, follow 'Caravan Route avoiding Sutton Bank' signs, through Ampleforth to site in 1 mile.*

An excellent, popular and spacious site with very good facilities, including a smart amenity block and good pitches. This friendly, immaculately maintained park is set in a quiet rural situation with lovely views over the North York Moors. Terraced on three levels and surrounded by mature trees, it caters particularly for families, with excellent play areas and space for ball games. Country walks and mountain bike trails start here, and attractive holiday homes are also available to hire. Please note that caravans are prohibited on the A170 at Sutton Bank between Thirsk and Helmsley.

Golden Square Caravan & Camping Park

Open: March to October (restricted service: November to 1 January statics only)
Last arrival: 21.00 **Last departure:** noon
Pitches: ; 30 hardstanding pitches; 50 seasonal pitches
Leisure:
Facilities:
Services:
Within 3 miles:

Additional site information: 12 acre site. Cars can be parked by caravans and tents. Awnings permitted. No skateboards, fires, Chinese lanterns or hover boards. No noise after 23.00. Microwave available, storage compound, table tennis, pool table, woodland walks, cycle trails. Bread and cakes available.

FACILITIES: Electric vehicle charging · Baths/Shower · Electric shaver sockets · Hairdryer · Ice pack facility · Baby facilities · Disabled facilities · Shop on site or within 200yds · BBQ area · Picnic area · WiFi · Internet access **SERVICES:** Electric hook-up · Launderette · Licensed bar · Calor Gas · Campingaz · Toilet fluid · Café/Restaurant · Fast Food/Takeaway · Battery charging · Motorhome service point · No credit or debit cards · Dogs permitted · No dogs

HELMSLEY continued

Foxholme Springs Touring Park
★★★★ 86%

tel: 01439 772336 **Gale Lane, Nawton YO62 7SD**
email: info@foxholmesprings.co.uk web: www.foxholmesprings.co.uk
dir: *From Helmsley, east on A170, signed Scarborough. Continue to Beadlam, in centre of village turn right into Gale Lane.*

Foxholme Springs is a quiet, adults-only park set in beautiful northern Ryedale countryside, with a pleasant open aspect to all pitches and views towards both the Yorkshire Wolds and the Howardian Hills Area of Outstanding Natural Beauty. The facilities are well maintained, and the site is ideal as a touring base or a place to relax. The stylish amenity block provides excellent decor, fixtures and fittings with the added benefit of good privacy options. Please note that caravans are prohibited on the A170 at Sutton Bank between Thirsk and Helmsley.

Open: Easter to 1st week of January **Last arrival:** 18.00 **Last departure:** noon

Pitches: * 🚐 from £35; 🚙 from £35 ⛺; 40 seasonal pitches

Facilities: 🏠 ⊙ 🚿 ✻ ♿

Services: 🔌 🗑 🚮 ⬇ 🔒 ⊘ 🅃

Within 3 miles: ⚓ ♘ 🛒

Additional site information: 13 acre site. Adults only. 🐕 Cars can be parked by caravans and tents. Awnings permitted.

HIGH BENTHAM   Map 18 SD66

Places to visit

Lancaster Maritime Museum, LANCASTER, LA1 1RB, 01524 382264
www.lancaster.gov.uk/sport-and-leisure/museums/maritime-museum

Lancaster City Museum, LANCASTER, LA1 1HT, 01524 64537
www.lancaster.gov.uk/sport-and-leisure/museums/city-museum

HIGH BENTHAM   Map 18 SD66

Premier Park

Riverside Caravan Park
★★★★★ 92%

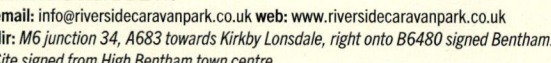

tel: 015242 61272 **LA2 7FJ**
email: info@riversidecaravanpark.co.uk web: www.riversidecaravanpark.co.uk
dir: *M6 junction 34, A683 towards Kirkby Lonsdale, right onto B6480 signed Bentham. Site signed from High Bentham town centre.*

A well-managed riverside park developed to a high standard, with level grass pitches set in avenues separated by trees, and there are excellent facilities for children who are made to feel as important as the adults. It has an excellent, modern amenity block, including a family bathroom, and a well-stocked shop, laundry and information room. The superb games room and adventure playground are hugely popular, and the market town of High Bentham is close by. Please note that this site does not accept tents. Bentham Golf Course with its 1922 Bar (within one mile) is also under same ownership with facilities available for Riverside customers.

Open: 14 February to 2 January **Last arrival:** 20.00 **Last departure:** noon

Pitches: 🚐 🚙; 27 hardstanding pitches; 50 seasonal pitches

Leisure: 🛝 ♠ 🎣

Facilities: 🏠 ⊙ 🚿 ♿ 💷 📶 💻

Services: 🔌 🗑 ⬇ 🔒 🅃

Within 3 miles: ⚓ ♘

Additional site information: 12 acre site. 🐕 Cars can be parked by caravans. Awnings permitted. No hoverboards, segways or drones. Chargeable permits for private fishing, discounted green fees at Bentham Golf Club.

Wenningdale Escapes
★★★★ 90% **GLAMPING ONLY**

tel: 015242 62455 **Robin Lane LA2 7AG**
email: hello@wenningdale.co.uk web: www.wenningdale.co.uk

Set within grounds adjacent to High Bentham Golf Club, this developing glamping destination is located in an Area of Outstanding Natural Beauty within easy reach of The Lakes and the Yorkshire Dales. Mature tree varieties of an arboretum standard combine with indigenous and cultivated plants to create an ambience of peace and tranquillity. In addition to stunning views, guests staying in the lodges and pods have the benefit of the golf course and driving range, and coffee and pastries are available in the Clubhouse, in addition to more substantial meals on certain days. Both pods and lodges are well spaced to create optimum privacy and in addition to stylish and comfortable interiors, outside seating and a communal barbecue area are also provided.

Open: All year **Last arrival:** 22.00 **Last departure:** 10.00

Accommodation available: 5 pods and 3 lodges

Changeover days: Monday and Friday

Additional site information: 70 acre site. 🐕

NORTH YORKSHIRE — ENGLAND

HUTTON-LE-HOLE Map 19 SE79

Places to visit

Nunnington Hall, NUNNINGTON, YO62 5UY, 01439 748283
www.nationaltrust.org.uk/nunnington-hall

Rievaulx Abbey, RIEVAULX, YO62 5LB, 01439 798228
www.english-heritage.org.uk/visit/places/rievaulx-abbey

Great for kids: Pickering Castle, PICKERING, YO18 7AX, 01751 474989
www.english-heritage.org.uk/visit/places/pickering-castle

Hutton-le-Hole Caravan Park
★★★★ 88%

tel: 01751 417261 **Westfield Lodge YO62 6UG**
email: stay@huttonleholecaravanpark.co.uk web: www.huttonleholecaravanpark.co.uk
dir: *From A170 at Keldholme follow Hutton-le-Hole signs. Approximately 2 miles, over cattle grid, left in 500 yards into Park Drive, site signed.*

A small, high quality park on a working farm in the North York Moors National Park. There is a choice of hardstanding or grass pitches within a well-tended area surrounded by hedges and shrubs. The purpose-built toilet block offers a good level of comfort and en suite family rooms. The pretty village with its facilities is a 10-minute walk away and the park is centrally located for visiting York, The Dales and other notable areas of interest. Two high quality lodges are also available for hire. For a glamping experience, three well-equipped bell tents and a shepherd's hut are located in a peaceful woodland with easy access to the amenity block. Please note, caravans are prohibited on the A170 at Sutton Bank between Thirsk and Helmsley.

Open: Easter to October **Last arrival:** 21.00 **Last departure:** noon
Pitches: ; 4 hardstanding pitches
Facilities:
Services:
Within 3 miles:
Additional site information: 5 acre site. Cars can be parked by caravans and tents. Awnings permitted. Boot, bike and dog washing area, farm walks.

KETTLEWELL Map 18 SD97

Places to visit

Grassington Folk Museum, GRASSINGTON, BD23 5AQ, 01756 753287
grassingtonfolkmuseum.org.uk

Great for kids: Kilnsey Park, KILNSEY, BD23 5PS, 01756 752150
kilnseypark.co.uk

Kettlewell Camping
★★★★ 80%

tel: 07930 379079 **Conistone Lane BD23 5RE**
email: info@kettlewellcamping.co.uk web: www.kettlewellcamping.co.uk
dir: *From roundabout on A65 (north of Skipton) take B6265 signed Grassington. Through Threshfield (do not turn right for Grassington). Road becomes B6160. In Kettlewell, first signed Scargill. Follow village brown tourist signs and not Google maps.*

Created from former farm fields, this rural camping site has stunning countryside views and is enclosed by well-maintained stone walls. It has the benefit of being just a few minutes' walk from Kettlewell with its craft shops, pubs, tea rooms and a village shop. A top-notch amenity block, fed by a bio-mass boiler, has underfloor heating and modern fixtures and fittings. It also includes a family room with shower, toilet and washbasin, and a dishwashing area. Free WiFi is available in the main field. A separate field, suitable for large families or groups, is also available in a more isolated location. There is also a field for The Duke of Edinburgh expeditions. Please note, there is no laundry at this site and is not licensed to take caravans.

Open: Easter to October half term (restricted service: only open from November to end March for special occasions) **Last arrival:** 20.30 **Last departure:** 11.00
Pitches:
Facilities:
Services:
Within 3 miles:
Additional site information: 0.6 acre site. Cars can be parked by tents. Awnings permitted. Quiet after 22.00. Fires permitted in raised fire pits only. Dogs must be kept on leads at all times. Separate field available for exclusive hire with private facilities.

KNARESBOROUGH Map 19 SE35

Places to visit

RHS Garden Harlow Carr, HARROGATE, HG3 1QB, 01423 565418
www.rhs.org.uk/gardens/harlow-carr

Aldborough Roman Site, ALDBOROUGH, YO51 9ES, 01423 322768
www.english-heritage.org.uk/visit/places/aldborough-roman-site

Kingfisher Caravan Park
★★★★ 83%

tel: 01423 869411 **Low Moor Lane, Farnham HG5 9JB**
email: enquiries@kingfisher-caravanpark.co.uk web: www.kingfisher-caravanpark.co.uk
dir: *From Knaresborough take A6055. Left in 1 mile towards Farnham, follow signs for Kingfisher. Park entrance on left.*

A large grassy site set in wooded, rural countryside with two beautiful lakes tucked away in the grounds. There is a small woodland path to walk dogs, who are welcome at the park. Whilst Harrogate, Fountains Abbey and York are within easy reach, visitors can, if they wish, just relax and enjoy the great variety of wildlife that can be seen here. The park has well-appointed holiday statics and caravan pitches, as well as a separate, flat tenting field with electric hook-ups.

Open: March to October **Last arrival:** 20.00 **Last departure:** 14.00
Pitches: ; 30 seasonal pitches
Leisure:
Facilities:
Services:
Within 3 miles:
Additional site information: 14 acre site. Cars can be parked by caravans and tents. Awnings permitted. No football.

FACILITIES: Electric vehicle charging Baths/Shower Electric shaver sockets Hairdryer Ice pack facility Baby facilities Disabled facilities Shop on site or within 200yds BBQ area Picnic area WiFi Internet access **SERVICES:** Electric hook-up Launderette Licensed bar Calor Gas Campingaz Toilet fluid Café/Restaurant Fast Food/Takeaway Battery charging Motorhome service point No credit or debit cards Dogs permitted No dogs

NABURN   Map 16 SE54

Places to visit

Clifford's Tower, YORK, YO1 9SA, 0370 333 1181
www.english-heritage.org.uk/visit/places/cliffords-tower-york

Fairfax House, YORK, YO1 9RN, 01904 655543
www.fairfaxhouse.co.uk

Naburn Lock Caravan Park
★★★★ 92%

tel: 01904 728697 **YO19 4RU**
email: mail@yorknaburnlock.com **web:** www.naburnlock.co.uk
dir: *From A64 (York Designer Outlet) take A19 (north), left signed Naburn onto B1222, site on right in 0.5 mile.*

Ideally situated near the River Ouse and within four miles of York's city centre, this friendly park is ideal for adults seeking countryside breaks; it is managed by enthusiastic owners. The well-surfaced pitches are arranged in small groups separated by mature hedges, and the heated facilities building is located at the centre of the park. The river towpath provides excellent walking and cycling opportunities, and the river bus to York leaves from a jetty beside the park.

Open: March to November **Last arrival:** 20.00 **Last departure:** 12.30
Pitches: 🚐 🚗 ⛺; 50 hardstanding pitches
Leisure: 🎣
Facilities: 🛁 ☉ 🚿 ✻ ♿ 🧺 🍳 WiFi 🖥
Services: 🔌 🗑 🧹 🛒 ⛽ 🧴 T
Within 3 miles: ∪

Additional site information: 7 acre site. Adults only. 🐕 Cars can be parked by caravans and tents. Awnings permitted. Quiet 23.00–07.00. River fishing.

NORTH STAINLEY   Map 19 SE27

Places to visit

Norton Conyers House & Gardens, RIPON, HG4 5EQ, 01765 640333
www.nortonconyers.org.uk

Theakston Brewery & Black Bull in Paradise Visitor Centre, MASHAM, HG4 4YD, 01765 680000
www.theakstons.co.uk/pages/visitor-centre

Great for kids: Lightwater Valley Family Adventure Park, NORTH STAINLEY, HG4 3HT, 01765 635321
lightwatervalley.co.uk

Sleningford Watermill Caravan Camping Park
★★★★ 88%

tel: 01765 635201 Sleningford Watermill Caravan and Camping Park, North Stainley HG4 3HQ
email: contact@sleningfordwatermill.co.uk **web:** www.sleningfordwatermill.co.uk
dir: *Follow site sign on A6108 between North Stainley and West Tanfield.*

An ideal site for nature-lovers. The old watermill and the River Ure make an attractive setting for Sleningford Watermill Caravan Camping Park that is run by two enthusiastic managers. The site is laid out in two areas and the pitches are in meadowland close to mature woodland. Back-to-nature opportunities include nature trails, bee gardens, wild bird listings and river walks. Canoeing and fly fishing are also available. There is a laundry room and a freezer.

Open: 1 April (or Easter weekend if in March) to 31 October **Last arrival:** 23.00
Last departure: 11.30 (late check-out available, subject to availability, up to 17.00)
Pitches: * 🚐 from £28; 🚗 from £28; ⛺ from £28; 8 hardstanding pitches; 49 seasonal pitches
Leisure: 🎣
Facilities: 🛁 ☉ 🚿 ✻ ♿ 🧺 🍳
Services: 🔌 🗑 🛒 🧴 T
Within 3 miles: 🚴 🏊

Additional site information: 20 acre site. 🐕 Cars can be parked by caravans and tents. Awnings permitted. No fires. Quiet after 23.00, no music after 22.00. Dogs must be kept on leads at all times. Information room, nature activity sheets, tree trail, fly-fishing (must bring own equipment), canoeing (must bring own equipment).

NORTHALLERTON   Map 19 SE3

Places to visit

Mount Grace Priory, House and Gardens, NORTHALLERTON, DL6 3JG, 01609 883494
www.english-heritage.org.uk/visit/places/mount-grace-priory

Great for kids: Thirsk Birds of Prey Centre, THIRSK, YO7 4EU, 01845 587522
www.falconrycentre.co.uk

Otterington Park
★★★★ 88%

tel: 01609 780656 Station Farm, South Otterington DL7 9JB
email: info@otteringtonpark.com **web:** www.otteringtonpark.com
dir: *From A168 midway between Northallerton and Thirsk onto unclassified road signed South Otterington. Site on right just before South Otterington.*

A neat park with superb rural views and within easy reach of both Northallerton and Thirsk. The park is split into two areas, both equipped with modern amenity blocks. Children can enjoy the two excellent play parks, and there are also nature trails, a dedicated dog exercise field, and a private fishing lake. Most of the pitches are for seasonal tourers, but there are also luxurious static lodges, and very good glamping facilities too; the camping pods are located in a separate naturally-screened area. The small on-site shop is well-stocked with a choice of essential goods.

Open: March to October **Last arrival:** 20.00 **Last departure:** noon
Pitches: 🏕; 62 hardstanding pitches
Additional site information: 42 acre site.

OSMOTHERLEY   Map 19 SE49

Places to visit

Mount Grace Priory, OSMOTHERLEY, DL6 3JG, 01609 883494
www.english-heritage.org.uk/visit/places/mount-grace-priory

Gisborough Priory, GUISBOROUGH, TS14 6HG
www.english-heritage.org.uk/visit/places/gisborough-priory

Great for kids: Thirsk Birds of Prey Centre, THIRSK, YO7 4EU, 01845 587522
www.falconrycentre.co.uk

NORTH YORKSHIRE 249 ENGLAND

OSMOTHERLEY
Map 19 SE49

AA CAMPSITE OF THE YEAR FOR NORTH EAST ENGLAND 2024–25

Premier Park

Cote Ghyll Caravan & Camping Park
★★★★★ 92%

tel: 01609 883425 **DL6 3AH**
email: hills@coteghyll.com web: www.coteghyll.com
dir: *Exit A19 on A684. Follow signs to Osmotherley. Left in village. Site 0.5 mile on right.*

A quiet site on the edge of moorland, close to the village. The park, which is served by two centrally located and well-equipped amenity blocks, is divided into terraces bordered by woodland. The only welcome distractions are the sounds of running water and birdsong. Mature trees, shrubs and seasonal floral displays create a relaxing and peaceful atmosphere, and the whole park is immaculately maintained. A superb combined reception and well-stocked shop is located at the entrance to the park. Cote Ghyll Mill near the park entrance serves cooked breakfasts and evening meals, to eat in or takeaway. There are two children's play areas and holiday statics for hire, as well as self-catering cottage/apartments.

Open: March to October **Last arrival:** 20.00 **Last departure:** noon
Pitches: ; 22 hardstanding pitches; 25 seasonal pitches
Leisure: **Facilities:**
Services: **Within 3 miles:**
Additional site information: 7 acre site. Cars can be parked by caravans and tents. Awnings permitted. Quiet after 22.00, no camp fires. Freshly baked breakfast produce available. Nature trail, woodland walk to reservoir.

PICKERING
Map 19 SE78

Places to visit
Pickering Castle, PICKERING, YO18 7AX, 01751 474989
www.english-heritage.org.uk/visit/places/pickering-castle

Great for kids: North Yorkshire Moors Railway, PICKERING, YO18 7AJ, 01751 472508
www.nymr.co.uk

Wayside Holiday Park

★★★★ 88% HOLIDAY PARK

tel: 01751 472608 & 07940 938517 Wrelton **YO18 8PG**
email: wrelton@waysideholidaypark.co.uk web: www.waysideholidaypark.co.uk
dir: *2.5 miles west of Pickering exit A170, follow signs to Wrelton.*

Located in the village of Wrelton, this well-maintained holiday park is divided into small paddocks by mature hedging. There is a choice of luxury static caravans and lakeside lodges, with an additional 13 luxurious lodges in the water garden area. A small library and laundry room are situated at the centre of the park. The village pub and restaurant are within a few minutes' walk of the park and there is plenty of interesting places to visit in the area. This is now a static and lodge park only.

Open: March to October
Facilities:
Within 3 miles:
Additional site information: 20 acre site.

NORTH YORKSHIRE

RIPON
Map 19 SE37

Places to visit
Fountains Abbey & Studley Royal, RIPON, HG4 3DY, 01765 608888
www.nationaltrust.org.uk/fountains-abbey-and-studley-royal-water-garden

Norton Conyers, RIPON, HG4 5EQ, 01765 640333
www.nortonconyers.org.uk

Great for kids: Thirsk Birds of Prey Centre, THIRSK, YO7 4EU, 01845 587522
www.falconrycentre.co.uk

Premier Park

Riverside Meadows Holiday Park
★★★★★ 84% HOLIDAY PARK

tel: 01765 602964 Ure Bank Top HG4 1JD
email: info@flowerofmay.com **web:** www.flowerofmay.com
dir: From A61 roundabout (north of bridge) in Ripon follow A6108 Leyburn and Masham signs. At next roundabout, 2nd exit into Ure Bank. Road becomes Ure Bank Top. Site at end of road.

This pleasant and peaceful site stands on high ground overlooking the River Ure, one mile from Ripon's town centre. The park has an excellent club with a bar and a games room, as well as two well-sized playgrounds on the outside. There are many walks to enjoy including those along the river, and free WiFi is available throughout the park. The touring site is open to seasonal customers only, allowing you to come and go as you please. Winter caravan storage can also be provided.

Open: Easter to October (restricted service: early and late season – bar open at weekends only) **Last arrival:** dusk **Last departure:** noon
Pitches: 🚐; 40 hardstanding pitches; 40 seasonal pitches
Leisure: ⚘ 🎣 ▢ ♫
Facilities: 🛁 ☉ 🅿 ✻ ♿ 🗑 🍴 🎪 WiFi
Services: 🔌 💧 🍽 🚐 ⬆ 🔒 📺
Within 3 miles: 🚶 🚴 🎠 🏊 ⛳ 🚂

Additional site information: 28 acre site. 🐕 No noise after midnight. Dogs accepted by prior arrangement only. Multi-ball sports court, dog walking track.

ROBIN HOOD'S BAY
Map 19 NZ90

Places to visit
Whitby Abbey, WHITBY, YO22 4JT, 01947 603568
www.english-heritage.org.uk/visit/places/whitby-abbey

Scarborough Castle, SCARBOROUGH, YO11 1HY, 01723 372451
www.english-heritage.org.uk/visit/places/scarborough-castle

Great for kids: Sea Life Scarborough, SCARBOROUGH, YO12 6RP, 01723 373414
www.visitsealife.com/scarborough

ROBIN HOOD'S BAY
Map 19 NZ90

Grouse Hill Caravan Park
★★★★ 91%

tel: 01947 880543 & 881230 Flask Bungalow Farm, Fylingdales YO22 4QH
email: info@grousehill.co.uk **web:** www.grousehill.co.uk
dir: From A171 (Whitby to Scarborough road), take loop road for Flask Inn (brown site sign).

A spacious family park on a south-facing slope with attractive, mostly level, terraced pitches. Situated in the North York Moors National Park, it is ideally located for visiting both the moors and east coast. The site has quality, solar-heated toilet blocks, a treatment plant to ensure excellent drinking water, security barriers, play areas (including an excellent woodland adventure play area), CCTV and WiFi. Heated wooden wigwams are available for hire. Please note that there are no hardstandings for tourers, only grass pitches, and this sloping site might be not suitable for visitors with mobility issues.

Open: March to October (restricted service: Easter to May – shop and reception reduced hours) **Last arrival:** 20.30 **Last departure:** noon
Pitches: 🚐 🚌 ⛺; see prices below; 30 hardstanding pitches; 20 seasonal pitches
Leisure: ⚘
Facilities: 🛁 ☉ 🅿 ✻ ♿ 🗑 WiFi
Services: 🔌 💧 🍽 ⬆ 🔒 ♻ 📺
Within 3 miles: 🚶 🎠

Additional site information: 14 acre site. 🐕 Cars can be parked by caravans and tents. Awnings permitted. No noise after 22.30. 8 family washrooms available.

Glamping available: Wooden wigwam cabins from £50.

Additional glamping information: All wigwams offer fridge, microwave, kettle, toaster, heater and picnic bench. Running Water wigwams also offer a toilet, TV, sink, table and four chairs. Cars can be parked by units

ROSEDALE ABBEY
Map 19 SE79

Places to visit
Pickering Castle, PICKERING, YO18 7AX, 01751 474989
www.english-heritage.org.uk/visit/places/pickering-castle

North Yorkshire Moors Railway, PICKERING, YO18 7AJ, 01751 472508
www.nymr.co.uk

Great for kids: Flamingo Land Resort, KIRBY MISPERTON, YO17 6UX, 0800 408 8840
www.flamingoland.co.uk

Rosedale Abbey Caravan Park
★★★★ 90%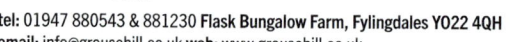

tel: 01751 417272 YO18 8SA
email: info@rosedaleabbeycaravanpark.co.uk
web: www.rosedaleabbeycaravanpark.co.uk
dir: From Pickering take A170 towards Sinnington for 2.25 miles. At Wrelton right onto unclassified road signed Cropton and Rosedale, 7 miles. Site on left in village.

Set in a sheltered valley in the centre of the North Yorkshire Moors National Park, this popular park is close to the pretty village of Rosedale Abbey. It is divided into separate areas for tents, tourers and statics. It has well-tended grounds, and continues to be upgraded by the enthusiastic owners. Two toilet blocks offer private, combined facilities. There are eight camping pods, all with electric hook-up, situated by the river and also five holiday cottages. In addition, there's a designated dog

PITCHES: 🚐 Caravans 🚌 Motorhomes ⛺ Tents 🏕 Glamping accommodation   LEISURE: 🏊 Indoor swimming pool 🏊 Outdoor swimming pool ⚘ Children's playground 🎣 Kids' club 🎾 Tennis court 🎱 Games room 📺 Separate TV room ⛳ golf course 🚩 Pitch n putt 🚣 Boats for hire 🚴 Bikes for hire 🎬 Cinema ♫ Entertainment 🎣 Fishing ⛳ Mini golf 🏄 Watersports 💪 Gym ⚽ Sports field 🐎 Stables 💆 Spa

walking area, children's playground and a small shop.

Open: March to October **Last arrival:** dusk **Last departure:** noon

Pitches: see prices below; 55 hardstanding pitches; 20 seasonal pitches

Leisure:

Facilities:

Services:

Within 3 miles:

Additional site information: 10 acre site. Cars can be parked by caravans and tents. Awnings permitted. No noise after 23.00. Dogs accepted by prior arrangement only. Freshly baked bread available.

Glamping available: Wooden pods from £40. **Changeover days:** Any day

Additional glamping information: Wooden pods; (sleep 5) maximum stay 2 nights (3 nights at bank holidays and in school holidays). Electricity, sockets, lighting, wooden decking included. 1 dog permitted per pod. Cars can be parked by units

SCARBOROUGH   Map 17 TA08

Places to visit

Scarborough Castle, SCARBOROUGH, YO11 1HY, 01723 372451
www.english-heritage.org.uk/visit/places/scarborough-castle

Great for kids: Sea Life Scarborough, SCARBOROUGH, YO12 6RP, 01723 373414
www.visitsealife.com/scarborough

AA SMALL CAMPSITE OF THE YEAR 2024–25

Killerby Old Hall Cottages & Caravan Site
★★★★ 87%

tel: 01723 583799 **Killerby Lane, Killerby YO11 3TW**
email: info@killerbyoldhall.co.uk **web:** www.killerbyoldhall.co.uk
dir: *From A165 between Scarborough and Filey, at Cayton Bay roundabout into Mill Lane towards Cayton. At T-junction left onto B1261 signed Filey. Site on left.*

A beautiful family-run site sheltered by mature trees and shrubs, located at the rear of The Old Hall, only 600 metres away from Cayton. The modern amenity blocks are well equipped and there's also a laundry room. All pitches are hardstanding with digital TV feed, and half are fully serviced. The outdoor children's play park is a special feature, and the indoor heated swimming pool can be booked for an additional charge. Meals and drinks can be enjoyed in the tastefully decorated Nine Eighty Bar & Bistro. Cottages and lakeside glamping lodges are also available for hire.

Open: 1 March to 2 January **Last arrival:** 19.00 **Last departure:** 11.00

Pitches: ; 47 hardstanding pitches

Leisure:

Facilities:

Services:

Additional site information: 13 acre site. Awnings permitted.

Glamping available: Wooden lodges.

Additional glamping information: Wooden lodges: sleep 4. Fully insulated, heated, double bed, bunk beds, smart TV, en suite.

SHERIFF HUTTON   Map 19 SE66

Places to visit

Kirkham Priory, KIRKHAM, YO60 7JS, 01653 618768
www.english-heritage.org.uk/visit/places/kirkham-priory

Sutton Park, SUTTON-ON-THE-FOREST, YO61 1DP, 01347 810249
www.sutton-park.co.uk

Great for kids: Castle Howard, MALTON, YO60 7DA, 01653 648333
www.castlehoward.co.uk

Premier Park

York Meadows Caravan Park
★★★★★ 79%

tel: 01347 878508 & 01439 788269 **York Road YO60 6QP**
email: reception@yorkmeadowscaravanpark.com
web: www.yorkmeadowscaravanpark.com
dir: *From York take A64 towards Scarborough. Left signed Flaxton and Sheriff Hutton. At West Lilling left signed Strensall. Site opposite junction.*

Peacefully located in open countryside and surrounded by mature trees, shrubs and wildlife areas, this park provides all level pitches and a modern, well-equipped amenity block with very good family rooms. Outdoor games such as draughts and snakes and ladders are available. A separate adjacent development contains luxury holiday homes.

Open: March to October **Last arrival:** 22.00 **Last departure:** noon

Pitches: ; 45 hardstanding pitches; 20 seasonal pitches

Leisure:

Facilities:

Services:

Within 3 miles:

Additional site information: 12 acre site. Cars can be parked by caravans and tents. Awnings permitted. No noise after 22.00, no skateboarding, hover boards, fires or Chinese lanterns. Fresh bread available. Outdoor table tennis.

ENGLAND 252 NORTH YORKSHIRE

STAINFORTH   Map 18 SD86

Places to visit
Malham National Park Centre, MALHAM, BD23 4DA, 01729 833200
www.yorkshiredales.org.uk/places/malham_national_park_centre

Knight Stainforth Hall Caravan & Campsite
★★★★ 92%

tel: 01729 822200 **BD24 0DP**
email: info@knightstainforth.com web: www.knightstainforth.co.uk
dir: *From west: A65 onto B6480 towards Settle, left before swimming pool signed Little Stainforth. From east: through Settle on B6480, over bridge, 1st right.*

Knight Stainforth Hall is a family park located near Settle and the River Ribble, which makes it an ideal base for walking or touring the beautiful Yorkshire Dales National Park. There is a modern amenity block with separate showers and toilets. Meals are served every day at The Knights Table café and restaurant, and essentials can be bought from the small shop section at reception. Fishing and WiFi are also available.

Open: March to mid January **Last arrival:** 22.00 **Last departure:** noon
Pitches: 🚐 🚙 ⛺; 30 hardstanding pitches
Leisure: /A ● /🎣 ⚽
Facilities: 🏠 ⊙ 🅿 ✻ ♿ 🪑 🍴 📶 💻
Services: 🔌 🗑 🚽 🍽 🧺 🧳 ⛽ 🧼 [T]
Within 3 miles: ⚓

Additional site information: 6 acre site. 🚗 Cars can be parked by caravans and tents. Awnings permitted. No groups of unaccompanied minors.

SUTTON-ON-THE-FOREST   Map 19 SE56

Places to visit
Sutton Park, SUTTON-ON-THE-FOREST, YO61 1DP, 01347 810249
www.statelyhome.co.uk

Treasurer's House, YORK, YO1 7JL, 01904 624247
www.nationaltrust.org.uk/treasurers-house-york

Great for kids: Jorvik Viking Centre, YORK, YO1 9WT, 01904 615505
www.jorvikvikingcentre.co.uk

Premier Park

Goosewood Holiday Park
★★★★★ 88% HOLIDAY PARK

tel: 01347 810829 **YO61 1ET**
email: nick@flowerofmay.com web: www.flowerofmay.com
dir: *From A1237 take B1363. In 5 miles turn right. Right again in 0.5 mile, site on right.*

A relaxing and immaculately maintained park with its own lake and seasonal fishing. It is set in attractive woodland just six miles north of York. Mature shrubs and stunning seasonal floral displays at the entrance create an excellent first impression and the well-located toilet facilities are kept spotlessly clean. The generous patio pitches, providing optimum privacy, are randomly spaced throughout the site, and in addition to an excellent outdoor children's play area, you will find an indoor swimming pool and spacious clubhouse with a games area, bar and bistro. There are holiday homes and lodges for hire, some with hot tubs.

Open: March to 2 January (restricted service: low season – shop, bar and pool reduced hours) **Last arrival:** dusk **Last departure:** noon
Pitches: 🚐 🚙; 50 hardstanding pitches; 35 seasonal pitches
Leisure: 🏊 /A ● /🎣
Facilities: 🏠 ⊙ 🅿 ✻ ♿ 🪑 🍴 🚮 📶
Services: 🔌 🗑 🚽 🍽 ⛽ 🔒 [T]
Within 3 miles: ⚓ 🍴

Additional site information: 20 acre site. 🚗 Cars can be parked by caravans. Awnings permitted. No noise after midnight. Dogs accepted by prior arrangement only. Multi-ball court.

THIRSK   Map 19 SE48

Places to visit
Monk Park Farm, THIRSK, YO7 2AG, 01845 421124
www.monkparkfarm.co.uk

Byland Abbey, COXWOLD, YO61 4BD, 0370 333 1181
www.english-heritage.org.uk/visit/places/byland-abbey

Great for kids: Thirsk Birds of Prey Centre, THIRSK, YO7 4EU, 01845 587522
falconrycentre.co.uk

Premier Park

Hillside Caravan Park
★★★★★ 89%

tel: 01845 537349 & 07711 643652 **Canvas Farm, Moor Road YO7 4BR**
email: info@hillsidecaravanpark.co.uk web: www.hillsidecaravanpark.co.uk
dir: *From Thirsk take A19 north, exit at Knayton sign. In 0.25 mile right (cross bridge over A19), through village. Site on left in approximately 1.5 miles.*

A high quality, spacious park with first-class facilities, set in open countryside. The striking sandstone amenity block houses the airy reception, shop and self-service coffee lounge, plus there's a dog-wash room, laundry, two excellent family rooms, and an accessible room. There are also six luxury camping pods for hire and the self-catering Granary Cottage and lodges. All the pitches are equipped with electric hook-ups, with a choice of grass or gravel; some luxurious, fully-serviced hardstanding superpitches are also available. This is an excellent base for walkers and for those wishing to explore the Thirsk area. There is a large field for ball games, and dogs are welcome. Please note, the park does not accept tents.

Open: 4 February to 4 January **Last arrival:** 21.00 **Last departure:** noon
Pitches: 🚐 🚙; 🏕 see prices below; 50 hardstanding pitches
Leisure: /A ☐ ⚽
Facilities: 🏠 ⊙ 🅿 ✻ ♿ 🪑 🍴 📶 💻
Services: 🔌 🗑 🧺 🔒 [T]
Within 3 miles: ⚓ ∪

Additional site information: 9 acre site. 🚗 Cars can be parked by caravans. Awnings permitted. Self service coffee lounge.

Glamping available: Wooden pods ('mega pods') from £45. **Changeover days:** Any day
Additional glamping information: Mega pods equipped with toilet, shower, hand basin, kitchenette, TV, kettle, toaster, microwave and fridge. Cars can be parked by units

---

PITCHES: 🚐 Caravans 🚙 Motorhomes ⛺ Tents 🏕 Glamping accommodation **LEISURE:** 🏊 Indoor swimming pool 🏊 Outdoor swimming pool /A Children's playground 🧸 Kids' club 🎾 Tennis court ● Games room ☐ Separate TV room ⛳ golf course 🏌 Pitch n putt 🚣 Boats for hire 🚲 Bikes for hire 🎬 Cinema 🎭 Entertainment 🎣 Fishing ⛳ Mini golf 🌊 Watersports 💪 Gym ⚽ Sports field ∪ Stables ♨ Spa

NORTH YORKSHIRE 253 ENGLAND

WEST KNAPTON
Map 19 SE87

Places to visit
Pickering Castle, PICKERING, YO18 7AX, 01751 474989
www.english-heritage.org.uk/visit/places/pickering-castle

North Yorkshire Moors Railway, PICKERING, YO18 7AJ, 01751 472508
www.nymr.co.uk

Great for kids: Eden Camp Modern History Museum, MALTON, YO17 6RT, 01653 697777
www.edencamp.co.uk

Wolds Way Caravan and Camping
★★★★ 85%

tel: 01944 728463 **West Farm YO17 8JE**
email: info@ryedalesbest.co.uk **web:** www.ryedalesbest.co.uk
dir: *Signed between Rillington and West Heslerton on A64 (Malton to Scarborough road). Site in 1.5 miles.*

A constantly improving park on a working farm in an elevated position on the Yorkshire Wolds, creating spectacular views of the surrounding Vale of Pickering. The carefully landscaped grounds are matched by modern, quality toilet and shower facilities that have good privacy options. This is an excellent area for walking, with The Wolds Way passing the site entrance, and a pleasant one and a half mile path leads to a lavender farm with a first-class coffee shop.

Open: March to October **Last arrival:** 22.30 **Last departure:** 19.00
Pitches: ; 5 hardstanding pitches
Facilities:
Services:
Within 3 miles:

Additional site information: 7.5 acre site. Cars can be parked by caravans and tents. Awnings permitted. Free use of microwave, toaster and TV. Drinks machine, fridge and freezer.

WHITBY
Map 19 NZ81

Places to visit
Whitby Abbey, WHITBY, YO22 4JT, 01947 603568
www.english-heritage.org.uk/visit/places/whitby-abbey

North Yorkshire Moors Railway, PICKERING, YO18 7AJ, 01751 472508
www.nymr.co.uk

WHITBY
Map 19 NZ81

Premier Park

Ladycross Plantation Caravan Park
★★★★★ 86%

tel: 01947 895502 **Egton YO21 1UA**
email: enquiries@ladycrossplantation.co.uk **web:** www.ladycross.co.uk
dir: *From A171 (Whitby to Teesside road) onto unclassified road (site signed).*

The unique forest setting creates an away-from-it-all feeling at this peaceful park, set in 95 acres of woodland and run by enthusiastic owners. The pitches are sited in clearings around two smartly appointed amenity blocks, which offer excellent facilities – underfloor heating, no-touch infra-red showers, cubicles, kitchen prep areas and laundry facilities. Luxurious oak lodges set in forest clearings are available for hire or sale and residents here can enjoy the park's own woodland walks. There's an open communal field for children to play on and for dogs to be exercised. The site is well placed for visiting Whitby and exploring the North York Moors.

Open: March to November **Last arrival:** 18.30 **Last departure:** noon
Pitches: ; 77 hardstanding pitches; 66 seasonal pitches
Facilities:
Services:
Within 3 miles:

Additional site information: 95 acre site. Cars can be parked by caravans. Awnings permitted. No noise after 22.00. Dogs must be kept on leads in all areas of the park.

FACILITIES: Electric vehicle charging Baths/Shower Electric shaver sockets Hairdryer Ice pack facility Baby facilities Disabled facilities Shop on site or within 200yds BBQ area Picnic area WiFi Internet access **SERVICES:** Electric hook-up Launderette Licensed bar Calor Gas Campingaz Toilet fluid Café/Restaurant Fast Food/Takeaway Battery charging Motorhome service point No credit or debit cards Dogs permitted No dogs

ENGLAND 254 NORTH YORKSHIRE

WYKEHAM
Map 17 SE98

Places to visit

Scarborough Castle, SCARBOROUGH, YO11 1HY, 01723 372451
www.english-heritage.org.uk/visit/places/scarborough-castle

Pickering Castle, PICKERING, YO18 7AX, 01751 474989
www.english-heritage.org.uk/visit/places/pickering-castle

Great for kids: Sea Life Scarborough, SCARBOROUGH, YO12 6RP, 01723 373414
www.visitsealife.com/scarborough

Platinum Park

St Helens in the Park
★★★★★

tel: 01723 862771 **YO13 9QD**
email: caravans@wykeham.co.uk **web:** www.sthelenscaravanpark.co.uk
dir: On A170 in village, 150 yards on left beyond Downe Arms Hotel towards Scarborough.

Set on the edge of the North York Moors National Park, this delightfully landscaped park is immaculately maintained and thoughtfully laid out; the stunning floral displays around the park are noteworthy. The conveniently located and very stylish amenity blocks offer excellent interiors and privacy options for each gender which are also ideally suitable for families. The site is divided into terraces with tree-screening that creates smaller areas including an adults' zone. There are 12 camping pods for hire, all with electricity and two have en suite shower rooms and small kitchens. There is also a luxurious, fully furnished lodge available too. A cycle route leads through to the surrounding Wykeham Estate and there is a short pathway to the Downe Arms Hotel. The licenced, dog-friendly café, with attractive alfresco garden and decking, provides light refreshments, and a superb Aqua Park water activity area is nearby.

Open: February to January (restricted service: shop/café open from April to October only) **Last arrival:** 20.30 (earliest arrivals 13.30) **Last departure:** 11.00
Pitches: 🚐 🚙 ⛺ 🏕 see prices below; 79 hardstanding pitches; 100 seasonal pitches
Leisure: 🛝 ☼
Facilities: 🚿 ⊙ 🚻 ✻ ♿ 🍳 🗑 🅿 🐕 WiFi 💻
Services: 🔌 🚰 🍽 🧺 ↕ 🛢 Ⓣ
Within 3 miles: 🚶 🎣 ⛳ ⛵ ◎ 🚃

Additional site information: 25 acre site. 🐕 Cars can be parked by caravans and tents. Awnings permitted. No noise after 22.00, no open fires. Dogs must be kept on a lead at all times and never left unattended, and exercised in designated area or off site only. Family and adult-only super pitches available, caravan storage; 3-acre dog exercise field.

Glamping available: Wooden pods from £25.

Additional glamping information: Wooden pods equipped with wall mounted heater, electric socket with USB ports, mirror, lights and blackout curtains. Beds and bed linen not provided. Cars can be parked by units.

YORK
Map 16 SE65

Places to visit

The York Dungeon, YORK, YO1 9RD, 01904 632599
www.thedungeons.com/york

York Brewery, MASHAM, HG4 4EN, 01765 680101
www.york-brewery.co.uk

Premier Park

York Caravan Park
★★★★★ 92%

tel: 01904 424222 **Stockton Lane YO32 9UB**
email: mail@yorkcaravanpark.com **web:** www.yorkcaravanpark.com

Located close to the inner ring road and ideally placed for touring the coast and visiting York city centre, this adults-only park provides generous, fully serviced pitches suitable for caravans and large motorhomes. The impressive amenity block provides very spacious unisex, combined showers with toilets and washbasins to supplement the general facilities, and a peaceful fishing lake is an added attraction. Mature trees and neat hedge divisions create additional privacy and both indigenous and cultivated flowers and shrubs create all year colour and interest. A pub is located a half-mile walk from the park and a major supermarket is also nearby. A regular bus service to the city centre stops at the park entrance.

Open: 15 March to 8 January **Last arrival:** 21.00 **Last departure:** 11.30
Pitches: 🚐 🚙; 55 seasonal pitches
Additional site information: 7 acre site. Adults only.

Premier Park

Flaxton Meadows
★★★★★ 88%

tel: 01904 393943 **York Lane, Flaxton YO60 7QZ**
email: hello@flaxtonmeadows.co.uk **web:** www.flaxtonmeadows.co.uk
dir: From York at roundabout take A64 towards Scarborough. Left signed Sheriff Hutton to Flaxton. In Flaxton opposite The Blacksmiths Arms turn left signed Strensall and York. (Do not turn into Cross Lane on right). Site further on, on left.

Flaxton Meadows is located in North Yorkshire's beautiful countryside, renowned for its wildlife and scenery. Bordered by rolling farmland and heathland and just eight miles out of York city centre, close to Castle Howard, the North York Moors, Helmsley, Scarborough and the east coast. The award-winning, eco-conscious Flaxton Meadows provides a peaceful retreat for those wishing to enjoy a natural environment, yet is within easy reach of a wide range of amenities. In addition to excellent touring and camping facilities, luxury lodges with hot tubs are also available.

Open: March to October **Last arrival:** 18.00 **Last departure:** 12.00
Pitches: 🚐 🚙 ⛺; 20 hardstanding pitches
Facilities: 🚿 ⊙ 🚻 ♿ WiFi
Services: 🔌 🚰 🍽 ↕ **Within 3 miles:** 🚶 🎣 🛒

Additional site information: 10 acre site. Adults only. 🐕 Cars can be parked by caravans. Awnings permitted. No noise after 22.00. No movement of vehicles between 23.00 and 07.00. No twin axle caravans, vans, trucks or sign written vehicles. Strictly no fires on site. No firepits. Only gas BBQs permitted. Dogs must be kept on short leads.

PITCHES: 🚐 Caravans 🚙 Motorhomes ⛺ Tents 🏕 Glamping accommodation **LEISURE:** 🏊 Indoor swimming pool 🏊 Outdoor swimming pool 🛝 Children's playground 🎪 Kids' club 🎾 Tennis court 🎱 Games room 📺 Separate TV room ⛳ golf course 🏌 Pitch n putt 🚣 Boats for hire 🚴 Bikes for hire 🎬 Cinema 🎵 Entertainment 🎣 Fishing ◎ Mini golf 🏄 Watersports 🏋 Gym ⚽ Sports field ⛵ Stables 💆 Spa

Rawcliffe Manor Caravan Park
★★★★ 85%

tel: 01904 640845 Manor Lane, Shipton Road YO30 5TZ
email: christine@lysanderarms.co.uk web: www.lysanderarms.co.uk
dir: *From roundabout junction of A1237 and A19, take A19 signed York, Clifton and Rawcliffe. 1st left into Manor Lane, follow brown camping signs.*

A lovely little adults-only site tucked away behind the Lysander Arms and located only minutes from the centre of York. Each of the 13 generously-sized pitches is fully serviced with an individual chemical disposal point, and the central toilet block is very airy, modern and spotlessly clean. The grounds have been imaginatively landscaped. The pub offers good food and the York Park & Ride facility is a 10-minute walk away.

Open: All year **Last arrival:** 18.00 **Last departure:** 11.00
Pitches: 13 hardstanding pitches
Leisure:
Facilities:
Services:
Within 3 miles:

Additional site information: 4.5 acre site. Adults only. Cars can be parked by caravans. Awnings permitted. No noise after 23.00. Chemical disposal points on each pitch.

Make your next UK holiday one to remember

Choose RatedTrips.com

SOUTH YORKSHIRE

WALES BAR
Map 16 SK48

Places to visit

Gulliver's Valley, Mansfield Road, WALES BAR S26 5QW
www.gulliversvalleyresort.co.uk

Wentworth Woodhouse, Wentworth, ROTHERHAM, S62 7TQ, 01226 351161
www.wentworthwoodhouse.org.uk

Premier Park

Waleswood Caravan and Camping Park
★★★★★ 92%

tel: 01709 808100 **Delves Lane, Waleswood S26 5RN**
email: booking@waleswood.co.uk **web:** www.waleswood.co.uk
dir: M1 Junction 31 to A57 towards Sheffield. Left at roundabout A618, right at traffic lights near the petrol station Waleswood/Delves Lane. Park on left in 0.5 miles. (Follow brown signs to Rother Valley Country Park but do not use main park entrance, instead turn at traffic lights Delves Lane off A618).

Waleswood is inside Rother Valley Country Park, and the elevated position commands stunning rural views. All pitches, many of which are fully serviced, are generously spaced to maximise comfort, while two amenity blocks offer modern facilities and good privacy options. The combined reception, licensed coffee shop and site shop has long opening hours. Dog friendly and children's play facilities are provided.

Waleswood Caravan and Camping Park

Open: All year **Last arrival:** 21.00 (later arrivals by prior arrangement) **Last departure:** noon

Pitches: 🚐 🚙 ⛺; 125 hardstanding pitches

Leisure: 🎪 🏓

Facilities: 🚿 🧺 😀 🚰 ♿ 💰 🍴 📶 💻

Services: 🔌 🗑 🍳 🍽 ⬇ 🚽

Within 3 miles: 🎣 ⛳ 🎢 🏊

Additional site information: 12.5 acre site. 🐕 Cars can be parked by caravans and tents. Awnings permitted. Dog walk, family and accessible changing facilities, licensed coffee shop, outdoor table tennis, outdoor table football, electric car charging points. 3 extra large pitches for RVs and longer motorhomes.

See advert below

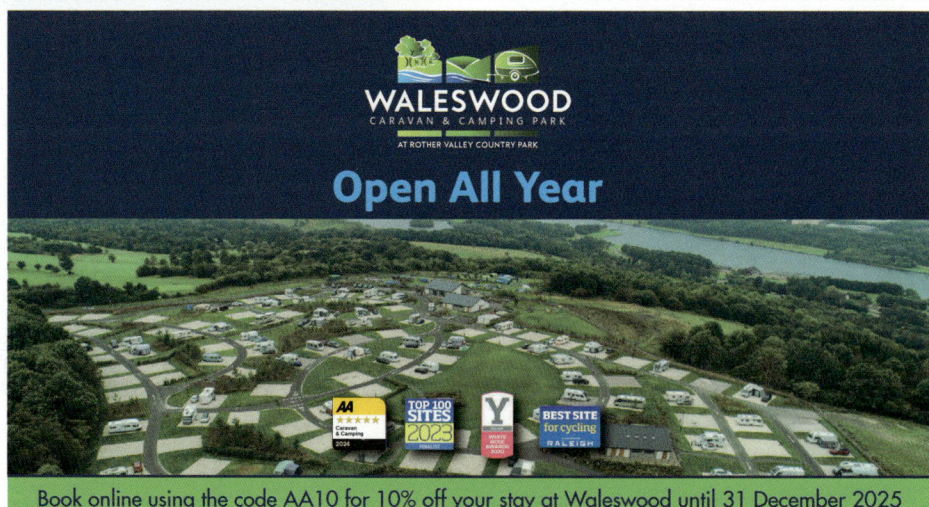

PITCHES: 🚐 Caravans 🚙 Motorhomes ⛺ Tents 🏕 Glamping accommodation **LEISURE:** 🏊 Indoor swimming pool 🏊 Outdoor swimming pool 🎪 Children's playground 👋 Kids' club 🎾 Tennis court 🎮 Games room 📺 Separate TV room ⛳ golf course 🏌 Pitch n putt ⛵ Boats for hire 🚲 Bikes for hire 🎬 Cinema 🎭 Entertainment 🎣 Fishing ⛳ Mini golf 🏄 Watersports 🏋 Gym ⚽ Sports field 🐴 Stables 💆 Spa

SOUTH YORKSHIRE 257 ENGLAND

WORSBROUGH
Map 16 SE30

Places to visit

Monk Bretton Priory, BARNSLEY, S71 5QD, 0370 333 1181
www.english-heritage.org.uk/visit/places/monk-bretton-priory

Millennium Gallery, SHEFFIELD, S1 2PP, 0114 278 2600
www.museums-sheffield.org.uk/museums/millennium-gallery/home

Great for kids: Magna Science Adventure Centre, ROTHERHAM, S60 1DX, 01709 720002
www.visitmagna.co.uk

Greensprings Touring Park
★★★★ 83%

tel: 01226 288298 **Rockley Abbey Farm, Rockley Lane S75 3DS**
email: greensprings_1@yahoo.co.uk web: greensprings-park.edan.io
dir: *M1 junction 36, A61 to Barnsley. Left after 0.25 mile signed Pilley. Site in 1 mile at bottom of hill.*

A secluded and very peaceful farm site amidst woods and farmland with access to several good local walks. There are two touring areas, one gently sloping. A modern amenity block is provided with good privacy options. There is no laundry room here, however, there is an indoor dishwashing area. Not far from the M1, this site is convenient for exploring the area's industrial heritage, as well as the beautiful Peak District and South Yorkshire market towns.

Open: April to October **Last arrival:** 21.00 **Last departure:** noon

Pitches: 🚐 🚙 ⛺; 30 hardstanding pitches; 22 seasonal pitches

Leisure: ⚽

Facilities: 🛁 ☺ ✻ ♿

Services: 🔌

Within 3 miles: ⬇ ✎ ∪ ◎ 🍴 🛍 🛒

Additional site information: 4 acre site. 🚗 Cars can be parked by caravans and tents. Awnings permitted.

FACILITIES: 🔌 Electric vehicle charging 🛁 Baths/Shower ☺ Electric shaver sockets 💇 Hairdryer ✻ Ice pack facility 👶 Baby facilities ♿ Disabled facilities 🛒 Shop on site or within 200yds 🍖 BBQ area 🧺 Picnic area WiFi WiFi 💻 Internet access **SERVICES:** 🔌 Electric hook-up 🧺 Launderette 🍷 Licensed bar ⛽ Calor Gas ⛽ Campingaz 🚾 Toilet fluid 🍽 Café/Restaurant 🍔 Fast Food/Takeaway 🔋 Battery charging 🚐 Motorhome service point 🚫 No credit or debit cards 🐕 Dogs permitted 🚫 No dogs

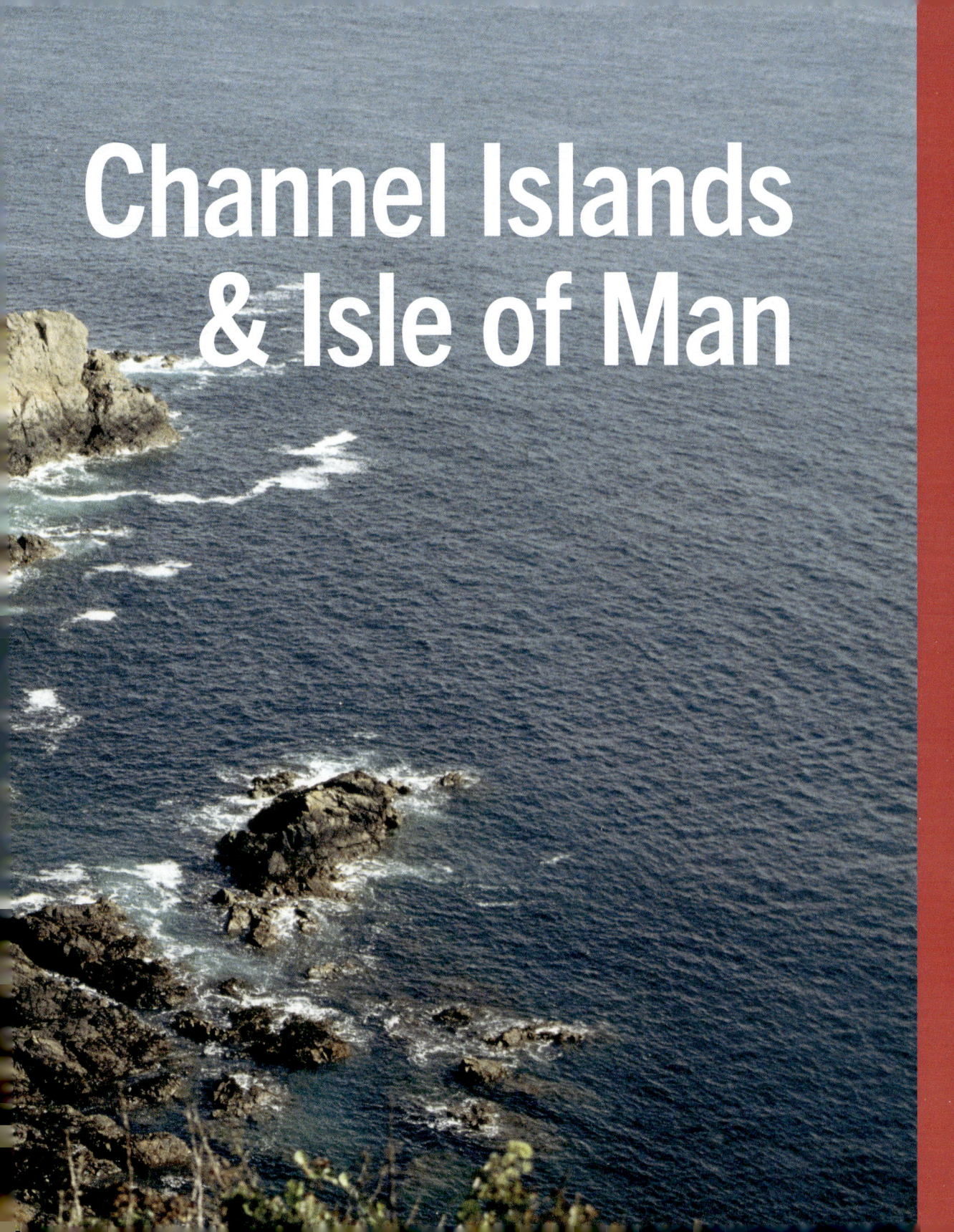

Channel Islands & Isle of Man

ENGLAND — GUERNSEY

GUERNSEY

ST SAMPSON Map 24

Places to visit

Sausmarez Manor, ST MARTIN, GY4 6SG, 01481 235571
www.sausmarezmanor.co.uk

Castle Cornet, ST PETER PORT, GY1 1AU, 01481 721657
www.museums.gov.gg

Le Vaugrat Camp Site
★★★   90%

tel: 01481 257468 **Route de Vaugrat GY2 4TA**
email: enquiries@vaugratcampsite.com **web:** www.vaugratcampsite.com
dir: *From main coast road on north-west of island, site signed at Port Grat Bay into Route de Vaugrat, near Peninsula Hotel.*

Overlooking the sea and set within the grounds of a lovely 17th-century house, this level, grassy park is backed by woodland, and is close to the lovely sandy beaches of Port Grat and Grand Havre. It is run by a welcoming family who pride themselves on creating magnificent floral displays. The facilities here are excellent and there are 18 electric hook-ups, plus several fully equipped tents for hire. A 'round the island' bus stops very close to the site. Motorhomes up to 6.9 metres are allowed on Guernsey – contact the site for details and a permit.

Open: May to mid September
Pitches: see prices below
Leisure:
Facilities:
Services:
Within 3 miles:

Additional site information: 6 acre site. Cars can be parked by caravans and tents. Awnings permitted. No pets.

Glamping available: Ready-erected tents from £53.

Additional glamping information: Ready-erected tents: beds, bedding (not towels) and cooking facilities are included. Electricity is not available. Cabanon Espace tents sleep 6. Bell tents sleep 3 (adults only). Cars can be parked by units

VALE Map 24

Places to visit

Guernsey Museum & Art Gallery, ST PETER PORT, GY1 1UG, 01481 726518
www.museums.gov.gg

Great for kids: Castle Cornet, ST PETER PORT, GY1 1AU, 01481 721657
www.museums.gov.gg/CastleCornet

La Bailloterie Camping
★★★★   88%

tel: 01481 243636 & 07781 103420 **GY3 5HA**
email: info@campinguernsey.com **web:** www.campinguernsey.com
dir: *Leave St Peter Port harbour and take the right turn at roundabout onto the seafront. At Halfway filter bear left into Vale Road following signs to Pembroke Bay. At the 3rd set of lights at Crossways, turn right into Braye Road. Site 1st left at sign.*

A pretty, rural site with one large touring field and a few small, well-screened paddocks. This delightful site has been privately run for over 50 years and offers good facilities in converted outbuildings, and a woodland walk has been created. There are two cabins, three safari glamping tents, a yurt and three pods (one with a double bed, the others with two singles). The beaches and a supermarket are a short walk away. Motorhomes up to 6.9 metres are allowed on Guernsey – contact the site for details and a permit.

Open: 15 May to 15 September **Last arrival:** 23.00 **Last departure:** 11.00
Pitches: see prices below
Leisure:
Facilities:
Services:
Within 3 miles:

Additional site information: 10 acre site. Cars can be parked by tents. Awnings permitted. Dogs by prior arrangement only, no dogs in safari tents or hired accommodation. Volleyball net, boules pitch, mini golf. Car hire can be arranged.

Glamping available: Safari tents from £25; Pods from £20; Yurt from £18.
Changeover days: Any day

Additional glamping information: Minimum stay 2 nights. Safari tents: prices per adult; family packages available. Pods: prices per adult, maximum 2 people, fully equipped with bedding. Yurt: fully equipped, no bedding. Cars can be parked by units

---

Make your next UK holiday one to remember

Choose RatedTrips.com

AA

HERM—JERSEY—ISLE OF MAN   ENGLAND

HERM

HERM   Map 24

Places to visit
St Tugal's Chapel, North Clifton, HERM, GY1 1JR, 01481 725 048
www.spurgeonchurch.org.uk/st-tuguals

Seagull Campsite
★★★★ 80%

tel: 01481 750000 **GY1 3HR**
email: campsitemanager@herm.com

Seagull Campsite is a well maintained grassy site offering fully-equipped camping in spacious 6-8 person tents on the idyllic tiny island of Herm. It's a special away-from-it-all location and the site enjoys stunning views of the sea and nearby islands. With a focus on families, there is a newly refurbished amenity bloack, a recreation field with a football pitch and you're just minutes from the coast path leading to Belvoir Bay. The island has a grocery store with an off licence. Herm is traffic free, so parking must be arranged with Trident Travel at St Peter Port, Guernsey, on 01481 721379, or ask when booking. Guests should check in at the information kiosk on the quay on arrival.

JERSEY

TRINITY   Map 24

Places to visit
Hamptonne Country Life Museum, ST LAWRENCE, JE3 1HS, 01534 863955
www.jerseyheritage.org/places-to-visit/hamptonne-country-life-museum

Mont Orgueil Castle, GOREY, JE3 6ET, 01534 853292
www.jerseyheritage.org/explore/find-a-place-to-visit/mont-orgueil-castle

Platinum Park

Durrell Wildlife Camp
★★★★★   GLAMPING ONLY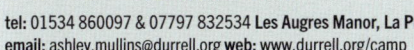

tel: 01534 860097 & 07797 832534 **Les Augres Manor, La Profonde Rue JE3 5BP**
email: ashley.mullins@durrell.org web: www.durrell.org/camp
dir: From St Helier take A8 to Trinity. At T-junction right signed Rozel and Jersey Zoo. Site on the right.

Part of Jersey Zoo, the camp consists of 12 canvas geo domes set in a beautifully landscaped area. Each dome, named after different Lemur species, is sited in its own separate area offering good privacy. Inside, is a king-size bed, two singles, a wood-burning stove and clothing storage space. Set on wooden decking, the domes have their own additional pod with high quality toilet, washbasin and shower plus a spacious fully-equipped kitchen. Table and chairs on the decking can be brought into the kitchen if the weather's not so good. Smaller tipis are available for extra guests or children. Guests have free, unlimited access to Jersey Zoo during its opening hours and can visit the excellent Café Firefly and Café Dodo, which both serve breakfasts and lunches and a variety of snacks. The whole holiday experience is quite magical.

Open: March to October **Last arrival:** 20.00 **Last departure:** 10.00
Facilities:
Within 3 miles:
Accommodation available: Geo domes from £140.
Changeover days: Any day
Additional site information: No pets. No noise after 23.00. Free entry into Jersey Zoo. Cars can be parked by units

ISLE OF MAN

KIRK MICHAEL   Map 24 SC39

Places to visit
Peel Castle, PEEL, IM5 1TB, 01624 843232
www.manxnationalheritage.im/our-sites/peel-castle

House of Manannan, PEEL, IM5 1TA, 01624 648090
www.manxnationalheritage.im/our-sites/house-of-manannan

Great for kids: Curraghs Wildlife Park, BALLAUGH, IM7 5EA, 01624 897323
www.curraghswildlifepark.im

Glen Wyllin Campsite
★★★ 84%

tel: 01624 878231 & 878836 **IM6 1AL**
email: tmdentith@manx.net web: www.glenwyllincampsite.co.uk
dir: From Douglas take A1 to Ballacraine, right at lights onto A3 to Kirk Michael. Left onto A4 signed Peel. Site 100 yards on right.

This site is set in a peaceful wooded glen with bridges over a babbling brook that divides the enclosed camping and touring areas, and where the only distractions are the welcome ones of running water and birdsong. A long gentle sloping tarmac road leads through the camping areas to a superb beach; a well-stocked shop and hot food takeaway service are additional features. Ready-erected tents are available and future plans include secluded lodges and yurts.

Open: mid April to mid September **Last departure:** noon
Pitches:
Leisure:
Facilities:
Services:
Within 3 miles:

Additional site information: 9 acre site. Cars can be parked by caravans and tents. Awnings permitted. No excess noise after midnight. Dogs must be kept under control.

Glamping available: Ready-erected tents.

Scotland

Scotland

With its remarkable, timeless beauty, jagged coastline and long and eventful history, Scotland is a country with something very special to offer. Around half the size of England, but with barely one fifth of its population and nearly 800 islands, the statistics alone are enough make you want to pack a suitcase and head north without hesitation.

The Scottish Borders region acts as a perfect introduction and is an obvious place to begin a tour of the country. The novelist and poet Sir Walter Scott was so moved by its remoteness and grandeur that he wrote: 'To my eye, these grey hills and all this wild border country have beauties peculiar to themselves. I like the very nakedness of the land; it has something bold and stern and solitary about it. If I did not see the heather at least once a year I think I should die.' Abbotsford, Scott's turreted mansion on the banks of the River Tweed near Melrose, re-opened to the public following a £12 million restoration programme.

Consisting of 1,800 square miles of dense forest, rolling green hills and the broad sweeps of heather that lifted Scott's spirits, this region is characterised by some of the country's most majestic landscapes. Adjacent to this region is Dumfries & Galloway, where, at Gretna Green on the border with England, eloping couples have tied the knot since Lord Hardwicke's Marriage Act came into force in 1754; it still can boast around 1,200 weddings a year. Travel north and you discover mile upon mile of open moorland and swathes of seemingly endless forest that stretch to the Ayrshire coast. At a crucial time in the country's history, it is fascinating to reflect on another momentous event in the story of Scotland when, following the signing of the Declaration of Arbroath in 1320, it became independent and was ruled by Robert the Bruce. Dumfries & Galloway is littered with the relics of his battles.

Not far from Dumfries is the cottage where Robert Burns, the Bard of Scotland, was born in 1759. This tiny white-washed dwelling, constructed of thatch and clay, was built by the poet's father two years earlier. In a 2009 poll, TV viewers voted Burns the 'Greatest ever Scot' and his song *Is there for Honest Poverty* opened the new Scottish Parliament in 1999. The cottage at Alloway is one of Scotland's most popular tourist attractions with a museum allowing the poet's collection of precious manuscripts, correspondence and artefacts to be housed in one building.

Scotland's two greatest cities, Glasgow and Edinburgh, include innumerable historic sites, popular landmarks and innovative visitor attractions. Edinburgh is home to the annual, internationally famous Military Tattoo; Glasgow, once the second city of the British Empire and yet synonymous with the dreadful slums and the grime of industry, has, in places, been transformed beyond recognition. The city hosted the Great Exhibitions of 1888 and 1901, was designated European City of Culture in 1990 and in 2014 became the setting for the highly successful Commonwealth Games.

To the north of Glasgow and Edinburgh lies a sublime landscape of tranquil lochs, fishing rivers, wooded glens and the fine cities of Perth and Dundee. There is also the superb scenery of The Trossachs, Loch Lomond and Stirling, which, with its handsome castle perched on a rocky crag, is Scotland's heritage capital. Sooner or later the might and majesty of the Cairngorms and the Grampians beckon, drawing you into a breathtakingly beautiful landscape of mountains and remote, rugged terrain. Scotland's isolated far north is further from many parts of England than a good many European destinations. Cape Wrath is Britain's most northerly outpost.

For many visitors, the Western Highlands is the place to go, evoking a truly unique and breathtaking sense of adventure. The list of island names seems endless — Skye, Mull, Iona, Jura, Islay — each with their own individual character and identity, and the reward of everlasting and treasured memories.

Rest and Be Thankful Pass near Arrochar ▷

ABERDEENSHIRE

HUNTLY — Map 23 NJ53

Places to visit

Leith Hall, Garden & Estate, RHYNIE, AB54 4NQ, 01464 831216
www.nts.org.uk/visit/places/leith-hall

Glenfiddich Distillery, DUFFTOWN, AB55 4DH, 01340 820373
www.glenfiddich.com

Premier Park

Huntly Castle Caravan Park
★★★★★ 90%

tel: 01466 794999 The Meadow AB54 4UJ
email: enquiries@huntlycastle.co.uk **web:** www.huntlycastle.co.uk
dir: *From Aberdeen on A96 to Huntly. 0.75 mile after roundabout (on outskirts of Huntly) right towards town centre, left into Riverside Drive.*

A quality parkland site within striking distance of the Speyside Malt Whisky Trail, the beautiful Moray coast and the Cairngorm Mountains. The park provides exceptional toilet facilities, and there are some fully serviced pitches. The attractive town of Huntly is only a five-minute walk away, with its ruined castle plus a wide variety of restaurants and shops.

Open: April to October **Last arrival:** 20.00 **Last departure:** noon
Pitches: 51 hardstanding pitches; 10 seasonal pitches
Leisure:
Facilities:
Services:
Within 3 miles:

Additional site information: 15 acre site. Cars can be parked by caravans and tents. Awnings permitted. No noise after 23.00.

KINTORE — Map 23 NJ71

Places to visit

Pitmedden Garden, PITMEDDEN, AB41 7PD, 01651 842352
www.nts.org.uk/visit/places/pitmedden-garden

Tolquhon Castle, TARVES, AB41 7LP, 01651 851286
www.historicenvironment.scot/visit-a-place/places/tolquhon-castle

Great for kids: Castle Fraser, SAUCHEN, AB51 7LD, 01330 833463
www.nts.org.uk/visit/places/castle-fraser

Hillhead Caravan Park
★★★★ 77%

tel: 01467 632809 **AB51 0YX**
email: enquiries@hillheadcaravan.com **web:** www.hillheadcaravan.com
dir: *From south: A96 at Broomhill Roundabout follow Kintore (and brown camping sign) onto B987. At mini-roundabout 1st left, immediately left signed Kemnay. Over A96, straight on at next roundabout, right signed Kintore. Site on right. From north: A96 at roundabout follow Kintore signs onto B987. 5th right into Forest Road. Over A96, 1st left to site on left.*

An attractive, nicely landscaped site, located on the outskirts of Kintore in the valley of the River Dee, with excellent access to forest walks and within easy reach of the many attractions in rural Aberdeenshire. The toilet facilities are of a high standard. There are good play facilities for smaller children plus a small café with TV and internet access.

Open: All year **Last arrival:** 21.00 **Last departure:** 13.00
Pitches: 17 hardstanding pitches; 10 seasonal pitches
Leisure:
Facilities:
Services:
Within 3 miles:

Additional site information: 1.5 acre site. Cars can be parked by caravans and tents. Awnings permitted. Caravan storage, accessories shop.

Make your next UK holiday one to remember

Choose RatedTrips.com

AA

ABERDEENSHIRE 267 SCOTLAND

MINTLAW   Map 23 NJ94

Places to visit

Aberdeenshire Farming Museum, MINTLAW, AB42 5FQ, 01771 624590
www.livelifeaberdeenshire.org.uk/museums/find-a-museum/aberdeenshire-farming-museum

Deer Abbey, OLD DEER, 0131 668 8600
www.historicenvironment.scot/visit-a-place/places/deer-abbey

Aden Caravan and Camping
★★★ 86%

tel: 077886 885435 & 01771 622071 **Station Road AB42 5FQ**
email: wardens@adencaravanandcamping.co.uk
web: www.adencaravanandcamping.co.uk
dir: From Mintlaw take A950 signed New Pitsligo and Aden Country Park. Site entrance is just inside entrance to Aden Country Park on right.

Situated adjacent to the 230-acre Aden Country Park, Aden Caravan and Camping is a small, tranquil site offering excellent facilities. It is ideally located for visiting the many tourist attractions in this beautiful north-east coastal area. The site is only a short drive from the busy fishing towns of Fraserburgh and Peterhead, and it is only an hour from Aberdeen's centre. This is an ideal spot for a short stay or a longer holiday, and there are camping pods and one disabled-adapted static for hire. The adjacent country park plays host to numerous events throughout the year, including pipe band championships, horse events and various ranger-run activities.

Open: 1 April (or Good Friday – whichever is first) to 31 October **Last arrival:** 20.00 **Last departure:** noon
Pitches: * from £30; from £30; from £8; 16 hardstanding pitches; 13 seasonal pitches
Leisure:
Facilities:
Services:
Within 3 miles:

Additional site information: 11.1 acre site. Cars can be parked by caravans and tents. Awnings permitted. 5mph onsite speed limit, reverse parking only, 1 vehicle per pitch only, gates closed overnight. Mobile chip van and ice cream van Friday evenings and some weekends
Glamping available: 3 wooden pods. **Changeover days:** Any day
Additional glamping information: Wooden pods sleep up to 4 people. Please see website for restrictions. Maximum of 2 dogs allowed at extra cost

STRACHAN   Map 23 NO69

Places to visit

Banchory Museum, BANCHORY, AB31 5SX, 01330 823367
www.livelifeaberdeenshire.org.uk/museums/find-a-museum/banchory-museum

Crathes Castle, Garden & Estate, CRATHES, AB31 5QJ, 01330 844525
www.nts.org.uk/visit/places/crathes-castle

Feughside Caravan Park
  87%

tel: 01330 850669 **AB31 6NT**
email: info@feughsidecaravanpark.co.uk web: www.feughsidecaravanpark.co.uk
dir: From Banchory take B974 to Strachan, 3 miles, take B976, 2 miles to Feughside B&B. Turn right after the B&B, caravan park on right. Reception 100 yards past entrance.

A small, well maintained family-run site, set amongst mature trees and hedges, located five miles from Banchory and with stunning views of Clachnaben Hill. The site is ideally suited to those wishing for a peaceful location that is within easy reach of scenic Royal Deeside.

Open: April to October **Last arrival:** 20.00 **Last departure:** noon
Pitches: ; 10 hardstanding pitches; 12 seasonal pitches
Leisure: **Facilities:**
Services: **Within 3 miles:**

Additional site information: 5.5 acre site. Cars can be parked by caravans and tents. Awnings permitted. Quiet after 22.00. No open fires. Pets to be on leads at all times and exercised outside the park.

TURRIFF   Map 23 NJ75

Places to visit

Fyvie Castle, Garden & Estate, TURRIFF, AB53 8JS, 01651 891266
www.nts.org.uk/visit/places/fyvie-castle

Turriff Caravan Park
★★★★ 84%

tel: 01888 562205 & 562943 **Station Road AB53 4ER**
email: info@turriffcaravanpark.com web: www.turriffcaravanpark.com
dir: On A947, south of Turriff.

Located on the outskirts of Turriff on the site of an old railway station, this site is owned by the local community. The pitches are level and the attractive landscaping is well maintained. The site also has a rally field. There is a large public park close to the site which has a boating pond and a large games park where the annual agricultural show is held. The town is only five minutes' walk through the park and has a good variety of shops. This is an ideal base for touring rural Aberdeenshire and the nearby Moray coastline with its traditional fishing villages.

Open: late March to end October **Last arrival:** 18.00 **Last departure:** 11.00
Pitches: ; 10 hardstanding pitches; 9 seasonal pitches
Leisure: **Facilities:**
Services: **Within 3 miles:**

Additional site information: 5 acre site. Cars can be parked by caravans and tents. Awnings permitted. No music or loud noise after 22.00. Reception open 09.00–13.00 and 16.00–18.00.

ANGUS

FOWLIS — Map 21 NO33

Places to visit

Camperdown Country Park, Coupar Angus Road, DD2 4TF, 01382 433710
www.dundeecity.gov.uk/service-area/neighbourhood-services/environment/camperdown-country-park

Great for kids: Camperdown Wildlife Centre, Camperdown Country Park, Coupar Angus Road, DD2 4TF, 01382 431811
www.camperdownwildlifecentre.co.uk

Piperdam Leisure Resort
★★★★ 91%

tel: 01382 585000 **Fowlis DD2 5LP**

email: piperdamguestservices@awayresorts.co.uk
web: www.awayresorts.co.uk/parks/scotland/piperdam
dir: *From A90 in Dundee take A923 signed Coupar Angus and Birkhill. Through Birkhill and Muirhead. Site entrance on left in approximately 3 miles..*

With serious investment and impressive plans in place, Away Resorts are gradually transforming this extensive holiday park that is set in 650 acres of beautiful Angus countryside. The resort has excellent facilities with investment to date showing very good results, especially in and around the bar and restaurant areas and the swimming pool. An array of lodge styles, sleeping 2 to 12 people, are currently being refurbished to very high standard – the best are located beside the stunning Piperdam Loch and have hot tubs and an indoor sauna. Guests have access to a wide range of on-site activities that include two golf courses, an indoor swimming pool, a sauna and steam room, beauty spa, tennis court, driving range, and a multi-functional activity barn for indoor games, sports, conferences and weddings.

Open: All year **Last arrival:** 22.00 **Last departure:** 12.00

Additional site information: 650 acre site.

ARGYLL & BUTE

CARRADALE — Map 20 NR83

Places to visit

Carradale Point Nature Reserve, Carradale, PA28 6SB, 0300 067 6650
www.forestryandland.gov.scot/visit/carradale

Saddell Abbey, Campbeltown, PA28 6RA,
www.undiscoveredscotland.co.uk/carradale/saddellabbey

CARRADALE — Map 20 NR83

Carradale Bay Caravan Park
★★★ 90%

tel: 01583 431665 **PA28 6QG**
email: info@carradalebay.com web: www.carradalebay.com
dir: *A83 from Tarbert towards Campbeltown, left onto B842 (Carradale road), right onto B879. Site in 0.5 mile.*

A beautiful, natural site on the sea's edge with superb views over Kilbrannan Sound to the Isle of Arran. Pitches are landscaped into small bays broken up by shrubs and bushes, and backed by dunes close to the long sandy beach. The toilet facilities are appointed to a very high standard. This is an environmentally-aware site that requires the use of green toilet chemicals – available on the site. Lodges and static caravans are available for holiday hire.

Open: April to September **Last arrival:** 22.00 **Last departure:** noon

Pitches: 🚐 🚍 Å

Facilities: ⊙ ⁂ ✳ ♿ 🛁 🛒 WiFi

Services: 🔌 🗑 T

Within 3 miles: ⬇ 🐟 U ≋ ✈

Additional site information: 8 acre site. Cars can be parked by caravans and tents. Awnings permitted.

GLENDARUEL — Map 20 NR98

Places to visit

Benmore Botanic Garden, BENMORE, PA23 8QU, 01369 706261
www.rbge.org.uk/visit/benmore-botanic-garden

Glendaruel Caravan Park
★★★ 86%

2024

tel: 01369 820267 **PA22 3AB**
email: mail@glendaruelcaravanpark.com web: www.glendaruelcaravanpark.com
dir: *A83 onto A815 to Strachur, 13 miles to site on A886. By ferry from Gourock to Dunoon take B836, then A886 for approximately 4 miles north. (Note: this route is not recommended for towing vehicles – 1:5 uphill gradient on B836).*

Glendaruel Gardens, with an arboretum, is the peaceful setting for this pleasant, well established wooded site in a valley surrounded by mountains. It is set back from the main road and screened by trees so that a peaceful stay is ensured. It has level grass and hardstanding pitches. A regular local bus service and a ferry at Portavadie (where there are retail outlets and eateries) make a day trip to the Mull of Kintyre a possibility. The Cowal Way, a long distance path, and a national cycle path pass the site. Static caravans and three 'little' camping bothies are available for hire.

Open: April to October **Last arrival:** 22.00 **Last departure:** noon

Pitches: 🚐 🚍 Å; 15 hardstanding pitches; 12 seasonal pitches

Leisure: ⚽

Facilities: ⊙ ⁂ ✳ 🛁 🛒 🛍 WiFi

Services: 🔌 🗑 🧺 🔒 ✂ T

Within 3 miles: 🐟

Additional site information: 6 acre site. Cars can be parked by caravans and tents. Awnings permitted. Sea trout and salmon fishing, woodland walks, 24-hour emergency phone.

SOUTH AYRSHIRE

BARRHILL — Map 20 NX28

Places to visit
Bargany Gardens, OLD DAILLY, KA26 9QL, 01465 871249
www.bargany.com

Barrhill Holiday Park
★★★★ 88%

tel: 01465 821355 **Barrhill Holiday Park, KA26 0PZ**
email: relax@barrhillholidaypark.com web: www.barrhillholidaypark.com
dir: *On A714 (Newton Stewart to Girvan road). 1 mile north of Barrhill.*

A small, friendly park in a tranquil rural location, screened from the A714 by trees. The park is terraced and well landscaped, and the high-quality amenity block includes disabled facilities. In addition to deluxe lodge pods with hot tubs, much longer, luxury pods have been added and these have the bonus of an inside shower. The local bus to Girvan stops at the site entrance. The site now has its own EV charger available to all residents and guests.

Open: March to January **Last arrival:** 22.00 **Last departure:** 10.00 (accommodation units) noon (touring)

Pitches: 🚐 🚍; ▲ see prices below; 20 hardstanding pitches

Leisure: ⚽

Facilities: 🖥 🛁 ☉ 🚿 ♿ 🍴 WiFi

Services: 🔌 🧺 🔋

Within 3 miles: ⚓ 🛒

Additional site information: 6 acre site. 🐕 Cars can be parked by caravans and tents. Awnings permitted. No noise after 23.00. Children's play park.

Glamping available: 10 wooden pods from £90 with hot tub; £153 for a 2 night stay (including a stargazer pod with a hot tub).
Changeover days: Any day, minimum 2 night stay

Additional glamping information: 10 have hot tubs, some have showers. Communal kitchen. Each pod has toilet, basin, microwave, TV, mini fridge, kettle, picnic table and fire pit. No glassware permitted in or around hot tubs. Hot tubs may not be used after 23.00. Cars can be parked by units

PRESTWICK — Map 20 NS32

Places to visit
Robert Burns Birthplace Museum, ALLOWAY, KA7 4PQ, 01292 443700
www.nts.org.uk/visit/places/robert-burns-birthplace-museum

Great for kids: Heads of Ayr Farm Park, ALLOWAY, KA7 4LD, 01292 441210
www.headsofayrfarmpark.co.uk

Prestwick Holiday Park
★★★ 85%

tel: 01292 479261 **Monkton, Prestwick KA9 1UH**
email: prestwickholidaypark@hotmail.co.uk web: www.prestwickholidaypark.co.uk
dir: *Site signed from A79 west of Glasgow Prestwick Airport..*

This holiday park is ideally located on the edge of Prestwick with good access to all major roads; Ayr and Troon are within easy reach and Glasgow is just 45 minutes away. For golfers and spectators it is in an ideal location between Royal Troon and the Prestwick Gold Club. Grass pitches benefit from good drainage and a few hardstandings are available. The site offers its own bar and restaurant with live entertainment on certain weekends.

DUMFRIES & GALLOWAY

ANNAN — Map 21 NY16

Places to visit
Ruthwell Cross, RUTHWELL, 0131 668 8600
www.historicenvironment.scot/visit-a-place/places/ruthwell-cross/history

Great for kids: Caerlaverock Castle, CAERLAVEROCK, DG1 4RU, 01387 770244
www.historicenvironment.scot/visit-a-place/places/caerlaverock-castle

Galabank Caravan & Camping Group
QUALITY ASSESSED

tel: 01461 203539 & 07999 344520 **North Street DG12 5DQ**
email: margaret.ramage@hotmail.com
web: www.annan.org.uk/accommodation/caravan-parks.html
dir: *Site access via North Street.*

A tidy, well-maintained grassy little park with spotless facilities close to the centre of town but with pleasant rural views, and skirted by the River Annan.

Open: March to October **Last departure:** noon

Pitches: 🚐 🚍 ▲

Facilities: 🛁 ☉ 🚿 🍴

Services: 🔌

Within 3 miles: ⚓ 🛒 🎯 🎱 🛍

Additional site information: 1 acre site. 🐕 Cars can be parked by caravans and tents. Awnings permitted. No commercial vehicles. Social club adjacent, washing machine and tumble dryer in ladies' block.

DUMFRIES & GALLOWAY

BRIGHOUSE BAY Map 20 NX64

Places to visit

MacLellan's Castle, KIRKCUDBRIGHT, DG6 4JD, 01557 331856
www.historicenvironment.scot/visit-a-place/places/maclellan-s-castle

Broughton House & Garden, KIRKCUDBRIGHT, DG6 4JX, 01557 330437
www.nts.org.uk/visit/places/broughton-house

Premier Park

Brighouse Bay Holiday Park
★★★★★ 90%

tel: 01557 870267 **DG6 4TS**
email: info@gillespie-leisure.co.uk **web:** www.gillespie-leisure.co.uk
dir: *From Gatehouse of Fleet take A755 towards Kirkcudbright, onto B727 (signed Borgue). Or from Kirkcudbright take A755 onto B727. Site signed in 3 miles.*

Brighouse Bay is a top class site with a country park feel that enjoys a marvellous coastal setting adjacent to the beach with superb views. The pitches have been imaginatively sculpted into the meadowland, where stone walls and hedges blend in with the site's mature trees. These features, together with excellent toilet facilities and the range of leisure activities, make this an excellent park for families who enjoy an active holiday. The site has an 18-hole golf course. Many of the facilities are at an extra charge. Wooden pods and self-catering units are available for hire.

Open: All year **Last arrival:** 20.00 **Last departure:** 11.00
Pitches: 🚐 🚗 ⛺; 🏠 see prices below; 100 hardstanding pitches; 50 seasonal pitches
Leisure:
Facilities:
Services:
Within 3 miles:

Additional site information: 120 acre site. Cars can be parked by caravans and tents. Awnings permitted. No noise after 22.30, no jet skis, 10mph speed limit on site. No open fires or fire pits. Dogs must be kept on leads. Mini golf, jacuzzi and toddler pool, slipway, sea angling, pony trekking (seasonal), mountain bike trails, indoor swimming pool, gym, games room, café and bar/restaurant. Slipway.

Glamping available: Wooden pods from £47.

Additional glamping information: Wooden pods: own camping equipment required but kettle, microwave, fridge, heating, lighting and exterior picnic seating provided. Minimum stay 3 nights. Cars can be parked by units

DALBEATTIE Map 21 NX86

Places to visit

Threave Garden & Estate, CASTLE DOUGLAS, DG7 1RX, 01556 502575
www.nts.org.uk/visit/places/threave-garden

Orchardton Tower, PALNACKIE, 0131 668 8600
www.historicenvironment.scot/visit-a-place/places/orchardton-tower

Glenearly Caravan Park
★★★★ 87%

tel: 01556 611393 **DG5 4NE**
email: glenearlycaravan@btconnect.com **web:** www.glenearlycaravanpark.co.uk
dir: *From Dumfries take A711 towards Dalbeattie. Site entrance after Edingham Farm on right (200 yards before boundary sign).*

Glenearly Caravan Park is an excellent small park in an open countryside setting. The park is located in 84 acres of farmland which has been carefully managed over the years to provide a peaceful and secluded location for a tranquil holiday. The attention to detail is superb with neatly kept grass, well tended borders and an excellent amenity block. There's a lochan and woodland plus a wildlife walk. Dalbeattie is a leisurely 10-minute walk away along a pedestrian path and the local bus passes the end of the farm road. The beautiful Solway coast is just five minutes away by car with Rockcliffe, Colvend and Kippford interesting places to explore. For the more adventurous, the mountain bike trails are numerous.

Open: All year **Last arrival:** 19.00 **Last departure:** noon
Pitches: 🚐 🚗 ⛺; 33 hardstanding pitches; 10 seasonal pitches
Leisure:
Facilities:
Services:
Within 3 miles:

Additional site information: 10 acre site. Cars can be parked by caravans and tents. Awnings permitted. No commercial vehicles. Table tennis, pool table.

DUMFRIES & GALLOWAY SCOTLAND

ECCLEFECHAN Map 21 NY17

Places to visit

Robert Burns House, DUMFRIES, DG1 2PS, 01387 255297
www.dgculture.co.uk/venue/robert-burns-house

Old Bridge House Museum, DUMFRIES, DG2 7BE, 01387 256904
www.dgculture.co.uk/venue/old-bridge-house-museum

Great for kids: Dumfries Museum, DUMFRIES, DG2 7SW, 01387 253374
www.dgculture.co.uk/venue/dumfries-museum

Premier Park

Hoddom Castle Caravan Park
★★★★★ 85%

tel: 01576 300251 **Hoddom DG11 1AS**
email: enquiries@hoddomcastle.co.uk **web:** www.hoddomcastle.co.uk
dir: *M74 junction 19, B725 signed Ecclefechan. At next roundabout left onto B7076. Right at crossroads in Ecclefechan, follow site signs. Left at T-junction onto B723. Right onto B725 to site. Or from Annan on B721 take B723 signed Lockerbie and follow site signs.*

A lovely, peaceful family park located close to Annan, with its large range of shops and eateries. There are three amenity blocks, one is adjacent to the reception in part of the old castle buildings. There are extensive grounds, with many walks including the Annan Way which borders the River Annan. The park is neatly divided into statics, seasonal tourers and touring pitches with a large area for tents, plus seven attractive wooden 'chill' pods and four Kelo huts for hire. Fishing, a 9-hole golf course and a large children's play area are available; the small restaurant and bar are open daily.

Open: Easter or April to October **Last arrival:** 22.00 **Last departure:** 13.00
Pitches: see prices below; 63 hardstanding pitches; 94 seasonal pitches
Leisure:
Facilities:
Services:
Within 3 miles:

Additional site information: 28 acre site. Cars can be parked by caravans and tents. Awnings permitted. No electric scooters, no gazebos, no fires, no noise after midnight.
Glamping available: Wooden pods, Kelo huts from £50.
Additional glamping information: Dogs permitted in some pods and Kelo huts only. Cars can be parked by units

GATEHOUSE OF FLEET Map 20 NX55

Places to visit

MacLellan's Castle, KIRKCUDBRIGHT, DG6 4JD, 01557 331856
www.historicenvironment.scot/visit-a-place/places/maclellans-castle

Cairnsmore of Fleet National Nature Reserve, GATEHOUSE OF FLEET, DG7 2BP, 01557 814435
www.nature.scot/enjoying-outdoors/scotlands-national-nature-reserves/cairns-more-fleet-national-nature-reserve

Premier Park

Auchenlarie Holiday Park
★★★★★ 93% HOLIDAY PARK

Best of British

tel: 01556 506200 **DG7 2EX**
email: enquiries@auchenlarie.co.uk **web:** www.swalwellholidaygroup.co.uk
dir: *Direct access from A75, 5 miles west of Gatehouse of Fleet.*

A well-organised family park set on cliffs overlooking Wigtown Bay, with its own sandy beach. The tenting area, on sloping grassland surrounded by mature trees, has its own sanitary facilities, while the marked caravan pitches are in paddocks, with open views and the provision of high quality toilets. The leisure centre includes a swimming pool, gym, solarium and soft play area, plus there is also an entertainment suite with live cabaret acts. There are static caravans and cottages to rent.

Open: mid February to October **Last arrival:** 20:00 **Last departure:** 10:00 (statics) noon (touring)
Pitches: 82 hardstanding pitches
Leisure:
Facilities:
Services:
Within 3 miles:

Additional site information: 32 acre site. Outdoor MUGA pitch, multiple outdoor play areas, soft play, evening entertainment venue

See advert on page 272

GATEHOUSE OF FLEET *continued*

Anwoth Caravan Site
★★★★ 87%

tel: 01557 814333 & 01556 506200 **DG7 2JU**
email: anwoth@outlook.com web: www.swalwellholidaygroup.co.uk/anwoth
dir: *From A75 into Gatehouse of Fleet, site on right towards Stranraer. Signed from town centre.*

A very high quality park in a peaceful sheltered setting within easy walking distance of the village, ideally placed for exploring the scenic hills, valleys and coastline. Grass, hardstanding and fully serviced pitches are available and guests may use the leisure facilities at the sister site, Auchenlarie Holiday Park.

Open: March to October **Last arrival:** 20.00 **Last departure:** noon

Pitches: 14 hardstanding pitches

Facilities: WiFi

Services:

Within 3 miles:

Additional site information: 2 acre site. Cars can be parked by caravans and tents. Awnings permitted.

See advert below

Auchenlarie
HOLIDAY PARK

An award winning, 5 star rated holiday park on the beautiful Dumfries & Galloway coastline

Fantastic facilities including a swimming pool, sauna, gym, arcade, restaurant, takeaway, entertainment suite, bars and Premier store

Anwoth
HOLIDAY PARK

A peaceful and tranquil holiday park on the doorstep of Gatehouse of Fleet

The perfect base to explore the Galloway Forest and the surrounding towns of Kirkcudbright, Castle Douglas, Newton Stewart and more

Swalwell Holiday Group • Gatehouse of Fleet • Castle Douglas • DG7 2EX
www.swalwellholidaygroup.co.uk   Tel. 01556 506 200

DUMFRIES & GALLOWAY 273 SCOTLAND

GRETNA Map 21 NY36

Places to visit

Carlisle Cathedral, CARLISLE, CA3 8TZ, 01228 548151
www.carlislecathedral.org.uk

Tullie House Museum & Art Gallery Trust, CARLISLE, CA3 8TP, 01228 618718
www.tulliehouse.co.uk

Great for kids: Carlisle Castle, CARLISLE, CA3 8UR, 01228 591922
www.english-heritage.org.uk/visit/places/carlisle-castle

King Robert the Bruce's Cave Caravan & Camping Park
★★★★ 81%

tel: 01461 800285 & 07779 138694 **Cove Estate, Kirkpatrick Fleming DG11 3AT**
email: enquiries@brucescave.co.uk **web:** www.brucescave.co.uk
dir: Exit A74(M) junction 21, follow Kirkpatrick Fleming signs, north through village, pass Station Inn, left at Bruce's Court. Over rail crossing to site.

The lovely wooded grounds of an old castle and mansion are the setting for this pleasant park. The mature woodland is a haven for wildlife; there is a riverside walk to Robert the Bruce's Cave and on-site coarse fishing is available. A toilet block, with en suite facilities, is especially useful to families. The site is convenient for the A74(M) and there is a good local bus service available nearby; the site is on a National Cycle Route.

Open: April to November (restricted service: November – shop closed, water restrictions) **Last arrival:** 20.00 **Last departure:** 13.00

Pitches: 10 hardstanding pitches; 60 seasonal pitches

Leisure:

Facilities:

Services:

Additional site information: 80 acre site. Cars can be parked by caravans and tents. Awnings permitted. No noise after 23.00. Dogs must be kept on leads at all times. First aid available.

KIRKCUDBRIGHT Map 20 NX65

Places to visit

The Stewartry Museum, KIRKCUDBRIGHT, DG6 4AQ, 01557 331643
www.dgculture.co.uk/venue/the-stewartry-museum-kirkcudbright

Tolbooth Art Centre, KIRKCUDBRIGHT, DG6 4JL, 01557 331556
www.dgculture.co.uk/venue/tolbooth-arts-centre-kirkcudbright

Great for kids: Broughton House & Garden, KIRKCUDBRIGHT, DG6 4JX, 01557 330437
www.nts.org.uk/visit/places/broughton-house

Premier Park

Seaward Holiday Park
★★★★★ 86%

tel: 01557 870267 **Dhoon Bay DG6 4TJ**
email: info@gillespie-leisure.co.uk **web:** www.gillespie-leisure.co.uk
dir: A711 to Kirkcudbright. In Kirkcudbright right onto A755 signed Borgue and Gatehouse of Fleet. Left onto B727 signed Borgue. Through Borgue to The Dhoon, site on left.

An attractive park with outstanding views over Kirkcudbright Bay which forms part of the Dee Estuary. Access to a sandy cove with rock pools is just across the road. Facilities are well organised and neatly kept, and the park offers a very peaceful atmosphere. The leisure facilities at the other Gillespie Parks are available to visitors at Seaward Holiday Park. There are five static homes and two mini lodges for hire.

Open: March to October (restricted service: March to Spring Bank Holiday and September to October – swimming pool closed) **Last arrival:** 20.00 **Last departure:** 11.00

Pitches: see prices below; 20 hardstanding pitches; 6 seasonal pitches

Leisure:

Facilities:

Services:

Within 3 miles:

Additional site information: 23 acre site. Cars can be parked by caravans and tents. Awnings permitted. No noise after 22.00, 10mph speed limit on site. No open fires or fire pits. No children in play area after 21.30. Sea angling.

Glamping available: Mini lodges from £49.

Additional glamping information: Mini lodges: own camping equipment required. Minimum stay 2 nights. No pets allowed. Cars can be parked by units

Make your next UK holiday one to remember

Choose RatedTrips.com

AA

FACILITIES: Electric vehicle charging Baths/Shower Electric shaver sockets Hairdryer Ice pack facility Baby facilities Disabled facilities Shop on site or within 200yds BBQ area Picnic area WiFi Internet access **SERVICES:** Electric hook-up Launderette Licensed bar Calor Gas Campingaz Toilet fluid Café/Restaurant Fast Food/Takeaway Battery charging Motorhome service point No credit or debit cards Dogs permitted No dogs

SCOTLAND — 274 — DUMFRIES & GALLOWAY

MOFFAT
Map 21 NT00

Places to visit

Moffat Museum, Harthope House, Churchgate, MOFFAT, DG10 9EG, 01683 220868
www.moffatmuseum.co.uk

Moffat Community Nature Reserve, MOFFAT DG10 9SF, 01683 220227
www.visitmoffat.co.uk/explore-moffat/moffat-community-nature-reserve

Moffat Manor Holiday Park
★★★★ 81%

tel: 01683 300313 Beattock **DG10 9RE**
email: zara.rowbotham@awayresorts.co.uk
web: www.awayresorts.co.uk/parks/scotland/moffat-manor
dir: *A74(M) junction 15, follow Dumfries, Beattock, Moffat signs. At roundabout follow Beattock signs. Through Beattock, under railway bridge, site entrance straight ahead.*

Moffat Manor Holiday Park is located just a few minutes' drive from the A74(M) but is in such a peaceful location that it is an ideal stopover for travellers heading north or south. The team are warm and welcoming, and there is a small shop for those essential items. The bar is popular and serves lite bites and snacks. A well-presented children's playground with a small zip wire, and a small loch for fishing are available. Further investment is planned for 2025.

Open: All year **Last arrival:** 22.00 **Last departure:** 12.00

Additional site information: 80 acre site.

PALNACKIE
Map 21 NX85

Places to visit

Orchardton Tower, PALNACKIE, 0131 668 8600
www.historicenvironment.scot/visit-a-place/places/orchardton-tower

Threave Garden & Estate, CASTLE DOUGLAS, DG7 1RX, 01556 502575
www.nts.org.uk/visit/places/threave-garden

Kippford View Holiday Park
★★★★ 86%

tel: 01557 870267 **DG7 1PF**
email: info@gillespie-leisure.co.uk web: www.gillespie-leisure.co.uk
dir: *On A711 (Dalbeattie to Auchencairn road). Site signed before Palnackie.*

Kippford View Holiday Park is a lovely caravan site situated within a short drive of the county town of Dalbeattie. It is ideally situated for exploring this particularly attractive area. Excellent investment over recent years has seen very good results. The site has a number of static homes set on level terraces, with mature planting, whilst the caravan and camping pitches are located on the lower area, near the outdoor heated pool. There are hardstanding pitches, grass pitches with electricity for tents and wooden pods.

Open: April to October (restricted service: April to Spring Bank Holiday and September to October – swimming pool closed) **Last arrival:** 20.00 **Last departure:** 11.30

Pitches: 16 hardstanding pitches; 2 seasonal pitches

Leisure:
Facilities: WiFi
Services:
Within 3 miles:

Additional site information: 9 acre site. Cars can be parked by caravans and tents. Awnings permitted. No noise after 23.00. Family games and TV room.

Glamping available: 2 wooden pods.

Additional glamping information: Cars can be parked by units

Make your next UK holiday one to remember

Choose RatedTrips.com

AA

PITCHES: Caravans Motorhomes Tents Glamping accommodation LEISURE: Indoor swimming pool Outdoor swimming pool Children's playground Kids' club Tennis court Games room Separate TV room golf course Pitch n putt Boats for hire Bikes for hire Cinema Entertainment Fishing Mini golf Watersports Gym Sports field Stables Spa

DUMFRIES & GALLOWAY 275 SCOTLAND

PORT WILLIAM
Map 20 NX34

Places to visit

Glenluce Abbey, GLENLUCE, DG8 0AF, 01581 300541
www.historicenvironment.scot/visit-a-place/places/glenluce-abbey

Whithorn Priory and Museum, WHITHORN, DG8 8PY, 01988 500700
www.historicenvironment.scot/visit-a-place/places/whithorn-priory-and-museum

Kings Green Caravan Site
★★★ 81%

tel: 01988 700489 & 700738 **South Street DG8 9SG**
email: kingsgreencaravanpark@gmail.com web: www.kingsgreencaravanpark.com
dir: *Direct access from A747 at junction with B7085 towards Whithorn.*

Located on the edge of Port William, with beautiful views across Luce Bay as far as the Isle of Man, this is a community run site which offers good facilities and large grass pitches, with direct access to the pebble shore where otters have been seen. The road which runs along the coast is relatively traffic free so does not detract from the tranquillity of this small site. Two public boat launches are available. There are several good shops in the village, and a local bus, with links to Whithorn, Garlieston and Newton Stewart, runs past the site.

Open: mid March to October **Last arrival:** 20.00 **Last departure:** noon

Pitches:

Facilities:

Services:

Within 3 miles:

Additional site information: 3 acre site. Cars can be parked by caravans and tents. Awnings permitted. No golf, no fireworks. Free book lending.

SANDHEAD
Map 20 NX04

Places to visit

Glenwhan Gardens, STRANRAER, DG9 8PH, 01581 400222
www.glenwhangardens.co.uk

Great for kids: Castle Kennedy Gardens, STRANRAER, DG9 8SL, 01776 702024
www.castlekennedygardens.com

Sands of Luce Holiday Park
★★★★ 93%

tel: 01776 830456 **Sands of Luce DG9 9JR**
email: info@sandsofluce.com web: www.sandsoflucholidaypark.co.uk
dir: *From south and east: left from A75 onto B7084 signed Drummore. Site signed at junction with A716. From north: A77 through Stranraer towards Portpatrick, 2 miles, follow A716 signed Drummore, site signed in 5 miles.*

This is a large, well-managed holiday park overlooking Luce Bay. It has a private boat launch and direct access to a wide sandy beach, which proves popular with kite surfers. The Lighthouse is a truly upmarket café, bar and pizzeria and The Barn leisure complex is an excellent facility at the park. Attached to The Lighthouse is the reception, and the staff at the bar can also handle arrivals and other enquiries; this arrangement significantly extends the checking in times. A wide range of entertainment, listed on daily planners, is on offer and includes kite flying, kite surfing, foraging and cooking, and entertainers for both adults and children. There is a regular bus that passes the park entrance, and Stranraer, the Mull of Galloway or Port Logan Botanical Gardens are not far away by car.

Open: March to January (restricted service: November to January – toilet block and shower closed) **Last arrival:** 20.00 **Last departure:** noon

Pitches: ; 20 hardstanding pitches

Leisure:

Facilities:

Services:

Within 3 miles:

Additional site information: 75 acre site. Cars can be parked by caravans and tents. Awnings permitted. No quad bikes. Owners must clear up after their dogs. Boat launching and storage. Indoor play area.

SANDYHILLS
Map 21 NX85

Places to visit

Threave Garden & Estate, CASTLE DOUGLAS, DG7 1RX, 01556 502575
www.nts.org.uk/visit/places/threave-garden

Orchardton Tower, PALNACKIE, 0131 668 8600
www.historicenvironment.scot/visit-a-place/places/orchardton-tower

Great for kids: Threave Castle, CASTLE DOUGLAS, DG7 1TJ, 07711 223101
www.historicenvironment.scot/visit-a-place/places/threave-castle

Sandyhills Bay Holiday Park
★★★★ 80%

tel: 01557 870267 **DG5 4NY**
email: info@gillespie-leisure.co.uk web: www.gillespie-leisure.co.uk
dir: *On A710, 7 miles from Dalbeattie, 6.5 miles from Kirkbean.*

A well maintained park in a superb location beside a beach, and close to many attractive villages. The level, grassy site is sheltered by woodland, and the south-facing Sandyhills Bay and beach, with their caves and rock pools, provide endless entertainment for all the family. The leisure facilities at Brighouse Bay are available to visitors to Sandyhills Bay. Two wooden pods and two wooden wigwams are on offer too.

Open: April to October **Last arrival:** 20.00 **Last departure:** 11.30

Pitches: ; see prices below; 9 hardstanding pitches

Leisure:

Facilities:

Services:

Within 3 miles:

Additional site information: 15 acre site. Cars can be parked by caravans and tents. Awnings permitted. No motorised scooters, jet skis or own quad bikes.

Glamping available: Wooden pods from £47; wooden wigwams from £45.

Additional glamping information: Wooden pods and wooden wigwams offer kettle, microwave, fridge with freezer compartment, toaster. Wooden wigwams also offer TV and are dog friendly (£3 a night). Cars can be parked by units

---

FACILITIES: Electric vehicle charging Baths/Shower Electric shaver sockets Hairdryer Ice pack facility Baby facilities Disabled facilities Shop on site or within 200yds BBQ area Picnic area WiFi Internet access **SERVICES:** Electric hook-up Launderette Licensed bar Calor Gas Campingaz Toilet fluid Café/Restaurant Fast Food/Takeaway Battery charging Motorhome service point No credit or debit cards Dogs permitted No dogs

STRANRAER
Map 20 NX06

Places to visit
Glenwhan Gardens, STRANRAER, DG9 8PH, 01581 400222
www.glenwhangardens.co.uk

Great for kids: Castle Kennedy Gardens, STRANRAER, DG9 8SL, 01776 702024
www.castlekennedygardens.com

Aird Donald Caravan Park
★★★★ 87%

tel: 01776 702025 London Road DG9 8RN
email: enquiries@aird-donald.co.uk web: www.aird-donald.co.uk
dir: *From A75 left on entering Stranraer (signed). Opposite school, site 300 yards.*

Aird Donald Caravan Park is a spacious touring site set behind mature trees and within a five-minute walk of Stranraer town centre at the head of Loch Ryan. It is an ideal base to tour the 'Rhins of Galloway', to visit Port Logan Botanic Gardens (half an hour's drive) or the Mull of Galloway Lighthouse (a 45-minute drive). It provides a very convenient stopover for the Cairnryan ferry to Ireland, but there's plenty to do in the area if staying longer. A 25-pitch rally field is available. There are also two well presented camping pods (camping barrels) for hire.

Open: All year (restricted service: October to March – tents not accepted. Laundry unavailable. Camping barrels unavailable.) **Last arrival:** 22.30 **Last departure:** 11.00

Pitches: from £23; from £20; from £10; 24 hardstanding pitches

Leisure:
Facilities:
Services:

Within 3 miles:

Additional site information: 12 acre site. Cars can be parked by caravans and tents. Awnings permitted. Transit or similar sized commercial vans, tippers or any class of commercial vehicles are not accepted. Covered cooking area for tents.

Glamping available: Camping barrels. Own bedding and cooking equipment required
Changeover days: Any day

Additional glamping information: Small Barrel – 2 adults, 2 children (maximum height 1.3 metres). Double bed, seating converts to 2 singles. Large Barrel – up to 5 average sized adults. No pets. Cars can be parked by units

Ryan Bay Caravan Park
★★★ 84%

tel: 01776 889458 Innermessan DG9 8QP
email: ryanbay@hagansleisure.co.uk
web: www.hagansleisure.co.uk/holidays/ryan-bay-holiday-residential-park-sw-scotland
dir: *Innermessan on A77, 2 miles north of Stranraer.*

Ryan Bay Caravan Park occupies an enviable position on the shores of Ryan Bay, within easy reach of Stranraer and the ferry terminal at Cairnryan for a day trip to Northern Ireland. It is also perfectly located for walking, fishing, watersports and exploring the scenic Dumfries & Galloway coast. Some premium pitches and static caravans are set beside the loch, making the most of the watery views, and this well-established park is popular with families, offering good children's facilities. Ryan Bay has an array of animals on the park including alpacas, pygmy goats, and a donkey.

Open: 1 March to 31 October **Last arrival:** 20.00 **Last departure:** 10.00

Pitches: ; 25 hardstanding pitches; 15 seasonal pitches

Leisure:
Facilities:
Services:
Within 3 miles:

Additional site information: 11 acre site. Cars can be parked by caravans and tents. Awnings permitted. Dogs must be kept on leads at all times. No noise after 22.00. 10mph speed limit

DUMFRIES & GALLOWAY—FIFE

WIGTOWN
Map 20 NX45

Places to visit

Whithorn Priory and Museum, WHITHORN, DG8 8PY, 01988 500700
www.historicenvironment.scot/visit-a-place/places/whithorn-priory-and-museum

Drumroamin Farm Camping & Touring Site
★★★ 91%

tel: 01988 840613 **1 South Balfern, Kirkinner DG8 9DB**
email: enquiry@drumroamin.co.uk web: www.drumroamin.co.uk
dir: *A75 towards Newton Stewart, onto A714 for Wigtown. Left on B7005 through Bladnock, A746 through Kirkinner. Take B7004 signed Garlieston, 2nd left opposite Kilsture Forest, site 0.75 mile at end of lane.*

Located near Wigtown and Newton Stewart, this is an easily accessible site for those wishing to stay in a rural location; it is an open and spacious site overlooking Wigtown Bay and the Galloway Hills. There is a large and separate tent field with a well-equipped day room, while the touring pitches can easily accommodate rally events. The toilets and other facilities are maintained in an exemplary manner. The sheltered camp kitchen proves very popular, especially in adverse weather; a drive-through motorhome service point is also available. The RSPB Crook of Baldoon reserve is a 10-minute walk away. There is a good bus service at the top of the road which goes to Newton Stewart, Wigtown and Whithorn.

Open: 1 April to 31 October **Last arrival:** 21.00 **Last departure:** noon (caravans 9.30)

Pitches:
Leisure:
Facilities:
Services:
Within 3 miles:

Additional site information: 5 acre site. Cars can be parked by caravans and tents. Awnings permitted. No camp fires, no noise after 22.00. Dogs must be kept on leads at all times. Ball games area. Sitting room with TV. Play park.

FIFE

ST ANDREWS
Map 21 NO51

Places to visit

St Andrews Castle, ST ANDREWS, KY16 9AR, 01334 477196
www.historicenvironment.scot/visit-a-place/places/st-andrews-castle

R&A World Golf Museum, ST ANDREWS, KY16 9AB, 01334 460046
www.worldgolfmuseum.com

Great for kids: St Andrews Aquarium, ST ANDREWS, KY16 9AS, 01334 474786
www.standrewsaquarium.co.uk

Platinum Park

Cairnsmill Holiday Park
★★★★★

tel: 01334 473604 **Largo Road KY16 8NN**
email: cairnsmill@aol.com web: www.cairnsmill.co.uk
dir: *A915 from St Andrews towards Lathones. In approximately 2 miles site on right.*

Hidden behind mature trees and hedging in open countryside on the outskirts of the historic university town of St Andrews, this top quality holiday park is ideally placed for visiting the nearby town and to explore further afield in Fife or across the Tay Bridge to the city of Dundee and beyond. The facilities on offer at this park are simply excellent and include a swimming pool complex, bar and café, games room and a soft play area, in addition to the various play areas located throughout the park. There is a small fishing lochan with a walkway leading towards the town and the botanical gardens. The toilet facilities are first class with two blocks for the touring area and a separate block for the tent field. The six rooms in a bunkhouse means that extended family and friends can holiday together. The local bus service stops at the park entrance.

Open: All year (restricted service: winter – prior bookings only) **Last arrival:** flexible **Last departure:** 11.00

Pitches: ; see prices below; 33 hardstanding pitches; 24 seasonal pitches
Leisure:
Facilities:
Services:
Within 3 miles:

Additional site information: 27 acre site. Cars can be parked by caravans and tents. Awnings permitted. No noise after midnight. 1 car per pitch. Electric car hire (seasonal). Car hire can be arranged.

Glamping available: 2 wooden pods from £40. **Changeover days:** Any day

Additional glamping information: Wooden pods (sleep 4) offer fridge, TV, microwave, toaster and kettle.

ST ANDREWS continued

Platinum Park

Craigtoun Meadows Holiday Park
★★★★★

tel: 01334 475959 **Mount Melville KY16 8PQ**
email: info@craigtounmeadows.co.uk **web:** www.craigtounmeadows.co.uk
dir: M90 junction 8, A91 to St Andrews. Just after Guardbridge right for Strathkinness. At 2nd crossroads left for Craigtoun.

Craigtoun Meadows is only a short drive from the centre of St Andrews which has numerous tourist attractions, from historic buildings and harbour aquarium to the wide, sandy beach where the famous scene from *Chariots of Fire* was filmed. The site is set in part of the Craigtoun Estate and the holiday homes and touring area are separated by mature woodland and shrubs — deer and red squirrels can be seen regularly in the neatly kept grounds. The generously sized, fully serviced pitches are very well spaced apart. In addition, the site offers four wooden pods called 'Little Lodges' that are located in a pretty setting. The centrally positioned amenity block provides private facilities including spacious showers and baths. St Andrews is 'the home of golf' so the numerous courses in the area prove a challenge for any golfer.

Craigtoun Meadows Holiday Park

Open: March to October (restricted service: March to Easter and September to October — shop closed, reduced opening hours at restaurant) **Last arrival:** 21.00 **Last departure:** 11.00

Pitches: see prices below; 56 hardstanding pitches; 12 seasonal pitches

Leisure:

Facilities: WiFi

Services:

Within 3 miles:

Additional site information: 32 acre site. Cars can be parked by caravans and tents. Awnings permitted. No groups of unaccompanied minors. No pets. Mini Golf, putting green, zip wire, all-weather football pitch

Glamping available: Little Lodges from £70. **Changeover days:** Any day

Additional glamping information: Little Lodges: stays from 1 night to 2 weeks. Fridge, freezer, microwave, kettle, toaster and TV provided. Bring own bedding and cutlery. Amenity building within 50 metres. Cars can be parked by units

See advert below

St Andrews, Fife KY16 8PQ • **Tel:** 01334475959
Web: craigtounmeadows.co.uk
Email: info@craigtounmeadows.co.uk

Craigtoun Meadows Holiday Park is a multi award winning park, 1 and a half miles from the centre of St Andrews which has numerous tourist attractions, from historic buildings, aquarium, castle and the wide, sandy beach where the running scene from the movie *Chariots of Fire* was filmed. The site is located next to the *Dukes Golf Course* and *Craigtoun Country Park* with its boating pond and many attractions for children. Our holiday homes, lodges, Little Lodges and touring area are separated by mature woodland and shrubs.

The grounds are very well maintained and a large area of woodland has been set aside as a natural habitat for wildlife, with deer, rabbits and squirrels being seen regularly. The well maintained amenity block is centrally located and provides private facilities, including spacious showers and baths. The pitches are very large, fully serviced and are exceptionally well spaced. Four wooden glamping pods, known as Little Lodges are a recent popular addition to the Touring area. St Andrews is 'the home of golf' so the numerous courses in the area are a challenge.

PITCHES: Caravans — Motorhomes — Tents — Glamping accommodation   **LEISURE:** Indoor swimming pool — Outdoor swimming pool — Children's playground — Kids' club — Tennis court — Games room — Separate TV room — golf course — Pitch n putt — Boats for hire — Bikes for hire — Cinema — Entertainment — Fishing — Mini golf — Watersports — Gym — Sports field — Stables — Spa

HIGHLAND

DUROR
Map 23 NM95

Places to visit
Glencoe Folk Museum, GLENCOE, PH49 4HS, 01855 811664
www.glencoemuseum.com

Achindarroch Touring Park
★★★ 85%

tel: 01631 740329 **Achindarroch Touring Park PA38 4BS**
email: stay@achindarrochtp.co.uk **web:** www.achindarrochtp.co.uk
dir: *A82 onto A828 at Ballachulish Bridge then towards Oban for 5.2 miles. In Duror, site on left, signed.*

Achindarroch Touring Park is a long-established, well-laid out park which continues to be maintained to a high standard by an enthusiastic and friendly family team. There is a well-appointed, heated toilet block and spacious all-weather pitches plus wooden camping pods for hire. The park is ideal for visits to Oban, Fort William and Glencoe and there is a wide variety of outdoor sports available in the area. There is a modern, luxury lodge for rental.

Open: 24 January to 16 January **Last arrival:** 19:00 **Last departure:** 11.00
Pitches: see prices below; 21 hardstanding pitches; 10 seasonal pitches
Facilities:
Services:
Within 3 miles:

Additional site information: 5 acre site. Cars can be parked by caravans and tents. Awnings permitted. See website for camp rules and regulations. Campers' kitchen with fridge, freezer, kettle, microwave.

Glamping available: Wooden pods from £40.

FORT WILLIAM
Map 22 NN17

Places to visit
West Highland Museum, FORT WILLIAM, PH33 6AJ, 01397 702169
www.westhighlandmuseum.org.uk

Ariundle Oakwood National Nature Reserve, FORT WILLIAM, PH33 6SW, 01397 704716
www.nature.scot/enjoying-outdoors/scotlands-national-nature-reserves/ariundle-oakwood-national-nature-reserve

FORT WILLIAM
Map 22 NN17

Glen Nevis Caravan & Camping Park
★★★★ 92%

tel: 01397 702191 **Glen Nevis PH33 6SX**
email: holidays@glen-nevis.co.uk **web:** www.glen-nevis.co.uk
dir: *From A82 (northern outskirts of Fort William) follow Glen Nevis signs at mini-roundabout. Site 2.5 miles on right.*

This is a large and very well maintained park, situated in Glen Nevis with easy access to the main footpath leading to Ben Nevis. Located a few miles from Fort William, the park is near Neptune's Staircase on the Caledonian Canal and the Great Glen. The site is divided into areas by beech hedges to give a sense of seclusion for caravan and motorhome users who have their own amenity blocks; tent campers have their own specific areas and large well-kept amenity blocks. To cater for those who are seeking a glamping experience, five luxury, wooden camping pods are offered – all have unrivalled views towards Ben Nevis. The park has a restaurant and café.

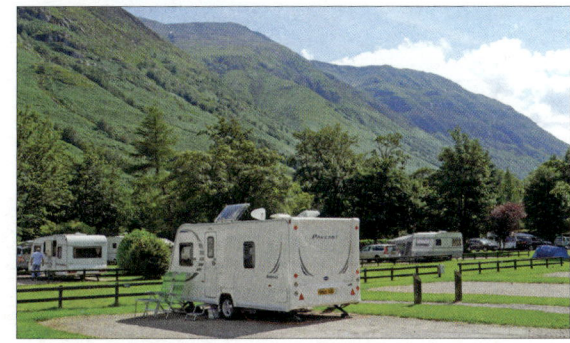

Open: 15 March to October (restricted service: March and October – limited restaurant facilities) **Last arrival:** 22.00 **Last departure:** noon
Pitches: see prices below; 150 hardstanding pitches
Leisure: **Facilities:**
Services: Within 3 miles:

Additional site information: 30 acre site. Cars can be parked by caravans and tents. Awnings permitted. Quiet from 23.00–08.00.

Glamping available: Wooden pods from £60.

Additional glamping information: Wooden pods: dogs by prior arrangement only. Cars can be parked by units

SCOTLAND — HIGHLAND–SOUTH LANARKSHIRE

GLENCOE Map 22 NN15

Places to visit
Glencoe Folk Museum, GLENCOE, PH49 4HS, 01855 811664
www.glencoemuseum.com

Invercoe Caravan & Camping Park
★★★★ 90%

tel: 01855 811210 **PH49 4HP**
email: holidays@invercoe.co.uk **web:** www.invercoe.co.uk
dir: *Exit A82 at Glencoe Hotel onto B863 for 0.25 mile.*

A level grass site set on the shore of Loch Leven, with excellent mountain views. The area is ideal for both walking and climbing, and also offers a choice of several freshwater and saltwater lochs. Convenient for the good shopping opportunities to be found in Fort William. There are a number of 'micro lodge' wooden pods for hire.

Open: All year **Last departure:** noon
Pitches:
Facilities:
Services:
Within 3 miles:

Additional site information: 5 acre site. Cars can be parked by caravans and tents. Awnings permitted. No large group bookings.

Glamping available: Wooden pods.

Additional glamping information: Cars can be parked by units

ULLAPOOL Map 22 NH19

Places to visit
Corrieshalloch Gorge National Nature Reserve, BRAEMORE, IV23 2PJ, 01445 781200
www.nts.org.uk/visit/places/corrieshalloch-gorge

Broomfield Holiday Park
★★★ 85%

tel: 01854 612020 **West Lane IV26 2UT**
email: sross@broomfieldhp.com **web:** www.broomfieldhp.com
dir: *Into Ullapool on A835, 1st right 1st left after harbour.*

Broomfield Holiday Park is set right on the water's edge of Loch Broom and the open sea, with lovely views of the Summer Isles. This clean, well maintained and managed park is close to the harbour and town centre with restaurants, bars and shops. The Ullapool ferry allows easy access to the Hebridean islands for day trips or longer visits.

Open: Easter or April to end September **Last arrival:** 19.30 **Last departure:** noon
Pitches: ; 102 hardstanding pitches
Leisure:
Facilities:
Services:
Within 3 miles:

Additional site information: 11 acre site. Cars can be parked by caravans and tents. Awnings permitted. No noise on the site from 10.00. Dogs must be on a leads at all times.

SOUTH LANARKSHIRE

ABINGTON Map 21 NS92

Places to visit
Museum of Lead Mining, WANLOCKHEAD, ML12 6UT, 01659 74387
www.leadminingmuseum.co.uk

Mount View Caravan Park
★★★ 84%

tel: 01864 502808 **ML12 6RW**
email: info@mountviewcaravanpark.co.uk
web: www.borderleisureparks.co.uk/mount-view
dir: *M74 junction 13, A702 south into Abington. Left into Station Road, over river and railway. Site on right.*

A delightfully maturing family park, surrounded by the Southern Uplands and handily located between Carlisle and Glasgow. It is an excellent stopover site for those travelling between Scotland and the south, and the West Coast Railway passes beside the park. Two pods are available for hire.

Open: March to October **Last arrival:** 20.45 **Last departure:** 11.30
Pitches: ; 42 hardstanding pitches; 18 seasonal pitches
Leisure:
Facilities:
Services:
Within 3 miles:

Additional site information: 5.5 acre site. Cars can be parked by caravans and tents. Awnings permitted. 5mph speed limit. Dogs must be exercised off site. Emergency phone.

Glamping available: 2 wooden pods

Additional glamping information: 2- and 4- berth pods. Own bedding and towels required.

PITCHES: Caravans Motorhomes Tents Glamping accommodation **LEISURE:** Indoor swimming pool Outdoor swimming pool Children's playground Kids' club Tennis court Games room Separate TV room golf course Pitch n putt Boats for hire Bikes for hire Cinema Entertainment Fishing Mini golf Watersports Gym Sports field Stables Spa

EAST LOTHIAN

DUNBAR — Map 21 NT67

Places to visit
Preston Mill & Phantassie Doocot, EAST LINTON, EH40 3DS, 01620 860426
www.nts.org.uk/visit/places/preston-mill

Great for kids: Tantallon Castle, NORTH BERWICK, EH39 5PN, 01620 892727
www.historicenvironment.scot/visit-a-place/places/tantallon-castle

Premier Park

Thurston Manor Leisure Park
★★★★★ 88%

tel: 01368 840643 **Innerwick EH42 1SA**
email: holidays@verdantleisure.co.uk **web:** www.thurstonmanor.co.uk
dir: 4 miles south of Dunbar, follow site signs from A1.

A pleasant park set in 250 acres of unspoilt countryside. The touring (no tents) and static areas of this large park are in separate areas. The main touring area occupies an open, level position, and the toilet facilities are modern and exceptionally well maintained. The park boasts a well-stocked fishing loch, a heated indoor swimming pool, steam room, sauna, jacuzzi, mini-gym and fitness room plus seasonal entertainment. There is a superb family toilet block. Fly fishing is available.

Open: 15 February to January **Last arrival:** 23.00 **Last departure:** 10.00
Pitches: 68 hardstanding pitches; 60 seasonal pitches
Leisure:
Facilities:
Services:

Additional site information: 175 acre site. Cars can be parked by caravans. Awnings permitted. Quiet after 23.00.

Belhaven Bay Caravan & Camping Park
★★★★ 91%

tel: 01368 865956 **Belhaven Bay EH42 1TU**
email: belhaven@meadowhead.co.uk **web:** www.meadowhead.co.uk
dir: A1 onto A1087 towards Dunbar. 1 mile to site in John Muir Park.

Belhaven Bay Caravan and Camping Park is located on the outskirts of Dunbar, this is a sheltered park within walking distance of the beach. There is a regular bus service to Dunbar where there is an East Coast Main Line railway station. The site is also convenient for the A1 and well placed for visiting the area's many seaside towns and various visitor attractions. There is a large children's play area. Six static caravans and three wooden wigwam pods are available for hire. This park is ideally located for the East Links Family Park, or if you like your fun in the water there's Foxlake Adventures.

Open: March to October **Last arrival:** 20.00 **Last departure:** noon
Pitches: 11 hardstanding pitches
Leisure: **Facilities:**
Services: **Within 3 miles:**

Additional site information: 40 acre site. Cars can be parked by caravans and tents. Awnings permitted. No rollerblades or skateboards, no open fires, no noise 23.00–07.00.
Glamping available: Wooden wigwams.

LONGNIDDRY — Map 21 NT47

Places to visit
Prestongrange Museum, PRESTONPANS, EH32 9RX, 0131 653 2904
www.eastlothian.gov.uk/info/210593/museums/11878/museums_in_east_lothian/4

Great for kids: Myreton Motor Museum, ABERLADY, EH32 0PZ, 07585 356931
www.myretonmotormuseum.co.uk

Premier Park

Seton Sands Holiday Village
★★★★★ 87% HOLIDAY PARK

tel: 01875 813333 **EH32 0QF**
email: setonsands@haven.com **web:** www.haven.com/parks/scotland/seton-sands
dir: A1 to A198 exit, take B6371 to Cockenzie. Right onto B1348. Site 1 mile on right.

Seton Sands is a well-equipped holiday park facing onto the Firth of Forth with mature landscaping. A dedicated entertainment team offers plenty of organised activities for children and there are pleasant bars, a show bar and a modern restaurant. It offers good sports and leisure facilities, including a multi-sports court, swimming pool, 9-hole golf course and a variety of play areas, so there's always plenty to do without leaving the park. The touring area offers fully-serviced pitches set in lovely landscaping with a dedicated on-site warden. There is a regular bus from the site entrance, which makes day trips to Edinburgh easy. 150 holiday homes are available for hire. Please note, this site does not accept tents.

Open: mid March to end October (restricted service: mid March to May and September to end October – facilities may be reduced) **Last arrival:** 22.00 **Last departure:** 10.00
Pitches: 40 hardstanding pitches
Leisure:
Facilities:
Services:
Within 3 miles:

Additional site information: 1.75 acre site. No commercial vehicles, no bookings by persons under 21 years unless a family booking. Maximum 2 dogs per booking, certain dog breeds banned.

WEST LOTHIAN

LINLITHGOW
Map 21 NS97

Places to visit

Linlithgow Palace, LINLITHGOW, EH49 7AL, 01506 842896
www.historicenvironment.scot/visit-a-place/places/linlithgow-palace

House of The Binns, LINLITHGOW, EH49 7NA, 01506 830175
www.nts.org.uk/visit/places/house-of-binns

Great for kids: Blackness Castle, LINLITHGOW, EH49 7NH, 01506 834807
www.historicenvironment.scot/visit-a-place/places/blackness-castle

Beecraigs Caravan & Camping Site
★★★★ 92%

tel: 01506 284516 & 284510 Beecraigs Country Park EH49 6PL
email: mail@beecraigs.com **web:** www.westlothian.gov.uk/stay-at-beecraigs
dir: M9 junction 3 (from east) or junction 4 (from west), A803 to Linlithgow. From A803 into Preston Road signed Beecraigs Country Park. Reception in visitor centre. (Note: Preston Road route is steep and winding).

Located on the hills above the town of Linlithgow with unrivalled views towards the Forth Bridges, Beecraigs Country Park has an excellent caravan and camping site, with two modern washrooms, large hardstanding pitches and a secluded tenting area, as well as two little lodges, sleeping 6 and 4 people, and cabins. There are extensive walks and cycle trails, a very large play area for children, a visitor centre, shop and café at the site entrance, and there are good road and train links nearby; the park is in an excellent location for exploring central Scotland, Edinburgh and Glasgow. For those who wish something simpler, boat trips are available from the local canal centre.

Open: All year (restricted service: 25 to 26 December and 1 to 2 January – no new arrivals) **Last arrival:** 22.00 **Last departure:** noon for caravans & tents, 10.00 for little lodges
Pitches: 23 hardstanding pitches
Leisure: **Facilities:**
Services: Within 3 miles:
Additional site information: 6 acre site. Cars can be parked by caravans. Awnings permitted. Site standards apply. Country Park facilities. WiFi available in and close to visitor centre. PC in visitor centre. Glass and general recycling
Glamping available: Cabins (Little Lodges)
Additional glamping information: Little Lodges sleep 4 or 6. Maximum 1 dog per unit. Use of shower block on site. Cars can be parked by units

PERTH & KINROSS

BLAIR ATHOLL
Map 23 NN86

Places to visit

Blair Castle & Gardens, BLAIR ATHOLL, PH18 5TL, 01796 481207
www.atholl-estates.co.uk/blair-castle

Killiecrankie, KILLIECRANKIE, PH16 5LQ, 01796 473233
www.nts.org.uk/visit/places/killiecrankie

Premier Park

Blair Castle Caravan Park
★★★★★ 92%

tel: 01796 481263 PH18 5SR
email: mail@blaircastlecaravanpark.co.uk
web: www.atholl-estates.co.uk/stay-with-us/caravan-park
dir: From A9 onto B8079 at Aldclune, follow to Blair Atholl. Site on right after crossing bridge in village.

An attractive site set in impressive seclusion within the Atholl Estate, surrounded by mature woodland and the River Tilt. Although a large park, the various groups of pitches are located throughout the extensive grounds, and each has its own sanitary block with all-cubicled facilities of a very high standard. There is a choice of grass pitches, hardstandings and fully serviced pitches. This park is particularly suitable for the larger type of motorhome. There are 13 wooden pods that each sleep two adults and two children.

Open: March to November **Last arrival:** 21.30 **Last departure:** noon
Pitches: see prices below; 184 hardstanding pitches; 67 seasonal pitches
Leisure:
Facilities:
Services:
Within 3 miles:
Additional site information: 9 acre site. Cars can be parked by caravans and tents. Awnings permitted. Family park, no noise after 23.00.
Glamping available: 10 wooden pods £35 (sleep 2 adults and 2 children).
Changeover days: Any day

PERTH & KINROSS 283 SCOTLAND

COMRIE
Map 21 NN72

Places to visit

Caithness Glass Visitor Centre, CRIEFF, PH7 4HQ, 01764 654014
www.caithnessglass.co.uk/visit-caithness-glass

Drummond Castle Gardens, MUTHILL, PH7 4HN, 01764 681433
www.drummondcastlegardens.co.uk

Twenty Shilling Wood Caravan Park
★★★ 83%

tel: 01764 670411 & 07502 298438 **A85 PH6 2JY**
email: info@twentyshillingwoodholidaypark.co.uk
web: www.twentyshillingwoodcaravanpark.co.uk
dir: *On A85, 0.5 mile west of Comrie towards St Fillans. Site opposite Tullybannocher Café.*

Situated on the outskirts of Comrie, this is a tranquil and mature site that offers terraced pitches in a well-maintained woodland setting which screens the site from the road. The facilities are clean and well maintained and the family owners are very helpful. It is ideally located for exploring the Perthshire countryside – there are stunning drives to beautiful lochs and charming rural villages such as Comrie, which is a short walk away. There is also a holiday home for hire. There are various hiking and cycling trails, for all levels of ability, that can be accessed from the site. Please note, tents are not accepted.

Open: 18 March to 20 October **Last arrival:** 21.00 **Last departure:** 18.00
Pitches: 🚐 🚗; 14 hardstanding pitches; 32 seasonal pitches
Leisure: /🅰\ 🔍
Facilities: 🏠 ☺ ℉ ✳ 🍽 WiFi
Services: 🔌 🗑 🧺 ⬇ 🔒 🗑
Within 3 miles: ⚓ ✏ 🛒

Additional site information: 10.5 acre site. 🚗 Cars can be parked by caravans. Awnings permitted. Booking advisable at all times. No noise after 23.00. Maximum of 2 dogs per pitch. Speed limit 10mph. Woodland walk. Kids' play park.

DUNKELD
Map 21 NO04

Places to visit

DUNKELD, PH8 0AN
www.nts.org.uk/visit/places/dunkeld

Loch of the Lowes, DUNKELD, PH8 0HH, 01350 727337
www.scottishwildlifetrust.org.uk/reserve/loch-of-the-lowes

Inver Mill Farm Caravan Park
★★★★ 87%

tel: 01350 727477 Inver **PH8 0JR**
email: admin@invermillfarm.com web: www.invermillfarm.com
dir: *A9 onto A822 then immediately right to Inver.*

Inver Mill Farm Caravan Park is a peaceful park on level former farmland, located on the banks of the River Braan and surrounded by mature trees and hills. The active resident owners keep the park in very good condition. It is close to Dunkeld and just a few minutes from the A9 which gives great transport links to the north and south. Further hardstandings were added in 2024, with all amenities refurbished too.

Open: March to October **Last arrival:** 21.00 (earliest 13.00) **Last departure:** noon
Pitches: 🚐 🚗 ⛺
Facilities: 🏠 ☺ ℉ ✳ ♿
Services: 🔌 🗑 🧺 ⬇ 🔒 ⊘
Within 3 miles: ⚓ ✏ 🛒

Additional site information: 5 acre site. 🚗 Cars can be parked by caravans and tents. Awnings permitted. Complete quiet from 23:00–08:00, 10mph speed limit. Fires are strictly forbidden but BBQs permitted. No dealers, traders or commercial vehicles.

PERTH
Map 21 NO12

Places to visit

Scone Palace, PERTH, PH2 6BD, 01738 552300
www.scone-palace.co.uk

Branklyn Garden, PERTH, PH12 7BB, 01738 625535
www.nts.org.uk/visit/places/branklyn-garden

Premier Park

Pathgreen Glamping
★★★★★ 93% GLAMPING ONLY

tel: 07840 769811 Path of Condie **PH2 9DW**
email: contact@pathgreenglamping.co.uk web: www.pathgreenglamping.co.uk
dir: *From Perth take B9112 towards Dunning. Road becomes B934. Cross railway line. In Dunning, at T-junction left signed Path of Condie. In approximately 4.5 miles left signed Path of Condie and Stronachie. Using postcode for sat nav is not recommended.*

Pathgreen Glamping enjoys a peaceful location with wonderful views and is an ideal location to base yourself for touring Perthshire. Luxury pods of different sizes offer a wealth of modern day comforts to make the stay a memorable one. Wood-burning hot tubs, hammocks or hanging swing seats allow you to make the most of the location regardless of the weather. Further pampering spa treatments are available too. WiFi coverage is available.

FACILITIES: 🔌 Electric vehicle charging 🛁 Baths/Shower ☺ Electric shaver sockets ℉ Hairdryer ✳ Ice pack facility 🍼 Baby facilities ♿ Disabled facilities 🛒 Shop on site or within 200yds 🍽 BBQ area 🌳 Picnic area WiFi WiFi 🌐 Internet access **SERVICES:** 🔌 Electric hook-up 🗑 Launderette 🍺 Licensed bar 🔒 Calor Gas ⊘ Campingaz 🚽 Toilet fluid ☕ Café/Restaurant 🍔 Fast Food/Takeaway 🔋 Battery charging ⬇ Motorhome service point 🚫 No credit or debit cards 🐕 Dogs permitted ⊗ No dogs

PITLOCHRY   Map 23 NN95

Places to visit
Edradour Distillery, PITLOCHRY, PH16 5JP, 01796 472095
www.edradour.com

Faskally Caravan Park
★★★★ 92%

tel: 01796 472007 **PH16 5LA**
email: info@faskally.co.uk **web:** www.faskally.co.uk
dir: *1.5 miles north of Pitlochry on B8019.*

A large park near Pitlochry, which is divided into smaller areas by mature trees and set within well-tended grounds. This family-owned site has two large amenity blocks and an entertainment complex with a heated swimming pool, bar, restaurant and indoor games area. There are numerous walks from the site and it is ideal for either a longer stay to explore the area or as a convenient stopover. A regular bus service is available at the site entrance. Please note, tent pitches are not available.

Open: 15 March to 31 October **Last arrival:** 23.00 **Last departure:** 11.00
Pitches: 45 hardstanding pitches
Leisure:
Facilities:
Services:
Within 3 miles:
Additional site information: 27 acre site. Cars can be parked by caravans. Awnings permitted.

Milton of Fonab Caravan Park
★★★★ 91%

tel: 01796 472882 **Bridge Road PH16 5NA**
email: info@fonab.co.uk **web:** www.fonab.co.uk
dir: *From south: on A924, pass petrol station on left, next left opposite Bell's Distillery into Bridge Road. Cross river, site on left. From north (and Pitlochry centre): on A924, under rail bridge, turn right opposite Bell's Distillery into Bridge Road.*

Milton of Fonab is a peaceful site on the banks of the River Tummel, close to Pitlochry. The site is very well maintained, with large pitches, good washrooms and a well-stocked shop, and it's an ideal base for exploring this scenic part of Perth & Kinross. The area is famous for the whisky industry, and Blair Athol distillery is a short walk from the site entrance, as is the Pitlochry Festival Theatre.

Open: 15 March to 31 October **Last arrival:** 21.00 **Last departure:** noon (touring) 10.00 (statics)
Pitches: 154 hardstanding pitches
Leisure:
Facilities:
Services:
Within 3 miles:
Additional site information: 15 acre site. Cars can be parked by caravans. Awnings permitted.

RENFREWSHIRE

BISHOPTON   Map 20 NS47

Places to visit
Finlaystone Country Estate, LANGBANK, PA14 6TJ, 01475 540505
www.finlaystone.co.uk

Premier Park

The Paddocks Touring Park
★★★★★ 93%

tel: 01505 864 333 **Ingliston Estate & Country Club, Old Greenock Road PA7 5PA**
email: helen@ingliston.com **web:** www.ingliston.com/thepaddocks
dir: *From M8 junction 29a follow Bishopton signs onto A8. Straight on at 2 roundabouts. Through Bishopton. At Chestnut Roundabout left signed Dargavel. Site entrance in 0.5 mile.*

The Paddocks Touring Park enjoys a fantastic location overlooking the Clyde and is within easy distance of Glasgow and Loch Lomond. As part of the Ingliston Estate and Country Club guests of The Paddocks have full use of the hotel's facilities. Pitches are fully serviced and of a generous size to cater for all sizes of motorhomes. Modern facilities including covered dishwashing and laundry, are on hand. Each pitch has its own outside bench and table with elevated views of the surrounding area.

SCOTTISH BORDERS

LAUDER   Map 21 NT54

Places to visit
Harmony Gardens (NT for Scotland), MELROSE, TD6 9LJ, 01896 822493
www.nts.org.uk/visit/places/harmony-garden

Thirlestane Castle Caravan & Camping Site
★★★ 90%

tel: 01578 718884 & 07976 231032 **Thirlestane Castle TD2 6RU**
email: info@thirlestanecastlepark.co.uk **web:** www.thirlestanecastlepark.co.uk
dir: *Signed from A68 and A697, just south of Lauder.*

Located on the outskirts of Lauder, close to the A68 and within the grounds of Thirlestane Castle, this is an ideal site from which to explore the many attractions in the Scottish Borders. The amenity block is immaculately maintained and the pitches are behind the estate boundary wall that provides a secluded and peaceful location. There are electric vehicle chargers and a regular bus service stops near the site entrance. The grounds are well maintained with colourful planters and co-ordinated signage throughout.

Open: April to October **Last arrival:** 20.00 **Last departure:** noon
Pitches: 30 hardstanding pitches; 55 seasonal pitches
Leisure:
Facilities:
Services: **Within 3 miles:**
Additional site information: 5 acre site. Cars can be parked by caravans and tents. Awnings permitted. Tourer storage facilities, discounted access to castle and grounds during opening hours.

STIRLING

BLAIRLOGIE — Map 21 NS89

Places to visit

Alloa Tower, ALLOA, FK10 1PL, 01259 211701
www.nts.org.uk/visit/places/alloa-tower

The National Wallace Monument, STIRLING, FK9 5LF, 01786 472140
www.nationalwallacemonument.com

Great for kids: Blair Drummond Safari & Adventure Park, BLAIR DRUMMOND, FK9 4UR, 01786 841456
www.blairdrummond.com

AA CAMPSITE OF THE YEAR FOR SCOTLAND 2024–25

Witches Craig Caravan & Camping Park
★★★★ 91%

tel: 01786 474947 **FK9 5PX**
email: info@witchescraig.co.uk web: www.witchescraig.co.uk
dir: *3 miles north-east of Stirling on A91 (Hillfoots to St Andrews road).*

In an attractive setting with direct access to the lower slopes of the dramatic Ochil Hills, Witches Craig Caravan & Camping Park is a well-maintained family-run park. The mature landscaping always displays lots of colour and is a tribute to the care and attention of the owners. The toilet block is immaculate, the touring pitches are all hardstanding and the tent field at the rear of the site is well drained. Many visitors return year after year. It is in the centre of 'Braveheart' country, with easy access to Stirling Castle and city centre as well the Wallace Monument. A regular bus stops at the site entrance. This is an ideal base from which to tour the central region of Scotland.

Open: April to October **Last arrival:** 20.00 **Last departure:** noon

Pitches: ; 60 hardstanding pitches; 6 seasonal pitches

Leisure:

Facilities:

Services:

Within 3 miles:

Additional site information: 5 acre site. Cars can be parked by caravans and tents. Awnings permitted. Food preparation area, cooking shelters, baby bath and changing area.

LUIB — Map 20 NN42

Places to visit

Ben Lawers National Nature Reserve, KILLIN, FK21 8TY, 01567 820988
www.nnr-scotland.org.uk/ben-lawers

Glen Dochart Holiday Park
★★★★ 79%

tel: 01567 820637 **FK20 8QT**
email: info@glendochart.co.uk web: www.glendochart-caravanpark.co.uk
dir: *On A85 (Oban to Stirling road) midway between Killin and Crianlarich.*

A small site located on the A85 some eight miles from Killin, with boating and fishing available on Loch Tay, and stunning views over the surrounded hills from tiered pitches. It is also convenient for Oban, Fort William and Loch Lomond. Hill walkers have direct access to numerous walks that suit all levels of ability, including the nearby Munro of Ben More. There is a regular bus service at the site entrance, and nearby Crianlarich provides access to the West Highland Railway, known as Britain's most scenic rail route, and also the West Highland Way. An ideal site as a stopover to the west coast or for a longer holiday.

Open: March to November **Last arrival:** 21.00 **Last departure:** noon

Pitches: ; 28 hardstanding pitches

Facilities:

Services:

Within 3 miles:

Additional site information: 15 acre site. Cars can be parked by caravans and tents. Awnings permitted.

Make your next UK holiday one to remember

Choose RatedTrips.com

AA

SCOTLAND
ISLE OF ARRAN—ISLE OF SKYE

SCOTTISH ISLANDS

ISLE OF ARRAN

KILDONAN — Map 20 NS02

Places to visit

Isle of Arran Heritage Museum, BRODICK, KA27 8DP, 01770 302636
www.arranmuseum.co.uk

Seal Shore Camping and Touring Site
★★★★ 90%

tel: 01770 820320 **KA27 8SE**
email: enquiries@campingarran.com **web:** www.campingarran.com
dir: *From ferry terminal in Brodick turn left, 12 miles, through Lamlash and Whiting Bay. Left to Kildonan, site on left.*

On the south coast of Arran and only 12 miles from the ferry at Brodick, this is a peaceful, family-run site with direct access to a sandy beach. There are fabulous views across the water to Pladda Island and Ailsa Craig, and an abundance of wildlife. The site is suited for all types of touring vehicles but caters very well for 'non-motorised' campers. The resident owner, also a registered fisherman, sells fresh lobsters and crabs, and on request will give fishing lessons on a small, privately owned lochan. There is an undercover barbecue, campers' kitchen, day room with TV, a wet suit dunk and shower that incorporates the dog wash area. A bus, which stops on request, travels around the island. There are two wooden pods for hire.

Open: March to October **Last arrival:** 21.00 **Last departure:** noon (pods 10:00)
Pitches: 🚐 🚗 ⛺ ; 🏠 see prices below; 16 hardstanding pitches
Leisure:
Facilities:
Services:
Within 3 miles:

Additional site information: 3 acre site. Cars can be parked by caravans (not available on all pitches). Awnings permitted. No fires, no gazebos, no noise after 22.00. Dog charge £1 per day. Small shop selling basic essentials. Car hire can be arranged.

Glamping available: 2 wooden pods from £40. **Changeover days:** Any day

Additional glamping information: No cooking or smoking in pods.

KILMORY — Map 20 NR92

Places to visit

Brodick Castle Garden & Country Park (NT for Scotland), BRODICK, KA27 8HY, 01770 302202
www.nts.org.uk/visit/places/brodick-castle

Lochranza Distillery, LOCHRANZA, KA27 8HJ, 01770 830264
www.arranwhisky.com

KILMORY — Map 20 NR92

Premier Park

Runach Arainn Glamping
★★★★★ 92% GLAMPING ONLY

tel: 01770 870515 **The Old Manse KA27 8PH**
email: runacharainn@gmail.com **web:** www.runacharainn.com
dir: *From ferry at Brodick, turn left onto A481 signed South and Lamlash. Through Lamlash and Whiting Bay. Approximately 9 miles to Kilmory. In Kilmory, 1st right, pass church to site.*

Runach Arainn, Gaelic for 'Secret Arran', lives up to its name – hidden away in a quiet and beautiful part of the Isle of Arran, just a 15-minute walk from a lovely beach. It offers superb 20ft-diameter Scottish-made yurts. Each of the three yurts has a private bathroom in an amenity building, and fire pits and outdoor cooking facilities are also available.

Open: February to November **Last arrival:** 22.00 **Last departure:** 10.00
Facilities:
Within 3 miles:

Accommodation available: Yurts from £90 per night.
Changeover days: Any day

Additional site information: 2 acre site. No stag or hen parties. Two yurts sleep 6; 1 yurt sleeps 4. Each has wood-burning stove (including oven and hob). Firewood. Dedicated private bathroom. Towels and bedding provided. Yurt field car-free with children's activities available. Yurts set around orchard and meadow.

ISLE OF SKYE

STAFFIN — Map 22 NG46

Staffin Camping & Caravanning
★★★ 86%

tel: 01470 562213 **IV51 9JX**
email: staffincampsite@btinternet.com **web:** www.staffincampsite.co.uk
dir: *On A855, 16 miles north of Portree. Turn right before 40mph signs.*

This site provides an ideal base to rest and appreciate the peace and tranquillity of the north of Skye. It is a large sloping grassy site with level hardstandings for motorhomes and caravans, some with electric and water points. The site has a good and very clean amenity block with heating and power showers, and a newly updated washing area with a table and TV. Nearby Staffin has a village store and a number of cafés, and meals are also served from The Hut here on certain days. Both sea and loch fishing are available nearby and the Trotternish Ridge and surrounding area offer spectacular hill walking opportunities. It is a relatively short, and spectacular, drive over the Quirang to reach the ferry terminal at Uig.

Open: 15 April to 10 October **Last arrival:** 20.00 **Last departure:** 11.00
Pitches: 🚐 🚗 ⛺ ; 20 hardstanding pitches; 20 seasonal pitches
Leisure:
Facilities:
Services:
Within 3 miles:

Additional site information: 2.5 acre site. Cars can be parked by caravans and tents. Awnings permitted. No music after 22.00. In wet weather it may not be possible to park cars by accomodation. Picnic tables, kitchen area, campers' bothy.

PITCHES: 🚐 Caravans 🚗 Motorhomes ⛺ Tents 🏠 Glamping accommodation **LEISURE:** Indoor swimming pool Outdoor swimming pool Children's playground Kids' club Tennis court Games room Separate TV room golf course Pitch n putt Boats for hire Bikes for hire Cinema Entertainment Fishing Mini golf Watersports Gym Sports field Stables Spa

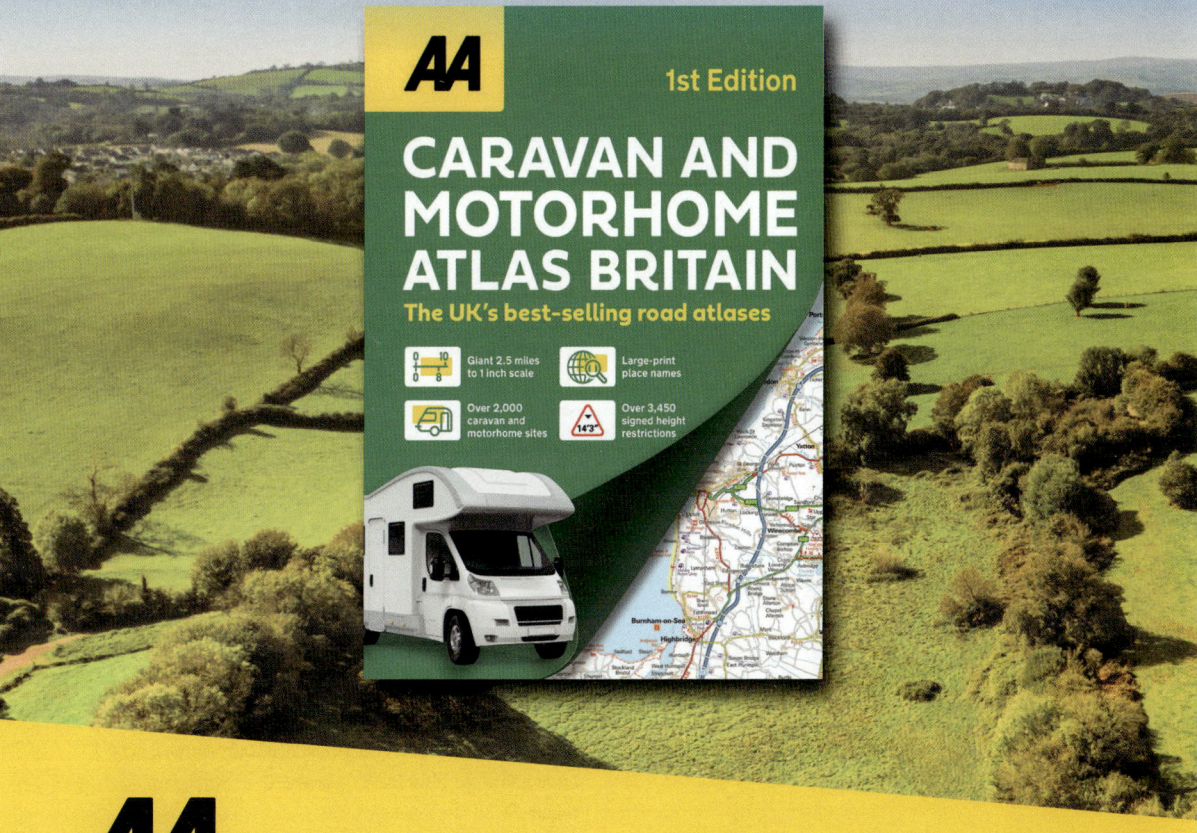

Wales

Wales

Wales – a place of myth and legend, a country loved passionately by actors and poets and male voice choirs, a land of rugged mountain grandeur and craggy, meandering coastline. Crossing the Severn Bridge, you sense at once you are entering a completely different country. The culture is different, so are the traditions and so are the physical characteristics. With its lush hills and dramatic headlands, it has echoes of other Celtic lands – most notably, Ireland and Scotland.

Wales's legacy of famous names from the world of the arts is truly impressive. Richard Burton hailed from the valleys in South Wales, Sir Anthony Hopkins originates from Port Talbot and Dylan Thomas was born over a century ago in a house on a hilltop street in Swansea. His birthplace in Cwmdonkin Drive can be hired for self-catering breaks and holidays and there is even the chance to sleep in the poet's tiny bedroom. Thomas described the house as 'a provincial villa…a small, not very well painted gateless house…very nice, very respective.'

Further west is the house where he lived in his final years. Thomas and his wife Caitlin moved to the Boat House at Laugharne, 40 miles from Swansea, in the spring of 1949. With its magnificent views across an expansive estuary, this was Dylan Thomas's perfect retreat and much of his creative writing was completed in the modest wooden shed on a bluff above the house. The Boat House is open to visitors and nearby Brown's Hotel, his favourite watering hole, offers the chance to relax and enjoy something to eat and drink.

On the Pembrokeshire coast, renowned for its beautiful beaches, is another, less familiar link with Dylan Thomas. The old fishing village of Lower Fishguard was home to a film unit of almost 100 people in the early months of 1971. Presided over by the film director Andrew Sinclair, filming of Thomas's classic play *Under Milk Wood* began, with Richard Burton and Peter O'Toole among the many film stars seen around the village. A young, virtually unknown Sir David Jason, also appeared in the film. Sinclair and his team built false fronts on the dock cottages and created an undertaker's parlour – among other work. The National Eisteddfod in Llangollen is one of the most important events in the Welsh cultural calendar, celebrating the country's long heritage of storytelling, music and poetry.

Think of Wales and you often think of castles. The formidable Caernarfon Castle, the setting for the investiture of the Prince of Wales (now King Charles) in 1969, stands in the northwest corner of the country. Harlech Castle was built around 1283 by Edward I and from it are seen the peaks of Snowdonia. This glorious region of towering summits and crags, which has the highest range of mountains in England and Wales and is now a National Park, has long attracted walkers and climbers. Edmund Hillary and his team rehearsed here for the first successful assault on Everest in 1953. However, Snowdonia is not just about mountain peaks. There are plenty of gentler alternatives, including an extensive network of lowland routes, forest trails and waymarked walks. Below Snowdon lies the historic village of Llanberis, one of the region's most popular attractions and ideally placed for touring Snowdonia. Another mountain resort is Betws-y-Coed, with a range of delightful walks exploring picturesque river scenery and pretty, pastoral uplands.

For the buzz and vibrancy of the city, Swansea and Cardiff cannot be beaten, the latter boasting a lively café culture, docklands-style apartments, a science discovery centre that's fun for all the family, and the internationally renowned Wales Millennium Centre (Canolfan Mileniwm Cymru). However, in terms of Welsh scenery, there is so much waiting to be discovered and explored; the grand, immensely varied landscape of the Brecon Beacons (Bannau Brycheiniog), and the gentler, pastoral acres of the Welsh Borders – among a host of beauty spots throughout Wales.

◁ *The Preseli Hills*

ISLE OF ANGLESEY

DULAS
Map 14 SH48

Places to visit

Din Lligwy Hut Group, LLANALLGO, 03000 252239
www.cadw.gov.wales/visit/places-to-visit/din-lligwy-hut-group

AA CAMPSITE OF THE YEAR FOR WALES & OVERALL WINNER 2024–25

Platinum Park

Tyddyn Isaf Caravan Park
★★★★★

tel: 01248 410203 **Lligwy Bay LL70 9PQ**
email: mail@tyddynisaf.co.uk web: www.tyddynisaf.co.uk
dir: *From A55 at Britannia Bridge take A5025 through Bellench to Moelfre roundabout. Take left exit signed Amlwch, to Brynrefail. In village turn right to Lligwy, follow park signs. The site is 0.5 mile on right.*

A beautifully situated and very spacious family park on rising ground adjacent to a sandy beach with magnificent views overlooking Lligwy Bay. A private footpath leads directly to the beach and there is an excellent nature trail around the park. The site has superb amenity blocks with most set up as private cubicles. High-speed WiFi is available at all pitches. Due to the undulating nature of the park, quality level pitches have been created ensuring stunning country views. The additions for 2024 were a brand new shop, a bistro offering alfresco dining, a modern gym and a business centre.

Open: End of April to September **Last arrival:** 20.00 **Last departure:** 11.00
Pitches: 🚐 🚍 ⛺; 60 hardstanding pitches; 50 seasonal pitches
Leisure: **Facilities:** **Services:** **Within 3 miles:**

Additional site information: 16 acre site. Cars can be parked by caravans and tents. Awnings permitted. No groups, loud music or open fires, maximum 3 units can be booked together. All-weather pitches, licensed coffee bar/takeaway, shop, baby changing unit, woodland walk, business centre, gym, footpath to beach.

MARIAN-GLAS
Map 14 SH58

Places to visit

Din Lligwy Hut Group, LLANALLGO, 03000 252239
www.cadw.gov.wales/visit/places-to-visit/din-lligwy-hut-group

Capel Lligwy, LLANALLGO, LL72 8LS, 03000 252239
www.cadw.gov.wales/visit/places-to-visit/capel-lligwy

Platinum Park

Home Farm Caravan Park
★★★★★

tel: 01248 410614 **LL73 8PH**
email: enq@homefarm-anglesey.co.uk web: www.homefarm-anglesey.co.uk
dir: *On A5025, 2 miles north of Benllech. Site 300 metres beyond church.*

A first-class park run with passion and enthusiasm, set in an elevated and secluded position sheltered by trees, and with good planting and landscaping. The peaceful rural setting affords views of farmland, the sea and the mountains of Snowdonia. The modern toilet blocks are spotlessly clean and well maintained, and there are excellent play opportunities for children both indoors and out. Facilities also include a visitors' parking area and a smart reception and shop. The area is blessed with sandy beaches, and the local pubs and shops cater for everyday needs. Please note that tents are not accepted.

Open: April to October **Last arrival:** 21.00 **Last departure:** noon
Pitches: 🚐 🚍; 65 hardstanding pitches
Leisure: **Facilities:** **Services:** **Within 3 miles:**

Additional site information: 12 acre site. Cars can be parked by caravans. Awnings permitted. No roller blades, skateboards or scooters.

RHÔS LLIGWY
Map 14 SH48

Places to visit

Din Lligwy Hut Group, LLANALLGO, 03000 252239
www.cadw.gov.wales/visit/places-to-visit/din-lligwy-hut-group

Capel Lligwy, LLANALLGO, LL72 8LS, 03000 252239
www.cadw.gov.wales/visit/places-to-visit/capel-lligwy

RHÔS LLIGWY
Map 14 SH48

Ty'n Rhos Caravan Park
★★★ 83%

tel: 01248 852417 Lligwy Bay, Moelfre LL72 8NL
email: robert@bodafonpark.co.uk web: www.bodafonpark.co.uk
dir: *Take A5025 from Benllech to Moelfre roundabout, right to T-junction in Moelfre. Left, approximately 2 miles, pass crossroads leading to beach, site 50 metres on right.*

A family park close to the beautiful beach at Lligwy Bay and cliff walks along the Heritage Coast, and historic Din Lligwy and the shops at picturesque Moelfre are nearby. All the touring pitches have water, electric hook-up and TV connections. Amenities, including toilets, showers and a laundry, are equipped with stylish fixtures and fittings. Excellent, more advanced WiFi coverage across the park is a recent upgrade. Please note that guests should register at Bodafon Caravan Park in Benllech where detailed directions will be given and pitches allocated.

Open: March to October **Last arrival:** 20.00 **Last departure:** 11.00
Pitches: 4 hardstanding pitches; 48 seasonal pitches
Facilities:
Services:
Within 3 miles:

Additional site information: 10 acre site. Cars can be parked by caravans and tents. Awnings permitted. No campfires, no noise after 23.00. Boat park.

CARMARTHENSHIRE

LLANDOVERY
Map 9 SN73

Places to visit
Dolaucothi, PUMSAINT, SA19 8US, 01558 650177
www.nationaltrust.org.uk/dolaucothi

Llandovery Caravan Park
★★★ 81%

tel: 01550 721065 Church Bank SA20 0DT
email: llandoverycaravanpark@gmail.com
web: www.llandovery-caravan-camping-park.co.uk
dir: *A40 from Carmarthen, over rail crossing, past junction with A483 (Builth Wells). Turn right for Llangadog, past church, 1st right signed Rugby Club and Camping.*

Within easy walking distance of the town centre and adjacent to the notable Llandovery Dragons Rugby Club, this constantly improving park is an ideal base for touring the Brecon Beacons (Bannau Brycheiniog) and many local attractions. Most pitches have both water and a hardstanding, and guests are welcome to use the popular on-site rugby club lounge bar.

Open: All year **Last arrival:** 20.00 **Last departure:** 20.00
Pitches: 60 seasonal pitches
Leisure:
Facilities:
Services:
Within 3 miles:

Additional site information: 8 acre site. Cars can be parked by caravans and tents. Awnings permitted.

NEWCASTLE EMLYN
Map 8 SN34

Places to visit
Cilgerran Castle, CILGERRAN, SA43 2SF, 03000 252239
www.cadw.gov.wales/visit/places-to-visit/cilgerran-castle

Castell Henllys Iron Age Fort, CRYMYCH, SA41 3UR, 01239 891319
www.pembrokeshirecoast.wales/castell-henllys

Premier Park

Cenarth Falls Resort Limited
★★★★★ 92%

tel: 01239 710345 Cenarth SA38 9JS
email: enquiries@cenarth-holipark.co.uk web: www.cenarth-holipark.co.uk
dir: *From Newcastle Emlyn on A484 towards Cardigan. Through Cenarth, site on right.*

Located close to the village of Cenarth where the River Teifi, famous for its salmon and trout fishing, cascades through the Cenarth Falls Gorge. With beautifully landscaped grounds and spotless amenities, the park also benefits from Coracles Health & Country Club with an indoor swimming pool, well-equipped gym, sauna and steam room, a bar serving evening meals (with a dog-friendly section), and a function room.

Open: March to November (restricted service: off-peak season – bar and meals available at weekends only) **Last arrival:** 20.00 **Last departure:** 11.00
Pitches: 27 hardstanding pitches
Leisure:
Facilities:
Services:
Within 3 miles:

Additional site information: 2 acre site. Cars can be parked by caravans and tents. Awnings permitted. No skateboards or hover boards. Pool table.

Afon Teifi Caravan & Camping Park
★★★★ 86%

tel: 01559 370532 Pentregagal SA38 9HT
email: contact@afonteifi.co.uk web: www.afonteifi.co.uk
dir: *Signed from A484, 2 miles east of Newcastle Emlyn.*

Set on the banks of the River Teifi, a famous salmon and sea trout river, this secluded, family-owned and run park has good views. It is only two miles from the market town of Newcastle Emlyn. The large amenity block is equipped with modern fixtures and fittings, and free WiFi is available throughout the park. Dog owners will especially appreciate the acres of land, including a river walk – here there are also benches to relax on and enjoy the sounds of the river and the birdsong.

Open: April to October **Last arrival:** 23.00
Pitches: 22 hardstanding pitches; 25 seasonal pitches
Leisure:
Facilities:
Services: **Within 3 miles:**

Additional site information: 6 acre site. Cars can be parked by caravans and tents. Awnings permitted. No noise after midnight, no bikes or scooters to be ridden after dark. Riverside and woodland walks.

CEREDIGION

ABERAERON Map 8 SN46

Places to visit

Llanerchaeron, ABERAERON, SA48 8DG, 01545 573010
www.nationaltrust.org.uk/llanerchaeron

Cae Hir Gardens, CRIBYN, SA48 7NG, 01570 471116
www.caehirgardens.com

Aeron Coast Caravan Park
★★★ 93%

tel: 01545 570349 **North Road SA46 0JF**
email: enquiries@aeroncoast.co.uk **web:** www.aeroncoast.co.uk
dir: *From Aberaeron on A487 (coast road) towards Aberystwyth. Filling station on left at entrance.*

A well-managed family holiday park on the edge of the attractive resort of Aberaeron, with direct access to the beach. All the spacious pitches are level. On-site facilities include an extensive outdoor pool complex, a multi-activity outdoor sports area, an indoor children's play area, a games room and an entertainment suite.

Open: March to October **Last arrival:** 23.00 **Last departure:** 11.00
Pitches: 🚐 🚗 ▲; 30 hardstanding pitches
Leisure: ≋ ⋀ ♨ ⊛ ▢ ♫ ♣
Facilities: 🏠 ☺ ↯ ✻ 📶 🖥
Services: 🔌 🔋 🍽 🍴 ⬇ 🔒 ⊘ 🅣
Within 3 miles: ✎ ∪ ⛴ 🏪

Additional site information: 22 acre site. 🚗 Cars can be parked by caravans and tents. Awnings permitted. Families only. No motorcycles.

NEW QUAY Map 8 SN35

Places to visit

Llanerchaeron, ABERAERON, SA48 8DG, 01545 573010
www.nationaltrust.org.uk/llanerchaeron

Premier Park

Quay West Holiday Park
★★★★★ 90% HOLIDAY PARK

tel: 01545 560477 **SA45 9SE**
email: quaywest@haven.com **web:** www.haven.com/quaywest
dir: *From Cardigan on A487 left onto A486 into New Quay. Or from Aberystwyth on A487 right onto B4342 into New Quay.*

This holiday park enjoys a stunning clifftop position overlooking picturesque New Quay and Cardigan Bay. It's an easy walk to a glorious sandy beach, and the all-action, on-site activities include heated swimming pools, SplashZone, football, archery and fencing (with professional tuition), the Aqua Bar and terrace and a kiddies' Pic 'n' Paint room. There is a good range of holiday caravans for hire.

Open: mid March to October
Holiday Homes: Sleep 8, Bedrooms 2, Bathrooms 1, Toilet 1, Microwave, Freezer, TV, Sky/Freeview, DVD player, WiFi, Linen included
Leisure: ≋ ⋧ ⋀ ✋ ♣
Facilities: 🛒

Additional site information: 🚗 The facilities provided in the holiday homes may differ depending on the grade. Most dog breeds accepted (please check when booking). Dogs must be kept on leads at all times.

CONWY

BETWS-YN-RHOS Map 14 SH97

Places to visit

Bodnant Garden, TAL-Y-CAFN, LL28 5RE, 01492 650460
www.nationaltrust.org.uk/bodnant-garden

Hunters Hamlet Caravan Park
★★★★ 85%

tel: 01745 832237 & 07721 552105 **Sirior Goch Farm LL22 8PL**
email: info@huntershamlet.co.uk **web:** www.huntershamlet.co.uk
dir: *From A55 (westbound), A547 junction 24 into Abergele. At 2nd lights turn left by George and Dragon pub, onto A548. 2.75 miles, right at crossroads onto B5381. Site 0.5 mile on left.*

A warm welcome is assured at this long established, family-run working farm park adjacent to the owners' Georgian farmhouse. Well-spaced pitches, including 15 with water, electricity and TV hook-up, are within two attractive hedge-screened grassy paddocks. The well-maintained amenity block includes unisex bathrooms. Please note, this site does not accept tents.

Open: March to October **Last arrival:** 22.00 **Last departure:** noon
Pitches: 🚐 🚗; 30 hardstanding pitches
Leisure: ⋀
Facilities: 🏠 ☺ ↯ ✻ ♿ 🚿 📶
Services: 🔌 🔋 🍴 ⬇
Within 3 miles: ⛳ ✎ 🏪

Additional site information: 2.5 acre site. 🚗 Cars can be parked by caravans. Awnings permitted. No football. Dogs must not be left unattended. Family bathroom.

KINMEL BAY
Map 14 SH97

Places to visit

Gwrych Castle, Llanddulas Road, Abergele, CONWY, LL22 8ET, 01745 826023
www.gwrychcastle.co.uk

Rhuddlan Castle, Castle St, RHUDDLAN, LL18 5AD, 03000 252239
www.cadw.gov.wales/visit/places-to-visit/castell-rhuddlan

Great for kids: Rhyl Miniature Railway, Central Station, Marine Lake, Wellington Road, RHYL, LL18 1AQ, 01352 759109
www.rhylminiaturerailway.co.uk

Golden Sands Holiday Park
★★★★ 88% **HOLIDAY PARK**

tel: 01745 343606 **Sandy Cove, Kinmel Bay LL18 5NA**
email: goldensandsguestservices@awayresorts.co.uk
web: www.awayresorts.co.uk/parks/north-wales/golden-sands

Golden Sands is a popular holiday park with direct access to sandy beaches and also within easy reach of Llandudno and historic Chester. It provides modern quality accommodation within stylish well-spaced static homes and chalets. A wide range of activities and attractions are suitable for all ages and include both adult and children's swimming pools in addition to excellent outdoor play areas.

Open: All year **Last arrival:** 22.00 **Last departure:** 10.00

LLANRWST
Map 14 SH86

Places to visit

Gwydir Uchaf Chapel, LLANRWST, 03000 252239
www.cadw.gov.wales/visit/places-to-visit/gwydir-uchaf-chapel

Trefriw Woollen Mills, TREFRIW, LL27 0NQ, 01492 640462
www.t-w-m.co.uk/visit

Great for kids: Conwy Valley Railway Museum, BETWS-Y-COED, LL24 0AL, 01690 710568
www.conwyrailwaymuseum.co.uk

Premier Park

Bron Derw Touring Caravan Park
★★★★★ 88%

tel: 01492 640494 **LL26 0YT**
email: bronderw@aol.com web: www.bronderw-wales.co.uk
dir: *A55 onto A470 for Betws-y-Coed and Llanrwst. In Llanrwst left into Parry Road signed Llanddoged. Left at T-junction, site signed at 1st farm entrance on right.*

A previous AA campsite award winner, Bron Derw, once a dairy farm, is beautifully landscaped with stunning floral displays and is surrounded by hills. The park has been built to a very high standard and is fully matured. All pitches are fully serviced, and there is a heated, stone-built toilet block with excellent and immaculately maintained facilities. The Parc Derwen adults-only field has 28 fully serviced pitches and its own designated amenity block. CCTV security cameras cover the whole park.

Open: 19 March to 31 October **Last arrival:** 21.00 **Last departure:** 11.00

Pitches: ; 48 hardstanding pitches; 17 seasonal pitches

Facilities:

Services:

Within 3 miles:

Additional site information: 4.5 acre site. Cars can be parked by caravans. Awnings permitted. Children must be supervised, no bikes, scooters or skateboards, no noise after 23.00.

LLANRWST continued

Bodnant Caravan Park
★★★★ 86%

tel: 01492 640248 Nebo Road LL26 0SD
email: ermin@bodnant-caravan-park.co.uk web: www.bodnant-caravan-park.co.uk
dir: From A470 in Llanrwst at lights take B5427 signed Nebo (opposite garage). Immediately right signed Nebo. Site 300 yards on right, opposite leisure centre.

This well maintained and stunningly attractive park is filled with flower beds, and the landscape includes trees and shrubberies. The statics are unobtrusively sited and the quality, spotlessly clean toilet blocks have fully serviced private cubicles. All caravan pitches are multi-service, and the tent pitches serviced. There is a separate playing and rally field and an adjacent farm with animals on show to keep children entertained. Victorian farming implements are on display around the touring fields.

Open: March to end October **Last arrival:** 20.00 **Last departure:** 11.00
Pitches: ; 34 hardstanding pitches
Facilities:
Services:
Within 3 miles:

Additional site information: 5 acre site. Cars can be parked by caravans and tents. Awnings permitted. No bikes, skateboards or camp fires, main gates locked 23.00–08.00 (pedestrian access only), no noise after 23.00.

DENBIGHSHIRE

PRESTATYN
Map 15 SJ08

Places to visit

Basingwerk Abbey, HOLYWELL, CH8 7GH, 03000 252239
www.cadw.gov.wales/visit/places-to-visit/basingwerk-abbey

Rhuddlan Castle, RHUDDLAN, LL18 5AD, 03000 252239
www.cadw.gov.wales/visit/places-to-visit/rhuddlan-castle

Premier Park

Presthaven Beach Holiday Park
★★★★★ 85% HOLIDAY PARK

tel: 01745 856471 Gronant LL19 9TT
email: presthavensands@haven.com
web: www.haven.com/parks/north-wales/presthaven
dir: A548 from Prestatyn towards Gronant. Site signed (Note: for sat nav use LL19 9ST).

Set beside two miles of superb sandy beaches and dunes (with donkeys on site at weekends), this constantly improving holiday park provides a wide range of both indoor and outdoor attractions. The small touring field at the park entrance offers all-electric pitches, most with hardstandings and a smart amenity block. The centrally located entertainment area includes two indoor swimming pools, excellent children's activities and a choice of eating outlets.

Open: mid March to end October (restricted service: mid March to May and September to end October – facilities may be reduced) **Last arrival:** 20.00 **Last departure:** 10.00
Pitches: ; 39 hardstanding pitches
Leisure:
Facilities:
Services:
Within 3 miles:

Additional site information: 21 acre site. No commercial vehicles, no bookings by persons under 21 years unless a family booking. Maximum 2 dogs per booking, certain dog breeds banned.

RHUALLT
Map 15 SJ07

Places to visit

Rhuddlan Castle, RHUDDLAN, LL18 5AD, 03000 252239
www.cadw.gov.wales/visit/places-to-visit/rhuddlan-castle

Penisar Mynydd Caravan Park
★★★★ 91%

tel: 01745 582227 & 07831 408017 Caerwys Road LL17 0TY
email: contact@penisarmynydd.co.uk web: www.penisarmynydd.co.uk
dir: From A55 junction 29 follow Dyserth and brown caravan signs. Site 500 yards on right.

A very tranquil, attractively laid-out park set in three grassy paddocks with a superb facilities block including a disabled room and dishwashing area. The majority of pitches are super pitches. Immaculately maintained throughout, the park is within easy reach of historic Chester and the seaside resort of Rhyl.

Open: All year **Last arrival:** 20.00 **Last departure:** noon (fee applies for later departures)
Pitches: ; 71 hardstanding pitches; 30 seasonal pitches
Leisure:
Facilities:
Services:
Within 3 miles:

Additional site information: 6.6 acre site. Cars can be parked by caravans and tents. Awnings permitted. No cycling, no fires. Rally area.

PITCHES: Caravans Motorhomes Tents Glamping accommodation **LEISURE:** Indoor swimming pool Outdoor swimming pool Children's playground Kids' club Tennis court Games room Separate TV room golf course Pitch n putt Boats for hire Bikes for hire Cinema Entertainment Fishing Mini golf Watersports Gym Sports field Stables Spa

FLINTSHIRE

HOLYWELL Map 15 SJ17

Haulfryn Caravan Park

★★★★ 84%

tel: 07986 435564 **Babell Road, Babell CH8 8PW**
email: info@haulfryncaravanpark.co.uk **web:** www.haulfryncaravanpark.co.uk
dir: *A55 junction 31 (from east follow Prestatyn A5151 signs, then Holywell A5026 signs. From west follow Holywell A5026 signs). At roundabout (BP garage and McDonalds can be seen) take A5026. Turn right for Gorsedd. In Gorsedd right opposite Druid Inn. 1.7 miles to site on left.*

Located on a former garden centre and nursery site and adjacent to a racecourse renowned in the late 1800s, this family park is located between the historic city of Chester and the popular Victorian resort of Llandudno. All pitches are well spaced and are fully serviced and include hardstandings. A stylish amenity block provides a combined kitchen and laundry and excellent modern shower and toilet facilities.

Open: 1 March to 1 November **Last arrival:** 20.00 **Last departure:** 11.00

Pitches: ; 29 hardstanding pitches

Facilities:

Services:

Within 3 miles:

Additional site information: 1.8 acre site. Cars can be parked by caravans. Awnings permitted. Dogs must be kept on leads at all times.

GWYNEDD

ABERSOCH Map 14 SH32

Places to visit

Plas-yn-Rhiw, PLAS YN RHIW, LL53 8AB, 01758 780219
www.nationaltrust.org.uk/plas-yn-rhiw

Beach View Caravan Park

★★★★ 87%

tel: 01758 712956 **Bwlchtocyn LL53 7BT**
email: beachviewabersoch4@gmail.com **web:** www.beachviewabersoch.co.uk
dir: *A499 to Abersoch. Through Abersoch and Sarn Bach. Straight on at crossroads, next left signed Porth Tocyn Hotel. Pass chapel. Left at next Porth Tocyn Hotel sign. Site on left.*

A long established clifftop park with stunning views of both the sea and the countryside. The grounds are immaculately maintained, and pitches are mainly hardstanding with good electric hook-ups. It is just a six-minute walk from the beach.

Open: mid March to mid October **Last arrival:** 21.00 **Last departure:** noon

Pitches: ; 47 hardstanding pitches; 40 seasonal pitches

Facilities:

Services:

Within 3 miles:

Additional site information: 4 acre site. Cars can be parked by caravans and tents. Awnings permitted. Families only.

Deucoch Touring & Camping Park

★★★★ 87%

tel: 01758 713293 & 07740 281770 **Sarn Bach LL53 7LD**
email: info@deucoch.com **web:** www.deucoch.com
dir: *From Abersoch take Sarn Bach road, at crossroads turn right, site on right in 800 yards.*

This is a colourful, sheltered site with stunning views of Cardigan Bay and the mountains that is situated just a mile from Abersoch and a long sandy beach. The friendly, enthusiastic, hands-on proprietors make year-on-year improvements to enhance their visitors' experience. Facilities include a superb chalet for dishwashing, outdoor hot showers for wetsuits, and a farmer's produce van delivers at weekends. An electric car charging point is also provided.

Open: March to October **Last arrival:** 18.00 **Last departure:** 11.00

Pitches: ; 10 hardstanding pitches

Leisure:

Facilities: WiFi

Services:

Within 3 miles:

Additional site information: 5 acre site. Cars can be parked by caravans and tents. Awnings permitted. Families only.

Bryn Bach Caravan & Camping Site

★★★★ 83%

tel: 07391 561160 & 07899 061737 **Tyddyn Talgoch Uchaf, Bwlchtocyn LL53 7BT**
email: brynbach@abersochcaravanandcamping.co.uk **web:** www.abersochcamping.co.uk
dir: *From Abersoch take Sarn Bach road for approximately 1 mile, turn left at sign for Bwlchtocyn. Follow signs to site, approximately 1 mile on left.*

Bryn Bach Caravan & Camping Site offers stunning views towards the beach and across the bay to the Snowdonia mountains, and a warm welcome is assured at this very well-maintained park on the outskirts of Abersoch. Pitch sizes are generous and a smart chalet houses the reception, a well-stocked shop and a cycle-hire facility. Quality family rooms are available in the amenity blocks and two glamping bell tents on spacious decking with scenic views are also available for hire.

Open: March to October **Last arrival:** 19.00 **Last departure:** 11.00

Pitches: * from £29; from £29; from £25; see prices below; 28 hardstanding pitches; 28 seasonal pitches

Leisure:

Facilities: WiFi

Services:

Within 3 miles:

Additional site information: 3.5 acre site. Cars can be parked by caravans and tents. Awnings permitted. No campfires, only breathable ground sheets permitted, children must return to pitch by 21.00. Boat/jet ski park.

Glamping available: Bell tents from £80

Additional glamping information: Bell tents: Family and couples only, no dogs allowed in tents. Heating and electricity included. Private BBQ and fridge. Cars can be parked by units

FACILITIES: Electric vehicle charging Baths/Shower Electric shaver sockets Hairdryer Ice pack facility Baby facilities Disabled facilities Shop on site or within 200yds BBQ area Picnic area WiFi WiFi Internet access **SERVICES:** Electric hook-up Launderette Licensed bar Calor Gas Campingaz Toilet fluid Café/Restaurant Fast Food/Takeaway Battery charging Motorhome service point No credit or debit cards Dogs permitted No dogs

WALES — GWYNEDD

ABERSOCH continued

Rhydolion
★★★ 77%

tel: 01758 712242 **Llangian LL53 7LR**
email: enquiries@rhydolion.co.uk **web:** www.rhydolion.co.uk/caravan_camping.htm
dir: From A499 take unclassified road to Llangian for 1 mile, left, through Llangian. Site 1.5 miles after road forks towards Hell's Mouth and Porth Neigwl.

A peaceful, small site with good views on a working farm close to the long sandy beach at Heels Mouth. The smart amenity block offers good privacy options for each gender and for families. Nearby Abersoch is a mecca for boat owners and watersports enthusiasts.

Open: March to October **Last arrival:** 22.00 **Last departure:** noon
Pitches: 🚐 🚗 ⛺
Leisure: ⚽
Facilities: ⊙ ✻
Services: 🔌 🔄 🛒
Within 3 miles: ⬇ ✏ ∪ ⚓ ≋ 🍴 💰

Additional site information: 1.5 acre site. 🚶 Cars can be parked by caravans and tents. Awnings permitted. Families and couples only. Dogs only accepted by prior arrangement. Fridge freezers and microwave available.

BALA — Map 14 SH93

Places to visit
Bala Lake Railway, Bala, LL23 7DD, 01678 540666
www.bala-lake-railway.co.uk

Tyn Cornel Camping
★★★ 83%

tel: 07859 431630 **Frongoch LL23 7NU**
email: booking@tyncornelcamping.co.uk **web:** www.tyncornelcamping.co.uk

A delightful riverside park with mountain views that is a popular base for those who enjoy kayaking and canoeing – The National White Water Centre is adjacent and there is a pleasant riverside walk to its café. Enthusiastic and hands-on managers deliver friendly service including a breakfast takeaway and bike hire. In addition to seasonal touring and camping pitches, glamping hire opportunities are available with two pods, a Lotus Belle tent and a geodome with night sky viewing.

Open: 25 March to 31 October **Last arrival:** 18.00 **Last departure:** noon
Pitches: 🚐 🚗 ⛺; 🏠 see prices below; 37 hardstanding pitches
Leisure: ⚽ ⊙ **Facilities:** 🏪 ✻ ♿ 🍴 WiFi 💻
Services: 🔌 🔄 **Within 3 miles:** ✏ ≋ 🍴 💰

Additional site information: 12 acre site. 🚶 Cars can be parked by caravans and tents. Awnings permitted.

Glamping available: 2 Lotus Belle tents from £65, 2 riverside pods £50, geodome
Changeover days: Any day

Additional glamping information: Lotus Belle tents: all kitchen equipment is provided. Gas stove, personal picnic bench, fire pit with a barbecue cooking griddle, lanterns, wood burning stove, double bed, bedding and towels. Riverside pods: electricity, lighting, heater, double bed. Geo dome: fully equipped. No dogs permitted.

BARMOUTH — Map 14 SH61

Places to visit
Harlech Castle, HARLECH, LL46 2YH, 03000 252239
www.cadw.gov.wales/visit/places-to-visit/harlech-castle

Cymer Abbey, PENRHYNDEUDRAETH, LL40 2HE, 03000 252239
www.cadw.gov.wales/visit/places-to-visit/cymer-abbey

Premier Park

Trawsdir Touring Caravans & Camping Park
★★★★★ 93%   *Best of British*

tel: 01341 280999 & 07798 520888 **Llanaber LL42 1RR**
email: enquiries@trawsdir.co.uk **web:** www.barmouthholidays.co.uk
dir: 3 miles north of Barmouth on A496, just past Nor Bar on right.

Well run by the owners, this quality park enjoys spectacular views to the sea and hills, and is very accessible for motor traffic. The facilities are appointed to a very high standard, and include spacious cubicles containing showers and washbasins, individual showers, smart toilets with sensor-operated flush and underfloor heating. Tents and caravans have their own designated areas divided by dry-stone walls (both have spacious fully serviced pitches). This site is very suitable for large recreational vehicles, and there are camping pods for hire. There is an excellent children's play area and an illuminated concrete dog walk that leads directly to the nearby pub, which offers takeaway pizza and fish suppers, in addition to restaurant meals. Fast WiFi is available throughout the park.

Open: March to January **Last arrival:** 17.00 **Last departure:** 11.00
Pitches: 🚐 🚗 ⛺; 🏠 see prices below; 70 hardstanding pitches; 30 seasonal pitches
Leisure: 🎪
Facilities: 🏪 ⊙ ✏ ✻ ♿ 🍴 🍽 🛋 WiFi
Services: 🔌 🔄 ⬇ 🛒 🧺 📺
Within 3 miles: ✏ ≋

Additional site information: 15 acre site. 🚶 Cars can be parked by caravans and tents. Awnings permitted. Families and couples only. Milk, bread etc available from reception, camping equipment available.

Glamping available: Wooden pods from £38.

Additional glamping information: Pet-friendly and no-pets-allowed pods available. Pods offer balcony area, BBQ, sea views and TV. Cars can be parked by units

GWYNEDD 299 WALES

Premier Park

Hendre Mynach Touring Caravan & Camping Park
★★★★★ 88%

tel: 01341 280262 Llanaber Road LL42 1YR
email: info@hendremynach.co.uk web: www.hendremynach.com
dir: *0.75 mile north of Barmouth on A496.*

A constantly improving site where the enthusiastic owners invest year on year to enhance the customer experience. Although there is a steep decent to the arrivals' area, staff are always on hand to assist. The beautifully maintained touring areas benefit from attractive hedge screening around the large well-spaced pitches that are equipped with water and TV hook-ups. Three camping pods, a duluxe, en suite camping pod, three shepherd's huts, three static caravans with dog friendly options and a holiday home are also available to rent. A well-stocked shop provides a wide range of food, beverages and caravan spares. There is direct access to the seafront which leads to the town centre and its many attractions.

Open: 1 March to 9 January (restricted service: Winter months – shop closed)
Last arrival: 20.30 **Last departure:** 10.30

Pitches: ; 85 hardstanding pitches; 10 seasonal pitches

Leisure:

Facilities:

Services:

Within 3 miles:

Additional site information: 10 acre site. Cars can be parked by caravans and tents. Awnings permitted. No open fires, no hard ball games. Play park; electric vehicle charging; dog wash.

Glamping available: 4 wooden pods, 3 shepherd's huts, deluxe glamping pod
Changeover days: Any day

Additional glamping information: Max 4 people in standard pods; 5 in deluxe pod. Bathroom/kitchen only in deluxe pod. Linen not supplied. Pet friendly. Cars can be parked by units

CAERNARFON
Map 14 SH46

Places to visit
Ffestiniog & Welsh Highland Railways, CAERNARFON, LL55 2YD, 01766 516000
www.festrail.co.uk

Great for kids: Caernarfon Castle, CAERNARFON, LL55 2AY, 03000 252239
www.cadw.gov.wales/visit/places-to-visit/caernarfon-castle

Riverside Camping
★★★★ 92%

tel: 01286 678781 Seiont Nurseries, Pont Rug LL55 2BB
email: info@riversidecamping.co.uk web: www.riversidecamping.co.uk
dir: *2 miles from Caernarfon on right of A4086 towards Llanberis, follow signs at entrance.*

Set in the grounds of a former garden centre and enjoying a superb location along the River Seiont, Riverside Camping is approached by an impressive tree-lined drive. Immaculately maintained by the owners, there is a mixture of riverside grassy pitches and fully serviced pitches for caravans and motorhomes. Hardstanding pitches have electric hook-up, water and TV connection but no drainage. In addition to the smart amenity blocks, other facilities include an excellent café/restaurant and volleyball and badminton courts; river fishing permits are also available. Four 'Riverside Cabans' with wood-burning stoves, picnic gardens and Japanese hot tubs, and two mountain-view, luxury tented lodges that include private saunas and sleep six people are offered for hire. This is a haven of peace close to Caernarfon and Snowdonia which offers some great walking opportunities.

Open: 14 March to October **Last arrival:** anytime **Last departure:** noon

Pitches: ; 16 hardstanding pitches; 10 seasonal pitches

Leisure:

Facilities:

Services:

Within 3 miles:

Additional site information: 5 acre site. Awnings permitted. No fires, no loud music. Debit cards accepted (no credit cards). Family shower room, undercover picnic area, table tennis, volleyball, basketball, mini-football pitch. Woodland dog walk.

Glamping available: Tented lodges. **Changeover days:** Monday and Friday

Additional glamping information: Tented lodges: beds, linen and towels provided, fully equipped. Woodburner, no electricity. Dogs accepted in 2 units only. No stag or hen groups.

CAERNARFON continued

Llys Derwen Caravan & Camping Site
★★★★ 88%

tel: 01286 673322 Ffordd Bryngwyn, Llanrug LL55 4AP
email: post@llysderwen.com web: www.llysderwen.co.uk
dir: *A55 junction 11 (follow Bangor (A5) and Llanberis signs). At roundabout left sign posted Betws y Coed (A5) and Llanberis (A4244). At next roundabout, second exit for Llanberis (A4244). At T-junction, turn right signed Caernarfon onto A4086. On entering the village of Llanrug, turn left at Y Glyntwrog pub, and the site entrance is 500 metres on right (just after the bungalows).*

On the outskirts of the village of Llanrug, three miles from Caernarfon on the way to Llanberis and Snowdon. A beautifully maintained site with enthusiastic owners who are constantly investing to improve the facilities. The amenity block is appointed to a high standard and the immaculately maintained grounds are planted with an abundance of colourful shrubs and seasonal flowers.

Llys Derwen Caravan & Camping Site

Open: March to October **Last arrival:** 22.00 **Last departure:** noon
Pitches: **Facilities:**
Services: **Within 3 miles:**
Additional site information: 4 acre site. Cars can be parked by caravans and tents. Awnings permitted. No open fires, no ball games, no noise after 22.00.

See advert below

LLYS DERWEN

Enjoy the adventure of a lifetime in wonderful North Wales. Book your holiday at the Award Winning Llys Derwen, our friendly Caravan, Touring Park and Campsite near Llanberis in Snowdonia. We are close to The Royal Town of Caernarfon, the University City of Bangor & home to the fastest Zip Line in the World 'Zip World'. Located near the foothills of Snowdon, our park is the perfect place for holidays and short breaks in the idyllic Welsh countryside. Get away from it all and reconnect with nature as you relax in one of our static caravans, your own touring van, motorhome or tent.

📍 Llys Derwen Caravan & Camping Site, Ffordd Bryngwyn, Llanrug, Caernarfon, Gwynedd LL55 4AP
📞 01286 673322
✉ post@llysderwen.com

PITCHES: Caravans Motorhomes Tents Glamping accommodation **LEISURE:** Indoor swimming pool Outdoor swimming pool Children's playground Kids' club Tennis court Games room Separate TV room golf course Pitch n putt Boats for hire Bikes for hire Cinema Entertainment Fishing Mini golf Watersports Gym Sports field Stables Spa

GWYNEDD 301 WALES

Plas Gwyn Caravan & Camping Park
★★★★ 86%

tel: 01286 672619 **Llanrug LL55 2AQ**
email: info@plasgwyn.co.uk **web:** www.plasgwyn.co.uk
dir: *A4086, 3 miles east of Caernarfon, site on right. Between River Seiont and Llanrug.*

A secluded park in an ideal location for visiting the glorious nearby beaches, historic Caernarfon, the attractions of Snowdonia and for walking opportunities. The site is set within the grounds of Plas Gwyn House, a Georgian property with colonial additions; the friendly owners constantly improve the facilities. There is a 'breakfast butty' service and fresh tea and coffee is available for delivery to individual pitches. All the pitches are fully serviced with water, electricity and waste water disposal and most have hardstandings. Three 'timber tents' (wooden pods) and five static caravans are also available for hire.

Open: March to October **Last arrival:** 22.00 **Last departure:** 11.30
Pitches: ; see prices below; 10 hardstanding pitches; 8 seasonal pitches
Facilities:
Services:
Within 3 miles:
Additional site information: 3 acre site. Cars can be parked by caravans and tents. Awnings permitted. Minimum noise 22.00 to midnight, complete quiet midnight to 08.00.
Glamping available: Wooden pods from £48.
Additional glamping information: Wooden pods: maximum of 4 people per unit. Cars can be parked by units

CRICCIETH   Map 14 SH43

Places to visit

Criccieth Castle, CRICCIETH, LL52 0DP, 03000 252239
www.cadw.gov.wales/visit/places-to-visit/criccieth-castle

Portmeirion, PORTMEIRION, LL48 6ER, 01766 770000
portmeirion.wales

Great for kids: Ffestiniog & Welsh Highland Railways, CAERNARFON, LL55 2YD, 01766 516000
www.festrail.co.uk

Eisteddfa
★★★★ 92%

tel: 01766 522696 **Eisteddfa Lodge, Pentrefelin LL52 0PT**
email: info@eisteddfapark.co.uk **web:** www.eisteddfapark.co.uk
dir: *From Porthmadog take A497 towards Criccieth. Approximately 3.5 miles, through Pentrefelin, site signed 1st right after Plas Gwyn Nursing Home.*

A quiet, secluded park on elevated ground, sheltered by the Snowdonia mountains and with lovely views of Cardigan Bay; Criccieth is nearby. The enthusiastic owners provide top-notch amenity blocks with good privacy options, especially for families. There's a field and play area, woodland walks, six superb slate-based hardstandings, a 'cocoon pod', and three static holiday caravans for hire, plus a three-acre coarse fishing lake adjacent to the park.

Open: March to October **Last arrival:** 22.30 **Last departure:** 11.00
Pitches: ; see prices below; 17 hardstanding pitches; 20 seasonal pitches
Leisure:
Facilities:

Services:
Within 3 miles:
Additional site information: 24 acre site. Cars can be parked by caravans and tents. Awnings permitted. No noise after 22.30. Baby bath available.
Glamping available: 1 cabin (cocoon pod) from £24.50.
Additional glamping information: Cars can be parked by unit

DINAS DINLLE   Map 14 SH45

Places to visit

Inigo Jones Slateworks, GROESLON, LL54 7UE, 01286 830242
www.inigojones.co.uk

Caernarfon Castle, CAERNARFON, LL55 2AY, 03000 252239
www.cadw.gov.wales/visit/places-to-visit/caernarfon-castle

Great for kids: Ffestiniog & Welsh Highland Railways, CAERNARFON, LL55 2YD, 01766 516000
www.festrail.co.uk

Premier Park

Dinlle Caravan Park
★★★★★ 93%

tel: 01286 830324 **LL54 5TW**
email: dinlle@thornleyleisure.co.uk **web:** www.thornleyleisure.co.uk/park/dinlle
dir: *From A487 at roundabout take A499 signed Pwllheli. Right at Caernarfon Airport and brown camping signs.*

A very accessible site adjacent to a sandy beach and with great views towards Snowdonia. Landscaping is particularly impressive with a colourful display of both cultivated and indigenous plants. All pitches have hardstandings with electricity and most are fully serviced. The man-made high banks create an effective wind break for campers and there are camping pods with decking and barbecue areas for hire. The tastefully furnished club room and bar creates a relaxing environment and the superb outdoor swimming pool has the benefit of an adjacent well-equipped gym. A golf club, nature reserve and Caernarfon Airworld Museum can be accessed from the beach road.

Open: March to November **Last arrival:** 22.00 **Last departure:** noon
Pitches: ; see prices below; 135 hardstanding pitches; 135 seasonal pitches
Leisure:
Facilities:
Services:
Within 3 miles:
Additional site information: 20 acre site. Cars can be parked by caravans and tents. Awnings permitted.
Glamping available: Wooden pods from £40. **Changeover days:** Any day
Additional glamping information: Wooden pods sleep 4. 1 double bed, 2 single beds. Minimum stay 2 nights. Cars can be parked by units

---

FACILITIES: Electric vehicle charging · Baths/Shower · Electric shaver sockets · Hairdryer · Ice pack facility · Baby facilities · Disabled facilities · Shop on site or within 200yds · BBQ area · Picnic area · WiFi · Internet access **SERVICES:** Electric hook-up · Launderette · Licensed bar · Calor Gas · Campingaz · Toilet fluid · Café/Restaurant · Fast Food/Takeaway · Battery charging · Motorhome service point · No credit or debit cards · Dogs permitted · No dogs

WALES — GWYNEDD

LLANDWROG
Map 14 SH45

Places to visit
Ffestiniog & Welsh Highland Railways, CAERNARFON, LL55 2YD, 01766 516000
www.festrail.co.uk

Great for kids: Caernarfon Castle, CAERNARFON, LL55 2AY, 03000 252239
www.cadw.gov.wales/visit/places-to-visit/caernarfon-castle

White Tower Holiday Park
★★★★ 96%

tel: 01286 830649 & 07802 562735 **LL54 5UH**
email: whitetowerholidaypark@gmail.com **web:** www.whitetowerpark.co.uk
dir: *From Caernarfon take A487 Porthmadog road. 1st right into Pant Road signed Llanfaglan and Saron. Site 3 miles on right.*

There are lovely views of Snowdonia from this park that is located just two miles from the beach at Dinas Dinlle. A very well maintained, quality amenity block provides good privacy options and all pitches are fully serviced. Popular features include a quality lounge bar with a family room and a games/TV room. A new outdoor swimming pool is being constructed for the 2025 season.

Open: March to 10 January (restricted service: March to mid May and September to November — bar closed weekdays) **Last arrival:** 23.00 **Last departure:** noon

Pitches: 50 hardstanding pitches; 50 seasonal pitches

Leisure:
Facilities:
Services:
Within 3 miles:

Additional site information: 9 acre site. Cars can be parked by caravans. Awnings permitted.

PORTHMADOG
Map 14 SH53

Places to visit
Portmeirion, PORTMEIRION, LL48 6ER, 01766 770000
portmeirion.wales

Great for kids: Ffestiniog & Welsh Highland Railways, CAERNARFON, LL55 2YD, 01766 516000
www.festrail.co.uk

Premier Park

Greenacres Holiday Park
★★★★★ 88% HOLIDAY PARK

tel: 01766 512781 **Black Rock Sands, Morfa Bychan LL49 9YF**
email: greenacres@haven.com **web:** www.haven.com/parks/north-wales/greenacres
dir: *From Porthmadog High Street follow Black Rock Sands signs between The Factory Shop and Post Office. Park 2 miles on left at end of Morfa Bychan.*

A quality holiday park on level ground just a short walk from Black Rock Sands, and set against a backdrop of Snowdonia National Park. All touring pitches are on hardstandings surrounded by closely-mown grass, and are near the entertainment complex. A full programme of entertainment, organised clubs, indoor and outdoor sports and leisure, pubs, shows and cabarets all add to a holiday experience here. A large shop with a bakery are useful amenities. The superb touring field has excellent fully serviced Euro pitches, extensive, colourful planting and a smart, well-equipped amenity block. The Marina Bar and club has facilities for all age groups.

Open: mid March to end October (restricted service: mid March to May and September to October — some facilities may be reduced) **Last arrival:** 22.00 **Last departure:** 10.00

Pitches: 45 hardstanding pitches

Leisure:
Facilities:
Services:
Within 3 miles:

Additional site information: 121 acre site. No commercial vehicles, no bookings by persons under 21 years unless a family booking, no open fires. Maximum 2 dogs per booking, certain dog breeds banned.

PITCHES: Caravans — Motorhomes — Tents — Glamping accommodation **LEISURE:** Indoor swimming pool — Outdoor swimming pool — Children's playground — Kids' club — Tennis court — Games room — Separate TV room — golf course — Pitch n putt — Boats for hire — Bikes for hire — Cinema — Entertainment — Fishing — Mini golf — Watersports — Gym — Sports field — Stables — Spa

PWLLHELI

Map 14 SH33

Places to visit

Lloyd George Museum, LLANYSTUMDWY, LL52 0SH, 01766 522071
www.gwynedd.llyw.cymru/en/Residents/Leisure-parks-and-events/Museums-and-the-Arts/The-Lloyd-George-Museum.aspx

Great for kids: Cricieth Castle, CRICCIETH, LL52 0DP, 03000 252239
www.cadw.gov.wales/visit/places-to-visit/criccieth-castle

Platinum Park

Hafan y Môr Holiday Park
★★★★★ HOLIDAY PARK

tel: 01758 612112 LL53 6HJ
email: hafanymor@haven.com web: www.haven.com/hafanymor
dir: *From Caernarfon take A499 to Pwllheli. A497 to Porthmadog. Park on right, approximately 3 miles from Pwllheli. Or from Telford, A5, A494 to Bala. Right for Porthmadog. Left at roundabout in Porthmadog signed Cricieth and Pwllheli. Park on left, 3 miles from Cricieth.*

Located between Pwllheli and Cricieth, and surrounded by mature trees that attract wildlife, this popular holiday centre provides a wide range of all-weather attractions. Activities include a sports hall, Dragon Lakes Outside Experiences, a large indoor swimming pool, a show bar and high-ropes activity. There are also great eating options – the stylish Coast House bistro, Cakery ice cream and cake parlour, the Pizza Deck with wood-fired pizzas, a beachside café, and the superb HMS Glendower bar over the bridge, and by The Splash Zone you'll find traditional fish and chips, Burger King® and Papa John's®. The touring area includes 75 fully serviced all-weather pitches and a top notch, air-conditioned amenity block.

Open: mid March to end October (restricted service: mid March to May and September to end October – reduced facilities) **Last arrival:** 21.00 **Last departure:** 10.00

Pitches: 75 hardstanding pitches

Leisure:

Facilities:

Services:

Within 3 miles:

Additional site information: 500 acre site. No commercial vehicles, no bookings by persons under 21 years unless a family booking. Maximum 2 dogs per booking, certain dog breeds banned.

Abererch Sands Holiday Centre
★★★ 84%

tel: 01758 612327 LL53 6PJ
email: enquiries@abererch-sands.co.uk web: www.abererch-sands.co.uk
dir: *On A497 (Porthmadog to Pwllheli road), 1 mile from Pwllheli.*

Glorious views of Snowdonia and Cardigan Bay can be enjoyed from Abererch Sands, a secure, family-run site adjacent to the railway station and four miles of sandy beach. The amenity block has stylish decor and modern, efficient fixtures and fittings. There are no handstanding pitches. A large, heated indoor swimming pool and children's play area make this an ideal family holiday venue.

Open: March to October **Last arrival:** 19.00 **Last departure:** noon

Pitches:

Leisure:

Facilities: WiFi

Services:

Within 3 miles:

Additional site information: 85 acre site. Cars can be parked by caravans and tents. Awnings permitted. Dogs must be kept on leads at all times. All pitches are grass.

Make your next UK holiday one to remember

Choose RatedTrips.com

FACILITIES: Electric vehicle charging Baths/Shower Electric shaver sockets Hairdryer Ice pack facility Baby facilities Disabled facilities Shop on site or within 200yds BBQ area Picnic area WiFi Internet access **SERVICES:** Electric hook-up Launderette Licensed bar Calor Gas Campingaz Toilet fluid Café/Restaurant Fast Food/Takeaway Battery charging Motorhome service point No credit or debit cards Dogs permitted No dogs

WALES 304 GWYNEDD

TALYBONT
Map 14 SH52

Places to visit
Cymer Abbey, PENRHYNDEUDRAETH, LL40 2HE, 03000 252239
www.cadw.gov.wales/visit/places-to-visit/cymer-abbey

Harlech Castle, HARLECH, LL46 2YH, 03000 252239
www.cadw.gov.wales/visit/places-to-visit/harlech-castle

Platinum Park

Islawrffordd Caravan Park
★★★★★

tel: 01341 247269 **LL43 2AQ**
email: info@islawrffordd.co.uk web: www.islawrffordd.co.uk
dir: *From A496 into Ffordd Glan-Mor towards sea, follow brown campsite sign. Over rail line, site on left.*

Situated on the coast between Barmouth and Harlech and within the Snowdonia National Park, this site has clear views of Cardigan Bay, the Llŷn Peninsula and the Snowdonia and Cader Idris mountain ranges. This is an excellent, family-run and family-friendly park that has seen considerable investment over recent years. Fully matured, the touring area boasts fully-serviced pitches, a superb toilet block with underfloor heating and top-quality fittings; there is private access to miles of sandy beach, adjacent to which is an excellent enclosed children's play area with imaginative, quality equipment to satisfy small children, including a pirate ship. An amenity block – The Cader Suite – has luxury, private bathrooms. A superb restaurant and bar, 'Nineteen57', offers both formal and relaxed areas for enjoying locally-sourced food.

Open: 14 February to 4 January **Last arrival:** 20.00 **Last departure:** noon
Pitches: 🚐 🚙; 75 hardstanding pitches; 50 seasonal pitches
Leisure: 🏊 ⛰ 🎮 **Facilities:** 🚻 ⊙ 🍴 ♿
Services: 🔌 🗑 🧺 🍴 🏪 🧳 ⬇ 🔒 ⌀ 🅃 **Within 3 miles:** 🏌 ⛴ 💰
Additional site information: 25 acre site. 🐕 Cars can be parked by caravans. Awnings permitted. Strictly families and couples only.

See advert opposite

TYWYN
Map 14 SH50

Places to visit
Talyllyn Railway, TYWYN, LL36 9EY, 01654 710472
www.talyllyn.co.uk

Castell y Bere, LLANFIHANGEL-Y-PENNANT, 03000 252239
www.cadw.gov.wales/visit/places-to-visit/castell-y-bere

Great for kids: King Arthur's Labyrinth, CORRIS, SY20 9RF, 01654 761584
www.kingarthurslabyrinth.co.uk

Barmouth Bay Holiday Park
★★★★ 88% HOLIDAY PARK

tel: 0330 053 7000 Talybont **LL43 2BJ**
web: www.awayresorts.co.uk/parks/north-wales/barmouth-bay

With a mountain backdrop and direct access to miles of sandy beaches, Barmouth Bay Holiday Park is an ideal location for escaping from the pressures of everyday life. Holiday homes are well spaced to create optimum privacy and the Indulgence range can include a rooftop garden area with stunning views. Interiors are well furnished and some come equipped with facilities for those less mobile. The impressive grounds enjoy colour and interest throughout the year, while entertainment and activities are for all ages.

Ynysymaengwyn Caravan Park
★★★★ 86%

tel: 01654 710684 **LL36 9RY**
email: rita@ynysy.co.uk web: www.ynysy.co.uk
dir: *On A493, 1 mile north of Tywyn, towards Dolgellau.*

A lovely park set in the wooded grounds of a former manor house, with designated nature trails through 13 acres of wildlife-rich woodland, scenic river walks, fishing and a sandy beach nearby. The attractive stone built amenity block is centrally heated, air conditioned and provides good privacy options; even the dogs have their own external warm shower. The park is ideal for families, and an indoor screened classroom and fairy trail has been created within the extensive woodland to maximise children's imagination and enjoyment.

Open: March to November **Last arrival:** 23.00 **Last departure:** noon
Pitches: 🚐 🚙 ⛺; 15 hardstanding pitches; 5 seasonal pitches
Leisure: ⛰ 🎣
Facilities: 🚻 ⊙ 🍴 ✳ ♿ 🪑 📶 💻
Services: 🔌 🗑 🧺 ⬇ 🔒 ⌀
Within 3 miles: 🚶 🏌 ⛳ 🛥 📅 💰
Additional site information: 4 acre site. 🐕 Cars can be parked by caravans and tents. Awnings permitted. Woodland walks. Fishing

---

PITCHES: 🚐 Caravans 🚙 Motorhomes ⛺ Tents 🏕 Glamping accommodation **LEISURE:** 🏊 Indoor swimming pool 🏊 Outdoor swimming pool ⛰ Children's playground 🎈 Kids' club 🎾 Tennis court 🎮 Games room 📺 Separate TV room ⛳ golf course 🏏 Pitch n putt 🚣 Boats for hire 🚴 Bikes for hire 🎬 Cinema 🎭 Entertainment 🎣 Fishing ⛳ Mini golf 🏄 Watersports 🏋 Gym 🏟 Sports field 🐎 Stables 💆 Spa

Islawrffordd Luxury Holiday Park

W: www.islawrffordd.co.uk   E: info@islawrffordd.co.uk   T: 01341 247269

In beautiful Barmouth, this 5 star luxury holiday park features static, seasonal and touring pitches and luxury holiday homes.

PARK FACILITIES INCLUDE:

- Heated indoor swimming pool with jacuzzi
- Amusement arcade with coffee shop and take away food
- Nineteen.57 restaurant and bar
- Luxury super euro pitches for touring caravans and motorhome
- Underfloor heated shower/washrooms and a launderette
- Private slipway to the beach and secure boat storage

FACILITIES: Electric vehicle charging or within 200yds · Baths/Shower · Electric shaver sockets · Hairdryer · Ice pack facility · Baby facilities · Disabled facilities · Shop on site · BBQ area · Picnic area · WiFi · Internet access   **SERVICES:** Electric hook-up · Launderette · Licensed bar · Calor Gas · Campingaz · Toilet fluid · Café/Restaurant · Fast Food/Takeaway · Battery charging · Motorhome service point · No credit or debit cards · Dogs permitted · No dogs

WALES — MONMOUTHSHIRE

MONMOUTHSHIRE

ABERGAVENNY — Map 9 SO21

Places to visit

Big Pit National Coal Museum, BLAENAVON, NP4 9XP, 0300 111 2333
museum.wales/bigpit

Hen Gwrt, LLANTILIO CROSSENNY, 03000 252239
www.cadw.gov.wales/visit/places-to-visit/hen-gwrt-moated-site

Wernddu Caravan Park
★★★★ 86%

tel: 01873 856223 **Old Ross Road NP7 8NG**
email: info@wernddu-golf-club.co.uk **web:** www.wernddu-golf-club.co.uk
dir: From A465, north of Abergavenny, take B4521 signed Skenfrith. Site on right in 0.25 mile.

Located north of the town centre, this former fruit farm, adjacent to a golf club and driving range, is managed by three generations of the same family, and has been transformed into an ideal base for those visiting the many nearby attractions. The well-spaced touring pitches have water, electricity and waste water disposal, and the smart modern amenity block provides very good privacy options. Site guests are welcome to use the golf club bar which also serves meals during the busy months; they are also eligible for half-price green fees.

Open: March to October **Last arrival:** 21.00 **Last departure:** noon

Pitches: 30 seasonal pitches

Leisure:

Facilities: WiFi

Services:

Within 3 miles:

Additional site information: 6 acre site. Adults only. Cars can be parked by caravans and tents. Awnings permitted. No fires. No noise after 23.00. 20 touring grass pitches. Driving range, bar

LLANVAIR DISCOED — Map 9 ST49

Places to visit

Chepstow Castle, CHEPSTOW, NP16 5EY, 03000 252239
www.cadw.gov.wales/visit/places-to-visit/chepstow-castle

Premier Park

Penhein Glamping
★★★★★ 94% GLAMPING ONLY

tel: 01633 400581 **Penhein NP16 6RB**
email: enquiries@penhein.co.uk **web:** www.penhein.co.uk/
dir: M48 junction 2, A446 towards Chepstow. 1st exit at roundabout onto A48 signed Caerwent. Approximately 8 miles, through Caerwent, right signed Llanvair Discoed. 1st right at village sign, immediately left into private drive. Site 1.5 miles.

Tucked away in secluded woodland surrounded by peaceful countryside, Penhein Glamping offers eight beautiful Alachigh (pronounced alla-cheeg) tents, that are cosy, warm and kitted out with everything you need for a holiday to remember. The sumptuous interiors have comfortable beds (a double, two truckle beds and a sofa bed for children), quality dining furniture, lanterns, a fully equipped kitchen with a cold-water sink, a large cool box and a wood-burning stove (wood provided). Each tent also has an en suite pod, with fully flushing toilet. Three of the tents have their own shower immediately outside, four of the tents have a dedicated shower in the shower block and the fifth tent is allocated the Victorian roll top bath. Outside each tent there is a fire pit for BBQs and carved tree-trunk seating. There are level bark pathways between the tents, and a 'Cheat's Kitchen' in the centre of the site, with microwave, cooking hobs, an honesty bar plus a freezer, as there's no electricity in the tents. The shower block has a drying room, underfloor heating, monsoon showers and a Victorian style roll-top bath. In addition, there's a communal tent with a wood-burning stove and a wildflower meadow for games. An impressive and spacious stretch marquee has been added for large group activities, with its own large fire pit outside for guests to gather around.

Open: March to November **Last arrival:** 22.00 **Last departure:** 11.00

Leisure:

Facilities:

Within 3 miles:

Accommodation available: 8 alachighs

Changeover days: Monday, Wednesday, Friday

Additional site information: 11 acre site. Adults only. No pets. 8-acre private wildflower and hay meadow, walks on large farm (woodlands and fields).

MONMOUTH — Map 10 SO51

Places to visit

Monmouth Castle, MONMOUTH, NP25 3BS, 03000 252239
www.cadw.gov.wales/visit/places-to-visit/monmouth-castle

The Kymin, MONMOUTH, NP25 3SF, 01874 625515
www.nationaltrust.org.uk/the-kymin

PITCHES: Caravans • Motorhomes • Tents • Glamping accommodation   **LEISURE:** Indoor swimming pool • Outdoor swimming pool • Children's playground • Kids' club • Tennis court • Games room • Separate TV room • golf course • Pitch n putt • Boats for hire • Bikes for hire • Cinema • Entertainment • Fishing • Mini golf • Watersports • Gym • Sports field • Stables • Spa

MONMOUTHSHIRE—PEMBROKESHIRE

MONMOUTH
Map 10 SO51

Rockfield Glamping
★★★★ 92% GLAMPING ONLY

tel: 07837 648315 Pendragon, Rockfield NP25 5QE
email: info@rockfieldglamping.com web: www.rockfieldglamping.com

Located on a working farm in a stunning landscape of undulating hills, quality, well spaced bell tents are strategically placed to maximise the excellent views. Interiors are furnished with a small wood-burning stove, efficient task lighting, quality beds and seating. Adjoining each tent is a stylishly converted horse box featuring a fully equipped private bathroom with smart fittings including a power shower over a bath. Drop the main door panel, relax in the bath and soak up the amazing rural views. A central campers' kitchen contains individual fridges and communal washing up and additional cooking facilities. The glamping area is a balance of neat lush grass and indigenous plants creating lots of colour with the added benefit of abundant wildlife; there are great play opportunities for children of all ages.

Open: 04 April to 02 October Last arrival: 21.00 Last departure: 10:30
Leisure: ⚽
Facilities: 🏠 🛁 🚿
Within 3 miles: 🎣 ⛵ 🚣 🏪 🏛 🛒
Accommodation available: 4 bell tents from £87.50
Changeover days: Monday to Friday or Friday to Monday
Additional site information: 2.5 acre site. 🐕 Football Pitch, Tree Swing, Zip Wire, Volleyball. Linen provided.

USK
Map 9 SO30

Places to visit
Caerleon Roman Fortress and Baths, CAERLEON, NP18 1AE, 03000 252239
www.cadw.gov.wales/visit/places-to-visit/caerleon-roman-fortress-and-baths

Big Pit National Coal Museum, BLAENAVON, NP4 9XP, 0300 111 2333
museum.wales/bigpit

Great for kids: Greenmeadow Community Farm, CWMBRAN, NP44 5AJ, 01633 647662
www.greenmeadowcommunityfarm.org.uk

Premier Park

Pont Kemys Caravan & Camping Park
★★★★★ 87%

tel: 01873 880688 & 07949 761376 Chainbridge NP7 9DS
email: info@pontkemys.com web: www.pontkemys.co.uk
dir: From Usk take B4598 towards Abergavenny. Approximately 4 miles, over river bridge, bear right, 300 yards to site. For other routes contact site for detailed directions.

A peaceful park adjacent to the River Usk, offering an excellent standard of toilet facilities with family rooms. The adults-only field benefits from large, fully serviced pitches with wide divisions for additional privacy, and a section of the park has fully serviced pitches; TV hook-up points are located across the site as reception is poor. The park is in a rural area with mature trees and country views, and attracts quiet visitors.

Open: March to October Last arrival: 21.00 Last departure: noon
Pitches: 🚐 🚗 ⛺; 29 hardstanding pitches; 25 seasonal pitches
Leisure: 🎱 ⚽
Facilities: 🏠 ☉ 🗡 ✻ ♿ 🍴 WiFi
Services: 🔌 🛢 🧺 🚽 🔒 ♻ 📺
Within 3 miles: 🎣 🚣 🛒

Additional site information: 8 acre site. 🐕 Cars can be parked by caravans and tents. Awnings permitted. No music. Mother and baby room, kitchen facilities for groups.

PEMBROKESHIRE

FISHGUARD
Map 8 SM93

Places to visit
Pentre Ifan Burial Chamber, NEWPORT, 03000 252239
www.cadw.gov.wales/visit/places-to-visit/pentre-ifan-burial-chamber

Great for kids: Sea Môr Aquarium, FISHGUARD, SA64 0DE, 01348 874737
www.seatrust.org.uk

Fishguard Bay Resort
★★★★ 90%

tel: 01348 811415 Garn Gelli SA65 9ET
email: enquiries@fishguardbay.com web: www.fishguardbay.com
dir: Accessed from A487. Turn at park sign onto single track road. (Note: if approaching Fishguard from Cardigan on A487 ignore sat nav to turn right).

Set high up on cliffs with outstanding views of Fishguard Bay, this site has the Pembrokeshire Coastal Path running right through its centre, so affording many opportunities for wonderful walks. The park is extremely well maintained, with a good toilet block, laundry and a well-stocked shop. There are glamping pods and studio lodges (with hot tubs) – all have superb sea views plus there's a 'pamper' pod for spa treatments.

Open: March to 9 January Last arrival: anytime Last departure: noon
Pitches: 🚐 🚗 ⛺; 🏠 see prices below; 10 hardstanding pitches
Facilities: 🏠 ☉ 🗡 ✻ 🍴 WiFi 💻
Services: 🔌 🛢 🧺 🚽 🔒 ♻ 📺
Within 3 miles: 🎣 ⛵ 🚣 🛒 🏪

Additional site information: 7 acre site. 🐕 Cars can be parked by caravans and tents. Awnings permitted. No commercial vehicles. Spa treatments.

Glamping available: 2 wooden pods from £55; 2 studio lodges from £85.
Changeover days: Any day

Additional glamping information: Wooden pods offer TV, fridge, BBQ, double sofa bed, 2 small bunk beds. Bedding is not included. Studio lodges offer TV, 2 double sofa beds, hot tub, BBQ area, decking, kitchen with fridge, microwave and shower and toilet. Cars can be parked by units

WALES 308 PEMBROKESHIRE

HAVERFORDWEST
Map 8 SM91

Places to visit
Llawhaden Castle, LLAWHADEN, 03000 252239
www.cadw.gov.wales/visit/places-to-visit/llawhaden-castle

Great for kids: Oakwood Theme Park, NARBERTH, SA67 8DE, 01834 815170
www.oakwoodthemepark.co.uk

Nolton Cross Caravan Park
★★★ 81%

tel: 01437 710701 & 07814 779020 **Nolton SA62 3NP**
email: info@noltoncross-holidays.co.uk web: www.noltoncross-holidays.co.uk
dir: *1 mile from A487 (Haverfordwest to St Davids road) at Simpson Cross, towards Nolton and Broadhaven.*

High grassy banks surround the touring area of this park adjacent to the owners' working farm. It is located on open ground above the sea and St Bride's Bay (within one and a half miles), and a shop is also provided. WiFi is available.

Open: March to December **Last arrival:** 22.00 **Last departure:** noon (Touring) 10.00 (static)
Pitches: 🚐 🚗 ⛺; 6 hardstanding pitches
Leisure: 🎠 **Facilities:** 🚻 ☉ ✲ 🌳 WiFi
Services: 🔌 🧺 🚮 ⬇ ⊘ T Within 3 miles: 🚶 🛒

Additional site information: 4 acre site. 🅿 Cars can be parked by caravans and tents. Awnings permitted. No youth groups. Pets must be kept on leads. Site shop open high season only.

ST DAVIDS
Map 8 SM72

Places to visit
St Davids Cathedral, ST DAVIDS, SA62 6RD, 01437 720202
www.stdavidscathedral.org.uk

St Davids Bishop's Palace, ST DAVIDS, SA62 6PE, 03000 252239
www.cadw.gov.wales/visit/places-to-visit/st-davids-bishops-palace

Premier Park

Caerfai Bay Caravan & Tent Park
★★★★★ 93%

tel: 01437 720274 **Caerfai Bay SA62 6QT**
email: info@caerfaibay.co.uk web: www.caerfaibay.co.uk
dir: *From Haverfordwest on A487 towards St Davids, left at roundabout into Caerfai Road (Ffordd Caerfai) signed Caerfai Bay. Or from Fishguard take A487 to St Davids. At St Davids speed restriction sign turn left into Glasfryn Road. At roundabout, second exit into Caerfai Road (Ffordd Caerfai). Site on right at end of road, before beach car park.*

Magnificent coastal scenery and an outlook over St Bride's Bay can be enjoyed from this delightful site, located just 300 yards from a bathing beach. The park offers good roadways, modern water points, solar-heated wetsuit shower rooms and excellent toilet facilities which include four family rooms. The lower field has been divided into separate dog-free and dog-friendly areas and low level lighting ensures a stunning night sky on cloud-free days.

Open: March to early November **Last arrival:** 21.00 **Last departure:** 11.00 (Touring); 09:30 (Static)
Pitches: 🚐 🚗 ⛺; 22 hardstanding pitches
Facilities: 🚻 ☉ ✲ ♿ WiFi 🔌
Services: 🔌 🧺 🚮 ⬇ 🔒 ⊘ T
Within 3 miles: 🚶 🛒

Additional site information: 10 acre site. 🅿 Cars can be parked by caravans and tents. Awnings permitted. Tent fields have dog friendly and non-dog areas, no skateboards or rollerblades, no audible devices after 22.00, quiet from 23.00. Local farm shop nearby is open from end May to end August.

PITCHES: 🚐 Caravans 🚗 Motorhomes ⛺ Tents 🏕 Glamping accommodation **LEISURE:** 🏊 Indoor swimming pool 🏊 Outdoor swimming pool 🎠 Children's playground 🧒 Kids' club 🎾 Tennis court 🎱 Games room 📺 Separate TV room ⛳ golf course 🏌 Pitch n putt ⛵ Boats for hire 🚲 Bikes for hire 🎬 Cinema 🎭 Entertainment 🎣 Fishing ⛳ Mini golf 🏄 Watersports 💪 Gym 🏟 Sports field 🐎 Stables ♨ Spa

PEMBROKESHIRE–POWYS WALES

Tretio Caravan & Camping Park
★★★ 83%

tel: 01437 781600 & 07814 588289 **SA62 6DE**
email: info@tretio.com web: www.tretio.com
dir: *From St Davids take A487 towards Fishguard, left at Rugby Football Club, straight on for 3 miles. Site signed, right to site.*

A warm welcome is assured at this long established family-orientated holiday destination in a rural location with superb country views and close to beautiful beaches. On-site facilities include a well-equipped amenity block and a very good children's play area. The small cathedral city of St Davids is only three miles away.

Open: March to October **Last arrival:** 20.00 **Last departure:** 11.00
Pitches: ; 1 hardstanding pitch; 8 seasonal pitches
Leisure: **Facilities:**
Services: **Within 3 miles:**

Additional site information: 6.5 acre site. Cars can be parked by caravans and tents. Awnings permitted. Quiet after 22.00. Climbing wall, play area.

TENBY   Map 8 SN10

Places to visit

Tudor Merchant's House, TENBY, SA70 7BX, 01646 623110
www.nationaltrust.org.uk/tudor-merchants-house

Tenby Museum & Art Gallery, TENBY, SA70 7BP, 01834 842809
www.tenbymuseum.org.uk

Great for kids: Colby Woodland Garden, AMROTH, SA67 8PP, 01646 623110
www.nationaltrust.org.uk/colby-woodland-garden

Premier Park

Kiln Park Holiday Centre
★★★★★ 86% **HOLIDAY PARK**

tel: 01834 844121 **Marsh Road SA70 8RB**
email: kilnpark@haven.com web: www.haven.com/parks/south-wales/kiln-park
dir: *Follow A477, A478 to Tenby for 6 miles. Then follow signs to Penally, site 0.5 mile on left.*

A large holiday complex complete with leisure and sports facilities and lots of entertainment for all the family. There are bars and cafés, including the stylish Harbwr Lights Bistro, and plenty of security features. This touring, camping and static site is on the outskirts of town, and it's only a short walk through dunes to the sandy beach. The modern amenity block provides a stylish interior with underfloor heating and superb fixtures and fittings.

Open: mid March to end October (restricted service: mid March to May and September to end October – some facilities may be reduced) **Last arrival:** dusk **Last departure:** 10.00
Pitches: ; 60 hardstanding pitches
Leisure:
Facilities:
Services: **Within 3 miles:**

Additional site information: 103 acre site. No commercial vehicles, no bookings by persons under 21 years unless a family booking, maximum 2 dogs per booking, certain dog breeds banned. Entertainment complex, bowling and putting green.

Well Park Caravan & Camping Site
★★★★ 83%

tel: 01834 842179 **New Hedges SA70 8TL**
email: enquiries@wellparkcaravans.co.uk web: www.wellparkcaravans.co.uk
dir: *A478 towards Tenby. At roundabout at Kilgetty follow Tenby and A478 signs. 3 miles to next roundabout, take 2nd exit, site 2nd right.*

An attractive, well-maintained park with good landscaping from trees, ornamental shrubs and flower borders. The amenities include a launderette and indoor dishwashing and an enclosed play area. The park is ideally situated between Tenby and Saundersfoot; Tenby is just a 15-minute walk away, or the town can be reached via a traffic-free cycle track.

Open: March to October (restricted service: March to mid June and mid September to October – bar may be closed) **Last arrival:** 22.00 **Last departure:** 11.00
Pitches: ; 30 hardstanding pitches; 50 seasonal pitches
Leisure: **Facilities:**
Services:
Within 3 miles:

Additional site information: 10 acre site. Cars can be parked by caravans and tents. Awnings permitted. Family groups only. 5mph speed limit. No noise after 23.00.

POWYS

BRECON   Map 9 SO02

Places to visit

Regimental Museum of The Royal Welsh, BRECON, LD3 7EB, 01874 613310
www.royalwelshmuseum.wales

Tretower Court and Castle, TRETOWER, NP8 1RF, 03000 252239
www.cadw.gov.wales/visit/places-to-visit/tretower-court-and-castle

---

Premier Park

Pencelli Castle Caravan & Camping Park
★★★★★ 94%

tel: 01874 665451 **Pencelli LD3 7LX**
email: pencelli@tiscali.co.uk web: www.pencelli-castle.com
dir: *A40 onto B4588 (2 miles east of Brecon), follow signs to Pencelli.*

Lying in the heart of the Brecon Beacons National Park, this charming park offers peace, beautiful scenery, high-quality facilities and a wildflower meadow. It is bordered by the Brecon and Monmouth Canal. The attention to detail is superb, and the well-equipped, heated toilets with en suite cubicles are matched by a drying room for clothes and boots, full laundry, and a shop. Super-fast WiFi is available throughout the park. Regular buses stop just outside the gate and go to Brecon, Abergavenny and Swansea.

Open: 15 February to December (restricted service: mid February to Easter and 30 October to November – shop closed) **Last arrival:** 22.00 **Last departure:** noon
Pitches: ; 40 hardstanding pitches
Leisure: **Facilities:**
Services: **Within 3 miles:**

Additional site information: 10 acre site. Only assistance dogs permitted. Cars can be parked by caravans and tents. Awnings permitted. No radios, music or camp fires.

FACILITIES: Electric vehicle charging · Baths/Shower · Electric shaver sockets · Hairdryer · Ice pack facility · Baby facilities · Disabled facilities · Shop on site or within 200yds · BBQ area · Picnic area · WiFi · Internet access **SERVICES:** Electric hook-up · Launderette · Licensed bar · Calor Gas · Campingaz · Toilet fluid · Café/Restaurant · Fast Food/Takeaway · Battery charging · Motorhome service point · No credit or debit cards · Dogs permitted · No dogs

BRONLLYS
Map 9 SO13

Places to visit
Regimental Museum of The Royal Welsh, BRECON, LD3 7EB, 01874 613310
www.royalwelshmuseum.wales

Anchorage Caravan Park
★★★★ 85%

tel: 01874 711246 **LD3 0LD**
email: info@anchoragecp.co.uk web: www.anchoragecp.co.uk
dir: *A40 to Brecon. At roundabout take A470 signed Hereford (this road becomes A438). Approximately 8 miles, at roundabout follow Bronllys signs. In Bronllys follow brown campsite signs.*

A well-maintained site with a choice of south-facing, sloping grass pitches and superb views of the Black Mountains, or a more sheltered lower area with a number of excellent super pitches. The site is a short distance from the watersports centre at Llangorse Lake.

Open: All year (restricted service: November to March – TV room closed)
Last arrival: 23.00 **Last departure:** 16.00
Pitches: ; 8 hardstanding pitches; 60 seasonal pitches
Leisure:
Facilities:
Services: Within 3 miles:

Additional site information: 8 acre site. Cars can be parked by caravans and tents. Awnings permitted. Hairdresser.

BUILTH WELLS
Map 9 SO05

Places to visit
RSPB Carngafallt, RHAYADER, LD6 5HW, 01654 700222
www.rspb.org.uk/reserves-and-events/reserves-a-z/carngafallt

Premier Park

Fforest Fields Caravan & Camping Park
★★★★★ 88%

tel: 01982 570452 Hundred House **LD1 5RT**
email: stay@fforestfields.co.uk web: www.fforestfields.co.uk
dir: *From town centre follow New Radnor signs on A481. 4 miles to signed entrance on right, 0.5 mile before Hundred House village. (Note: if using sat nav, entrance is not centred on post code).*

This is a constantly improving, sheltered park surrounded by magnificent scenery and an abundance of wildlife. The spacious pitches are well laid out to create optimum privacy, and the excellent eco-friendly amenity block is fuelled by a biomass boiler and solar panels. The glamping field, with superb lake and country views, contains four yurts that have electricity, adjacent pod kitchens and a centrally located toilet; this all adds up to a genuine 'away from it all' experience. The Bar and Fforest café specialises in local produce and the lake is popular with wild swimmers. The historic town of Builth Wells and The Royal Welsh Showground are just four miles away.

Fforest Fields Caravan & Camping Park

Open: Easter to New Year **Last arrival:** 21.00 **Last departure:** 18.00
Pitches: ; see prices below; 30 hardstanding pitches
Leisure:
Facilities:
Services:
Within 3 miles:

Additional site information: 15 acre site. Cars can be parked by caravans and tents. Awnings permitted. No loud music. Quiet after 23.00. Dogs must be kept on leads at all times. Fridges, microwave, electric kettle and phone-charging available.

Glamping available: 4 yurts from £120. **Changeover days:** Monday, Friday

Additional glamping information: Yurts sleep 4. Minimum stay 2 nights. Double bed (two single beds optional), wood-burning stove, wooden floors, decking area, fully-equipped kitchen pod. Off-grid – solar power only. 2 dogs permitted (additional deposit required).

CHURCHSTOKE
Map 15 SO29

Places to visit
Montgomery Castle, MONTGOMERY, SY15 6HN, 03000 252239
www.cadw.gov.wales/visit/places-to-visit/monmouth-castle

Premier Park

Daisy Bank Caravan Park
★★★★★ 85%
tel: 01588 620471 Snead SY15 6EB
email: enquiries@daisy-bank.co.uk web: www.daisy-bank.co.uk
dir: *On A489, 2 miles east of Churchstoke.*

Peacefully located between Craven Arms and Churchstoke and surrounded by rolling hills, this idyllic, adults-only park offers generously sized, fully serviced pitches; some with superb country views – all are situated in attractive areas. The immaculately maintained amenity blocks provide smart, modern fittings and excellent privacy options. Camping pods, a pitch and putt course and WiFi are also available.

Open: All year **Last arrival:** 20.00 **Last departure:** noon
Pitches: see prices below; 64 hardstanding pitches; 30 seasonal pitches
Leisure:
Facilities:
Services:
Additional site information: 7 acre site. Adults only. Cars can be parked by caravans and tents. Awnings permitted. Caravan storage.
Glamping available: Camping pods from £35 night **Changeover days:** Any day
Additional glamping information: Electric heater, electric light, BBQ, table and chairs provided. Guests must bring their own bed and bedding. Cars can be parked by units

CRICKHOWELL — Map 9 SO21

Places to visit

Tretower Court and Castle, TRETOWER, NP8 1RF, 03000 252239
www.cadw.gov.wales/visit/places-to-visit/tretower-court-and-castle

Big Pit National Coal Museum, BLAENAVON, NP4 9XP, 0300 111 2333
museum.wales/bigpit

CRICKHOWELL — Map 9 SO21

Riverside Caravan & Camping Park
★★★★ 85%
tel: 01873 810397 New Road NP8 1AY
email: riversidecaravanpark@outlook.com web: www.riversidecaravanscrickhowell.co.uk
dir: *On A4077, well signed from A40.*

Within a few minutes' walk of the river and town centre with its excellent shopping and eating choices, is this all-level park. It is surrounded by mature hedges and trees to create privacy and has an excellent amenity block with stylish decor, underfloor heating, modern fixtures and fittings and very good privacy options.

Open: March to October **Last arrival:** 21.00 **Last departure:** 11.00
Pitches:
Facilities:
Services:
Within 3 miles:
Additional site information: 3.5 acre site. Adults only. Cars can be parked by caravans and tents. Awnings permitted. No fires, no noise after 22.00. Large canopied area for cooking, drying clothes, etc.

Make your next UK holiday one to remember

Choose RatedTrips.com

AA

FACILITIES: Electric vehicle charging | Baths/Shower | Electric shaver sockets | Hairdryer | Ice pack facility | Baby facilities | Disabled facilities | Shop on site or within 200yds | BBQ area | Picnic area | WiFi | Internet access **SERVICES:** Electric hook-up | Launderette | Licensed bar | Calor Gas | Campingaz | Toilet fluid | Café/Restaurant | Fast Food/Takeaway | Battery charging | Motorhome service point | No credit or debit cards | Dogs permitted | No dogs

WALES 312 POWYS

LLANDRINDOD WELLS Map 9 SO06

Places to visit
RSPB Carngafallt, RHAYADER, LD6 5HW, 01654 700222
www.rspb.org.uk/reserves-and-events/reserves-a-z/carngafallt

Disserth Caravan & Camping Park
★★★★ 84%

tel: 01597 860277 **Disserth, Howey LD16NL**
email: disserthcaravan@btconnect.com **web:** www.disserth.biz
dir: *1 mile from A483, between Newbridge-on-Wye and Howey, by church. Follow brown signs from A483 or A470.*

By a 13th-century church, this is a delightfully secluded and predominantly adult park that sits in a beautiful valley on the banks of the River Ithon, a tributary of the River Wye. It has a small bar which is open at weekends and during busy periods. The amenity block and laundry are appointed to a high standard and provide good privacy options. The site offers a shepherd's hut and a wooden 'morphPod' for hire.

Open: 1 March to 31 October **Last arrival:** sunset **Last departure:** noon
Pitches: ; see prices below; 12 hardstanding pitches
Leisure:
Facilities:
Services:
Within 3 miles:

Additional site information: 4 acre site. Cars can be parked by caravans and tents. Awnings permitted. Quiet after 22.00. Maximum 2 pets. No fires. No play area or equipment. Private trout fishing.

Glamping available: Wooden pod from £40; shepherd's hut from £40
Changeover days: Any day

Additional glamping information: Wooden pod offers twin beds; Shepherd's hut offers microwave, fridge, kettle, heating, pull-down double bed and private shower and toilet. Cars can be parked by units

LLANGORS Map 9 SN98

Places to visit
Regimental Museum of The Royal Welsh, BRECON, LD3 7EB, 01874 613310
www.royalwelshmuseum.wales

Great for kids: Tretower Court and Castle, TRETOWER, NP8 1RF, 03000 252239
www.cadw.gov.wales/visit/places-to-visit/tretower-court-and-castle

Lakeside Caravan Park
★★★★ 88%

tel: 01874 658226 **LD3 7TR**
email: reception@llangorselake.co.uk **web:** www.llangorselake.co.uk
dir: *Exit A40 at Bwlch onto B4560 towards Llangorse. Site signed towards lake in Llangorse village.*

Surrounded by spectacular mountains and set close to Llangorse Lake, with mooring and launching facilities, this is a must-do holiday destination for lovers of outdoor pursuits, from walking to watersports, and even pike fishing for which the lake is renowned. The hedge- or tree-screened touring areas provide generously-sized pitches and the amenity blocks offer very good privacy options. There's a well-stocked shop, bar and café, with a takeaway, under the same ownership.

Open: Easter or 3rd weekend in March to end of October (restricted service: March to May and September to October – reduced opening hours in bar) **Last arrival:** 21.00
Last departure: 11.00

Pitches: ; 16 hardstanding pitches
Leisure:
Facilities:
Services:
Within 3 miles:

Additional site information: 2 acre site. Cars can be parked by caravans and tents. Awnings permitted. No open fires, noise to be kept to a minimum after 23.00. No dogs permitted in hire caravans. Boat hire in summer.

PITCHES: Caravans Motorhomes Tents Glamping accommodation **LEISURE:** Indoor swimming pool Outdoor swimming pool Children's playground Kids' club Tennis court Games room Separate TV room golf course Pitch n putt Boats for hire Bikes for hire Cinema Entertainment Fishing Mini golf Watersports Gym Sports field Stables Spa

POWYS 313 WALES

LLANIDLOES
Map 9 SN98

Places to visit

Bryntail Lead Mine Buildings, LLANIDLOES, 03000 252239
www.cadw.gov.wales/visit/places-to-visit/bryntail-lead-mine-buildings

Gilfach Nature Reserve, RHAYADER, LD6 5LF, 01597 823298
www.rwtwales.org/nature-reserves/gilfach

Premier Park

Red Kite Touring and Lodge Park
★★★★★ 88%

tel: 01686 412122 Van Road SY18 6NG
email: info@redkitetouringpark.co.uk web: www.redkitetouringpark.co.uk
dir: *From roundabout on A470 at Llanidloes take B4518 signed Penffordd-las Staylittle. At next roundabout take 3rd exit signed Machynlleth. Over river. 1st left (B4518) signed Penffordd-las Staylittle. Pass Clywedog Riverside Holiday Home Park on left, site in approximately 100 yards.*

Within 15 minutes' walk of the historic town centre, this stunningly located park has been created on undulating hills and fields, which include two lakes, one being a habitat for newts. All pitches are fully serviced to include a green chemical disposal point and TV hook-up, and the superb amenity block with underfloor heating provides excellent fixtures and fittings coupled with privacy options for both men and women. Please note, this is an adults-only park.

Open: March to January **Last arrival:** 19.00 **Last departure:** 11.00
Pitches: 🚐 🚍; 66 hardstanding pitches; 15 seasonal pitches
Leisure: ✏
Facilities: 🛁 ⊙ 🗲 ✻ ♿ 🎪 WiFi
Services: 🔌 🧺 ⛽ 🔒 🚽
Within 3 miles: ⛳ 🛒

Additional site information: 20 acre site. Adults only. 🐕 Cars can be parked by caravans. Awnings permitted. Enclosed dog run, dog wash. Car hire can be arranged.

See advert opposite

MIDDLETOWN
Map 15 SJ31

Places to visit

Powis Castle and Garden, WELSHPOOL, SY21 8RF, 01938 551944
www.nationaltrust.org.uk/powis-castle-and-garden

Bank Farm Caravan Park
★★★★ 84%

tel: 01938 570526 & 07753 685260 SY21 8EJ
email: bankfarmcaravans@yahoo.co.uk web: www.bankfarmcaravans.co.uk
dir: *13 miles west of Shrewsbury, 5 miles east of Welshpool on A458.*

A very attractive park located between Welshpool and Shrewsbury, ideally located for visiting many attractions. The grounds are sheltered by a mountain forest backdrop and landscaping is superb with an excellent display of topiary, neat hedges and colourful seasonal shrubs complemented by both indigenous and cultivated plants to ensure an all-year colourful presentation. The main touring field has a high quality amenity block with excellent decor, fixtures and fittings, and a private family room is an additional benefit. Two quality static caravans are also available for hire. An adjacent play field with quality equipment makes this an ideal location for families.

Open: March to October **Last arrival:** 20.00
Pitches: 🚐 🚍 ⛺
Leisure: 🎱 🎯 ✏
Facilities: 🛁 ⊙ ✻ ♿ 🎪 WiFi
Services: 🔌 🧺 🍴 🔒

Additional site information: 2 acre site. 🐕 Cars can be parked by caravans and tents. Awnings permitted. Coarse fishing, jacuzzi, snooker room.

WALES — SWANSEA

SWANSEA

OXWICH
Map 8 SS48

Places to visit

Castell Oxwich, OXWICH, SA3 1ND, 03000 252239
www.cadw.gov.wales/visit/places-to-visit/oxwich-castle

Oxwich National Nature Reserve, OXWICH, SA3 1LR, 0300 065 3000
www.naturalresources.wales/days-out/places-to-visit/south-west-wales/oxwich-national-nature-reserve/?lang=en

Greenways of Gower Premier Leisure Park
★★★ 85%
tel: 01792 391203 **SA3 1LY**
email: info@greenwaysleisure.co.uk
web: www.premierleisureparks.com/our-holiday-parks/greenways-of-gower

Set in a superb location overlooking Oxwich Bay on the Gower Peninsula, this popular park offers 160 well drained grass pitches and caters for tents and small camper vans. The central toilet/shower facilities are spotlessly maintained and include a dedicated, fully serviced cubicle for the less able visitor. Good security is provided by a barrier and CCTV. There is a bar and an undercover outside seating area where customers can enjoy a wood-fired pizzas from the unique Pizza Bus.

Greenways of Gower Premier Leisure Park

Open: 1 April to 30 September **Last arrival:** 21.00 **Last departure:** noon
Pitches: * ▲ from £23
See advert below

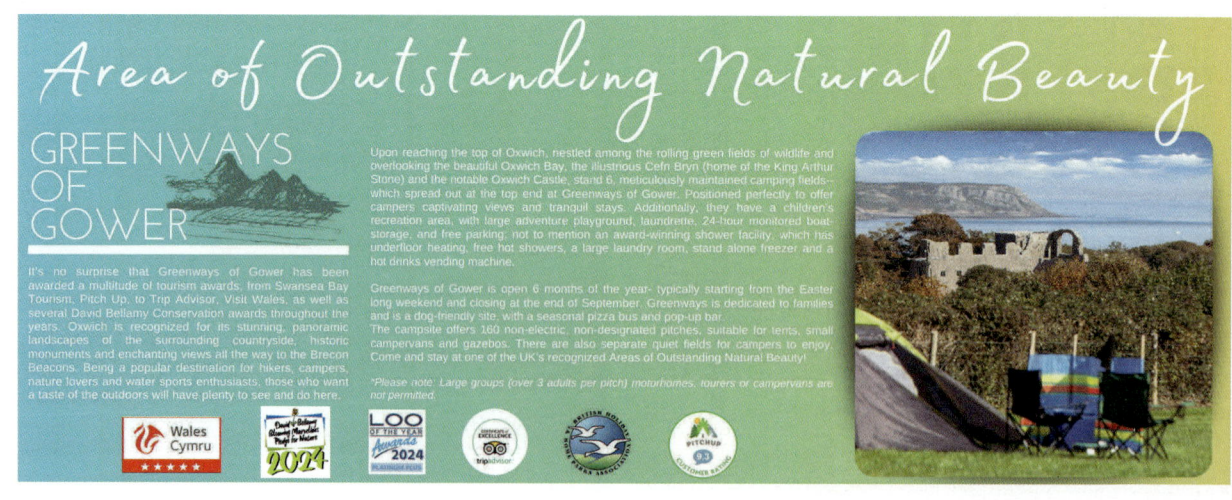

PITCHES: Caravans Motorhomes Tents Glamping accommodation **LEISURE:** Indoor swimming pool Outdoor swimming pool Children's playground Kids' club Tennis court Games room Separate TV room golf course Pitch n putt Boats for hire Bikes for hire Cinema Entertainment Fishing Mini golf Watersports Gym Sports field Stables Spa

PORT EYNON
Map 8 SS48

Places to visit

Weobley Castle, LLANRHIDIAN, SA3 1HB, 03000 252239
www.cadw.gov.wales/visit/places-to-visit/weobley-castle

Gower Heritage Centre, PARKMILL, SA3 2EH
www.gowerheritagecentre.co.uk

Great for kids: Oxwich Castle, OXWICH, SA3 1ND, 03000 252239
www.cadw.gov.wales/visit/places-to-visit/oxwich-castle

Skysea Camping & Caravan Park
★★★★ 87%

tel: 01792 390795 **SA3 1NL**
email: booking@porteynon.com **web:** www.porteynon.com
dir: *A4118 to Port Eynon, site adjacent to beach.*

Set in an unrivalled location alongside the safe sandy beach of Port Eynon on the Gower Peninsula, this popular park is an ideal family holiday spot; it is also close to an attractive village with pubs and shops. The lush green sloping ground has been partially terraced to create excellent sea views and the luxurious amenity blocks provide superb fixtures and fittings combined with good privacy and family options.

Open: All year **Last arrival:** 22.00 **Last departure:** 15.00
Pitches: 🚐 🚗 ⛺
Facilities: ⊙ ♿ 💲 WiFi
Services: 🔌 🗑 ⛽ 🚽 🐕 T
Within 3 miles: ✎ ⛵ 🏊

Additional site information: 12 acre site. 🐕 Cars can be parked by caravans and tents. Awnings permitted.

RHOSSILI
Map 8 SS48

Places to visit

Weobley Castle, LLANRHIDIAN, SA3 1HB, 03000 252239
www.cadw.gov.wales/visit/places-to-visit/weobley-castle

Gower Heritage Centre, PARKMILL, SA3 2EH
www.gowerheritagecentre.co.uk

Great for kids: Oxwich Castle, OXWICH, SA3 1ND, 03000 252239
www.cadw.gov.wales/visit/places-to-visit/oxwich-castle

RHOSSILI
Map 8 SS48

Pitton Cross Caravan & Camping Park
★★★ 91%

tel: 01792 390593 **Pitton SA3 1PT**
email: admin@pittoncross.co.uk **web:** www.pittoncross.co.uk
dir: *2 miles west of Scurlage on B4247, on the left.*

Surrounded by farmland close to Rhossili Bay, Pitton Cross is divided by hedging into paddocks, with hardstandings for motorhomes available. Some areas are deliberately left uncultivated, resulting in colourful displays of wild flowers. Dogs are welcome and WiFi is available across park. Rhossili Beach, popular with surfers, and the Welsh Coastal Path are nearby. Paragliding on Rhossili Downs is possible too.

Open: All year (restricted service: November to March – no bread or milk)
Last arrival: 21.00 **Last departure:** 11.00
Pitches: 🚐 🚗 ⛺; 27 hardstanding pitches
Leisure: 🎱
Facilities: 🛁 ⊙ ✂ ❄ ♿ 💲 🍴 WiFi
Services: 🔌 🗑 🐕 🚽 T
Within 3 miles: ✎ 🏊

Additional site information: 7 acre site. 🐕 Cars can be parked by caravans and tents. Awnings permitted. Quiet at all times. Charcoal BBQs must be off ground, no fire pits or log burning. Leisure park for children up to 12 years. Dogs must be kept on leads at all times, including pitch side. Pay as you go WiFi, disc golf (enquire at reception/shop).

WALES 316 SWANSEA—WREXHAM

SWANSEA   Map 9 SS69

Places to visit
Swansea Museum, SWANSEA, SA1 1SN, 01792 653763
www.swanseamuseum.co.uk

Great for kids: Plantasia Tropical Zoo, SWANSEA, SA1 2AL, 01792 474555
www.plantasiaswansea.co.uk

Riverside Caravan Park
★★★★   81% HOLIDAY PARK

tel: 01792 775587 Ynys Forgan Farm, Morriston SA6 6QL
email: reception@riversidewansea.com web: www.riversidewansea.com
dir: *M4 junction 45 follow Swansea signs. Before joining A4067 turn left into private road signed to site.*

A large and busy park close to the M4 but in a quiet location beside the River Taw. This friendly, family orientated site has a licensed club and bar with a full high-season entertainment programme. There is a choice of eating outlets – the clubhouse restaurant, takeaway and chip shop. The park has a good indoor pool.

Open: All year (restricted service: in winter months – pool and club closed)
Last arrival: midnight **Last departure:** noon
Pitches:
Leisure:
Facilities:
Services:
Within 3 miles:

Additional site information: 5 acre site. Dogs by prior arrangement only, no aggressive breeds permitted. Fishing on site by arrangement.

WREXHAM

EYTON   Map 15 SJ34

Places to visit
Erddig, WREXHAM, LL13 0YT, 01978 355314
www.nationaltrust.org.uk/erddig

Chirk Castle, CHIRK, LL14 5AF, 01691 777701
www.nationaltrust.org.uk/chirk-castle

Platinum Park

Plassey Holiday Park
★★★★★

tel: 01978 780277 The Plassey LL13 0SP
email: enquiries@plassey.com web: www.plassey.com
dir: *From A483 at Bangor-on-Dee exit onto B5426 for 2.5 miles. Site entrance signed on left.*

A lovely park set in several hundred acres of quiet farm and meadowland in the Dee Valley. The superb toilet facilities include individual cubicles for total privacy and security, while the Edwardian farm buildings have been converted into a super restaurant, coffee shop, beauty studio and various craft outlets. There is plenty here to entertain the whole family, from scenic walks and a swimming pool to free fishing and use of the 9-hole golf course. For a memorable glamping experience there is a choice of large safari tents or Studio Lodges complete with en suite facilities and private hot tubs.

Open: February to December **Last arrival:** 20.00 **Last departure:** noon
Pitches: see prices below; 85 hardstanding pitches; 60 seasonal pitches
Leisure:
Facilities:
Services:
Within 3 miles:

Additional site information: 10 acre site. Cars can be parked by caravans and tents. Awnings permitted. No footballs or skateboards. No noise after 23.00. Badminton, table tennis, driving range.

Glamping available: 10 wooden pods (plodges) from £110 per night; 4 safari tents from £95 per night. **Changeover days:** Monday and Friday

Additional glamping information: Wooden pods (plodges) and safari tents: minimum stay 3 nights. Pods and safari tents fully furnished and equipped with hot tubs.

Make your next UK holiday one to remember

Choose RatedTrips.com

PITCHES: Caravans Motorhomes Tents Glamping accommodation **LEISURE:** Indoor swimming pool Outdoor swimming pool Children's playground Kids' club Tennis court Games room Separate TV room golf course Pitch n putt Boats for hire Bikes for hire Cinema Entertainment Fishing Mini golf Watersports Gym Sports field Stables Spa

WREXHAM 317 WALES

OVERTON
Map 15 SJ34

Premier Park

The Trotting Mare Caravan Park
★★★★★ 88%

tel: 01978 711963 **LL13 0LE**
email: info@thetrottingmare.co.uk web: www.thetrottingmare.co.uk
dir: *From Oswestry towards Whitchurch take A495. In Ellesmere take A528 towards Overton. Site on left. Or from Wrexham take A525 signed Whitchurch. In Marchwiel turn right onto A528 towards Overton. Through Overton to Ellesmere A528, site on right.*

Located between Overton-on-Dee and Ellesmere, this adults-only touring park is quietly located behind the Trotting Mare pub. The majority of pitches are fully serviced, and creative landscaping and a free coarse-fishing lake are additional benefits. A superb amenity block is served by a bio-mass boiler and equipped with contemporary decor and top-notch fixtures and fittings. Stylish holiday lets are also available.

Open: All year **Last arrival:** 20.00 **Last departure:** noon

Pitches: 43 hardstanding pitches

Leisure:

Facilities:

Services:

Within 3 miles:

Additional site information: 4.2 acre site. Adults only. Cars can be parked by caravans and tents. Awnings permitted. No commercial vehicles, no open fires, no gas bottles outside caravan or awning, no bikes, no ball games, no noise after 23.00. Car hire can be arranged.

FACILITIES: Electric vehicle charging Baths/Shower Electric shaver sockets Hairdryer Ice pack facility Baby facilities Disabled facilities Shop on site or within 200yds BBQ area Picnic area WiFi Internet access **SERVICES:** Electric hook-up Launderette Licensed bar Calor Gas Campingaz Toilet fluid Café/Restaurant Fast Food/Takeaway Battery charging Motorhome service point No credit or debit cards Dogs permitted No dogs

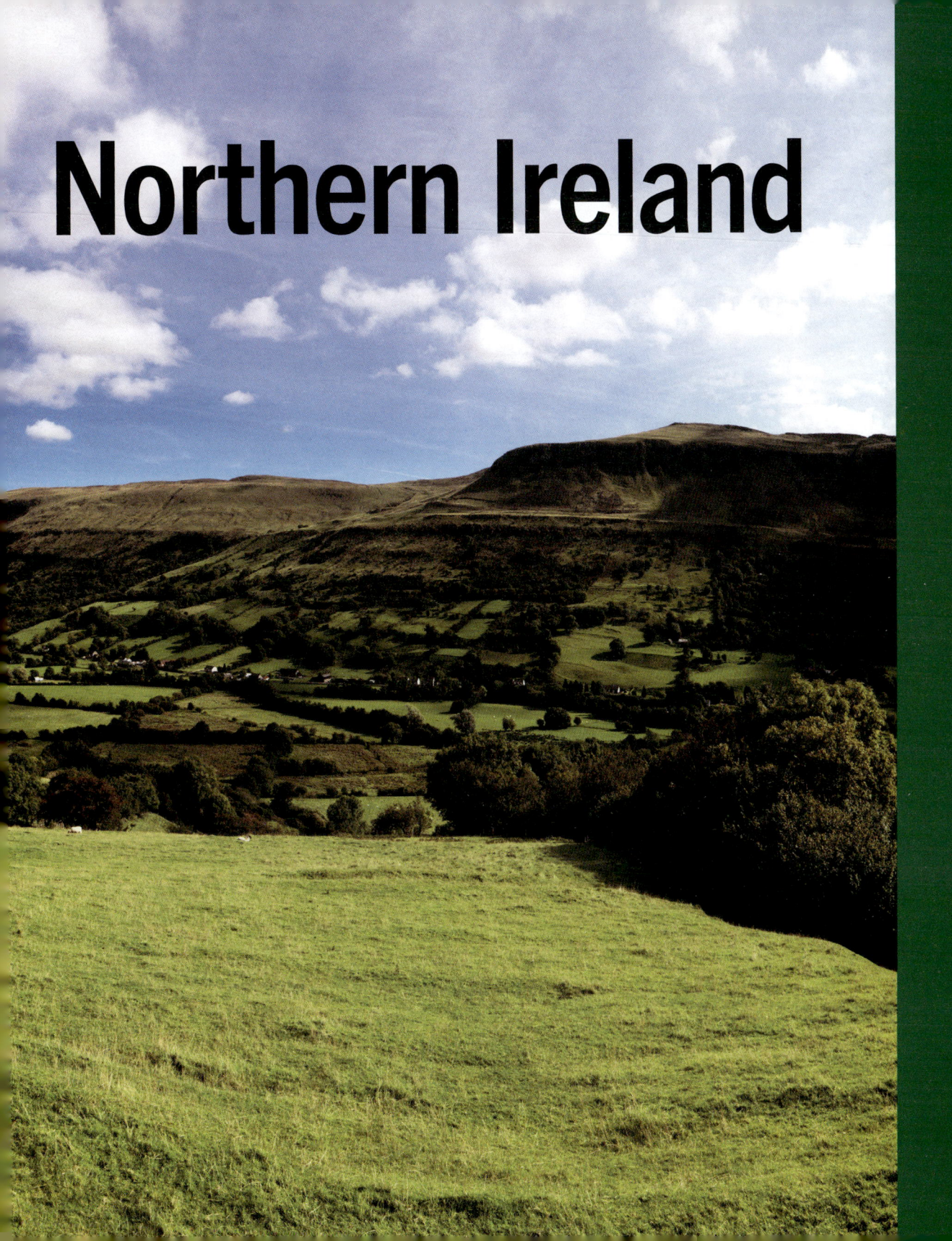

Northern Ireland

COUNTY ANTRIM

ANTRIM — Map 1 D5

Places to visit

Antrim Round Tower, ANTRIM, BT41 1BL 028 9082 3207
www.discovernorthernireland.com/things-to-do/antrim-round-tower-p674961

Great for kids: Belfast Zoo, BELFAST, BT36 7PN, 028 9077 6277
www.belfastcity.gov.uk/zoo/home

Six Mile Water Caravan Park
★★★★ 84%

tel: 028 9034 0024 Lough Road BT41 4DG
email: sixmilewater@antrimandnewtownabbey.gov.uk
web: www.antrimandnewtownabbey.gov.uk/caravanpark
dir: From A6 (Dublin road) into Lough Road signed Antrim Forum and Loughshore Park. Site at end of road on right.

This is a peaceful touring site, surrounded by trees and mature hedges, that is part of a large municipal park with boating and outdoor sports opportunities; it is also adjacent to a golf club and within easy walking distance of Antrim and The Forum Leisure Complex. All the generously spaced pitches have hardstandings and electric hook-ups and in addition to a well-equipped amenity block, a lounge is also available.

Open: March to October (restricted service: February and December – open at weekends)
Last arrival: 21.00 **Last departure:** noon
Pitches: 🚐 🚗 ⛺; 37 hardstanding pitches
Leisure:
Facilities:
Services:
Within 3 miles:

Additional site information: 9.61 acre site. Cars can be parked by caravans and tents. Awnings permitted. Maximum stay 7 nights. No noise between 22.00–08.00. Watersports, angling stands.

BALLYCASTLE — Map 1 D6

Places to visit

Carrick-a-Rede Rope Bridge, CARRICK-A-REDE, BT54 6LS, 028 2073 1855
www.nationaltrust.org.uk/carrick-a-rede

Bushmills Distillery, BUSHMILLS, BT57 8XH, 028 2073 3218
www.bushmills.eu/distillery

Premier Park

Causeway Coast Holiday Park
★★★★★ 88% HOLIDAY PARK

tel: 028 2076 2550 & 07720 464465 21 Clare Road BT54 5DB
email: causewaycoast@hagansleisure.co.uk web: www.hagansleisure.co.uk
dir: From A44 in Ballycastle follow Portrush sign (A2). 1st right into Moyle Road. At T-junction right into Clare Road.

In an elevated location close to the seafront with views of Ballycastle Bay and Rathlin Island, this bustling holiday park is ideally located for visiting the many attractions along this unspoilt coastline including the Giant's Causeway just 15 minutes away. Facilities include a pub, a well-equipped indoor swimming pool with slide and an outdoor play area. Most of the grassed touring pitches have an electric supply. Please note that the site does not have hardstandings and tents are not accepted.

Open: March to October **Last arrival:** 23.00 **Last departure:** 10.00
Pitches: 🚐 🚗
Leisure:
Facilities:
Services:
Within 3 miles:

Additional site information: 28 acre site. Quiet time 22.00–07.00, no children out after 23.00.

Make your next UK holiday one to remember

Choose RatedTrips.com

AA

BUSHMILLS

Map 1 D6

Places to visit

Bushmills Distillery, BUSHMILLS, BT57 8XH, 028 2073 3218
www.bushmills.eu/distillery

Premier Park

Ballyness Caravan Park

★★★★★ 93%

tel: 028 2073 2393 **40 Castlecatt Road BT57 8TN**
email: info@ballynesscaravanpark.com **web:** www.ballynesscaravanpark.com
dir: *0.5 mile south of Bushmills on B66, follow signs.*

A peacefully located, quality park with superb toilet and other facilities, on farmland beside St Columb's Rill which is the stream that supplies the famous Bushmills Distillery which is close by. The site has fully serviced, hardstanding pitches, free WiFi, an indoor games barn, play park and football field, a centrally heated amenity building, an 8-acre dog walk and wildlife ponds. It is close to the Giant's Causeway, and within walking distance to local shops, pubs and restaurants. The Causeway Rambler bus stops at the site en route to the north coast attractions.

Open: 14 March to 2 November **Last arrival:** 21.00 **Last departure:** noon
Pitches: 49 hardstanding pitches
Leisure:
Facilities:
Services:
Within 3 miles:
Additional site information: 36 acre site. Cars can be parked by caravans. Awnings permitted. Library, accessories shop, 8 acre dog walk and wildlife ponds.

BELFAST

DUNDONALD

Map 1 D5

Places to visit

Mount Stewart, NEWTOWNARDS, BT22 2AD, 028 4278 8387
www.nationaltrust.org.uk/mount-stewart

Giant's Ring, BELFAST, BT8 8LE, 028 9082 3207
www.discovernorthernireland.com/things-to-do/giants-ring-p674861

Great for kids: Belfast Zoo, BELFAST, BT36 7PN, 028 9077 6277
www.belfastcity.gov.uk/zoo/home

Dundonald Touring Caravan Park

★★★★ 84%

tel: 028 9080 9123 & 9080 9129 **111 Old Dundonald Road BT16 1XT**
email: dundonaldcaravanpark@lisburncastlereagh.gov.uk
web: www.dundonaldcaravanpark.com
dir: *From Belfast city centre follow M3 and A20 to City Airport. Then A20 to Newtownards, follow signs to Dundonald and Ulster Hospital. At hospital right at sign for Dundonald Ice Bowl. Follow to end, turn right, Ice Bowl on left, follow signs for caravan park.*

A purpose-built site in a quiet corner of Dundonald Leisure Park on the outskirts of Belfast. This peaceful park provides excellent, well-spaced, fully serviced pitches and is ideally located for touring County Down and exploring the capital. In the winter it offers an 'Aire de Service' for motorhomes and caravans with their own hygiene facilities.

Open: mid March to October **Last arrival:** 23.00 **Last departure:** noon
Pitches: ; 22 hardstanding pitches
Facilities:
Services:
Within 3 miles:
Additional site information: 1.5 acre site. Cars can be parked by caravans and tents. Awnings permitted. No commercial vehicles or vans permitted (including any on tow). Dundonald International Ice Bowl, adjacent to the park, offers bowling, indoor play area, olympic-size ice rink (additional charges apply).

COUNTY FERMANAGH

BELCOO — Map 1 C5

Places to visit

Florence Court, ENNISKILLEN, BT92 1DB, 028 6634 8249
www.nationaltrust.org.uk/florence-court

IRVINESTOWN

Premier Park

Rushin House Caravan Park
★★★★★ 88%

tel: 028 6638 6519 **Holywell BT93 5DU**
email: enquiries@rushinhouse.com web: www.rushinhouse.com
dir: *From Enniskillen take A4 west for 13 miles to Belcoo. Right onto B52 towards Garrison for 1 mile. Site signed.*

This park occupies a scenic location overlooking Lough MacNean, close to the picturesque village of Belcoo, and is the result of meticulous planning and execution. There are 24 very generous, fully serviced pitches standing on a terrace overlooking the lough, with additional tenting pitches below; all are accessed via well-kept, wide tarmac roads. Facilities include a lovely, well-equipped play area and a hard surface, fenced five-a-side football pitch. There is a slipway providing boat access to the lough and, of course, fishing; there is an access path to the lake that is suitable for less mobile visitors to use. The excellent toilet facilities are purpose-built and include family rooms.

Open: mid March to October (restricted service: November to March — Aire de Service facilities available) **Last arrival:** 21.00 **Last departure:** 13.00
Pitches: 38 hardstanding pitches
Leisure:
Facilities:
Services:
Within 3 miles:

Additional site information: 5 acre site. Cars can be parked by caravans. Awnings permitted. Lakeside walk.

IRVINESTOWN — Map 1 C5

Places to visit

Castle Coole, ENNISKILLEN, BT74 6JY, 028 6632 2690
www.nationaltrust.org.uk/castle-coole

Castle Balfour, LISNASKEA, BT92 0JE, 028 9082 3207
www.discovernorthernireland.com/Castle-Balfour-Lisnaskea-Enniskillen-P2901

IRVINESTOWN — Map 1 C5

Castle Archdale Caravan Park & Camping Site
★★★★ 86%

tel: 028 6862 1333 **Lisnarick BT94 1PP**
email: info@castlearchdale.com web: www.castlearchdale.com
dir: *From Irvinestown take B534 signed Lisnarick. Left onto B82 signed Enniskillen. In approximately 1 mile right by church, site signed.*

This park is located within the grounds of Castle Archdale Country Park on the shores of Lough Erne which boasts stunning scenery, forest walks and also war and wildlife museums. The site is ideal for watersport enthusiasts with its marina and launching facilities. Also on site there's a shop, licensed restaurant, takeaway and play park. There are fully serviced, hardstanding pitches, and glamping pods.

Open: April to October (restricted service: April to June and September to October — shop and bar closed on weekdays) **Last departure:** noon
Pitches: 150 hardstanding pitches
Leisure:
Facilities:
Services:
Within 3 miles:

Additional site information: 11 acre site. Cars can be parked by caravans and tents. Awnings permitted. No open fires, no noise after 23.00. Table tennis, woodland walk, cycling trail. Car hire can be arranged.

Glamping available: wooden pods. No dogs permitted

COUNTY TYRONE

DUNGANNON — Map 1 C5

Places to visit

The Argory (NT), DUNGANNON, BT71 6NA, 028 8778 4753
www.nationaltrust.org.uk/visit/northern-ireland/the-argory

Dungannon Park
★★★★ 88%

tel: 028 8772 8690 & 03000 132132 **Moy Road BT71 6DY**
email: parks@midulstercouncil.org web: www.midulstercouncil.org/dungannonpark
dir: *M1 junction 15, A29 towards Dungannon, left at 2nd lights.*

Set within the magnificent public Dungannon Park, with a fishing lake, cricket ground and regular concerts during the summer months, this family-friendly caravan park provides excellent, fully serviced pitches and a stylish, well-equipped amenity block. The attractive coffee shop is a real benefit.

Open: March to October **Last arrival:** 20.00 **Last departure:** noon
Pitches: 24 hardstanding pitches
Leisure:
Facilities:
Services:
Within 3 miles:

Additional site information: 4 acre site. Cars can be parked by caravans and tents. Awnings permitted. No noise between 22.00–08.00, no generators, no commercial vehicles, speed limit 10mph, no dishwashing in toilet block. Dogs must be kept on leads.

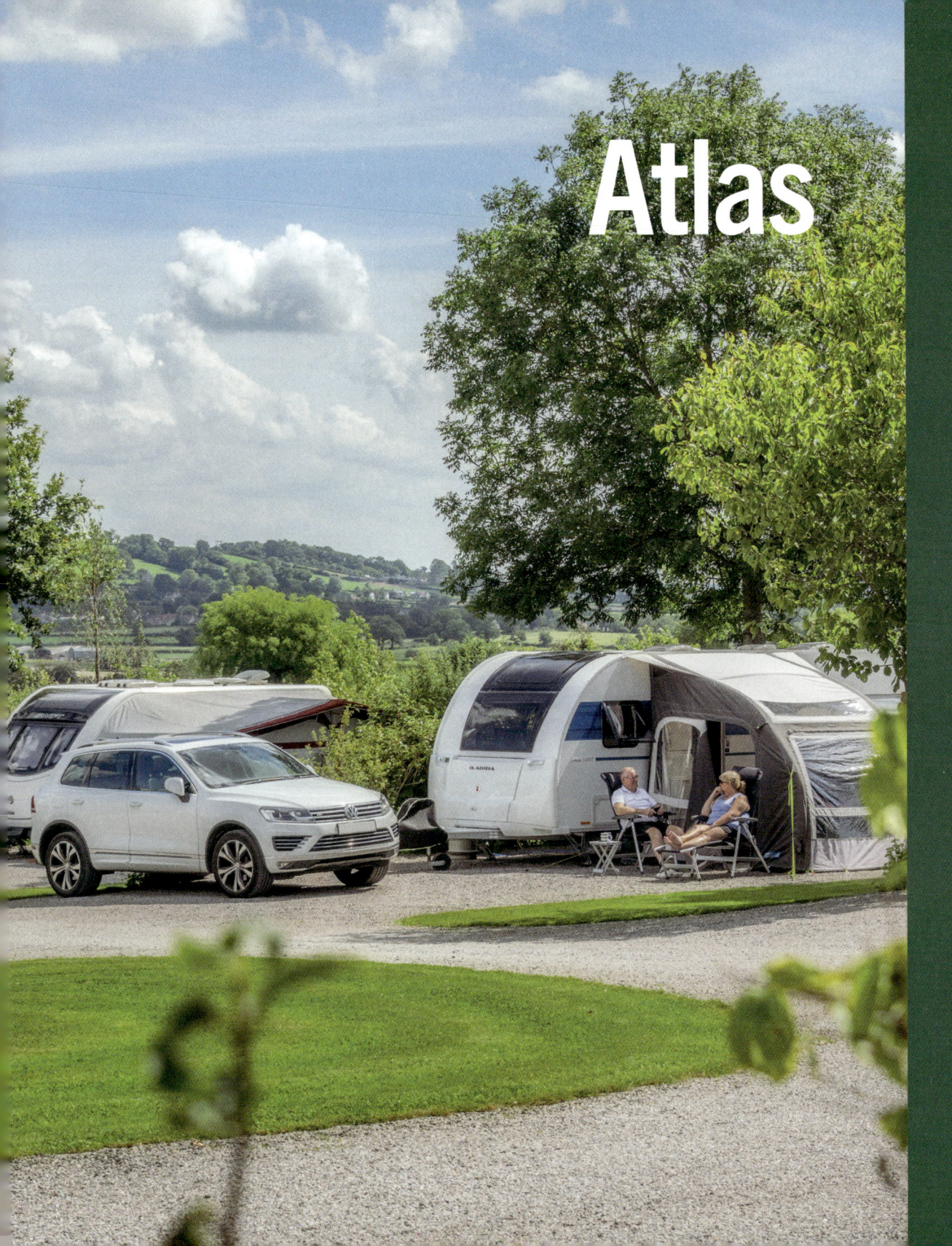

Atlas

COUNTY MAPS

England
1. Bedfordshire
2. Berkshire
3. Bristol
4. Buckinghamshire
5. Cambridgeshire
6. Greater Manchester
7. Herefordshire
8. Hertfordshire
9. Leicestershire
10. Northamptonshire
11. Nottinghamshire
12. Rutland
13. Staffordshire
14. Warwickshire
15. West Midlands
16. Worcestershire

Scotland
17. City of Glasgow
18. Clackmannanshire
19. East Ayrshire
20. East Dunbartonshire
21. East Renfrewshire
22. Perth & Kinross
23. Renfrewshire
24. South Lanarkshire
25. West Dunbartonshire

Wales
26. Blaenau Gwent
27. Bridgend
28. Caerphilly
29. Denbighshire
30. Flintshire
31. Merthyr Tydfil
32. Monmouthshire
33. Neath Port Talbot
34. Newport
35. Rhondda Cynon Taf
36. Torfaen
37. Vale of Glamorgan
38. Wrexham

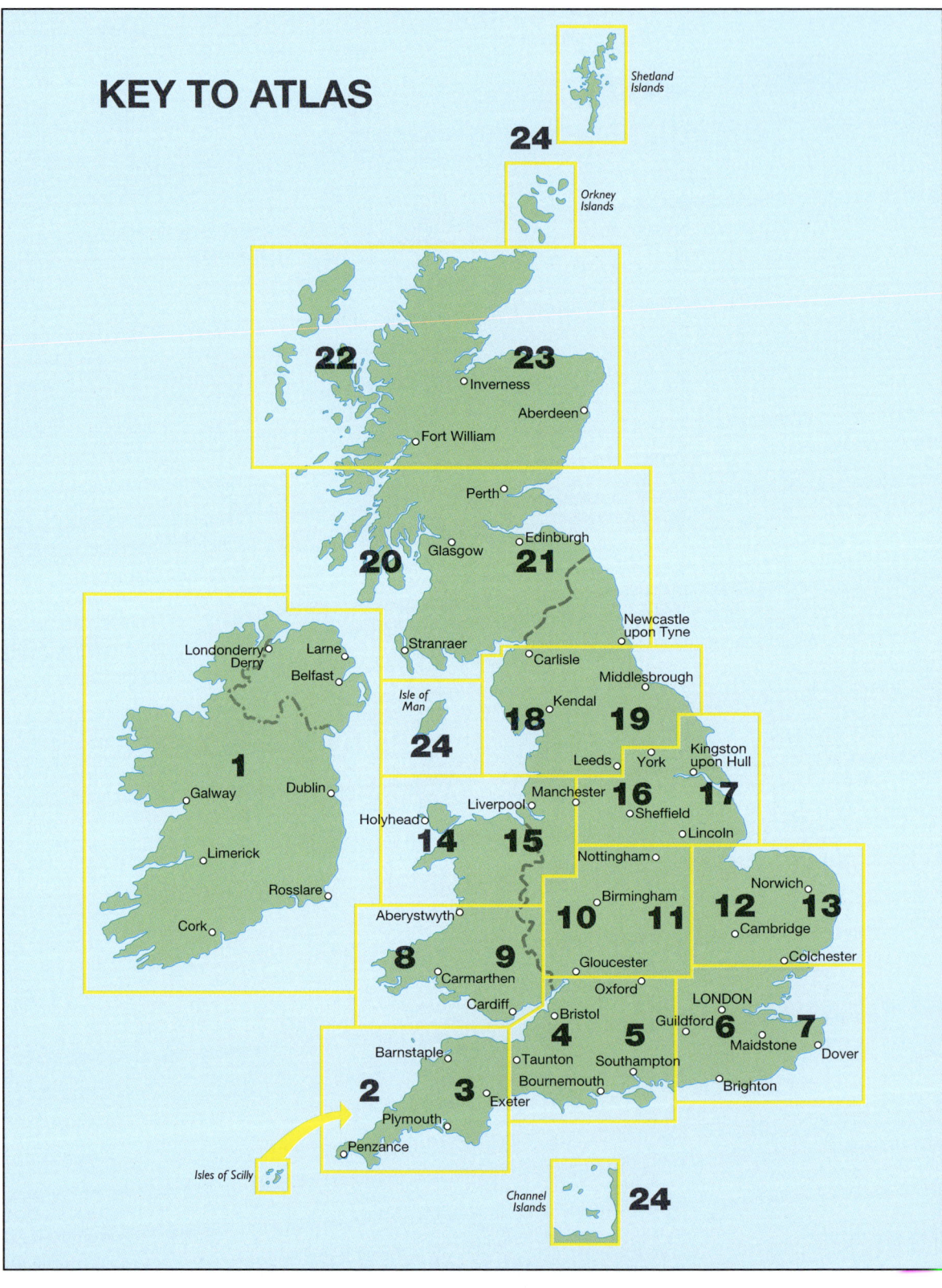

For continuation pages refer to numbered arrows

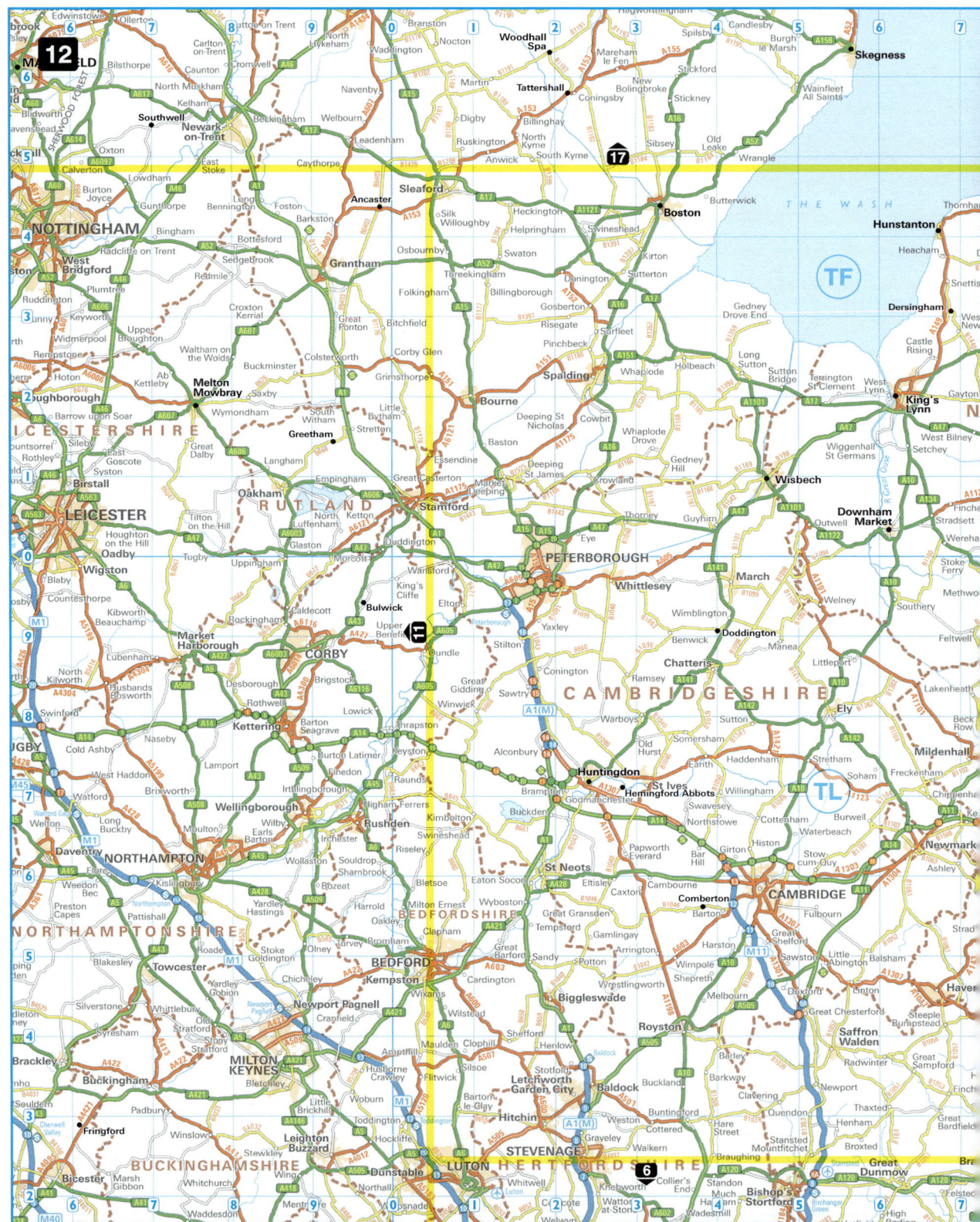

For continuation pages refer to numbered arrows

For continuation pages refer to numbered arrows

Index

A

ABERAERON
Aeron Coast Caravan Park 294

ABERGAVENNY
Wernddu Caravan Park 306

ABERSOCH
Beach View Caravan Park 297
Bryn Bach Caravan & Camping Site 297
Deucoch Touring & Camping Park 297
Rhydolion 298

ABINGTON
Mount View Caravan Park 280

ACASTER MALBIS
Moor End Farm 238

ALLERSTON
Vale of Pickering Caravan Park 239

ALNE
Alders Caravan Park 240

AMBLESIDE
Hawkshead Hall Farm 92
Skelwith Fold Caravan Park 92

ANCASTER
Woodland Waters 174

ANNAN
Galabank Caravan & Camping Group 269

ANTRIM
Six Mile Water Caravan Park 320

ARUNDEL
Ship & Anchor Marina 227

ASHBOURNE
Rivendale Lodge Retreat 103

ASHBURTON
Parkers Farm Holiday Park 108
River Dart Country Park 108

ASHFORD
Broadhembury Caravan & Camping Park 162

ASHTON
Boscrege Caravan & Camping Park 58

ASKRIGG
Cherish Glamping 240

AXMINSTER
Andrewshayes Holiday Park 109
Hawkchurch Resort & Spa 108

B

BAKEWELL
Greenhills Holiday Park 103

BALA
Tyn Cornel Camping 298

BALLYCASTLE
Causeway Coast Holiday Park 320

BAMBURGH
Glororum Caravan Park 191
Waren Caravan & Camping Park 191

BANBURY
Barnstones Caravan & Camping Site 196

BARMOUTH
Hendre Mynach Touring Caravan & Camping Park 299
Trawsdir Touring Caravans & Camping Park 298

BARNARD CASTLE
Pecknell Farm Caravan Park 150

BARNEY
The Old Brick Kilns 182

BARNS GREEN
Sumners Ponds Fishery & Campsite 227

BARNSTAPLE
Hallsdown Farm Touring Park 109

BARRHILL
Barrhill Holiday Park 269

BARROW-IN-FURNESS
South End Caravan Park 93

BATH
Bath Mill Lodge Retreat 206

BATTLE
Senlac Wood 226

BELCOO
Rushin House Caravan Park 322

BELFORD
South Meadows Caravan Park 192

BELLINGHAM
Bellingham Camping & Caravanning Club Site 192

BELTON
Rose Farm Touring & Camping Park 182
Wild Duck Holiday Park 183

BERKELEY
Hogsdown Farm Caravan & Camping Park 152

BERRYNARBOR
Mill Park Touring Caravan & Camping Park 110

BERWICK ST JAMES
Stonehenge Campsite & Glamping Pods 231

BERWICK-UPON-TWEED
Berwick Holiday Park 193
Haggerston Castle Holiday Park 193
Ord House Country Park 193

BETWS-YN-RHOS
Golden Sands Holiday Park 295
Hunters Hamlet Caravan Park 294
Kinmel Bay 295

BEWALDETH
Keswick Reach Lodge Retreat 93

BIDEFORD
Adventure Camping 110

BISHOP SUTTON
Bath Chew Valley Caravan Park 206

BISHOPTON
The Paddocks Touring Park 284

BLACKPOOL
Marton Mere Holiday Village 164

BLACKWATER
Trevarth Holiday Park 58

BLAIR ATHOLL
Blair Castle Caravan Park 282

BLAIRLOGIE
Witches Craig Caravan & Camping Park 285

BLANDFORD FORUM
The Inside Park 132

BODMIN
Mena Farm: Touring, Camping, Glamping 59

BOLTON-LE-SANDS
Bay View Holiday Park 165
Red Bank Farm 166

BOSTON
Long Acres Touring Park 174
Orchard Park 174

INDEX

BRANDESBURTON
Blue Rose Caravan and Country Park 236
Dacre Lakeside Park 236

BRANSGORE
Harrow Wood Farm Caravan Park 154

BRAUNTON
Lobb Fields Caravan & Camping Park 111

BREAN
Holiday Resort Unity 207
Northam Farm Holiday Park 208
Warren Farm Holiday Centre 206

BRECON
Pencelli Castle Caravan & Camping Park 309

BRIDESTOWE
Bridestowe Caravan Park 111

BRIDGETOWN
Exe Valley Caravan Site 208

BRIDGNORTH
Stanmore Hall Touring Park 199

BRIDLINGTON
Fir Tree Caravan Park 236

BRIDPORT
Freshwater Beach Holiday Park 133
Highlands End Holiday Park 132

BRIGHOUSE BAY
Brighouse Bay Holiday Park 270

BRIGHSTONE
Grange Farm 158

BROADWOODWIDGER
Roadford Lake 112

BRONLLYS
Anchorage Caravan Park 310

BRYHER (ISLES OF SCILLY)
Bryher Camp Site 59

BUCKFASTLEIGH
Beara Farm Caravan & Camping Site 112

BUDE
Upper Lynstone Caravan Park 61
Willow Valley Holiday Park 61
Wooda Farm Holiday Park 60

BUILTH WELLS
Fforest Fields Caravan & Camping Park 310

BULWICK
New Lodge Farm Caravan & Camping Site 190

BUNGAY
Outney Meadow Caravan Park 220

BURNHAM DEEPDALE
Deepdale Camping & Rooms 183

BUSHMILLS
Ballyness Caravan Park 321

BUXTON
Beech Croft Farm Caravan and Camping Park 103
Lime Tree Park 104

C

CAERNARFON
Llys Derwen Caravan & Camping Site 300
Plas Gwyn Caravan & Camping Park 301
Riverside Camping 299

CAISTER-ON-SEA
Caister-on-Sea Holiday Park 183

CAISTOR
Caistor Lakes 175
Wolds View Country Park 175

CAMELFORD
Lakefield Caravan Park 61

INDEX

CAPERNWRAY
Old Hall Caravan Park 166

CARLISLE
Green Acres Caravan Park 94

CARLYON BAY
Carlyon Bay Caravan & Camping Park 62

CARNFORTH
Marsh House Holiday Park 166

CARRADALE
Carradale Bay Caravan Park 268

CARTMEL
Greaves Farm Caravan Park 94

CASTLE CARY
Hadspen Glamping 209

CERNE ABBAS
Giants Head Caravan & Camping Park 133

CHACEWATER
Chacewater Park 63
Killiwerris Touring Park 63

CHARMOUTH
Manor Farm Holiday Centre 136
Monkton Wyld Holiday Park 135
Newlands Holidays 136

CHEDDAR
Cheddar Woods Resort & Spa 209

CHELTENHAM
Briarfields Motel & Touring Park 153

CHICHESTER
Concierge Camping 228
Concierge Glamping 229

CHIDEOCK
Golden Cap Holiday Park 136

CHIPPENHAM
Plough Lane Touring Caravan Site 232

CHOP GATE
Lordstones Country Park 241

CHRISTCHURCH
Meadowbank Holidays 137

CHURCH LANEHAM
Trentfield Farm 195

CHURCHSTOKE
Daisy Bank Caravan Park 311

CIRENCESTER
Mayfield Park 153

CLAYHIDON
Kingsmead Centre Camping 112

CLEETHORPES
Cleethorpes Beach 175

CLIPPESBY
Clippesby Hall 184

CLYST ST MARY
Crealy Theme Park & Resort 113

COCKERHAM
Moss Wood Caravan Park 167

CODDINGTON
Manor Wood Country Caravan Park 53

COMBE MARTIN
Newberry Valley Park 113

COMBERTON
Highfield Farm Touring Park 50

COMRIE
Twenty Shilling Wood Caravan Park 283

CONSTABLE BURTON
Constable Burton Hall Caravan Park 241

COOMBE BISSETT
Summerlands Caravan Park 232

CORFE CASTLE
Norden Farm Touring Caravan and Camping Site 137
Woodyhyde Camp Site 138

COVERACK
Little Trevothan Camping and Caravan Park 63

COWSLIP GREEN
Brook Lodge Farm Camping & Caravan Park 210

CRANTOCK (NEAR NEWQUAY)
Quarryfield Holiday Park 64
Treago Farm Caravan Site 64

CRICCIETH
Eisteddfa 301

CRICKHOWELL
Riverside Caravan & Camping Park 311

CROMER
Forest Park 184
Manor Farm Caravan & Camping Site 184

CROOKLANDS
Waters Edge Caravan Park 94

CROYDE
Bay View Farm Caravan & Camping Park 114

CUMWHITTON
Cairndale Caravan Park 95

D

DALBEATTIE
Glenearly Caravan Park 270

DARTMOUTH
Woodlands Grove Caravan & Camping Park 114

DAWLISH
Cofton Holidays 115
Lady's Mile Holiday Park 115

DELAMERE
Fishpool Farm Caravan Park 53

DERSINGHAM
Pinecones Caravan and Camping 185

DINAS DINLLE
Dinlle Caravan Park 301

DODDINGTON
Fields End Water Caravan Park & Fishery 51

DOWNHAM MARKET
Lakeside Caravan Park & Fisheries 186

DREWSTEIGNTON
Woodland Springs Adult Touring Park 116

DULAS
Tyddyn Isaf Caravan Park 292

DULVERTON
Wimbleball Lake 211

DUNBAR
Thurston Manor Leisure Park 281
Belhaven Bay Caravan & Camping Park 281

DUNDONALD
Dundonald Touring Caravan Park 321

DUNGANNON
Dungannon Park 322

DUNKELD
Inver Mill Farm Caravan Park 283

DUNWICH
Haw Wood Farm Caravan Park 220

DUROR
Achindarroch Touring Park 279

E

EAST WORLINGTON
Yeatheridge Farm Caravan Park 116

ECCLEFECHAN
Hoddom Castle Caravan Park 271

EXFORD
Westermill Farm Holidays Ltd 211

EYTON
Plassey Holiday Park 316

F

FAKENHAM
Norfolk Coast Caravan & Camping at Fakenham Racecourse 186

FALMOUTH
Tregedna Farm Touring Caravan & Tent Park 64

FAR ARNSIDE
Hollins Farm Holiday Park 168

FELIXSTOWE
Peewit Caravan Park 221

FERNDOWN
St Leonards Farm Caravan & Camping Park 139

FILEY
Blue Dolphin Holiday Park 243
Crows Nest Caravan Park 242
Filey Brigg Touring Caravan & Country Park 243
Flower of May Holiday Park 241
Orchard Farm Holiday Park 242
Primrose Valley Holiday Park 242
Reighton Sands Holiday Park 242

FINCHAMPSTEAD
California Chalet & Touring Park 50

FISHGUARD
Fishguard Bay Resort 307

FLAMBOROUGH
Thornwick Bay Holiday Village 237

FLEETWOOD
Cala Gran Holiday Park 168

FLOOKBURGH
Lakeland Leisure Park 95

FORT WILLIAM
Glen Nevis Caravan & Camping Park 279

FOWLIS
Piperdam Leisure Resort 268

FRESHWATER
Heathfield Farm Camping 158

FRINGFORD
Glebe Leisure 197

FRODSHAM
Lady Heyes Holiday Park 54

FROME
Seven Acres Caravan & Camping Site 211

G

GARSTANG
Bridge House Marina & Caravan Park 169

GATEHOUSE OF FLEET
Anwoth Caravan Site 272
Auchenlarie Holiday Park 271

GISBURN
Hedgerow Luxury Glamping 170

GLASTONBURY
Isle of Avalon Touring Caravan Park 212
Old Oaks Touring & Glamping 212

GLENCOE
Invercoe Caravan & Camping Park 280

GLENDARUEL
Glendaruel Caravan Park 268

GREAT YARMOUTH
Ormesby Grange Tents & Touring 187
Seashore Holiday Park 187

GREENHALGH
Charoland Farm Caravan Site 170

GREETHAM
In The Stix 199
Rutland Caravan & Camping 199

GRETNA
King Robert the Bruce's Cave Caravan & Camping Park 273

H

HALTWHISTLE
Herding Hill Farm, Glamping site 194
Herding Hill Farm Touring & Camping Site 194

HARBURY
Harbury Fields 231

HARROGATE
Harrogate Caravan Park 244
High Moor Farm Park 244
Ripley Caravan Park 243
Rudding Holiday Park 244
Shaws Trailer Park 245

HARTINGTON
Bank House Farm 104

HASTINGS & ST LEONARDS
Combe Haven Holiday Park 226

HAVERFORDWEST
Nolton Cross Caravan Park 308

HAYLE
Atlantic Coast Holiday Park 65
Riviere Sands Holiday Park 65
Treglisson Touring Park 65

HELMSLEY
Foxholme Springs Touring Park 246
Golden Square Caravan & Camping Park 245

HELSTON
Polladras Holiday Park 65
Skyburriowe Farm 66

HEMINGFORD ABBOTS
Quiet Waters Caravan Park 51

HENLEY-ON-THAMES
Swiss Farm Touring & Camping 197

HERM
Seagull Campsite 261

HEXHAM
Hexham Racecourse Caravan Site 195

HIGH BENTHAM
Riverside Caravan Park 246
Wenningdale Escapes 246

HODDESDON
Lee Valley Caravan Park, Dobbs Weir 155

HOLDITCH
Mallinson's Woodland Retreat 140

HOLLESLEY
Run Cottage Touring Park 221

HOLMROOK
Seven Acres Caravan Park 95

HOLSWORTHY
Headon Farm Caravan Site & Storage 117
Noteworthy Farm Caravan and Campsite 117

HOLYWELL
Haulfryn Caravan Park 297

HOLYWELL BAY
Trevornick 66

HONEYBOURNE
Ranch Caravan Park 233

HOPE
Pindale Farm Outdoor Centre 104

HOPTON ON SEA
Hopton Holiday Village 187

HUNSTANTON
Searles Leisure Resort 188

HUNTINGDON
Huntingdon Boathaven & Caravan Park 52

HUNTLY
Huntly Castle Caravan Park 266

HUTTON-LE-HOLE
Hutton-le-Hole Caravan Park 247

I

ILFRACOMBE
Sunnymead Farm Camping & Touring Site........................... 117

IRVINESTOWN
Castle Archdale Caravan Park & Camping Site 322

K

KENNACK SANDS
Silver Sands Holiday Park 66

KENNFORD
Kennford International Holiday Park 118

KENTISBEARE
Forest Glade Holiday Park 118

KESWICK
Burns Farm Caravan, Camping & Glamping 97
Castlerigg Hall Caravan & Camping Park 96

KETTLEWELL
Kettlewell Camping 247

KILDONAN
Seal Shore Camping and Touring Site.................................. 286

KILKHAMPTON
Upper Tamar Lake 66

KILMORY
Runach Arainn Glamping 286

KINGSBRIDGE
Island Lodge Caravan & Camping Site................................ 120
Parkland Caravan and Camping Site 119

KING'S LYNN
King's Lynn Caravan and Camping Park 188

KINTORE
Hillhead Caravan Park.. 266

KIRKBY LONSDALE
New House Caravan Park 97
Woodclose Caravan Park 97

KIRKCUDBRIGHT
Seaward Holiday Park 273

KIRK MICHAEL
Glen Wyllin Campsite 261

KNARESBOROUGH
Kingfisher Caravan Park 247

L

LACOCK
Piccadilly Caravan Park 232

LANCASTER
New Parkside Farm Caravan Park 170

LANGWORTH
Barlings Country Holiday Park 176

LAUDER
Thirlestane Castle Caravan & Camping Site....................... 284

LEISTON
Cakes & Ale.. 222

LEYSDOWN-ON-SEA
Priory Hill... 162

LINLITHGOW
Beecraigs Caravan & Camping Site.................................... 282

INDEX

LITTLEBOROUGH
Hollingworth Lake Caravan Park 154

LLANDOVERY
Llandovery Caravan Park 293

LLANDRINDOD WELLS
Disserth Caravan & Camping Park 312

LLANDWROG
White Tower Holiday Park 302

LLANGORS
Lakeside Caravan Park 312

LLANIDLOES
Red Kite Touring and Lodge Park 313

LLANRWST
Bodnant Caravan Park 296
Bron Derw Touring Caravan Park 295

LLANVAIR DISCOED
Penhein Glamping 306

LONDON E4
Lee Valley Campsite, Sewardstone 178

LONDON N9
Lee Valley Camping and Caravan Park, Edmonton 179

LONGNIDDRY
Seton Sands Holiday Village 281

LONGNOR
Longnor Wood Holiday Park 217

LOOE
Tencreek Holiday Park 67

LOSTWITHIEL
Eden Valley Holiday Park 67

LUDLOW
Westbrook Park 200

LUIB
Glen Dochart Holiday Park 285

LYME REGIS
Shrubbery Touring Park 140

LYNEAL
Fernwood Caravan Park 200

LYNTON
Lynmouth Holiday Retreat 120

LYTHAM ST ANNES
Eastham Hall Holiday Park 171

M

MABLETHORPE
Golden Sands Holiday Park 176
Kirkstead Holiday Park 176

MANSFIELD
Tall Trees Touring Park 196

MARDEN
Tanner Farm Touring Caravan & Camping Park 163

MARIAN-GLAS
Home Farm Caravan Park 292

MARTOCK
Southfork Caravan Park 212

MAWGAN PORTH
Trevarrian Holiday Park 68

MEALSGATE
Larches Caravan Park 97

MELTON MOWBRAY
Eye Kettleby Lakes 173

MERSEA ISLAND
Fen Farm Caravan Site 151
Waldegraves Holiday Park 151

MIDDLETOWN
Bank Farm Caravan Park 313

MINTLAW
Aden Caravan and Camping 267

MODBURY
Moor View Touring Park 121
Pennymoor Camping & Caravan Park 121

MOFFAT
Moffat Manor Holiday Park 274

MONMOUTH
Rockfield Glamping 307

MORTEHOE
North Morte Farm Caravan & Camping Park 121

N

NABURN
Naburn Lock Caravan Park 248

NETHER WASDALE
Church Stile Farm & Holiday Park 98

NEWBRIDGE
The Orchards Holiday Caravan Park 159

NEWCASTLE EMLYN
Afon Teifi Caravan & Camping Park 293
Cenarth Falls Resort Limited 293

NEW QUAY
Quay West Holiday Park 294

NEWQUAY
Hendra Holiday Park 68
Monkey Tree Holiday Park 69
Porth Beach Holiday Park 69
Riverside Holiday Park 70
Trebellan Park 70
Treloy Touring Park 68
Trenance Holiday Park 70
Trencreek Holiday Park 69

NORTHALLERTON
Otterington Park 248

NORTH STAINLEY
Sleningford Watermill Caravan Camping Park 248

NORTH WALSHAM
Two Mills Touring Park 189

NORTHWICH
Belmont Camping 54

O

OSMOTHERLEY
Cote Ghyll Caravan & Camping Park 249

OVERTON
The Trotting Mare Caravan Park 317

OXWICH
Greenways of Gower Premier Leisure Park 314

P

PADSTOW
The Retreats @ Padstow Holiday Park 71

PAGHAM
Church Farm Holiday Park 230

PAIGNTON
Beverley Park Caravan & Camping Park 122
Whitehill Country Park 122

PALNACKIE
Kippford View Holiday Park 274

PATTERDALE
Sykeside Camping & Caravan Park 98

PENTEWAN
Heligan Caravan & Camping Park 71

PERRANPORTH
Perran Sands Holiday Park 71
Tollgate Farm Caravan & Camping Park 72

PERTH
Pathgreen Glamping 283

PICKERING
Wayside Holiday Park 249

PITLOCHRY
Bishopton 284
Faskally Caravan Park 284
Milton of Fonab Caravan Park 284

PLYMOUTH
Riverside Caravan Park 123

POLPERRO
Great Kellow Farm 72

POLZEATH
Gunvenna Holiday Park 72
Southwinds Caravan & Camping Park 73
Tristram Caravan & Camping Park 73

POOLE
Rockley Park 141
South Lytchett Manor Caravan & Camping Park 141

POOLEY BRIDGE
Hillcroft Park 99
Park Foot Holiday Park 99
Waterfoot Caravan Park 99

PORLOCK
Burrowhayes Farm Caravan & Camping Site & Riding Stables 213

PORTESHAM
Portesham Dairy Farm Campsite 141

PORT EYNON
Skysea Camping & Caravan Park 315

PORTHMADOG
Greenacres Holiday Park 302

PORTHTOWAN
Porthtowan Tourist Park 73

PORTREATH
Landal Gwel an Mor 73
Tehidy Holiday Park 74

PORTSCATHO
Trewince Farm Touring Park 75

PORT WILLIAM
Kings Green Caravan Site 275

PRESTATYN
Presthaven Beach Holiday Park 296

PRESTWICK
Prestwick Holiday Park 269

PRIDDY
Cheddar Mendip Heights Camping & Caravanning Club Site 213

PUNCKNOWLE
Home Farm Caravan and Campsite 142

PWLLHELI
Abererch Sands Holiday Centre 303
Hafan y Môr Holiday Park 303

R

REDRUTH
Cambrose Touring Park 76
Globe Vale Holiday Park 75
Lanyon Holiday Park 76
Stithians Lake Country Park 77

RHÔS LLIGWY
Ty'n Rhos Caravan Park 293

RHOSSILI
Pitton Cross Caravan & Camping Park 315

RHUALLT
Penisar Mynydd Caravan Park 296

RIDDINGS
Riddings Wood Holiday Park 105

RIPLEY
Golden Valley Caravan & Camping Park 105

RIPON
Riverside Meadows Holiday Park 250

ROBIN HOOD'S BAY
Grouse Hill Caravan Park 250

ROCHESTER
Kent Coast Leisure Park 163

ROSE
Higher Hendra Park 77

ROSEDALE ABBEY
Rosedale Abbey Caravan Park 250

ROSLISTON
Beehive Woodland Lakes 105

RUDSTON
Thorpe Hall Caravan & Camping Site 237

RUTHERNBRIDGE
Ruthern Valley Holidays 77

RUYTON-XI-TOWNS
Riverside Cabins 200

RYDE
Whitefield Forest Touring Park 159

S

ST AGNES
Beacon Cottage Farm Touring Park 78
Presingoll Farm Caravan & Camping Park 78

ST ANDREWS
Cairnsmill Holiday Park 277
Craigtoun Meadows Holiday Park 278

ST AUSTELL
Court Farm Campsite 79
River Valley Holiday Park 79

ST BLAZEY GATE
Doubletrees Farm 79

ST COLUMB MAJOR
Trewan Hall 80

ST DAVIDS
Caerfai Bay Caravan & Tent Park 308
Tretio Caravan & Camping Park 309

ST HILARY
Wayfarers Caravan & Camping Park 80

ST IVES
Ayr Holiday Park 81
Higher Penderleath Caravan & Camping Park 83
Polmanter Touring Park 82
Trevalgan Touring Park 82

ST JUST [NEAR LAND'S END]
Roselands Caravan and Camping Park 83
Trevaylor Caravan & Camping Park 84

ST JUST-IN-ROSELAND
Trethem Mill Touring Park 84

ST LEONARDS
Back of Beyond Touring Park 142

ST MARY'S (ISLES OF SCILLY)
Garrison Campsite 84

ST MERRYN (NEAR PADSTOW)
Atlantic Bays Holiday Park 85
Carnevas Holiday Park 85
Tregavone Touring Park 85

ST OSYTH
The Orchards Holiday Park 152

ST SAMPSON
Le Vaugrat Camp Site 260

SALCOMBE
Bolberry House Farm Caravan & Camping Park 124
Higher Rew Caravan & Camping Park 124
Karrageen Caravan & Camping Park 123

SALISBURY
Coombe Touring Park 233

SAMPFORD PEVERELL
Minnows Touring Park 124

SANDHEAD
Sands of Luce Holiday Park 275

SANDYHILLS
Sandyhills Bay Holiday Park 275

SAXMUNDHAM
Marsh Farm Caravan Site 223

SCARBOROUGH
Killerby Old Hall Cottages & Caravan Site 251

SCRATBY
Scratby Hall Caravan Park 189

SELSEY
Warner Farm 230

SENNEN
Trevedra Farm Caravan & Camping Site 85

SHANKLIN
Ninham Country Holidays 160

SHERIFF HUTTON
York Meadows Caravan Park 251

SHREWSBURY
Beaconsfield Holiday Park 201
Cartref Caravan & Camping 202
Love2Stay Shrewsbury 202
Oxon Hall Touring Park 202
Stoney Acres Luxury Holiday Park 202
Sunnyside Farm Caravan Park & Fishery 203
Walnut Cottage Holiday Park 203

SIDDINGTON
Capesthorne Hall 54

SIDMOUTH
Oakdown Holiday Park 125
Salcombe Regis Caravan & Camping Park 125

SILLOTH
Hylton Caravan Park 100
Solway Holiday Village 100
Stanwix Park Holiday Centre 100

SILVERDALE
Silverdale Holiday Park 172

SIXPENNY HANDLEY
Church Farm Caravan & Camping Park 143

SKEGNESS
Chapel Fields Holiday Park 177
Eastview Caravan Park 177
Skegness Holiday Park 176

SKELMERSDALE
The Secret Garden Glamping 172

SKIPSEA
Skirlington Leisure Park 237

SLIMBRIDGE
Tudor Caravan & Camping 153

SOUTH MOLTON
Riverside Caravan & Camping Park 126

SOUTHPORT
Willowbank Holiday Home & Touring Park 179

SOUTHWELL
New Hall Farm Touring Park 196

SPARKFORD
Long Hazel Park 214

SPROATLEY
Burton Constable Holiday Park & Arboretum 238

STAFFIN
Staffin Camping & Caravanning 286

STAINFORTH
Knight Stainforth Hall Caravan & Campsite 252

STANDLAKE
Lincoln Farm Park Oxfordshire 198

STANHOE
The Rickels Caravan & Camping Park Ltd 190

STOKE GABRIEL
Higher Well Farm Holiday Park 127

STRACHAN
Feughside Caravan Park 267

STRANRAER
Aird Donald Caravan Park 276
Ryan Bay Caravan Park 276

SUMMERCOURT
Carvynick Holiday Park 86

SUTTON-ON-THE-FOREST
Goosewood Holiday Park 252

SWANAGE
Acton Field Camping Site 144
Ulwell Holiday Park 143

SWANSEA
Riverside Caravan Park 316

T

TALYBONT
Islawrffordd Caravan Park 304

TATTERSHALL
Willow Holt Caravan Park 177

TAUNTON
Ashe Farm Camping & Caravan Site 215
Cornish Farm Touring Park 214

TAVISTOCK
Harford Bridge Holiday Park 128
Langstone Manor Camping & Caravan Park 128
Woodovis Park 127

TELFORD
Severn Gorge Park 203

TENBY
Kiln Park Holiday Centre 309
Well Park Caravan & Camping Site 309

THIRSK
Hillside Caravan Park 252

THORNTON
Waters Edge Country Park 173

THREE LEGGED CROSS
Woolsbridge Manor Farm Caravan Park 144

TORQUAY
Widdicombe Farm Touring Park 128

TRINITY
Durrell Wildlife Camp 261

TRURO
Cosawes Park 87
Summer Valley Touring Park 87

TURRIFF
Turriff Caravan Park 267

TYWYN
Barmouth Bay Holiday Park 304
Ynysymaengwyn Caravan Park 304

U

ULLAPOOL
Broomfield Holiday Park 280

ULVERSTON
Bardsea Leisure Park 101

USK
Pont Kemys Caravan & Camping Park 307

V

VALE
La Bailloterie Camping 260

W

WADEBRIDGE
The Laurels Holiday Park 87
Little Bodieve Holiday Park 87

WALES BAR
Waleswood Caravan and Camping Park 256

WAREHAM
Birchwood Tourist Park 146
East Creech Farm Campsite 146
Ridge Farm Camping & Caravan Park 147
Wareham Forest Tourist Park 145

WARSASH
Dibles Park 155

WATCHET
Doniford Bay Holiday Park 215

WATERGATE BAY
Watergate Bay Touring Park 88

WATERMILLOCK
The Quiet Site 101
The Quiet Site Glamping 101
Ullswater Holiday Park 102

WELLS
Wells Touring Park 215

WENTNOR
The Green Caravan Park 203

WEST KNAPTON
Wolds Way Caravan and Camping 253

WESTON-SUPER-MARE
Country View Holiday Park 216

WEYMOUTH
Bagwell Farm Touring Park 148
East Fleet Farm Touring Park 147
Littlesea Holiday Park 148
Pebble Bank Caravan Park 149
Rosewall Camping 149
Sea Barn Farm Camping Park 149
Seaview Holiday Park 148
West Fleet Holiday Farm 149
Weymouth Bay Holiday Park 147

WHITBY
Ladycross Plantation Caravan Park 253

WHITE CROSS
Piran Meadows Resort and Spa 89

WHITEGATE
Lamb Cottage Caravan Park 55

WHITSTABLE
Homing Park 164

WIDEMOUTH BAY
Penhalt Farm Holiday Park 89

WIGTOWN
Drumroamin Farm Camping & Touring Site 277

WINDERMERE
Park Cliffe Camping & Caravan Estate 102

WINSFORD
Halse Farm Caravan & Camping Park 216

WISBECH
Little Ranch Leisure 52

WIVELISCOMBE
Waterrow Touring Park 217

INDEX

WOLVEY
Wolvey Villa Farm Caravan & Camping Park 231

WOODBRIDGE
Moon & Sixpence 223

WOODHALL SPA
Petwood Caravan Park 178
Woodhall Country Park 177

WOOL
Whitemead Caravan Park 150

WOOLACOMBE
Easewell Farm Holiday Village 129
Golden Coast Holiday Park 129
Twitchen House Holiday Village 129

WOOTTON BRIDGE
Kite Hill Farm Caravan & Camping Park 161
Woodside Bay Lodge Retreat 160

WORSBROUGH
Greensprings Touring Park 257

WYKEHAM
St Helens in the Park 254

Y

YORK
Flaxton Meadows 254
Rawcliffe Manor Caravan Park 255
York Caravan Park 254

Notes

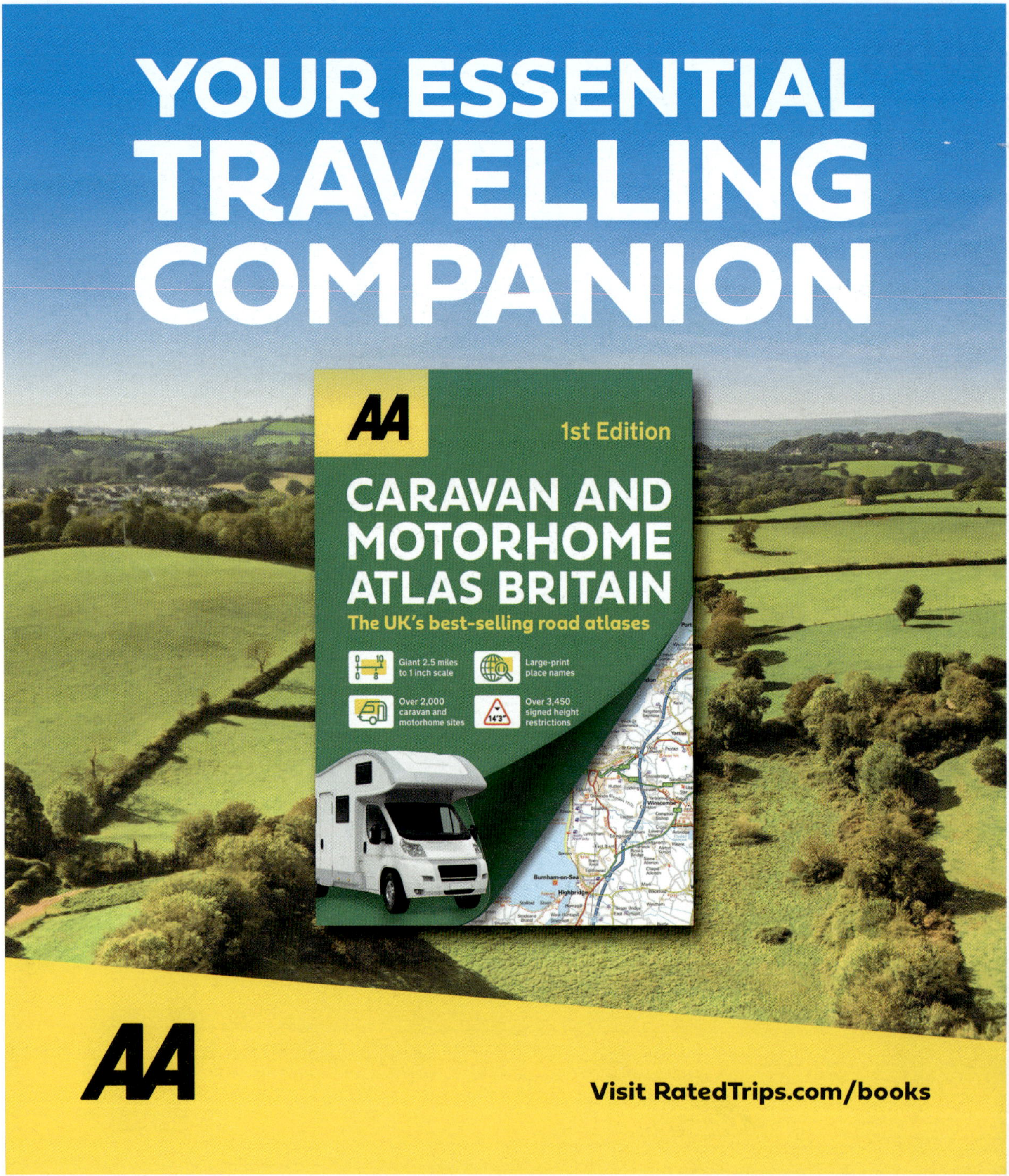
YOUR ESSENTIAL
TRAVELLING
COMPANION
AA
1st Edition
CARAVAN AND MOTORHOME ATLAS BRITAIN
The UK's best-selling road atlases
Giant 2.5 miles to 1 inch scale
Large-print place names
Over 2,000 caravan and motorhome sites
Over 3,450 signed height restrictions
AA
Visit RatedTrips.com/books

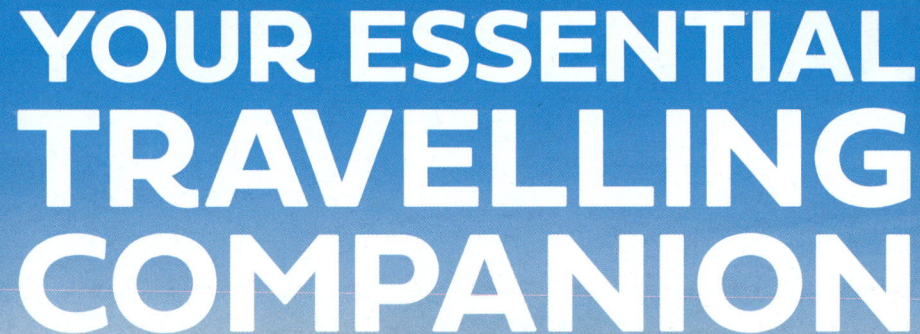